THE PURITANS

VOLUME I

*the text of this book is printed
on 100% recycled paper*

Mr. Richard Mather.

Reproduced from Increase Mather's *The Life and Death of . . .*
Richard Mather.

THE PURITANS

VOLUME I Revised Edition

PERRY MILLER

AND

THOMAS H. JOHNSON

Bibliographies Revised for the Torchbook Edition

by George McCandlish

HARPER TORCHBOOKS ❦ THE ACADEMY LIBRARY

HARPER & ROW, PUBLISHERS, NEW YORK

FOR

SAMUEL ELIOT MORISON

Liberali liberaliter instituendi

✒ FOREWORD

Jonathan Edwards cautioned himself in his Notes on Natural Science: "What is prefatorial, not to write in a distinct preface, or introduction, but in the body of the work; then I shall be sure to have it read by every one." The editors of the following selections have been mindful of his warning, and they here need merely to say that the volume portrays the Puritans who settled New England and those of the next two generations who lived there. The focus of the work has been Puritanism in the seventeenth century, when the word had a comparatively definite meaning, and in only one respect has any effort been made to trace the modifications of it in the eighteenth century. The selections from the writings of Jonathan Mayhew have been included for the purpose of giving a continuous view of political theory. Otherwise the consistent aim has been restriction to what might be called "pure" Puritanism, leaving later ramifications to be traced out elsewhere. It has for that reason been thought wise to leave the greatest of all Puritan intellectuals, Jonathan Edwards, to be studied in the context of his different intellectual environment.

To the end that the elusive terms Puritan and Puritanism should be clearly defined, at least in so far as they apply to the colonizers of America and their spiritual descendants, the selections have been grouped into chapters;—divisions which most naturally provide opportunity for discussion of all phases of Puritan ways and ideas, with such emphasis, selectivity, and proportion as seem representative and true. The General Introduction attempts to view Puritanism as a whole: to mete its boundaries, fix its location, supply guides to its monuments, and establish that unity which so clearly runs in Puritan thought, expression, and manners.

It has seemed best to let the Puritans speak for themselves as much as possible, for they were not a reticent people, nor were they wanting in ideas. As Ælfric remarked in the foreword to his *Lives of the Saints:* "We say nothing new in this work, for it all stood written long ago, albeit laymen did not know it." Much that the Puritans wrote has been deservedly forgotten, but the dust has gathered as well upon the works of some who, when brought into the light of the present, appear to have been powerful instruments in working out the social and political, as well as the religious and cultural, destiny of America. It therefore seemed wiser to give in general ample passages from a few pivotal documents, rather than to go wide afield in an effort merely to extend the list of Puritan writers. The editors are aware that no American today can read a Puritan work without having a definite opinion of the author, and they in their turn have not been reticent in the introductory portions about speaking their minds; yet the larger purpose has been to supply enough of the Puritan literature itself to let each reader judge for himself.

The texts throughout follow the earliest edition, or the most accurately printed when the first seems inadvisable. Spelling and punctuation are reproduced exactly, except that the modern "s" has been uniformly adopted, and obvious printers' errors corrected. It should be stated that the map of New England which forms the end-papers of the volume, while based mainly upon the accurate surveys of more recent times, has been constructed to show certain features of the coast-lines and harbors as indicated by a study of many old maps, some of them published near the close of the Puritan period.

The editors have collaborated closely, and each has contributed something to almost every section; but the major task of preparation and annotation was divided, and final responsibility for expression of opinion must rest as follows: "The Puritan Way of Life" in the General Introduction, and Chapters I, II, III, and V are the work of Perry Miller; "The Puritans as Literary Artists" in the General Introduction, and Chapters IV, VI, VII, VIII, and IX are the work of Thomas H. Johnson.

First of all the editors wish to express their gratitude to Professor Harry Hayden Clark, the general editor of the series of which this volume is a part. It was he who first proposed the idea of the undertaking, and his assistance and encouragement have been constant and generous. They also wish to thank the Librarians and the staffs of Harvard College Library, Boston Public Library, the Massachusetts Historical Society, Princeton University Library, and New York Public Library for innumerable courtesies, always graciously extended. The demands on Mr. Gerald D. McDonald, Head of the Reserve Room of the last named institution, have been especially importunate, and always met with unfailing skill. Dr. Erdman Harris and Mr. Hugh King Wright have been good enough to read through and offer helpful suggestions about the chapters of the text prepared by Thomas H. Johnson. Perry Miller is indebted to Professor F. O. Matthiessen for his generous assistance in reading the introductory material and advising in the whole construction of the volume; he has also profited largely from the help of Professor David Prall, Dr. Richard B. Schlatter, and Mr. Edmund S. Morgan. To Catherine Rice Johnson and Elizabeth Williams Miller the debt is truly immense, for without their help the book could hardly have reached completion.

The editors' reliance upon the work of Professor Samuel Eliot Morison is testified by the frequent citation of his name in the Introduction and the notes; but the debt goes even further, and is acknowledged elsewhere.

P. M.
T. H. J.

CONTENTS

Volume I

GENERAL INTRODUCTION

Chapter I

HISTORY 81

Chapter II

THE THEORY OF THE STATE AND OF SOCIETY 181

Chapter III

THIS WORLD AND THE NEXT

Readings

Volume II

Chapter IV

MANNERS, CUSTOMS, AND BEHAVIOR . . . 379

Readings

Chapter V

Chapter VI

Chapter VII

LITERARY THEORY 665

Readings

Contents xv

Illustrations

Volume I

Volume II

The Map of New England has been prepared especially for this volume. The page of Taylor's manuscript is reproduced through the courtesy of Yale University Library. All the other reproductions are by courtesy of the Massachusetts Historical Society.

Cowass - Indian name applied to a stretch of the upper Connecticut R. Later known as "Great Intervale."

Blaxton's Point, Noddle's Island, Tompson's Island, Castle Island, Governor's Island, Isle of Slate - all within Boston Bay.

Salisbury
Merrimac
Haverhill
Merrimac
Newbury
PLUM ISLAND
N. Andover
Rowley
CAPE ANN
Andover Topsfield
ESSEX
Agawam
Ipswich
Wenham
Gloucester
Salem Village
Danvers
Beverly
Manchester
Billerica
Reading
Salem
Marblehead
Woburn
Lynn
Malden
Medford
Winnissimmet
Newtown
Cambridge
Chelsea
Charlestown
Watertown
SUFFOLK
Boston
Brookline
Roxbury
Dorchester
Milton
Mt. Wollaston
Merry Mount
Hingham
Dedham
Braintree
Wessagusett
Weymouth
Scituate
Medfield

MASSACHUSETTS BAY

Northfield
Turners Falls
Deerfield
MASSA
Hatfield
Hadley
Northampton
Brookfield
Westfield
Agawam
Springfield
Enfield
Kingston
Simsbury
Windsor
NEW YORK
Newtown
Hartford
Farmington
Pyquag
Wethersfield
PEQUOT
CONNECTICUT
Colchester
Middletown
Norwich
Wallingford
Haddam
COUNTRY
Pequot Gro
New London
New Haven
E. Haven
Branford
Guilford
Killingworth
Saybrook
Lyme
Paugassett
Derby
Stratford
Milford
Fairfield
LONG ISLAND SOUND
Norwalk
Stamford
Greenwich
Rye
Southold
GARDINER'S
SHELTER
NEW
HORS NECK
Setauket
Sag Harbor
Fire Place
East Hampton
East Chester
New Rochelle
SPUYTEN DUYVIL
KINGSBRIDGE
Westchester
Oyster Bay
Huntington
Southampton
JERSEY
Flushing
BOWERY
Hempstead
New Amsterdam
New York
Gravesend
GREAT BAY
STATEN ISLAND

A Scale of Miles
4 8 12 16 20 24 28 32 36

A MAP OF
NEW ENGLAND

"... done in the best Pattern that could be had, which being in some places defective, it made the others less exact: yet doth it sufficiently shew the Scituation of the Countrey, and conveniently well the distance of Places."

from map published in 1677 by Wm. Hubbard.

—— The Journey of Madam Knight

.... Portion of Long Island under Connecticut jurisdiction until 1664

- - - - - - Present-day state boundaries

❧ INTRODUCTION

I. THE PURITAN WAY OF LIFE

1. The Puritan in His Age

PURITANISM may perhaps best be described as that point of view, that philosophy of life, that code of values, which was carried to New England by the first settlers in the early seventeenth century. Beginning thus, it has become one of the continuous factors in American life and American thought. Any inventory of the elements that have gone into the making of the "American mind" would have to commence with Puritanism. It is, indeed, only one among many: if we should attempt to enumerate these traditions, we should certainly have to mention such philosophies, such "isms," as the rational liberalism of Jeffersonian democracy, the Hamiltonian conception of conservatism and government, the Southern theory of racial aristocracy, the Transcendentalism of nineteenth-century New England, and what is generally spoken of as frontier individualism. Among these factors Puritanism has been perhaps the most conspicuous, the most sustained, and the most fecund. Its role in American thought has been almost the dominant one, for the descendants of Puritans have carried at least some habits of the Puritan mind into a variety of pursuits, have spread across the country, and in many fields of activity have played a leading part. The force of Puritanism, furthermore, has been accentuated because it was the first of these traditions to be fully articulated, and because it has inspired certain traits which have persisted long after the vanishing of the original creed. Without some understanding of Puritanism, it may safely be said, there is no understanding of America.

Yet important as Puritanism has undoubtedly been in shaping the nation, it is more easily described than defined. It figures frequently in controversy of the last decade, very seldom twice with exactly the same connotation. Particularly of recent years has it become a hazardous feat to run down its meaning. In the mood of revolt against the ideals of previous generations which has swept over our period, Puritanism has become a shining target for many sorts of marksmen. Confusion becomes worse

confounded if we attempt to correlate modern usages with anything that can be proved pertinent to the original Puritans themselves. To seek no further, it was the habit of proponents for the
repeal of the Eighteenth Amendment during the 1920's to dub
Prohibitionists "Puritans," and cartoonists made the nation familiar with an image of the Puritan: a gaunt, lank-haired kill-
joy, wearing a black steeple hat and compounding for sins he
was inclined to by damning those to which he had no mind.
Yet any acquaintance with the Puritans of the seventeenth century will reveal at once, not only that they did not wear such
hats, but also that they attired themselves in all the hues of the
rainbow, and furthermore that in their daily life they imbibed
what seem to us prodigious quantities of alcoholic beverages, with
never the slightest inkling that they were doing anything sinful.
True, they opposed drinking to excess, and ministers preached
lengthy sermons condemning intoxication, but at such pious ceremonies as the ordination of new ministers the bill for rum, wine,
and beer consumed by the congregation was often staggering.
Increase Mather himself—who in popular imagination is apt to
figure along with his son Cotton as the arch-embodiment of the
Puritan—said in one of his sermons:

Drink is in it self a good creature of God, and to be received
with thankfulness, but the abuse of drink is from Satan; the wine
is from God, but the Drunkard is from the Devil.[1]

Or again, the Puritan has acquired the reputation of having
been blind to all aesthetic enjoyment and starved of beauty;
yet the architecture of the Puritan age grows in the esteem of
critics and the household objects of Puritan manufacture, pewter
and furniture, achieve prohibitive prices by their appeal to discriminating collectors. Examples of such discrepancies between
the modern usage of the word and the historical fact could be
multiplied indefinitely.[2] It is not the purpose of this volume to
engage in controversy, nor does it intend particularly to defend
the Puritan against the bewildering variety of critics who on
every side today find him an object of scorn or pity. In his life
he neither asked nor gave mercy to his foes; he demanded only
that conflicts be joined on real and explicit issues. By examining

---

[1] *Wo to Drunkards* (Cambridge, 1673), p. 4.
[2] Cf. Kenneth B. Murdock, "The Puritan Tradition in American Literature,"
The Reinterpretation of American Literature (New York, 1928), chap. V.

his own words it may become possible to establish, for better or for worse, the meaning of Puritanism as the Puritan himself believed and practiced it.

Just as soon as we endeavor to free ourselves from prevailing conceptions or misconceptions, and to ascertain the historical facts about seventeenth-century New Englanders, we become aware that we face still another difficulty: not only must we extricate ourselves from interpretations that have been read into Puritanism by the twentieth century, but still more from those that have been attached to it by the eighteenth and nineteenth. The Puritan philosophy, brought to New England highly elaborated and codified, remained a fairly rigid orthodoxy during the seventeenth century. In the next age, however, it proved to be anything but static; by the middle of the eighteenth century there had proceeded from it two distinct schools of thought, almost unalterably opposed to each other. Certain elements were carried into the creeds and practices of the evangelical religious revivals, but others were perpetuated by the rationalists and the forerunners of Unitarianism. Consequently our conception of Puritanism is all too apt to be colored by subsequent happenings; we read ideas into the seventeenth century which belong to the eighteenth, and the real nature of Puritanism can hardly be discovered at all, because Puritanism itself became two distinct and contending things to two sorts of men. The most prevalent error arising from this fact has been the identification of Puritanism with evangelicalism in many accounts, though in histories written by Unitarian scholars the original doctrine has been almost as much distorted in the opposite direction.

Among the evangelicals the original doctrines were transformed or twisted into the new versions of Protestantism that spawned in the Great Awakening of the 1740's, in the succeeding revivals along the frontier and through the back country, in the centrifugal speculations of enraptured prophets and rabid sects in the nineteenth century. All these movements retained something of the theology or revived something of the intensity of spirit, but at the same time they threw aside so much of authentic Puritanism that there can be no doubt the founding fathers would vigorously have repudiated such progeny. They would have had no use, for instance, for the camp meeting and the revivalist orgy; "hitting the sawdust trail" would have been an action exceedingly distasteful to the most ardent among them.

What we know as "fundamentalism" would have been completely antipathetic to them, for they never for one moment dreamed that the truth of scripture was to be maintained in spite of or against the evidences of reason, science, and learning. The sects that have arisen out of Puritanism have most strikingly betrayed their rebellion against the true spirit of their source by their attack upon the ideal of a learned ministry; Puritans considered religion a very complex, subtle, and highly intellectualized affair, and they trained their experts in theology with all the care we would lavish upon preparing men to be engineers or chemists. For the same reasons, Puritans would object strenuously to almost all recent attempts to "humanize" religion, to smooth over hard doctrines, to introduce sweetness and light at the cost of hardheaded realism and invincible logic. From their point of view, to bring Christ down to earth in such a fashion as is implied in statements we sometimes encounter—that He was the "first humanitarian" or that He would certainly endorse this or that political party—would seem to them frightful blasphemy. Puritanism was not only a religious creed, it was a philosophy and a metaphysic; it was an organization of man's whole life, emotional and intellectual, to a degree which has not been sustained by any denomination stemming from it. Yet because such creeds have sprung from Puritanism, the Puritans are frequently praised or blamed for qualities which never belonged to them or for ideas which originated only among their successors and which they themselves would have disowned.

On the other hand, if the line of development from Puritanism tends in one direction to frontier revivalism and evangelicalism, another line leads as directly to a more philosophical, critical, and even skeptical point of view. Unitarianism is as much the child of Puritanism as Methodism. And if the one accretion has colored or distorted our conception of the original doctrine, the other has done so no less. Descendants of the Puritans who revolted against what they considered the tyranny and cruelty of Puritan theology, who substituted taste and reason for dogma and authority and found the emotional fervor of the evangelicals so much sound and fury, have been prone to idealize their ancestors into their own image. A few decades ago it had become very much the mode to praise the Puritans for virtues which they did not possess and which they would not have considered virtues at all. In the pages of liberal historians, and above all in the speeches of Fourth of July orators, the Puritans have been hymned as the pioneers of religious liberty, though nothing was ever farther from their designs; they have been hailed as the forerunners of democracy, though if they were, it was quite beside their intention; they have been invoked in justification for an economic philosophy of free competition and laissez-faire, though they themselves believed in government regulation of business, the fixing of just prices, and the curtailing of individual profits in the interests of the welfare of the whole.[1]

The moral of these reflections may very well be that it is dangerous to read history backwards, to interpret something that was by what it ultimately became, particularly when it became several things. In order that the texts presented in this volume may be read for their proper meaning, it is necessary that the student divest himself as far as possible of those preconceptions which have been established only in later times, and approach the Puritans in terms of their own background. Only thus can we hope to understand what Puritanism was, or what it became and why. The Puritan had his defects, certainly, and he had his virtues, but the defects of one century may become the virtues of another, and what is considered commendable at one time may be viewed with horror by later generations. It is not easy to restrain one's own prejudices and to exercise the sort of historical imagination that is required for the understanding of a portion of the past according to its own intentions before we allow ourselves to judge it by our own standards. The Puritans were not a bashful race, they could speak out and did; in their own words they have painted their own portraits, their majestic strength and their dignity, their humanity and solidity, more accurately than any admirer has been able to do; and also they have betrayed the motes and beams in their own eyes more clearly than any enemy has been able to point them out.

2. The Spirit of the Age

Puritanism began as an agitation within the Church of England in the latter half of the sixteenth century. It was a movement for reform of that institution, and at the time no more

---

[1] See below p. 384. In 1639, John Cotton condemned as a "false principle" the assertion "that a man might sell as dear as he can, and buy as cheap as he can," and Mr. Robert Keayne was fined £200 by the General Court and admonished by the church of Boston for making a profit of sixpence or more in the shilling (*Winthrop's Journal*, ed. J. K. Hosmer [New York, 1908], I, 315–318).

constituted a distinct sect or denomination than the advocates
of an amendment to the Constitution of the United States constitute a separate nation. In the 1530's the Church of England
broke with the Pope of Rome. By the beginning of Elizabeth's
reign it had proceeded a certain distance in this revolt, had become Protestant, had disestablished the monasteries and corrected
many abuses. Puritanism was the belief that the reform should be
continued, that more abuses remained to be corrected, that practices still survived from the days of Popery which should be renounced, that the Church of England should be restored to the
"purity" of the first-century Church as established by Christ
Himself. In the 1560's, when the advocates of purification first acquired the name of Puritans, no one, not even the most radical,
knew exactly how far the process was to go or just what the
ultimate goal would be; down to the days of Cromwell there
was never any agreement on this point, and in the end this
failure of unanimity proved the undoing of English Puritanism.
Many Puritans desired only that certain ceremonies be abolished
or changed. Others wanted ministers to preach more sermons,
make up their own prayers on the inspiration of the moment
rather than read set forms out of a book. Others went further
and proposed a revision of the whole form of ecclesiastical government. But whatever the shade or complexion of their Puritanism,
Puritans were those who wanted to continue a movement which
was already under way. Their opponents, whom we shall speak
of as the Anglicans—though only for the sake of convenience,
because there was at that time not the remotest thought on either
side of an ultimate separation into distinct churches, and Puritans
insisted they were as stoutly loyal to the established institution
as any men in England—the Anglicans were those who felt that
with the enthronement of Elizabeth and with the "Elizabethan
Settlement" of the Church, things had gone far enough. They
wanted to call a halt, just where they were, and stabilize at that
point.

Thus the issue between the two views, though large enough,
still involved only a limited number of questions. On everything
except matters upon which the Puritans wanted further reformation, there was essential agreement. The Puritans who settled
New England were among the more radical—though by no means
the most radical that the movement produced—and even before their migration in 1630 had gone to the lengths of formu-

lating a concrete platform of church organization which they wished to see instituted in England in place of the episcopal system. Joining battle on this front gave a sufficiently extended line and provided a vast number of salients to fight over; the gulf between the belief of these Puritans and the majority in the Church of England grew so wide that at last there was no bridging it at all. But notwithstanding the depth of this divergence, the fact still remains that only certain specific questions were raised. If we take a comprehensive survey of the whole body of Puritan thought and belief as it existed in 1630 or 1640, if we make an exhaustive enumeration of ideas held by New England Puritans, we shall find that the vast majority of them were precisely those of their opponents. In other words, Puritanism was a movement toward certain ends within the culture and state of England in the late sixteenth and early seventeenth centuries; it centered about a number of concrete problems and advocated a particular program. Outside of that, it was part and parcel of the times, and its culture was simply the culture of England at that moment. It is necessary to belabor the point, because most accounts of Puritanism, emphasizing the controversial tenets, attribute everything that Puritans said or did to the fact that they were Puritans; their attitudes toward all sorts of things are pounced upon and exhibited as peculiarities of their sect, when as a matter of fact they were normal attitudes for the time. Of course, the Puritans acquired their special quality and their essential individuality from their stand on the points actually at issue, and our final conception of Puritanism must give these concerns all due importance. Yet if first of all we wish to take Puritan culture as a whole, we shall find, let us say, that about ninety per cent of the intellectual life, scientific knowledge, morality, manners and customs, notions and prejudices, was that of all Englishmen. The other ten per cent, the relatively small number of ideas upon which there was dispute, made all the difference between the Puritan and his fellow-Englishmen, made for him so much difference that he pulled up stakes in England, which he loved, and migrated to a wilderness rather than submit them to apparent defeat. Nevertheless, when we come to trace developments and influences on subsequent American history and thought, we shall find that the starting point of many ideas and practices is as apt to be found among the ninety per cent as among the ten. The task of defining Puritanism and giving an account of its culture resolves itself, therefore, into isolating first of all the larger features which were not particularly or necessarily Puritan at all, the elements in the life and society which were products of the time and place, of the background of English life and society rather than of the individual belief or peculiar creed of Puritanism.

Many of the major interests and preoccupations of the New England Puritans belong to this list. They were just as patriotic as Englishmen who remained at home. They hated Spain like poison, and France only a little less. In their eyes, as in those of Anglicans, the most important issue in the Western world was the struggle between Catholicism and Protestantism. They were not unique or extreme in thinking that religion was the primary and all-engrossing business of man, or that all human thought and action should tend to the glory of God. John Donne, Dean of St. Paul's, preached in London, "all knowledge that begins not, and ends not with his glory, is but a giddy, but a vertiginous circle, but an elaborate and exquisite ignorance"; [1] the content, though not the style, of the passage might just as well come from any Puritan preacher. Both the Anglican and the Puritan were at one in conceiving of man as sinful, they both beheld him chained and enslaved by evil until liberated by the redeeming grace of Christ. They both believed that the visible universe was under God's direct and continuous guidance, and that though effects seemed to be produced by natural causes—what at that time were called "secondary causes"—the actual government of the minutest event, the rise of the sun, the fall of a stone, the beat of the heart, was under the direct and immediate supervision of God. This conception, a fundamental one in the Puritan view of the world, was no more limited to them than their habits of eating and drinking. John Donne said:

The very calamities are from him; the deliverance from those calamities much more. All comes from God's hand; and from his hand, by way of hand-writing, by way of letter, and instruction to us. And therefore to ascribe things wholly to nature, to fortune, to power, to second causes, this is to mistake the hand, not to know God's hand; but to acknowledge it to be God's hand, and not to read it, to say that it is God's doing, and not to consider, what God intends in it, is as much a slighting of God, as the other. [2]

[1] Donne, *Works*, ed. Henry Alford (London, 1839), I, 278.
[2] *Ibid.*, p. 120.

A New England parson later in the century would preach in exactly the same vein:

His hand has made and framed the whole Fabrick of Heaven & Earth. He hath hung out the Globe of this World; hung the Earth upon nothing; drawn over the Canopy of the Heavens; laid the foundation of the earth in its place; Created that Fountain and Center of Light, Heat, & Influence in this lower World, the *Sun.* . . . The whole Administration of Providence in the Upholding and Government of all created Beings, in a way of highest Wisdom and exact Order, it is *all* His work. . . . Those notable changes in the World in the promoting or suppressing, exalting or bringing down of Kingdoms, Nations, Provinces or Persons, they are all wrought by Him. . . . The Yearly seasons, also Seed-time and Harvest, Summer and Winter, binding up and covering the earth with Frost, Ice and Snow, and the releasing and renewing of the face of the Earth again, it's His work.[1]

The great Anglican preacher said, "Even in natural things all the reason of all that is done is the power and the will of him who infused that virtue into that creature,"[2] and the president of Harvard College preached a sermon on God's governing through the natural causes that might well have taken Donne's utterance for its text (cf. pp. 350–367).

In its major aspects the religious creed of Puritanism was neither peculiar to the Puritans nor different from that of the Anglicans. Both were essentially Protestant; both asserted that men were saved by their faith, not by their deeds. The two sides could agree on the general statement that Christians are bound to believe nothing but what the Gospel teaches, that all traditions of men "contrary to the Word of God" are to be renounced and abhorred. They both believed that the marks of a true church were profession of the creed, use of Christ's sacraments, preaching of the word—Anglican sermons being as long and often as dull as the Puritan—and the union of men in profession and practice under regularly constituted pastors. The Puritans always said that they could subscribe the doctrinal articles of the Church of England; even at the height of the controversy, even after they had left England rather than put up with what they considered its abominations, they always took care to insist that the Church of England was a "true" church, not Anti-Christ as was the Church

[1] William Adams, *God's Eye on the Contrite* (Boston, 1685), pp. 6–7.
[2] Donne, *Works*, I, 33.

of Rome, that it contained many saints, and that men might find salvation within it. Throughout the seventeenth century they read Anglican authors, quoted them in their sermons, and even reprinted some of them in Boston.

The vast substratum of agreement which actually underlay the disagreement between Puritans and Anglicans is explained by the fact that they were both the heirs of the Middle Ages. They still believed that all knowledge was one, that life was unified, that science, economics, political theory, aesthetic standards, rhetoric and art, all were organized in a hierarchical scale of values that tended upward to the end-all and be-all of creation, the glory of God. They both insisted that all human activity be regulated by that purpose. Consequently, even while fighting bitterly against each other, the Puritans and Anglicans stood shoulder to shoulder against what they called "enthusiasm." The leaders of the Puritan movement were trained at the universities, they were men of learning and scholars; no less than the Anglicans did they demand that religion be interpreted by study and logical exposition; they were both resolute against all pretences to immediate revelation, against all ignorant men who claimed to receive personal instructions from God. They agreed on the essential Christian contention that though God may govern the world, He is not the world itself, and that though He instills His grace into men, He does not deify them or unite them to Himself in one personality. He converses with men only through His revealed word, the Bible. His will is to be studied in the operation of His providence as exhibited in the workings of the natural world, but He delivers no new commands or special revelations to the inward consciousness of men. The larger unanimity of the Puritans and the Anglicans reveals itself whenever either of them was called upon to confront enthusiasm. The selections given in this volume include Governor John Winthrop's account of the so-called Antinomian affair, the crisis produced in the little colony by the teachings of Mistress Anne Hutchinson in 1636 and 1637 (pp. 129–136). Beneath the theological jargon in which the opinions of this lady appear we can see the substance of her contention, which was that she was in direct communication with the Godhead, and that she therefore was prepared to follow the promptings of the voice within against all the precepts of the Bible, the churches, reason, or the government of Massachusetts Bay. Winthrop relates how the magistrates and the ministers defended the community against this perversion of the doctrine of regeneration, but the tenor of his condemnation would have been duplicated practically word for word had Anne Hutchinson broached her theories in an Anglican community. The Anglicans fell in completely with the Puritans when both of them were confronted in the 1650's by the Quakers. All New England leaders saw in the Quaker doctrine of an inner light, accessible to all men and giving a perfect communication from God to their inmost spirits, just another form of Anne Hutchinson's blasphemy. John Norton declared that the "light of nature" itself taught us that "madmen acting according to their frantick passions are to be restrained with chaines, when they can not be restrained otherwise." [1] About the same time George Hickes, Dean of Worcester, was advocating that Quakers be treated likewise in England, and he ended a sermon upon them by calling them "Imposters, or enthusiasts, and Blasphemers of the Holy Ghoast." [2] Enthusiasts, whether Antinomian or Quaker, were proposing doctrines that threatened the unity of life by subduing the reason and the intellect to the passions and the emotions. Whatever their differences, Puritans and Anglicans were struggling to maintain a complete harmony of reason and faith, science and religion, earthly dominion and the government of God. When we immerse ourselves in the actual struggle, the difference between the Puritan and the Anglican may seem to us immense; but when we take the vantage point of subsequent history, and survey religious thought as a whole over the last three centuries, the two come very close together on essentials. Against all forms of chaotic emotionalism, against all over-simplifications of theology, learning, philosophy, and science, against all materialism, positivism or mechanism, both were endeavoring to uphold a symmetrical union of heart and head without impairment of either. By the beginning or middle of the next century their successors, both in England and America, found themselves no longer capable of sustaining this unity, and it has yet to be re-achieved today, if achieved again it ever can be. The greatness of the Puritans is not so much that they conquered a wilderness, or that they carried a religion into it, but that they carried a religion which, narrow and starved though it may have been in some respects, deficient

[1] *The Heart of N-England Rent at the Blasphemies of the Present Generation* (Cambridge, 1659), p. 39.
[2] Paul Elmer More and Frank Leslie Cross, *Anglicanism* (1935), pp. 68, 84.

in sensuous richness or brilliant color, was nevertheless indis-
solubly bound up with an ideal of culture and learning. In contrast to all other pioneers, they made no concessions to the forest,
but in the midst of frontier conditions, in the very throes of
clearing the land and erecting shelters, they maintained schools
and a college, a standard of scholarship and of competent writing,
a class of men devoted entirely to the life of the mind and of
the soul.

Because the conflict between the Puritans and the Churchmen
was as much an intellectual and scholarly issue as it was emotional,
it was in great part a debate among pundits. This is not to say
that passions were not involved; certainly men took sides because
of prejudice, interest, irrational conviction, or for any of the motives that may incite the human race to conflict. The disagreement finally was carried from the field of learned controversy to
the field of battle. There can be no doubt that many of the people
in England, or even in New England, became rabid partisans and
yet never acquired the erudition necessary to understand the intricate and subtle arguments of their leaders. A great number,
perhaps even a majority, in both camps were probably not intelligent or learned enough to see clearly the reasons for the
cause they supported. Thomas Hooker, the clerical leader of the
settlement of Connecticut—and therefore the dominant figure in
that community—said frankly, "I can speak it by experience, that
the meaner ordinary sort of people, it is incredible and uncon-
ceiveable, what Ignorance is among them." [1] This being the case,
we who are today being made all too familiar with the horrors
of the art of "popularization," can only marvel at how little allowance the divines made for the ignorance or the simplicity of
the average man in the addresses and sermons they delivered to
him. It is true, several Anglicans began to feel, after the dispute
became acrimonious, that the wind of doctrine ought perhaps to
be tempered to the uneducated lamb; the authorities ordered
parish priests not to discuss the more difficult points of specula-

[1] *The Soules Preparation for Christ* (London, 1632), p. 70; the sermons in this volume
were delivered in England, so that Hooker was here speaking of the level of knowledge
among the English people, which was of course much lower than among the select
group that settled New England; New England Puritans were undoubtedly much
more skilled in following the logic of theology, and they received a thorough and
lifelong course of instruction in Sunday sermons and Thursday lectures. Even so, as
Winthrop points out in describing the Antinomian agitation, the debate on the theology
soon got over the heads of the many (p. 131).

tion before all the people.[1] The Puritans would not show their
people any such mercy. They endeavored to assist the feebler
understandings of their congregations by using the simplest and
most comprehensible style, by employing a schematic organization for their sermons, with heads and subheads so clearly marked
that earnest listeners could take notes and study the points during the week, and by eschewing Latin quotations or glittering
phrases that might distract attention from content to form. But
these were the only sort of crutches that Puritan ministers would
allow to the rank and file for helping them over the hard parts
of divinity. Of course many texts from scripture permitted sermons
that were relatively simple and ethical, but others raised per-
plexing enigmas, discussion of which the Medieval Church had
restricted to the schools; Puritans took each kind as it came and
did not flinch from struggling in the pulpit with the difficult
ones any more than from expounding the more obvious. Thomas
Hooker told his people that they were responsible for acquiring a certain amount of knowledge if they expected to be saved:

Its with an ignorant sinner in the midst of all means as with a
sick man remaining in an Apothecaries shop, ful of choycest
Medicines in the darkest night: though there be the choycest of
all receipts at hand, and he may take what he needs, yet because
he cannot see what he takes, and how to use them, he may kill
himself or encrease his distempers, but never cure any disease.[2]

The wonder is that by and large the populace did yield their
judgments to those who were supposed to know, respected learning and supported it, sat patiently during two- and three-hour
sermons while ministers expounded the knottiest and most recon-

---

[1] The Anglican disposition to refrain from discussing the unfathomable mysteries
of the creed before the laity was reinforced by a strategic consideration; the people
enjoyed listening to highly technical discussions of subtle points and flocked to Puritan
sermons for that reason. The English officials believed that Puritan sermons simply
inflamed popular passions without elevating the public intelligence, and therefore
endeavored to restrict the discussion of unanswerable questions. As the controversy
widened the leading Anglicans turned against the theology of rigorous predestination
and reprobation—which had been generally accepted by the first bishops of Elizabeth's
reign—and identified Puritan theology with the Puritan program in church and state;
the effect on the Puritans was to make them all the more determined that no subject,
no matter how involved, should be kept out of the pulpits, and that the people should
be lifted by main force to the highest possible pitch of understanding. Particularly
were they resolved that predestination should be thoroughly thrashed out for the
benefit of the populace.

[2] *The Application of Redemption* (London, 1659), pp. 89–90; these sermons were delivered in Connecticut.

dite of metaphysical texts. The testimony of visitors, travelers, and memoirs agrees that during the Puritan age in New England the common man, the farmer and merchant, was amazingly versed in systematic divinity. A gathering of yeomen and "hired help" around the kitchen fire of an evening produced long and unbelievably technical discussions of predestination, infant damnation, and the distinctions between faith and works. In the first half of the seventeenth century the people had not yet questioned the conception of religion as a difficult art in which the authority of the skilled dialectician should prevail over the inclinations of the merely devout. This ideal of subjection to qualified leadership was social as well as intellectual. Very few Englishmen had yet broached the notion that a lackey was as good as a lord, or that any Tom, Dick, or Harry, simply because he was a good, honest man, could understand the Sermon on the Mount as well as a Master of Arts from Oxford, Cambridge, or Harvard. Professor Morison has shown that the life of the college in New England was saved by the sacrifice of the yeomen farmers, who contributed their pecks of wheat, wrung from a stony soil, taken from their none too opulent stores, to support teaching fellows and to assist poor scholars at Harvard College, in order that they and their children might still sit under a literate ministry "when our present Ministers shall lie in the Dust." [1]

When we say that the majority of the people in the early seventeenth century still acceded to the dictation of the learned in religion and the superior in society, we must also remark that the Puritan leaders were in grave danger of arousing a revolt against themselves by their very own doctrines. Puritans were attacking the sacerdotal and institutional bias which had survived in the Church of England; they were maintaining a theology that brought every man to a direct experience of the spirit and removed intermediaries between himself and the deity. Yet the authority of the infallible church and the power of the bishops had for centuries served to keep the people docile. Consequently when the Puritan leaders endeavored to remove the bishops and to deny that the Church should stand between God and man, they ran the hazard of starting something among the people that might get out of hand. Just as the Puritan doctrine that men were saved by the infusion of God's grace could lead to the An-

[1] Morison, _The Founding of Harvard College_ (1935), p. 318; _Harvard College in the Seventeenth Century_, p. 28.

tinomianism of Mrs. Hutchinson, and often did warrant the simple in concluding that if they had God's grace in them they needed to pay no heed to what a minister told them, so the Puritan contention that regenerate men were illuminated with divine truth might lead to the belief that true religion did not need the assistance of learning, books, arguments, logical demonstrations, or classical languages. There was always a possibility that Puritanism would raise up a fanatical anti-intellectualism, and against such a threat the Puritan ministers constantly braced themselves. It was no accident that the followers of Mrs. Hutchinson, who believed that men could receive all the necessary instructions from within, also attacked learning and education, and came near to wrecking not only the colony but the college as well.[1] Edward Johnson, stout militia captain of the town of Woburn, and no intellectual, set forth the anguish of soul through which he passed while the citizens of Boston were under the spell of "Jezebel" (p. 158); he was particularly shocked to hear one of the heretics say flatly, "I had rather hear such a one that speakes from the meere motion of the spirit, without any study at all, then any of your learned Scollers, although they may be fuller of Scripture." [2] Puritanism was forever giving rise to such rebellions against its own ideal of learned religion; the experience of Massachusetts with the Hutchinsonians in the 1630's was only a premonition of what England was to encounter in the 1650's, when the Civil Wars generated not one form of Antinomianism but a thousand. Anabaptists and Fifth Monarchy men then began to vaunt that an ignorant man inspired with the spirit made a better preacher than one who had attended the "cob-webbed Universities," and in the disturbed state of society found an opportunity to spread their dangerous opinions among the people. The true Puritans were forced to resort to repressive measures to save Puritanism itself. Oliver Cromwell was the most liberal of seventeenth-century Puritan leaders; it is his eternal glory that he did not confront with the sword all the zealots who ran riot over the land, but strove to work out a scheme of toleration for as many of them as would behave with civil decency. But even Cromwell had to draw the line somewhere, and he drew it when the upsurge of popular religious frenzies turned against the universities and the learned ministry. His assumption of the dic-

[1] Morison, *The Founding of Harvard College*, chap. XIII.
[2] *The Wonder-working Providence*, ed. J. F. Jameson (New York, 1910), p. 128.

tatorship in 1653, unlike later seizures of arbitrary power, was
prompted in great part by his determination to protect a sober
and instructed clergy and the universities from an assault by
the lunatic fringe in his own party.[1] Cromwell's New England
brethren thoroughly sympathized with his efforts, but they thought
he had invited the trouble by allowing ignorant men to preach
at all; they looked upon his policy of toleration as the sole stain
upon the otherwise flawless record of the pre-eminent warrior
saint of the age. They were determined to run no such risks in
their communities. They would have the rabble entirely submissive to the intellectual aristocracy, even though many or all of
the mass were supposedly saints of God.

Both Cromwell and the New England leaders were face to face
with a problem as old as the history of the Christian Church.
Throughout the Middle Ages there had been such stirrings among
the people as those to which Mrs. Hutchinson or the Fifth Monarchy Men gave voice. The great scholastic synthesis always remained incomprehensible to the vulgar, who demanded to be fed
again and again with the sort of religious sustenance they craved.
The Reformation drew upon these suppressed desires. Common
men turned Protestant primarily because Protestantism offered
them a religion which more effectively satisfied their spiritual
hunger. Yet in Europe theologians and metaphysicians retained
the leadership and kept Protestantism from becoming merely an
emotional outburst. They supplied it with a theology which,
though not so sophisticated as scholastic dogma, was still equipped
with a logic and organon of rational demonstration. Though
Protestantism can be viewed as a "liberation" of the common
man, it was far from being a complete emancipation of the individual. It freed him from many intellectual restraints that had
been imposed by the Church, but it did not give him full liberty
to think anything he pleased; socially it freed him from many
exactions, but it did not permit him to abandon his traditional
subjection to his social and ecclesiastical superiors. The original
settlers of New England carried this Protestantism intact from
Europe to America. Except for the small band that was driven
into exile with Anne Hutchinson, and one or two other groups
of visionaries who also were hustled across the borders into Rhode
Island, the rank and file did follow their leaders, meekly and
reverently. Captain Johnson probably represents the average lay-

[1] David Masson, *The Life of John Milton* (London, 1877), IV, 566 ff.

man's loyalty to the clergy. The New England "theocracy" was simply a Protestant version of the European social ideal, and except for its Protestantism was thoroughly medieval in character.

It was only as the seventeenth century came to a close that the imported structure began to show the strain. In Europe social tradition had conspired with the ministers to check enthusiasts in religion and "levellers" in society; in England the authorities, whether Anglican or Puritan, royal or Cromwellian, were able to suppress the assault upon the scholarly and aristocratic ideal. In America the character of the people underwent a change; they moved further into the frontier, they became more absorbed in business and profits than in religion and salvation, their memories of English social stratification grew dim. A preacher before the General Court in 1705 bewailed the effects of the frontier in terms that have been echoed by "Easterners" for two hundred years and more; men were no longer living together, he said, in compact communities, under the tutelage of educated clergymen and under the discipline of an ordered society, but were taking themselves into remote corners "for worldly conveniences." "By that means [they] have seemed to bid defiance, not only to Religion, but to Civility it self: and such places thereby have become Nurseries of Ignorance, Prophaneness and Atheism." [1] In America the frontier conspired with the popular disposition to lessen the prestige of the cultured classes and to enhance the social power of those who wanted their religion in a more simple, downright and "democratic" form, who cared nothing for the refinements and subtleties of historic theology. Not until the decade of the Great Awakening did the popular tendency receive distinct articulation through leaders who openly renounced the older conception, but for half a century or more before 1740 its obstinate persistence can be traced in the condemnations of the ministers.

The Puritan leaders could withstand this rising tide of democracy only by such support as the government would give them—which became increasingly less after the new charter of 1692 took away from the saints all power to select their own governors and divorced the state and church—or else by the

---

[1] Joseph Easterbrooks, *Abraham the Passenger* (Boston, 1705), p. 3; cf. Increase Mather as early as 1677: "People are ready to run wild into the woods again and to be as Heathenish as ever, if you do not prevent it" (*A Discourse Concerning the Danger of Apostacy* [Boston, 1679], 2d ed., 1685, p. 104).

sheer force of their personalities. As early as the 1660's and 70's
we can see them beginning to shift their attentions from mere
exposition of the creed to greater and greater insistence upon
committing power only to men of wisdom and knowledge. William
Hubbard in an election sermon of 1676 told the citizens that piety
alone in a ruler was not enough; magistrates should be such "as
by the benefit of natural parts Experience, Education, and study,
have advantage above others to be acquainted with the affairs
of the world abroad, as well as with the Laws and Customes of
their own people at home." [1] By the beginning of the eighteenth
century the task of buttressing the classified society, maintaining
the rule of the well-trained and the culturally superior both in
church and society seems to have become the predominant concern of the clergy. Sermon after sermon reveals that in their
eyes the cause of learning and the cause of a hierarchical, dif-
ferentiated social order were one and the same. For example,
Ebenezer Pemberton, who was a tutor at Harvard College and
then colleague minister with Samuel Willard at the Old South
Church, delivered a funeral sermon upon the death of the Honourable John Walley, member of the council and judge, in 1711.
Judge Walley, said Pemberton, rendered his country great service; there are various ways in which the country can be served.
One of them is by the promotion of "good literature":

This is necessary for the true prosperity and happiness of a
people. *Greece* and *Rome* are more renowned for the flourishing
state of learning in them, than for their arms. This has for ever
been in highest esteem among civilized nations. . . . The more of
good literature civil rulers are furnished with, the more capable
they are to discharge their trust to the honour and safety of their
people. And learning is no less necessary, as an ordinary medium
to secure the glory of Christ's visible kingdom. Without a good
measure of this the truth can't be explained, asserted and demonstrated; nor errors detected and the heretick baffled . . . When
ignorance and barbarity invade a generation, their glory is laid
in the dust; and the ruin of all that is great and good among them
will soon follow. [2]

A second way in which the welfare of the nation is served is by
each and every person's keeping to his proper station:

[1] *The Happiness of a People* (Boston, 1676), p. 28.
[2] *Sermons and Discourses on Several Occasions* (London, 1727), pp. 212–213.

This intends that we keep within the *line* and *place*, that providence has set us . . . We must not without God's call quit our post, thrust our selves into *anothers province*, with a conceit that *there* we may best serve, and promote the good of the world. But herein observe the will of God by keeping to the service that belongs to our station, which providence has made our peculiar business. Thus every man is to serve his generation by moving in his own orb; and discharging those offices that belong to that order that the government of heaven has assigned him to.[1]

Leadership by the learned and dutiful subordination of the unlearned—as long as the original religious creed retained its hold upon the people these exhortations were heeded; in the eighteenth century, as it ceased to arouse their loyalties, they went seeking after gods that were utterly strange to Puritanism. They demanded fervent rather than learned ministers and asserted the equality of all men.

Thus Puritanism appears, from the social and economic point of view, to have been a philosophy of social stratification, placing the command in the hands of the properly qualified and demanding implicit obedience from the uneducated; from the religious point of view it was the dogged assertion of the unity of intellect and spirit in the face of a rising tide of democratic sentiment suspicious of the intellect and intoxicated with the spirit. It was autocratic, hierarchical, and authoritarian. It held that in the intellectual realm holy writ was to be expounded by right reason, that in the social realm the expounders of holy writ were to be the mentors of farmers and merchants. Yet in so far as Puritanism involved such ideals it was simply adapting to its own purposes the ideals of the age. Catholics in Spain and in Spanish America pursued the same objectives, and the Puritans were no more rigorous in their application of an autocratic standard than King Charles himself endeavored to be—and would have been had he not been balked in the attempt.

3. *Puritan Humanism*

There is another body of assumptions, besides those underlying the Puritan philosophy of religion and of religious learning, which Puritans shared in common with Anglicans and even with Catholics. They were the heirs not only of medieval Christianity and of the Reformation, but also of the Renaissance—they were

[1] *Ibid.*, pp. 220–221.

humanists. They were students of the recently revived and re-
discovered classical literature, and they shared in the reinvigoration of mind and spirit which that literature inspired in Western
Europe. Their theology undoubtedly stood in the way of un-
restricted appreciation, yet in the amount of Greek and Roman
writing they could enjoy and utilize, they fell very little short of
the most liberal of Anglican scholars. That a Puritan writer could
be no less devoted to classical literature than his opponent, in
spite of his theology, is demonstrated most conspicuously by John
Milton. The miraculous fusion of Puritanism and Hellenism which
he achieved is unique only in his grandeur of expression; the same
combination of religious dogma with the classics, of Protestant
theology and ancient morality, was the aim of the curriculum
at Harvard College, and it was sustained, though on a rudi-
mentary or pedestrian level, in the sermons of Yankee parsons
throughout the seventeenth century.

The humanist learning had already become a regular part of
the studies in the English Universities when the men who were
to be ministers and magistrates in New England matriculated
there. Those institutions were no longer training students solely
for the ministry; they were also training men to be scholars in
the classics, or even to be simply "gentlemen." [1] The same trinity
of intentions was continued at Harvard. Tutor William Brattle
declared in a college oration in 1689, "Liberali liberaliter instituendi"—that is, "Gentlemen must be educated like gentlemen." [2] Just how extensive a role the classics played in Puritan
education can best be seen by a reading of the chapters on the
subject in Professor Morison's history of Harvard College.[3] It is
enough to say here that study of the arts and sciences and of good
literature was among the purposes of education in New England
as well as the learning of theology. The General Court itself
went on record, in the name of all the citizens and presumably
without dissent from the other inhabitants of Massachusetts, that
though learning, "namely, skill in the tongues & liberall artes,"
might not be absolutely necessary "for the beinge of a common
wealth & churches, yet we conceive that the judgment of the
godly wise, it is beyond all question, not only laudable, but necessary for the beinge of the same." [4] In a sermon of 1677, Increase

[1] Morison, *The Founding of Harvard College*, pp. 50 ff.
[2] Morison, *Harvard College in the Seventeenth Century*, p. 165.
[3] *Ibid.*, chaps. VII–XIV.
[4] *Massachusetts Records*, ed. N. B. Shurtleff (Boston, 1853–1854), III, 279.

Mather told the legislature that they must take care of the schools
and the college, "that so there might be able instruments raised
up for the propagating of Truth in succeeding Generations. And
some have well & truly observed, that the Interest of Religion
and good Literature, hath risen and fallen together." [1] Mather's
conception of what constitutes "good literature" might not coin-
cide with what we mean by the phrase, but it would include a
knowledge of the poetry, drama, and history of the ancient world,
and an ability to write sentences which would not appear utterly
contemptible when compared with those of classical authors.

Thanks to the labors of Professor Morison, we may now rest
assured that the Puritans of New England were the disciples of
Erasmus and Colet. The question with which we are concerned
in the present context is what part of the Puritan mentality must
be put down to their participation in the humanist tradition.
How much of what Puritans said and did, how much of their
belief and their judgment, is to be attributed not so much to
their Puritanism as to their education? Latin and Greek contributed more to the Puritan mind than a method of pedagogy
or an exercise in grammar. When these tongues were the foundation of the training for an A.B., and when there existed no alternative S.B. by which, as Dean Briggs remarked, the college
could graduate a man with a sealed certification that he was
totally ignorant of them, then it was inevitable that Puritan
thought would appropriate some ideas from Hesiod or Horace,
some wisdom from Plato, or even some wit from Plautus.

From the evidence afforded by Puritan sermons and polemics
it seems clear that the tendency of the humanist culture was to
accentuate the element of rationalism, to enlarge the sphere of
competence of the natural reason even when not inspired with
God's special grace. Neither the Puritans nor the most anti-
Puritanical bishops in the early seventeenth century would have
entertained for a moment the idea that merely natural training,
civilized morality, and gentlemanly culture could get a man to
heaven; both would have admitted that many souls can be and
are saved without such embellishments. But they both would
have agreed that, by and large, men who are called by God
will heed the summons all the better if they know Latin, Greek,
and Hebrew. John Cotton said that if knowledge is but an empty
speculation or a mere collection of facts it will bring forth no

---

[1] *A Discourse Concerning the Danger of Apostasy*, pp. 100–101.

"heat"; but though "knowledge is no knowledge without zeal," on the other hand it is equally true that "zeale is but a wilde-fire without knowledge." [1] The great heathen moralists, particularly the Stoics, above all Seneca and Plutarch, [2] inculcated a system of ethics that was in effect so close to the precepts of Puritanism that the divines could never find it in their hearts to envisage these noble heathens languishing in the same Hell to which they consigned the minions of Anti-Christ and the deluded followers of Mistress Hutchinson, any more than Dante could confine Vergil to the Inferno. Increase Mather reveals significantly the alacrity with which a Puritan theologian made room on his shelves for the books of pagan Greece and Rome:

Some among the Heathen have been notable *Moralists*, such as *Cato*, *Seneca*, Aristides, &c. And although we must not say that their Morality saved them, yet it was not altogether unprofitable to them, for God did therefore reward them with many outward blessings, and they did thereby escape many temporal Judgements, which otherwise would have befallen them: And they had more quietness in their own spirits, then otherwise would have been, being freed from those stinging Accusations of Conscience, which more profane sinners, that usually have an Hell in their Consciences, are daily tormented with. Moreover, their punishment in another world will not be so great, as of those that have been of a vicious Conversation. [3]

Hence in the sermons of Puritan ministers, side by side with passages of scripture, appear examples of the wisdom of Greece, episodes from the lives of Plutarch, tart sayings from Aristophanes,

---

[1] *Christ the Fountaine of Life* (London, 1651), p. 145.

[2] For the estimation in which Plutarch in particular was held, see the commendations of Cotton Mather (p. 169) and the citations made by John Wise (pp. 260–261). There is no better way of perceiving how the lamb of classical culture could lie down with the lion of Puritan theology than by reading Plutarch's *Lives*, then available to all literate men in the great translation of Sir Thomas North. Compare, for example, the Puritan theory of nature with the attitude expressed in Plutarch's remarks in the life of Pericles on the two approaches to natural phenomena of Lampon the diviner and Anaxagoras the philosopher; Lampon interprets the discovery of a ram with one horn as a portent, while Anaxagoras splits open the skull to demonstrate a natural cause for the monstrosity; Plutarch comments that the wise man will say both were right, one finding the cause by which it was produced, the other the end for which it was designed. There could be no better statement of the Puritan theory of the concurrence of God's determination and the secondary cause, or no better exposition of the Puritan attitude toward "divine providences." Seneca was so congenial to the Puritan temper that scholars strained to the limit the tradition that he had been in correspondence with St. Paul and was secretly a Christian.

[3] *Wo to Drunkards*, p. 15.

hard realism from Thucydides. Plato serves as an authority for the principles of society, subordinated of course to the Word of God, but agreeing with it nevertheless; and when a minister, painting the splendors of future bliss, wants to make clear to his auditors that the sorrows and tribulations of this life will then seem sweet in retrospect, he can find no better words to project into the Christian heaven than those of the Roman Vergil, "Haec olim meminisse Juvabit." [1] Some of the clergy carried their veneration of classical precedents to lengths that seemed dangerous to less venturesome Puritans. When Nathaniel Ward was invited by the deputies to deliver the election sermon in 1641, he grounded "his propositions much upon the old Roman and Grecian governments" (cf. p. 205). John Winthrop, the governor, thought this a little unnecessary, and protested that Christians ought to stick to the Bible and not go hunting for lessons in "those heathen commonwealths." The ministers apparently hastened to reassure him that such a mode of reasoning was perfectly orthodox; the Reverend Thomas Shepard, minister at Cambridge, wrote to him, "Your apprehensions agaynst reading & learning heathen authors, I perswade myselfe were suddenly suggested," and told him that if he would impart his objections to Brother Dunster, the president of Harvard College, they would readily be answered. [2]

The remarkable fact concerning the mental life of these Puritans is that more of them did not share Winthrop's apprehensions. Every appeal to classical models, every invocation of wisdom which men had achieved without the assistance of grace, was in effect a confession that they did not believe man was hopelessly corrupt or too abysmally sinful. Every such passage was by implication an acknowledgment that natural reason had its place in the scheme of things, and a respectable place, that natural man, employing reason, was not quite a contemptible worm. Elnathan Chauncy, when a student at Harvard in the late 1650's, copied into his commonplace book a passage from van Helmont's *Ternary of Paradoxes* which ran thus:

Truth and the rational soule are twins. For so uncessant a magnetisme or congenerous love doth the soule hold unto the truth, that she can Know no reall or permanent satisfaction, in the fruition of any other object. [3]

[1] Jonathan Mitchell, *A Discourse of the Glory To which God hath called Believers* (London, 1677), pp. 128–129.
[2] *Collections of the Massachusetts Historical Society*, Ser. 4, VII, 272.
[3] Morison, *Harvard College in the Seventeenth Century*, p. 130.

Truly, if the Puritans had been as they are often pictured, merely dogmatic Calvinists, holding a brutal and ironclad theory of innate depravity and original sin, the young student would have been playing with fire even to have let his eyes rest upon such a passage. But his jotting down this aphorism was nothing startling in the life of a Puritan. That man was, however much deformed by sin and passion, essentially a rational and responsible being was just as much an axiom of their thought as that he needed to wait upon God for the special grace that would bring him to salvation. How they reconciled the two beliefs is a complicated story, but for the moment it is necessary to make clear that the conception of man as competent to judge on the basis of his innate reason was perfectly acceptable in Puritan thought, and that it was confirmed and sustained by the influence of classical literature. [1] John Cotton said that reason flows from the soul of man and is an inherent part of it; we learn much by experience and education, he said, "yet there is also an essentiall wisdome in us, namely, our Reason which is natural." [2] William Hubbard spoke to the General Court of "Reason, our most faithful and best Councellour." [3] The first body of College Laws at Harvard required the student to be able not merely to read Scripture, but "to Resolve them Logically." [4] It was not enough for the Puritan minister to read his text and apply it as the mood or the spirit

[1] Among the theses defended at Harvard commencements there appear frequently "Voluntas est libera" (The will is free, e.g. 1653 Theses Physicae No. 15) and other enhancements of human ability, such as "An discrimen boni & mali à lege Naturae cognoscatur" (Whether discrimination of good and evil may be known by the light of nature, 1663 Quaestiones No. 3), "An Homo sit Causa libera suarum Actionum" (May man be the free cause of his own actions, 1669 Quaestiones No. 2) affirmed by John Richardson, "Anima Rationalis Creatur" (The soul is created rational, 1670 Theses Physicae No. 8), "An notitia Dei sit homini naturalis" (Whether the conception of God may be natural to man, 1679 Quaestiones No. 2) affirmed by Thomas Brattle, and again by Samuel Russell (1684 Quaestiones No. 6), "An Cognitio Dei sit Homini Naturalis" (Whether cognition of God may be natural to man, 1693 Quaestiones No. 5) affirmed by Joseph Whiting, "An Detur Actio humana involuntaria" (Whether there exists involuntary human action, 1704 Quaestiones No. 16) denied by Ephraim Woodbridge. (See Morison, *Harvard College in the Seventeenth Century*, Appendix B.) These are picked at random, but they demonstrate that, along with the theological conception of man as bound in sin and dependent upon divine grace, there flourished also the conception of man as responsible, free to choose between good and evil, naturally imbued with at least the glimmerings of some good principles.
[2] *A Practical Commentary . . . upon The First Epistle Generall of John* (London, 1656), p. 8.
[3] *The Happiness of a People*, p. 32.
[4] Morison, *The Founding of Harvard College*, p. 337.

dictated; interpretation of scripture was an abstruse art, to be learned with diligence, to be employed with caution, and to be regulated by the immutable laws of right reason and infallible logic. There is a vast difference between this point of view and the evangelical Protestantism which so largely replaced it in subsequent centuries. To define that difference—the actual antagonism of the two—is not easy, because the evangelicals arrayed their thought in theological terms which to our undiscriminating eyes seem almost identical; yet the difference can be dramatized at once if we compare the use made of scripture in the ordinary revival sermon with the manner in which the Puritan minister declared that scripture was to be interpreted:

Sapience or Wisdome properly belongs to Syllogistical Judgement, and is a virtue of the Understanding, whereby a man discerns the dependance of things, and how one follows upon another. [It] imports in it a laying of things together in a Syllogistical way. Hence when men reason amiss, and conclude that which is not virtually contained in the Premises, or make wrong inferences, they are said to Paralogize themselves. . . . Wisdome lyes in the *Rational Application* of general Rules of Scripture to our selves and our own conditions, and in the *induction of particulars*, and due Reasoning from it.[1]

The "enthusiast" who rushes from his helter-skelter reading into some crack-brained interpretation, or the exuberant fanatic who, without the training of the scholar, the critic, the logician, and the linguist, jumps to the conclusion that he as well as any man can read and understand the word of God—these men "paralogize themselves." There was hardly a greater sin in the Puritan decalogue.

The remark of John Cotton which we have just quoted, that an essential wisdom dwells within us which is natural reason, if read hastily may seem a dull platitude, but Cotton's putting it in precisely these terms made it a very vital sentence. For to define human reason in this manner was to take sides in a great intellectual revolution that had been fought all over Europe during the previous century. The combined force of the Protestant revolt against the Papacy and of the humanistic protest against the barbarities of the Dark Ages had inspired a widespread rejection of the authority and method of scholasticism. Protestant and humanist altered their allegiance to that magnificent structure

[1] Urian Oakes, *New-England Pleaded with* (Cambridge, 1673), pp. 11–12.

which the medieval schoolmen had erected as a monument to
the marriage of reason and faith, the Protestant because the
system was identified in his mind with Catholicism, the humanist because it had become decayed, lopsided, and fantastic. The
humanist criticism was the more pertinent. The beautiful symmetry of the scholastic philosophy, as it exists in the work of
Thomas Aquinas, had been destroyed and perverted by the lesser
lights of the fifteenth century; in the eyes of intelligent men,
scholasticism by 1500 had become a pointless game of farfetched
logic-chopping, the deductive process gone mad, a construction
of syllogisms for the sake of syllogisms, and an elaborate trick of
speaking nonsense through a series of intellectual handsprings.
Puritan and Anglican ministers were at one in their condemnation of the schoolmen. John Donne said that in order to define
ignorance, "the schools have made so many divisions, and subdivisions, and re-divisions, and post-divisions of ignorance, that
there goes as much learning to understand ignorance, as knowledge." [1] John Cotton fulminated against "the subtilty and sophistry of the School-men, suppressing the reading of the Scriptures,
and mixing Philosophy with Divinity, that they might as well
have studied a point of *Aristotle* as their divinity, and make as
good use of the one as of the other." [2] In understanding Puritan
thought, we must remember that much of it was conditioned,
like all Protestantism, by its active hostility to a method of thinking which, having prevailed for several centuries, was now believed to be prostituted to the ambitions of the Papacy, and
become the source of all the mischief and "superstition" in the
Church of Rome. [3]

Yet for men in that period to purge their minds entirely of
scholasticism was almost impossible, for in many fields there
existed nothing else to turn to. In so far as scholasticism was a
defence of the Church of Rome, the Puritans could push it aside
and set up the Bible. But in so far as scholasticism was a theory
of physics and of the natural constitution of the world, it was
more difficult for them to scuttle it, because, though they of course
did not know it, they lived during that hiatus in scientific history
when the old was disappearing but the new had not yet sufficiently emerged. Puritans were cordial enough to the new science

[1] *Works*, I, 536.
[2] *An Exposition upon The Thirteenth Chapter of the Revelation* (London, 1656), p. 27.
[3] Cf. Morison, *Harvard College in the Seventeenth Century*, pp. 130–131.

as it did emerge during the seventeenth century, but when New England was founded and Harvard College begun, though the literary culture of Humanism had been successfully absorbed into the Puritan intellect, the mathematical method had not yet been established to supply a coherent account of the natural universe. Consequently, in physics the Puritan retained his scholasticism, and only gradually abandoned it as the triumph of Newtonian physics became assured.[1] But the important point is this: absurd as scholasticism may seem to one familiar with modern science, futile as may seem its explanations by means of qualities and quiddities, rather than of quantities and motions, still to any one who had yet to learn the newer hypotheses, scholastic physics gave an account of the natural world which was at any rate orderly, sensible, regular, and causal. Oakes's sermon on the efficacy of divine providence (pp. 350–367) is still speaking of natural processes in scholastic language, and the point of his discourse is that God can interrupt or reverse the laws of physics, and that even when they operate undisturbed they produce only effects ordered by God; yet the inference throughout is that in ordinary life, day in and day out, the processes of nature follow regular and predictable laws. That the Puritans in their conception of physics retained the terminology and notions of scholasticism was an inevitable result of their living when and where they did; that they retained of scholasticism primarily its physics meant that there was no essential connection between scholastic science and religious dogma, so that, although some of the more conservative were reluctant to change, Puritans on the whole were quite willing to abandon the old theories for the new when the new had proved their case. The theological moral of the natural world seemed to such a man as Oakes the same, whether the natural world were explained as forms and substances, or as atoms and motion.

It was in the realm of logic that the revolt against scholasticism left the most important mark upon Puritan culture. The Protestant, reinforced by the humanist, or rather by his own humanism, found that scholasticism had become a stagnant and barren way of thinking, it had become over-subtle, irresponsible, formal; the new learning demanded that rational men go about thinking in straightforward, commonsense terms, that they go directly to the point and keep out of the tangled labyrinth of scholastic involu-

[1] *Ibid.*, pp. 224–251.

tions. Various churches and various groups of scholars devised
their own methods for replacing the logic of the schoolmen, but
for the Puritans of New England there was one man above all
to whom they looked for guidance in the management of reason
—the great French Protestant, a martyr in the St. Bartholomew
massacre, Petrus Ramus.[1]

Ramus, as his name was Latinized, or Pierre de la Ramée as
he was christened, was as much a figure in the Protestant world
of the 1630's as Charles Darwin in the scientific world of the
1930's. He was the great discoverer and formulator in the preceding century of a method that seemed to promise liberation from
the tyranny of outworn notions, and he seemed to have inaugurated a new era in the history of thought. Ramus electri-
fied the learned in 1536 by maintaining, as his Master of Arts thesis,
that "all that Aristotle has said is forged," which was equivalent to saying that the doctors and professors of the Church had
been wasting their time, because the scholastic discipline was
based upon Aristotle. To make good his word, Ramus spent the
rest of his life producing a staggering array of books on almost
every major subject, to show in each field wherein Aristotelian
and scholastic doctrine had been wrong, and wherein the correct
method should consist. Ramus was primarily a humanist: he did
not become converted to Protestantism until 1561, but his assas-
sination enshrined him forever in Protestant sentiment. What
Protestantism found most valuable in his voluminous work was
his logic; it was carried by his disciples to England, was particularly cultivated at the University of Cambridge, and so became the standard method followed by the New England divines
in their reasoning and in their sermonizing. They naturally carried
it to New England, and though at Harvard College the scholastic
method was also taught [2]—on the theory that ministers needed
to know all doctrines, even if only to refute them—the Ramean
method was the one approved. In the course of the century the
mathematical method of the new science, the method of Descartes,
and the inductive method of Baconian investigation became
known, and Puritans maintained a hospitable mind toward
them all.[3] They were able to do so in large part because the
teaching of Ramus was, as it now seems to us, a preparation

[1] Cf. Morison, *Harvard College in the Seventeenth Century*, pp. 185–190.
[2] *Ibid.*, p. 193.
[3] *Ibid.*, pp. 167, 168; cf. p. 721.

for that of Descartes, and the inferences from it proved friendly to what turned out to be the new science.

Ramus seemed to men of the Renaissance to offer liberation, simplification, and clarity. To them he seemed to have been raised up, as though by divine providence, to combine in one personality the three dominant characters of the age, humanist, Protestant, and logician; not only to Puritans but to humanists like Sir Philip Sidney he promised liberation from the gloomy cave of scholastic metaphysics into the spacious meadows of classical literature. He put into the hands of Protestant divines and scholars dialectical spears with which they could pierce the metaphysical armor of the Catholic champions. One of his principal contentions was that logical processes and figures were to be illustrated from classical poets, orators, and historians rather than from works of technical disputation; [1] for example, in order to show how dissimilar qualities may be compared, Ramus does not erect a hypothetical contrast of abstractions but employs the contrast made in a famous love lyric of Catullus between suns and the lives of lovers, that suns are able to die and to rise again, but for lovers, when the brief light of life fails, there remains but perpetual night.[2] Logic taught in this manner inevitably became fresh and exhilarating; it formed new and intoxicating alliances with rhetoric and classical scholarship. Puritan writers were logicians to a man, and Puritan sermons were severely logical in structure, but all according to the logic of Ramus, which was a relatively simple, clear-cut, and commonsense system, and one which furthermore furnished good authority for the study and even for the quotation of Catullus and Vergil in order to elucidate the fine points of divinity.

Ramus was able to assert that the principles of logic were embodied in the writings of poets, because he went upon the assumption that a simple and comprehensible order permeated the universe. Great writers, speaking out of their inward being, were speaking from nature herself, and through them, he said, nature reveals herself. "Science ought, therefore, to study the lessons that are innate in select minds . . . and upon them as a model should formulate the rules for those who desire to reason well." [3] His

---

[1] Petrus Ramus, *Dialecticae Libri Duo* (London, 1669), p. 50.

[2] *Ibid.*, p. 22.

[3] Frank P. Graves, *Peter Ramus and the Educational Reformation of the Sixteenth Century* (New York, 1912), pp. 145–147.

logic is a typically Renaissance product in that it was intended not
so much for proof and analysis as for assertion. It will not stand
up under the rigorous scrutiny of a modern logician; it could
not even survive once it came into competition with Locke. Yet
it was ideally adapted to the times, because it cleared away the
rubbish of scholasticism and yet did not challenge but rather
strengthened the authoritarianism that was still as essential to
a Renaissance philosophy of religion as it had been to a medieval.[1]
The Ramean logic was an instrument for setting forth only received truth, simply and concisely, and Ramus himself compressed
the essential outlines into sixty pages. It was a short cut to demonstration, resting squarely and firmly upon the conviction that the
world is a comprehensible logical structure to which the mind
of man, in spite of the fall of Adam and human corruption, almost exactly corresponds.[2]

Though the Ramean logic was actually much less of a depar-

[1] Hardin Craig, *The Enchanted Glass* (Oxford, 1936), pp. 140–146, 149–151, 156–
158, 198–202.
[2] Ramus's textbook, *Dialecticae Libri Duo*, first published 1556, frequently republished
in England, was used continuously in seventeenth-century New England, and was
supplemented by his other works. The *Dialecticae* was published in England with a
commentary by William Temple, 1584, but it was generally read by English students
bound up with *Commentarii* by George Downame (first delivered as lectures in 1590),
which provide the best text for study of the full implications of the system. It can also
be read in brief form in Milton's *Artis Logicae, plenior institutio, at Petri Rami methodum
concinnata*, published in 1672, reprinted *Works*, ed. John Mitford (London, 1851),
VII, 1–185, and in other editions of Milton. At Harvard Milton's work was used, and
an earlier handbook, Marcus Friedrich Wendelin, *Logicae institutiones tironum adolescentium
captui accommodatae*, 1654. For versions in English the best examples are Abraham
Fraunce, *The Lawiers Logike*, 1588, and Alexander Richardson, *The Logicians School-
Master*, 1657, a commentary that circulated in manuscript at both Cambridges for
several decades before it was printed. However, the student of New England history
can best review the system in Samuel Johnson's *Technologia Sive Technometria*, a manuscript summary by Johnson when an undergraduate at Yale, and published with an
excellent introduction and a translation in *Samuel Johnson*, ed. Herbert and Carol
Schneider (New York, 1929), II, 57–95. Johnson completed the manuscript on November 11, 1714, and in a later note on the margin records that by November 11, 1715,
"I was wholly changed to the New Learning," by which he means the logic and
philosophy of John Locke. Among the more conservative New England divines the
Ramean logic died a more lingering death, but by the time of Jonathan Edwards'
active career it had generally expired, and with it had gone the philosophy of original
Puritanism. Edwards' Calvinism is Calvinism harmonized as far as possible with
Locke; the Calvinism of early New England was colored by a totally different metaphysic. Of the general accounts of Ramus the best are still the articles in Bayle's
Dictionary or in Charles Waddington, *Ramus, Sa vie, ses écrits, et ses opinions* (Paris,
1855); cf. also Frank P. Graves, *Peter Ramus and the Educational Reformation of the Sixteenth Century;* for the influence of Ramus at Cambridge University, cf. J. B. Mul-
linger, *History of Cambridge*, II, 406–411.

ture from Aristotle than Ramists pretended, and though Ramus' own knowledge of Plato was very imperfect, the basic premise of his system was a Platonic conception: that the world is a copy or material counterpart of an ordered hierarchy of ideas existing in the mind of God.[1] All that logic need do, therefore, is to draw up an account of how things follow one another in nature, and if the account corresponds to the way things actually are, men can safely act upon it.[2] The generalized concepts of the mind, the principles of "art," are not human constructions, not mere hypotheses or useful categories, but eternal and inviolable ideas, the authentic realities upon which the world is constructed. Truth therefore becomes for the Ramist, and through him for the Puritan, clear-eyed perception of immutable essences, beauty becomes correspondence to them, virtue becomes conformity to them. The method of discovering them is inward; they exist not only in nature but in the human intelligence, and though much study and caution are necessary in deriving them from the mind, since the mind is corrupted by sin, and the rules of logic must always preside over the formulating of them, still the soul contains an intuitive knowledge of the eternal truths, which truths also govern the world.[3]

The Ramean logic therefore was not so much what we think of as logic as it was a grouping of all the ideas, sensations, causes, and perceptions in the world, laying them out in a simple and symmetrical pattern, so that a diagram of the logic with its divisions and subdivisions was practically a blueprint of the universe. It was a simple scheme, but it was also, Ramus insisted, true and useful. Indeed, his emphasis was possibly more upon its utility than upon its simplicity or truth, and there were many dialectical

[1] For the impact of Plato on Ramus, see Waddington, pp. 24–27, 35; in the sixteenth century he was called "the French Plato" (Graves, p. 92). Of course the "Platonic" conception of a world built upon ideas or exempla in the mind of God was part and parcel of the Christian tradition, and Puritans held it as much because of Augustine as because of Ramus; but since they already entertained the fundamental belief, Ramus' logic was all the more acceptable to them.

[2] Cf. "Ars igitur naturam sibi propositam semper habeat, exercitatio artem" (Art therefore always pre-supposes nature, as exercise does art), Waddington, p. 368.

[3] Ramus said that man has in himself naturally the power to know all things, and that when he sets before his eyes the art of thinking according to these innate universal concepts, it will show him as in a mirror the universal and generalized images of all things, so that he can then recognize by them the singular species and find a place for every thing in the cosmology, though Ramus adds that many examples, hard work, and long usage are necessary to polish the mirror before it will be able to supply the images of the universals (Waddington, p. 370).

Gordian knots which he endeavored to cut rather than untangle, so that the permanent value of his contribution to the science of thought is not great. But the very utility of his system assured men of the early seventeenth century that it must be true, and Puritans seized upon it avidly. Ramus believed that he derived the guiding principle of his groupings and classifications from Plato, the principle of "dichotomy," that is, that all ideas and things go in pairs, like the animals into the ark, because the world is symmetrical. Thus logic itself is divided into halves, in the first of which individual ideas or arguments are formulated, in the second put together in axioms and doctrines, just as grammar is divided into "etymology," the study of words, and "syntax," the putting of words together in sentences. Ideas in turn are divided into two sorts, those which establish themselves to our own experience and those which rest upon the authority of a witness, as do facts in history or the assertions of the Bible. The task of the logician (and the preacher must be a logician) was that of arranging everything in pairs under the proper rubrics. Thinking was not conceived as a method by which we compose our knowledge discovery by discovery, but as the unveiling of an ideal form. Knowledge was a schedule to be filled in, and this end, it seemed to Ramus and the Puritans, was best accomplished by pairing every idea and object with its counterpart, sun with moon, man with woman, cause with effect, subject with adjunct. When all existence was thus systematized, the problem of seeing the architecture of the whole, of grasping the diagram of the universe, became relatively simple. It consisted merely of arranging the pairs so that the more general came before the specific, the genus before the species, the important before the subsidiary. The final function of logic, as Ramus taught it, was "method." "That great and famous Martyr of France, *Peter Ramus*, held forth the light to others," said Increase Mather, and by that light he discovered the proper manner "wherein Scriptural Definitions and Distributions, expressing the Sum of the only true Christian Religion, are methodically disposed, according to the golden Rules of Art." [1] In defining the intellectual character of the New England Puritans, we must always exercise caution about calling them Calvinists. John Calvin's metaphysics were still Aristotelian and scholastic; New Englanders had thrown aside

---

[1] Preface to James Fitch, *The first Principles of the Doctrine of Christ* (Boston, 1679), Sig. A2, verso.

much of the philosophy which is implied at every point in Calvin's theology, and had taken up a system of which the implications were quite different.

The most striking example of the difference can be seen in the uses to which the Ramists put the logical procedures historically known as "disjunction" and "hypothesis." When Ramus had arrayed all things and all ideas in pairs, he found that while some pairs harmonize with each other, as do cause and effect, others ·set up oppositions, as do night and day, true and false, in and out. Therefore he provided a large place in his plan for serried ranks of opposites or contraries, all of which he classified according to his system of dichotomies. His principal English commentator admitted freely that the doctrine of diversities was to be found only in Ramus,[1] but in a fashion characteristic of the Ramists, asserted that if the example of reason and experience were observed, the necessity for the doctrine would become clear at once. The reason other logicians had conspired against it, he said, was that scholastic logic had been enslaved by the syllogism, and the Aristotelians had striven to confine all thinking processes to the three figures of the syllogism as defined by Aristotle. Thus one of the chief grudges of the Ramists against Aristotle was the tyranny of the syllogism; Ramus assigned it a very minor role in his "method," where it served upon occasion merely to clear up individual arguments, so that they could be placed in their proper place in the grand sequence. As he debased the syllogism, he exalted the doctrine of contraries; ideas could be immediately distinguished by setting them against their opposites; a good could be defined by placing it against the corresponding evil, and thus sounder conclusions could be reached in the twinkling of an eye than in whole centuries of fruitless disputation with the cumbersome form of the syllogism.[2]

Ramus did not limit the doctrine of opposites to single ideas. If the principle of instantaneous recognition of contraries by the human mind would serve to sort out particular ideas and words, it would serve as well for more complex alternatives, for immediate adjudication between opposing doctrines as well as between opposing words. The Renaissance logician did not distinguish be-

[1] "Diversorum doctrina ab omnibus praeter Ramum Logicis omissa est," George Downame, *Commentarii* (London, 1669), p. 129.

[2] For the scheme of opposites, disparates, and contraries, see Ramus, *Dialecticae*, pp. 10–14; Milton, *Artis Logicae*, pp. 36–54; Johnson, *Technologia*, pp. 74–76.

tween a fact, an idea, or a doctrine to the extent of treating them
as different logical counters; an opposition could be set up between black and white, bad and good, salvation by works and
salvation by faith. In each case the mind was simply called upon
to say which of the two corresponded to the divine order. The
way to test the truth of a statement was to ask oneself a question:
it is either thus and so or it is not, which? Or else the way was
to suppose it true and see if it would prove itself, by saying, if
it is so, then such and such must follow, and if such and such is
true, then the statement must be true. The methods of disjunction and hypothesis probably take their origin from Plato, whether
or not Ramus derived them from him. They are certainly methods
that follow obviously from a belief in the Platonic world, where
all things are ranged in a hierarchy of ideas and the philosophical
problem is to sort the genus into species and the species into sub-
species. The Ramists proclaimed that Ramus' rehabilitation of
disjunction and hypothesis was his greatest contribution to logic;
Ramus himself insisted that they be elevated to the title of "syllogisms"; calling the three conventional Aristotelian syllogisms
"simple" ones, he denominated disjunction and hypothesis "composite." He remarked that "composite" syllogisms were the ones
men actually used most frequently, and that this fact alone justified the dignity with which he invested them.[1] His English ex-
positor was still more aggressive; admitting that the authority of
Aristotle was opposed to composite syllogisms, Downame exultantly
declared that nevertheless Aristotle himself used them again and
again, once in the very passage in which he denied their validity,
that furthermore the practice of the best writers and above all
of the Bible itself thoroughly exonerated them.[2] Therefore if the
Holy Ghost thought by means of composite syllogisms, students
of Ramus considered that they were free to employ them on
every occasion, and New England divines believed that a conclusion established by their aid was as strong as one confirmed
by Holy Writ.

If we turn to a Puritan textbook, written according to the
"golden rules" of art as taught by Petrus Ramus, we can perceive what the Ramean revolution in logic meant in practice.
For example, in the book for the preface of which Increase Mather
wrote the praise of Ramus already quoted, the author, James

[1] Ramus, *Dialecticae*, pp. 44–46; Johnson, *Technologia*, pp. 93–95.
[2] Downame, *Commentarii*, p. 448.

Fitch, pastor at Norwich, Connecticut, discusses the question whether the world was created or is eternal. The scholastic way of settling this inquiry would have been through the syllogism; a schoolman might argue, for example, all temporal things are made, the world is a temporal thing, ergo, the world is made.[1] He would seek to rehearse Aristotle's complicated argument for the first unmoved mover of all things, and would spend much time refuting all other propositions. But the disciple of Ramus puts all this aside as superfluous and inconclusive. He says that by using demonstrations of this sort it would be equally easy to prove that there is a continuous and eternal succession of motions, with no necessity for a first unmoved mover. Instead of employing "simple" syllogisms, the Ramist invokes the "composite" and solves the disjunctive by the hypothetical. He asks himself the question, the world was either made or not made, which? Then he answers himself to his own complete satisfaction: if it was not made, then there was no cause for its being, there is no design in it, no end for which it exists, and any man in his senses knows that these are absurd conclusions. Ergo, the world was made. Then he continues his self-interrogation, it was either made by God, or it made itself. Hypothesis demonstrates at once that the second alternative is untenable, and so the Ramist triumphantly concludes that God must have made it.[2]

Undoubtedly the Ramean logic was much too facile, and when it was employed by shallow minds that were utterly unskilled in the more noble if more tortuous logic of the schoolmen, it produced a breed of disputants so fascinated by their own logic-chopping they could not see the open fallacies in their method. Yet whether the Ramean logic was a good one or a bad one does not concern us; historically speaking, the importance of such reasoning as that of James Fitch is its recurrent appeal to an innate, *a priori* knowledge. He does not attempt to establish an invincible case in the void, but to establish a case which no human being in possession of his wits can deny. The syllogism strikes

---

[1] It is interesting to note that the greatest of the scholastics found the assertion of this very proposition impossible to establish by rational demonstration and was constrained to rest his case with a demonstration that no arguments for the negative were any better than those for the affirmative (St. Thomas Aquinas, *Summa Contra Gentiles*, Bk. II, chaps. XXXI–XXXVIII); where the Angelic Doctor treads cautiously through many pages of his most wary reasoning, the Puritan pastor confidently rushes in to "prove" the point in a paragraph.

[2] James Fitch, *The first Principles*, p. 17.

downward vertically, so to speak, driving the mind before it,
where disjunction extends horizontally for the contemplation of
self-reflecting intelligence. The Ramean logic is the logic of a
Humanist, the conclusions come from within, they are not reached
by piling one brick upon another in a shaky and top-heavy sequence, but by the prompt and decisive arbitration of the natural
reason between two possibilities. Puritan preachers and disputants
would use the syllogism wherever they found it profitable; more
often they would establish their points by the use of disjunction,
by ruling out the alternative which all men, on the strength of
their native intelligence, would be compelled to admit could not
hold water.[1]

Thus when John Cotton spoke of an "essentiall wisdome in
us, namely, our Reason which is natural," he was speaking from
his Ramean training. What such an assumption might lead to
in a man's philosophy can readily enough be seen, at least in
broad outline. For if the way to test the truth of things is by the
measure of a rationality implicit in man, then there must be an
inherent rationality in things, in the mind, in the order of the
universe; only if this is so can a careful examination of the in-

[1] The rule of disjunction was crystallized into a number of convenient aphorisms
which practitioners of the logic repeatedly cited as the ultimate in human wisdom.
Thus Milton says, improving on Ramus, "Itaque ex altero affirmato alterum negatur"
(Thus by the one affirmed the other is negated), or "Ex affirmatione unius, necessario
sequitur negatio alterius" (From affirmation of the one there follows necessarily
negation of the other), *Artis Logicae*, pp. 40–41. Johnson has it, "Hic etiam fictum
arguet alterum verum" (For this being a fiction argues the other true), *Technologia*,
p. 76. Samuel Willard, giving a young scholar directions for studying for the ministry,
tells him that he must learn the wrong doctrines as well as the right ones, reduce all
to their proper heads and ascertain their opposites; he then quotes the Ramean commonplace, "Quibus Argumentis Veritas astruitur, iisdem Falsitas destruitur" (By the
same arguments with which truth is established, falsity is destroyed), *Brief Directions
to a Young Scholar Designing the Ministry* (Boston, 1735), p. 4. How disjunction was used
in actual sermons can be illustrated from Willard's method of proving that the righteousness of Christ is merely "imputed" to the elect for their legal justification and not
"infused" directly into them, as the Antinomians claimed: "That the individual and
personal Righteousness of Christ cannot be infused into a Believer, is a truth so plain
and necessary, that to assert the contrary, is to speak a contradiction, and therefore if
it be any way ours, it must needs be imputed to us. Everyone that knows anything of
the nature of things" knows that the acts of one man cannot be infused into another,
but, Willard says, "on the other hand, this is a notion that is very well agreeing with
common reason, that another did such a thing for this man, such as one paid a Debt for
him," *A Brief Discourse of Justification* (Boston, 1686), p. 65. Thus, thanks to Ramus'
doctrine of opposites and his glorification of "composite" syllogisms, the actual arbiter
in New England theology, time and time again, was not Calvin, not even the Bible, so
much as it was "plain and necessary truth," the "nature of things," or "common
reason."

tellect, a checking of all propositions by the instinctive knowledge
of the soul, result in finding the true propositions. Therefore the
way to avoid "paralogizing" yourself is to consult, with scrupulous
care and dispassionate honesty, the essential wisdom within yourself, which, being natural and true, will enable you to reason
correctly.[1] The material world is transitory and deceptive, the
passions of men ebb and flow, men make mistakes, accidents
happen, and God can override or turn aside all natural processes;
but something eternal and immutable does exist, and by that we
must live. There are a number of propositions, fitting together
into a harmonious whole, upon which things are built, to which
they correspond, which they must follow, which they do follow
even when to earthly eyes they seem to be accidental and for-
tuitous. The sum total of these eternal propositions, the completed
system of truth, exists only in the mind of God, but that it does
exist we know, because we in small part share in it; some of the
divine truth does exist in our minds. In the counsel of God, so
the argument runs—a clear consequence of this Ramean position
—there must be this "idea or pattern of well acting"; hence God
in acting follows it of his own free choice, and he therefore must
create his creatures in accordance with this pattern; "and that
wisdome in the creatures is imprinted, and is the impression or
Image of it." Hence the "rules of art," the rules that God follows
in organizing and governing the world, the rules that enable us
to tell which of the disjunctive alternatives must be wrong and
which is clearly right, these rules of art must be eternal, though all
material objects which exemplify them are transitory and illusory.
Though men are unstable and life is full of pitfalls, there is a divine
wisdom that governs and controls all. "The definitions of things
are eternal Truths, whatever becomes of the things themselves." [2]
    There can be no doubt that this way of thinking is a species

---

[1] Cf. "An Dentur Ideae innatae" (Whether there exist innate ideas), affirmed by
John Whiting at the Commencement of 1703 (Quaestiones No. 2), Morison, *Harvard
College in the Seventeenth Century*, Appendix B.

[2] Fitch, *The first Principles*, p. 15. Cf. among the Harvard theses: "Veritas est con-
formitas intellectus cum re" (Truth is intellectual conformity with fact, 1643 Theses
Metaphysicae No. 5); "Artium praecepta sunt aeternae veritatis" (The precepts of the
arts are of eternal truth, 1653 Theses Technologicae No. 3); "Utrum Detur Idaea
omnium Entium in primo Ente" (Whether there exists an idea of all beings in the
primary being, 1664 Quaestiones No. 2) affirmed by Nathaniel Chauncy; "Non ab
artifice Ars, sed ab arte artifex creatur" (The art is not created by the artisan, but the
artisan by the art, 1678 Theses Technologicae No. 13); "Idea est res percepta, prout
est in intellectu objective" (An idea is a thing perceived, as it is objectively in the

of Platonism. It is a method of establishing the pre-existence of ideas, or of a divine pattern, to which the world roughly conforms and by which all movement and contingency are to be ex-

intellect, 1687 Theses Technologicae No. 2); "Praecepta Artium non formamus, sed formata invenimus" (We do not form the precepts of the arts, but come upon them formed, 1693 Theses Technologicae No. 5). Samuel Johnson began his summary of the system with the central doctrine of the Ramean logic: "Artem suos reflectere radios in intellectum intelligentis creaturae ab antiquissimes, ideoque cum intelligente creatura reflexum suum habere ortum manifeste apparet . . ." (It is manifest that art has reflected its rays into the intellect of intelligent creatures from greatest antiquity, and therefore has its reflex origin in the intelligent creature); he distinguishes between "art," i.e., logic, as it exists in the mind of God, which he calls "archetypal" and describes as the idea of things decreed in the divine intelligence, and art as it exists in the visible world, which he calls "typal" and describes as manifesting itself on the one hand in the ideas impressed upon the creature and on the other in the rules gathered from the actions and operations of things by the senses, observations and experience (Johnson, *Technologia*, pp. 58–68). Josiah Flynt, graduating in 1664, published the almanac for 1666 and presented therein an argument similar to that already quoted from James Fitch concerning the creation of the world; here in the one publication designed for popular consumption the citizens of Massachusetts Bay were given a succinct statement of Puritan Platonism:

". . . The *Divine Idea* (If I speak in the dialect of some learned and pious) being God contemplating himself as imitable in the creatures fabrick, or as it were capable to receive the impression of the *Image* or *Vestigium* of those divine perfections which were in himself; it follows that whatever perfection was eminently in God, and the creature was Analogically capable of, was according to divine wisdome expressed (for otherwise the *Idea* or *Exemplar* would not have been consentaneous to the τό πραττόμενον)" (Morison, *Harvard College in the Seventeenth Century*, p. 278).

Note the decisive use of disjunction in the last sentence. The πραττόμενον means roughly the achieving, the realization, the passing over of the ideal into actualization. It was this Platonic conception of a realm of eternal and pure ideas passing into realization in a realm of matter which made possible the Puritan hierarchy of values—from those of sense to those of Reason, from those of Reason to those of Faith. Thus Fitch expounded it:

"Reason in a believer is a means to let in a light and good beyond Reason, that as the senses are means to present the Reason in things to the Reason of man, although Reason is above Sense, so Reason is a means to present a divine good unto Faith, though that divine good is above Reason, but as Reason can use the *Prattomenon* of the Rule of Sense, (namely) that which is effected by it, so Faith can use the Prattomenon of the Rule of Reason, that which is effected by it, and yet these are distinct arts, and have distinct Objects, and distinct lights" (*The first Principles*, p. 4). For the philosophical significance of Platonism in the thought of the early seventeenth century, see Etienne Gilson, *Études sur le Role de la pensée médiéval dans la formation du système Cartésien*, especially pp. 30–36, 48, 193–201. To characterize the Puritans as "Platonists" may create more confusion than clarification, because Platonism has come to be a battleground of interpretation; yet if we accept Platonism in the definition of Dean Inge— "the conception of an unseen world, of which the visible world is but a pale copy"—we can list the Puritans in that camp. This is, of course, to say no more than that they were in the main stream of Christian tradition; in order to determine what special species of the Platonic genus we may call New England Puritanism we must consider the actual background, the modifying influences of the environment, with the "climate of opinion" in the seventeenth century, and the climate, meteorological and mental, of the new world. But it should be noted that if Puritanism is Platonic in that plained. The Ramean logic might be said to be one of the several forms in which Platonism was revived in the Renaissance and enlisted in the humanists' and the theologians' battle with scholasticism. But without pursuing the philosophical problem too far afield, we can for the moment rest with this reflection, that the humanist strain in Puritan culture, represented by the classical authors and the logic of Petrus Ramus, made for the conception of a fundamental rationality in the universe and in the mind of man. Because the Puritans were humanists, they could not rest in a belief that God's decrees were nothing but arbitrary fiats. They held that God was indeed sovereign and absolute lord, but not entirely a capricious, ruthless, unpredictable tyrant. They held that man was indeed caught in the toils of sin, but they did not hold that he was so empty a creature that he needed to be filled with grace in any such crude fashion as a toy balloon is filled with air. In his fallen state he still can test the validity of reasons and reach a vision, if only a sort of distant perception, of the serene order that really prevails. The grace of God, which is a special and additional imparting of His spirit to man, whose reason is already endowed with some inklings of the divine nature, this grace is not some emotional cataclysm, an attack of the jerks, an agitation "with Antick and uncouth motions." [1] On the contrary it is an elevation of reason, a freshening and quickening of the understanding; it is an imparting to man of that spark of imagination and that breadth of insight whereby he can at last perceive in part, and apprehend in the rest, the essential unity of life, and the essential reasonableness of things. As a great Puritan preacher put it, John Preston, who was the Master of Emmanuel College at Cambridge, England, and who was looked upon as one of their chief intellectual progenitors by New Englanders, divine grace "elevateth reason, and makes it higher, it makes it see further than reason could, it is contrary indeed to corrupt reason, but to reason that is right reason, it is not contrary, only it raiseth it higher: And therefore faith teacheth nothing contrary to sense and reason." [2] Thomas Hooker told his congregations that conversion made "things appear as they be," that the regenerate man is the man who at last understands

---

it was occupied with the detemporalized hierarchy of ideas, it is not that sort of Platonism that looks upon the visible world as mere illusion, utterly unreal, or absolutely evil.

[1] Norton, *Heart of N-England Rent*, p. 6.
[2] *The Cuppe of Blessing* (London, 1633), p. 13.

what he already knows, or could have known, in his reason:
"look what the truth determines, reason approves, and Conscience witnesseth . . . Such judg not by outward appearance
as it is the guise of men of corrupt minds, but upon experience,
that which they have found and felt in their own hearts." [1] At
the end of the century a Puritan minister is still insisting, "Spiritual
Light received in Conversion, strengthens the reason of men, and
makes the law of nature more legible." [2] A few decades more,
and there would be ministers who insisted that spiritual light was
something entirely different from the reason of man and quite
other than the law of nature; and consequently other ministers
would reply that in that case spiritual light must be insanity,
and that if they had to choose they preferred the reason of men
and the law of nature. The seamless garment of Puritanism thus
was rent, and the edifice erected by the founders in order to
justify God's ways to man was riven in two; in the one half came
to dwell those who no longer made any effort to *justify* God's ways,
and in the other those who preferred to set up the ways of man
for approbation and imitation by the divinity.

In this fashion, then, Puritanism attempted to appropriate the
heritage of humanism and to embody it in a system of Christian
belief and a theological conception of the world. It did not turn
its back upon the new literary learning, as it did not turn its
back upon the still newer scientific learning that burgeoned during
the century. Puritanism was an outgrowth of the advanced culture
of its day; its basic ideas as to the function of the human mind
and the responsibilities of the human soul were common to Chris-
tendom at the time, its fundamental doctrines were common to
Protestantism at the time, the texture and range of its learning
were common to educated opinion of the time, its struggle to
maintain homogeneity in religious thought, to unify religion and
knowledge, was common to all devout and intelligent men of the
time. Thinking men were all in one way or another still dominated by the medieval tradition of unity, and could break away
from the scholastic formulation of that unity only by endeavoring to achieve another formulation in more satisfactory terms.
The chief elements in Puritan culture, therefore, the foundations
of Puritan thought, "ninety per cent" of its ideas, roughly speaking, are to be accounted for by a study of the age and background.

[1] *The Application of Redemption*, p. 557.
[2] Solomon Stoddard, *The Danger of Speedy Degeneracy* (Boston, 1705), p. 11.

But we are still left with the question: What then was the essence of Puritanism, apart from beliefs and opinions common to others in the period, what was this precious "ten per cent" that made the difference? What particular devices did the Puritans employ in formulating the unity of knowledge and religion which divided them sharply and fatally from the Anglicans? For if the war between the Puritans and the Church of England was an engagement between men who, from our point of view at least, were agreed on the larger assumptions, the concrete issue must be narrowed down to a difference of deduction from those premises. The evidence of history goes to show that the bitterest and most furious combats are generally fought between those who agree on fundamentals, for there is no greater annoyance that a man can suffer than attack from persons who accord with him in the main, but who apply his principles to conclusions utterly foreign to his liking. Puritanism started from the background and the beliefs we have been outlining; it then worked its way to certain concrete applications, and it was these specific deductions that made Puritanism Puritanical.

4. *The Essential Issue*

Where Puritanism and the Church of England at last parted company, after marching abreast over so immense a terrain, may conveniently be illustrated if we begin with a statement of William Laud himself, the Archbishop of Canterbury and the archfoe of the Puritans, whose head they finally chopped off. In 1622 Laud, then Bishop of London, held a conference with a Jesuit, in the course of which he drew up an excellent statement of the position of the Church of England. Inevitably the nub of this debate was the authority of scripture, and Laud set forth the grounds upon which the Protestant, believing still in the unity of reason and faith, maintaining the harmony of knowledge and belief, could nevertheless anchor his whole system to the arbitrary word of God, to the ukase of revelation handed down from on high by the absolute Tsar of the universe. The Catholic was arguing that if the authority of the Universal Church were disowned, the Bible would prove an inadequate substitute, because the Bible would become subject to interpretation, no two men would agree on what it meant, Protestantism would split into a hundred differing sects, each one twisting Biblical meanings to suit its own

convenience, and thus scripture would lose all the necessary attributes of an authority. Laud answered that there was no danger
of this happening in Protestant thought, because the authority
of the Bible was established by a logical necessity. In every science,
he said, certain principles outside its own limits must be supplied
before the science can proceed; geometry must be built upon
a priori axioms, that the whole is greater than the part, etc.
The basic principles of the sciences are "given" in the natural
reason—exactly as Ramus demonstrates. But in divinity, which
is the science of the divine, the basic principles must come from
the divine, and therefore must be given, if at all, by God. Consequently, unless Protestants abandoned theology entirely, which
was not possible for Laud to imagine, they would always proceed in the science of theology upon divine axioms, laid down
by God, believed exactly as all axioms are believed, because,
though they cannot be demonstrated to be true, yet no thinking
can go on unless they are true. The axioms enacted by God are
accepted by faith. The Bible is believed, not on the authority of
any Church, but because it must be believed; nothing will "prove"
that the scripture is divine, it must be believed to be divine.
But there are, however, some natural or rational testimonies helping to establish the fact that scripture is divinely inspired; these
considerations do not prove it, but they help to convince men.
These are: the tradition of the Church, the testimony of other ages,
consent of many men, the harmony of the prophets, the success
Biblical teachings have enjoyed in the world, the constancy and
consistency of the doctrine, the inward light and excellency of the
text. Hence, though the authority of scripture cannot be proved,
and is basically a matter of faith, rational arguments may be
used, for "grace is never planted but in a reasonable creature,
and proves by the very seat which it hath taken up that the end
it hath is to be spiritual eye-water, to make reason see what 'by
nature only it cannot,' but never to blemish reason in that which
it can, 'comprehend.' " [1]

Now taking this argument just as it stands, any Puritan would
gladly have subscribed to it. He might not stress the tradition
of the Church quite so emphatically as Laud did among the rational confirmations of the authority of scripture; but that scripture was to be accepted by faith, and yet no violence to be done
to reason, that reason actually proved the necessity for the faith

[1] More and Cross, *Anglicanism*, pp. 97–103.

and endorsed it with almost infallibly convincing testimonies—this was the argument of the Puritan as well as of the bishop. But the Puritan then and there challenged the bishop to be as good as his word. If the bishop submitted to the Bible as God's word, received it by faith and reinforced his faith with rational convictions—very well then, let him accept it and act accordingly. Let him not, once he has established its authority, then turn about and explain away a good part of it, invent reasons to prove that only some portions are God's law, that the Bible is not binding in every point on which it speaks, but merely on some few. If the Bible declares God is three persons in one, let that be believed, said the Puritan; if the Bible says that wigs are an abomination unto the Lord, let that also be believed.

And there the Anglican protested, and the fight commenced. For to him it seemed absurd to imagine that God, the sovereign of sovereigns, would take the time, would demean himself, to tell men whether or not they should wear wigs. He could not imagine that everything in the Bible, every incidental history, every minute circumstance, was intended by God to be universally and literally binding on all men. God had inspired the book in order that the fundamental and comprehensive truths of religion might be set down; he had inspired individual men at particular times and places to write it, and they had written in their particular dialects and told a great many things that were of only temporary importance. The difference between the Anglican and the Puritan, then, was that the Puritan thought the Bible, the revealed word of God, was the word of God from one end to the other, a complete body of laws, an absolute code in everything it touched upon; the Anglican thought this a rigid, doctrinaire, and utterly unjustifiable extension of the authority of scripture. The Puritan held that the Bible was sufficiently plain and explicit so that men with the proper learning, following the proper rules of deduction and interpretation, could establish its meaning and intention on every subject, not only in theology, but in ethics, costume, diplomacy, military tactics, inheritances, profits, marriages, and judicial procedure. The Anglican position, set forth supremely in Richard Hooker's *Of the Laws of Ecclesiastical Polity*, was simply that the Bible is God's revealed word only on the broad principles of the Christian religion, that in all minor matters, God has not intended to set up ironclad rules for men, but to leave them to the discretion of their reason, to the considerations of circumstance and propriety, to the determinations of proportion and decency. In His providence, in His government of events, through the reason He has instilled in man, through the law which governs nature, God can and does teach men; in the Bible He is concerned only with those things which they could not otherwise learn from these sources.

Let them with whom we have hitherto disputed consider well, how it can stand with reason to make the bare mandate of sacred Scripture the only rule of all good and evil in the actions of mortal men. The testimonies of God are true, the testimonies of God are perfect, the testimonies of God are all sufficient unto that end for which they were given. Therefore accordingly we do receive them, we do not think that in them God hath omitted anything needful unto his purpose, and left his intent to be accomplished by our devisings.[1]

If the Puritan contention were correct, that the Bible is the supreme and absolute law, says the Anglican Hooker, then the law of nature and the law of reason would be effectually abrogated; they would become useless, because we would need to search scripture at every juncture and would never dare trust ourselves to decide anything on any other grounds. "In every action of common life to find out some sentence clearly and infallibly setting before our eyes what we ought to do, (seem we in Scripture never so expert) would trouble us more than we are aware." [2] The Anglican was accusing the Puritan of narrow-minded literalism, pointing out that if he had the effrontery to assume that his and only his interpretation of scripture was correct, and to set himself up as dictator to all other men on a host of points upon which God intended men to follow their own discretion, custom or political expediency, then the Puritan was guilty of arrogance and pride. "This Disciplinarian humor," said one bishop, "which will admit no latitude in religion, but makes each nicety a fundamental, and every private opinion an article of Faith." [3] Another Anglican cleric said that to give men the power of saying what scripture does and does not mean makes them "to be as much lawgivers to the Church by their uncontrolable law-interpreting, as any Pope or enthusiast can or need

[1] Book II, chap. VIII, par. 5.
[2] *Ibid.*, par. 6.
[3] More and Cross, *Anglicanism*, p. 80.

pretend to be." [1] The Puritan replied, in effect, that if the Anglican said that the Bible was the word of God, and then put aside anything in the Bible which he did not like by saying this or that particular law or precedent was peculiar to the historical circumstances and was not part of the eternal law of the Christian religion, then it was certainly the Anglican who was setting himself up to be the lawgiver and the tyrant; he was perverting the law of God to his own purposes by sophistry and fine distinctions, he did not really believe in the Bible at all, he was playing fast and loose with it and was no better than a skeptic or an atheist.

If the dispute had remained a merely academic one whether the authority of the Bible extended as far as the wearing or not wearing of wigs or hoop petticoats, New England would have remained somewhat longer in the possession of the Indians. But one of the most important discoveries made by the Puritan in his study of scripture was that it contained the perfect constitution for the organization of the visible church. [2] The Anglican denied this, and Richard Hooker wrote his book on the "laws" of ecclesiastical polity to prove that there were many kinds of laws which men were to follow in different connections, and that in ecclesiastical government they were not to follow the Bible at all, because Christ had left the form of the church to be determined by political considerations, by the particular traditions of each country, and by the principles of aesthetic judgment. Thus the argument involved very important elements in the state and society; conservatives, satisfied with things as they were, saw in Puritan radicalism a serious threat to the vested interests; those dissatisfied with the *status quo* welcomed for social as well as for religious reasons the Puritan condemnation of the episcopal hierarchy, with its wealth, its monopoly of advantages, and its alliance with the Court and the aristocracy. Political passions and economic grievances increased the tension. In the 1640's both sides appealed to the sword and the God of battles, but before the actual outbreak had come, when Charles I had dismissed his parliament and was apparently launched upon an era of absolute rule by and with the aid of the bishops, a small band of particularly earnest Puritans, fearing that the divine church polity could never be established in England, secured a charter from the king giving them title to land in Massachusetts Bay. They moved

[1] *Ibid.*, p. 91.
[2] Perry Miller, *Orthodoxy in Massachusetts* (Cambridge, 1933), chap. II.

themselves and their families thither, in order that under a government of their own constituting, the form of church government
ordained by Christ might be set up, and His faithful saints might
worship him in the precise manner He had decreed.

At this point certain doubts might justifiably arise in the mind
of the reader concerning what has just been said about the Puritan
emphasis upon reason and scholarship. If after all the Puritan
erected the Bible into a hard and fast body of arbitrary law,
then it might seem that the function of his reason must amount
to the very inferior one of deducing concrete applications from
a miscellaneous collection of arbitrary dicta, and his scholarship
simply consist in the administration of a number of imposed
statutes. Certainly, it was to this that Richard Hooker felt the
role of the intellect would be reduced if the Puritan had his
way, and the fact of the matter is that in many cases, in such
unimaginative and pedantic Puritans as Cotton Mather, the
solemn invocation of scriptural sanctions for decisions about the
minutiae of daily life became nothing short of ludicrous. But
Cotton Mather was a case for a psychiatrist in any event, and
is not, fortunately, very representative of Puritanism as a whole,
a fact which it is hoped these selections will make clear. The
Puritan's attitude toward the Bible was called fanatical by his
opponents, but it was not the worship of the book in a naïve or
infatuated spirit. It was an acceptance of the Bible as revealed
law from an absolute sovereign, but the law of that sovereign
was not therefore erected against all reason, science, and natural
wisdom. Puritanism was not, as we have said, "fundamentalism";
its conflict with the Church of England was, on the purely intellectual side, a difference in definition concerning the spheres
of reason and faith, and of their connection.

As we attempt to ascertain the difference, we should remember
that from now on it becomes increasingly difficult to speak of the
Anglican argument as though one train of thought were common
to all apologists for the Church of England, at that time or at
any time since. The very freedom which Richard Hooker allowed
to the reason and the intelligence made possible a variety of
attitudes; Churchmen differed among themselves concerning how
much or how little of the Bible was to be accounted the eternal
law of God, or how much weight was to be given to the other sanctions of thought and conduct, whether more to the law or to reason
or to the traditions of the Church. But if we take Hooker, and

47

Introduction

Introduction

Introduction

some one of his successors in the moderate and well-considered vein, Jeremy Taylor for instance, and look upon them as representative, simply because they avoided the extremes either of the "high-church" party of Laud, or of the "low-church" party of Ussher, we may safely compare them with the Puritans in order to define more precisely the exact nature of the Puritan thought.

From the description we have already given of Richard Hooker's volume, it becomes clear that he is stressing the multiformity of the revelation of God's will. As though the divinity were a great light, a sun of illumination, various rays emanate in various directions, each of them a partial revelation of his character. One of these rays is the law of reason, one the law of nature, one the conception of beauty, one His daily providence; and among these rays another one, important indeed, but only one among the others, is the Bible. This is no doubt an over-simplified statement of Hooker's very subtle position, but it will serve; it is the idea which, in one way or another, underlies almost all Anglican thinking in the seventeenth century, and it is the belief above all others that the Puritans could never swallow.

In a portentous volume called *Ductor Dubitantium*,[1] a guide for troubled consciences in some 1400 pages, published by Jeremy Taylor in 1659, this liberal and eloquent clergyman, occupying the leisure forced upon him by the reign of Oliver Cromwell, deliberately devised for the Church of England a book of practical divinity, a manual for the solution of ethical puzzles, because, for one reason, the Puritans, with their direct application of Scripture to the affairs of ordinary life, had seemed far to excel the Anglican divines in casuistical writing.[2] Before entering into particular cases, Taylor endeavored to demonstrate how first of all men might ascertain the regulations to which their consciences should conform. The measure and rule should be, he says, the law of God, but the law of God is not promulgated merely and solely in the Bible; it is also to be found in the law of nature, in the articles to which all nations have consented, in

---

[1] Vols. IX and X of *Works*, under general editorship of Reginald Heber, edited by Alexander Taylor (London, 1851).

[2] Taylor cites as his predecessors in this sort of divinity the work of William Perkins, William Ames, and Johann Heinrich Alsted; Perkins and Ames were English Puritans, both much read in America; Ames was intimately associated with many of the founders of Massachusetts and the book to which Taylor refers, Ames's *De Conscientia*, was the Puritan manual of casuistry throughout the seventeenth century. A comparison of this volume with Taylor's will tell the whole story of the two types of minds. Alsted was a Calvinist professor at Herborn and at Weissemburg, the author of a great encyclopedia

right reason, in laws ecclesiastical and civil, in popular proverbs, and in the wisdom of great poets.[1] The larger number of the rules which men are to obey, Taylor insists, come from these sources; the number to be derived from the Bible should be kept down to the bare minimum of those essential truths which cannot be learned from the other instructors, and the validity of much of scripture, at least in morality, is actually that it expresses felicitously what the other texts already have taught. "The best portions of scripture, even the law of Jesus Christ, which in moral things is the eternal law of nature, is written in our hearts, is reason, and that wisdom to which we cannot choose but assent." [2] The fundamental discriminations of right and wrong are such that all men must acknowledge them, "so long as a man is in his wits, and hath the natural use of reason." [3] The natural man, unless he is insane or diseased, can and does grasp these fundamentals; [4] most of his mistakes come in the application, where he is misled through ignorance or by evil customs. The way to correct him is not to bring down upon him the crushing weight of a pretended Biblical condemnation, but to discover the province in which his error lies, whether in reason or nature or civil law, and to put him to rights according to the legislation of that domain. "Every thing must be derived from its own fountain." [5]

Against this method of instructing men's consciences, Taylor continues, the Puritans protest because they say it puts reason before the Bible, and they offer instead to draw up a set of rules straight from the Bible to cover almost all moral problems. They say that we must not start with what is reasonable, and then find that the law of Christ is like unto it, but with the law of Christ, and then we must abide by it, whether it seems reasonable or not. This, says Taylor, is to make a separation between what is reasonable and what is revealed. That such a discrepancy can even imaginably exist Taylor denies emphatically.[6] He will admit that human reason is below God and cannot understand all that God is, but everything that God reveals to men must be

---

of the arts and of a summa of cases of conscience (1628), standard works of reference in New England (Morison, *Harvard College in the Seventeenth Century*, p. 158). The *Ductor Dubitantium*, therefore, is doubly interesting for our purposes, since it was written to supply what Taylor thought were the deficiencies in works which were the received authority in New England.

[1] *Ibid.*, IX, 13.   [4] *Ibid.*, pp. 29, 34.
[2] *Ibid.*, p. 69.   [5] *Ibid.*, p. 60.
[3] *Ibid.*, p. 41.   [6] *Ibid.*, pp. 67–68.

comprehensible to the reason, for the reason of man must come from the same God who gives the revelation. "If reason cannot consent to it when it is told of it, then it is nothing, it hath no being, it hath no possibility." [1] Therefore one cannot say of any proposition, it is against scripture and therefore against reason, "because reason is before revelation, and that this is revealed by God must be proved by reason"; but if we will define carefully and accurately what is reasonable, we are then empowered to assert that what is against reason must, *ipse facto*, be against the word of God. For, says Taylor in conclusion,

when both sides agree that these are the words of God, and the question of faith is concerning the meaning of the words, nothing is an article of faith, or a part of religion, but what can be proved by reason to be the sense and intentions of God. Reason is never to be pretended against the clear sense of scripture, because by reason it is that we came to perceive that to be the clear sense of scripture.[2]

Taylor's argument is a permutation upon the theme announced by Richard Hooker. He is asserting the primacy of an eternal reason, which finds expression in nature, in the human intellect, experience, civil law, proverbs, and poetry; it also finds expression in the Bible. In order that there may be no conflict between the Bible and other manifestations of the immutable wisdom, Biblical teachings must be held to a minimum, and those few entertained as much as possible not because the Bible says so, but because they are clearly consistent with what men learn from all the sources of knowledge available to them.

If we now turn to the Puritan side of the debate, we shall find that Taylor's opponents have one all-important consideration to advance against his seductive pleading. If men had remained as they had been created, if they had retained the pristine innocence of creation fresh from the hand of God, then everything that Taylor says would be true. But the fact of the matter is—and by "fact" the Puritan meant not only in Christian theology but in experience—something has happened to mankind. History proves, and daily events confirm, that men are not naturally noble, reasonable, honest, kind, decent, or intelligent. Taylor's whole structure of moral instruction derived by the reasonable

---

[1] *Ibid.*, p. 71.
[2] *Ibid.*, p. 74.

being from natural and reasonable preceptors leaves out of account what John Cotton called "mans perverse subtilty in inventing wayes of backsliding." [1] Let human beings go free amid nature, let them read the poets and memorize the proverbs, induce them to examine their hearts for an instinctive knowledge of right and wrong, teach them what the wise and good of all nations have agreed on, and what will be the result? The same old chronicle of meanness and cruelty, bloodshed and robbery, hatred and betrayal, blunder and stupidity, which passes under the name of history. From such sources some men, like Socrates or Plutarch, may learn virtue and self-control, but only on the basis of calculation; the vast majority are totally incapable of leading the life of reason if they have only reason to inspire them. No man who knows a hawk from a handsaw can doubt for a moment "the depravation of nature, in the blindnesse of our minds: who are so far from discerning spiritual things . . . that we cannot rightly judge of moral or civil things." [2] If men are to act by the laws of right reason and in harmony with the laws of nature, they need something more than a knowledge of the laws; they must be infused with a power to keep and observe them, and only the grace of God can give it to them. Thomas Shepard said that there is a sort of knowledge which some men have "from the book of creation, some by power of education, some by the light of the law . . . some by the letter of the gospel, and so men may know much and speak well. . . ." But over against this there is quite another kind of knowledge which only the elect can acquire, whereby they "see things in another manner; to tell you how, they can not; it is the beginning of light in heaven." [3] The Puritan would not doubt that Taylor's method was admirable and his book a tribute to his own nobility of character, but the facts of life being what they are, his way of dealing with sin simply will not work; make the truth as clear as he may to the mind of man, and man "will bend the Truth to his mind though hee breake it." Thomas Hooker of Connecticut directly opposed Richard Hooker of Bishopshorne by insisting that the latter's splendid galleon of stately reason will wreck itself upon the shoals of human perversity:

[1] *A Briefe Exposition with Practicall Observations upon The Whole Book of Ecclesiastes* (London, 1654), p. 160.
[2] *Ibid.*, p. 131.
[3] *Works*, ed. John A. Albro (Boston, 1853), II, 235.

Though arguments be never so plaine, and Scriptures never so pregnant; yet a carnall wretch will carry himselfe against all, and say, it is not my judgement, I am not of that mind.[1]

The morality of mere right reason and behavior regulated by judicious analysis will not hold up very far or very long; it is not enough:

There is a weakness, impotencie and insufficiencie in the understanding to reach this right discovery of sin, for however there remaynes so much glimmering in the twilight of Natural reason, and so much sensibleness in the stupid benummedness of the corrupt conscience of a carnal man, that it can both see and sensibly check for some grosser evil, or some such sins, or venom of sin, as crosseth his own peace and Comfort, or those ends which he sets up as the chiefest good at which he aymes, but to search into the entrales of sin, and discern the spiritual composition of the accursed nature thereof, he can in no wise attayn this by all the labor and light he hath.[2]

In the Puritan view, which the Puritan pointed out was undeniably corroborated by the evidence of human affairs, men needed the aid of God to achieve what the innocent Jeremy Taylor naïvely assumed was their natural capacity.

But, it should be noted, the Puritan does not deny that truth can be discovered in nature, poetry, right reason, and the consent of nations. He does not deny that these things are emanations of God's wisdom and that from them men may gain all manner of valuable instruction. He does not doubt that there is a light of nature, which, he says, "consists in common principles imprinted upon the reasonable soul, by nature," and that man naturally inclines his assent to certain fundamental truths, not only such truths as that the whole is greater than the part, but that there is a God, that parents are to be honored, and that there is a great difference between what is good and what is bad. As we have seen, the whole methodology of Puritan logic, following the example of Ramus, was built upon the inner monitor that can tell which of any two alternatives is the right one. The discoveries of the natural reason are useful to men "as a help whence they might seek after God" and "for the preservation of humane society." What the Puritan does insist on is that the

---

[1] Thomas Hooker, *The Soules Humiliation* (London, 1638), pp. 147–148.
[2] Thomas Hooker, *The Application of Redemption*, pp. 43–44.

natural man, if left to himself, will not read the lessons of nature
and reason correctly. "The little light that there is, is much miscarried[;] whilest it is managed by the reigning influence of the
power of darkness the Judgment is corrupt as well as the will,
whose corruption perverts the exercise of the faculty of reason."
Therefore God must draw up for man in black and white an exhaustive and authoritative code of laws, where he can find them
in terms adapted to his imperfect and benighted state, in clear
and unmistakable bold-faced type:

Star-light cannot make it, otherwise then night. The light of
nature since the fall, compared with the light of the image of God,
before the fall, hath not the proportion of Star-light, to the bright
Sun-light at noon-day. This indeed is but darkness. But, if compared with the light of the Gospell, it is worse then gross darkness.[1]

The laws of the Gospel, drawn up under these considerations,
cannot be limited to a few fundamentals, but must be numerous
enough to cover all the essential contingencies of life. Man was
once left free to learn from reason and nature, and promptly
abused the privilege; he must now submit his comprehension to
the instituted law before he be allowed to seek meanings once
more in the natural world. "Almost all the sin and misery that
hath filled the World, hath broke in at this door, hearkning to
reason against Institution." [2] The Biblical institution must fill
the place man made empty through his own folly, and since he
has thrown away his ability to profit from natural wisdom, he
must have an explicit law imposed upon him.

Thus when we pursue the difference between the attitude of
the Anglican and the Puritan toward the authority of scripture,
we come upon a deeper difference in their attitude toward man.
The Puritan believes as much as his opponent that the will of
God is exhibited in the world of nature and in the processes of
right reason, but in order for man to perceive it, there must be
something added to him.

True it is that the Lord fills Heaven and Earth with his presence, yea, the Heaven of Heavens is not able to contain him.
His infinite Being is every where, and one and the same every
where in regard of himself; because his being is most simple, and

[1] Norton, *Heart of N-England Rent*, pp. 12–13.
[2] Samuel Mather, *A Testimony from the Scripture against Idolatry & Superstition* (Cambridge, 1670), p. 16.

not subject to any shadow of change, being all one with himself. Yet he is said to take up his abode in a special manner, when he doth put forth the peculiar expression of his Work.[1]

There must be the spark, the quickening insight, the subtle and inward genius, which makes all the difference between the men who see and understand and know, and ordinary men who live from hand to mouth, never pierce below surface meanings, and never achieve self-mastery and direction. It is not merely ignorance that condemns the run of mortals to their fate; the man of unenlightened learning is in the same fix: "Let a man live the life of reason, and so as that he can discourse never so wisely and judiciously, and that he can converse with all sorts of men, and transact businesses in great dexterity, yet it is but a dead life." [2] The spark, when it does come, is not the revelation of new and undreamed-of truths, it is not the discovery of any hitherto unknown facts. It is a reinvigoration of the inner man, it is inspiration, ecstasy: "it leaves an impression upon the most inward motions of the soul, as they meet with God in the most retired and refined actions thereof." [3] It is not merely a correct teaching of the mind or judgment, it is "a renewall of the whole soule of a man, the disposition and inclination of the whole must be changed and altered." [4] All the ideas, all the doctrines, all the reasons can be known before a man becomes regenerate, but known only with the mind, not with the heart. An unregenerate man, following the dictates of nature and cultivating the virtues celebrated in the poets, may perform many separate good actions, but these will not come "from an inward soul or principle of life," just as, says Thomas Shepard in a metaphor characteristically Puritan in its middle-class homeliness:

he that had beer given him, when milk and wine and sugar were put into it to mend it, said, the wine is good, and the milk is good, but the beer is bad; so profession, affection is good, but the heart, the man, is bad.[5]

By the grace of God, the Puritan meant the insight which sees at last what has been before the eyes all along; as though one had listened many times to a piece of music which to his ears

---

[1] Thomas Hooker, *The Application of Redemption*, pp. 3–4.

[2] John Cotton, *The way of Life* (London, 1641), p. 301.

[3] Thomas Hooker, *A Comment upon Christ's last Prayer In the Seventeenth of John* (London, 1656), p. 88.

[4] Cotton, *Christ the Fountaine of Life*, p. 98.

[5] *Works*, II, 282–283.

was meaningless, and then suddenly its form becomes clear to him and for the first time he really hears it, not merely with his ears, but with his whole being. Regeneration is such a comprehension of the world in a flash of vision, and it therefore "exceeds, and over-flies the most Eagle-sighted Apprehensions of any Natural Man in the World." [1] Only those who have experienced it will be able to understand aright the law of nature or be able to guide the steps of reason.

If the plight of man in the world is thus desperate, how absurd to erect his reason into a yardstick for what must be true in the reason of God, how fantastic to assert that if human reason cannot conceive a thing, then the thing is nothing, "hath no possibility"! It is the most insidious form of arrogance to proclaim that what seems reasonable and just on earth, in time and space, must also be binding in infinity, outside the realm of time and space, on God, who dwells in regions undecipherable to our discourse. Undoubtedly, the Puritans would answer Taylor's ultimate point, God *is* reasonable and just, but not necessarily in *our* terms. If He accommodates Himself to *our* notions of what is equitable, it is His gracious condescension. The finite cannot legislate for infinitude; our reason, though partaking of the divine nature, partakes of it only in part, and is not sufficiently universal to warrant our saying that what is absurd to it cannot be part of faith. Reason is not before Revelation. We do not prove the authority of scripture by testing it with reasonable laws formulated beforehand; we find out first what scripture means by exegesis, etymology, comparison of texts, analysis of words, logical deductions and inferences. Our premises are not secured by approaching the Bible convinced beforehand that what is contrary to reason cannot be contained there, or that what is against the light of nature cannot possibly be intended, but the Bible itself gives us the premises of reason. The light of reason is "an effect proceeding from the word." [2] We do not test the Bible by nature, but nature by the Bible. It is in this sense that the Puritan achieved, or thought he had achieved, the unity of faith and intellect, dogma and reason. Reason is the implement for the interpretation of given principles, and grace is the implement for the direction of reason. But reason does not discover fundamental principles in itself. The regenerate intellect does not fetch up truth from

[1] Thomas Hooker, *A Comment upon Christ's last Prayer*, p. 443.
[2] Norton, *Heart of N-England Rent*, p. 13.

its own depths, like water from a well, but is filled with truth from the fountain of scripture. Thomas Hooker thus summarized the union of the three factors, scripture, reason, and grace, into the moment of supreme insight which was the goal of all Puritan aspiration and the inspiration for all Puritan theory:

The godly doe not onely apprehend the meaning of the words in the Scripture, and are able to discourse of the reasons therein contained, but they discern also the spiritualnesse of the work of grace, that is discovered in the same. Observe it: There being, first, the Word of God set down in his book, and then reasons that goe along with it, and lastly, a spirituall work of grace, that God hath made known in those reasons; the Saints of God alone see the spiritualnesse of the work that is manifested and communicated in that reason there set down . . . Take but an Apple, there is never a man under heaven can tell what tast it is of, whether sweet or soure, untill he have tasted of it; he seeth the colour and the quantity of it, but knoweth not the tast.[1]

Therefore Jeremy Taylor speaks from a purely external and formal knowledge when he says that we are to prove by reason whether any proposition is revealed by God. Reasons are there indeed, good reasons and bad reasons; the saints of God understand the right reasons and why they are right, exactly as a man knows the taste of an apple. The certitude is neither irrational conviction nor mere rational demonstration, but both at once. Jeremy Taylor is arguing that a body of truth exists, of which the Bible is one expression. The Puritan is arguing that the source of truth is the Bible, read with the eye of grace, and therefore rationally understood. Reason does not prove the sense and intention of God, as Taylor says, but the sense and intention of God instruct the reason. For the Puritan, reason does not make clear the sense of scripture, but the clear sense of scripture creates the reason.

5. *Estimations*

The Puritan attitude toward the Bible, to the extent that it was a preservation of intellectual values within the dogmatism, may elicit our hearty approbation. But when we come to the content of the dogma, to what the Puritan insisted the Bible did teach, and to what he expected the regenerate man to find reasonable,

[1] "Culpable Ignorance, or the Danger of Ignorance under Meanes," pp. 189–216 in *The Saints Dignitie* (London, 1651), pp. 208–209.

in short, when we come to Puritan theology, many persons encounter an insuperable stumbling block to an unqualified approval of Puritan thinking. Not only does the conventional picture of the Puritan creed seem exceedingly unattractive to twentieth-century taste, but the idea of theology in any form is almost equally objectionable. In most secondary accounts Puritans are called Calvinists, and then and there discussion of their intellectual life ceases. Dr. Holmes's "One-Hoss Shay" is deemed a sufficient description.

It is true, the Puritans were Calvinists, if we mean that they more or less agreed with the great theologian of Geneva. They held, that is, that men had fallen into a state of sin, that in order to be saved they must receive from God a special infusion of grace, that God gives the grace to some and not to others out of His own sovereign pleasure, and that therefore from the beginning of time certain souls were "predestined" to heaven and the others sentenced to damnation. But if the New Englanders were Calvinists, it was because they happened to agree with Calvin; they approved his doctrine not because he taught it, but because it seemed inescapably indicated when they studied scripture or observed the actions of men. The sinfulness of the average man was a fact that could be empirically verified, and in itself demonstrated that he needed divine grace in order to be lifted above himself; the men who did receive what they thought was an influx of grace learned by experience that only in such an ecstasy of illumination did truth become thoroughly evident and completely understandable. Obviously the experience was given to relatively few men; therefore God, who is outside time and who is omniscient, must have known from the beginning of time who would and who would not achieve it. This is the law of life; some men are born rich and some poor, some intelligent and some stupid, some are lucky and others unfortunate, some are happy and some melancholy, some are saved and some are not. There is no reason but that God so ordained it.

The Lord to shew the soveraign freedom of his pleasure, that he may do with his own what he wil, and yet do wrong to none, he denyes pardon and acceptance to those who seek it with some importunity and earnestness . . . and yet bestowes mercy and makes known himself unto some *who never sought him*.[1]

---

[1] Thomas Hooker, *The Application of Redemption*, p. 299.

Puritan theology, therefore, is simply a statement in dogmatic guise of a philosophy of life, wherein it is held on the one hand that men must act by reason and abide by justice, and strive for an inward communication with the force that controls the world, but on the other hand that they must not expect that force always to be cribbed and confined by their conceptions of what is reasonable and just. There is an eternal obligation upon men to be equitable, fair, and good, but who can say that any such morality is also binding on the universe? There are certain amenities which men must observe in their dealings with men, but who can say that they must also be respected by the tiger, by the raging storm, by the lightning, or by the cancer? It is only when the theology of "predestination" is seen in these less technical terms that its vitality as a living faith and its strength as a sustaining philosophy become comprehensible.

But the theology of New England was not simply Calvinism, it was not a mere reduplication of the dogmas of the *Institutes*. What New Englanders believed was an outgrowth, as we have seen, of their background, which was humanistic and English, and it was conditioned by their particular controversy with the Church of England. Simon-pure Calvinism is a much more dogmatic, anti-rational creed than that of the Congregational parsons in Massachusetts. The emigrants went to New England to prove that a state and a church erected on the principles for which they were agitating in England would be blessed by God and prosper. The source of the New England ideology is not Calvin, but England, or more accurately, the Bible as it was read in England, not in Geneva.

Though, of course, the controversy in England was a political, social, and economic one, it was also the intellectual dispute we have outlined. We might summarize it at this point by saying that in order to harmonize reason and scripture, the Anglican endeavored to reduce the doctrines imposed by scripture to the barest minimum; the Puritan extended scripture to cover the whole of existence and then set himself to prove the content of all scripture essentially reasonable. Only with this definition of origins and tendencies in mind can we read Puritan theology aright. In order to demonstrate that the content of scripture was comprehensible to reason, the Puritan theorists worked out a substantial addition to the theology of Calvinism which in New England was quite as important as the original doctrine. This ad-

dition or elaboration of the Calvinist doctrine is generally called
the "Covenant Theology," or the "Federal Theology." There is
no necessity here for examining it in detail.[1] It was a special way
of reading scripture so that the books assembled in the Bible
could all be seen to make sense in the same way. The doctrine
held that after the fall of man, God voluntarily condescended to
treat with man as with an equal and to draw up a covenant or
contract with His creature in which He laid down the terms and
conditions of salvation, and pledged Himself to abide by them.
The covenant did not alter the fact that those only are saved
upon whom God sheds His grace, but it made very clear and
reasonable how and why certain men are selected, and prescribed
the conditions under which they might reach a fair assurance of
their own standing. Above all, in the covenant God pledged Himself not to run athwart human conceptions of right and justice;
God was represented while entering the compact as agreeing to
abide by certain human ideas. Not in all respects, not always,
but in the main. I have said that any Puritan would have subscribed to Laud's argument concerning the authority of scripture;
it is now necessary to add that if called upon to discuss the question himself, the Puritan would not go about it in the same way.
He would not make a distinction between testimonies brought
in from another realm of experience besides faith, between rational confirmations and the act of belief, but he would begin
with scripture itself, the object of faith and the measure of reason.
His principal argument for the satisfaction of the reason would
be that once the Bible is believed by faith, it appears wholly
and beautifully rational; it contains a consistent doctrine, that of
the covenant, which makes it at once the source of belief and
the fountain of reason.

To find equivalents in modern terms for the ideas we have
been discussing is well-nigh impossible. To translate seventeenth-
century issues into twentieth-century phrases, when they cannot
possibly mean the same things, is to forego any accurate understanding of them. The results of modern historical investigation
and textual criticism have made fantastic, even for those who
believe the scripture to be the word of God, acceptance of it in
anything like the spirit of the seventeenth century. But if we
cannot find a common denominator for equating the ideas of the

[1] Cf. Perry Miller, "The Marrow of Puritan Divinity," *Publications of the Colonial
Society of Massachusetts*, XXXII, 247–300.

Puritans with ideas of today, we may possibly get at them by understanding the temperament, the mood, the psychology that underlay the theories. If Puritanism as a creed has crumbled, it can be of only antiquarian significance to us, but if Puritanism is also a state of mind, it may be something closer home.

There is probably no admirer of Puritanism so blindly devoted that he will not find the Anglican apologists in some respects much more attractive. The richness of their culture, the catholicity of their taste, the calmness of their temper, the well-controlled judgment, the mellow piety, and above all the poetry of Richard Hooker and Jeremy Taylor are qualities which unhappily are not too conspicuous in the pages reprinted in this volume. There is an air about these men of breadth and wisdom, they do not labor under terrific and incessant pressure, they are not always taut under the critical scrutiny of an implacable taskmaster. Simple humanity cries at last for some relief from the interminable high seriousness of the Puritan code, the eternal strenuousness of self-analysis, and the never-ending search of conscience. Though it is a great mistake to think the Puritans could not forget their theology and enjoy themselves, and though Nathaniel Ward proves that they could possess a rollicking sense of humor, the general impression conveyed by Puritan writing is that of men who lived far too uninterruptedly upon the heights of intensity. Perhaps the most damning feature of their intensity was that it could become, over a period of time, as conventional and as stereotyped as worldliness itself. Thomas Shepard, telling the story of his conversion (pp. 471–472), has a vivid and living sense of the eternal presence of God, but Samuel Sewall, moralizing over God's grace while feeding his chickens (p. 511), is at best quaintly amusing, and when he bears down with the authority of scripture on the question of wigs he becomes tiresome, as Madam Winthrop undoubtedly felt (p. 526). There was almost always an element of narrowness, harshness, and literal-mindedness associated with Puritanism, enough to justify some of the criticisms of the bishops and some of the condemnations that have been made on the Puritan spirit in more recent times.

The strength of Puritanism was its realism. If we may borrow William James's frequently misleading division of the human race into the two types of the "tough-minded" and the "tender-minded," and apply it with caution, it may serve our purposes. Though there were undoubtedly men in the Church of England, such as John Donne, whom we would have to describe as "tough," and a number of Puritans who would fit the description of "tender," yet in the main Anglicans such as Hooker and Taylor are quite clearly on the side of the more tender-minded, while the Puritan mind was one of the toughest the world has ever had to deal with. It is impossible to conceive of a disillusioned Puritan; no matter what misfortune befell him, no matter how often or how tragically his fellowmen failed him, he would have been prepared for the worst, and would have expected no better. At the same time, there was nothing of the fatalist about him; as so often happens in the history of thought, the believers in a supreme determining power were the most energetic of soldiers and crusaders. The charge of Cromwell's Ironsides was, on that particular score, proof positive of the superiority of the Puritan over the Anglican, and the Indians of New England learned to their very great sorrow how vehement could be the onset of troops who fought for a predestined victory. There was nothing luke-warm, halfhearted, or flabby about the Puritan; whatever he did, he did with zest and gusto. In that sense we might say that though his life was full of anguish of spirit, he nevertheless enjoyed it hugely. Existence for him was completely dramatic, every minute was charged with meaning. And when we come to an end of this roll call of characteristics, the one which yet remains the most difficult to evoke was his peculiar balance of zeal and enthusiasm with control and wariness. In his inner life he was overwhelmingly preoccupied with achieving a union with the divine; in his external life he was predominantly concerned with self-restraint. Compare, for example, these two passages from Thomas Hooker: the first in the vein of subjective rapture:

So, I would have you do, loose your selves, and all ordinances, and creatures, and all that you have, and do, in the Lord Christ. How is that? Let all bee swallowed up, and let nothing be seene but a Christ . . . As it is with the Moone and Starres, when the Sunne comes, they loose all their light, though they are there in the heavens still; and as it is with rivers, they all goe into the Sea, and are all swallowed up of the Sea: and yet there is nothing seene but the Sea . . . So let it bee with thy Soule, when thou wouldest finde mercy and grace.[1]

And then this admonition:

[1] *The Soules Humiliation*, p. 77.

I know there is wilde love and joy enough in the world, as there is wilde Thyme and other herbes, but we would have garden love and garden joy, of Gods owne planting.[1]

No wonder the Puritan has been something of a puzzlement and a trial to the Gentiles. He was a visionary who never forgot that two plus two equals four; he was a soldier of Jehovah who never came out on the losing side of a bargain. He was a radical and a revolutionary, but not an anarchist; when he got into power he ruled with an iron hand, and also according to a fundamental law. He was a practical idealist with a strong dash of cynicism; he came to New England to found the perfect society and the kingdom of the elect—and never expected it to be perfect, but only the best that fallible men could make. His creed was the revealed word of God and his life was the rule of moderation; his beliefs were handed down from on high and his conduct was regulated by expediency. He was a doctrinaire and an opportunist. Truth for him had been written down once and for all in a definitive, immutable, complete volume, and the covers closed to any further additions; thereupon he devoted all the energies he could spare from more immediate tasks to scholarship and interpretation. He lived in the world according to the principles that must govern this world, with an ever-present sense that they were only for the time being and that his true home was elsewhere. "There is," said John Cotton, "another combination of vertues strangely mixed in every lively holy Christian, And that is, Diligence in worldly businesses, and yet deadnesse to the world; such a mystery as none can read, but they that know it." The Puritan ideal was the man who could take all opportunities, lose no occasions, "and bestir himselfe for profit," and at the same time "bee a man dead-hearted to the world." He might wrest New England from the Indians, trade in the seven seas, and speculate in lands; "yet his heart is not set upon these things, he can tell what to doe with his estate when he hath got it." [2]

The most serious of charges laid against the Puritans has been their supposed deficiency in aesthetic perceptions. Because they did not want men to fix their veneration upon worldly things, they had no use for sculpture, distrusted the arts when they were prized merely for their sensuous appeal, were contemptuous of

[1] *The Soules Implantation* (London, 1637), p. 158.
[2] *Christ the Fountaine of Life*, pp. 119–120.

the beautiful ritual and ornamentation of the Church of England.
The poet George Herbert, defending the habiliment of his church
against what he thought the trappings of the Church of Rome,
found the plainness of Puritan worship going much too far in the
other direction:

> She in the valley is so shie
> Of dressing that her hair doth lie
>   About her eares;
> While she avoids her neighbour's pride,
> She wholly goes on th'other side,
>   And nothing wears.[1]

The New Model Army has incurred infamy with posterity for
hacking to pieces the furnishings of cathedrals. But the asperity of
the Puritan discipline and the Puritan distrust of merely sensuous
beauty did not mean that the Puritan was without an aesthetic
of his own, or that he was hostile to beauty. John Preston defined beauty in characteristic Puritan fashion: "Beauty that consists in a conformity of all the parts"; [2] Thomas Hooker said
that sin "defaceth the beautiful frame, and that sweet correspondence and orderly usefulness the Lord first implanted in the order
of things." [3] The Puritan conceived of beauty as order, the order
of things as they are, not as they appear, as they are in pure and
abstract conception, as they are in the mind of God. He spoke
of his church polity, his bare, crude churches, without altars or
choirs, foursquare and solid, as lovely; they were so to him because they incarnated the beauty of the one polity Christ had
ordained. His conception of the beautiful was, like Plato's, the
efficient order of things; in that sense, he held indeed that beauty
is truth, and truth beauty, though he did not think that was quite
all he needed to know in life.

When the historian thus attempts to consider Puritanism in
all its ramifications, he finds himself at the end hesitating to deliver judgment upon it, or to be wholly satisfied that it has passed
into the limbo of anthologies. Certainly we can look upon the
disappearance of some features with no regrets, and only deplore
some others where they still survive. We have had enough of
the Puritan censoriousness, its tendency to make every man his
brother's keeper. When the Puritan habit of probing into the soul

[1] *Works*, ed. George Herbert Palmer (New York, 1905), III, 103.
[2] *The New Creature* (London, 1633), p. 52.
[3] *The Application of Redemption*, p. 59.

has degenerated into the "New England conscience"—where it is apt to remain as a mere feeling that everything enjoyable is sinful—then the ridicule heaped upon Puritan inhibitions becomes a welcome antidote. Certainly many amenities of social life have increased in New England, and in America, in direct proportion as Puritanism has receded. But while we congratulate ourselves upon these ameliorations, we cannot resist a slight fear that much of what has taken the place of Puritanism in our philosophies is just so much failure of nerve. The successors of Puritanism, both the evangelicals and the rationalists, as we survey them today, seem to have been comparatively sentimental, to have lacked a stomach for reality. The optimism and cheerfulness to which the revolters against Puritanism turned now threaten to become rather a snare and a delusion than a liberation. "Science" tells us of a world of stark determinism, in which heredity and environmental conditioning usurp the function of the Puritan God in predestining men to ineluctable fates. It is, indeed, true that the sense of things being ordered by blind forces presents a different series of problems than does the conception of determination by a divine being; no matter how unintelligible the world might seem to the Puritan, he never lost confidence that ultimately it was directed by an intelligence. Yet even with this momentous difference in our imagination of the controlling power, the human problem today has more in common with the Puritan understanding of it than at any time for two centuries: how can man live by the lights of humanity in a universe that appears indifferent or even hostile to them? We are terribly aware once more, thanks to the revelation of psychologists and the events of recent political history, that men are not perfect or essentially good. The Puritan description of them, we have been reluctantly compelled to admit, is closer to what we have witnessed than the description given in Jeffersonian democracy or in transcendentalism. The Puritan accounted for these qualities by the theory of original sin; he took the story of the fall of man in the Garden of Eden for a scientific, historical explanation of these observable facts. The value of his literature today cannot lie for us in his explanation; if there is any, it must rest in the accuracy of his observations.

II. The Puritans as Literary Artists

The tenets of Puritan faith obstructed any clear formulation of general aesthetic theory. Puritans saw images of divine things in the world about them, and drew analogies between the beautiful objects and the perfect archetype which they conceived as existing in the mind of God. William Hubbard spoke thus:

In a curious piece of Architecture, that which first offers it self to the view of the beholder, is the beauty of the structure, the proportion that one piece bears to another, wherein the skill of the Architect most shews it self. But that which is most Admirable in sensitive and rational beings, is that inward principle, seated in some one part, able to guid[e] the whole, and influence all the rest of the parts, with an apt and regular motion, for their mutual good and safety.[1]

The emphasis is theological. Hubbard has in mind the "remains of God's Image"—that is, the remnant of the regulative power which God had originally created in perfection in the human understanding by which the will is informed and directed, and the passions balanced and utilized. Beauty is the order and harmony which God established, and art is useful only so far as the exercise of it may shape man's spirit to a better understanding of the divine purpose. Reason and emotion were given man to perceive the end for which God created the world, and if properly controlled they lead to the highest virtue. In such a scheme beauty is postulated as reason and faith conjoined; therefore to single out music, statuary, painting, drama, and the dance as subjects for considered appraisal,—to assign to such purely sensuous phenomena more than a negligible rank in the teleological scheme, would have been grossly unbefitting.

Yet within the duly proportioned framework the spoken and written word deserved considered analysis, for "The Wise Man saith, Words in season are as Apples of Gold in Pictures of Silver, or fitness of words (well tuning them) is the grace of them, and puts wheels to the Chariots to carry them to the mind. . . ."[2] Nicholas Noyes gave a further clue to the Puritan approach:

[1] *The Happiness of a People*, p. 11.

[2] William Hubbard, *The Benefits Of a Well-Ordered Conversation* (Boston, 1684), beginning of preface. Samuel Willard's *A Compleat Body of Divinity* (Boston, 1726) is a compendium of orthodox Puritan theology as he had preached it in the 1680's and 1690's. On pp. 27–33 he gives attention to the service of rhetoric in preaching.

> Nor thine, nor thy Books credit, would I raise,
> Within the gates thine own works thee shall praise
> Or suffer for 't: For good Books now adayes
> Like virtue practice need, but no man's praise.[1]

Noyes's point of view is typical of Puritan critical theory in that he does not seek to glorify literature or proclaim its laws, but rather to emphasize the fitness of a "plain style" which had been the badge of Puritan writers for a century. Even before New England was founded, the Puritans had advocated a prose, simple, clear, and restrained; fit to satisfy the reason, not charm the fancy; to instruct, not rouse the passions. "Painful" Perkins, fellow of Christ College, Cambridge, was a Puritan whose evangelical fervor made him one of the most influential leaders of New England thought. He had written, in a manual of sermonizing that was the recognized authority in New England, that "the Minister may, yea and must privately use at his libertie the arts, Philosophy, and variety of reading, whilest he is in framing his sermon: but he ought in publike to conceale all these from the people. . . ." [2] Thomas Hooker warned such of his readers as might find the manner of his discourse "too *Logical, or Scholasticall*, in regard of the *terms*" he used:

> That plainesse and perspicuity, both for matter and manner of expression, are the things, that I have conscientiously indeavoured in the whole debate: for I have ever thought writings that come abroad, they are not to dazle, but direct the apprehension of the meanest, and I have accounted it the chiefest part of Judicious learning, to make a hard point easy and familiar in explication.[3]

Although Puritans cultivated a studied simplicity, we would stray quite from the truth if we imagined they countenanced prose that was flat and awkward. The audience helped to prevent a minister from neglecting good form, for the Puritan listener "esteemed that preaching best wherein was most of God, least of man, when vain flourishes of wit, and words were declined . . . yet could he distinguish between studied plainness, & negligent rudeness. . . .[4] There were several motives which led the

---

[1] *Ibid.*, commendatory verses, sig. A 2ᵛ and A 3.

[2] William Perkins, *The Art of Prophecying* (*Works*, 1631), II, 670.

[3] *A Survey of the Summe of Church-Discipline* (London, 1648), preface, sig. b.

[4] John Geree, *The Character of an old English Puritan, Or Non Conformist* (London, 1646), p. 2.

Puritans to develop an intentional style—one which, though plain, was reached by conscious purpose. Their ministers were not so dull as to think that careless oratory or illogical analysis would hold the respect of an educated laity, nor did they intend that the uneducated among their people should be allowed to respect a slipshod utterance. They wrote voluminously and with high dedication; the art of writing well therefore was assiduously cultivated that both the intellect and the emotions might be stirred to the fullest response. One of the greatest preachers in the first quarter of the century, Richard Sibbes, whose works were widely read in New England, enunciated one part of the Puritan theory of style in writing the preface for a fellow Puritan's book:

But because the way to come to the heart is often to pass through the fancy, therefore this godly man studied by lively representations to help men's faith by the fancy. It was our Saviour Christ's manner of teaching to express heavenly things in an earthly manner; and it was the study of the wise man, Solomon, becoming a preacher, to find out pleasant words, or words of delight.[1]

Sibbes here reveals that the source for much that is actually dramatic in Puritan writing was the Bible,—the model which justified an indulgence in rhetorical flourishes even though plainness and perspicuity were being exalted at the expense of form and finish.

However, had the Puritan style derived entirely from Biblical models, it would have lacked the hard-driving logic, the analytical and reasoned exposition, the close-knit structure which are its distinguishing characteristics. William Ames's textbook of theology was the standard work used at Harvard and Yale down to the middle of the eighteenth century; Ames defended the plain style, speaking both as logician and preacher, and his example influenced every sermon delivered in New England:

The drinesse of the style, and harshnesse of some words will be much blamed by the same persons [as those who object to the logical structure]. But I doe profer to exercise my selfe in that heresie, that when it is my purpose to Teach, I thinke I should not say that in two words which may be said in one, and that that key is to be chosen which doth open best, although it be of wood, if there be not a golden key of the same efficacy.[2]

---

[1] *Complete Works*, ed. Alexander B. Grosart (Edinburgh, 1862), I, ci.
[2] *The Marrow of Sacred Divinity* (London, 1643), sig. A 4ᵛ.

But economy of words was not to mean ineffective delivery; the plain style was not intended to become a dull style. As Ames instructed his students on another page:

Men are to be pricked to the quick, that they may feele in every one of them that the Apostle saith, namely that the Word of the Lord is a two edged sword, that peirceth into the inward thoughts and affections, and goeth through unto the joyning together of the bones and marrow. Preaching therefore ought not to be dead, but lively and effectuall, so that an unbeliever coming into the Congregation of the faithfull he ought to be affected, and as it were digged through with the very hearing of the Word, that he may give glory to God.[1]

It is not fair to judge Puritan prose on the basis of the pamphlet wars engaged in by the Marprelates, or by William Prynne or John Milton, wherein too frequently the attacks are violent, the issue trivial, and the language harsh and coarse. The Puritans left to posterity a full harvest of sermons and tracts, histories, biographies, and journals. If much appears disproportionately argued or exhaustively analyzed, we have the writers' expressed purpose to "direct the apprehension of the meanest." The Puritan ideal might be phrased roughly in this fashion: enough rhetoric to pass through the fancy to the heart, but never so much that the apprehension of the simple or the earnest should be dazzled. Thomas Hooker pointed to the evil consequences that followed upon a too ornate sermon style:

I have sometime admired at this: why a company of Gentlemen, yeomen and poore women, that are scarcely able to know their A. B. C. yet they have a Minister to speake Latine, Greeke, and Hebrew, and to use the Fathers, when it is certain, they know nothing at all. The reason is, because all this stings not, they may sit and sleepe in their sinnes, and goe to hell hoodwinckt, never awakened.[2]

Many features of Puritan writing, which from a purely literary point of view might seem to be faults, were deliberately cultivated in order to achieve greater clarity or more certain effectiveness with the particular audience addressed. No doubt, too, occasional carelessness of structure in Puritan tracts can be charged to the insatiable demand for theological discussion, which sometimes betrayed a Puritan minister into offering his wares before

---

[1] *Ibid.*, p. 159.
[2] *The Soules Preparation* (London, 1632), p. 66.

he gave them adequate trimming. Certain sterile characteristics
are common to Anglican literature as well: the pedantry of
learned quotation, and the unrelieved syllogistic method. In manner also there are many similarities between Anglican and Puritan
style. To the extent that any writer of the second quarter of the
seventeenth century was heir to Elizabethan word-consciousness,
to the flavor of the Geneva Bible—the most popular version for
a hundred years—he inherited a love of figure and ornament which
the King James version itself drew upon.

But there are well marked differences. The Anglican love of
solemn ritual, of tradition and hierarchy is often reflected in a
suavity of diction which the Puritans scorned. Furthermore, the
Anglicans did not share the Puritans' veneration for the Bible as
the sole approach to the spiritual life; therefore they drew more
consciously upon their classical culture and wide reading to enrich their style and vary their rhetorical effects. Anglican sermons
less often attempt to convince the reason by clear logic and coherent summary than to stir the imagination. In constructing
their sentences, modeled upon Latin, they strove for the harmony of Ciceronian periods—a rhetorical effect which Puritans
looked upon as "more sauce than meat." "I professe it is beyond
my care to please the nicenesse of mens palates, with any quaint-
nesse of language," Thomas Hooker remarks, adding: "It was a
cavill cast upon *Hierom* that in his writings he was *Ciceronianus
non Christianus*." [1] Anglicans unlike Puritans, made use of ornament for its own sake; they elaborated metaphors and illustra-
tions for the purpose of enriching their prose. Let these selections,
taken at random from the works of three great Anglican preachers,
serve to illustrate the point: [2]

And it falls out very often, that some one Father, of Strong
reputation and authority in his time, doth snatch and swallow
some probable interpretation of Scripture: and then digesting it
into his Homilies, and applying it in dehortations, and encouragements, as the occasions and diseases of his Auditory, or his age
require, and imagining thereupon delightfull and figurative in-
sinuations, and setting it to the Musique of his style, (as every man

---

[1] *A Survey of the Summe*, sig. 4ᵛ. Hooker refers to Erasmus's Life of St. Jerome
included in the Complete Works of the church father (9 vols., Basel, 1516–1520).

[2] The first is John Donne, *Biathanatos* [*ca.* 1610] (London, 1646), p. 206; the second,
Lancelot Andrewes, "Sermons of the Resurrection," delivered Easter Sunday, April
13, 1623, in *Ninety-Six Sermons* (Anglo-Catholic Library, 5 vols., Oxford, 1841–1843),
III, 75, 76; the third, Jeremy Taylor, *The Golden Grove* (London, 1656), pp. 24, 25.

which is accustomed to these Meditations, shall often finde in himselfe such a spirituall wontonnesse, and devout straying into such delicacies,) that sense which was but probable, growes necessary, and those who succeed had rather enjoy his wit, then vexe their owne; as often times we are loath to change or leave off a counterfeit stone, by reason of the well setting thereof.

By this meanes, I thinke, it became so generally to be beleeved, that the fruit which *Eve* eat was an Apple; And that *Lots* wife was turned to a pillar of Salt; And that *Absalon* was hanged by the haire of the head; And that *Iephthe* killed his Daughter; And many other such, which grew currant, not from an evidence in the Text, but because such an acceptation, was most usefull, and applyable. Of this number, *Iudas* case might be.

You see how Christs garments came to be "red." Of the wine-press that made them so we have spoken, but not of the colour itself. A word of that too. It was His colour at His Passion. They put Him in purple; then it was His weed itself, and so He made it more with the dye of His own blood. And the same colour He is now in again at His rising. Not with His own now, but with the blood of the wounded Edomites, whom treading under His feet, their blood bestained Him and His apparel. So one and the same colour at both; dying and rising in red; but with difference as much as is between His own as His enemies' blood . . .

The tincture, I say, first of our sin original, dyed in the wool; and then again of our sins actual, dyed in the cloth too. Twice dyed; so was Christ twice . . . So was it meet for crimson sinners to have a crimson Saviour; a Saviour of such a colour it behoved us to have . . . Yea, He died and rose again both in our colours, that we might die and rise too in His. We fall now again upon the same point in the colours we did before in the cups. He to drink the sour vinegar of our wild grapes, that we might drink His sweet in the cup of blessing. O cup of blessing, may we say of this cup! *O stolam formosam*, of that colour! *Illi gloriosam, nobis fructuosam;* 'glorious to Him, no less fruitful to us.' He in Mount Golgotha like to us, that we in Mount Tabor like to Him. This is the substance of our rejoicing in this colour.

Jesus Christ being taken by the Rulers of the Jews, bound and derided, buffeted and spit upon, accused weakly and persecuted violently; at last, wanting matter and pretences to condemn him, they asked him of his Person and Office; and because he affirmed that great Truth, which all the world of good men long'd for, that he was the *Messias*, and designed to sit *at the right hand of the Majesty on high*, they resolved to call it *Blasphemy*, and delivered him over to *Pilate*, and by importunity and threats, forced him against his Conscience, to give him up to be scourged, and then to be Crucified. The Souldiers therefore mocking him with a robe and reed, and pressing a Crown of thorns upon his head, led him to the place of his death; compelling him to bear his Cross, to which they presently nail'd him; on which for three hours he hang'd in extreme torture, being a sad spectacle of the most afflicted, and the most innocent person of the whole warld.

Putting aside individual idiosyncrasies for the moment, we observe certain tendencies which are common to all three selections: an eloquence which is achieved by such rhythmic periods, mannered ingenuity, grammatical subtleties, and tortuous language as rob the prose of any sense of urgency while conveying through the rich, sometimes extravagant, fancy a poetic delicacy. It seems to be the authors' conscious aim to stir the reader through the wealth and variety of ornaments, through balance, antithesis, and alliteration, through word-pairs and verbal conceits. The Puritans, on the other hand, adopted plainness to give the application of their sermons more force and directness; there is ready use of figure in their sermons, but the intent is less to enrich the color of the prose than to vitalize the point at issue, to intensify the concreteness, or clarify the doctrine. Perhaps the four examples [1] here set forth will serve to point the case:

Learn wee then hereby, every one of us to judge our selves and our families, and to teach every person to judge themselves, as at other times, so more especially in the dayes of their humiliation, and when they come to renew their promises and vowes with their God. If *David* were not able to say that his house were perfect with God, what then may we say? we have not that means which he had, such Teachers to instruct us, such guides whereby we might be brought forward, neither are wee compassed about with Prophets in a land of uprightnesse; where shall we finde an house that walks with God as *David* did? that growes as the tender grasse, and is as the Sun without cloud? We are therefore to charge our selves with our follies and failings, and to humble our selves for them, whether it be towards God, or towards one another: wee should consider how wee are failing in the true feare of

[1] The first is John Cotton, *The Covenant of Gods free Grace* (London, 1645), p. 7; the second, Thomas Shepard, *The Clear Sun-shine of the Gospel* (London, 1648), p. 37; the third, Urian Oakes, *New-England Pleaded with*, p. 34; the fourth, Samuel Willard, *The Child's Portion* (Boston, 1684), pp. 226, 227 (selection from sermon entitled "All Plots against God and his People Detected and Defeated").

God, how subject we are to eye-service, and although wee can do little in reforming kingdomes and nations, yet we may take care for our own houses, wee may judge our selves and our families in our manifold failings, we may judge our selves for our high-mindednesse, drousinesse in good duties, for our evill slow heart to get hold of any spirituall thing, for our customary performances.

Thus you have a true, but somewhat rent and ragged relation of these things; it may be most sutable to the story of naked and ragged men: my desire is that no mans Spectacles may deceive him, so as to look upon these things either as bigger or lesser, better or worser then they are; which all men generally are apt to doe at things at so great distance, but that they may judge of them as indeed they are, by which truth they see here exprest in the things themselves. I knowe that some thinke that all this worke among them is done and acted thus by the *Indians* to please the *English*, and for applause from them; and it is not unlikely but 'tis in many, who doe but blaze for a time; but certainly 'tis not so in all, but that the power of the Word hath taken place in some, and that inwardly and effectually, but how far savingly time will declare, and the reader may judge of, by the story it self of these things.

Nor am I so Severe, or Morose, as to exclaim against this or that Fashion, provided it carry nothing of Immodesty in it, or Contrariety to the Rules of Moral Honesty. The civil Custome of the place where we live is that which must regulate in this case. But when persons spend more time in trimming their Bodies then their Souls, that you may say of them (as a Worthy Divine wittily speaks) that they are like the *Cinamon Tree*, nothing good but the *Bark:* When they go beyond what their State and Condition will allow, that they are necessitated to run into Debt, and neglect works of mercy and charity, or exact upon others in their dealings, that they may maintain their Port and Garb; or when they exceed their Rank and Degree (whereas one end of Apparel is to distinguish and put a difference between persons according to their Places and Conditions) and when the Sons and Daughters of *Sion* are proud and haughty in their Carriage and Attire in an humbling time, when the *Church* is brought low, *Ierusalem* and *Iudah* is in a Ruinous Condition, and the Lord calls to deep Humiliation: This is very displeasing to God, and both Scripture and Reason condemn it. These are the most gross, and fantastical, and foolish buddings of Pride.

The Web which they [the wicked] have been for a long while in weaving, God will unravel in a moment: He will shortly muster up his Forces and draw out his Armies into the Field, and call together the Fowls of Heaven to his great Supper which he shall provide for them, where he will give them to eat of *the flesh of Kings* . . . Rev. 19.17. This is the work which he hath undertaken to do, and will certainly accomplish it throughly, who hath written on his Vesture, and on his Thigh, KING OF KINGS, AND LORD OF LORDS. And since the case stands thus, what is there then remaining more for us to do, but to be the Lord's Remembrancers. Not ceasing day nor night to be earnestly and importunately putting him in mind of his Covenant, his Name, and Glory? and in Faith pray to him in the behalf of his poor, despised, and abused Church, which is as a Lilly among the Thornes, that he would remember and not forget, or grow unmindful of the Congregation which he hath purchased of old, and arise to save those that are as sheep prepared to the slaughter, and appointed to dy: And when we have thus done, and in a way of so doing, there is nothing more but to sit and wait to see the Salvation of the Lord.

Let two good Puritans frame the idea in their own words— incidentally, in words embodying the very art they recommend: [1]

It is a good saying of one, that the Reading of many diverse heads without some interlaced meditations, is like eating of Marrow without bread. But he that shall take time to Pause upon what he reads (especially where great Truths are but in a few words hinted at) with intermixed meditations and ejaculations suitable to the matter in hand, shall find such Truths concisely delivered, to be like marrow and fatness, whereof a little goes far, and does feed and nourish much.

Those who came to New England to establish a *"Plantation Religious"* were gentlemen for whom a way to "truth" lay in advancement of learning, if not encyclopædic, then discriminating. The Puritan believed that any serious, intelligent work is a transcript of life, and necessary to an understanding of that life, whether conveyed by way of history, poetry, or exegesis. "Hee resolved well that said, Books and friends would I have few and choice," said William Morton,[2] and the sense of life as an art extends to the art of literary expression. A consciousness of style

---

[1] John Wise and Jonathan Mitchell, preface to Samuel Whiting, *A Discourse of the Last Judgement* (Cambridge, 1664), sig. A8.
[2] Preface to John Cotton, *The way of Life*, opening sentence.

was present from the first,[1] bred into schoolboys who did little except imitate and absorb the rhetorical exellencies of classical writers. Clearly, however, the Puritans admired the direct exposition and lucid argument of their models, not the elaborate rhetorical constructions. Roger Williams apologized to Lady Vane the Younger for "the *forme* and *stile* [which] I know will seem to this refined *age*, too rude and barbarous."[2] As a group the Puritans were in revolt against the oratorical flights, the flashing rockets of Pistolese which they had doubtless observed in the writings of the late Elizabethans. Nathaniel Ward's "world of words" was out of fashion even as he coined them. They would have seemed out of place in the writings of any preacher;—that a Puritan should affect them is curious in the extreme:

. . . when I heare a nugiperous Gentledame inquire what dresse the Queen is in this week; what the nudiustertian fashion of the Court; I mean the very newest: with egge to be in it in all haste, what-ever it be; I look at her as the very gizzard of a trifle, the product of a quarter of a cypher, the epitome of nothing. . . .[3]

Such glittering phrases lost caste among all Puritans after 1630, for they looked upon "high style," with its definite conventions, as "Exotic Words" that led to "Carnal wisdome."[4] Some who had been trained in the Anglican tradition changed their views of style as they swung over to the Puritan faith. Cotton Mather tells of the struggle which John Cotton underwent:

And that which added unto the Reputation, thus raised for him, was an University Sermon, wherein sinning more to preach *Self* than *Christ*, he used such Florid Strains, as extremely recommended him unto *the most*, who relished the *Wisdom of Words* above the *Words of Wisdom;* Though the pompous Eloquence of that Sermon, afterwards gave such a Distast unto his own *Reverend Soul*, that with a Sacred Indignation he threw his Notes into the Fire . . .
But although he had been Educated in the *Peripatetick* way, yet like the other *Puritans* of those times, he rather affected the *Ramaean* Discipline; and chose to follow the Methods of the Excel-

---

[1] See E. F. Bradford, "Conscious Art in Bradford's *History of Plymouth Plantation*," *New England Quarterly*, I (1928), 133–157; F. O. Matthiessen, "Michael Wigglesworth, a Puritan Artist," *ibid.*, pp. 491–504.

[2] *Experiments of Spiritual Life & Health* (London, 1652), p. iv.

[3] *The Simple Cobler* . . . (London, 1647), pp. 24, 25.

[4] Increase Mather, *The Life* . . . *of* . . . *Mr. Richard Mather* (Cambridge, 1670), p. 85. See also pp. 489–496 following.

lent *Ramus*, who like *Justin* of old vvas not only a *Philosopher*, but a
Christian, and a *Martyr* also; rather than the more Empty, Trifling,
Altercative Notions, to which the Works of the Pagan *Aristotle*
derived unto us, through the Mangling Hands of the Apostate
Prophyrie, have Disposed his Disciples . . .¹

The turn to plainness was thus established in Puritan America
from the beginning, and the controversies over style carried on
in England were but slightly reflected in the colonies. On two
occasions in particular ministers took opportunity to express opinions on literary art: The funeral sermon offered them a chance
to pay critical tribute to the writings of the departed,² and the
sermon preached at the ordination of a young pastor furnished
occasion to theorize on oratory and literary composition:

When instead of conveying his Ideas and Sense of Things in
plain and natural Words and Expressions, the minister [makes]
use of the Jargon of Logic and Metaphysics, or amuses [the audi-
tors] with Hebrew, Greek, Latin or French Names; or soars above
them in Flights of Poetry, and Flourishes of Rhetorick; or goes
into the other Extream of using indecent and homely Phrases,
such as savour of the Mobb or the Play-house, he gives Offence.³

Our discussion so far has been limited to theories of style in
sermon literature. The Puritan historians were as scrupulous as
the ministers in preserving the amenities of a plain, lucid style.
Governor Bradford opened "Of Plimmoth Plantation" by saying that he is about to narrate events "The which I shall en-
deuor to manefest in a plaine stile; with singuler regard unto yᵉ
simple trueth in all things." ⁴ The remark is characteristic of

¹ Cotton Mather, *Johannes in Eremo* (Boston, 1695), pp. 52, 53; *idem, Magnalia*,
Bk. III, chap. 1, p. 15. Ramus' reform of logic was accompanied by a reform of
rhetoric, in both cases in the direction of simplicity and clarity. The two studies went
hand in hand, the Puritans embracing the logic of Ramus and the rhetorical principles of Ramus' disciple, Omer Talon; while the Anglican preachers in the main
clung to the traditional Aristotelian logic and scholastic rhetoric. See also Samuel
Eliot Morison, *Harvard College in the Seventeenth Century*, pp. 172–187.

² See Benjamin Colman, *The Prophet's Death Lamented* . . . (Boston, 1723), p. 32
(sermon for Increase Mather); John Barnard, *Elijah's Mantle* . . . (Boston, 1724),
p. 36 (sermon for Ezekiel Cheever); Eliphalet Adams, *A Funeral Discourse* . . . (New
London, 1724), sig. K 3ᵛ (sermon for Gurdon Saltonstall).

³ Ebenezer Turell, *Ministers should carefully avoid giving Offence in any Thing* (Boston,
1740), p. 14. For similar ideas, see Cotton Mather, *Parentator* . . . (Boston, 1724),
p. 215; Samuel Mather, *The Life of . . . Cotton Mather* . . . (Boston, 1729), pp. 33, 34;
Nathaniel Appleton, *Superior Skill and Wisdom* . . . (Boston, 1737), p. 26; William
Cooke, *The great Duty of Ministers* . . . (Boston, 1742), p. 7.

⁴ MS (*ca.* 1650) in Massachusetts State Library, Boston. From Facsimile, ed. J. A.
Doyle, (London, 1896).

Renaissance critical theory in so far as it shows the author dedicating himself to the exposition of moral truth. Bradford's nephew, drawing heavily upon his uncle's work, acknowledged that he has "more solicitously followed the truth of things" than "studied quaintness in expressions." [1] When Thomas Sprat came to write the history of the Royal Society of London, he described the practice which that body had demanded of its members. We might almost say that Sprat's words give an official sanction to a manner of writing which the Puritans for many years had approved and adopted:

And, in few words, I dare say that, of all the Studies of men, nothing may be sooner obtain'd than this vicious abundance of *Phrase*, this trick of *Metaphors*, this volubility of *Tongue*, which makes so great a noise in the World. . . .
[The members of the Royal Society] have therefore been most rigorous in putting in execution the only Remedy that can be found for this *extravagance*, and that has been a constant Resolution to reject all amplifications, digressions, and swellings of style; to return back to the primitive purity and shortness, when men deliver'd so many *things* almost in an equal number of *words*. They have exacted from all their members a close, naked, natural way of speaking, positive expressions, clear senses, a native easiness, bringing all things as near the Mathematical plainness as they can, and preferring the language of Artizans, Countrymen, and Merchants, before that of Wits or Scholars. [2]

Colonial secular writers continued to advocate the method which had been most serviceable. Daniel Gookin says that his narrative is "not clothed in elegancy of words and accurate sentences," since, he concludes, "I have endeavoured all plainness that I can, that the most vulgar capacity might understand." [3] It was a point of view carried into the eighteenth century with little variation. [4]

As expressions of critical theory passed from the rationalistic

[1] William Morton, *New-Englands Memoriall* (Cambridge, 1669), preface.
[2] *The History of the Royal-Society of London* (1667), section XX, in J. E. Spingarn, *Critical Essays of the Seventeenth Century* (Oxford, 1908), II, 117, 118.
[3] *Historical Collections of the Indians in New England* (preface dated November, 1674), in *Collections of the Massachusetts Historical Society*, first series, I (1792), 141–226; see also James Allen, *New-Englands choicest Blessing* (Boston, 1679), preface.
[4] See Howard M. Jones, "American Prose Style: 1700–1770," *Huntington Library Bulletin*, No. 6 (1934), pp. 115–151. See also Benjamin Colman, preface to Samuel Penhallow, *The History of the Wars of New-England* (Boston, 1726); Cotton Mather, *Magnalia* (1702), "General Introduction."

philosophers—men like Sprat, for instance—to such appreciators
of literature as Dryden and Addison, and as the magazines sprang
up in the first quarter of the eighteenth century to give general
access to literary expression, the changes in literary fashions are
reflected by Puritans. They wished to escape the criticism, now
being leveled at them, that they were a provincial stock, out of the
current of public taste in England, concerned merely with abstract
theology. As early as 1708 Cotton Mather discourses of classical
writers in the manner of the English essayists.[1] When Jonathan
Belcher, the governor's son, was an undergraduate at Harvard
(1725–1730), he kept in his commonplace book many pages of
extracts from *The Spectator* and *The Guardian*, from Blackwall,
Rapin, and Halifax on critical and aesthetic theories. They leave
no doubt of the influence upon one young Puritan of the current English literary modes. Even the pious and cantankerous
governor, no author himself, voiced gracious tribute to a study
of belles lettres in the educational scheme of his son in the many
letters he wrote to the young man who was studying law in England soon after 1730.[2] After 1722 a change is observable in literary
taste, brought about in part by the decreasing isolation of New
England from current trends abroad. As the second quarter of
the century approached, nearly all tastes that may be labeled
Puritan were rapidly adapting themselves to the English modes.
No work on style was exerting more universal influence than
Fénelon's *Dialogues on Eloquence*, wherein the archbishop of Cam-
bray averred that he thought "the whole Art of Oratory may be
reduc'd to *proving*, *painting*, and *raising* the *Passions*"; it should
reach the heart, not merely stir the imagination.[3] His point of view
found ready adherents among the coming generation, and to the
extent it was adopted indicates that the earlier Puritan feeling—
that consciousness of style should be concealed—was undergoing
change. Cotton Mather leaves no doubt that the public was developing a finicky sensitivity to style:

[1] *Corderius Americanus* (Boston, 1708), sig. A2; see *idem, Just Commemorations* (Boston,
1715), p. ii.
[2] *The Belcher Papers*, 2 vols., in *Collections of the Massachusetts Historical Society*, sixth
series, VI, VII (1893, 1894); for example, I, 125–129, 180–187, 197–205.
[3] *Dialogues . . .* (London, 1722), p. 74. See Thomas Prince, preface to Thomas
Hooker, *The Poor Doubting Christian* (Boston, 1743), p. 13. In England Dennis was
an advocate of emotion in the pulpit as contrasted with "correctness"; so also was
Thomas Blackwall. For a recent discussion of the eighteenth-century view of the
"Passions," see "The Sublime and the Pathetic," in Samuel H. Monk, *The Sublime:
A Study of Critical Theories in XVIII-Century England* (New York, 1935), chap. III.

The blades that set up for critics . . . appear to me, for the most part, as contemptible as they are a supercilious generation. For indeed no two of them have the same stile; and they are as intolerably cross-grained, and severe in their censures upon one another, as they are upon the rest of mankind . . . There is much talk of a florid stile obtaining among the pens that are most in vogue; but how often would it puzzle one, even with the best glasses to find the flowers! . . . After all, every man will have his own stile.[1]

At no point does the literary thought of the Puritans reflect the trend of the times more exactly than in their views of poetry. When Milton, searching for a worthy epic theme, finally chose to write on the fall of man, he was himself but following a trail that had been already blazed. Davenant had said that poetry "is as all good Arts subservient to Religion,"[2] and Abraham Cowley, greatly admired for his learning, had begun *Davideis*, a sacred epic. The famous preface to Cowley's *Poems* remarks that "he who can write a *prophane Poem well* may write a *Divine one better*."[3] Puritans were agreed that subjects other than moral and divine were unworthy of serious treatment. It was as inheritors of the Renaissance and of the metaphysicals that Puritans conceived of poetry as a learning or a moral philosophy directed toward the highest ends within the conception of man; and believing such, they viewed mere versifying as a pleasant accomplishment for leisure hours. The Puritans who compiled the Bay Psalm Book saying that "Gods Altar needs not our pollishing";[4] the men who "attended Conscience rather then Elegance, fidelity rather then poetry,"[5] were in part tacitly acknowledging their inadequacy as poets, not belittling the power of verse—into which, after all, they were fashioning their thoughts. More influential and learned men than Wigglesworth had furnished precedent for his remark that he would traffic with

> No Toyes nor Fables (Poets wonted Crimes) . . .
> For I do much abominate
> To call the Muses to mine aid:
> Which is th' Unchristian use, and trade
> Of some that Christians would be Thought. . . .[6]

---

[1] *Manuductio ad Ministerium* (Boston, 1726), pp. 44–46.
[2] Preface to *Gondibert* (1650), ed. Spingarn, *op. cit.*, II, 48.
[3] *Ibid.* (1656), p. 90.   [4] Conclusion to preface.
[5] Prefatory poem to Wigglesworth, *Day of Doom*, sig. xx3ᵛ.
[6] *Ibid.*, sig. B1, B2.

To none of the founders would Addison's conception of poetry as an indulgence of the imagination,—a relaxation by which we are "cheared and delighted with agreeable sensations," have been adequate. But as fashions changed, as the bonds between the colonies and England became closer, the Puritans inevitably were affected, for they more and more reflected the trends in England. Thoughtful Puritans essayed verses often enough, and recommended poetic composition as good training for the young; but enthusiasm for poetry as a means of expressing great truths in exalted moods gave place to urbane appreciation of verse as a social accomplishment. Such a concept indicates that strictly Puritan theories were on the wane, even though the Bible remained the fountain of inspiration for some time to come. For simon-pure Puritans David ever remained the "Divine *Poet*," for he "derived his *Inspiration* not from *Parnassus*, but from *Zion*, the Mount of God." [1]

It is as writers of prose that the Puritans' literary art finally must be judged. Prose was the vehicle for their finest thoughts; it was the one by which they assisted a whole people to a realization of the powerful idiom at hand for all men to use. They were men who valued learning highly, who talked and wrote voluminously, and of whose style it may be said, as of their colleagues in England, that "while to the Royal Society must be given the honour of definitely hallmarking the new style, to the more temperate among the Puritan preachers belongs the praise of having demonstrated to large masses of the nation, learned and unlearned, the possibilities of a simple, straightforward, unencumbered prose." [2] It is impossible, furthermore, to escape the conviction that all who wrote were conscious of the importance of style, and that most of them adhered to some model. Many left record of their theories. The ornate fashion of Samuel Lee and Samuel Chandler is as unrepresentative of Puritan theory of style as Jonathan Edwards's youthful remark that he would scant it altogether.[3] The problem of poetic composition seldom absorbed their attention, but in so far as they were gentlemen trained in the manners of their day they were alert to the changes of taste,

[1] Thomas Walter, *The Sweet Psalmist of Israel* (Boston, 1722), p. 2.
[2] W. Fraser Mitchell, *English Pulpit Oratory from Andrewes to Tillotson* (London, 1932), p. 275.
[3] S. E. Dwight, *The Life of President Edwards* (New York, 1829), p. 601. See also John Webb's funeral sermon for Peter Thacher, *The Duty of Survivers* (Boston, 1739), p. 27, for a similar opinion.

and adapted themselves, especially in the later Puritan era, to the current modes. Prose, on the other hand, was the vehicle for their ripest thoughts and their deepest emotions. A flat, awkward, cumbrous style is rarely encountered in their treatises or sermons; the color of their rhetoric was absorbed from the world they knew about them—the sea, the market place, the moods of nature. In the hands of such men as John Cotton, Thomas Hooker, Increase Mather, or John Wise the style is seldom commonplace; frequently distinguished:—they lived in an age when devotional literature and sermons were a staple diet, when current preaching fashions were shaping literary taste. It should also be remembered that the Puritans who guided the thought of their day were never merely sectarian in their reading. The Bible was the great font of Puritan inspiration and the model for their style, yet behind the Bible was the common heritage of Renaissance learning and Elizabethan enthusiasm. The Puritans more than others shaped that learning and enthusiasm to the idiom of language with a clarity, directness, grace, and freedom from eccentricity that rendered incalculable service to English prose.

Letter of John Winthrop to His Wife. (For text, see p. 465.)

HISTORY

IN THE 1660's and 1670's, as the last survivors of the first generation were dying off, and the ministers felt that the religious ardor of their successors was noticeably cooling, preachers before the General Court of Massachusetts frequently called for the composition of a history of New England. They hoped that a chronicle of the deeds of the fathers would arouse the emulation of the sons, and that a recital of the favors which God had already bestowed upon the colony would incite the present inhabitants to a determination to merit still more of them. They strove to arrest the general declension from the original ideals, upon which we have already commented (pp. 17–19), by adducing the testimonies of divine approbation evident in the history of the commonwealth. Thus in 1673 Urian Oakes dwelt at length upon this theme:

Hath God essayed to go and take him a part of a Nation from the midst of a Nation, by temptations, by signs, by wonders, by a mighty hand & by an out-stret[c]hed arm, according to all that the Lord your God hath done for you before your eyes? God hath shewn us almost unexampled unparall[el]ed mercy. And it were very well if there were a memorial of these things faithfully drawn up, and transmitted to Posterity . . . It is our great duty to be the Lords *Remembrancers* or *Recorders* . . . that the mercies of the Lord (that hath allured us into this wilderness, spoken comfortably to us and dealt bountifully with us therein) may be faithfully registred in our hearts, and remem-bred by us. It is a desireable thing, that all the loving kindnesses of God, and his singular favours to this poor and despised out cast might be Chronicled and communicated (in the History of them) to succeeding Ages; that the memory of them may not dy and be extinct, with the present Generation.[1]

The call for a history of Massachusetts Bay was redoubled after 1669, when Nathaniel Morton published a history of Plymouth, *New England's Memoriall*. The General Court at last paid the Reverend William Hubbard £50 for having composed a corresponding vol-ume for Massachusetts, declaring, "it hath binn thought necessary, & a duty incumbent vpon vs to take due notice of all occurrances & passages of Gods providence towards the people of this jurisdiction since their first arrivall in these parts." [2] Hubbard pocketed the money,

---

[1] *New-England Pleaded with* (Cambridge, 1673), p. 23.
[2] *Massachusetts Records*, V, 279, 378, 394.

but can hardly be said to have earned it. Neither his nor Morton's work contributed anything worth much in itself; the chief value of both books came from the fact that the authors had access to un-published manuscripts by the two great governors of the colonies at the time of the respective settlements. Morton and Hubbard did little more than plagiarize from the *History of Plymouth Plantation* of William Bradford, and from the journal of John Winthrop. In spite of the ministerial demand, two of the three masterpieces of New England historiography were not printed until the nineteenth century, and the third, Cotton Mather's *Magnalia*, was not issued until 1701.

For our purposes, however, the important point about Oakes's para-graph is not its failure to get results, but the philosophy of history that it contains, either explicitly or by implication. He puts a some-what exaggerated emphasis upon the use of history in arousing a lethargic generation, but even so he gives an excellent statement of what the Puritan conceived to be the function of an historian and from what point of view the narrative should be arranged. History is a memorial of the mercies of God, so that posterity may know them, remember them, and hymn His praises. The history of New England is history *par excellence*, for the mercies of God have been shown in New England above all other portions of the globe. History is not only philosophy teaching by example, but theology exemplified.

During the seventeenth century there was carried on in learned circles a debate between the "ancients" and the "moderns," between scholars who believed that the ancients, being closer to the date of creation, were inevitably of a stronger and more original genius than was any longer possible, and those who believed that genius could flourish as well in modern centuries as in classical. This dispute, being largely a literary one, did not much interest the Puritans, but had they taken sides in it, they would certainly have supported the mod-ernists' contention. They would not have been swayed by a prefer-ence for modern literature over the ancient, but would have been determined by their fundamental belief in divine providence. To them all human affairs have always been under the continuous direction of God; history is the record of His incessant supervision, and there can be no real decline or fluctuation of God's power. The past is a drama, written, directed, produced and prompted by God. It must, therefore, be as full of meaning at one time as at another. The natural world, the customs of men, the abilities of statesmen, all purely physical aspects of existence do not vary in kind from one era to another: "In Civil matters there be the like manners of men now as of old;

the like causes and successes of warre and peace &c. whence the knowledge of History of former times is so much behovefull." It is therefore wrong to prefer "elder times before the present." Nature has not decayed; great authors of the past are indeed to be read, but we are "not to approve all their sayings and doings, as best." At whatever moment we happen to live, God has called upon us to achieve "a wise consideration of our present times."[1]

Consequently for the Puritan writer of history there is always a two-fold consideration determining his attitude toward his material, and sometimes the one reflection seems almost contradictory to the other. On the one hand, everything that has happened, disaster as well as triumph, the minutest event as well as the greatest, has been under divine control. God is not a being of whims or caprices, He is not less powerful at one moment than at another; therefore in a certain sense any event is just as significant as any other. But on the other hand, God regulates the universe for distinct ends; He does not work without purpose, and history should be seen as a long revelation of divine intentions. Therefore the first function of the historian is to relate everything that has happened, to exclude nothing, to erect no standards or criteria on a purely human basis. He must not sort out his materials, suppress some facts and accentuate others, because they conform to patterns he has himself constructed, such as economic interest, national characteristics, literary forms. Yet at the same time the historian is not merely to relate what has happened, but to interpret it. He must show wherein events have fulfilled God's purposes whenever the purposes can be ascertained. He must pass judgment on men accordingly as they served the divine design. On the first score he is not to exploit personality for the sake of personality, as the modern biographer does, but on the second he is to estimate all men from the one absolute standard, as Bradford estimates his dear friend Elder Brewster, or as Cotton Mather does John Eliot. Because every minutest happening, every fortune of war, every chance coincidence, is arranged by God, the Puritan historian does not elide minor incidents or incidental stories if their meaning is clear. In the midst of telling the broad movements or major crises he can always stop, as Bradford does, to relate "a spetiall work of Gods providence," and John Winthrop, putting into his *Journal* the material he intended ultimately to use in a formal history, finds that the rescue of the wife of one Dalkin, "dwelling near Medford," by clinging to her dog's

[1] John Cotton, *A Briefe Exposition . . . upon . . . Ecclesiastes* (London, 1654), pp. 21, 129–132.

tail, is intrinsically as important as the whole episode of the Antinomian turmoil. In reading histories of Puritan authorship it is
necessary that we always remember the vast difference between their
intentions and those of modern writers. The Puritan would feel that
the points of view assumed by a twentieth-century scholar are determined solely by the writer's place in time and space, and therefore
temporary, fallacious, and partial. Yet where the modern researcher
feels bound to tell all the facts, not to generalize before exhaustive
investigation, the Puritan has no hesitancy in sifting his material,
placing emphases, omitting facts, generalizing upon any single piece
of evidence, interpreting every action by one explicit standard. The
guiding principle of his art is the extent to which anything can be
made to illustrate clearly the operation of God's will. The contemporary
historian would stress the economic and social inducement for the
migration to New England; Thomas Shepard is concerned only with
showing that in 1630 God Himself was engineering the opportunity
and thereby ordering men to seize upon it.

Consequently two distinct characteristics reveal themselves when we
come to the study of Puritan historiography. In the first place, the
art of history, as practiced by Puritans, is bound to be specific and
concrete, bound to stay close to the particular happening and episode; it is apt to be anecdotal, for the design of the whole is the will
of God, which always emerges of itself if each step of the procedure
is adequately noted and interpreted. In the second place, it is also a
didactic art; nothing is to be told for its own sake alone; if any portion
of history yields no meanings, it is either to be presented as a problem
yet to be solved, like some obscure passage in scripture, or else it is
to be ignored entirely. Above all, no explanations which rest merely
upon natural or secondary causation, on mere economic motives,
political expediency, accidental circumstance, the character of this
or that man—no such explanations are to be accepted as final. God's
will is the ultimate reason why things fall out one way rather than
another, although God does work through natural causes; His will is
intelligent, and the task of the historian is to discover, as far as the
evidence will permit, the conscious and deliberate direction which lies
behind all events.

Puritan history was posited upon the assumption of an eternal same-
ness in things, their perpetual control by the same agency for the same
ends. Yet there was no denial that surfaces varied from age to age,
that if the essential configurations were identical, the particular
manifestations could show a vast difference from one century to an-

other. The unity within variety for which Puritan thinkers sought in all other fields of speculation and study was also the objective of the Puritan historian, and he, not less than the theologian, strove not to lose sight of the one in the many or to over-simplify the particulars in establishing the universal. Thus John Cotton explained the historical process:

The principal cause of all passages in the world: which is not mans weaknesse, or goodnesse, but chiefly the wise and strong and good providence of God: who presenteth every age with a new stage of acts and actors . . . And if a Poet would not present his spectators but with choyce variety of matters, how much lesse God? [1]

So New England chroniclers had first to demonstrate that their narratives exemplified once more the eternal and immutable regulations of providence, and then to indicate the particular and individual character of their own age. And when they came to this latter consideration, they explained history by what they believed to be the all-engrossing concern of the sixteenth and seventeenth centuries, the Reformation. Though all ages are under God's government, and one age should teach as much about him as any other, or equally exhibit his majesty, still some ages achieve greater exhibitions of his power than less fortunate ones. Next to the period in which Christ himself had lived, the Puritans believed that the hundred years since Luther nailed his theses on the cathedral door at Wittenberg were the most fraught with meaning of all human history.

Truth is the Daughter of time, was the saying of old, and our daily experience gives in evidence and proof hereof, to every mans ordinary observation. Only as in other births, so here, the barrennesse and fruitfullnesse of severall ages, depend meerly upon Gods good pleasure, who opens and shuts the womb of truth from bearing, as he sees fit, according to the counsell of his own will.

Not that there is any change in the truth, but the alteration grows, according to mens apprehensions, to whom it is more or lesse discovered, according to Gods most just judgement, and their own deservings. [2]

Clearly the Protestant movement had come about because men's apprehensions had been enabled to discover more of the truth than at any time since the Apostles; and as the Reformation was a continuous movement away from the Church of Rome toward the pure discipline established by Christ, the pure doctrine taught by scripture, and the

---

[1] John Cotton, *A Briefe Exposition . . . upon . . . Ecclesiastes* (London, 1654), p. 131.
[2] Thomas Hooker, *A Survey of the Summe of Church-Discipline* (London, 1648), A2 recto.

society built, politically and socially as well as ecclesiastically, upon divine enactments, New England was the culmination of the Reformation, the climax of world history, the ultimate revelation through events of the objective toward which the whole of human activity had been tending from the beginning of time. Winthrop preached to the emigrants during the voyage that the eyes of the world would be upon them, that they would be as a city set upon a hill for all to observe (p. 199); Captain Edward Johnson imagined that Christ himself had drawn up the "commission" for the migration; Cotton Mather modestly admitted that the churches in New England were not perfect, but that they were the best the world had yet achieved. The inspiration for the writing of histories by pious New Englanders was consequently twofold: not only to exhibit the truth as shown in the course of the world under God's providence, but to establish the climax of that course in the Reformation, of which New England was the supreme and purest embodiment.

Of course, there were many persons in the world, particularly in England, who did not agree with the New Englanders' idea of their own importance. The Anglicans naturally would not believe that any form of Puritanism was the logical result of the Reformation; Puritans who believed in the Presbyterian rather than the Congregational polity said all the discreditable things they could think of concerning New England, the soil, the climate, the inhabitants, and the practices; those Puritans who turned eventually to a philosophy of toleration attacked the New England Way for its tyranny and cruelty; Puritans who stayed at home to fight the King accused their brethren in America of having run away from danger. In order to maintain their view of history, with their contention that it had come to a peak in their own experiment, New England historians had to present the story of settlement and conquest, of ecclesiastical triumph and political institution, as they saw it. And sometimes the spokesmen for New England did not have time to tell the whole story, but were forced to take up their pens in answer to specific charges and to plead special cases against the particular reproaches.

In the selections given in this chapter there are examples of both formal history and occasional polemic. Higginson's pamphlet was sent back from Salem, to which an advance guard of the Massachusetts Bay Company had gone out in 1629; it was an advertising tract defending the region from the charge of being a barren desert, made against it by enemies of the enterprise. There are some respects in which Puritans writing about their own history are amazingly impartial; since they viewed whatever had happened as God's doing, they could suppress or twist facts only by running the danger of blaspheming God's work. But in the heat of controversy, or to score a point against mortal adversaries, they were strongly tempted to exaggerate, to put the best possible face on some rather dubious matters. Those who have lived in and with the climate of New England may very justifiably feel that good parson Higginson allowed his enthusiasm to run away with his judgment on that score. Thomas Shepard and John Allin wrote their book in direct answer to an attack upon the New England churches. In the late 1630's a group of Presbyterian Puritans had sent over a list of nine embarrassing questions concerning ecclesiastical practices. John Davenport had been commissioned to answer them, which he had done in the name of the ministers and the elders; in 1643 his manuscript was published in London, and because just at that moment the furious controversy between English Independents and Presbyterians was flaring up, Davenport's work was assailed with unanimity by the Presbyterians. One of these, John Ball, was an author much read and admired in New England for his theological writings, and his attack upon the New England church polity was exceedingly distressing to the ministers; Shepard and Allin were commissioned to reply to Ball's attack upon Davenport's answers to the original nine questions—thus did religious controversy lengthen out from book to book in the seventeenth century. Ball not only assailed the form of church organization, but raised the cry that those who fled to New England were deserters, that they had been afraid to stay in England and fight the good fight. The preface to the book, probably written by Shepard alone—for it has all the marks of his very individual style—reviews in masterly fashion the history of the settlement, and is perhaps the best surviving statement in their own terms of the intentions of the Massachusetts leaders.

The works of Bradford, Johnson, and Cotton Mather were written as full-dress, comprehensive histories, and the *Journal* of John Winthrop was undoubtedly a repository of jottings out of which he intended to compose a formal narrative. Of all the writings by New England Puritans in the seventeenth century, Bradford's *History* is the pre-eminent work of art. No other document so perfectly incarnates the Puritan ideal of the simple and plain style, is so filled with the deep feeling of religious dedication, so perfectly masters the rhythms of Biblical prose, so fluently handles the imagery of the devotional life, or so reveals the solid, broad, and generous aspects of the Puritan character. But in reading these pages, the student should remember that William Bradford was not quite a Puritan in the meaning in which the term is generally used in this volume. The true Puritan was a member of the Church of England, whose whole effort while in England was to remain within the Church and secure the mastery of it; he belonged to a strong, wealthy, organized, and powerful interest, led by important politicians and learned clergymen. Bradford was a Separatist, one of a small and earnest band of simple souls, all of humble station, who were quite incapable of containing their religion within the fine distinctions by which the Puritans endeavored to stay in the Church at the same time that they were in deadly combat with the authorities. The persons who made up the "Pilgrim" company were home-spun, hard-working farmers from Nottinghamshire and Lincolnshire; their minister, John Robinson, was a university man, and Elder Brewster had spent a couple of years at Cambridge, but otherwise they were men instructed only in the Bible and in simplicity of spirit. They had openly broken with the Church of England, and proceeded to set up a completely "separate" body. No government in Europe at that epoch would have tolerated the existence of such a society, outside and independent of the established institution, and it is no wonder that the bishops and the sheriffs of England got after this congregation with vehemence. Holland alone of all Europe would offer an asylum to these people, though not so much because the Dutch believed in toleration as because the Separatists were theologically good Calvinists, as were the Dutch. Robinson's congregation, escaping to Holland, lived there for several years, until the reasons which Bradford enumerates persuaded many of them to undertake a settlement in America. Robinson did not come with the first settlers in 1620, and died before his intended removal; the community was without funds, entirely self-supporting, too small and insignificant to be noticed by the English authorities. Bradford's history is the history of simple folk, directly inspired by a religious ideal, working out the will of God by themselves, amid incredible hardship. They underwent privation because they were absolutely confident that they were obeying the direct behests of God Himself, and that through all miseries and anguish He was watching over them and testing their fidelity. The *History of Plymouth Plantation* is the story of that ordeal, told by the man who was the leader and whose simple strength and rugged integrity were the mainstays of the community. Plymouth was a minute, relatively insignificant community, completely overshadowed by Massachusetts Bay from 1630 on, and ultimately absorbed into it by the royal charter of 1692. The leaders of Massachusetts Bay were aggressive, educated, philosophical; Plymouth was pious, struggling, and desired chiefly to be let alone. But though Bradford is not, for these reasons, altogether representative of the Puritan mind in its intellectualized and metaphysical form, he might by that very fact be said to be the essence of the Puritan. The soaring passage in which he contemplates the plight of the settlers at the moment of landing, in November, 1620, and affirms the faith in the might of which they confronted the desolate shore and the murderous climate is the masterpiece of all Puritan eloquence. No other writer will lead us so directly to the core of Puritanism as Bradford, none with such charm, generosity, largeness of spirit, with such calm assurance and massive strength will so completely reveal the essential frame of mind, the type of character, the quality of life that underlay the theology.

The *Journal* of John Winthrop lacks the form and beauty of Bradford's history by the very necessities of the case. It was a day-by-day, or at any rate month-by-month, chronicle of the adventure at Massachusetts Bay, put down in rare minutes of leisure by the outstanding leader of the expedition and the man upon whose shoulders rested the larger part of the responsibility for success or failure. Had he ever found opportunity to make a coherent history he would undoubtedly have polished the style and systematized the presentation. But even as a journal his volume frequently achieves genuine literary merit, and reveals completely the character and prowess of the Puritan statesman. In sharp contrast to Bradford, Winthrop came of distinctly aristocratic stock; his grandfather had been a wealthy clothier in the reign of Henry VIII, who obtained the manor of Groton in Suffolk when the monasteries were dispossessed; his father was a university man, a famous lawyer, who added to the family fortunes. John Winthrop himself attended Trinity College, Cambridge, though he left without taking a degree. Before he migrated to New England he was a country squire, a justice of the peace, an attorney and a member of the Inner Temple. When he left England it was at the sacrifice of a career already launched, a secure social position, a background of wealth, influence, and leisure. He came to New England determined that the experiment should succeed, and it did; if he is not as eloquent in voicing the religious inspiration as Bradford, none the less the motive was in him as intensely and as powerfully.

Edward Johnson was one of the citizens, not one of the humblest, but representative of the rank and file. The title of his book, *The Wonder-working Providence of Sions Saviour in New England*, is in itself a confession of the Puritan philosophy of history; the story of New

England is to him a protracted evidence of the assistance of God, the same God who protected Israel of old, and who still works wonders for men by his providence—whenever they will coöperate with Him in the right spirit. He is a slighter figure than either Winthrop or Bradford, and writes in a much more ornate, windy, and verbose style. Even at his most inflated moments he is not without a certain charm, however, and the zest for living which so conspicuously marked the writings of Elizabethan England had not yet died out in him.

Of Cotton Mather the most remarkable fact is that one small head could carry all he knew. He writes as a member of the third generation in New England, the grandson of Richard Mather, the son of Increase, the inheriting figure in what had become the outstanding dynasty of ministerial rule in the colony. The deep passions of the founding generation had become more regular and lukewarm in his day; times were changing, and the early Puritan creed was crumbling all about him. Though he himself contributed to the change in many respects, though he himself fought the more hidebound conservatives on the question of inoculation for smallpox, his life was generally motivated by an attempt to keep the hands of the clock at the same hour they had indicated when his grandfather had preached at Dorchester. His great history, the *Magnalia Christi Americana*, "the great achievements of Christ in America," was in large part designed to revive fading piety, as demanded in the sermon of Urian Oakes. He did not succeed in this objective, but he did manage to bring together within the covers of one Gargantuan book almost the whole account of Puritan thought and action in seventeenth-century America. He spattered his pages with his amazing erudition, and earned himself the description of pedant, but he also summarized a century of experience.

WILLIAM BRADFORD, 1590–1657

[William Bradford was born in Austerfield, of Yorkshire yeoman stock; inheriting a "comfortable" sum from his father, who died in his childhood, he might well have grown into a substantial, solid farmer, had he not at the age of twelve become a serious reader of the Bible and been driven by his religious convictions, in opposition to the wishes of his family, to join the group who met at the house of William Brewster in Scrooby. With John Robinson as minister, these persons organized a Separatist church in 1606, fled to Amsterdam in 1609, and then to Leyden, where Bradford supported himself as a fustian weaver and say worker. During these years he must have read extensively in theological literature. He was a leader in the migration to New England and was elected Governor of the Plymouth colony upon the death of John Carver in April, 1621. He served in that office for thirty out of his remaining thirty-six years, without salary until 1639 and thereafter for £20 a year. He exercised almost complete discretionary power, proved himself on every occasion shrewd, firm, and generous. In his old age he undertook the study of Hebrew, in order to see "the ancient oracles of God in their native beauty." In the inventory of his estate there was a red waistcoat, a great silver "beer bowle," and a violet cloak. He commenced writing the *History* in 1630, probably finished it about 1650. This text is from the *History of Plymouth Plantation*, ed. Worthington C. Ford (Massachusetts Historical Society, Boston, 1912), 2 vols : I, 16–18, 21–22, 24–25, 28–35, 53–60, 149–158, 189–196, 239–246, 299–303, 362–367; II, 45–58, 161–164, 308–310, 342–353. For further bibliography see this edition, or the article by Samuel Eliot Morison in *The Dictionary of American Biography*.]

HISTORY OF PLIMOTH PLANTATION

WHEN as by the travell, and diligence of some godly, and zealous preachers, and Gods blessing on their labours; as in other places of the land, so in the North parts, many became inlightened by the word of God; and had their ignorance and sins discovered unto them, and begane by his grace to reforme their lives, and make conscience of their wayes. The worke of God was no sooner manifest in them; but presently they were both scoffed and scorned by the prophane multitude, and the ministers urged with the yoak of subscription, or els must be silenced; and the poore people were so vexed with apparators, and pursuants, and the comissarie courts, as truly their affliction was not smale; which, notwithstanding, they bore sundrie years with much patience, till they were occasioned (by the continuance and encrease of these troubles, and other means which the Lord raised up in those days) to see further into things by the light of the word of God. How not only these base and beggerly ceremonies were unlawfull; but also that the lordly and tiranous power of the prelates ought not to be submitted unto; which thus (contrary to the freedome of the gospell,) would load and burden mens consciences; and by their compulsive power make a prophane mixture of persons, and things in the worship of God. . . .

So many therfore (of these proffessors) as saw the evill of these things, (in thes parts,) and whose harts the Lord had touched with heavenly zeale for his trueth; they shooke of this yoake of Antichristian bondage. And as the Lords free people, joyned them selves (by a covenant of the Lord) into a church estate, in the felowship of the Gospell, to walke in all his wayes, made known, or to be made known unto them (according to their best endeavours) whatsoever it should cost them, the Lord assisting them. And that it cost them something this ensewing historie will declare. . . .

But after these things; they could not long continue in any peaceable condition; but were hunted and persecuted on every side, so as their former afflictions were but as flea-bitings in comparison of these which now came upon them. For some were taken and clapt up in prison, others had their houses besett and watcht night and day, and hardly escaped their hands; and the most were faine to flie and leave their howses and habitations, and the means of their livelehood. Yet these and many other sharper things which afterward befell them, were no other then they looked for, and therfore were the better prepared to bear them by the assistance of Gods grace and spirite; yet seeing them selves thus molested, and that ther was no hope of their continuance ther, by a joynte consente they resolved to goe into the Low-Countries, wher they heard was freedome of Religion for all men; as also how sundrie from London, and other parts of the land, had been exiled and persecuted for the same cause, and were gone thither; and lived at Amsterdam, and in other places of the land. . . .

Being thus constrained to leave their native soyle and countrie, their lands and livings, and all their freinds and famillier acquaintance, it was much, and thought marvelous by many. But to goe into a countrie they knew not (but by hearsay) wher they must learne a new language, and get their livings they knew not how, it being a dear place, and subjecte to the misseries of warr, it was by many thought an adventure almost desperate, a case intolerable, and a misserie worse then death. Espetially seeing they were not acquainted with trads nor traffique (by which that countrie doth subsiste) but had only been used to a plaine countrie life, and the inocente trade of husbandrey. But these things did not dismay them (though they did some times trouble them) for their desires were sett on the ways of god, and to injoye his ordinances; but they rested on his providence, and knew whom they had beleeved. Yet this was not all, for though they could not stay, yet were they not suffered to goe, but the ports and havens were shut against them, so as they were faine to seeke secrete means of conveance, and to bribe and fee the mariners, and give exterordinarie rates for their passages. And yet were they often times betrayed (many of them) and both they and their goods intercepted and surprised, and therby put to great trouble and charge, of which I will give an instance or tow, and omitte the rest.

Ther was a large companie of them purposed to get passage at Boston in Lincoln-shire, and for that end had hired a shipe wholy to them selves, and made agreement with the maister to be ready at a certaine day, and take them and their goods in, at a conveniente place, wher they accordingly would all attende in readines. So after long waiting, and large expences (though he kepte not day with them) yet he came at length and tooke them in, in the night. But when he had them and their goods abord, he betrayed them, haveing before hand complotted with the serchers and other officers so to doe. Who tooke them, and put them into open boats, and ther rifled and ransaked them, searching them to their shirts for money, yea even the women furder then became modestie; and then caried them back into the towne, and made them a spectackle and wonder to the multitude, which came flocking on all sids to behould them. Being thus first, by the chatch-poule officers, rifled, and stripte of their money, books, and much other goods; they were presented to the majestrates, and messengers sente to informe the lords of the Counsell of them; and so they were commited to ward. Indeed the majestrats used them courteously, and shewed them what favour they could; but could not deliver them, till order came from the Counsell-table. But the issue was that after a months imprisonmente, the greatest parte were dismiste, and sent to the places from whence they came; but 7. of the principall were still kept in prison, and bound over to the Assises.

The nexte spring after, ther was another attempte made by some of these and others, to get over at an other place. And it so fell out, that they light of a Dutchman at Hull, having a ship of his owne belonging to Zealand; they made agreemente with him, and acquainted him with their condition, hoping to find more faithfullnes in him, then in the former of their owne nation; he bad them not fear, for he would doe well enough. He was (by appointment) to take them in betweene Grimsbe and Hull, wher was a large commone a good way distante from any towne. Now aganst the prefixed time, the women and children, with the goods, were sent to the place in a small barke, which they had hired for that end; and the men were to meete them by land. But it so fell out, that they were ther a day before the shipe came, and the sea being rough, and the women very sicke, prevailed with the seamen to put into a creeke hardby, wher they lay on ground at lowwater. The nexte morning the shipe came, but they were fast, and could not stir till aboute noone; In the mean time (the shipe maister, perceiving how the matter was) sente his boate to be getting the men abord whom he saw ready, walking aboute the shore. But after the first boat full was gott abord, and she was ready to goe for more, the mᵣ espied a greate company (both horse and foote) with bills, and gunes, and other weapons (for the countrie was raised to take them). The Dutch-man seeing that, swore (his countries oath), "sacremente"; and having the wind faire, waiged his Ancor, hoysed sayles, and away. But the poore-men which were gott abord, were in great distress for their wives, and children, which they saw thus to be taken, and were left destitute of their helps; and them selves also, not having a cloath to shifte them with, more then they had on their baks, and some scarce a peney aboute them, all they had being abord the barke. It drew tears from their eyes, and any thing they had they would have given to have been a shore againe; but all in vaine, ther was no remedy, they must thus sadly part. . . .

The rest of the men that were in greatest danger, made shift to escape away before the troope could surprise them; those only staying that best might, to be assistante unto the women. But pitifull it was to see the heavie case of these poore women in this distress; what weeping and crying on every side, some for their husbands, that were caried away in the ship as is before related. Others not knowing what should become of them, and their litle ones; others againe melted in teares, seeing their poore litle ones hanging aboute them, crying for feare, and quaking with could. Being thus aprehended, they were hurried from one place to another, and from one justice to another, till in the ende they knew not what to doe with them; for to imprison so many women and innocent children for no other cause (many of them) but that they must goe with their husbands; semed to be unreasonable and all would crie out of them; and to send them home againe was as difficult, for they aledged (as the trueth was) they had no homes to goe to, for they had either sould, or otherwise disposed of their houses, and livings. To be shorte, after they had been thus turmolyed a good while, and conveyed from one constable to another, they were glad to be ridd of them in the end upon any termes; for all were wearied and tired with them. Though in the mean time they (poore soules) indured miserie enough; and thus in the end necessitie forste a way for them. . . . And in the end, notwithstanding all these stormes of opposition, they all gatt over at length, some at one time and some at an other, and some in one place, and some in

[handwritten at top: analogy to Christian soul's perilous journey + arrival at safe harbor.]

an other, And mete togeather againe according to their desires, with no small rejoycing. . . .

After they had lived in this citie about some 11. or 12. years, (which is the more observable being the whole time of that famose truce between that state and the Spaniards,) and sundrie of them were taken away by death; and many others begane to be well striken in years (the grave mistris Experience haveing taught them many things) those prudent governours, with sundrie of the sagest members begane both deeply to apprehend their present dangers, and wisely to foresee the future, and thinke of timly remedy. In the agitation of their thoughts, and much discours of things hear aboute, at length they began to incline to this conclusion, of remooval to some other place. Not out of any newfanglednes, or other such like giddie humor, by which men are oftentimes transported to their great hurt, and danger. But for sundrie weightie and solid reasons; some of the cheefe of which I will hear breefly touch. And first, they saw and found by experience the hardnes of the place and countrie to be such, as few in comparison would come to them; and fewer that would bide it out, and continew with them. For many that came to them, and many more that desired to be with them; could not endure that great labor and hard fare, with other inconveniences which they underwent and were contented with. But though they loved their persons, approved their cause, and honoured their sufferings, yet they left them as it weer weeping, as Orpah did her mother in law Naomie; or as those Romans did Cato in Utica, who desired to be excused and borne with, though they could not all be Catoes. For many, though they desired to injoye the ordinances of God in their puritie, and the libertie of the gospell with them, yet (alass) they admitted of bondage—with deanger of conscience, rather than to indure these hardships; yea, some preferred, and chose the prisons in England, rather then this libertie in Holland, with these afflictions. But it was thought that if a better, and easier place of living, could be had, it would draw many, and take away these discouragments. Yea, their pastor would often say, that many of those who both wrote, and preached now against them, if they were in a place, wher they might have libertie and live comfortably, they would then practise as they did.

2^{ly}. They saw, that though the people generally, bore all these difficulties very cherfully, and with a resolute courage, being in the best, and strength of their years, yet old age began to steale on many of them, (and their great and continuall labours, with other crosses and sorrows, hastened it before the time) so as it was not only probably thought, but apparently seen, that within a few years more, they would be in danger to scatter (by necessities pressing them) or sinke under their burdens, or both. And therfore according to the devine proverb, that a wise man seeth the plague when it cometh, and hideth him selfe, Pro. 22. 3., so they like skillfull and beaten souldiers were fearfull, either to be intrapped or surrounded by their enimies, so as they should neither be able to fight nor flie. And therfor thought it better to dislodge betimes to some place of better advantage and less danger, if any such could be found.

Thirdly; As necessitie was a taskmaster over them, so they were forced to be such, not only to their servants (but in a sorte) to their dearest children; the which as it did not a litle wound the tender harts of many a loving father, and mother; so it produced likwise sundrie sad and sorowful effects. For many of their children, that were of best dispositions, and gracious Inclinations (haveing lernde to bear the yoake in their youth) and willing to bear parte of their parents burden, were (often times) so oppressed with their hevie labours, that though their minds were free and willing, yet their bodies bowed under the weight of the same, and became decreped in their early youth; the vigor of nature being consumed in the very budd as it were. But that which was more lamentable, and of all sorowes most heavie to be borne, was that many of their children, by these occasions, and the great licentiousness of youth in that countrie, and the manifold temptations of the place, were drawne away by evill examples into extravagante and dangerous courses, getting the raines off their neks, and departing from their parents. Some became souldiers, others tooke upon them farr viages by sea, and other some worse courses, tending to dissolutnes and the danger of their soules, to the great greefe of their parents and dishonour of God. So that they saw their posteritie would be in danger to degenerate and be corrupted.

Lastly, (and which was not least), a great hope, and inward zeall they had of laying some good foundation, or (at least to make some way therunto) for the propagating, and advancing the gospell of the kingdom of Christ in those remote parts of the world; yea, though they should be but even as stepping-stones, unto others for the performing of so great a work.

These, and some other like reasons, moved them to undertake this resolution of their removall; the which they afterward prosecuted with so great difficulties, as by the sequell will appeare.

The place they had thoughts on, was some of those vast and un-

peopled countries of America, which are frutfull, and fitt for habitation; being devoyd of all civill inhabitants; wher ther are only salvage,
and brutish men, which range up and downe, litle otherwise then the
wild beasts of the same. This proposition being made publike, and
coming to the scaning of all; it raised many variable opinions amongst
men, and caused many fears, and doubts amongst them selves. Some
from their reasons, and hopes conceived, laboured to stirr up and incourage the rest to undertake, and prosecute the same; others againe
out of their fears, objected against it, and sought to diverte from it;
aledging many things, and those neither unreasonable, nor unprob-
able. As that it was a great designe, and subjecte to many unconceivable perills, and dangers; as, besids the casulties of the seas (which
none can be freed from) the length of the vioage was such, as the
weake bodys of women and other persons worne out with age and
traville (as many of them were) could never be able to endure. And
yet if they should, the miseries of the land, which they should be exposed unto, would be to hard to be borne; and lickly, some, or all
of them togeither, to consume, and utterly to ruinate them. For ther
they should be liable to famine, and nakednes, and the wante in a
maner of all things. The chang of aire, diate, and drinking of water,
would infecte their bodies with sore sickneses, and greevous diseases.
And also those which should escape or overcome these difficulties,
should yett be in continuall danger of the salvage people; who are
cruell, barbarous, and most trecherous, being most furious in their
rage, and merciles wher they overcome; not being contente only to
kill, and take away life, but delight to tormente men in the most bloodie
manner that may be; fleaing some alive with the shells of fishes, cutting
of the members, and joynts of others by peesmeale, and broiling on
the coles, eate the collops of their flesh in their sight whilst they live;
with other cruelties horrible to be related. And surely it could not
be thought but the very hearing of these things could not but move
the very bowels of men to grate within them, and make the weake
to quake, and tremble. It was furder objected, that it would require
greater summes of money to furnish such a voiage (and to fitt them
with necessaries) then their consumed estats would amounte too; and
yett they must as well looke to be seconded with supplies, as presently
to be transported. Also many presidents of ill success, and lamentable
misseries befalne others, in the like designes, were easie to be found,
and not forgotten to be aledged. Besides their owne experience, in
their former troubles, and hardships in their removall into Holand;
and how hard a thing it was for them to live in that strange place,

though it was a neighbour countrie, and a civill and rich comone wealth.

It was answered, that all great, and honourable actions, are accompanied with great difficulties; and must be both enterprised, and overcome with answerable courages. It was granted the dangers were great, but not desperate; the difficulties were many, but not invincible. For though their were many of them likly, yet they were not cartaine; it might be sundrie of the things feared might never befale; others by providente care and the use of good means, might in a great measure be prevented; and all of them (through the help of God) by fortitude, and patience, might either be borne, or overcome. True it was, that such atempts were not to be made and undertaken without good ground, and reason; not rashly, or lightly as many have done for curiositie, or hope of gaine, etc. But their condition was not ordinarie; their ends were good and honourable; their calling lawfull, and urgente; and therfore they might expecte the blessing of God in their proceding. Yea, though they should loose their lives in this action, yet might they have comforte in the same, and their endeavors would be honourable. . . .

These troubls being blowne over, and now all being compacte togeather in one shipe, they put to sea againe with a prosperus winde, which continued diverce days togeather, which was some incouragmente unto them; yet according to the usuall maner many were afflicted with seasicknes. And I may not omite hear a spetiall worke of Gods providence. Ther was a proud and very profane yonge man, one of the sea-men, of a lustie, able body, which made him the more hauty; he would allway be contemning the poore people in their sicknes, and cursing them dayly with greevous execrations, and did not let to tell them, that he hoped to help to cast halfe of them over board before they came to their jurneys end, and to make mery with what they had; and if he were by any gently reproved, he would curse and swear most bitterly. But it plased God before they came halfe seas over, to smite this yong man with a greeveous disease, of which he dyed in a desperate maner, and so was him selfe the first that was throwne overbord. Thus his curses light on his owne head; and it was an astonishmente to all his fellows, for they noted it to be the just hand of God upon him.

After they had injoyed faire winds and weather for a season, they were incountred many times with crosse winds, and mette with many feirce stormes, with which the shipe was shroudly shaken, and her upper works made very leakie; and one of the maine beames in the

midd ships was bowed and craked, which put them in some fear
that the shipe could not be able to performe the vioage. So some of
the cheefe of the company, perceiveing the mariners to feare the suffi-
siencie of the shipe, as appeared by their mutterings, they entred into
serious consulltation with the m^r and other officers of the ship, to
consider in time of the danger; and rather to returne then to cast
them selves into a desperate and inevitable perill. And truly ther was
great distraction and differance of opinion amongst the mariners them
selves; faine would they doe what could be done for their wages sake,
(being now halfe the seas over,) and on the other hand they were
loath to hazard their lives too desperately. But in examening of all
opinions, the m^r and others affirmed they knew the ship to be stronge
and firme under water; and for the buckling of the maine beame,
ther was a great iron scrue the passengers brought out of Holland,
which would raise the beame into his place; the which being done,
the carpenter and m^r affirmed that with a post put under it, set firme
in the lower deck, and otherways bounde, he would make it sufficiente.
And as for the decks and uper workes they would calke them as well
as they could, and though with the workeing of the ship they would
not longe keepe stanch, yet ther would otherwise be no great danger,
if they did not overpress her with sails. So they commited them selves
to the will of God, and resolved to proseede. In sundrie of these
stormes the winds were so feirce, and the seas so high, as they could
not beare a knote of saile, but were forced to hull, for diverce days
togither. And in one of them, as they thus lay at hull, in a mighty
storme, a lustie yonge man (called John Howland) coming upon some
occasion above the grattings, was, with a seele of the shipe throwne
into [the] sea; but it pleased God that he caught hould of the top-
saile halliards, which hunge over board, and rane out at length; yet
he held his hould (though he was sundrie fadomes under water) till
he was hald up by the same rope to the brime of the water, and then
with a boat hooke and other means got into the shipe againe, and his
life saved; and though he was something ill with it, yet he lived many
years after, and became a profitable member both in church and
commone wealthe. In all this viage ther died but one of the passengers,
which was William Butten, a youth, servant to Samuell Fuller, when
they drew near the coast. But to omite other things, (that I may be
breefe,) after longe beating at sea they fell with that land which is
called Cape Cod; the which being made and certainly knowne to be
it, they were not a litle joyfull. After some deliberation had amongst
them selves and with the m^r of the ship, they tacked aboute and re-

solved to stande for the southward (the wind and weather being faire)
to finde some place aboute Hudsons river for their habitation. But
after they had sailed that course aboute halfe the day, they fell amongst
deangerous shoulds and roring breakers, and they were so farr in-
tangled ther with as they conceived them selves in great danger; and
the wind shrinking upon them withall, they resolved to bear up againe
for the Cape, and thought them selves hapy to gett out of those dangers
before night overtooke them, as by Gods providence they did. And the
next day they gott into the Cape-harbor wher they ridd in saftie. A
word or too by the way of this cape; it was thus first named by Capten
Gosnole and his company, Anº: 1602, and after by Capten Smith
was caled Cape James; but it retains the former name amongst seamen.
Also that pointe which first shewed those dangerous shoulds unto them,
they called Pointe Care, and Tuckers Terrour; but the French and
Dutch to this day call it Malabarr, by reason of those perilous shoulds,
and the losses they have suffered their.

Being thus arived in a good harbor and brought safe to land, they
fell upon their knees and blessed the God of heaven, who had brought
them over the vast and furious ocean, and delivered them from all
the periles and miseries therof, againe to set their feete on the firme
and stable earth, their proper elemente. And no marvell if they were
thus joyefull, seeing wise Seneca was so affected with sailing a few
miles on the coast of his owne Italy; as he affirmed, that he had rather
remaine twentie years on his way by land, then pass by sea to any
place in a short time; so tedious and dreadfull was the same unto him.

But hear I cannot but stay and make a pause, and stand half amased
at this poore peoples presente condition; and so I thinke will the reader
too, when he well considers the same. Being thus passed the vast ocean,
and a sea of troubles before in their preparation (as may be remembred
by that which wente before), they had now no freinds to wellcome
them, nor inns to entertaine or refresh their weatherbeaten bodys, no
houses or much less townes to repaire too, to seeke for succoure. It
is recorded in scripture as a mercie to the apostle and his shipwraked
company, that the barbarians shewed them no smale kindnes in refreshing them, but these savage barbarians, when they mette with
them (as after will appeare) were readier to fill their sids full of arrows
then otherwise. And for the season it was winter, and they that know
the winters of that cuntrie know them to be sharp and violent, and
subjecte to cruell and feirce stormes, deangerous to travill to known
places, much more to serch an unknown coast. Besides, what could
they see but a hidious and desolate wildernes, full of wild beasts and

Pisgah - mountain which Moses goes up on to view the promised land.

wasn't what they had expected - the promised land is heaven only

willd men? and what multituds ther might be of them they knew not. Nether could they, as it were, goe up to the tope of Pisgah, to vew from this willdernes a more goodly cuntrie to feed their hops; for which way soever they turnd their eys (save upward to the heavens) they could have litle solace or content in respecte of any outward objects. For summer being done, all things stand upon them with a wether-beaten face; and the whole countrie, full of woods and thickets, repre-sented a wild and savage heiw. If they looked behind them, ther was the mighty ocean which they had passed, and was now as a maine barr and goulfe to seperate them from all the civill parts of the world. If it be said they had a ship to sucour them, it is trew; but what heard they daly from the m^r and company? but that with speede they should looke out a place with their shallop, wher they would be at some near distance; for the season was shuch as he would not stirr from thence till a safe harbor was discovered by them wher they would be, and he might goe without danger; and that victells consumed apace, but he must and would keepe sufficient for them selves and their returne. Yea, it was muttered by some, that if they gott not a place in time, they would turne them and their goods ashore and leave them. Let it also be considred what weake hopes of supply and succoure they left behinde them, that might bear up their minds in this sade condi-tion and trialls they were under; and they could not but be very smale. It is true, indeed, the affections and love of their brethren at Leyden was cordiall and entire towards them, but they had litle power to help them, or them selves; and how the case stode betweene them and the marchants at their coming away, hath allready been declared. What could now sustaine them but the spirite of God and his grace? May not and ought not the children of these fathers rightly say: *Our faithers were Englishmen which came over this great ocean, and were ready to perish in this willdernes; but they cried unto the Lord, and he heard their voyce, and looked on their adversitie, etc. Let them therfore praise the Lord, because he is good, and his mercies endure for ever. Yea, let them which have been re-deemed of the Lord, shew how he hath delivered them from the hand of the op-pressour. When they wandered in the deserte willdernes out of the way, and found no citie to dwell in, both hungrie, and thirstie, their sowle was over-whelmed in them. Let them confess before the Lord his loving kindnes, and his wonderfull works before the sons of men.* . . .

[1620] I shall a litle returne backe and begine with a combination made by them before they came ashore, being the first foundation of their govermente in this place; occasioned partly by the discontented and mutinous speeches that some of the strangers amongst them had let fall from them in the ship; That when they came a shore they would use their owne libertie; for none had power to command them, the patente they had being for Virginia, and not for New-england, which belonged to an other Goverment, with which the Virginia Company had nothing to doe. And partly that shuch an acte by them done (this their condition considered) might be as firme as any patent, and in some respects more sure.

The forme was as followeth.

In the name of God, Amen. We whose names are under-writen, the loyall subjects of our dread soveraigne Lord, King James, by the grace of God, of Great Britaine, Franc, and Ireland king, defender of the faith, etc., haveing undertaken, for the glorie of God, and advancemente of the Christian faith, and honour of our king and countrie, a voyage to plant the first colonie in the Northerne parts of Virginia, doe by these presents solemnly and mutualy in the presence of God, and one of another, covenant and combine our selves togeather into a civill body politick, for our better ordering and preservation and furtherance of the ends aforesaid; and by vertue hearof to enacte, constitute, and frame such just and equall lawes, ordinances, acts, constitutions, and offices, from time to time, as shall be thought most meete and convenient for the generall good of the Colonie, unto which we promise all due submission and obedience. In witnes wherof we have hereunder subscribed our names at Cap-Codd the 11. of November, in the year of the raigne of our soveraigne lord, King James, of England, France, and Ireland the eighteenth, and of Scotland the fiftie fourth. Anᵒ: Dom. 1620.

After this they chose, or rather confirmed, Mr. John Carver (a man godly and well approved amongst them) their Governour for that year. And after they had provided a place for their goods, or comone store, (which were long in unlading for want of boats, foulnes of winter weather, and sicknes of diverce,) and begune some small cottages for their habitation, as time would admitte, they mette and consulted of lawes and orders, both for their civill and military Govermente, as the necessitie of their condition did require, still adding therunto as urgent occasion in severall times, and as cases did require.

In these hard and difficulte beginings they found some discontents and murmurings arise amongst some, and mutinous speeches and carriags in other; but they were soone quelled and overcome by the wisdome, patience, and just and equall carrage of things by the Govʳ and better part, which clave faithfully togeather in the maine. But that which was most sadd and lamentable was, that in 2. or 3. moneths time halfe of their company dyed, espetialy in Jan: and February, being the depth of winter, and wanting houses and other comforts; being infected with the scurvie and other diseases, which this long vioage and their inacomodate condition had brought upon them; so as ther dyed some times 2. or 3. of a day, in the foresaid time; that of 100. and odd persons, scarce 50. remained. And of these in the time of most distres, ther was but 6. or 7. sound persons, who, to their great comendations be it spoken, spared no pains, night nor day, but with abundance of toyle and hazard of their owne health, fetched them woode, made them fires, drest them meat, made their beads, washed their lothsome cloaths, cloathed and uncloathed them; in a word, did all the homly and necessarie offices for them which dainty and quesie stomacks cannot endure to hear named; and all this willingly and cherfully, without any grudging in the least, shewing herein their true love unto their freinds and bretheren. A rare example and worthy to be remembred. Tow of these 7. were Mr. William Brewster, ther reverend Elder, and Myles Standish, ther Captein and military comander, unto whom my selfe, and many others, were much beholden in our low and sicke condition. And yet the Lord so upheld these persons, as in this generall calamity they were not at all infected either with sicknes, or lamnes. And what I have said of these, I may say of many others who dyed in this generall vissitation, and others yet living, that whilst they had health, yea, or any strength continuing, they were not wanting to any that had need of them. And I doute not but their recompence is with the Lord. . . .

[1621] After the departure of this ship, [the *Fortune*] (which stayed not above 14. days,) the Gover and his assistante haveing disposed these late commers into severall families, as they best could, tooke an exacte accounte of all their provissions in store, and proportioned the same to the number of persons, and found that it would not hould out above 6. months at halfe alowance, and hardly that. And they could not well give less this winter time till fish came in againe. So they were presently put to half alowance, one as well as an other, which begane to be hard, but they bore it patiently under hope of supply.

Soone after this ships departure, the great people of the Narigansets, in a braving maner, sente a messenger unto them with a bundl of arrows tyed aboute with a great sneak-skine; which their interpretours tould them was a threatening and a chaleng. Upon which the Govr, with the advice of others sente them a round answere, that if they had rather have warre then peace, they might begine when they would; they had done them no wrong, neither did they fear them, or should they find them unprovided. And by another messenger sente the sneake-skine back with bulits in it; but they would not receive it, but sent it back againe. But these things I doe but mention, because they are more at large allready put forth in printe, by Mr. Winslow, at the requeste of some freinds. And it is like the reason was their owne ambition, who, (since the death of so many of the Indeans,) thought to dominire and lord it over the rest, and conceived the English would be a barr in their way, and saw that Massasoyt took sheilter allready under their wings.

But this made them the more carefully to looke to them selves, so as they agreed to inclose their dwellings with a good strong pale, and make flankers in convenient places, with gates to shute, which were every night locked, and a watch kept and when neede required ther was also warding in the day time. And the company was by the Captaine and the Govr advise, devided into 4. squadrons, and every one had ther quarter apoynted them, unto which they were to repaire upon any suddane alarme. And if ther should be any crie of fire, a company were appointed for a gard, with muskets, whilst others quenchet the same, to prevent Indean treachery. This was accomplished very cherfully, and the towne impayled round by the begining of March, in which evry family had a prety garden plote secured. And herewith I shall end this year. Only I shall remember one passage more, rather of mirth then of waight. One the day called Chrismasday, the Govr caled them out to worke, (as was used,) but the most of this new-company excused them selves and said it wente against their consciences to work on that day. So the Govr tould them that if they made it mater of conscience, he would spare them till they were better informed. So he led-away the rest and left them; but when they came home at noone from their worke, he found them in the streete at play, openly; some pitching the barr and some at stoole-ball, and shuch like sports. So he went to them, and tooke away their implements, and tould them that was against his conscience, that they should play and others worke. If they made the keeping of it mater of devotion, let them kepe their houses, but ther should be no gameing or revelling in the streets. Since which time nothing hath been atempted that way, at least openly. . . .

[1623] They begane to thinke how they might raise as much corne as they could, and obtaine a beter crope then they had done, that they might not still thus languish in miserie. At length, after much debate of things, the Govr (with the advise of the cheefest amongst them) gave way that they should set corne every man for his owne perticuler, and in that regard trust to them selves; in all other things to goe on in the generall way as before. And so assigned to every family a parcell of land, according to the proportion of their number for that end, only for present use (but made no devission for inheritance), and ranged all boys and youth under some familie. This had very good success; for it made all hands very industrious, so as much more corne was planted then other waise would have bene by any means the Govr or any other could use, and saved him a great deall of trouble, and gave farr better contente. The women now wente willingly into the feild, and tooke their litle-ons with them to set corne, which before would aledg weaknes, and inabilitie; whom to have compelled would have bene thought great tiranie and oppression.

The experience that was had in this commone course and condition, tried sundrie years, and that amongst godly and sober men, may well evince the vanitie of that conceite of Platos and other ancients, applauded by some of later times;—that the taking away of propertie, and bringing in communitie into a comone wealth, would make them happy and florishing; as if they were wiser then God. For this comunitie (so farr as it was) was found to breed much confusion and discontent, and retard much imployment that would have been to their benefite and comforte. For the yong-men that were most able and fitte for labour and service did repine that they should spend their time and streingth to worke for other mens wives and children, with out any recompence. The strong, or man of parts, had no more in devission of victails and cloaths, then he that was weake and not able to doe a quarter the other could; this was thought injuestice. The aged and graver men to be ranked and equalised in labours, and victails, cloaths, etc., with the meaner and yonger sorte, thought it some indignite and disrespect unto them. And for mens wives to be commanded to doe servise for other men, as dresing their meate, washing their cloaths, etc., they deemd it a kind of slaverie, neither could many husbands well brooke it. Upon the poynte all being to have alike, and all to doe alike, they thought them selves in the like condition, and one as good as another; and so, if it did not cut of those relations that God hath set amongest men, yet it did at least much diminish and take of the mutuall respects that should be preserved amongest them. And would have bene worse if they had been men of another condition. Let none objecte this is men's corruption, and nothing to the course it selfe. I answer, seeing all men have this corruption in them, God in his wisdome saw another course fiter for them. . . .

[1624] With the former letter write by Mr. Sherley, there were sente sundrie objections concerning which he thus writeth. "These are the cheefe objections which they that are now returned make against you and the countrie. I pray you consider them, and answer them by the first conveniencie." These objections were made by some of those that came over on their perticuler and were returned home, as is before mentioned, and were of the same suite with those that this other letter mentions.

I shall here set them downe, with the answers then made unto them, and sent over at the returne of this ship; which did so confound the objecters, as some confessed their falte, and others deneyed what they had said, and eate their words, and some others of them have since come over againe and heere lived to convince them selves sufficiently, both in their owne and other mens judgments.

1. obj. was diversitie aboute Religion. Ans: We know no such matter, for here was never any controversie or opposition, either publicke or private, (to our knowledg,) since we came.

2. ob: Neglecte of familie duties, one the Lords day.

Ans. We allow no such thing, but blame it in our selves and others; and they that thus reporte it, should have shewed their Christian love the more if they had in love tould the offenders of it, rather then thus to reproach them behind their baks. But (to say no more) we wish them selves had given better example. . . .

5. ob: Many of the perticuler members of the plantation will not work for the generall.

Ans: This allso is not wholy true; for though some doe it not willingly, and other not honestly, yet all doe it; and he that doth worst gets his owne foode and something besids. But we will not excuse them, but labour to reforme them the best we cane, or else to quitte the plantation of them.

6. ob: The water is not wholsome.

Ans: If they mean, not so wholsome as the good beere and wine in London, (which they so dearly love,) we will not dispute with them; but els, for water, it is as good as any in the world, (for ought we knowe,) and it is wholsome enough to us that can be contente therwith.

7. ob: The ground is barren and doth bear no grasse.

Ans: It is hear (as in all places) some better and some worse; and if they well consider their words, in England they shall not find such grasse in them, as in their feelds and meadows. The catle find grasse, for they are as fatt as need be; we wish we had but one for every hundred that hear is grase to keep. Indeed, this objection, as some other. are ridiculous to all here which see and know the contrary.

8. ob: The fish will not take salt to keepe sweete.

Ans: This is as true as that which was written, that ther is scarce a foule to be seene or a fish to be taken. Things likly to be true in a cuntrie wher so many sayle of ships come yearly a fishing; they might as well say, there can no aile or beere in London be kept from sowering.

9. ob: Many of them are theevish and steale on from an other.

Ans: Would London had been free from that crime, then we should not have been trobled with these here; it is well knowne sundrie have smarted well for it, and so are the rest like to doe, if they be taken.

10. ob: The countrie is anoyed with foxes and woules.

Ans: So are many other good cuntries too; but poyson, traps, and other such means will help to destroy them.

11. ob: The Dutch are planted nere Hudsons Bay, and are likely to overthrow the trade.

Ans: They will come and plante in these parts, also, if we and others doe not, but goe home and leave it to them. We rather commend them, then condemne them for it.

12. ob: The people are much anoyed with muskeetoes.

Ans: They are too delicate and unfitte to begine new-plantations and collonies, that cannot enduer the biting of a muskeeto; we would wish such to keepe at home till at least they be muskeeto proofe. Yet this place is as free as any, and experience teacheth that the more the land is tild, and the woods cut downe, the fewer ther will be, and in the end scarse any at all. . . .

[1628] Aboute some 3. or 4. years before this time, ther came over one Captaine Wolastone, (a man of pretie parts,) and with him 3. or 4. more of some eminencie, who brought with them a great many servants, with provissions and other implments for to begine a plantation; and pitched them selves in a place within the Massachusets, which they called, after their Captains name, Mount-Wollaston. Amongst whom was one Mr. Morton, who, it should seeme, had some small adventure (of his owne or other mens) amongst them; but had litle respecte amongst them, and was sleghted by the meanest servants. Haveing continued ther some time, and not finding things to answer their expectations, nor profite to arise as they looked for, Captaine Wollaston takes a great part of the sarvants, and transports them to Virginia, wher he puts them of at good rates, selling their time to other men; and writs back to one Mr. Rassdall, one of his cheefe partners, and accounted their marchant, to bring another parte

of them to Verginia likewise, intending to put them of ther as he had
done the rest. And he, with the consente of the said Rasdall, appoynted
one Fitcher to be his Livetenante, and governe the remaines of the
plantation, till he or Rasdall returned to take further order theraboute.
But this Morton abovesaid, haveing more craft then honestie, (who
had been a kind of petiefogger, of Furnefells Inne,) in the others ab-
sence, watches an oppertunitie, (commons being but hard amongst
them,) and gott some strong drinck and other junkats, and made
them a feast; and after they were merie, he begane to tell them, he
would give them good counsell. You see (saith he) that many of your
fellows are carried to Virginia; and if you stay till this Rasdall returne,
you will also be carried away and sould for slaves with the rest. Therfore I would advise you to thruste out this Levetenant Fitcher; and
I, having a parte in the plantation, will receive you as my partners
and consociats; so may you be free from service, and we will converse,
trad, plante, and live togeather as equalls, and supporte and protecte
one another, or to like effecte. This counsell was easily received; so
they tooke oppertunitie, and thrust Levetenante Fitcher out a dores,
and would suffer him to come no more amongst them, but forct him
to seeke bread to eate, and other releefe from his neigbours, till he
could gett passage for England. After this they fell to great licen-
ciousnes, and led a dissolute life, powering out them selves into all
profanenes. And Morton became lord of misrule, and maintained (as
it were) a schoole of Athisme. And after they had gott some good
into their hands, and gott much by trading with the Indeans, they
spent it as vainly, in quaffing and drinking both wine and strong
waters in great exsess, and, as some reported, 10 *li.* worth in a morning.
They allso set up a Maypole, drinking and dancing aboute it many
days togeather, inviting the Indean women, for their consorts, dancing
and frisking togither, (like so many fairies, or furies rather,) and worse
practises. As if they had anew revived and celebrated the feasts of the
Roman Goddes Flora, or the beasly practieses of the madd Bac-
chinalians. Morton likwise (to shew his poetrie) composed sundry
rimes and verses, some tending to lasciviousnes, and others to the
detraction and scandall of some persons, which he affixed to this idle
or idol May-polle. They chainged allso the name of their place, and
in stead of calling it Mounte Wollaston, they call it Meriemounte, as
if this joylity would have lasted ever. But this continued not long,
for after Morton was sent for England, (as follows to be declared,)
shortly after came over that worthy gentlman, Mr. John Indecott,
who brought over a patent under the broad seall, for the govermente

of the Massachusets, who visiting those parts caused that May-polle to be cutt downe, and rebuked them for their profannes, and admonished them to looke ther should be better walking; so they now, or others, changed the name of their place againe, and called it Mounte-Dagon.

Now to maintaine this riotous prodigallitie and profuse excess, Morton, thinking him selfe lawless, and hearing what gaine the French and fishermen made by trading of peeces, powder, and shotte to the Indeans, he, as the head of this consortship, begane the practise of the same in these parts; and first he taught them how to use them, to charge, and discharg, and what proportion of powder to give the peece, according to the sise or bignes of the same; and what shotte to use for foule, and what for deare. And having thus instructed them, he imployed some of them to hunte and fowle for him, so as they became farr more active in that imploymente then any of the English, by reason of ther swiftnes of foote, and nimblnes of body, being also quick-sighted, and by continuall exercise well knowing the hants of all sorts of game. So as when they saw the execution that a peece would doe, and the benefite that might come by the same, they became madd, as it were, after them, and would not stick to give any prise they could attaine too for them; accounting their bowes and arrowes but bables in comparison of them. . . .

This Morton having thus taught them the use of peeces, he sould them all he could spare; and he and his consorts detirmined to send for many out of England, and had by some of the ships sente for above a score. The which being knowne, and his neigbours meeting the Indeans in the woods armed with guns in this sorte, it was a terrour unto them, who lived straglingly, and were of no strenght in any place. And other places (though more remote) saw this mischeefe would quietly spread over all, if not prevented. Besides, they saw they should keep no servants, for Morton would entertaine any, how vile soever, and all the scume of the countrie, or any discontents, would flock to him from all places, if this nest was not broken; and they should stand in more fear of their lives and goods (in short time) from this wicked and deboste crue, then from the salvages them selves.

So sundrie of the cheefe of the stragling plantations, meeting togither, agreed by mutuall consente to sollissite those of Plimoth (who were then of more strength then them all) to joyne with them, to prevent the further grouth of this mischeefe, and suppress Morton and his consortes before they grewe to further head and strength. Those that joyned in this acction (and after contributed to the charge of sending him for England) were from Pascataway, Namkeake, Winisimett, Weesagascusett, Natasco, and other places wher any English were seated. Those of Plimoth being thus sought too by their messengers and letters, and waying both their reasons, and the commone danger, were willing to afford them their help; though them selves had least cause of fear or hurte. So, to be short, they first resolved joyntly to write to him, and in a freindly and neigborly way to admonish him to forbear these courses, and sent a messenger with their letters to bring his answer. But he was so highe as he scorned all advise, and asked who had to doe with him; he had and would trade peeces with the Indeans in dispite of all, with many other scurillous termes full of disdaine. They sente to him a second time, and bad him be better advised, and more temperate in his termes, for the countrie could not beare the injure he did; it was against their comone saftie, and against the king's proclamation. He answerd in high terms as before, and that the kings proclaimation was no law; demanding what penaltie was upon it. It was answered, more then he could bear, his majesties displeasure. But insolently he persisted, and said the king was dead and his displeasure with him, and many the like things; and threatened withall that if any came to molest him, let them looke to them selves, for he would prepare for them. Upon which they saw ther was no way but to take him by force; and having so farr proceeded, now to give over would make him farr more hautie and insolente. So they mutually resolved to proceed, and obtained of the Govr of Plimoth to send Captaine Standish, and some other aide with him, to take Morton by force. The which accordingly was done; but they found him to stand stifly in his defence, having made fast his dors, armed his consorts, set diverse dishes of powder and bullets ready on the table; and if they had not been over armed with drinke, more hurt might have been done. They sommaned him to yeeld, but he kept his house, and they could gett nothing but scofes and scorns from him; but at length, fearing they would doe some violence to the house, he and some of his crue came out, but not to yeeld, but to shoote; but they were so steeld with drinke as their peeces were to heavie for them; him selfe with a carbine (over charged and allmost halfe fild with powder and shote, as was after found) had thought to have shot Captaine Standish; but he stept to him, and put by his peece, and tooke him. Neither was ther any hurte done to any of either side, save that one was so drunke that he rane his owne nose upon the pointe of a sword that one held before him as he entred the house; but he lost but a litle of his hott blood. Morton they brought away to Plimoth, wher he was kepte, till a ship went from the Ile of Shols for England, with which he was sente to the Counsell of New-England; and letters writen to give them information of his course and cariage; and also one was sent at their commone charge to informe their Ho^{rs} more perticulerly, and to prosecute against him. But he foold of the messenger, after he was gone from hence, and though he wente for England, yet nothing was done to him, not so much as rebukte, for ought was heard; but returned the nexte year. Some of the worst of the company were disperst, and some of the more modest kepte the house till he should be heard from. But I have been too long about so unworthy a person, and bad a cause. . . .

[1633] Mr. Roger Williams (a man godly and zealous, having many precious parts, but very unsettled in judgmente) càme over first to the Massachusets, but upon some discontente left that place, and came hither, (wher he was friendly entertained, according to their poore abilitie,) and exercised his gifts amongst them, and after some time was admitted a member of the church; and his teaching well approoved, for the benefite wherof I still blese God, and am thankfull to him, even for his sharpest admonitions and reproufs, so farr as they agreed with truth. He this year begane to fall into some strang oppinions, and from opinion to practise; which caused some controversie betweene the church and him, and in the end some discontente on his parte, by occasion wherof he left them some thing abruptly. Yet after wards sued for his dismission to the church of Salem, which was granted, with some caution to them concerning him, and what care they ought to have of him. But he soone fell into more things ther, both to their and the goverments troble and disturbance. I shall not need to name perticulers, they are too well knowen now to all, though for a time the church here wente under some hard censure by his occasion, from some that afterwards smarted them selves. But he is to be pitied, and prayed for, and so I shall leave the matter, and desire the Lord to shew him his errors, and reduse him into the way of truth, and give him a setled judgment and constancie in the same; for I hope he belongs to the Lord, and that he will shew him mercie. . . .

[1642] Marvilous it may be to see and consider how some kind of wickednes did grow and breake forth here, in a land wher the same was so much witnesed against, and so narrowly looked unto, and severly punished when it was knowne; as in no place more, or so much, that I have known or heard of; insomuch as they have been somewhat censured, even by moderate and good men, for their severitie in punish-

ments. And yet all this could not suppress the breaking out of sundrie
notorious sins, (as this year, besids other, gives us too many sad presidents and instances,) espetially drunkennes and unclainnes; not only
incontinencie betweene persons unmaried, for which many both men
and women have been punished sharply enough, but some maried
persons allso. But that which is worse, even sodomie and bugerie,
(things fearfull to name,) have broak forth in this land, oftener then
once. I say it may justly be marveled at, and cause us to fear and
tremble at the consideration of our corrupte natures, which are so
hardly bridled, subdued, and mortified; nay, cannot by any other
means but the powerfull worke and grace of Gods spirite. But (besids
this) one reason may be, that the Divell may carrie a greater spite
against the churches of Christ and the gospell hear, by how much the
more they indeaour to preserve holynes and puritie amongst them,
and strictly punisheth the contrary when it ariseth either in church
or comone wealth; that he might cast a blemishe and staine upon
them in the eyes of [the] world, who use to be rash in judgmente. I
would rather thinke thus, then that Satane hath more power in these
heathen lands, as som have thought, then in more Christian nations,
espetially over Gods servants in them.

2. An other reason may be, that it may be in this case as it is with
waters when their streames are stopped or dammed up, when they
gett passage they flow with more violence, and make more noys and
disturbance, then when they are suffered to rune quietly in their owne
chanels. So wikednes being here more stopped by strict laws, and the
same more nerly looked unto, so as it cannot rune in a comone road
of liberty as it would, and is inclined, it searches every wher, and at
last breaks out wher it getts vente.

3. A third reason may be, hear (as I am verily perswaded) is not
more evills in this kind, nor nothing nere so many by proportion, as
in other places; but they are here more discoverd and seen, and made
publick by due serch, inquisition, and due punishment; for the churches
looke narrowly to their members, and the magistrats over all, more
strictly then in other places. Besids, here the people are but few in
comparison of other places, which are full and populous, and lye
hid, as it were, in a wood or thickett, and many horrible evills by that
means are never seen nor knowne; wheras hear, they are, as it were,
brought into the light, and set in the plaine feeld, or rather on a hill,
made conspicuous to the veiw of all. . . .

[1643] I am to begine this year whith that which was a mater of
great saddnes and mourning unto them all. Aboute the 18. of Aprill

dyed their Reve^d Elder, and my dear and loving friend, Mr. William Brewster; a man that had done and suffered much for the Lord Jesus and the gospells sake, and had bore his parte in well and woe with this poore persecuted church above 36. years in England, Holand, and in this wildernes, and done the Lord and them faithfull service in his place and calling. And notwithstanding the many troubls and sorrows he passed throw, the Lord upheld him to a great age. He was nere fourskore years of age (if not all out) when he dyed. He had this blesing added by the Lord to all the rest, to dye in his bed, in peace, amongst the mids of his freinds, who mourned and wepte over him, and ministered what help and comforte they could unto him, and he againe recomforted them whilst he could. His sicknes was not long, and till the last day therof he did not wholy keepe his bed. His speech continued till somewhat more then halfe a day, and then failed him; and aboute 9. or 10. a clock that evning he dyed, without any pangs at all. A few howers before, he drew his breath shorte, and some few minuts before his last, he drew his breath long, as a man falen into a sound slepe, without any pangs or gaspings, and so sweetly departed this life unto a better.

I would now demand of any, what he was the worse for any former sufferings? What doe I say, worse? Nay, sure he was the better, and they now added to his honour. *It is a manifest token* (saith the Apostle, 2. Thes: 1. 5, 6, 7.) *of the righ[t]eous judgmente of God that ye may be counted worthy of the kingdome of God, for which ye allso suffer; seing it is a righteous thing with God to recompence tribulation to them that trouble you: and to you who are troubled, rest with us, when the Lord Jesus shall be revealed from heaven, with his mighty angels.* 1. Pet. 4. 14. *If you be reproached for the name of Christ, hapy are ye, for the spirite of glory and of God resteth upon you.* What though he wanted the riches and pleasurs of the world in this life, and pompous monuments at his funurall? yet the memoriall of the just shall be blessed, when the name of the wicked shall rott (with their marble monuments). Pro: 10. 7.

I should say something of his life, if to say a litle were not worse then to be silent. But I cannot wholy forbear, though hapily more may be done hereafter. After he had attained some learning, viz. the knowledg of the Latine tongue, and some insight in the Greeke, and spent some small time at Cambridge, and then being first seasoned with the seeds of grace and vertue, he went to the Courte, and served that religious and godly gentlman, Mr. Davison, diverce years, when he was Secretary of State; who found him so discreete and faithfull as he trusted him above all other that were aboute him, and only

imployed him in all matters of greatest trust and secrecie. He esteemed him rather as a sonne then a servante, and for his wisdom
and godlines (in private) he would converse with him more like a
freind and familier than a maister. He attended his m^r when he was
sente in ambassage by the Queene into the Low-Countries, in the Earle
of Leicesters time, as for other waighty affaires of state, so to receive
possession of the cautionary townes, and in token and signe therof the
keyes of Flushing being delivered to him, in her ma^{tis} name, he kepte
them some time, and committed them to this his servante, who kept
them under his pilow, on which he slepte the first night. And, at his
returne, the States honoured him with a gould chaine, and his maister
committed it to him, and commanded him to wear it when they arrived in England, as they ridd thorrow the country, till they came to
the Courte. He afterwards remained with him till his troubles, that
he was put from his place aboute the death of the Queene of Scots;
and some good time after, doeing him manie faithfull offices of servise
in the time of his troubles. Afterwards he wente and lived in the
country, in good esteeme amongst his freinds and the gentle-men of
those parts, espetially the godly and religious. He did much good in
the countrie wher he lived, in promoting and furthering religion, not
only by his practiss and example, and provocking and incouraging
of others, but by procuring of good preachers to the places theraboute,
and drawing on of others to assiste and help forward in such a worke;
he him selfe most comonly deepest in the charge, and some times above
his abillitie. And in this state he continued many years, doeing the
best good he could, and walking according to the light he saw, till
the Lord reveiled further unto him. And in the end, by the tirrany
of the bishops against godly preachers and people, in silenceing the
one and persecuting the other, he and many more of those times
begane to looke further into things, and to see into the unlawfullnes
of their callings, and the burthen of many anti-christian corruptions,
which both he and they endeavored to cast of; as they allso did, as
in the begining of this treatis is to be seene. After they were joyned
togither in comunion, he was a spetiall stay and help unto them.
They ordinarily mett at his house on the Lords day, (which was a
manor of the bishops,) and with great love he entertained them when
they came, making provission for them to his great charge. He was
the cheefe of those that were taken at Boston, and suffered the greatest
loss; and of the seven that were kept longst in prison, and after bound
over to the assises. Affter he came into Holland he suffered much
hardship, after he had spente the most of his means, haveing a great

charge, and many children; and, in regard of his former breeding
and course of life, not so fitt for many imployments as others were,
espetially such as were toylesume and laborious. But yet he ever bore
his condition with much cherfullnes and contentation. Towards the
later parte of those 12. years spente in Holland, his outward condition
was mended, and he lived well and plentifully; for he fell into a way
(by reason he had the Latine tongue) to teach many students, who
had a disire to lerne the English tongue, to teach them English; and
by his method they quickly attained it with great facilitie; for he drew
rules to lerne it by, after the Latine maner; and many gentlemen,
both Danes and Germans, resorted to him, as they had time from
other studies, some of them being great mens sonnes. He also had
means to set up printing, (by the help of some freinds,) and so had
imploymente inoughg, and by reason of many books which would
not be alowed to be printed in England, they might have had more
then they could doe. But now removeing into this countrie, all these
things were laid aside againe, and a new course of living must be
framed unto; in which he was no way unwilling to take his parte,
and to bear his burthen with the rest, living many times without
bread, or corne, many months together, having many times nothing
but fish, and often wanting that also; and drunke nothing but water
for many years togeather, yea, till within 5. or 6. years of his death.
And yet he lived (by the blessing of God) in health till very old age.
And besids that, he would labour with his hands in the feilds as long
as he was able; yet when the church had no other minister, he taught
twise every Saboth, and that both powerfully and profitably, to the
great contentment of the hearers, and their comfortable edification;
yea, many were brought to God by his ministrie. He did more in this
behalfe in a year, then many that have their hundreds a year doe in
all their lives. For his personall abilities, he was qualified above many;
he was wise and discreete and well spoken, having a grave and deliberate utterance, of a very cherfull spirite, very sociable and pleasante
amongst his freinds, of an humble and modest mind, of a peaceable
disposition, under vallewing him self and his owne abilities, and some
time over valewing others; inoffencive and innocente in his life and
conversation, which gained him the love of those without, as well as
those within; yet he would tell them plainely of their faults and evills,
both publickly and privatly, but in such a maner as usually was well
taken from him. He was tender harted, and compassionate of such as
were in miserie, but espetialy of such as had been of good estate and
ranke, and were fallen unto want and poverty, either for goodnes

and religions sake, or by the injury and oppression of others; he would say, of all men these deserved to be pitied most. And none did more offend and displease him then such as would hautily and proudly carry and lift up themselves, being rise from nothing, and haveing litle els in them to comend them but a few fine cloaths, or a litle riches more then others. In teaching, he was very moving and stirring of affections, also very plaine and distincte in what he taught; by which means he became the more profitable to the hearers. He had a singuler good gift in prayer, both publick and private, in ripping up the hart and conscience before God, in the humble confession of sinne, and begging the mercies of God in Christ for the pardon of the same. He always thought it were better for ministers to pray oftener, and devide their prears, then be longe and tedious in the same (excepte upon sollemne and spetiall occasions, as in days of humiliation and the like). His reason was, that the harte and spirits of all, espetialy the weake, could hardly continue and stand bente (as it were) so long towards God, as they ought to doe in that duty, without flagging and falling of. For the govermente of the church, (which was most proper to his office,) he was carfull to preserve good order in the same, and to preserve puritie, both in the doctrine and comunion of the same; and to supress any errour or contention that might begine to rise up amongst them; and accordingly God gave good success to his indeavors herein all his days, and he saw the fruite of his labours in that behalfe. But I must breake of, having only thus touched a few, as it were, heads of things.

I cannot but here take occasion, not only to mention, but greatly to admire the marvelous providence of God, that notwithstanding the many changes and hardships that these people wente throwgh, and the many enemies they had and difficulties they mette with all, that so many of them should live to very olde age! It was not only this reve^d mans condition, (for one swallow maks no summer, as they say,) but many more of them did the like, some dying aboute and before this time, and many still living, who attained to 60. years of age, and to 65. diverse to 70. and above, and some nere 80. as he did. It must needs be more than ordinarie, and above naturall reason, that so it should be; for it is found in experience, that chaing of aeir, famine, or unholsome foode, much drinking of water, sorrows and troubls, etc., all of them are enimies to health, causes of many diseaces, consumers of naturall vigoure and the bodys of men, and shortners of life. And yet of all these things they had a large parte, and suffered deeply in the same. They wente from England to Holand, wher they found both worse air and dyet then that they came from; from thence (induring a long imprisonmente, as it were, in the ships at sea) into New-England; and how it hath been with them hear hath allready beene showne; and what crosses, troubls, fears, wants, and sorrowes they had been lyable unto, is easie to conjecture; so as in some sorte they may say with the Apostle, 2. Cor: 11. 26, 27. they were *in journeyings often, in perils of waters, in perills of robers, in perills of their owne nation, in perils among the heathen, in perills in the willdernes, in perills in the sea, in perills among false breethern; in wearines and painfullnes, in watching often, in hunger and thirst, in fasting often, in could and nakednes.* What was it then that upheld them? It was Gods vissitation that preserved their spirits. Job. 10. 12. *Thou hast given me life and grace, and thy vissitation hath preserved my spirite.* He that upheld the Apostle upheld them. *They were persecuted, but not forsaken, cast downe, but perished not.* 2. Cor: 4. 9. *As unknowen, and yet knowen; as dying, and behold we live; as chastened, and yett not kiled.* 2. Cor: 6. 9. God, it seems, would have all men to behold and observe such mercies and works of his providence as these are towards his people, that they in like cases might be incouraged to depend upon God in their trials, and also blese his name when they see his goodnes towards others. Man lives not by bread only, Deut: 8. 3. It is not by good and dainty fare, by peace, and rest, and harts ease, in injoying the contentments and good things of this world only, that preserves health and prolongs life. God in such examples would have the world see and behold that he can doe it without them; and if the world will shut ther eyes, and take no notice therof, yet he would have his people to see and consider it. Daniell could be better liking with pulse then others were with the kings dainties. Jaacob, though he wente from one nation to another people, and passed thorow famine, fears, and many afflictions, yet he lived till old age, and dyed sweetly, and rested in the Lord, as infinite others of Gods servants have done, and still shall doe, (through Gods goodnes,) notwithstanding all the malice of their enemies: *when the branch of the wicked shall be cut of before his day,* Job. 15. 32. *and the bloody and deceitfull men shall not live out halfe their days.* Psa: 55. 23.

THOMAS SHEPARD, 1605–1649

[Thomas Shepard, one of the great preachers in the first generation of New England Puritans, was born in Towcester, the son of a grocer. He entered pensioner at Emmanuel College, Cambridge, receiving his B.A. in 1624, his M.A. in 1627. He was a lecturer in Essex until silenced by Bishop Laud in 1630, then served as tutor and chaplain in the family of Sir Richard Darley in Yorkshire, where he married. He sailed for New England in 1634, was driven back by a storm and remained in hiding until the next spring, when he was successful in reaching America. Chosen minister at Cambridge, he immediately became one of the clerical leaders of the colony, being particularly energetic in suppressing the Antinomians. His first wife died in 1636, and he married a daughter of Thomas Hooker. His works enjoyed a great reputation in their day, one of them, *The Sincere Convert*, running to twenty editions between 1641 and 1812. For biography and discussion of his work, see Samuel Eliot Morison, *Builders of the Bay Colony*. This text is from *A Defence of the Answer made unto the Nine Questions or Positions sent from New-England against the reply thereto by Mr. John Ball* (London, 1648), pp. 3–9. The book was written in collaboration with John Allin, 1596–1671, minister at Dedham from 1639, though the preface is probably the work of Shepard alone.]

A DEFENCE OF THE ANSWER

LET us intreat all the Godly wise, to consider and look back upon the season of this great enterprise,[1] undertaken by us, and the manner of our proceedings in it, with the admirable workings of Gods Providence first and last about it; and we think (though we were silent) they may easily satisfie themselves, whether this was of God or men, a sinfull neglect of the Cause of Christ, or a manifest attestation to the truth, by open profession against Corruptions of Worship in use, and for the necessity of reformation of the Church; and that confirmed by no small degree of sufferings for the same. For was it not a time when humane Worship and inventions were growne to such an intolerable height, that the consciences of Gods saints and servants inlightened in the truth could no longer bear them? was not the power of the tyrannicall Prelates so great, that like a strong Current carryed all down streame before it, what ever was from the law, or otherwise set in their way? Did not the hearts of men generally faile them? Where was the people to bee found that would cleave to their godly Ministers in their sufferings, but rather thought it their descretion, to provide for their owne quiet and safety? Yea, when some freely in zeale of the Truth preached or professed against the corruptions of the times, did not some take offence at it, judge it rashnesse, and to bee against all rules of discretion, who since are ready to censure us for deserting the Cause? Many then thought, it

[1] Superior figures through individual selections refer to correspondingly numbered notes at the back of the volume.

is an evill time, the prudent shall hold their peace, and might wee not say, this is not our resting place? And what would men have us doe in such a case? Must wee study some distinctions to salve our Consciences in complying with so manifold corruptions in Gods Worship? or should wee live without Gods ordinances, because wee could not partake in the corrupt administration thereof? or content our selves to live without those ordinances of Gods Worship and Communion of Saints which hee called us unto, and our soules breathed after? or should wee forsake the publique Assemblies, and joyne together in private separated Churches? how unsufferable it would then have been, the great offence that now is taken at it, is a full evidence.[2] And if in Cities, or some such great Townes that might have been done, yet how was it possible for so many scattered Christians all over the Countrey? It is true, we might have suffered, if wee had sought it, wee might easily have found the way to have filled the Prisons, and some had their share therein. But whether wee were called thereunto, when a wide doore was set open of liberty otherwise; and our witnesse to the truth, (through the malignant policy of those times) could not bee open before the world, but rather smothered up in close prisons or some such wayes, together with our selves, wee leave to bee considered. Wee cannot see but the rule of Christ to his Apostles and Saints, and the practise of Gods Saints in all ages, may allow us this liberty as well as others, to fly into the Wildernesse from the face of the Dragon. But if it had been so, that the Godly Ministers and Christians that fled to *New-England*, were the most timorous and faint hearted of all their Brethren, that stayed behinde, and that those sufferings were nothing in comparison of their Brethrens (for why should any boast of sufferings?) yet who doth not know that the Spirit who gives various gifts, and all to profit withall, in such times doth single out every one to such worke, as hee in wisdome intends to call them unto? And whom the Lord will honour by suffering for his Cause, by imprisonment, &c. hee gives them spirits suitable thereto: whom the Lord will reserve for other service, or imploy in other places, hee inclines their hearts rather to fly, giving them an heart suitable to such a condition. It is a case of Conscience frequently put, and oft resolved by holy *Bradford*, *Peter Martyr*, *Philpot*, and others, in Queene *Maries* bloody dayes, viz. Whether it was lawfull to flee out of the Land: To which their anwer was, that if God gave a spirit of courage and willingnesse to glorifie him by sufferings, they should stay; but if they found not such a spirit they might lawfully fly, yea, they advised them thereunto. Those Servants of Christ, though full of the spirit of glory, and of Christ to outface the greatest persecuters in profession of the Truth, unto the death, yet did not complaine of the cowardize of such as fled, because they deserted them and the Cause, but rather advised divers so to doe, and rejoyced when God gave liberty to their brethren to escape with their lives to the places of liberty, to serve the Lord according to his Word. Neither were those faithfull Saints and servants of God uselesse and unprofitable in the Church of God that fled from the bloody Prelates. The infinite and onely wise God hath many workes to doe in the World, and hee doth by his singular Providence give gifts to his Servants, and disposeth them to his Worke as seemeth best to himselfe. If the Lord will have some to beare witnesse by imprisonments, dismembring, &c. wee honour them therein; if hee will have others instrumentall to promote reformation in *England,* wee honor them, and rejoyce in their holy endeavours, praying for a blessing upon themselves and labours. And what if God will have his Church and the Kingdome of Christ goe up also in these remote parts of the world, that his Name may bee known to the Heathen, or whatsoever other end hee hath, and to this end will send forth a company of weake-hearted Christians, which dare not stay at home to suffer, why should wee not let the Lord alone, and rejoyce that Christ is preached howsoever, and wheresoever? And who can say that this work was not undertaken and carryed on with sincere and right ends, and in an holy serious manner, by the chiefe and the body of such as undertooke the same? The Lord knows whether the sincere desires of worshipping himselfe according to his will, of promoting and propagating the Gospel, was not in the hearts of very many in this enterprise; and hee that seeth in secret, and rewardeth openly, knows what prayers and teares have been poured out to God by many alone, and in dayes of fasting and prayer of Gods servants together, for his counsell, direction, assistance, blessing in this worke: How many longings and pantings of heart have been in many after the Lord Jesus, to see his goings in his Sanctuary, as the one thing their soules desired and requested of God, that they might dwell in his house for ever; the fruit of which prayers and desires this liberty of *New-England* hath been taken to bee, and thankfully received from God. Yea, how many serious consultations with one another, and with the faithfull Ministers, and other eminent servants of Christ, have been taken about this worke, is not unknowne to some; which cleares us from any rash heady rushing into this place, out of discontent, as many are ready to conceive. Wee will here say nothing of the persons whose hearts the Lord stirred up in this businesse; surely all were not rash, weake-spirited, inconsiderate of what they left behinde, or of what it was to goe into a Wildernesse. But if it were well knowne and considered, or if wee were able to expresse and recount the singular workings of divine Providence, for the bringing on of this worke, to what it is come unto, it would stop the mouths of all that have not an heart to accuse and blaspheme the goodnesse of God in his glorious workes: whatever many may say or think, wee beleeve after-times will admire and adore the Lord herein, when all his holy ends, and the wayes he hath used to bring them about shall appeare. Look from one end of the heaven to another, whether the Lord hath assayed to do such a Worke as this in any Nation, so to carry out a people of his owne from so flourishing a State, to a wildernesse so far distant, for such ends, and for such a worke: Yea, and in few yeares hath done for them, as hee hath here done for his poore despised people. When wee looke back and consider what a strange poise of spirit the Lord hath laid upon many of our hearts, wee cannot but wonder at our selves, that so many, and some so weak and tender, with such cheerfulnesse and constant resolutions against so many perswasions of friends, discouragements from the ill report of this Countrey, the straits, wants, and tryalls of Gods people in it, &c. yet should leave our accommodations and comforts, should forsake our dearest relations, Parents, brethren, Sisters, Christian friends, and acquaintances, overlooke all the dangers and difficulties of the vast Seas, the thought whereof was a terrour to many, and all this to go to a wildernesse, where wee could forecast nothing but care and temptations, onely in hopes of enjoying Christ in his Ordinances, in the fellowship of his people; was this from a stupid senslesnesse or desperate carelesnesse what became of us or ours? or want of naturall affections to our deare Countrey, or nearest relations? No surely, with what bowells of compassion to our deare Countrey; with what heart-breaking affections, to our deare relations, and Christian friends many of us at least came away, the Lord is witnesse. What shall we say of the singular Providence of God bringing so many Ship-loads of his people, through so many dangers, as upon Eagles wings, with so much safety from yeare to yeare? The fatherly care of our God in feeding and cloathing so many in a Wildernesse, giving such healthfulnesse and great increase of posterity? what shall wee say of the Worke it selfe of the kingdome of Christ? and the form of a Common-wealth erected in a Wildernesse, and in so few yeares brought to that state, that scarce the like can bee seen in any of our English Colonies in the richest places of this *America*, after many more

years standing? That the Lord hath carryed the spirits of so many
of his people through all their toylsome Labour, wants, difficulties,
losses, &c. with such a measure of chearfulnesse and contentation?
But above all wee must acknowledge the singular pity and mercies
of our God, that hath done all this and much more for a people so
unworthy, so sinfull, that by murmurings of many, unfaithfulnesse in
promises, oppressions, and other evils which are found among us,
have so dishonoured his Majesty, exposed his worke here to much
scandall and obloquie, for which wee have cause for ever to bee
ashamed, that the Lord should yet owne us, and rather correct us in
mercy, then cast us off in displeasure, and scatter us in this Wildernesse, which gives us cause with Mich. 7. to say, *Who is a God like our
God, that pardoneth iniquities, and passeth by the transgressions of the remnant of his heritage; even because he delighteth in mercy?* Though we be a
people of many weaknesses and wants, yet wee acknowledge our God
to have been to us a God of many mercies, in respect of that sweet
peace which he hath taken away from so many Nations, yet continuing
the same to us; in respect also of that liberty wee have in Gods house,
the blessed Ministery of the Word, the sweet unity and communion of
Gods Churches and Ministers, increase and multiplication of Churches,
Christian government in the Common-wealth, and many other mercies
wee enjoy, but especially the gracious presence of Christ to many of
our soules in all these. But wee will not insist much upon this subject,
being perswaded it is in the consciences and hearts of many of our
dear Countrey-men to thinke that we should be an object of love
and tendernesse to that State and people, by whose Laws and unkind usages we were driven out into a wildernesse, rather then to
bee judged as desertors of our Brethren, and the Cause of Christ in
hand: with whom (excuse us if we now speak plainly) it had been
far more easie unto many of us to have suffered, then to have adventured hither upon the wildernesse sorrows wee expected to have
met withall; though we must confesse the Lord hath sweetned it
beyond our thoughts, and utmost expectations of prudent men.

FRANCIS HIGGINSON, 1586–1630

[Francis Higginson was born in Claybrook, Leicestershire, where
his father was vicar; he took his B.A. at Jesus College, Cambridge, 1610,
his M.A. in 1613. He succeeded his father at Claybrook, 1615, and
from 1617 to 1627 was lecturer at St. Nicholas. Under the influence
of Thomas Hooker he became a Puritan and was deprived for non-con-

formity. When proceedings were commenced against him in the High Commission he was engaged by the Massachusetts Bay Company and sent with the first body of settlers to Salem, 1629, where he was chosen teacher of the church and where he died of a hectic fever, August 6, 1630, leaving a widow and seven children. He wrote an account of the voyage to New England, and shortly before his death despatched back the manuscript of *New-Englands Plantation*, published by the Company in London in 1630. This text is from the first edition, pp. B1 verso–B2 recto, C1 recto–C2 verso.]

NEW–ENGLANDS PLANTATION

IT BECOMMETH not a Preacher of Truth to be a Writer of Falshood in any degree: and therefore I haue beene carefull to report nothing of *New-England* but what I haue partly seene with mine owne Eyes, and partly heard and enquired from the Mouthes of verie honest and religious person, who by liuing in the Countrey a good space of time haue had experience and knowledge of the state thereof, & whose testimonies I doe beleeue as my selfe.

First therefore of the Earth of *New-England* and all the appurtenances thereof: It is a Land of diuers and sundry sorts all about *Masathulets* Bay, and at *Charles* Riuer is as fat blacke Earth as can be seene any where: and in other places you haue a clay soyle, in other grauell, in other sandy, as it is all about our Plantation at *Salem*, for so our Towne is now named, *Psal. 76. 2.*

The forme of the Earth here in the superficies of it is neither too flat in the plainnesse, nor too high in Hils, but partakes of both in a mediocritie, and fit for Pasture, or for Plow or Meddow ground, as Men please to employ it: though all the Countrey be as it were a thicke Wood for the generall, yet in diuers places there is much ground cleared by the *Indians*, and especially about the Plantation: and I am told that about three miles from vs a Man may stand on a little hilly place and see diuers thousands of acres of ground as good as need to be, and not a Tree in the same. It is thought here is good Clay to make Bricke and Tyles and Earthen-Pots as needs to be. At this instant we are setting a Bricke-Kill on worke to make Brickes and Tyles for the building of our Houses. For Stone, here is plentie of Slates at the Ile of Slate in *Masathulets* Bay, and Lime-stone, Free-stone, and Smooth-stone, and Iron-stone, and Marble-stone also in such store, that we haue great Rockes of it, and a Harbour hard by. Our Plantation is from thence called Marble-harbour. . . .

Of the Aire of New-England with the Temper
and Creatures in it.

The Temper of the Aire of *New-England* is one speciall thing that commends this place. Experience doth manifest that there is hardly a more healthfull place to be found in the World that agreeth better with our English Bodyes. Many that haue beene weake and sickly in old *England*, by comming hither hane beene thoroughly healed and growne healthfull and strong. For here is an extraordinarie cleere and dry Aire that is of a most healing nature to all such as are of a Cold, Melancholy, Flegmatick, Reumaticke temper of Body. None can more truly speake hereof by their owne experience then my selfe. My Friends that knew me can well tell how verie sickly I haue been and continually in Physick, being much troubled with a tormenting paine through an extraordinarie weaknesse of my Stomacke, and aboundance of Melancholicke humors; but since I came hither on this Voyage, I thanke God I haue had perfect health, and freed from paine and vomitings, hauing a Stomacke to digest the hardest and coursest fare who before could not eat finest meat; and whereas my Stomacke could onely digest and did require such drinke as was both strong and stale, now I can and doe oftentimes drink *New-England* water verie well; and I that haue not gone without a Cap for many yeeres together, neither durst leaue off the same, haue now cast away my Cap, and doe weare none at all in the day time: and whereas beforetime I cloathed my selfe with double cloathes and thicke Wastcoats to keepe me warme, euen in the Summer time, I doe now goe as thin clad as any, onely wearing a light Stuffe Cassocke vpon my Shirt and Stuffe Breeches of one thicknesse without Linings. Besides, I haue one of my Children that was formerly most lamentably handled with sore breaking out of both his hands and feet of the Kings-Euill, but since he came hither he is verie well ouer hee was, and there is hope of perfect recouerie shortly, euen by the verie wholesomnesse of the Aire, altering, digesting and drying vp the cold and crude humors of the Body: and therefore I thinke it is a wise course for all cold complections to come to take Physicke in *New-England:* for a sup of *New-Englands* Aire is better then a whole draft of old *Englands* Ale.

In the Summer time in the midst of *July* and *August*, it is a good deale hotter then in old *England:* and in Winter, *January* and *February* are much colder as they say: but the Spring and Autumne are of a middle temper.

Fowles of the Aire are plentifull here, and of all sorts as we haue in *England* as farre as I can learne, and a great many of strange Fowles which we know not. Whilst I was writing these things, one of our Men brought home an Eagle which he had killed in the Wood: they say they are good meat. Also here are many kinds of excellent Hawkes, both Sea Hawkes and Land Hawkes: and my selfe walking in the Woods with another in company, sprung a Partridge so bigge that through the heauinesse of his Body could fly but a little way: they that haue killed them, say they are as bigge as our Hens. Here are likewise aboundance of Turkies often killed in the Woods, farre greater then our English Turkies, and exceeding fat, sweet and fleshy, for here they haue aboundance of feeding all the yeere long, as Straw-berries, in Summer all places are full of them, and all manner of Berries and Fruits. In the Winter time I haue seene Flockes of Pidgeons, and haue eaten of them: they doe flye from Tree to Tree as other Birds doe, which our Pidgeons will not doe in *England:* they are of all colours as ours are, but their wings and tayles are farr longer, and therefore it is likely they fly swifter to escape the terrible Hawkes in this Countrey. In Winter time this Countrey doth abound with wild Geese, wild Duckes, and other Sea Fowle, that a great part of winter the Planters haue eaten nothing but roastmeat of diuers Fowles which they haue killed. . . .

Though it be here somthing cold in the winter, yet here we haue plentie of Fire to warme vs, and that a great deale cheaper then they sell Billets and Faggots in *London:* nay, all *Europe* is not able to afford to make so great Fires as *New-England.* A poore Seruant here that is to possesse but 50 Acres of Land, may afford to giue more wood for Timber and Fire as good as the world yeelds, then many Noble Men in *England* can afford to doe. Here is good liuing for those that loue good Fires.

JOHN WINTHROP, 1588–1649

[The Winthrop family was decidedly one of importance in Suffolk, where John Winthrop's grandfather, a wealthy clothier, acquired the manor of Groton in 1544; his father, Adam Winthrop, was a suc-cessful lawyer and was auditor for St. John's and Trinity Colleges, Cambridge, from 1594 to 1609. John Winthrop entered pensioner at Trinity College, March, 1603, but left in less than two years when he was married at the age of seventeen. As justice of the peace and lord of Groton Manor he was a man of consequence; he was attorney of the Court of Wards, 1626, and admitted of the Inner Temple, 1628. An intense Puritan from his youth, he was profoundly discouraged

about the future of religion in England; losing his attorneyship, he
became interested in the Massachusetts Bay Company and was one
of the twelve signatories to the agreement drawn up at Cambridge,
August 26, 1629, promising to migrate to New England if the charter
could be transferred and the government established there. Elected
governor on October 26, he superintended the departure, and sailed,
March, 1630, on the *Arbella*. He first settled at Charlestown, but moved
to Boston in 1631. In most of the remaining years of his life he was either
governor or deputy governor of the colony, at all times its leading
citizen and most influential personage. He supported the banishment of
Williams, fought the Antinomians, and guided the community through
several crises in the 1640's. *Life and Letters*, by Robert C. Winthrop
(Boston, 1869); Samuel Eliot Morison, *Builders of the Bay Colony*. The
Journal, sometimes called *The History of New England*, was begun at
Southampton when the expedition was about to set sail, and was
kept up intermittently until his death. This text is from the edition by
James Savage (Boston, 1825), 2 vols.]

JOURNAL

Landing at Salem, June 12, 1630.] About four in the morning we
were near our port. We shot off two pieces of ordnance, and
sent our skiff to Mr. Peirce his ship (which lay in the harbor, and had
been there [blank] days before). About an hour after, Mr. Allerton [1]
came aboard us in a shallop as he was sailing to Pemaquid. As we
stood towards the harbor, we saw another shallop coming to us; so
we stood in to meet her, and passed through the narrow strait between
Baker's Isle and Little Isle, and came to an anchor a little within
the islands.

After Mr. Peirce came aboard us, and returned to fetch Mr. Endecott,[2] who came to us about two of the clock, and with him Mr. Skelton [3] and Capt. Levett. We that were of the assistants, and some other
gentlemen, and some of the women, and our captain, returned with
them to Nahumkeck,[4] where we supped with a good venison pasty
and good beer, and at night we returned to our ship, but some of the
women stayed behind.

In the mean time most of our people went on shore upon the land
of Cape Ann, which lay very near us, and gathered store of fine
strawberries.

An Indian came aboard us and lay there all night. . . .

[February 10, 1631.] The frost brake up; and after that, though we had many snows and sharp frost, yet they continued not, neither were the waters frozen up as before. It hath been observed, ever since this bay was planted by Englishmen, viz., seven years, that at this day the frost hath broken up every year.

The poorer sort of people (who lay long in tents, etc.) were much afflicted with the scurvy, and many died, especially at Boston and Charlestown; but when this ship came and brought store of juice of lemons, many recovered speedily. It hath been always observed here, that such as fell into discontent, and lingered after their former conditions in England, fell into the scurvy and died. . . .

[October 11, 1631.] The governor,[5] being at his farm house at Mistick, walked out after supper, and took a piece in his hand supposing he might see a wolf, (for they came daily about the house, and killed swine and calves, etc.;) and, being about half a mile off, it grew suddenly dark, so as, in coming home, he mistook his path, and went till he came to a little house of Sagamore John, which stood empty. There he stayed, and having a piece of match in his pocket, (for he always carried about him match and a compass, and in summer time snake-weed,) he made a good fire near the house, and lay down upon some old mats, which he found there, and so spent the night, sometimes walking by the fire, sometimes singing psalms, and sometimes getting wood, but could not sleep. It was (through God's mercy) a warm night; but a little before day it began to rain, and, having no cloak, he made shift by a long pole to climb up into the house. In the morning, there came thither an Indian squaw, but perceiving her before she had opened the door, he barred her out; yet she stayed there a great while essaying to get in, and at last she went away, and he returned safe home, his servants having been much perplexed for him, and having walked about, and shot off pieces, and hallooed in the night, but he heard them not. . . .

[January 18, 1636.] Mr. Vane[6] and Mr. Peter,[7] finding some distraction in the commonwealth, arising from some difference in judgment, and withal some alienation of affection among the magistrates and some other persons of quality, and that hereby factions began to grow among the people, some adhering more to the old governor, Mr. Winthrop, and others to the late governor, Mr. Dudley,[8]—the former carrying matters with more lenity, and the latter with more severity,—they procured a meeting, at Boston, of the governor, deputy, Mr. Cotton, Mr. Hooker, Mr. Wilson,[9] and there was present Mr. Winthrop, Mr. Dudley, and themselves; where, after the Lord had been sought, Mr. Vane declared the occasion of this meeting, (as is before noted,) and the fruit aimed at, viz. a more firm and friendly uniting of minds, etc., especially of the said Mr. Dudley and Mr. Winthrop, as those upon whom the weight of the affairs did lie, etc., and therefore desired all present to take up a resolution to deal freely and openly with the parties, and they each with other, that nothing might be left in their breasts, which might break out to any jar or difference hereafter, (which they promised to do). Then Mr. Winthrop spake to this effect: that when it pleased Mr. Vane to acquaint him with what he had observed, of the dispositions of men's minds inclining to the said faction, etc., it was very strange to him, professing solemnly that he knew not of any breach between his brother Dudley and himself, since they were reconciled long since, neither did he suspect any alienation of affection in him or others from himself, save that, of late, he had observed, that some new comers had estranged themselves from him, since they went to dwell at Newtown; and so desired all the company, that, if they had seen any thing amiss in his government or otherwise, they would deal freely and faithfully with him, and for his part he promised to take it in good part, and would endeavor, by God's grace, to amend it. Then Mr. Dudley spake to this effect: that for his part he came thither a mere patient, not with any intent to charge his brother Winthrop with any thing; for though there had been formerly some differences and breaches between them, yet they had been healed, and, for his part, he was not willing to renew them again; and so left it to others to utter their own complaints. Whereupon the governor, Mr. Haynes,[10] spake to this effect: that Mr. Winthrop and himself had been always in good terms, etc.; therefore he was loath to give any offence to him, and he hoped that, considering what the end of this meeting was, he would take it in good part, if he did deal openly and freely, as his manner ever was. Then he spake of one or two passages, wherein he conceived, that [he] dealt too remissly in point of justice; to which Mr. Winthrop answered, that his speeches and carriage had been in part mistaken; but withall professed, that it was his judgment, that in the infancy of plantation, justice should be administered with more lenity than in a settled state, because people were then more apt to transgress, partly of ignorance of new laws and orders, partly through oppression of business and other straits; but, if it might be made clear to him, that it was an error, he would be ready to take up a stricter course. Then the ministers were desired to consider of the question by the next morning, and to set down a rule in the case. The next morning, they delivered their several reasons, which all sorted to this conclusion, that strict discipline, both in criminal offences and in martial affairs, was more needful in plantations than in a settled state, as tending to the honor and safety of the gospel. Wherepon Mr. Winthrop acknowledged that he was convinced, that he had failed in over much lenity and remissness, and would endeavor (by God's assistance) to take a more strict course hereafter. . . .

[WINTHROP'S ACCOUNT OF THE ANTINOMIAN CRISIS]

[October 21, 1636.] One Mrs. Hutchinson, a member of the church of Boston, a woman of a ready wit and bold spirit, brought over with her two dangerous errors: 1. That the person of the Holy Ghost dwells in a justified person. 2. That no sanctification can help to evidence to us our justification.—From these two grew many branches; as, 1. Our union with the Holy Ghost, so as a Christian remains dead to every spiritual action, and hath no gifts nor graces, other than such as are in hypocrites, nor any other sanctification but the Holy Ghost himself.[11]

There joined with her in these opinions a brother of hers, one Mr. Wheelwright,[12] a silenced minister sometimes in England.

[October 25.] The other ministers in the bay, hearing of these things, came to Boston at the time of a general court, and entered conference in private with them, to the end they might know the certainty of these things; that if need were, they might write to the church of Boston about them, to prevent (if it were possible) the dangers, which seemed hereby to hang over that and the rest of the churches. At this conference, Mr. Cotton was present, and gave satisfaction to them, so as he agreed with them all in the point of sanctification, and so did Mr. Wheelwright; so as they all did hold, that sanctification did help to evidence justification. The same he had delivered plainly in public, divers times; but, for the indwelling of the person of the Holy Ghost, he held that still, as some others of the ministers did, but not union with the person of the Holy Ghost, (as Mrs. Hutchinson and others did,) so as to amount to a personal union . . .

[November 17.] The governor, Mr. Vane, a wise and godly gentleman, held, with Mr. Cotton and many others, the indwelling of the person of the Holy Ghost in a believer, and went so far beyond the rest, as to maintain a personal union with the Holy Ghost; but the deputy,[13] with the pastor [14] and divers others, denied both; and the question proceeded so far by disputation, (in writing, for the peace sake of the church, which all were tender of,) as at length they could not find the person of the Holy Ghost in scripture, nor in the primitive churches three hundred years after Christ. So that, all agreeing in the chief matter of substance, viz. that the Holy Ghost is God, and that he doth dwell in the believers, (as the Father and Son both are said also to do,) but whether by his gifts and power only, or by any other manner of presence, seeing the scripture doth not declare it,— it was earnestly desired, that the word person might be forborn, being a term of human invention, and tending to doubtful disputation in this case . . .

[December 10.] At this court the elders of the churches were called, to advise with them about discovering and pacifying the differences among the churches in point of opinion. The governor having declared the occasion to them, Mr. Dudley desired, that men would be free and open, etc. Another of the magistrates spake, that it would much further the end they came for, if men would freely declare what they held different from others, as himself would freely do, in what point soever he should be opposed. The governor said, that he would be content to do the like, but that he understood the ministers were about it in a church way, etc., which he spake upon this occasion: the ministers had met, a little before, and had drawn into heads all the points, wherein they suspected Mr. Cotton did differ from them, and had propounded them to him, and pressed him to a direct answer, affirmative or negative, to every one; which he had promised, and taken time for. This meeting being spoke of in the court the day before, the governor took great offence at it, as being without his privity, etc., which this day Mr. Peter told him as plainly of, (with all due reverence,) and how it had sadded the ministers' spirits, that he should be jealous of their meetings, or seem to restrain their liberty, etc. The governor excused his speech, as sudden and upon a mistake. Mr. Peter told him also, that before he came, within less than two years since, the churches were in peace, etc. The governor answered, that the light of the gospel brings a sword, and the children of the bondwoman would persecute those of the freewoman. Mr. Peter also besought him humbly to consider his youth, and short experience in the things of God, and to beware of peremptory conclusions, which he perceived him to be very apt unto. . . .

Mr. Wilson made a very sad speech of the condition of our churches, and the inevitable danger of separation, if these differences and alienations among brethren were not speedily remedied; and laid the blame upon these new opinions risen up amongst us, which all the magistrates, except the governor and two others, did confirm, and all the ministers but two. . . .

The speech of Mr. Wilson was taken very ill by Mr. Cotton and others of the same church, so as he and divers of them went to admonish him. But Mr. Wilson and some others could see no breach of rule, seeing he was called by the court about the same matter with the rest of the elders, and exhorted to deliver their minds freely and faithfully, both for discovering the danger, and the means to help; and the things he spake of were only in general, and such as were under a common fame. And being questioned about his intent, he professed he did not mean Boston church, nor the members thereof, more than others. But this would not satisfy, but they called him to answer publicly, [December] 31; and there the governor pressed it violently against him, and all the congregation, except the deputy and one or two more, and many of them with much bitterness and reproaches; but he answered them all with words of truth and soberness, and with marvellous wisdom. It was strange to see, how the common people were led, by example, to condemn him in that, which (it was very probable) divers of them did not understand, nor the rule which he was supposed to have broken; and that such as had known him so long, and what good he had done for that church, should fall upon him with such bitterness for justifying himself in a good cause; for he was a very holy, upright man, and for faith and love inferior to none in the country, and most dear to all men. The teacher joined with the church in their judgment of him, (not without some appearance of prejudice,) yet with much wisdom and moderation. They were eager to proceed to present censure, but the teacher staid them from that, telling them he might not do it, because some opposed it, but gave him a grave exhortation. The next day Mr. Wilson preached, notwithstanding, and the Lord so assisted him, as gave great satisfaction, and the governor himself gave public witness to him. . . .

[January 20, 1637.] The differences in the said points of religion increased more and more, and the ministers of both sides (there being only Mr. Cotton of one party) did publicly declare their judgments in some of them, so as all men's mouths were full of them. And there being, 12 mo. [February] 3, a ship ready to go for England, and many passengers in it, Mr. Cotton took occasion to speak to them about the differences, etc., and willed them to tell our countrymen, that all the strife amongst us was about magnifying the grace of God; one party seeking to advance the grace of God within us, and the other to advance the grace of God towards us, (meaning by the one justification, and by the other sanctification;) and so bade them tell them, that, if there were any among them that would strive for grace, they should come hither; and so declared some particulars. Mr. Wilson spake after him, and declared, that he knew none of the elders or brethren of the churches, but did labor to advance the free grace of God in justification, so far as the word of God required; and spake also about the doctrine of sanctification, and the use and necessity, etc., of it; by occasion whereof no man could tell (except some few, who knew the bottom of the matter) where any difference was: which speech, though it offended those of Mr. Cotton's party, yet it was very seasonable to clear the rest, who otherwise should have been reputed to have opposed free grace. Thus every occasion increased the contention, and caused great alienation of minds; and the members of Boston (frequenting the lectures of other ministers) did make much disturbance by public questions, and objections to their doctrines, which did any way disagree from their opinions; and it began to be as common here to distinguish between men, by being under a covenant of grace or a covenant of works, as in other countries between Protestants and papists. . . .

[March 9.] Mr. Wheelwright, one of the members of Boston, preaching at the last fast, inveighed against all that walked in a covenant of works, as he described it to be, viz., such as maintain sanctification as an evidence of justification, etc. and called them antichrists, and stirred up the people against them with much bitterness and vehemency. For this he was called into the court, and his sermon being produced, he justified it, and confessed he did mean all that walk in such a way. Whereupon the elders of the rest of the churches were called, and asked whether they, in their ministry, did walk in such a way. They all acknowledged they did. So, after much debate, the court adjudged him guilty of sedition, and also of contempt, for that the court had appointed the fast as a means of reconciliation of the differences, etc., and he purposely set himself to kindle and increase them. The governor and some few more (who dissented) tendered a protestation, which, because it wholly justified Mr. Wheelwright, and condemned the proceedings of the court, was rejected. The church of Boston also tendered a petition in his behalf, justifying Mr. Wheelwright's sermon. The court deferred sentence till the next court, and advised with the ministers, etc., whether they might enjoin his silence, etc. They answered, that they were not clear in that point, but desired rather, that he might be commended to the church of Boston to take care of him, etc., which accordingly was done, and he enjoined to appear at the next court. Much heat of contention was this court between the opposite parties; so as it was moved, that the next court might be kept at Newtown. . . .[15]

[May 17.] Our court of elections was at Newtown. So soon as the court was set, being about one of the clock, a petition was preferred by those of Boston. The governor would have read it, but the deputy said it was out of order; it was a court for elections, and those must first be despatched, and then their petitions should be heard. Divers others also opposed that course, as an ill precedent, etc.; and the petition, being about pretence of liberty, etc., (though intended chiefly for revoking the sentence given against Mr. Wheelwright,) would have spent all the day in debate, etc.; but yet the governor and those of that party would not proceed to election, except the petition was read. Much time was already spent about this debate, and the people crying out for election, it was moved by the deputy, that the people should divide themselves, and the greater number must carry it. And so it was done, and the greater number by many were for election. But the governor and that side kept their place still, and would not proceed. Whereupon the deputy told him, that, if he would not go to election, he and the rest of that side would proceed. Upon that, he came from his company, and they went to election; and Mr. Winthrop was chosen governor, Mr. Dudley deputy and Mr. Endecott of the standing council; and Mr. Israel Stoughton and Mr. Richard Saltonstall were called in to be assistants; and Mr. Vane, Mr. Coddington, and Mr. Dummer, (being all of that faction,) were left quite out.

There was great danger of a tumult that day; for those of that side grew into fierce speeches, and some laid hands on others; but seeing themselves too weak, they grew quiet. They expected a great advantage that day, because the remote towns were allowed to come in by proxy; but it fell out, that there were enough beside. . . .

[August 30.] The synod,[16] called the assembly, began at Newtown. There were all the teaching elders through the country, and some new come out of England, not yet called to any place here, as Mr. Davenport,[17] etc.

The assembly began with prayer, made by Mr. Shepherd, the pastor of Newtown. Then the erroneous opinions, which were spread in the country, were read, (being eighty in all: [18]) next the unwholesome expressions; then the scriptures abused. Then they chose two moderators for the next day, viz., Mr. Buckly and Mr. Hooker, and these were continued in that place all the time of the assembly. There were about eighty opinions, some blasphemous, others erroneous, and all unsafe, condemned by the whole assembly; whereto near all the elders, and others sent by the churches, subscribed their names; but some few liked not subscription, though they consented to the condemning of them. . . .

[November 1.] There was great hope that the late general assembly would have had some good effect in pacifying the troubles and dissensions about matters of religion; but it fell out otherwise. For though Mr. Wheelwright and those of his party had been clearly confuted and confounded in the assembly, yet they persisted in their opinions, and were as busy in nourishing contentions (the principal of them) as before. Whereupon the general court, being assembled in the 2 of the 9th month [November], and finding, upon consultation, that two so opposite parties could not contain in the same body, without apparent hazard of ruin to the whole, agreed to send away some of the principal; . . . Then the court sent for Mr. Wheelwright, and, he persisting to justify his sermon, and his whole practice and opinions, and refusing to leave either the place or his public exercisings, he was disfranchised and banished. Upon which he appealed to the king, but neither called witnesses, nor desired any act to be made of it. The court told him, that an appeal did not lie; for by the king's grant we had power to hear and determine without any reservation,[19] etc. So he relinquished his appeal, and the court gave him leave to go to his house, upon his promise, that, if he were not gone out of our jurisdiction within fourteen days, he would render himself to one of the magistrates.

The court also sent for Mrs. Hutchinson, and charged her with divers matters, as her keeping two public lectures every week in her house, whereto sixty or eighty persons did usually resort, and for reproaching most of the ministers (viz., all except Mr. Cotton) for not preaching a covenant of free grace, and that they had not the seal of the spirit, nor were able ministers of the New Testament; which were clearly proved against her, though she sought to shift it off. And, after many speeches to and fro, at last she was so full as she could not contain, but vented her revelations;[20] amongst which this was one, that she had it revealed to her, that she should come into New England, and should here be persecuted, and that God would ruin us and our posterity, and the whole state, for the same. So the court proceeded and banished her; but, because it was winter, they committed her to a private house, where she was well provided, and her own friends and the elders permitted to go to her, but none else. . . .

After this, many of the church of Boston, being highly offended with the governor for this proceeding, were earnest with the elders to have him called to account for it; but they were not forward in it, and himself, understanding their intent, thought fit to prevent such a public disorder, and so took occasion to speak to the congregation to this effect:—

. . . He did nothing in the cases of the brethren, but by the advice and direction of our teacher and other of the elders. For in the oath, which was administered to him and the rest, etc., there was inserted, by his advice, this clause,—In all causes wherein you are to give your vote, etc., you are to give your vote as in your judgment and conscience you shall see to be most for the public good, etc.; and so for his part he was persuaded, that it would be most for the glory of God, and the public good, to pass sentence as they did.

He would give them one reason, which was a ground for his judgment, and that was, for that he saw, that those brethren, etc., were so divided from the rest of the country in their judgment and practice, as it could not stand with the public peace, that they should continue amongst us. So, by the example of Lot in Abraham's family, and after Hagar and Ishmael, he saw they must be sent away. . . .

[March 1, 1638.] While Mrs. Hutchinson continued at Roxbury, divers of the elders and others resorted to her, and finding her to persist in maintaining those gross errors beforementioned, and many others, to the number of thirty or thereabout, some of them wrote to the church at Boston, offering to make proof of the same before the church, etc., [March] 15; whereupon she was called, (the magistrates being desired to give her license to come,) and the lecture was appointed to begin at ten. . . . When she appeared, the errors were read to her. . . . These were also clearly confuted, but yet she held her own; so as the church (all but two of her sons) agreed she should be admonished, and because her sons would not agree to it, they were admonished also.

Mr. Cotton pronounced the sentence of admonition with great solemnity, and with much zeal and detestation of her errors and pride of spirit.[21] The assembly continued till eight at night, and all did acknowledge the special presence of God's spirit therein; and she was appointed to appear again the next lecture day. . . .

[March 22.] Mrs. Hutchinson appeared again; (she had been licensed by the court, in regard she had given hope of her repentance, to be at Mr. Cotton's house, that both he and Mr. Davenport might have the more opportunity to deal with her;) and the articles being again read to her, and her answer required, she delivered it in writing, wherein she made a retractation of near all, but with such explanations and circumstances as gave no satisfaction to the church; so as she was required to speak further to them. Then she declared, that it was just with God to leave her to herself, as he had done, for her slighting his ordinances, both magistracy and ministry; and confessed that what she had spoken against the magistrates at the court (by way of revelation) was rash and ungrounded; and desired the church to pray for her. This gave the church good hope of her repentance; but when she was examined about some particulars, as that she had denied inherent righteousness, etc., she affirmed that it was never her judgment; and though it was proved by many testimonies, that she had been of that judgment, and so had persisted, and maintained it by argument against divers, yet she impudently persisted in her affirmation, to the astonishment of all the assembly. So that, after much time and many arguments had been spent to bring her to see her sin, but all in vain, the church, with one consent, cast her out. Some moved to have her admonished once more; but, it being for manifest evil in matter of conversation, it was agreed otherwise; and for that reason also the sentence was denounced by the pastor, matter of manners belonging properly to his place.

After she was excommunicated, her spirits, which seemed before to be somewhat dejected, revived again, and she gloried in her sufferings, saying, that it was the greatest happiness, next to Christ, that ever befel her. Indeed, it was a happy day to the churches of Christ here, and to many poor souls, who had been seduced by her, who, by what they heard and saw that day, were (through the grace of God) brought off quite from her errors, and settled again in the truth. . . .

After two or three days, the governor sent a warrant to Mrs. Hutchinson to depart this jurisdiction before the last of this month, according to the order of court, and for that end set her at liberty from her former constraint, so as she was not to go forth of her own house till her departure; and upon the 28th she went by water to her farm at the Mount, where she was to take water, with Mr. Wheelwright's wife and family, to go to Pascataquack; but she changed her mind, and went by land to Providence, and so to the island in the Naragansett Bay, which her husband and the rest of that sect had purchased of the Indians, and prepared with all speed to remove unto. For the court had ordered, that, except they were gone with their families by such a time, they should be summoned to the general court. . . .

[September 25, 1638.] The court, taking into consideration the great disorder general through the country in costliness of apparel, and following new fashions, sent for the elders of the churches, and conferred with them about it, and laid it upon them, as belonging to them, to redress it, by urging it upon the consciences of their people, which they promised to do. But little was done about it; for divers of the elders' wives, etc., were in some measure partners in this general disorder. . . .

[May 26, 1639.] Mr. Hooker being to preach at Cambridge, the governor and many others went to hear him, (though the governor did very seldom go from his own congregation upon the Lord's day). He preached in the afternoon, and having gone on, with much strength of voice and intention of spirit, about a quarter of an hour, he was at a stand, and told the people, that God had deprived him both of his strength and matter, etc., and so went forth, and about half an hour after returned again, and went on to very good purpose about two hours. . . .

[December 15, 1640.] About this time there fell out a thing worthy of observation. Mr. Winthrop the younger, one of the magistrates, having many books in a chamber where there was corn of divers sorts, had among them one wherein the Greek testament, the psalms and the common prayer were bound together. He found the common prayer eaten with mice, every leaf of it, and not any of the two other touched, nor any other of his books, though there were above a thousand.

[April 13, 1641.] A godly woman of the church of Boston, dwelling sometimes in London, brought with her a parcel of very fine linen of great value, which she set her heart too much upon, and had been at charge to have it all newly washed, and curiously folded and pressed, and so left it in press in her parlor over night. She had a negro maid went into the room very late, and let fall some snuff of the candle upon the linen, so as by the morning all the linen was burned to tinder, and the boards underneath, and some stools and a part of the wainscot burned, and never perceived by any in the house, though some lodged in the chamber over head, and no ceiling between. But it pleased God that the loss of this linen did her much good, both in taking off her heart from worldly comforts, and in preparing her for a far greater affliction by the untimely death of her husband, who was slain not long after at Isle of Providence.

[September 15, 1641.] A great training at Boston two days. About 1200 men were exercised in most sorts of land service; yet it was ob-

served that there was no man drunk, though there was plenty of wine
and strong beer in the town, not an oath sworn, no quarrel, nor any
hurt done.[22]

[September 22, 1642.] The sudden fall of land and cattle, and the
scarcity of foreign commodities, and money, etc., with the thin access
of people from England, put many into an unsettled frame of spirit,
so as they concluded there would be no subsisting here, and accordingly they began to hasten away, some to the West Indies, others to
the Dutch, at Long Island, etc., (for the governor there invited them
by fair offers,) and others back for England. . . .

. . . They fled for fear of want, and many of them fell into it, even
to extremity, as if they had hastened into the misery which they feared
and fled from, besides the depriving themselves of the ordinances and
church fellowship, and those civil liberties which they enjoyed here;
whereas, such as staid in their places, kept their peace and ease, and
enjoyed still the blessing of the ordinances, and never tasted of those
troubles and miseries, which they heard to have befallen those who
departed. Much disputation there was about liberty of removing for
outward advantages, and all ways were sought for an open door to
get out at; but it is to be feared many crept out at a broken wall.
For such as come together into a wilderness, where are nothing but
wild beasts and beastlike men, and there confederate together in civil
and church estate, whereby they do, implicitly at least, bind themselves to support each other, and all of them that society, whether
civil or sacred, whereof they are members, how they can break from
this without free consent, is hard to find, so as may satisfy a tender
or good conscience in time of trial. Ask thy conscience, if thou wouldst
have plucked up thy stakes, and brought thy family 3000 miles, if
thou hadst expected that all, or most, would have forsaken thee there.
Ask again, what liberty thou hast towards others, which thou likest
not to allow others towards thyself; for if one may go, another may,
and so the greater part, and so church and commonwealth may be
left destitute in a wilderness, exposed to misery and reproach, and all
for thy ease and pleasure, whereas these all, being now thy brethren,
as near to thee as the Israelites were to Moses, it were much safer for
thee, after his example, to choose rather to suffer affliction with thy
brethren, than to enlarge thy ease and pleasure by furthering the
occasion of their ruin. . . .

[July 5, 1643.] There arose a sudden gust at N. W. so violent for
half an hour, as is blew down multitudes of trees. It lifted up their
meeting house at Newbury, the people being in it. It darkened the

air with dust, yet through God's great mercy it did no hurt, but only killed one Indian with the fall of a tree.

[January 18, 1644.] The 18th of this month two lights were seen near Boston, (as is before mentioned,) and a week after the like was seen again. A light like the moon arose about the N. E. point in Boston, and met the former at Nottles Island, and there they closed in one, and then parted, and closed and parted divers times, and so went over the hill in the island and vanished. Sometimes they shot out flames and sometimes sparkles. This was about eight of the clock in the evening, and was seen by many. About the same time a voice was heard upon the water between Boston and Dorchester, calling out in a most dreadful manner, boy, boy, come away, come away: and it suddenly shifted from one place to another a great distance, about twenty times. It was heard by divers godly persons. About 14 days after, the same voice in the same dreadful manner was heard by others on the other side of the town towards Nottles Island.

These prodigies having some reference to the place where Captain Chaddock's pinnace was blown up a little before, gave occasion of speech of that man who was the cause of it, who professed himself to have skill in necromancy, and to have done some strange things in his way from Virginia hither, and was suspected to have murdered his master there; but the magistrates here had not notice of him till after he was blown up. This is to be observed that his fellows were all found, and others who were blown up in the former ship were also found, and others also who have miscarried by drowning, etc., have usually been found, but this man was never found. . . .

[March 21, 1644.] One Dalkin and his wife dwelling near Meadford coming from Cambridge, where they had spent their Sabbath, and being to pass over the river at a ford, the tide not being fallen enough, the husband adventured over, and finding it too deep, persuaded his wife to stay a while, but it raining very sore, she would needs adventure over, and was carried away with the stream past her depth. Her husband not daring to go help her, cried out, and thereupon his dog, being at his house near by, came forth, and seeing something in the water, swam to her, and she caught hold on the dog's tail, so he drew her to the shore and saved her life.

[July 15, 1644.] A poor man of Hingham, one Painter, who had lived at New Haven and at Rowley and Charlestown, and been scandalous and burdensome by his idle and troublesome behavior to them all, was now on the sudden turned anabaptist, and having a child born, he would not suffer his wife to bring it to the ordinance of baptism, for she was a member of the church, though himself were not. Being presented for this, and enjoined to suffer the child to be baptized, he still refusing, and disturbing the church, he was again brought to the court not only for his former contempt, but also for saying that our baptism was antichristian; and in the open court he affirmed the same. Whereupon after much patience and clear conviction of his error, etc., because he was very poor, so as no other but corporal punishment could be fastened upon him, he was ordered to be whipped, not for his opinion, but for reproaching the Lord's ordinance, and for his bold and evil behavior both at home and in the court. He endured his punishment with much obstinacy, and when he was loosed, he said boastingly, that God had marvellously assisted him. Whereupon two or three honest men, his neighbors, affirmed before all the company, that he was of very loose behavior at home, and given much to lying and idleness, etc. Nor had he any great occasion to gather God's assistance from his stillness under the punishment, which was but moderate, for divers notorious malefactors had showed the like, and one the same court.

[April 13, 1645.] Mr. Hopkins, the governor of Hartford upon Connecticut, came to Boston, and brought his wife with him, (a godly young woman, and of special parts,) who was fallen into a sad infirmity, the loss of her understanding and reason, which had been growing upon her divers years, by occasion of her giving herself wholly to reading and writing, and had written many books. Her husband, being very loving and tender of her, was loath to grieve her; but he saw his error, when it was too late. For if she had attended her household affairs, and such things as belong to women, and not gone out of her way and calling to meddle in such things as are proper for men, whose minds are stronger, etc., she had kept her wits, and might have improved them usefully and honorably in the place God had set her. He brought her to Boston, and left her with her brother, one Mr. Yale, a merchant, to try what means might be had here for her. But no help could be had.

[April 13, 1645.] The wars in England kept servants from coming to us, so as those we had could not be hired, when their times were out, but upon unreasonable terms, and we found it very difficult to pay their wages to their content, (for money was very scarce). I may upon this occasion report a passage between one of Rowley and his servant. The master, being forced to sell a pair of his oxen to pay his servant his wages, told his servant he could keep him no longer, not knowing how to pay him the next year. The servant answered, he would serve him for more of his cattle. But how shall I do (saith the master) when all my cattle are gone? The servant replied, you shall then serve me, and so you may have your cattle again.[23]

[July 3, 1645.] Divers free schools were erected, as at Roxbury (for maintenance whereof every inhabitant bound some house or land for a yearly allowance forever) and at Boston (where they made an order to allow forever 50 pounds to the master and an house and 30 pounds to an usher, who should also teach to read and write and cipher, and Indians' children were to be taught freely, and the charge to be by yearly contribution, either by voluntary allowance, or by rate of such as refused, etc., and this order was confirmed by the general court . . . Other towns did the like, providing maintenance by several means.

[July, 1646.] Great harm was done in corn (especially wheat and barley) in this month by a caterpillar, like a black worm about an inch and a half long. They eat up first the blades of the stalk, then they eat up the tassels, whereupon the ear withered. It was believed by divers good observers, that they fell in a great thunder shower, for divers yards and other bare places, where not one of them was to be seen an hour before, were presently after the shower almost covered with them, besides grass places where they were not so easily discerned. They did the most harm in the southern parts, as Rhode Island, etc., and in the eastern parts in their Indian corn. In divers places the churches kept a day of humiliation, and presently after the caterpillars vanished away.

[September 20, 1646.] There fell a sad affliction upon the country this year, though it more particularly concerned New Haven and those parts. A small ship of about 100 tons set out from New Haven in the middle of the eleventh month last (the harbor there being so frozen, as they were forced to hew her through the ice near three miles). She was laden with pease and some wheat, all in bulk, with about 200 West India hides, and store of beaver, and plate, so as it was estimated in all at 5000 pounds. There were in her about seventy persons, whereof divers were of very precious account, as Mr. Grigson, one of their magistrates, the wife of Mr. Goodyear, another of their magistrates, (a right godly woman,) Captain Turner, Mr. Lamberton, master of the ship, and some seven or eight others, members of the church there. The ship never went voyage before, and was very crank-sided, so as it was conceived, she was overset in a great tempest, which happened soon after she put to sea, for she was never heard of after. . . .

[June 28, 1648.] There appeared over the harbor at New Haven, in the evening, the form of the keel of a ship with three masts, to which were suddenly added all the tackling and sails, and presently after, upon the top of the poop, a man standing with one hand akimbo under his left side, and in his right hand a sword stretched out toward the sea. Then from the side of the ship which was from the town arose a great smoke, which covered all the ship, and in that smoke she vanished away; but some saw her keel sink into the water. This was seen by many, men and women, and it continued about a quarter of an hour. . . .

[June 4, 1647.] An epidemical sickness was through the country among Indians and English, French and Dutch. It took them like a cold, and a light fever with it. Such as bled or used cooling drinks died; those who took comfortable things, for most part recovered, and that in few days. Wherein a special providence of God appeared, for not a family, nor but few persons escaping it, had it brought all so weak as it did some, and continued so long, our hay and corn had been lost for want of help; but such was the mercy of God to his people, as few died, not above forty or fifty in the Massachusetts, and near as many at Connecticut. But that which made the stroke more sensible and grievous, both to them and to all the country, was the death of that faithful servant of the Lord, Mr. Thomas Hooker, pastor of the church in Hartford, who, for piety, prudence, wisdom, zeal, learning, and what else might make him serviceable in the place and time he lived in, might be compared with men of greatest note; and he shall need no other praise: the fruits of his labors in both Englands shall preserve an honorable and happy remembrance of him forever.

[June 14.] In this sickness the governor's wife, daughter of Sir John Tindal, Knight, left this world for a better, being about fifty-six years of age: a woman of singular virtue, prudence, modesty, and piety, and specially beloved and honored of all the country.

[August 15, 1648.] The synod [24] met at Cambridge by adjournment from the (4) [June] last. Mr. Allen of Dedham preached out of Acts 15, a very godly, learned, and particular handling of near all the doctrines and applications concerning that subject with a clear discovery and refutation of such errors, objections, and scruples as had been raised about it by some young heads in the country.

It fell out, about the midst of his sermon, there came a snake into the seat, where many of the elders sate behind the preacher. It came in at the door where people stood thick upon the stairs. Divers of the elders shifted from it, but Mr. Thomson, one of the elders of Braintree, (a man of much faith,) trode upon the head of it, and so held it with his foot and staff with a small pair of grains, until it was killed. This being so remarkable, and nothing falling out but by divine providence, it is out of doubt, the Lord discovered somewhat of his mind in it. The serpent is the devil; the synod, the representative of the churches of Christ in New England. The devil had formerly and lately attempted their disturbance and dissolution; but their faith in the seed of the woman overcame him and crushed his head.

EDWARD JOHNSON, 1598–1672

[Edward Johnson, born in Canterbury, was brought up to the trade of joiner, married in 1618, and emigrated to Boston in 1630. He went back to England for his wife and seven children, and returned to New England in the midst of the Antinomian crisis. He settled at Charlestown in 1636; in 1640 he became one of the founders of Woburn, where he remained a leading citizen for the remainder of his life, serving as proprietor, clerk, selectman, militia captain, deputy to the General Court. He was Speaker of the House of Deputies in 1655, and was employed by the government as surveyor of the boundaries and inspector of arms and ammunitions. He commenced writing his history in 1650; it was published anonymously in London in 1654. This text is from *Wonder-Working Providence of Sions Saviour in New England.* ed. J. F. Jameson (New York, 1910). For discussion see this edition, or that of William Frederick Poole (Andover, 1867).]

WONDER-WORKING PROVIDENCE OF SIONS SAVIOUR

BEING A RELATION OF THE FIRST PLANTING IN NEW ENGLAND, IN THE YEARE, 1628.

BOOK I.

CHAP. I.

THE SAD CONDITION OF ENGLAND, WHEN THIS PEOPLE REMOVED.

WHEN *England* began to decline in Religion, like luke-warme *Laodicea*, and instead of purging out Popery, a farther compliance was sought not onely in vaine Idolatrous Ceremonies, but also in prophaning the Sabbath, and by Proclamation throughout their Parish churches, exasperating lewd and prophane persons to celebrate a Sabbath like the Heathen to *Venus*, *Baccus* and *Ceres;* [1]

in so much that the multitude of irreligious lascivious and popish affected persons spred the whole land like *Grashoppers*, in this very time Christ the glorious King of his Churches, raises an Army out of our *English* Nation, for freeing his people from their long servitude under usurping Prelacy; and because every corner of *England* was filled with the fury of malignant adversaries, Christ creates a New *England* to muster up the first of his Forces in; Whose low condition, little number, and remotenesse of place made these adversaries triumph, despising this day of small things, but in this hight of their pride the *Lord Christ* brought sudden, and unexpected destruction upon them. Thus have you a touch of the time when this worke began.

Christ Jesus intending to manifest his Kingly Office toward his Churches more fully than ever yet the Sons of men saw, even to the uniting of *Jew* and *Gentile* Churches in one Faith, begins with our *English* Nation (whose former reformation being vere imperfect) doth now resolve to cast down their false foundation of Prelacy, even in the hight of their domineering dignity. And therefore in the yeere 1628, he stirres up his servants as the Heralds of a King to make this proclamation for Voluntiers, as followeth.

Oh yes! oh yes! oh yes! *All you the people of Christ that are here Oppressed, Imprisoned and scurrilously derided, gather yourselves together, your Wives and little ones, and answer to your severall Names as you shall be shipped for his service, in the Westerne World, and more especially for planting the united Collonies of new* England; *Where you are to attend the service of the King of Kings, upon the divulging of this Proclamation by his Herralds at Armes.* Many (although otherwise willing for this service) began to object as followeth:

Can it possible be the mind of Christ, (who formerly inabled so many Souldiers of his to keepe their station unto the death here) that now so many brave Souldiers disciplined by Christ himselfe the Captaine of our salvation, should turne their backs to the disheartning of their Fellow-Souldiers, and losse of further opportunity in gaining a greater number of Subjects to Christs Kingdome?

Notwithstanding this Objection, It was further proclaimed as followeth: What Creature, wilt not know that Christ thy King crusheth with a rod of Iron, the Pompe and Pride of man, and must he like man cast and contrive to take his enemies at advantage? No, of purpose hee causeth such instruments to retreate as hee hath made strong for himselfe: that so his adversaries glorying in the pride of their power, insulting over the little remnant remaining, Christ causeth them to be cast downe suddenly forever, and wee find in stories reported, Earths Princes have passed their Armies at need over Seas and deepe Torrents. Could *Cæsar* so suddenly fetch over fresh forces from *Europe* to *Asia*, *Pompy* to foyle? How much more shall Christ who createth all power, call over this 900 league Ocean at his pleasure, such instruments as he thinks meete to make use of in this place, from whence you are now to depart, but further that you may not delay the Voyage intended, for your full satisfaction, know this is the place where the Lord will create a new Heaven, and a new Earth in, new Churches, and a new Common-wealth together; Wherefore,

Chap. II.

The Commission of the People of Christ shipped for New England, and first of their gathering into Churches.

Attend to your Commission, all you that are or shall hereafter be shipped for this service, yee are with all possible speed to imbarque your selves, and as for all such Worthies who are hunted after as *David* was by *Saul* and his Courtiers, you may change your habit and ship you with what secrecy you can, carrying all things most needfull for the Voyage and service you are to be imployed in after your landing. But as soone as you shall be exposed to danger of tempestious Seas, you shall forthwith shew whose servants you are by calling on the Name of your God, sometimes by extraordinary seeking his pleasing Face in times of deepe distresse, and publishing your Masters will, and pleasure to all that Voyage with you, and that is his minde to have purity in Religion preferred above all dignity in the world; your Christ hath commanded the Seas they shall not swallow you, nor Pyrates imprison your persons, or possesse your goods. At your landing see you observe the Rule of his Word, for neither larger nor stricter Commission can hee give by any, and therefore at first filling the Land whither you are sent, with diligence, search out the mind of God both in planting and continuing Church and civill Government, but be sure they be distinct, yet agreeing and helping the one to the other; Let the matter and forme of your Churches be such as were in the Primitive Times (before *Antichrists* Kingdome prevailed) plainly poynted out by Christ and his Apostles, in most of their Epistles to be neither Nationall nor Provinciall, but gathered together in Covenant of such a number as might ordinarily meete together in one place, and built of such living stones as outwardly appeare Saints by calling. You are also to ordaine Elders in every Church, make you use of such as

Christ hath indued with the best gifts for that end, their call to Office shall be mediate from you, but their authority and commission shall be immediate from Christ revealed in his word; which, if you shall slight, despise or contemne, hee will soone frustrate your call by taking the most able among you to honour with an everlasting Crown; whom you neglected to honour on Earth double as their due, or he will carry them remote from you to more infant Churches. You are not to put them upon anxious Cares for their daily Bread, for assuredly (although it may now seeme strange) you shall be fed in this Wildernesse, whither you are to goe, with the flower of Wheate and Wine shall be plentifull among you (but be sure you abuse it not) these Doctrines delivered from the Word of God imbrace, and let not Satan delude you by perswading their learned skill is unnecessary, soone then will the Word of God be slighted as translated by such, and you shall be left wildred with strange Revelations of every phantastick brain. . . .

Chap. XII.

Of the voluntary banishment, chosen by this People of Christ, and their last farewell taken of their Country and Friends.

And now behold the severall Regiments of these Souldiers of *Christ*, as they are shipped for his service in the *Western* World, part thereof being come to the Towne and Port of *Southamptan* in *England*, where they were to be shipped, that they might prosecute this designe to the full, one Ship called the *Eagle*, they wholy purchase, and many more they hire, filling them with the seede of man and beast to sow this yet untilled Wildernesse withall, making sale of such Land as they possesse, to the great admiration of their Friends and Acquaintance, who thus expostulate with them, What, will not the large income of your yearly revenue content you, which in all reason cannot chuse but be more advantagious both to you and yours, then all that Rocky Wildernesse, whither you are going, to run the hazard of your life? Have you not here your Tables filled with great variety of Foode, your Coffers filled with Coyne, your Houses beautifully built and filled with all rich Furniture? (or otherwise) have you not such a gainfull Trade as none the like in the Towne where you live? Are you not inriched daily? Are not your Children very well provided for as they come to years? (nay) may you not here as pithily practise the two chiefe Duties of a Christian (if Christ give strength) namely Mortification and Sanctification as in any place of the World? What helps can you have there that you must not carry from hence? With bold resolvednesse these stout Souldiers of Christ reply; as Death, the King of terror with all his dreadfull attendance inhumane and barbarous, tortures doubled and trebled by all the infernal furies have appeared but light and momentany to the Souldiers of *Christ Iesus*, so also the Pleasure, Profits and Honours of this World set forth in their most glorious splendor, and magnitude by the alluring Lady of Delight, proffering pleasant embraces, cannot intice with her *Syren* Songs, such Souldiers of Christ, whose aymes are elevated by him, many Millions above that brave Warrier *Vlysses*.

Now seeing all can be said will but barely set forth the immoveable Resolutions that Christ continued in these men; Passe on and attend with teares, if thou hast any, the following discourse, while these Men, Women and Children are taking their last farwell of their Native Country, Kindred, Friends and Acquaintance, while the Ships attend them; Many make choise of some solitary place to eccho out their bowell-breaking affections in bidding their Friends farwell, deare friends (sayes one) as neare as my owne soule doth thy love lodge in my brest, with thought of the heart-burning Ravishments, that thy Heavenly speeches have wrought: my melting soule is poured out at present with these words, both of them had their farther speach strangled from the depth of their inward dolor, with breast-breaking sobs, till leaning their heads each on others shoulders, they let fall the salt-dropping dews of vehement affection, striving to exceede one another, much like the departure of *David* and *Jonathan:* having a little eased their hearts with the still streames of Teares, they recovered speech againe. Ah! my much honoured friend, hath Christ given thee so great a charge as to be Leader of his People into that far remote, and vast Wildernesse, I, oh, and alas thou must die there and never shall I see thy Face in the flesh againe, wert thou called to so great a taske as to passe the pretious Ocean, and hazard thy person in Battell against thousands of Malignant Enemies there? there were hopes of thy return with triumph, but now after two three, or foure moneths spent with daily expectation of swallowing Waves, and cruell Pirates, you are to be Landed among barbarous *Indians*, famous for nothing but cruelty, where you are like to spend your days in a famishing condition for a long space; Scarce had he uttered this, but presently hee lockes his friend fast in his armes, holding each other thus for some space of time, they weepe againe, But as *Paul* to his beloved flock: the other replies what doe you weeping and breaking my heart? I am now prest for the service of our *Lord Christ*, to re-build the most glorious Edifice

of Mount *Sion* in a Wildernesse, and as *John* Baptist, I must cry prepare yee the way of the Lord, make his paths strait, for behold hee
is comming againe, hee is comming to destroy *Antichrist*, and give the
whore double to drinke the very dregs of his wrath.

Then my deare friend unfold thy hands, for thou and I have much
worke to doe, I and all Christian Souldiers the World throughout,
then hand in hand they leade each other to the Sandy-banks of the
brinish Ocean, when clenching their hands fast, they unloose not til
inforced to wipe their watery-eyes, whose constant streames forced a
watery-path upon their Cheekes, which to hide from the eyes of others
they shun society for a time, but being called by occasion, whose
bauld back-part none can lay hold one; They thrust in among the
throng now ready to take Ship, where they beheld the like affections
with their own among divers Relations, Husbands and Wives with mutuall consent are now purposed to part for a time 900 Leagues asunder,
since some providence at present will not suffer them to goe together,
they resolve their tender affections shall not hinder this worke of Christ,
the new Married and betrothed man, exempt by the Law of God
from war, now will not claime their priviledge, but being constrained
by the Love of Christ, lock up their naturall affections for a time,
till the Lord shall be pleased to give them a meeting in this *Westerne*
World, sweetly mixing it with spirituall love, in the meane time many
Fathers now take their yong *Samuells*, and give them to this service
of Christ all their Lives. Brethren, Sisters, Unkles, Nephewes, Neeces,
together with all Kindred of bloud that binds the bowells of affection
in a true Lovers knot, can now take their last farewell, each of other,
although naturall affection will still claime her right, and manifest her
selfe to bee in the body by looking out at the Windowes in a mourne-
full manner among this company, thus disposed doth many Reverend
and godly Pastors of Christ present themselves, some in a Seamans
Habit,[2] and their scattered sheepe comming as a poore Convoy loftily
take their leave of them as followeth, what dolefull dayes are these,
when the best choise our Orthodox Ministers can make is to take up
a perpetuall banishment from their native soile, together with their
Wives and Children, wee their poore sheepe they may not feede, but
by stoledred should they abide here. *Lord Christ*, here they are at thy
command, they go, this is the doore thou hast opened upon our
earnest request, and we hope it shall never be shut: for *Englands* sake
they are going from *England* to pray without ceasing for *England*, O
England! thou shalt finde *New England* prayers prevailing with their
God for thee, but now woe alas, what great hardship must these our

indeared Pastors indure for a long season, with these words they lift up their voyces and wept, adding many drops of salt liquor to the ebbing Ocean; Then shaking hands they bid adue with much cordiall affection to all their Brethren, and Sisters in Christ, yet now the Scorne and Derision of those times, and for this their great enterprise counted as so many crackt-braines, but Christ will make all the earth know the wisdome he hath indued them with, shall over-top all the humane policy in the World, as the sequell wee hope will shew; Thus much shall suffice in generall to speak of their peoples farewell they tooke from time to time of their Country and Friends. . . .

Chap. XVII.

Of the first leading of these People of Christ, when the Civill Government was Established.

But to goe on with the Story, the 12 of *July* or thereabout 1630. these Souldiers of *Christ* first set foote one this *Westerne* end of the World; where arriveing in safety, both Men, Women and Children. On the North side of *Charles* River, they landed neare a small Island, called *Noddells* Island, where one Mr. *Samuel Mavereck* then living, a man of a very loving and curteous behaviour, very ready to entertaine strangers, yet an enemy to the Reformation in hand, being strong for the Lordly Prelaticall power one this Island, he had built a small Fort with the helpe of one Mr. *David Tompson*, placing therein foure Murtherers to protect him from the *Indians*. About one mile distant upon the River ran a small creeke, taking its Name from Major Gen. *Edward Gibbons*, who dwelt there for some yeares after; One the South side of the River one a point of Land called *Blaxtons* point, planted Mr. *William Blaxton*, of whom we have former spoken: to the South-East of him, neare an Island called *Tompsons* Island lived some few Planters more, these persons were the first Planters of those parts, having some small Trading with the *Indians* for *Beaver*-Skins, which moved them to make their aboade in those parts, whom these first Troopes of *Christs* Army, found as fit helpes to further their worke. At their arrivall those small number of Christians gathered at *Salem*, greatly rejoycing and the more, because they saw so many that came chiefly for promoting the great Work of *Christ* in hand, the Lady *Arrabella* [3] and some other godly Women aboad at *Salem*, but their Husbands continued at *Charles* Town, both for the settling the civill Government, and gathering another Church of *Christ*. The first Court was holden aboard the *Arrabella* the 23. of *August*. When the much

honoured *John Wintrope* Esq. was chosen Governour for the remainder
of that yeare, 1630. Also the worthy *Thomus Dudly* Esq. was chosen
Deputy Governour, and Mr. *Simon Brodestreet* Secretary, the people
after their long Voyage were many of them troubled with the *Scurvy*,
and some of them died: the first station they tooke up was at *Charles.*
Towne, where they pitched some Tents of Cloath, other built them
small Huts, in which they lodged their Wifes and Children. The first
beginning of this worke seemed very dolorous; First for the death of
that worthy personage *Izaac Johnson* Esq. whom the Lord had indued
with many pretious gifts, insomuch that he was had in high esteeme
among all the people of God, and as a chiefe Pillar to support this
new erected building. He very much rejoyced at his death, that the
Lord had been pleased to keepe his eyes open so long, as to see one
Church of *Christ* gathered before his death, at whose departure there
was not onely many weeping eyes, but some fainting hearts, fearing
the fall of the present worke. For future Remembrance of him mind
this *Meeter*.

Izaac Johnson Esquire, beloved of Christ and his people, and one of
    the Magistrates of *New England*.

What mov'd thee on the Seas upon such toyle with Lady-taking;
    Christs drawing love all strength's above, when way for his hee's making.
Christ will have thee example be, honoured with's graces, yeilding
    His Churches aid, foundation laid, now new one Christ a building.
Thy Faith, Hope, Love, Joy, Meeknesse prove improved for thy Lord,
    As he to thee, to people be, in Government accord.
Oh! people why, doth Christ deny this worthies life to lengthen?
    Christ onely trust, Johnsons *turnd dust, and yet hee's crownd and strengthend.*

The griefe of this people was further increased by the sore sicknesse
which befell among them, so that almost in every Family Lamentation,
Mourning, and woe was heard, and no fresh food to be had to cherish
them, it would assuredly have moved the most lockt up affections to
Teares no doubt, had they past from one Hut to another, and beheld
the piteous case these people were in, and that which added to their
present distresse was the want of fresh water, for although the place
did afford plenty, yet for present they could finde but one Spring,
and that not to be come at, but when the tide was downe, which
caused many to passe over to the South-side of the River, where they
afterward erected some other Townes, yet most admirable it was to
see with what Christian courage many of these Souldiers of *Christ*
carried it amidst all these calamities, and in *October*, the Governour

Deputy and Assistants, held their second Court on the South-side of the River; Where they then began to build, holding correspondency with *Charles* Towne, as one and the same.

At this Court many of the first Planters came, and were made free, yet afterward none were admitted to this fellowship, or freedome, but such as were first joyned in fellowship with some one of the Churches of *Christ*, their chiefest aime being bent to promote his worke altogether. The number of Freemen this yeare was 110. or thereabout. . . .

CHAP. XXIX.

OF THE LORDS REMARKABLE PROVIDENCE TOWARD HIS INDEARED
SERVANTS M. NORTON AND MR. SHEPHERD.

Now my loving Reader, let mee lead thee by the hand to our Native Land, although it was not intended to speake in particulars of any of these peoples departure from thence, purposing a generall relation should serve the turne, yet come with mee and behold the wonderous worke of *Christ* in preserving two of his most valiant Souldiers, namely Mr. *John Norton*,[4] and that soule ravishing Minister Mr. *Thomas Shepheard*, who came this yeare to *Yarmouth* to ship themselves for *New England*, where the people of God resorted privately unto them to hear them Preach, during the time of their aboade the Enemies of Christs Kingdome were not wanting to use all meanes possible to intrap them, in which perilous condition they remained about two months, waiting for the Ships readinesse, in which time some persons eagerly hunting for Mr. *Thomas Shepheard*, began to plot (for apprehending of him) with a Boy of sixteene or seventeene yeares of Age, who lived in the House where hee Lodged to open the doore for them at a certaine houre in the night; But the Lord Christ, who is the Shepheard of *Israel* kept a most sure watch over his indeared servants, for thus it befell, the sweet words of grace falling from the of lips of this Reverend and godly Mr. *Thomas Shepheard* in the hearing of the Boy (the Lords working withall) hee was perswaded this was an holy man of God, and therefore with many troubled thoughts, began to relate his former practice, although hee had a great some of money promised him, onely to let them in at the houre and time appointed; but the Boy, the more neere the time came, grew more pensive and sad, insomuch that his Master taking notice thereof began to question him about the cause of his heavinesse, who being unwilling to reveale the matter, held of from confessing a long time, till by urgent and insinuating search of his godly Master, with teares hee tells that

on such a night hee had agreed to let in Men to apprehend the godly
Preacher. The good Man of the house forthwith gave notice thereof
unto them, who with the helpe of some well-affected persons was
convay'd away by boate through a back Lane, the men at the time
appointed came to the house, where finding not the doore open (when
they lifted up the Latch) as they expected, they thrust their staves
under it to lift it from the hookes, but being followed by some persons,
whom the good man of the house had appointed for that end: yet
were they boulstred out in this their wicked act by those who set them
one worke. Notwithstanding they were greatly ashamed when they
mist of their end.

But the Lord Christ intending to make his *New England* Souldiers
the very wonder of this Age, brought them into greater straites, that
this *Wonder working Providence* might the more appeare in their deliverance, for comming a shipboard, and hoiseing saile to accomplish
their Voyage, in little time after they were tossed and sore beaten with
a contrary winde, to the losse of the Ships upper worke, with which
losse and great perill they were driven back againe, the *Lord Christ*
intending to confirme their Faith in shewing them, that although they
were brought back, as it were into the mouth of their enemies, yet
hee could hide them from the hand of the Hunter, for the space of
six moneths longer or thereabout, even till the Spring of the yeare
following, at which time (God willing) you shall hear of them againe,
in the meane time the Master, and other Sea men made a strange
construction of the sore storme they met withall, saying, their Ship
was bewitched, and therefore made use of the common Charme
ignorant people use, nailing two red hot horseshoos to their maine
mast. But assuredly it was the *Lord Christ*, who hath command both
of Winds and Seas, and now would have his poeple know he hath
delivered, and will deliver from so great a death. . . .

Chap. XXXVI.

Of the laborious worke Christs people have in planting this wildernesse, set forth in the building the Towne of Concord, being the first in-land Towne.

Now because it is one of the admirable acts of Christ Providence
in leading his people forth into these Westerne Fields, in his providing of Huts for them, to defend them from the bitter stormes this
place is subject unto, therefore here is a short Epitome of the manner
how they placed downe their dwellings in this Desart Wildernesse,

the Lord being pleased to hide from the Eyes of his people the difficulties they are to encounter withall in a new Plantation, that they might not thereby be hindered from taking the worke in hand; upon some inquiry of the *Indians,* who lived to the North-west of the Bay, one Captaine *Simon Willard* being acquainted with them, by reason of his Trade, became a chiefe instrument in erecting this Town, the land they purchase of the *Indians,* and with much difficulties traveling through unknowne woods, and through watery scrampes, they discover the fitnesse of the place, sometimes passing through the Thickets, where their hands are forced to make way for their bodies passage, and their feete clambering over the crossed Trees, which when they missed they sunke into an uncertaine bottome in water, and wade up to the knees, tumbling sometimes higher and sometines lower, wearied with this toile, they at end of this meete with a scorching plaine, yet not so plaine, but that the ragged Bushes scratch their legs fouly, even to wearing their stockings to their bare skin in two or three houres; if they be not otherwise well defended with Bootes, or Buskings, their flesh will be torne: (that some being forced to passe on without further provision) have had the bloud trickle downe at every step, and in the time of Summer the Sun casts such a reflecting heate from the sweet Ferne, whose scent is very strong so that some herewith have beene very nere fainting, although very able bodies to undergoe much travell, and this not to be indured for one day, but for many, and verily did not the Lord incourage their naturall parts (with hopes of a new and strange discovery, expecting every houre to see some rare sight never seene before) they were never able to hold out, and breake through: but above all, the thirsting desires these servants of Christ have had to Plant his Churches, among whom the forenamed Mr. *Jones* shall not be forgotten.

> *In Desart's depth where Wolves and Beares abide,*
> *There* Jones *sits down a wary watch to keepe,*
> *O're Christs deare flock, who now are wandered wide;*
> *But not from him, whose eyes ne're close with sleepe.*
> *Surely it sutes thy melancholly minde,*
> *Thus solitary for to spend thy dayes,*
> *Much more thy soule in Christ content doth finde,*
> *To worke for him, who thee to joy will raise.*
> *Leading thy son to Land, yet more remote,*
> *To feede his flock upon this Westerne wast:*
> *Exhort him then Christs Kingdome to promote;*
> *That he with thee of lasting joyes may tast.*

Yet farther to tell of the hard labours this people found in Planting this Wildernesse, after some dayes spent in search, toyling in the day time as formerly is said; like true *Jacob*, its they rest them one the Rocks where the night takes them, their short repast is some small pittance of Bread, if it hold out, but as for Drinke they have plenty, the Countrey being well watered in all places that yet are found out, their farther hardship is to travell, sometimes they know not whether, bewildred indeed without sight of Sun, their compasse miscarrying in crouding through the Bushes, they sadly search up and down for a known way, the *Indians* paths being not above one foot broad, so that a man may travell many dayes and never find one. But to be sure the directing Providence of Christ hath beene better unto them than many paths, as might here be inserted, did not hast call my Pen away to more waighty matters; yet by the way a touch thus, it befell with a servant maide, who was travelling about three or foure miles from one Towne to another, loosing her selfe in the Woods, had very diligent search made after her for the space of three dayes, and could not possible be found, then being given over as quite lost, after three dayes and nights, the Lord was pleased to bring her feeble body to her own home in safety, to the great admiration of all that heard of it. This intricate worke no whit daunted these resolved servants of Christ to goe on with the worke in hand, but lying in the open aire, while the watery Clouds poure down all the night season, and sometimes the driving Snow dissolving on their backs, they keep their wet cloathes warme with a continued fire, till the renewed morning give fresh opportunity of further travell; after they have thus found out a place of aboad, they burrow themselves in the Earth for their first shelter under some Hill-side, casting the Earth aloft upon Timber; they make a smoaky fire against the Earth at the highest side, and thus these poore servants of Christ provide shelter for themselves, their Wives and little ones, keeping off the short showers from their Lodgings, but the long raines penetrate through, to their great disturbance in the night season: yet in these poore *Wigwames* (they sing Psalmes, pray and praise their God) till they can provide them houses, which ordinarily was not wont to be with many till the Earth, by the Lords blessing, brought forth Bread to feed them, their Wives and little ones, which with sore labours they attaine every one that can lift a hawe to strike it into the Earth, standing stoutly to their labours, and teare up the Rootes and Bushes, which the first yeare beares them a very thin crop, till the soard of the Earth be rotten, and therefore they have been forced to cut their bread very thin for a long season. But the Lord is pleased to provide for them great store of Fish in the spring time, and especially Alewives about the bignesse of a Herring, many thousands of these, they used to put under their *Indian* Corne, which they plant in Hills five foote asunder, and assuredly when the Lord created this Corne, hee had a speciall eye to supply these his peoples wants with it, for ordinarily five or six graines doth produce six hundred.

As for flesh they looked not for any in those times (although now they have plenty) unlesse they could barter with the *Indians* for Venison or Rockoons, whose flesh is not much inferiour unto Lambe, the toile of a new Plantation being like the labours of *Hercules* never at an end, yet are none so barbarously bent (under the *Mattacusets* especially) but with a new Plantation they ordinarily gather into Church-fellow-ship, so that Pastors and people suffer the inconveniences together, which is a great meanes to season the sore labours they undergoe, and verily the edge of their appetite was greater to spirituall duties at their first comming in time of wants, than afterward: many in new Plantations have been forced to go barefoot, and bareleg, till these latter dayes, and some in time of Frost and Snow: Yet were they then very healthy more then now they are: in this Wildernesse-worke men of Estates speed no better than others, and some much worse for want of being inured to such hard labour, having laid out their estate upon cattell at five and twenty pound a Cow, when they came to winter them with in-land Hay, and feed upon such wild Fother as was never cut before, they could not hold out the Winter, but ordinarily the first or second yeare after their comming up to a new Plantation, many of their Cattell died, especially if they wanted Salt-marshes: and also those, who supposed they should feed upon Swines flesh were cut short, the Wolves commonly feasting themselves before them, who never leave neither flesh nor bones, if they be not scared away before they have made an end of their meale, as for those who laid out their Estate upon Sheepe, they speed worst of any at the beginning (al-though some have sped the best of any now) for untill the Land be often fed with other Cattell Sheepe cannot live; And therefore they never thrived till these latter dayes; Horse had then no better successe, which made many an honest Gentleman travell a foot for a long time, and some have even perished with extreame heate in their travells: as also the want of English graine, Wheate, Barly and Rie proved a sore affliction to some stomacks, who could not live upon *Indian* Bread and water, yet were they compelled to it till Cattell increased, and the Plowes could but goe: instead of Apples and Peares, they had

Pomkins and Squashes of divers kinds, their lonesome condition was very grievous to some, which was much aggravated by continuall feare of the *Indians* approach, whose cruelties were much spoken of, and more especially during the time of the *Peqot* wars.

Thus this poore people populate this howling Desart, marching manfully on (the Lord assisting) through the greatest difficulties, and sorest labours that ever any with such weak means have done. . . .

Chap. LXII.

Of sad effects of the pitifull and errionous Doctrines broached by the Sectuaries.

The number of these infectious persons increasing now, haveing drawn a great party on their side, and some considerable persons they grow bold, and dare question the sound and wholesome truths delivered in publick by the Ministers of *Christ*. Their Church-meetings are full of Disputes in points of difference, and their love-Feasts are not free from spots, in their Courts of civill Justice some men utter their Speeches in matters of Religion very ambiguously, and among all sorts of persons a great talke of new light, but verily it proved but old darknesse, such as sometime overshadowed the City of *Munster;* [5] But blessed be the *Lord Christ*, who now declared himselfe to be a helpe at hand for his poore *New England* Churches, being now in their infancy, whose condition at present was very dolorous, and full of difficulties, insomuch that the better part of this new transported people stood still many of them gazing one upon another, like Sheepe let loose to feed on fresh pasture, being stopped and startled in their course by a Kennell of devouring Wolves. The weaker sort wavered much, and such as were more growne Christians hardly durst discover the truth they held one unto another, the fogs of errour increasing the bright beames of the glorious Gospell of our *Lord Christ* in the Mouth of his Ministers could not be discerned through this thick mist by many, and that sweete refreshing warmth that was formerly felt from the spirits influence, was now turned (in these Erronists) to a hot inflamation of their owne conceited Revelations, ulcerating and bringing little lesse then frenzy or madnesse to the patient, the Congregation of the people of God began to be forsaken, and the weaker Sex prevailed so farre, that they set up a Priest of their own Profession and Sex, who was much thronged after, abominably wresting the Scriptures to their own destruction: this Master-piece of Womens wit, drew many Disciples after her, and to that end boldly insinuated her selfe into the favour of none of the meanest, being also backed with the Sorcery of a second, who had much converse with the Devill by her own confession, and did, to the admiration of those that heard her, utter many speeches in the Latine Tongue, as it were in a trance. . . .

Oh yee *New England* Men and Women, who hath bewitched you that you should not obey the truth? And indeed Satan, to make sure worke with semblance of Preaching the Doctrine of Free-gree by his instruments, makes shew of out-bidding all the Orthodox, and godly Ministers in the Countrey, pretending their Preaching to be but a Covenant of workes, supposing by this meanes to silence them without a Bishop, and lest the civill power should stand up for their aid, they threaten them with the high displeasure of Christ for persecuting his people, which as they said these erronious persons with their new light, were the onely Men and Women that were pure Gospell Preachers. Thus the poore people of Christ, who kept close to his antient truths invironed with many straites, having expended their Estates to voyage far through the perillous Seas, that their eyes might behold their Teachers, and that they might injoy the protection of a godly civill Government, began to deeme themselves in a more dolorous condition then when they were in the Commissaries Court, and Prelates Prisons, the hideous waves in which their brittle Barques were sometimes covered, as they passed hither, were nothing so terrible in the apprehension of some as was this floud of errors violently beating against the bankes of Church and civill Government, the wants of this Wildernesse, and pinching penury in misse of Bread, put them to no such paine by gnawing on their empty stomacks, with feare of famishing, as did the misse of the Administration of Christ in his Word and Ordinances, leaving the soule in a languishing condition for want of a continuall supply of *Christ* in his Graces.

CHAP. LXIII.

OF THE SORROWFULL CONDITION OF THE PEOPLE OF CHRIST, WHEN THEY WERE INCOUNTRED WITH THESE ERRONISTS AT THEIR FIRST LANDING.

But to end this dismall yeare of sixteene hundred thirty six, take here the sorrowfull complaint of a poore Soule in misse of its expectation at landing, who being incountered with some of these Erronists at his first landing, when he saw that good old way of *Christ* rejected by them, and hee could not skill in that new light, which was the common theame of every mans Discourse, hee betooke him to a narrow

Indian path, in which his serious Meditations soone led him, where none but sencelesse Trees and eccohing Rocks make answer to his heart-easeing mone. Oh quoth he where am I become, is this the place where those Reverend Preachers are fled, that *Christ* was pleased to make use of to rouse up his rich graces in many a drooping soule; here I have met with some that tell mee, I must take a naked *Christ*. Oh, woe is mee if *Christ* be naked to mee, wherewith shall I be cloathed, but methinks I most wonder they tell me of casting of all godly sorrow for sin as unbeseeming a Soule, that is united to *Christ* by Faith, and there was a little nimbled tongued Woman among them, who said she could bring me acquainted with one of her own Sex that would shew me a way, if I could attaine it, even Revelations, full of such ravishing joy that I should never have cause to be sorry for sinne, so long as I live, and as for her part shee had attained it already: a company of legall Professors, quoth she lie poring on the Law which *Christ* hath abolished, and when you breake it then you breake your joy, and now no way will serve your turne, but a deepe sorrow. These and divers other expressions intimate unto men, that here I shall finde little increase in the Graces of *Christ*, through the hearing of his word Preached, and other of his blessed Ordinances. Oh cunning Devill, the *Lord Christ* rebuke thee, that under pretence of a free and ample Gospell shuts out the Soule from partaking with the Divine Nature of *Christ*, in that mysticall Union of his Blessed Spirit creating, and continuing his Graces in the Soule: my deare *Christ*, it was thy worke that moved me hither to come, hoping to finde thy powerfull presence in the Preaching of the Word, although administred by sorry men, subject to like infirmities with others of Gods people, and also by the glasse of the Law, to have my sinfull corrupt nature discovered daily more and more, and my utter inabillity of any thing that is good, magnifying hereby the free grace of *Christ;* who of his good will and pleasure worketh in us to will, and to doe working all our works in us, and for us.

But here they tell me of a naked *Christ*, what is the whole life of a Christian upon this Earth? But through the power of *Christ* to die to sinne, and live to holinesse and righteousnesse, and for that end to be diligent in the use of meanes: at the uttering of this word he starts up from the greene bed of his complaint with resolution to hear some one of these able Ministers Preach (whom report had so valued) before his will should make choyce of any one principle, though of crossing the broade Seas back againe, then turning his face to the Sun, he steered his course toward the next Town,[6] and after some small travell hee came to a large plaine, no sooner was hee entred thereon, but hearing the sound of a Drum he was directed toward it by a broade beaten way, following this rode he demands of the next man he met what the signall of the Drum ment, the reply was made they had as yet no Bell to call men to meeting; and therefore made use of a Drum, who is it, quoth hee, Lectures at this Towne. The other replies, I see you are a stranger, new come over, seeing you know not the man, it is one Mr. *Shepheard*, verily quoth the other you hit the right, I am new come over indeed, and have been told since I came most of your Ministers are legall Preachers, onely if I mistake not they told me this man Preached a finer covenant of workes then the other, but however, I shall make what hast I can to heare him. Fare you well, then hasting thither hee croudeth through the thickest, where having stayed while the glasse was turned up twice, the man was metamorphosed, and was faine to hang down the head often, least his watry eyes should blab abroad the secret conjunction of his affections, his heart crying loud to the Lords ecchoing answer, to his blessed spirit, that caused the Speech of a poore weake pale complectioned man to take such impression in his soule at present, by applying the word so aptly, as if hee had beene his Privy Counseller, cleering Christs worke of grace in the soule from all those false Doctrines, which the erronious party had afrighted him withall, and now he resolves (the Lord willing) to live and die with the Ministers of *New England;* whom hee now saw the Lord had not onely made zealous to stand for the truth of his Discipline, but also of the Doctrine, and not to give ground one inch. . . .

Book III.

Chap. XII.

Of the time of the fall of Antichrist, and the increase of the Gentile Churches, even to the provoking of the twelve Tribes to submit to the kingdom of Christ.

It hath been the longing expectation of many, to see that notable and wonderfull worke of the Lord Christ, in casting down that man of sin who hath held the whole world (of those that profess any Christ) under his Lordly power, while the true professors of Christ have hardly had any appearance to the eye of the world; first, take notice the Lord hath an assured set time for the accomplishment of this work, which is set down in his word, although more darkly to be understood;

wherefore the reverend Ministers of Christ, for these many yeers have
studied and laboured for the finding it out, and that holy man of God
Mr. *John Cotton*, among many other, hath diligently searched for the
Lords mind herein, and hath declared some sudden blow to be given
to this blood-thirsty monster: but the Lord Christ hath unseparably
joyned the time, meanes, and manner of this work together, and
therefore all men that expect the day, must attend the means: for such
hath been and is the absurdity of many, that they make semblance
of a very zealous affection to see the glorious work of our Lord Christ
herein, and yet themselves uphold, or at least side with those that
uphold some part of Antichrists kingdome: and therefore the lordly
Prelacy may pray for his fall till their lungs are spent, and their
throats grow dry. But while they have a seeming shew (and hardly
that) to oppose his doctrines, they themselves in the mean time, make
use of his power to advance themselves to honour: as also in these
dayes there are divers desperate, blasphemous, and erronious persons,
whose consciences and their own self-will are unseparable companions;
these are very hot in their own apprehensions to prosecute the work;
but in the mean time, they not only batter down the truths of Christ,
and his own Ordinances and Institutions, but also set up that part
of Antichrists kingdom, which hath formerly had a great blow already,
even his deceiveable and damnable doctrines: for as one badg of the
beast is to be full of blasphemies, so are they, and these take unto
themselves seven spirits worse then the former, making the latter end
worse then the beginning, as this story may testifie: and some stories
in our native country much more. But to come to the time of Antichrists fall; and all that expect it may depend upon the certainty of
it: yea it may be boldly said that the time is come, and all may see
the dawning of the day: you that long so much for it, come forth and
fight: who can expect a victory without a battel? the lordly Prelates
that boasted so much of these great atcheivements in this work, are fled
into holes and corners: *Familists, Seekers, Antinomians* and *Anabaptists*,
they are so ill armed, that they think it best sleeping in a whole skin,
fearing that if the day of battell once go on, they shall fall among
Antichrists Armies: and therefore cry out like cowards, If you will
let me alone, and I will let you alone; but assuredly the Lord Christ
hath said, *He that is not with us, is against us:* there is no room in his
Army for toleratorists.[7] But some will say, We will never believe the
day is come, till our eyes behold *Babylon* begirt with Souldiers. I pray
be not too hasty; hath not the Lord said, *Come out of her my people?*
&c, surely there is a little space left for this, and now is the time, seeing

the Lord hath set up his standerd of resort: now, *Come forth of her, and be not partakers of her sins:* now is the time, when the Lord hath assembled his Saints together; now the Lord will come and not tarry. As it was necessary that there should be a *Moses* and *Aaron*, before the Lord would deliver his people and destroy *Pharaoh* left they should be wildred indeed in the Wilderness; so now it was needfull, that the Churches of Christ should first obtain their purity, and the civill government its power to defend them, before Antichrist come to his finall ruine: and because you shall be sure the day is come indeed, behold the Lord Christ marshalling of his invincible Army to the battell: some suppose this onely to be mysticall, and not literall at all: assuredly the spirituall fight is chiefly to be attended, and the other not. neglected, having a neer dependancy one upon the other, especially at this time; the Ministers of Christ who have cast off all lording power over one another, are created field-Officers, whose Office is extravagant in this Army, chiefly to encourage the fighting Souldiers, and to lead them on upon the enemy in the most advantagious places, and bring on fresh supplies in all places of danger, to put the sword of the spirit in their Souldiers hands: but Christ (who is their general) must onely enable them to use it aright: to give every Souldier in charge that they watch over one another, to see that none meddle with the execrable things of Antichrist, and this to be performed in every Regiment throughout the Army: and not one to exercise dominion over the other by way of superiority: for Christ hath appointed a parity in all his Regiments, *&c.* let them beware that none go apart with rebellious *Korah.* And further, behold, Kings, Rulers, or Generals of Earths Armies, doth Christ make use of in this day of battell, the which he hath brought into the field already also; who are appointed to defend, uphold, and maintain the whole body of his Armies against the insolent, beastly, and bloody cruelty of their insatiable enemies, and to keep order that none do his fellow-Souldier any wrong, nor that any should raise a mutiny in the hosts. Notwithstanding all this, if any shall say, they will not believe the day is come till they see them ingage battell with Antichrist; Verily, if the Lord be pleased to open your eyes, you may see the beginning of the fight, and what success the Armies of our Lord Christ have hitherto had: the Forlorne hopes of Antichrists Army, were the proud Prelates of *England:* the Forlorne of Christs Armies, were these *N. E.* people, who are the subject of this History, which encountring each other for some space of time, ours being overpowered with multitude, were forced to retreat to a place of greater safety, where they waited for a fresh opportunity to ingage with the main battell of Antichrist, so soon as the Lord shall be pleased to give a word of Command. Immediately upon this success, the Lord Christ was pleased to command the right Wing of his Army, to advance against the left Wing of Antichrist: where in his former forlorn hopes of proud Prelates lay: these by our right Wing had their first pay (for that they had done to our forlorne before) being quite overthrown and cut in peices by the valiant of the Lord in our right Wing, and still remain fighting. Thus far of the battell of Antichrist, and the various success: what the issue will be, is assuredly known in the generall already. *Babylon* is fallen, the God of truth hath said it; then who would not be a Souldier on Christs side, where is such a certainty of victory? nay I can tell you a farther word of encouragement, every true-hearted Souldier that falls by the sword in this fight, shall not lye dead long, but stand upon his feet again, and be made partaker of the triumph of this Victory: and none can be overcome, but by turning his back in fight. And for a word of terrour to the enemy, let them know, Christ will never give over the raising of fresh Forces, till they are overthrown root and branch. And now you antient people of *Israel* look out of your Prison grates, let these Armies of the Lord Christ Jesus provoke you to acknowledge he is certainly come, I and speedily he doth come to put life into your dry bones: here is a people not onely praying but fighting for you, that the great block may be removed out of the way, (which hath hindered hitherto) that they with you may enjoy that glorious resurrection-day, the glorious nuptials of the Lamb: when not only the Bridegroom shall appear to his Churches both of *Jews* and *Gentiles*, (which are his spouse) in a more brighter aray then ever heretofore, but also his Bride shall be clothed by him in the richest garments that ever the Sons of men put on, even the glorious graces of Christ Jesus, in such a glorious splendor to the eyes of man, that they shall see and glorifie the Father of both Bridegroom and Bride.

COTTON MATHER, 1663–1728

[Cotton Mather's very name is a proclamation of his standing in seventeenth-century New England; the grandson of John Cotton, and of Richard Mather, the first minister of Dorchester, the son of Increase Mather, minister of the North Church in Boston and President of Harvard College, Cotton was born in the clerical purple. Educated at home by his very learned father, at the age of twelve he entered Harvard, where it is said he was better liked by his tutors than by his

EVIDENCE OF LOOSENING STYLE ① interjection of lengthy passages in Latin + Greek — allusions to classical literature ② stylistic show off metaphors to church history p. 176 ③ opening is like an epic poem's invocation.

fellow students. He took his M.A. in 1681, was ordained the colleague of his father in 1685 and married his first wife in 1686; along with his father he soon became a leader of orthodox opinion in eastern Massachusetts. He was active in the Revolution of 1689, and was made Fellow of Harvard College in 1690. After 1700 the Mathers suffered many reverses; when Increase was forced out of Harvard College Cotton, not being chosen President as he had expected he would be, resigned his fellowship. Governor Dudley was his enemy; his last days were embittered by the restriction of his influence, the insanity of his third wife, the profligacy of his favourite son. He was an indefatigable worker, publishing some five hundred books, tracts, and pamphlets, corresponding with learned men all over Europe, contributing to the *Transactions* of the Royal Society, to which he was elected in 1713. In 1721 he and his father made a heroic fight for smallpox inoculation against the enraged hostility of the majority of the citizens. For biography cf. Barrett Wendell, *Cotton Mather the Puritan Priest* (New York, 1891). This text is from *Magnalia Christi Americana; or, the Ecclesiastical History of New England* (London, 1702).]

A GENERAL INTRODUCTION

§. 1. I write the *Wonders* of the CHRISTIAN RELIGION, flying from the *Depravations* of *Europe*, to the *American Strand:* And, assisted by the Holy Author of that *Religion*, I do, with all Conscience of *Truth*, required therein by Him, who is the *Truth* it self, Report the *Wonderful Displays* of His Infinite Power, Wisdom, Goodness, and Faithfulness, wherewith His Divine Providence hath *Irradiated* an *Indian Wilderness.*

INVOCATION OF EPIC POEM !

I Relate the *Considerable Matters*, that produced and attended the First Settlement of COLONIES, which have been Renowned for the Degree of REFORMATION, Professed and Attained by *Evangelical Churches*, erected in those *Ends of the Earth:* And a *Field* being thus prepared, I proceed unto a Relation of the *Considerable Matters* which have been acted thereupon.

I first introduce the *Actors*, that have, in a more exemplary manner served those *Colonies;* and give *Remarkable Occurrences*, in the exemplary LIVES of many *Magistrates*, and of more *Ministers*, who so *Lived*, as to leave unto Posterity, *Examples* worthy of *Everlasting Remembrance.*

I add hereunto; the *Notables* of the only *Protestant University*, that ever *shone* in that Hemisphere of the *New World;* with particular Instances of *Criolians*,[1] in our *Biography*, provoking the *whole World*, with vertuous Objects of Emulation.

I introduce then, the *Actions* of a more Eminent Importance, that have signalized those *Colonies;* Whether the *Establishments*, directed by their *Synods;* with a Rich Variety of *Synodical* and *Ecclesiastical* Determinations; or, the *Disturbances*, with which they have been from all sorts of *Temptations* and *Enemies* Tempestuated; and the *Methods* by which they have still weathered out each *Horrible Tempest.*

And into the midst of these *Actions*, I interpose an entire *Book*, wherein there is, with all possible Veracity, a *Collection* made, of *Memorable Occurrences*, and amazing *Judgments* and *Mercies*, befalling many *particular Persons* among the People of *New-England*.

Let my Readers expect all that I have promised them, in this *Bill of Fair;* and it may be they will find themselves entertained with yet many other *Passages*, above and beyond their Expectation, deserving likewise a room in *History:* In all which, there will be nothing but the *Author's* too mean way of preparing so great Entertainments, to Reproach the Invitation.

§. 2. The Reader will doubtless desire to know, what it was that

> ——*tot Volvere casus* ⟵ "Drove forth the
> *Insignes Pietate Viros, tot adire Labores,* eminent pious heroes
> *Impulerit.*[2]   to withstand so many
> fortunes, to undertake the
> labors"

And our *History* shall, on many fit Occasions which will be therein offered, endeavour, with all *Historical* Fidelity and Simplicity, and with as little Offence as may be, to satisfie him. The Sum of the Matter is, That from the very Beginning of the REFORMATION in the *English Nation*, there hath always been a Generation of *Godly Men*, desirous to pursue the *Reformation of Religion, according to the Word of God, and the Example of the best Reformed Churches;* and answering the Character of *Good Men*, given by *Josephus*, in his Paraphrase on the words of *Samuel* to *Saul*, μηδὲν ἄλλο πραχθήσεσθαι καλῶς ὑφ' ἑαυτῶν νομίζοντες ἢ ὅτι ἂν ποιήσωσι τοῦ Θεοῦ κεκελευκότος. *They think they do nothing Right in the Service of God, but what they do according to the Command of God.* And there hath been another Generation of Men, who have still employed the *Power* which they have generally still had in their Hands, not only to stop the Progress of the Desired *Reformation*, but also, with Innumerable Vexations, to Persecute those that most Heartily wished well unto it. There were many of the *Reformers*, who joyned with the Reverend JOHN FOX,[3] in the *Complaints* which he then entred in his *Martyrology*, about the *Baits of Popery* yet left in the Church; and in his *Wishes, God take them away, or ease us from them, for God knows, they be the Cause of much Blindness and Strife amongst Men!* They Zealously decreed the *Policy* of complying always with the *Ignorance* and *Vanity* of the *People;* and cried out earnestly for *Purer Administrations* in the House of God, and more *Conformity* to the *Law of Christ,* and *Primitive Christianity:* While others would not hear of going any further than the *First Essay* of *Reformation.* 'Tis very certain, that the *First Reformers* never intended, that what *They* did, should be the *Absolute Boundary* of *Reformation,* so that it should be a Sin to proceed any further; as, by their own going beyond *Wicklift,*[4] and *Changing* and *Growing* in their own *Models* also, and the Confessions of *Cranmer,* with the *Scripta Anglicana* of *Bucer,* and a thousand other things, was abundantly demonstrated. But after a Fruitless Expectation, wherein the truest Friends of the *Reformation* long waited, for to have that which *Heylin* [5] himself owns to have been the Design of the *First Reformers,* followed as it should have been, a Party very unjustly arrogating to themselves, the Venerable Name of, *The Church of* England, by Numberless Oppressions, grievously *Smote those their Fellow-Servants.* Then 'twas that, as our Great OWEN [6] hath expressed it, *Multitudes of Pious, Peaceable Protestants, were driven, by their Severities, to leave their Native Country, and seek a Refuge for their Lives and Liberties, with Freedom, for the Worship of God, in a Wilderness, in the Ends of the Earth.*

§. 3. It is the History of these PROTESTANTS, that is here attempted: PROTESTANTS that highly honoured and affected *The Church of* ENGLAND, and humbly Petition to be a *Part* of it: But by the Mistake of a few powerful *Brethren,* driven to seek a place for the Exercise of the *Protestant Religion,* according to the Light of their Consciences, in the Desarts of *America.* And in this Attempt I have proposed, not only to preserve and secure the Interest of *Religion,* in the Churches of that little Country NEW-ENGLAND, so far as the Lord Jesus Christ may please to Bless it for that End, but also to offer unto the Churches of the *Reformation,* abroad in the World, some small *Memorials,* that may be serviceable unto the Designs of *Reformation,* whereto, I believe, they are quickly to be awakened. I am far from any such Boast, concerning these Churches, *That they have Need of Nothing,* I wish their *Works* were more *perfect before God.* Indeed, that which *Austin* called *The Perfection of Christians,* is like to be, until the Term for the *Antichristian Apostasie* be expired, *The Perfection of Churches* too; *Ut Agnoscant se nunquam esse perfectas.*[7] Nevertheless, I perswade my self, that *so far as they have attained,* they have given *Great Examples* of the *Methods* and *Measures,* wherein an *Evangelical Reformation* is to be prosecuted, and of the *Qualifications* requisite in the Instruments that are to prosecute it, and of the *Difficulties* which may be most likely to obstruct it, and the most likely *Directions* and *Remedies* for those Obstructions. It may be, 'tis not possible for me to do a greater Service unto the Churches on the *Best Island* of the Universe, than to give a distinct Relation of those *Great Examples* which have been occurring among Churches of *Exiles*, that were driven out of that *Island*, into an horrible *Wilderness*, meerly for their being Well-willers unto the *Reformation*. When that Blessed Martyr *Constantine* was carried, with other Martyrs, in a *Dung-Cart*, unto the place of Execution, he pleasantly said, *Well, yet we are a precious Odour to God in Christ*. Tho' the *Reformed Churches* in the *American Regions*, have, by very Injurious Representations of their Brethren (all which they desire to Forget and Forgive!) been many times thrown into a *Dung-Cart;* yet, as they have been a *precious Odour to God in Christ*, so, I hope, they will be a *precious Odour* unto *His People;* and not only *Precious*, but *Useful* also, when the *History* of them shall come to be considered. A *Reformation of the Church* is coming on, and I cannot but thereupon say, with the dying *Cyrus* to his Children in *Xenophon*, Ἐκ τῶν προγεγεννημένων μανθάνετε, αὐτὴ γὰρ ἀρίστη διδασκαλία. *Learn from the things that have been done already, for this is the best way of Learning*. The Reader hath here an Account of *The Things that have been done already*. *Bernard* upon that Clause in the *Canticles*, [*O thou fairest among Women*] has this ingenious Gloss, *Pulchram, non omnimode quidem, sed pulchram inter mulieres eam docet, videlicet cum Distinctione, quatenus ex hoc amplius reprimatur, & sciat quid desit sibi*.[8] Thus I do not say, That the Churches of *New-England* are the most *Regular* that can be; yet I do say, and am sure, That they are very like unto those that were in the *First Ages* of Christianity. And if I assert, That in the *Reformation* of the Church, the State of it in those *First Ages*, is to be not a little considered, the Great *Peter Ramus*,[9] among others, has emboldened me. For when the Cardinal of *Lorrain*, the *Mæcenas* of that Great Man, was offended at him, for turning *Protestant*, he replied, *Inter Opes illas, quibus me ditasti, has etiam in æternum recordabor, quod Beneficio, Poessiacæ Responsionis tuæ didici, de Quindecim a Christo sæculis, primum vere esse aureum, Reliqua, quo longius abscederent esse nequiora, atque deteriora: Tum igitur cum fieret optio, Aureum sæculum delegi*.[10] In short, The *First Age* was the *Golden Age:* To return unto *That*, will make a Mǎn a *Protestant*, and I may add, a *Puritan*. 'Tis possible, That our Lord Jesus Christ carried some Thousands of *Reformers* into the Retirements of an *American Desart*, on purpose, that, with an opportunity granted unto many of his Faithful Servants, to enjoy the precious *Liberty* of their *Ministry*, tho' in the midst of many *Temptations* all their days, He might there, *To* them first, and then *By* them, give a *Specimen* of many Good Things, which He would have His

Churches elsewhere aspire and arise unto: And *This* being done, He knows not whether there be not *All done*, that *New-England* was planted for; and whether the Plantation may not, soon after this, *Come to Nothing*. Upon that Expression in the Sacred Scripture, *Cast the unprofitable Servant into Outer Darkness*, it hath been imagined by some, That the *Regiones Exteræ* [11] of *America*, are the *Tenebræ Exteriores*,[12] which the *Unprofitable* are there condemned unto. No doubt, the Authors of those Ecclesiastical Impositions and Severities, which drove the English Christians into the *Dark Regions* of *America*, esteemed those *Christians* to be a very *unprofitable* sort of Creatures. But behold, ye *European* Churches. There are *Golden Candlesticks* [more than *twice Seven times Seven!*] in the midst of this *Outer Darkness:* Unto the *upright* Children of *Abraham*, here hath arisen *Light in Darkness*. And let us humbly speak it, it shall be *Profitable* for you to consider the *Light*, which from the midst of this *Outer Darkness*, is now to be Darted over unto the other side of the *Atlantick Ocean*. But we must therewithal ask your Prayers, that these *Golden Candlesticks* may not *quickly* be *Removed out of their place!*

§. 4. But whether *New England* may *Live* any where else or no, it must *Live* in our *History!*

HISTORY, in general, hath had so many and mighty Commendations from the Pens of those Numberless Authors, who, from *Herodotus* to *Howel*,[13] have been the professed Writers of it, that a tenth part of them Transcribed, would be a Furniture for a *Polyanthea in Folio*.[14] We, that have neither liberty, nor occasion, to quote those Commendations of *History*, will content our selves with the Opinion of one who was not much of a *profess'd Historian*, expressed in that passage, whereto all Mankind subscribe, *Historia est Testis temporum, Nuntia vetustatis, Lux veritatis, vita memoriæ, magistra vita*.[15] But of all *History* it must be confessed, that the *Palm* is to be given unto *Church History;* wherein the *Dignity*, the *Suavity*, and the *Utility* of the *Subject* is transcendent. I observe, that for the Description of the *whole World* in the Book of *Genesis*, that *First-born of all Historians*, the great *Moses*, implies but *one* or *two* Chapters, whereas he [e]mpl[oyes], it may be *seven times* as many Chapters, in describing that one little *Pavilion, The Tabernacle*. And when I am thinking, what may be the Reason of this *Difference*, methinks it intimates unto us, That the *Church* wherein the Service of God is performed, is much more *Precious* than the *World*, which was indeed created for the Sake and Use of the *Church*. 'Tis very certain, that the greatest Entertainments must needs occur in the History of the *People*, whom the *Son* of God hath *Redeemed* and *Purified* unto himself, as a *Peculiar People*, and whom the *Spirit* of God, by *Supernatural Operations* upon their Minds, does cause to live like *Strangers* in *this World*, conforming themselves unto the *Truths* and *Rules* of his Holy Word, in Expectation of a *Kingdom*, whereto they shall be in another and a better *World* advanced. Such a *People* our Lord Jesus Christ hath procured and preserved in all Ages *visible;* and the Dispensations of his *wonderous Providence* towards this People (for, *O Lord, thou do'st lift them up, and cast them down!*) their Calamities, their Deliverances, the Dispositions which they have still discovered, and the considerable *Persons* and *Actions* found among them, cannot but afford Matters of *Admiration* and *Admonition*, above what any other Story can pretend unto: 'Tis nothing but *Atheism* in the Hearts of Men, that can perswade them otherwise. Let any Person of good Sense peruse the History of *Herodotus*, which, like a River taking Rise, where the *Sacred Records* of the *Old Testament* leave off, runs along smoothly and sweetly, with Relations that sometimes perhaps want an *Apology*, down until the *Grecians* drive the *Persians* before them. Let him then peruse *Thucydides*, who from *Acting* betook himself to *Writing*, and carries the ancient State of the *Grecians*, down to the twenty first Year of the *Peloponnesian Wars* in a manner, which *Casaubon* judges to be *Mirandum potius quam imitandum*,[16] Let him next Revolve *Xenophon*, that *Bee* of *Athens*, who continues a Narrative of the *Greek Affairs*, from the *Peloponnesian Wars*, to the Battle of *Mantinea*, and gives us a *Cyrus* into the bargain, at such a rate, that *Lipsius* reckons the Character of a *Suavi, Fidus & Circumspectiis Scriptor*,[17] to belong unto him. Let him from hence proceed unto *Diodorus Siculus*, who, besides a rich Treasure of *Egyptian, Assyrian, Lybian* and *Grecian*, and other *Antiquities*, in a Phrase, which according to *Photius's* Judgment, is ἱστορίᾳ μάλιστὰ, πρεπούσῃ, *of all most becoming an Historian*, carries on the Thread begun by his Predecessors, until the End of the Hundred and nineteenth *Olympiad;* and where he is defective, let it be supplied from *Arianus*, from *Justin*, and from *Curtius*, who in the relish of *Colerus* is, *Quovis melle dulcior*.[18] Let him hereupon consult *Polybius*, and acquaint himself with the Birth and Growth of the *Roman Empire*, as far as 'tis described, in *Five* of the *Forty* Books composed by an Author, who with a Learned *Professor of History* is, *Prudens Scriptor, si quis alius*.[19] Let him now run over the Table of the *Roman* Affairs, compendiously given by *Lucius Florus*, and then let him consider the Transactions of above three hundred Years reported by *Dionysius Halicarnassæus*, who, if the Censure of *Bodin* may be taken, *Græcos omnes & Latinos superasse videatur*.[20] Let him from hence pass to *Livy*, of whom the famous Critick says,

Hoc solum ingenium (de Historicis Loquor) populus Romanus par Imperio suo habuit,[21] and supply those of his *Decads* that are lost, from the best Fragments of Antiquity, in others (and especially *Dion* and *Salust*) that lead us on still further in our way. Let him then proceed unto the Writers of the *Cesarean* times, and first revolve *Suetonius*, then *Tacitus*, then *Herodian*, then a whole Army more of *Historians*, which now crowd into our *Library;* and unto all the rest, let him not fail of adding the Incomparable *Plutarch*, whose Books they say, *Theodore Gaza* preferred above any in the World, next unto the Inspired Oracles of the *Bible:* But if the Number be still too little to satisfie an *Historical Appetite*, let him add *Polyhistor* unto the number, and all the *Chronicles* of the following Ages. After all, he must sensibly acknowledge, that the two short Books of *Ecclesiastical History*, written by the Evangelist *Luke*, hath given us more *glorious Entertainments*, than all these voluminous Historians if they were put all together. The *Atchievements* of one *Paul* particularly, which that Evangelist hath *Emblazon'd*, have more *True Glory* in them, than all the Acts of those Execrable *Plunderers* and *Murderers*, and irresistible *Banditti* of the World, which have been dignified with the Name of *Conquerors*. *Tacitus* counted *Ingentia bella, Expugnationes urbium, fusos captosque Reges*,[22] the Ravages of *War*, and the glorious *Violences*, whereof great Warriors make a wretched Ostentation, to be the *Noblest Matter* for an *Historian*. But there is a *Nobler*, I humbly conceive, in the planting and forming of *Evangelical Churches*, and the *Temptations*, the *Corruptions*, the *Afflictions*, which assault them, and their *Salvations* from those Assaults, and the Exemplary *Lives* of those that Heaven employs to be Patterns of *Holiness* and *Usefulness* upon Earth: And unto such it is, that I now invite my Readers; Things, in comparison whereof, the Subjects of many other Histories, are of as little weight, as the Questions about Z, the last Letter of our Alphabet, and whether H is to be pronounced with an Aspiration, where about whole Volumes have been written, and of no more Account, than the Composure of *Didymus*.[23] But for the *manner* of my treating this *Matter*, I must now give some account unto him.

§. 5. *Reader!* I have done the part of an *Impartial Historian*, albeit not without all occasion perhaps, for the Rule which a worthy Writer, in his *Historica*, gives to every Reader, *Historici Legantur cum Moderatione & venia, & cogitetur fieri non posse ut in omnibus circumstantiis sint Lymei*.[24] *Polybius* complains of those *Historians*, who always made either the *Carthagenians* brave, and the *Romans* base, or *è contra*, in all their Actions, as their *Affection* for their own *Party* led them. I have endeavoured, with all *good Conscience*, to decline this writing meerly for a *Party*, or doing like the Dealer in History, whom *Lucian* derides, for always calling the Captain of his own Party an *Achilles*, but of the adverse Party a *Thersites:* Nor have I added unto the just Provocations for the Complaint made by the Baron *Maurier*,[25] That the *greatest part of Histories* are but so many *Panegyricks* composed by *Interested Hands*, which *elevate Iniquity to the Heavens*, like *Paterculus*, and like *Machiavel*, who propose *Tiberius Cesar*, and *Cesar Borgia*, as Examples fit for *Imitiation*, whereas *True History* would have Exhibited them as Horrid *Monsters* as very *Devils*. 'Tis true, I am not of the Opinion, that one cannot merit the Name of an *Impartial Historian*, except he write bare *Matters of Fact*, without all *Reflection;* for I can tell where to find this given as the Definition of *History*, *Historia est rerum gestarum, cum laude aut vituperatione, Narratio:*[26] And if I am not altogether a *Tacitus*, when *Vertues* or *Vices* occur to be Matters of *Reflection*, as well as of *Relation*, I will, for my Vindication, appeal to *Tacitus* himself, whom *Lipsius* calls one of the *Prudentest* (tho' *Tertullian*, long before, counts him the *Lyingest*) of them who have Inriched the World with *History:* He says, *Præcipuum munus Annalium reor, ne virtutes sileantur, utque pravis Dictis, Factisque ex posteritate & Infamia metus sit.*[27] I have not *Commended* any Person, but when I have really judg'd, not only *That* he *Deserved* it, but also that it would be a Benefit unto Posterity to know, Wherein he deserved it: And my Judgment of *Desert*, hath not been *Biassed*, by Persons being of my own particular Judgment in matters of *Disputation*, among the Churches of God. I have been as willing to wear the Name of *Simplicius Verinus*,[28] throughout my whole undertaking, as he that, before me, hath assumed it: Nor am I like Pope *Zachary*, impatient so much as to hear of any *Antipodes*.[29] The Spirit of a *Schlusselbergius*,[30] who falls foul with Fury and Reproach on all who differ from him; The Spirit of an *Heylin*,[5] who seems to count no Obloquy too hard for a *Reformer;* and the Spirit of those (*Folio-writers* there are, some of them, in the English Nation!) whom a Noble Historian Stigmatizes, as, *Those Hot-headed, Passionate Bigots, from whom, 'tis enough, if you be of a Religion contrary unto theirs, to be defamed, condemned and pursued with a thousand Calumnies*. I thank Heaven I Hate it with all my Heart. But how can the *Lives* of the *Commendable* be written without *Commending* them? Or, is that Law of *History* given in one of the eminentest pieces of *Antiquity* we now have in our hands, wholly antiquated, *Maxime proprium est Historiæ, Laudem rerum egregie gestarum persequi?*[31] Nor have I, on the other side, forbore to mention many *Censurable* things, even in the Best of my Friends, when the things, in my opinion, were *not Good;* or so bore away for *Placentia*, in the course of our Story, as to pass by *Verona;* [32] but been mindful of the Direction which *Polybius* gives to the Historian, *It becomes him that writes an History, sometimes to extol Enemies in his Praises, when their praise-worthy Actions bespeak it, and at the same time to reprove the best Friends, when their Deeds appear worthy of a reproof; in-as much as History is good for nothing, if Truth (which is the very Eye of the Animal) be not in it.* Indeed I have thought it my duty upon all accounts, (and if it have proceeded unto the degree of a *Fault,* there is, it may be, something in my *Temper* and *Nature,* that has betray'd me therein) to be more sparing and easie, in thus mentioning of *Censurable* things, than in my *other Liberty:* A writer of *Church-History,* should, I know, be like the *builder of the Temple,* one of the *Tribe* of *Naphthali;* and for this I will also plead my *Polybius* in my Excuse; *It is not the Work of an Historian, to commemorate the Vices and Villanies of Men, so much as their just, their fair, their honest Actions: And the Readers of History get more good by the Objects of their Emulation, than of their Indignation.* Nor do I deny, that tho' I cannot approve the Conduct of *Josephus,* (whom *Jerom* not unjustly nor ineptly calls, *The Greek Livy*) when he left out of his *Antiquities,* the Story of the *Golden Calf,* and I don't wonder to find *Chamier,* and *Rivet,*[33] and others, taxing him for his *Partiality* towards his Country-men; yet I have left unmentioned some *Censurable Occurrences* in the *Story* of our *Colonies,* as things no less *Unuseful* than *Improper* to be raised out of the Grave, wherein *Oblivion* hath now buried them; lest I should have incurred the *Pasquil* bestowed upon Pope *Urban,* who employing a *Committee* to Rip up the *Old Errors* of his Predecessors, one clap'd a pair of Spurs upon the heels of the Statue of St. *Peter;* and a Label from the Statue of St. *Paul* opposite thereunto, upon the Bridge, ask'd him, *Whither he was bound?* St. *Peter* answered, *I apprehend some Danger in staying here; I fear they'll call me in Question for denying my Master.* And St. *Paul* replied, *Nay, then I had best be gone too, for they'll question me also, for Persecuting the Christians before my Conversion.*[34] Briefly, My Pen shall Reproach none, that can give a Good Word unto any Good Man that is not of their *own Faction,* and shall *Fall out* with none, but those that can *Agree* with no body else, except those of their own *Schism.* If I draw any sort of Men with *Charcoal,* it shall be, because I remember a notable passage of the *Best Queen* that ever was in the World, our late Queen *Mary.* Monsieur *Juvien,* that he might Justifie the Reformation in *Scotland,* made a very black Representation of their old Queen *Mary;* for which, a certain *Sycophant* would have incensed our Queen *Mary* against that Reverend Person, saying, *Is it not a Shame that this Man, without any Consideration for your Royal Person, should dare to throw such Infamous Calumnies upon a Queen, from whom your Royal Highness is descended?* But that Excellent Princess replied, *No, not at all; Is it not enough that by fulsome Praises great Persons be lull'd asleep all their Lives; But must Flattery accompany them to their very Graves? How should they fear the Judgment of Posterity, if Historians be not allowed to speak the Truth after their Death?* But whether I do my self *Commend,* or whether I give my Reader an opportunity to *Censure,* I am careful above all things to do it with *Truth;* and as I have considered the words of *Plato, Deum indigne & graviter ferre, cum quis ei similem hoc est, virtute præstantem, vituperet, aut laudet contrarium:* [35] So I have had the *Ninth Commandment* of a greater *Law-giver* than *Plato,* to preserve my care of *Truth* from first to last. If any Mistake have been any where committed, it will be found meerly *Circumstantial,* and wholly *Involuntary;* and let it be remembred, that tho' no *Historian* ever merited better than the Incomparable *Thuanus,*[36] yet learned Men have said of *his* Work, what they never shall truly say of *ours,* that it contains *multa falsissima & indigna.*[37] I find *Erasmus* himself mistaking *One* Man for *Two,* when writing of the Ancients. And even our own English Writers too are often mistaken, and in Matters of a very late Importance, as *Baker,* and *Heylin,* and *Fuller,* (professed Historians) tell us, that *Richard Sutton,* a single Man, founded the *Charter-House;* whereas his Name was *Thomas,* and he was a married Man. I think I can Recite such Mistakes, it may be *Sans* Number occurring in the most credible Writers; yet I hope I shall *commit* none such. But altho' I thus challenge, as my due, the Character of an *Impartial,* I doubt I may not challenge *That* of an *Elegant Historian.* I cannot say, whether the *Style,* wherein this *Church-History* is written, will please the Modern *Criticks:* But if I seem to have used ἁπλουστάτῃ συντάξει γραφῆς,[38] a Simple, Submiss, Humble *Style,* 'tis the same that *Eusebius* affirms to have been used by *Hegesippus,* who, as far as we understand, was the first Author (after *Luke*) that ever composed an entire Body of *Ecclesiastical History,* which he divided into *Five Books,* and Entitled, ὑπομνήματα των ἐκκλησιαστικῶν πραξεων.[39] Whereas *others,* it may be, will reckon the *Style* Embellished with too much of *Ornament,* by the multiplied References to other and former Concerns, closely couch'd, for the Observation of the *Attentive,* in almost every Paragraph; but I must confess, that I am of his mind who said, *Sicuti sal modice cibis aspersus Condit, & gratiam saporis addit, ita si paulum Antiquitatis admiscueris, Oratio fit venustior.*[40] And I have seldom seen that Way of Writing faulted, but by those, who, for a certain odd Reason, sometimes find fault, *That the Grapes are not ripe.* These *Embellishments* (of which yet I only—

Veniam pro laude peto [41]) are not the puerile Spoils of *Polyanthea's;* but I should have asserted them to be as choice *Flowers* as most that occur in Ancient or Modern Writings, almost unavoidably putting themselves into the Authors Hand, while about his Work, if those words of *Ambrose* had not a little frighted me, as well as they did *Baronius, Unumquemque Fallunt sua scripta.* [42] I observe that Learned Men have been so terrified by the Reproaches of *Pedantry*, which little Smatterers at Reading and Learning have, by their *Quoting Humours* brought upon themselves, that, for to avoid all Approaches towards that which those Feeble Creatures have gone to imitate, the best way of Writing has been most injuriously deserted. But what shall we say? The Best way of Writing, under Heaven, shall be the Worst, when *Erasmus* his Monosyllable Tyrant will have it so! [43] And if I should have resign'd my self wholly to the Judgment of *others*, What way of Writing to have taken, the Story of the two Statues made by *Policletus* tells me, what may have been the Issue: He contrived one of them according to the Rules that best pleased himself, and the other according to the Fancy of every one that look'd upon his Work: The former was afterwards Applauded by all, and the latter Derided by those very Persons who had given their Directions for it. As for such *Unaccuracies* as the *Critical* may discover, *Opere in longo*, [44] I appeal to the *Courteous*, for a favourable Construction of them; and certainly they will be favourably Judged of, when there is considered the *Variety* of my *other Employments*, which have kept me in continual Hurries, I had almost said, like those of the *Ninth Sphere*, for the few Months in which this Work has been *Digesting*. It was a thing well thought, by the wise Designers of *Chelsey-Colledge*, wherein able *Historians* were one sort of Persons to be maintained; That the Romanists do in one Point condemn the Protestants; for among the Romanists, they don't burden their *Professors* with any *Parochial Incumbrances;* but among the *Protestants*, the very same *Individual* Man must *Preach, Catechize*, Administer the *Sacraments*, Visit the Afflicted, and manage all the parts of *Church-Discipline;* and if any *Books* for the Service of Religion, be written, Persons thus *extreamly incumbred* must be the Writers. Now, of all the Churches under Heaven, there are none that expect so much *Variety* of Service from their Pastors, as those of *New-England;* and of all the Churches in *New-England*, there are none that require more, than those in *Boston*, the Metropolis of the English *America;* whereof *one* is, by the Lord Jesus Christ, committed unto the Care of the unworthy Hand, by which this *History* is compiled. Reader, Give me leave humbly to mention, with him in *Tully, Antequam de Re, Pauca de Me!* [45] Constant *Sermons*, usually more than once, and perhaps three or four times, in a Week, and all the other Duties of a *Pastoral Watchfulness*, a very *large Flock* has all this while demanded of me; wherein, if I had been furnished with as many *Heads* as a *Typheus*, as many *Eyes* as an *Argos*, and as many *Hands* as a *Briareus*, I might have had Work enough to have employ'd them all; nor hath my *Station* left me free from Obligations to spend very much time in the *Evangelical Service* of *others* also. It would have been a great *Sin* in me, to have *Omitted*, or *Abated*, my Just Cares, to *fulfil my Ministry in these things*, and in a manner *Give my self wholly to them.* All the time I have had for my *Church-History*, hath been perhaps only, or chiefly, that, which I might have taken else for less profitable Recreations; and it hath all been done by *Snatches.* My Reader will not find me the Person intended in his *Littany*, when he says, *Libera me ab homine unius Negotis:* [46] Nor have I spent *Thirty Years* in shaping this my *History*, as *Diodorus Siculus* did for his, (and yet both *Bodinus* and *Sigonius* complain of the Σφαλματα[47] attending it.) But I wish I could have enjoy'd entirely for this Work, one quarter of the little more than *Two Years* which have roll'd away since I began it; whereas I have been forced sometimes wholly to throw by the Work whole Months together, and then resume it, but by a stolen hour or two in a day, not without some hazard of incurring the *Title* which *Coryat* put upon his History of his Travels, *Crudities hastily gobbled up in five Months.* *Protogenes* being seven Years in drawing a Picture, *Apelles* upon the sight of it, said, *The Grace of the Work was much allay'd by the length of the Time.* Whatever else there may have been to take off the *Grace of the Work*, now in the Readers hands, (whereof the *Pictures* of Great and Good Men make a considerable part) I am sure there hath not been the *length of the Time* to do it. Our English Martyrologer, counted it a sufficient *Apology*, for what Meanness might be found in the first Edition of his *Acts and Monuments*, that it was *hastily rashed up in about fourteen Months:* And I may Apologize for this Collection of our *Acts and Monuments*, that I should have been glad, in the little more than *Two Years* which have ran out, since I enter'd upon it, if I could have had one half of *About fourteen Months* to have entirely devoted thereunto. But besides the *Time*, which the *Daily Services* of *my own* first, and then many *other* Churches, have necessarily call'd for, I have lost abundance of precious *Time*, thro' the feeble and broken State of my *Health*, which hath unfitted me for *Hard Study;* I can do nothing to purpose at *Lucubrations.* And yet, in this *Time* also of the two or three Years last past, I have not been excused from the further Diversion of *Publishing* (tho' not so many as they say *Mercurius Trismegistus* did, yet) more than a *Score* of other *Books*, upon a copious Variety of other Subjects, besides the composing of several more, that are not yet published. . . . My Reader sees, why I commit the Fault of a περιαυτία,[48] which appears in the mention of these Minute-passages; 'tis to excuse whatever other Fault of In-accuracy, or Inadvertency, may be discovered in an History, which hath been a sort of Rapsody made up (like the Paper whereon 'tis written!) with many little Rags, torn from an Employment, multi-farious enough to overwhelm one of my small Capacities. . . .

§. 6. I hope 'tis a right Work that I have done; but we are not yet arrived unto the *Day, wherein God will bring every Work into Judgment* (the Day of the *Kingdom* that was promised unto *David*) and a Son of *David* hath as Truly as Wisely told us, that until the arrival of that Happy Day, this is one of the *Vanities* attending Humane Affairs; *For a right VVork a Man shall be envied of his Neighbour.* It will not be so much a Surprise unto me, if I should live to see our *Church-History* vexed with *Anie-mad-versions* of Calumnious Writers, as it would have been unto *Virgil,* to read his *Bucolicks* reproached by the *Antibucolica* of a *Nameless Scribbler,* and his *Æneids* travestied by the *Æneidomastix* of *Carbilius:* Or *Herennius* taking pains to make a Collection of the *Faults,* and *Faustinus* of the *Thefts,* in his incomparable Composures: Yea, *Pliny,* and *Seneca* themselves, and our *Jerom,* reproaching him, as a Man of no Judgment, nor Skill in Sciences; while *Pædianus* affirms of him, that he was himself, *Usque adeo invidiæ Expers, ut si quid erudite dictum inspiceret alterius, non minus gauderet ac si suum-esset.*[49] How should a Book, no better laboured than this of ours, escape *Zoilian* Outrages, when in all Ages, the most exquisite Works have been as much vilified, as *Plato's* by *Scaliger,* and *Aristotle's* by *Lactantius?* In the time of our K. *Edward* VI. there was an Order to bring in all the Teeth of St. *Apollonia,* which the People of his one Kingdom carried about them for the Cure of the *Tooth ach;* and they were so many, that they almost fill'd a Tun. Truly *Envy* hath as many *Teeth* as Madam *Apol-lonia* would have had, if all those pretended Reliques had been really hers. And must all these *Teeth* be fastned on thee, *O my Book?* It may be so! And yet the *Book,* when ground between these *Teeth,* will prove like *Ignatius* in the *Teeth* of the furious Tygers, *The whiter Manchet for the Churches of God.* The greatest and fiercest Rage of *Envy,* is that which I expect from those IDUMÆANS,[50] whose Religion is all Ceremony, and whose Charity is more for them who deny the most Essential things in the Articles and Homilies of the Church of *England,* than for the most Conscientious Men in the World, who manifest their being so, by their Dissent in some little Ceremony: Or those Persons whose Hearts are notably expressed in those words used by one of them ('tis *Howel* in his *Familiar Letters*, Vol. 1. Sect. 6. Lett. 32.) *I rather pitty, than hate, Turk or Infidel, for they are of the same Metal, and bear the same Stamp, as I do, tho' the Inscriptions differ; If I hate any, 'tis those Schismaticks that puzzle the sweet Peace of our Church; so that I could be content to see an Anabaptist go to Hell on a Brownists Back.* The Writer whom I last quoted, hath given us a Story of a young Man in *High-Holbourn*, who being after his death Dissected, there was a Serpent with divers tails, found in the left Ventricle of his Heart. I make no question, that our Church-History will find some Reader disposed like that Writer, with an Heart as full of Serpent and Venom as ever it can hold: Nor indeed will they be able to hold, but the Tongues and Pens of those angry Folks, will scourge me as with Scorpions, and cause me to feel (if I will feel) as many Lashes as *Cornelius Agrippa* [51] expected from their Brethren, for the Book in which he exposed their Vanities. . . .

Reader, I also expect nothing but *Scourges* from that Generation, to whom the *Mass-book* is dearer than the *Bible*. But I have now likewise confessed another Expectation, that shall be my Consolation under all. They tell us, That on the highest of the *Capsian* Mountains in *Spain*, there is a Lake, whereinto if you throw a Stone, there presently ascends a Smoke, which forms a dense Cloud, from whence issues a Tempest of Rain, Hail, and horrid Thunder-claps, for a good quarter of an hour. Our Church-History will be like a Stone cast into that Lake, for the furious Tempest which it will raise among some, whose Ecclesiastical Dignities have set them, as on the top of Spanish Mountains. The Catholick Spirit of Communion wherewith 'tis written, and the Liberty which I have taken, to tax the Schismatical Impositions and Persecutions of a Party, who have always been as real Enemies to the English Nation, as to the Christian and Protestant Interest, will certainly bring upon the whole Composure, the quick Censures of that Party, at the first cast of their look upon it. In the Duke of *Alva's* Council of twelve Judges, there was one *Hessels* a *Flemming*, who slept always at the Trial of Criminals, and when they wak'd him to deliver his Opinion, he rub'd his Eyes, and cry'd, between sleeping and waking, *Ad patibulum! ad Patibulum!* To the Gallows with 'em! (And, by the way, this Blade was himself, at the last, condemned unto the Gallows, without an Hearing!) As quick Censures must this our Labour expect from those who will not bestow waking thoughts upon the Representations of Christianity here made unto the World; but have a Sentence of Death always to pass, or at least,

Wish, upon those Generous Principles, without which, 'tis impossible
to maintain the Reformation: And I confess, I am very well content,
that this our Labour takes the Fate of those Principles: Nor do I
dissent from the words of the Excellent *VVhitaker* upon *Luther, Fœlix
ille, quem Dominus eo Honore dignatus est, ut Homines nequissimos suos
haberet inimicos.*[52] But if the old Epigrammatist, when he saw Guilty
Folks raving Mad at his Lines, could say—

> *Hoc volo; nunc nobis carmina nostra placent:* [53]

Certainly an Historian should not be displeased at it, if the Enemies
of Truth discover their Madness at the true and free Communications
of his History; and therefore the more Stones they throw at this Book,
there will not only be the more Proofs, that it is a Tree which hath
good Fruits growing upon it, but I will build my self a Monument
with them, whereon shall be inscribed, that Clause in the Epitaph of
the Martyr *Stephen:*

> *Excepit Lapides, cui petra Christus erat:* [54]

Albeit perhaps the *Epitaph*, which the old *Monks* bestow'd upon
Wickliff, will be rather endeavour'd for me, (*If I am thought worth one!*)
by the Men, who will, with all possible *Monkery*, strive to stave off the
approaching *Reformation*.[55]
But since an Undertaking of this Nature, must thus encounter so
much Envy, from those who are under the Power of the *Spirit that
works in the Children of Unperswadeableness*, methinks I might perswade
my self, that it will find another sort of Entertainment from those
Good Men who have a better Spirit in them: For, as the Apostle
James hath noted, (so with Monsieur *Claude* I read it) *The Spirit
that is in us, lusteth against Envy;* and yet even in *us* also, there will be
the *Flesh*, among whose Works, one is *Envy*, which will be *Lusting*
against the *Spirit*. All Good Men will not be satisfied with every
thing that is here set before them. In my own Country, besides a
considerable number of loose and vain Inhabitants risen up, to
whom the Congregational Church-Discipline, which cannot Live well,
where the Power of Godliness dyes, is become distastful for the Purity
of it; there is also a number of eminently Godly Persons, who are
for a Larger way,[56] and unto these my Church-History will give distast, by the things which it may happen to utter, in favour of that
Church-Discipline on some few occasions; and the Discoveries which
I may happen to make of my Apprehensions, that *Scripture*, and *Reason*,
and *Antiquity* is for it; and that it is not far from a glorious Resurrec-

tion. But that, as the Famous Mr. *Baxter*, after Thirty or Forty Years hard Study, about the true Instituted Church-Discipline, at last, not only own'd, but also invincibly prov'd, That it is *The Congregational;* so, The further that the *Unprejudiced Studies* of Learned Men proceed in this Matter, the more generally the *Congregational Church-Discipline* will be pronounced for. On the other side, There are some among us, who very strictly profess the *Congregational Church-Discipline*, but at the same time they have an unhappy Narrowness of Soul, by which they confine their value and Kindness too much unto their own Party; and unto those my *Church History* will be offensive, because my Regard unto our own declared Principles, does not hinder me from giving the Right hand of Fellowship unto the valuable Servants of the Lord Jesus Christ, who find not our Church-Discipline as yet agreeable unto their present Understandings and Illuminations. If it be thus in my own Country, it cannot be otherwise in That whereto I send this account of my own. Briefly, as it hath been said, That if all *Episcopal* Men were like Archbishop *Usher*,[57] and all *Presbyterians* like *Stephen Marshal*,[58] and all *Independents* like *Jeremiah Burroughs*,[59] the Wounds of the Church would soon be healed; my Essay to carry that Spirit through this whole Church-History, will bespeak Wounds for it, from those that are of another Spirit. And there will also be in every Country those Good Men, who yet have not had the Grace of Christ so far prevailing in them, as utterly to divest them of that piece of Ill Nature which the Comedian resents, *In homine Imperito, quo nil quicquam Injustius, quia nisi quod ipse facit, nil recte factum putat.*[60]

However, All these things, and an hundred more such things which I think of, are very small Discouragements for such a Service as I have here endeavoured. I foresee a Recompence, which will abundantly swallow up all Discouragements! It may be *Strato* the Philosopher counted himself well recompensed for his Labours, when *Ptolomy* bestow'd fourscore Talents on him. It may be *Archimelus* the Poet counted himself well recompensed, when *Hiero* sent him a thousand Bushels of Wheat for one little Epigram: And *Saleius* the Poet might count himself well recompensed, when *Vespasian* sent him twelve thousand and five hundred *Philippicks;* and *Oppian* the Poet might count himself well recompensed, when *Caracalla* sent him a piece of Gold for every Line that he had inscribed unto him. As I live in a Country where such Recompences never were in fashion; it hath no Preferments for me, and I shall count that I am well Rewarded in it, if I can escape without being heavily Reproached, Censured and Condemned, for what I have done: So I thank the Lord, I should exceedingly Scorn all such mean Considerations, I seek not out for Benefactors, to whom these Labours may be Dedicated: There is ONE to whom all is due! From Him I shall have a Recompence: And what Recompence? The Recompence, whereof I do, with inexpressible Joy, assure my self, is this, *That these my poor Labours will certainly serve the Churches and Interests of the Lord Jesus Christ.* And I think I may say, That I ask to live no longer, than I count a Service unto the Lord Jesus Christ, and his Churches, to be it self a glorious Recompence for the doing of it. When *David* was contriving to build the House of God, there was that order given from Heaven concerning him, *Go tell* David, *my Servant.* The adding of *that* more than *Royal Title* unto the Name of *David*, was a sufficient Recompence for all his Contrivance about the House of God. In our whole *Church-History*, we have been at work for the House of the Lord Jesus Christ, (Even that *Man* who is the *Lord God*, and whose *Form* seems on that occasion represented unto His *David*.) And herein 'tis Recompence enough, that I have been a *Servant* unto that heavenly Lord. The greatest *Honour*, and the sweetest *Pleasure*, out of *Heaven*, is to Serve our Illustrious Lord JESUS CHRIST, who hath *loved us, and given himself for us;* and unto whom it is infinitely reasonable that we should *give our selves*, and all that we *have* and *Are:* And it may be the *Angels* in *Heaven* too, aspire not after an higher Felicity.

Unto thee, therefore, O thou Son of God, and King of Heaven, and Lord of all things, whom all the Glorious Angels of Light, unspeakably love to Glorifie; I humbly offer up a poor History of Churches, which own thee alone for their Head, and Prince, and Law-giver; Churches which thou hast purchas'd with thy own Blood, and with wonderful Dispensations of thy Providence hitherto protected and preserved; and of a People which thou didst Form for thy self, to shew forth thy Praises. I bless thy great Name, for thy inclining of me to, and carrying of me through, the Work of this History: I pray thee to sprinkle the Book of this History with thy Blood, and make it acceptable and profitable unto thy Churches, and serve thy Truths and Ways among thy People, by that which thou hast here prepared; for 'tis THOU *that hast prepar'd it for them.* Amen.

Quid sum? Nil. Quis sum? Nullus. Sed Gratia CHRISTI, *Quod sum, quod Vivo, quodque Laboro, facit.*[61]

THE
SIMPLE COBLER
OF
AGGAVVAM in AMERICA.

WILLING
To help 'mend his Native Country, lamentably tattered, both in the upper-Leather
and sole, with all the honest stitches he can take.

And as willing never to bee paid for his work,
by Old English wonted pay.

It is his Trade to patch all the year long, gratis.

Therefore I pray Gentlemen keep your purses.

By *Theodore de la Guard.*

In rebus arduis ac tenui spe, fortissima quaeque consilia tutissima sunt. Cic.

In English,
When bootes and shoes are torne up to the lefts,
Coblers must thrust their awles up to the hefts.

This is no time to feare *Apelles gramm:*
Ne Sutor quidem ultra crepidam.

LONDON,
Printed by *J. D. & R. I.* for *Stephen Bowtell*, at the signe of the
Bible in Popes Head-Alley, 1647.

Title Page of Nathaniel Ward's *The Simple Cobler.*

Chapter II

THE THEORY OF THE STATE AND OF
SOCIETY

I T HAS often been said that the end of the seventeenth and the beginning of the eighteenth century mark the first real break with
the Middle Ages in the history of European thought. Even though
the Renaissance and Reformation transformed many aspects of the
Western intellect, still it was not until the time of Newton that the
modern scientific era began; only then could men commence to regard life in this world as something more than preparation for life
beyond the grave. Certainly if the eighteenth century inaugurated the
modern epoch in natural sciences, so also did it in the political and
social sciences. For the first time since the fall of the Roman Empire
religion could be separated from politics, doctrinal orthodoxy divorced
from loyalty to the state, and the citizens of a nation permitted to
worship in diverse churches and to believe different creeds without
endangering the public peace. Various factors contributed to effecting
this revolution; the triumph of scientific method and of rationalism
made impossible the older belief that government was of divine origin;
the rise of capitalism, of the middle class, and eventually of democracy, necessitated new conceptions of the rôle of the state. Social
leadership in England and America was assumed by a group of gentlemen who were, by and large, deists or skeptics, and to them all religious issues had become supremely boring. At the same time the
churches themselves, particularly the newer evangelical denominations,
were swinging round to a theology that made religious belief the subjective experience of individual men, entirely unrelated to any particular political philosophy or social theory.

In order to understand Puritanism we must go behind these eighteenth-century developments to an age when the unity of religion and
politics was so axiomatic that very few men would even have grasped
the idea that church and state could be distinct. For the Puritan
mind it was not possible to segregate a man's spiritual life from his
communal life. Massachusetts was settled for religious reasons, but as
John Winthrop announced, religious reasons included "a due forme
of Government both ciuill and ecclesiasticall," and the civil was quite
as important in his eyes as the ecclesiastical. Only in recent years has
it become possible for us to view the political aspects of Puritanism
with something like comprehension and justice. For two centuries our

social thinking has been dominated by ideas which were generated in the course of a sweeping revolt against everything for which the Puritans stood; the political beliefs of the Puritans were forgotten, or, if remembered at all, either deplored or condemned as unfortunate remnants of medievalism. Puritanism has been viewed mainly as a religious and ethical movement. But of late years the standards of the eighteenth century have for the first time come under serious criticism and in many quarters are showing the strain. In these circumstances the social philosophy of Puritanism takes on a new interest, and quite possibly becomes for us the most instructive and valuable portion of the Puritan heritage.

The Puritan theory of the state began with the hypothesis of original sin. Had Adam transmitted undiminished to his descendants the image of God in which he had been created, no government would ever have been necessary among men; they would all then have done justice to each other without the supervision of a judge, they would have respected each other's rights without the intervention of a policeman. But the Bible said—and experience proved—that since the fall, without the policeman, the judge, the jail, the law, and the magistrate, men will rob, murder, and fight among themselves; without a coercive state to restrain evil impulses and administer punishments, no life will be safe, no property secure, no honor observed. Therefore, upon Adam's apostasy, God Himself instituted governments among men. He left the particular form to be determined by circumstance—this was one important human art on which the Puritans said the Bible was *not* an absolute and imperious lawgiver—but He enacted that all men should be under some sort of corporate rule, that they should all submit to the sway of their superiors, that no man should live apart from his fellows, that the government should have full power to enforce obedience and to inflict every punishment that the crimes of men deserved.

There was a strong element of individualism in the Puritan creed; every man had to work out his own salvation, each soul had to face his maker alone. But at the same time, the Puritan philosophy demanded that in society all men, at least all regenerate men, be marshaled into one united array. The lone horseman, the single trapper, the solitary hunter was not a figure of the Puritan frontier; Puritans moved in groups and towns, settled in whole communities, and maintained firm government over all units. Neither was the individualistic business man, the shopkeeper who seized every opportunity to enlarge his profits, the speculator who contrived to gain wealth at the expense of his fellows, neither were these typical figures of the original Puritan society. The most obvious lesson of the selections printed herein is that Puritan opinion was at the opposite pole from Jefferson's feeling that the best government governs as little as possible. The theorists of New England thought of society as a unit, bound together by inviolable ties; they thought of it not as an aggregation of individuals but as an organism, functioning for a definite purpose, with all parts subordinate to the whole, all members contributing a definite share, every person occupying a particular status. "Society in all sorts of humane affaires is better then Solitariness," said John Cotton.[1] The society of early New England was decidedly "regimented." Puritans did not think the state was merely an umpire, standing on the side lines of a contest, limited to checking egregious fouls, but otherwise allowing men free play according to their abilities and the breaks of the game. They would have expected the rule of "laissez-faire" to result in a reign of rapine and horror. The state to them was an active instrument of leadership, discipline, and, wherever necessary, of coercion; it legislated over any or all aspects of human behavior, it not merely regulated misconduct but undertook to inspire and direct all conduct. The commanders were not to trim their policies by the desires of the people, but to drive ahead upon the predetermined course; the people were all to turn out as they were ordered, and together they were to crowd sail to the full capacity of the vessel. The officers were above the common men, as the quarter-deck is above the forecastle. There was no idea of the equality of all men. There was no questioning that men who would not serve the purposes of the society should be whipped into line. The objectives were clear and unmistakable; any one's disinclination to dedicate himself to them was obviously so much recalcitrancy and depravity. The government of Massachusetts, and of Connecticut as well, was a dictatorship, and never pretended to be anything else; it was a dictatorship, not of a single tyrant, or of an economic class, or of a political faction, but of the holy and regenerate. Those who did not hold with the ideals entertained by the righteous, or who believed God had preached other principles, or who desired that in religious belief, morality, and ecclesiastical preferences all men should be left at liberty to do as they wished— such persons had every liberty, as Nathaniel Ward said, to stay away from New England. If they did come, they were expected to keep their opinions to themselves; if they discussed them in public or attempted to act upon them, they were exiled; if they persisted in re-

[1] *A Briefe Exposition . . . upon . . . Ecclesiastes* (London, 1654), p. 85.

turning, they were cast out again; if they still came back, as did four
Quakers, they were hanged on Boston Common. And from the Puritan
point of view, it was good riddance.

These views of the nature and function of the state were not peculiar to the Puritans of New England; they were the heritage of the
past, the ideals, if not always the actuality, of the previous centuries.
That government was established by God in order to save depraved
men from their own depravity had been orthodox Christian teaching
for centuries; that men should be arranged in serried ranks, inferiors
obeying superiors, was the essence of feudalism; that men should live
a social life, that profit-making should be restrained within the limits
of the "just price," that the welfare of the whole took precedence
over any individual advantage, was the doctrine of the medieval
church, and of the Church of England in the early seventeenth century. Furthermore, in addition to these general principles, there were
two or three more doctrines in the New England philosophy which
also were common to the age and the background. All the world at
that moment believed with them that the church was to be maintained and protected by the civil authority, and a certain part of the
world was contending that government was limited by fundamental
law and that it took its origin from the consent of the people.

Every respectable state in the Western world assumed that it could
allow only one church to exist within its borders, that every citizen
should be compelled to attend it and conform to its requirements,
and that all inhabitants should pay taxes for its support. When the
Puritans came to New England the idea had not yet dawned that a
government could safely permit several creeds to exist side by side
within the confines of a single nation. They had not been fighting in
England for any milk-and-water toleration, and had they been offered
such religious freedom as dissenters now enjoy in Great Britain they
would have scorned to accept such terms. Only a hypocrite, a person
who did not really believe what he professed, would be content to
practice his religion under such conditions. The Puritans were assured that they alone knew the exact truth, as it was contained in
the written word of God, and they were fighting to enthrone it in
England and to extirpate utterly and mercilessly all other pretended
versions of Christianity. When they could not succeed at home, they
came to America, where they could establish a society in which the
one and only truth should reign forever. There is nothing so idle as
to praise the Puritans for being in any sense conscious or deliberate
pioneers of religious liberty—unless, indeed, it is still more idle to

berate them because in America they persecuted dissenters from their beliefs after they themselves had undergone persecution for differing with the bishops. To allow no dissent from the truth was exactly the reason they had come to America. They maintained here precisely what they had maintained in England, and if they exiled, fined, jailed, whipped, or hanged those who disagreed with them in New England, they would have done the same thing in England could they have secured the power. It is almost pathetic to trace the puzzlement of New England leaders at the end of the seventeenth century, when the idea of toleration was becoming more and more respectable in European thought. They could hardly understand what was happening in the world, and they could not for a long time be persuaded that they had any reason to be ashamed of their record of so many Quakers whipped, blasphemers punished by the amputation of ears, Antinomians exiled, Anabaptists fined, or witches executed. By all the lights which had prevailed in Europe at the time the Puritans had left, these were achievements to which any government could point with pride. In 1681 a congregation of Anabaptists, who led a stormy and precarious existence for several years in Charlestown, published an attack upon the government of Massachusetts Bay; they justified themselves by appealing to the example of the first settlers, claiming that like themselves the founders had been nonconformists and had fled to New England to establish a refuge for persecuted consciences. When Samuel Willard, minister of the Third Church in Boston, read this, he could hardly believe his eyes; he hastened to assure the authors that they did not know what they were talking about:

I perceive they are mistaken in the design of our first Planters, whose business was not Toleration; but were professed Enemies of it, and could leave the World professing they *died no Libertines*. Their business was to settle, and (as much as in them lay) secure Religion to Posterity, according to that way which they believed was of God.[1]

For the pamphlet in which Willard penned these lines Increase Mather wrote an approving preface. Forty years later, he and his son Cotton participated in the ordination of a Baptist minister in Boston, and he then preached on the need for harmony between differing sects. But by that time much water had gone under the bridge, the old charter had been revoked, there was danger that the Church of England might be made the established church of the colonies, theology had

[1] *Ne Sutor ultra Crepidam* (Boston, 1681), p. 4.

come to be of less importance in men's minds than morality, the tone of the eighteenth century was beginning to influence opinion—even in Boston. Increase was old and weary. Puritanism, in the true sense of the word, was dead.

Of course, the whole Puritan philosophy of church and state rested upon the assumption that the word of God was clear and explicit, that the divines had interpreted it correctly, and that no one who was not either a knave or a fool could deny their demonstrations. Ergo, it seemed plain, those who did deny them should be punished for being obstinate. John Cotton said that offenders should not be disciplined for their wrong opinions, but for persisting in them; he said that Roger Williams was not turned out of Massachusetts for his conscience, but for sinning against his own conscience. Roger Williams and John Cotton debated the question of "persecution" through several hundred pages; after they had finished, I think it is very doubtful whether Cotton had even begun to see his adversary's point. And still today it is hard to make clear the exact grounds upon which Roger Williams became the great apostle of religious liberty. Williams was not, like Thomas Jefferson, a man to whom theology and divine grace had become stuff and nonsense; on the contrary he was pious with a fervor and passion that went beyond most of his contemporaries. So exalted was his conception of the spiritual life that he could not bear to have it polluted with earthly considerations. He did not believe that any man could determine the precise intention of scripture with such dreadful certainty as the New England clergy claimed to possess. Furthermore, it seemed to him that even if their version were true, submission to truth itself was worth nothing at all when forced upon men by the sword. Williams evolved from an orthodox Puritan into the champion of religious liberty because he came to see spiritual truth as so rare, so elevated, so supernal a loveliness that it could not be chained to a wordly establishment and a vested interest. He was a libertarian because he contemned the world, and he wanted to separate church and state so that the church would not be contaminated by the state; Thomas Jefferson loved the world and was dubious about the spirit, and he sought to separate church and state so that the state would not be contaminated by the church. But John Cotton believed the state and church were partners in furthering the cause of truth; he knew that the truth was clear, definite, reasonable, and undeniable; he expected all good men to live by it voluntarily, and he was sure that all men who did not do so were obviously bad men. Bad men were criminals, whether their offense was theft or a belief in the "inner light," and they should be punished. Moses and Aaron, the priest and the statesman, were equally the viceregents of God, and the notion that one could contaminate the other was utter insanity.

The two other ideas which we have noted as being derived from the background of the age, rule by fundamental law and social compact, were the special tenets of English Puritanism. For three decades before the settlement of Massachusetts the Puritan party in England had been working hand in glove with the Parliament against the King. The absolutist Stuarts were allied with the bishops, and the Puritan agitator and the Parliamentary leader made common cause against them both. As a result of this combination, the Puritan theorists had taken over the essentials of the Parliamentary conception of society, the contention that the power of the ruler should be exercised in accordance with established fundamental law, and that the government should owe its existence to a compact of the governed. Because these ideas were strategically invaluable in England, they became ingrained in the Puritan consciousness; they were carried to New England and were preached from every pulpit in the land.

The Puritans did not see any conflict between them and their religious intentions. In New England the fundamental law was the Bible. The magistrates were to have full power to rule men for the specific purposes to which the society was dedicated; but they as well as their subordinates were tied to the specific purposes, and could not go beyond the prescribed limits. The Bible was clear and definite on the form of the church, on the code of punishments for crimes, on the general purposes of social existence; its specifications were binding on all, magistrates, ministers, and citizens. Consequently, the Puritans did not find it difficult to conclude that in those matters upon which the Bible left men free to follow their own discretion, the society itself should establish basic rules. The New England leaders and the people frequently disagreed as to what these rules were, or as to how detailed they should be made, but neither side ever doubted that the community must abide by whatever laws had been enacted, either by God or by the state. The government of New England was, as we have said, a dictatorship, but the dictators were not absolute and irresponsible. John Cotton was the clerical spokesman for the Massachusetts rulers, but he stoutly demanded "that all power that is on earth be limited."

The belief that government originated in the consent of the governed was equally congenial to the Puritan creed. The theology is often enough described as deterministic, because it held that men were predestined to heaven or hell; but we are always in danger of forgetting that the life of the Puritan was completely voluntaristic. The natural man was indeed bound in slavery to sin and unable to make exertions toward his own salvation; but the man into whose soul grace had been infused was liberated from that bondage and made free to undertake the responsibilities and obligations of virtue and decency. The holy society was erected upon the belief that the right sort of men could of their own free will and choice carry through the creation and administration of the right sort of community. The churches of New England were made up of "saints," who came into the church because they wanted membership, not because they were born in it, or were forced into it, or joined because of policy and convention. Though every resident was obliged to attend and to pay taxes for the support of the churches, no one became an actual member who did not signify his strong desire to be one. The saints were expected to act positively because they had in them a spirit of God that made them capable of every exertion. No doubt the Puritans maintained that government originated in the consent of the people because that theory was an implement for chastening the absolutism of the Stuarts; but they maintained it also because they did not believe that any society, civil or ecclesiastical, into which men did not enter of themselves was worthy of the name.

Consequently, the social theory of Puritanism, based upon the law of God, was posited also upon the voluntary submission of the citizens. As men exist in nature, said Thomas Hooker, no one person has any power over another; "there must of necessity be a mutuall ingagement, each of the other, by their free consent, before by any rule of God they have any right or power, or can exercise either, each towards the other." This truth appears, he argues, from all relations among men, that of husband and wife, master and servant; there must be a compact drawn up and sealed between them.

From *mutuall acts* of consenting and ingaging each of other, there is an impression of *ingagement* results, as a *relative bond*, betwixt the contractours and confederatours, wherein the *formalis ratio*, or *specificall nature* of the covenant lieth, in all the former instances especially *that of* corporations. So that however it is true, the rule bindes such to the duties of their places and relations, yet it is certain, it requires that they should *first freely ingage* themselves in such covenants, and *then* be carefull to fullfill such duties. A man is allowed freely to make choice of his wife, and she of her husband, before they need or should perform the duties of husband and wife one towards another.[1]

[1] *A Survey of the Summe of Church-Discipline* (London, 1648), Part I, p. 69.

The rules and regulations of society, the objectives and the duties, are erected by God; but in a healthy state the citizens must first agree to abide by those regulations, must first create the society by willing consent and active participation.

These ideas, of a uniform church supported by the civil authority, of rule by explicit law, of the derivation of the state from the consent of the people, were transported to New England because they were the stock ideas of the time and place. What the New England Puritans added of their own was the unique fashion in which they combined them into one coherent and rounded theory. The classic expression of this theory is the speech on liberty delivered by John Winthrop to the General Court in 1645. In that year Winthrop was serving as lieutenant governor, and as such was a justice of the peace; a squabble broke out in the town of Hingham over the election of a militia officer; Winthrop intervened, committing one faction for contempt of court when they would not give bond to appear peaceably before the legislature and let the affair be adjudicated. Some of the citizens were enraged, and the lower house of the General Court impeached Winthrop for exceeding his commission and going beyond the basic law of the land. He was tried and acquitted; thereupon he pronounced this magnificent oration, setting before the people the unified theory of the Puritan commonwealth.

As he expounds it, the political doctrine becomes part and parcel of the theological, and the cord that binds all ideas together is the covenant. The New England divines had already refashioned the original theology of Calvinism to bring it more into accord with the disposition of Englishmen, their most important addition being their statement of the relationship between the elect and God in the form of a covenant. As they saw it, when a man received the spirit of God, he availed himself of his liberty to enter a compact with the Deity, promising to abide by God's laws and to fulfill God's will to the best of his ability. In turn God guaranteed him redemption. A regenerate man was thus by definition committed by his own plighted word to God's cause, not only in his personal life and behaviour, but in church affairs and in society. Winthrop argues that individuals, in a natural state, before grace has been given them, are at absolute liberty to do anything they can, to lie, steal, murder; obviously he is certain that natural men, being what they are, will do exactly these things unless prevented. But when men become regenerate they are then at "liberty" to do only what God commands. And God commands certain things for the group as a whole as well as for each individual. Regenerate men, therefore, by the very fact of being regenerate, come together, form churches and a state upon explicit agreements, in which they all promise to live with one another according to the laws and for the purposes of God. Thus the government is brought into being by the act of the people; but the people do not create just any sort of government, but the one kind of government which God has outlined. The governors are elected by the people, but elected into an office which has been established by God. God engenders the society by acting through the people, as in nature He secures His effects by guiding secondary causes; the collective will of regenerate men, bound together by the social compact, projects and continues the will of God into the state. As John Davenport expressed it, "In regular actings of the creature, God is the first Agent; there are not two several and distinct actings, one of God, another of the People: but in one and the same action, God, by the Peoples suffrages, makes such an one Governour, or Magistrate, and not another." [1] So, when men have made a covenant with God they have thereby promised Him, in the very terms of that agreement, to compact among themselves in order to form a holy state in which His discipline will be practiced. As one of the ministers phrased it:

Where the Lord sets himselfe over a people, he frames them unto a willing and voluntary subjection unto him, that they desire nothing more then to be under his government . . . When the Lord is in Covenant with a people, they follow him not forcedly, but as farre as they are sanctified by grace, they submit willingly to his regiment. [2]

When men have entered these covenants, first with God, then with each other in the church and again in the state, they have thrice committed themselves to the rule of law and the control of authority. Winthrop can thus insist that though the government of Massachusetts is bound by fundamental law, and though it takes its rise from the people, and though the people elect the officials, still the people's liberty in Massachusetts consists in a "liberty to that only which is good, just and honest." By entering the covenant with God, and the covenant with each other, the citizens renounce all natural liberty, surrender the right to seek for anything that they themselves might lust after, and retain only the freedom that "is maintained and exercised in a way of subjection to authority."

The theory furnishes an excellent illustration of the intellectual ideal

---

[1] *A Sermon Preach'd at The Election . . . May 19th 1669* ([n. p.], 1670), in *Publications of the Colonial Society of Massachusetts*, X, 6.

[2] Peter Bulkeley, *The Gospel-Covenant* (London, 1651), pp. 219–220.

toward which all Puritan thought aspired; in the realm of government as of nature, the Puritan thinker strove to harmonize the determination of God with the exertion of men, the edicts of revelation with the counsels of reason and experience. On one side, this account exhibits the creation of society as flowing from the promptings and coaction of God; on the other side it attributes the origination to the teachings of nature and necessity. The social compact may be engineered by God, but it is also an eminently reasonable method of bringing a state into being. Delimitation of the ruler's power by basic law may be a divine ordinance to restrain the innate sinfulness of men, but it is also a very natural device to avoid oppression and despotism; the constitution may be promulgated to men from on high, but it is in fact very much the sort which, had they been left to their own devices, they might have contrived in the interests of efficiency and practicality. Men might conceivably have come upon the erection of governments through explicit compacts, in which they incorporated certain inviolable regulations and a guarantee of rights, quite as much by their own intelligence as by divine instruction. As always in Puritan thought, there was no intention to discredit either source, but rather to integrate the divine and the natural, revelation and reason, into a single inspiration. "Power of Civil Rule, by men orderly chosen, is Gods Ordinance," said John Davenport, even if "It is from the Light and Law of Nature," because "the Law of Nature is God's Law." [1] The Puritan state was thus from one point of view purely and simply a "theocracy"; God was the sovereign, His fiats were law and His wishes took precedence over all other considerations; the magistrates and ministers were His viceroys. But from another point of view, the Puritan state was built upon reason and the law of nature; it was set up by the covenant of the people, the scope of its power was determined by the compact, and the magistrates and ministers were the commissioned servants of the people.

As this theory stands on paper it is, like so many edifices erected by the Puritan mind, almost perfect. When it was realized in practice, however, there were at least two difficulties that soon became apparent. For one, not all the people, even in New England, were regenerate; in fact, the provable elect were a minority, probably no more than one fifth of the total population. But this did not dismay the original theorists, for they had never thought that mere numerical majorities proved anything. Consequently, though the social compact furnished the theoretical basis of society in New England, neverthe-

[1] *A Sermon Preach'd at The Election*, p. 4.

less it was confined to the special few; the election of officers and the
passing of laws was given to those only who could demonstrate their
justification and sanctification. The Congregational system, with its
membership limited to those who had proved before the church that
they possessed the signs of grace, offered a ready machinery for win-
nowing the wheat from the chaff. Therefore, under the first charter
the suffrage in Massachusetts was limited to the church members. In
Connecticut the franchise was not officially restrained in this fashion,
but other means served as well to keep the electorate pure and orthodox. The "citizens," as they were called, elected delegates to the
General Court, chose judges, and passed laws. The others, the "inhabitants," had equality before the law, property rights, police protection; they were taxed no more than the citizens or submitted to
no indignities, but they were allowed no voice in the government or
in the choice of ministers, and only by the mere force of numbers
gained any influence in town meetings.

The restriction of the franchise to church membership seemed to
solve the first difficulty confronted by the Puritan theorists. But in
time it only brought them face to face with the second and more
serious problem: the whole structure of theory which Winthrop outlined in his speech, and which the sermons of Mitchell, Stoughton,
and Hubbard reiterated, fell apart the moment the "citizens" were
no longer really and ardently holy. Just as soon as the early zeal began
to die down, and the distinction between the citizens and the inhabitants became difficult to discern, then the purely naturalistic,
rational, practical aspect of the political theory became detached from
the theological, began to stand alone and by itself. As the religious
inspiration waned, there remained no reason why all the people should
not be held partners to the social compact; the idea that God worked
His ends through the covenant of the people grew vague and obscure,
while the notion that all the people made the covenant for their own
reasons and created the state for their own purposes took on more
and more definite outlines. As toleration was forced upon the colonies
by royal command, or became more estimable as religious passions
abated, the necessity for the social bond being considered a commit-
ment of the nation to the will of God disappeared. Instead, men perceived the charms and usefulness of claiming that the compact had
been an agreement of the people, not to God's terms, but to their
own terms. The divine ordinance and the spirit of God, which were
supposed to have presided over the political process, vanished, leaving
a government founded on the self-evident truths of the law of nature,

brought into being by social compact, instituted not for the glory of God, but to secure men's "inalienable rights" of life, liberty, and the pursuit of happiness. Until Jefferson rewrote the phrase, the three interests which were to be furthered and guaranteed by the government were more candidly summarized as life, liberty—and property.

The sermon of Samuel Willard, delivered in the 1690's, betrays the merest beginnings of the change from the theological version of political principle to the purely rational and naturalistic variant, but the real revolution in the thought was first decisively proclaimed by the Reverend John Wise. He wrote his pamphlet in defence of church government only; he was aroused by a proposal that had been tentatively suggested several years previously among a group of Boston ministers, that the local autonomy of individual congregations had perhaps been carried too far and that possibly a more centralized administration would help check the degeneration of the religious spirit. Wise wrote his vindication of the Congregational system in order to demolish this ecclesiastical proposal, but in working out the philosophy of church government he had to overhaul the fundamentals of all government. The revolution he inaugurated in the thinking of New England consisted in the very organization of his book; where the early defenders of the church system discussed the Biblical and rational arguments together, or forced them to coalesce into one argument, Wise deliberately separated them into two distinct and independent chapters. He compressed into the first section of his book a recital of all the passages of scripture that had been held to substantiate the Congregational system, and then hurried on to the argument from unaided natural wisdom. The radicalism of his pamphlet is compressed into one sentence, into his suggestion that the scheme of government might be said to have originated with nature and reason, and only subsequently to have "obtained the Royal Approbation." Where the early writers had maintained that government springs from the action of God upon the reason, Wise separates divine commands and the dictates of reason into independent sources, and establishes a direct line of communication with God through the natural reason, without any real necessity for consulting scripture. Instead of the unity of early Puritan theory, this account is actually out-and-out rationalism, and the function of the Bible is reduced to supplying a secondary confirmation of the reasonable. From Wise to the philosophy of the Declaration of Independence is a clear and inevitable progress. Barnard and Mayhew mark further steps in that development, and with Mayhew the right of revolution, the right to resist the government when

it oversteps the limits established by the social compact and the fundamental law, becomes the most important doctrine in the theory. With
Jonathan Mayhew the separation of God's will from man's is complete; or rather, with him, the divine will has been made over into
the image of the human. The purposes of society are no longer the
deity's, but the subject's; the advantages to be derived from corporate
existence are no longer salvation, but the well-being of the citizen.
The power of the Puritan God, and of the English King, is bound
by the terms of this compact and by the basic law; we are by now
certain that God will respect the law we have agreed upon, but as
for the King—if he impose a tax on tea to which we do not ourselves
consent, and if we thereupon resist him, "even to the dethroning him,"
we are not criminals, but have only taken "a reasonable way" of
vindicating our natural rights.

JOHN WINTHROP, 1588–1649

[For Winthrop's life see p. 124. "A Modell of Christian Charity"
was delivered as a lecture or lay-sermon to the passengers aboard the
Arbella on the voyage to New England; it follows the standard sermon
form, asserting a doctrinal truth, supporting it with reasons, applying
it to the case in hand. The text is from *Winthrop Papers*, Vol. II (Massachusetts Historical Society, Boston, 1931).

"A Defence of an Order of Court" was written to silence Henry
Vane. During the strain of the Antinomian crisis, when the authorities
had good reason to fear an insurrection of the Hutchinsonians, the
General Court passed a law that no immigrant should be allowed to
remain in Massachusetts Bay unless one of the magistrates gave him
a permit. The immediate purpose of the law was obviously to prevent
the Hutchinsonians from receiving further reinforcements. Vane, who
had just been turned out of the governorship (p. 133), called this act
"tyranny." Winthrop defended it with the following tract; Vane replied with a longer document, and Winthrop answered in a still longer
argument. The text is from Thomas Hutchinson, *A Collection of Papers
Relating to the History of Massachusetts Bay* (Boston, 1769), pp. 63–71.

The selections from the *Journal* illustrate the workings of the Puritan
state. Winthrop's speech, delivered to the General Court immediately
after he had been acquitted in a trial for exceeding his magisterial
authority, is the classic expression of Puritan political theory. The text
is from the edition of James Savage (Boston, 1825), I, 300–302, 322–
323, II, 35, 228–230.]

A MODELL OF CHRISTIAN CHARITY

Written
On Boarde the Arrabella,
On the Attlantick Ocean.
By the Honorable John Winthrop Esquire.

In His passage, (with the great Company of Religious people, of which Christian Tribes he was the Brave Leader and famous Governor;) from the Island of Great Brittaine, to New-England in the North America.

Anno 1630.

CHRISTIAN CHARITIE.

A Modell Hereof.

GOD ALMIGHTIE in his most holy and wise providence hath soe disposed of the Condicion of mankinde, as in all times some must be rich some poore, some highe and eminent in power and dignitie; others meane and in subieccion.

The Reason Hereof.

1. Reas: *First*, to hold conformity with the rest of his workes, being delighted to shewe forthe the glory of his wisdome in the variety and differance of the Creatures and the glory of his power, in ordering all these differences for the preservacion and good of the whole, and the glory of his greatnes that as it is the glory of princes to haue many officers, soe this great King will haue many Stewards counting himselfe more honoured in dispenceing his guifts to man by man, then if hee did it by his owne immediate hand.

2. Reas: *Secondly*, That he might haue the more occasion to manifest the worke of his Spirit: first, vpon the wicked in moderateing and restraineing them: soe that the riche and mighty should not eate vpp the poore, nor the poore, and dispised rise vpp against their superiours, and shake off theire yoake; 2ly in the regenerate in exerciseing his graces in them, as in the greate ones, theire loue mercy, gentlenes, temperance etc., in the poore and inferiour sorte, theire faithe patience, obedience etc:

3. Reas: Thirdly, That every man might haue need of other, and from hence they might be all knitt more nearly together in the Bond of brotherly affeccion: from hence it appeares plainely that noe man is made more honourable then another or more wealthy etc., out of

any perticuler and singuler respect to himselfe but for the glory of his
Creator and the Common good of the Creature, Man; Therefore God
still reserues the propperty of these guifts to himselfe as Ezek: 16. 17.
he there calls wealthe his gold and his silver etc. Prov: 3. 9. he claimes
theire seruice as his due honour the Lord with thy riches etc. All
men being thus (by divine providence) rancked into two sortes, riche
and' poore; vnder the first, are comprehended all such as are able to
liue comfortably by theire owne meanes duely improued; and all
others are poore according to the former distribution. There are two
rules whereby wee are to walke one towards another: Justice and
Mercy. These are allwayes distinguished in theire Act and in theire
obiect, yet may they both concurre in the same Subiect in eache
respect; as sometimes there may be an occasion of shewing mercy to
a rich man, in some sudden danger of distresse, and allsoe doeing of
meere Justice to a poor man in regard of some perticuler contract
etc. There is likewise a double Lawe by which wee are regulated in
our conversacion one towardes another: in both the former respects,
the lawe of nature and the lawe of grace, or the morrall lawe or the
lawe of the gospell, to omitt the rule of Justice as not propperly belonging to this purpose otherwise then it may fall into consideracion
in some perticuler Cases: By the first of these lawes man as he was
enabled soe withall [is] commaunded to loue his neighbour as himselfe vpon this ground stands all the precepts of the morrall lawe,
which concernes our dealings with men. To apply this to the works
of mercy this lawe requires two things first that every man afford his
help to another in every want or distresse Secondly, That hee performe this out of the same affeccion, which makes him carefull of his
owne good according to that of our Saviour Math: [7. 12.] Whatsoever
ye would that men should doe to you. This was practised by Abraham
and Lott in entertaineing the Angells and the old man of Gibea.

The Lawe of Grace or the Gospell hath some differance from the
former as in these respectes first the lawe of nature was giuen to man
in the estate of innocency; this of the gospell in the estate of regeneracy:
2ly, the former propounds one man to another, as the same fleshe and
Image of god, this as a brother in Christ allsoe, and in the Communion of the same spirit and soe teacheth vs to put a difference
betweene Christians and others. Doe good to all especially to the household of faith; vpon this ground the Israelites were to putt a difference
betweene the brethren of such as were strangers though not of the
Canaanites. 3ly. The Lawe of nature could giue noe rules for dealeing
with enemies for all are to be considered as freinds in the estate of

innocency, but the Gospell commaunds loue to an enemy. proofe[:]
If thine Enemie hunger feede him; Loue your Enemies doe good to
them that hate you Math: 5. 44.

This Lawe of the Gospell propoundes likewise a difference of seasons
and occasions there is a time when a christian must sell all and giue
to the poore as they did in the Apostles times. There is a tyme allsoe
when a christian (though they giue not all yet) must giue beyond theire
abillity, as they of Macedonia. Cor: 2. 6. likewise community of perills
calls for extraordinary liberallity and soe doth Community in some
speciall seruice for the Churche. Lastly, when there is noe other meanes
whereby our Christian brother may be releiued in this distresse, wee
must help him beyond our ability, rather then tempt God, in putting
him vpon help by miraculous or extraordinary meanes. . . .

1. For the persons, wee are a Company professing our selues fellow
members of Christ, In which respect onely though wee were absent
from eache other many miles, and had our imploymentes as farre
distant, yet wee ought to account our selues knitt together by this
bond of loue, and liue in the exercise of it, if wee would haue comforte
of our being in Christ, this was notorious in the practise of the Christians
in former times, as is testified of the Waldenses [1] from the mouth of
one of the adversaries Aeneas Syluius, mutuo [solent amare] penè
antequam norint, they vse to loue any of theire owne religion even
before they were acquainted with them.

2ly. for the worke wee haue in hand, it is by a mutuall consent
through a speciall overruleing providence, and a more then an ordinary approbation of the Churches of Christ to seeke out a place of
Cohabitation and Consorteshipp vnder a due forme of Government
both ciuill and ecclesiasticall. In such cases as this the care of the
publique must oversway all private respects, by which not onely conscience, but meare Ciuill pollicy doth binde vs; for it is a true rule
that perticuler estates cannott subsist in the ruine of the publique.

3ly. The end is to improue our liues to doe more seruice to the Lord
the comforte and encrease of the body of christe whereof wee are members that our selues and posterity may be the better preserued from the
Common corrupcions of this euill world to serue the Lord and worke
out our Salvacion vnder the power and purity of his holy Ordinances.

4ly for the meanes whereby this must bee effected, they are 2fold,
a Conformity with the worke and end wee aime at, these wee see are
extraordinary, therefore wee must not content our selues with vsuall
ordinary meanes whatsoever wee did or ought to haue done when
wee liued in England, the same must wee doe and more allsoe where

wee goe: That which the most in theire Churches maineteine as a truthe in profession onely, wee must bring into familiar and constant practice,[2] as in this duty of loue wee must loue brotherly without dissimulation, wee must loue one another with a pure hearte feruently wee must beare one anothers burthens, wee must not looke onely on our owne things, but allsoe on the things of our brethren, neither must wee think that the lord will beare with such faileings at our hands as hee dothe from those among whome wee haue liued. . . .

Thus stands the cause betweene God and vs, wee are entered into Covenant with him for this worke, wee haue taken out a Commission, the Lord hath giuen vs leaue to drawe our owne Articles wee haue professed to enterprise these Accions vpon these and these ends, wee haue herevpon besought him of favour and blessing: Now if the Lord shall please to heare vs, and bring vs in peace to the place wee desire, then hath hee ratified this Covenant and sealed our Commission, [and] will expect a strickt performance of the Articles contained in it, but if wee shall neglect the observacion of these Articles which are the ends wee haue propounded, and dissembling with our God, shall fall to embrace this present world and prosecute our carnall intencions seekeing great things for our selues and our posterity, the Lord will surely breake out in wrathe against vs be revenged of such a periured people and make vs knowe the price of the breache of such a Covenant.[3]

Now the onely way to avoyde this shipwracke and to provide for our posterity is to followe the Counsell of Micah, to doe Justly, to loue mercy, to walke humbly with our God, for this end, wee must be knitt together in this worke as one man, wee must entertaine each other in brotherly Affeccion, wee must be willing to abridge our selues of our superfluities, for the supply of others necessities, wee must vphold a familiar Commerce together in all meekenes, gentlenes, patience and liberallity, wee must delight in eache other, make others Condicions our owne reioyce together, mourne together, labour, and suffer together, allwayes haueing before our eyes our Commission and Community in the worke, our Community as members of the same body, soe shall wee keepe the vnitie of the spirit in the bond of peace, the Lord will be our God and delight to dwell among vs, as his owne people and will commaund a blessing vpon vs in all our wayes, soe that wee shall see much more of his wisdome power goodnes and truthe then formerly wee haue beene acquainted with, wee shall finde that the God of Israell is among vs, when tenn of vs shall be able to resist a thousand of our enemies, when hee shall make vs a prayse and glory, that men shall say of succeeding plantacions: the lord make it like

that of New England: for wee must Consider that wee shall be as a
<u>Citty vpon a Hill,</u> the eies of all people are vppon vs; soe that if wee
shall deale falsely with our god in this worke wee haue vndertaken
and soe cause him to withdrawe his present help from vs, wee shall
be made a story and a by-word through the world, wee shall open
the mouthes of enemies to speake euill of the wayes of god and all
professours for Gods sake; wee shall shame the faces of many of gods
worthy seruants, and cause theire prayers to be turned into Cursses
vpon vs till wee be consumed out of the good land whether wee are
goeing: And to shutt vpp this discourse with that exhortacion of Moses
that faithfull seruant of the Lord in his last farewell to Irsaell Deut. 30.
Beloued there is now sett before vs life, and good, deathe and euill
in that wee are Commaunded this day to loue the Lord our God, and
to loue one another to walke in his wayes and to keepe his Com-
maundements and his Ordinance, and his lawes, and the Articles of
our Covenant with him that wee may liue and be multiplyed, and
that the Lord our God may blesse vs in the land whether wee goe to
possesse it: But if our heartes shall turne away soe that wee will not
obey, but shall be seduced and worshipp . . . other Gods our pleasures,
and proffitts, and serue them; it is propounded vnto vs this day, wee
shall surely perishe out of the good Land whether wee passe over this
vast Sea to possesse it;

> Therefore lett vs choose life,
> that wee, and our Seede,
> may liue; by obeyeing his
> voyce, and cleaueing to him,
> for hee is our life, and
> our prosperity.

A DEFENCE OF AN ORDER OF COURT MADE IN THE YEAR 1637.

A Declaration of the Intent and Equitye of the Order made at the
last Court, to this effect, that none should be received to inhabite
within this Jurisdiction but such as should be allowed by some of
the Magistrates.

FOR CLEARING of such scruples as have arisen about this order, it is
to be considered, first, what is the essentiall forme of a common
weale or body politic such as this is, which I conceive to be this—The
consent of a certaine companie of people, to cohabite together, under
one government for their mutual safety and welfare. . . .

It is clearly agreed, by all, that the care of safety and wellfare was the original cause or occasion of common weales and of many familyes subjecting themselves to rulers and laws; for no man hath lawfull power over another, but by birth or consent, so likewise, by the law of proprietye, no man can have just interest in that which belongeth to another, without his consent.

From the premises will arise these conclusions.

1. No common weale can be founded but by free consent.

2. The persons so incorporating have a public and relative interest each in other, and in the place of their cohabitation and goods, and laws, &c. and in all the means of their wellfare so as none other can claime priviledge with them but by free consent.

3. The nature of such an incorporation tyes every member thereof to seeke out and entertaine all means that may conduce to the well-fare of the bodye, and to keepe off whatsoever doth appeare to tend to theire damage.

4. The wellfare of the whole is [not] to be put to apparent hazard for the advantage of any particular members.

From these conclusions I thus reason.

1. If we heere be a corporation established by free consent, if the place of our cohabitation be our owne, then no man hath right to come into us &c. without our consent.

2. If no man hath right to our lands, our government priviledges, &c. but by our consent, then it is reason we should take notice of before we conferre any such upon them.

3. If we are bound to keepe off whatsoever appears to tend to our ruine or damage, then may we lawfully refuse to receive such whose dispositions suite not with ours and whose society (we know) will be hurtfull to us, and therefore it is lawfull to take knowledge of all men before we receive them.

4. The churches take liberty (as lawfully they may) to receive or reject at their discretion; [4] yea particular towns make orders to the like effect; why then should the common weale be denied the like liberty and the whole more restrained than any parte? . . .

10. Seeing it must be granted that there may come such persons (suppose Jesuits, &c.) which by consent of all ought to be rejected, it will follow that this law (being only for notice to be taken of all that come to us, without which we cannot avoyd such as indeed are to be kept out) is no other but just and needfull, and if any should be rejected that ought to be received, that is not to be imputed to the

law, but to those who are betrusted with the execution of it. And herein is to be considered, what the intent of the law is, and by consequence, by what rule they are to walke, who are betrusted with the keeping of it. The intent of the law is to preserve the wellfare of the body; and for this ende to have none received into any fellowship with it who are likely to disturbe the same, and this intent (I am sure) is lawful and good. Now then, if such to whom the keeping of this law is committed, be persuaded in theire judgments that such a man is likely to disturbe and hinder the publick weale, but some others who are not in the same trust, judge otherwise, yet they are to follow theire owne judgments, rather then the judgments of others who are not alike interested: As in tryall of an offender by a jury; the twelve men are satisfied in their consciences, upon the evidence given, that the party deserves death: but there are 20 or 40 standers by, who conceive otherwise, yet is the jury bound to condemn him according to their owne consciences, and not to acquit him upon the different opinion of other men, except theire reasons can convince them of the errour of theire consciences, and this is according to the rule of the Apostle, Rom. 14. 5. Let every man be fully persuaded in his own mynde.

If it be objected, that some prophane persons are received and others who are religious are rejected, I answer 1st, It is not knowne that any such thinge hath as yet fallen out. 2, Such a practice may be justifiable as the case may be, for younger persons (even prophane ones) may be of lesse danger to the common weale (and to the churches also) than some older persons, though professors of religion: for our Saviour Christ when he conversed with publicans, &c. sayth that such were nearer the kingdom of heaven than the religious pharisees, and one that is of large parts and confirmed in some erronious way, is likely to doe more harme to church and common weale, and is of lesse hope to be reclaymed, then 10 prophane persons, who have not yet beene hardened, in the contempt of the meanes of grace.

Lastly, Whereas it is objected that by this law, we reject good christians and so consequently Christ himselfe: I answer 1st, It is not knowne that any christian man hath beene rejected. 2, A man that is a true christian, may be denyed residence among us, in some cases, without rejecting Christ, as admitt a true christian should come over, and should maintaine community of goods, or that magistrates ought not to punish the breakers of the first table,[5] or the members of churches for criminal offences: or that no man were bound to be subject to those lawes or magistrates to which they should not give an explicite consent, &c. I hope no man will say, that not to receive such an one, were to reject Christ; for such opinions (though being maintained in simple ignorance, they might stand with a state of grace yet) they may be so dangerous to the publick weale in many respects, as it would be our sinne and unfaithfullness to receive such among us, except it were for tryall of theire reformation, I would demand then in the case in question (for it is bootelesse curiosity to refrayne openesse in things publick) whereas it is sayd that this law was made of purpose to keepe away such as are of Mr. Wheelwright his judgment (admitt it were so which yet I cannot confesse) where is the evill of it? If we conceive and finde by sadd experience that his opinions are such, as by his own profession cannot stand with externall peace, may we not provide for our peace, by keeping of such as would strengthen him, and infect others with such dangerous tenets? and if we finde his opinions such as will cause divisions, and make people looke at their magistrates, ministers and brethren as enemies to Christ and Antichrists, &c. were it not sinne and unfaithfullness in us, to receive more of those opinions, which we allready finde the evill fruite of: Nay, why doe not those who now complayne joyne with us in keeping out of such, as well as formerly they did in expelling Mr. Williams for the like, though lesse dangerous? Where this change of theire judgments should arise I leave to themselves to examine, and I earnestly entreate them so to doe, and for this law let the equally mynded judge, what evill they finde in it, or in the practice of those who are betrusted with the execution of it.

JOURNAL

MAY 22, 1639.] The court, finding the number of deputies to be much increased by the addition of new plantations, thought fit, for the ease both of the country and the court, to reduce all towns to two deputies. This occasioned some to fear, that the magistrates intended to make themselves stronger, and the deputies weaker, and so, in time, to bring all power into the hands of the magistrates; so as the people in some towns were much displeased with their deputies for yielding to such an order. Whereupon, at the next session, it was propounded to have the number of deputies restored; and allegations were made, that it was an infringement of their liberty; so as, after much debate, and such reasons given for diminishing the number of deputies, and clearly proved that their liberty consisted not in the number, but in the thing, divers of the deputies, who came with intent to reverse the last order, were, by force of reason, brought to uphold it; so that, when it was put to the vote, the last order for two deputies only was confirmed. Yet, the next day, a petition was brought to the court from the freemen of Roxbury, to have the third deputy restored. Whereupon the reasons of the court's proceedings were set down in writing, and all objections answered, and sent to such towns as were unsatisfied with this advice, that, if any could take away those reasons, or bring us better for what they did desire, we should be ready, at the next court, to repeal the said order.

The hands of some of the elders (learned and godly men) were to this petition, though suddenly drawn in, and without due consideration, for the lawfulness of it may well be questioned: for when the people have chosen men to be their rulers, and to make their laws, and bound themselves by oath to submit thereto, now to combine together (a lesser part of them) in a public petition to have any order repealed, which is not repugnant to the law of God, savors of resisting an ordinance of God; for the people, having deputed others, have no power to make or alter laws, but are to be subject; and if any such order seem unlawful or inconvenient, they were better prefer some reasons, etc., to the court, with manifestation of their desire to move them to a review, than peremptorily to petition to have it repealed, which amounts to a plain reproof of those whom God hath set over them, and putting dishonor upon them, against the tenor of the fifth commandment.

There fell out at this court another occasion of increasing the people's jealousy of their magistrates, viz.: One of the elders, being present with those of his church, when they were to prepare their votes for the election, declared his judgment, that a governor ought to be for his life, alleging for his authority the practice of all the best commonwealths in Europe, and especially that of Israel by God's own ordinance. But this was opposed by some other of the elders with much zeal, and so notice was taken of it by the people, not as a matter of dispute, but as if there had been some plot to put it in practice, which did occasion the deputies, at the next session of this court, to deliver in an order drawn to this effect: That, whereas our sovereign lord, King Charles, etc., had, by his patent, established a governor, deputy and assistants, that therefore no person, chosen a counsellor for life, should have any authority as a magistrate, except he were chosen in the annual elections to one of the said places of magistracy established by the patent. . . . That which led those of the council to yield to this desire of the deputies was, because it concerned themselves, and they did more study to remove these jealousies out of the people's

heads, than to preserve any power or dignity to themselves above
others; . . . And here may be observed, how strictly the people would
seem to stick to their patent, where they think it makes for their advantage, but are content to decline it, where it will not warrant such
liberties as they have taken up without warrant from thence, as appears in their strife for three deputies, etc., when as the patent allows
them none at all, but only by inference. . . .[6]

[September 4, 1639.] The people had long desired a body of laws,
and thought their condition very unsafe, while so much power rested
in the discretion of magistrates. Divers attempts had been made at
former courts, and the matter referred to some of the magistrates and
some of the elders; but still it came to no effect; for, being committed
to the care of many, whatsoever was done by some, was still disliked
or neglected by others. At last it was referred to Mr. Cotton and
Mr. Nathaniel Warde, etc., and each of them framed a model, which
were presented to this general court, and by them committed to the
governor and deputy and some others to consider of, and so prepare
it for the court in the 3d month next. Two great reasons there were,
which caused most of the magistrates and some of the elders not to
be very forward in this matter. One was, want of sufficient experience
of the nature and disposition of the people, considered with the condition of the country and other circumstances, which made them conceive, that such laws would be fittest for us, which should arise pro
re nata upon occasions, etc., and so the laws of England and other
states grew, and therefore the fundamental laws of England are called
customs, consuetudines. 2. For that it would professedly transgress
the limits of our charter, which provide, we shall make no laws repugnant to the laws of England, and that we were assured we must
do. But to raise up laws by practice and custom had been no trans-
gression; as in our church discipline, and in matters of marriage, to
make a law, that marriages should not be solemnized by ministers,
is repugnant to the laws of England; but to bring it to a custom by
practice for the magistrates to perform it, is no law made repugnant,
etc. At length (to satisfy the people) it proceeded, and the two models
were digested with divers alterations and additions, and abbreviated and
sent to every town, to be considered of first by the magistrates and
elders, and then to be published by the constables to all the people, that
if any man should think fit, that any thing therein ought to be altered,
he might acquaint some of the deputies therewith against the next court.[7]

[June 21, 1641.] Some of the freemen, without the consent of the
magistrates or governor, had chosen Mr. Nathaniel Ward to preach

at this court, pretending that it was a part of their liberty. The governor (whose right indeed it is, for till the court be assembled the freemen are but private persons) would not strive about it, for though it did not belong to them, yet if they would have it, there was reason to yield it to them. . . . In his sermon he delivered many useful things, but in a moral and political discourse, grounding his propositions much upon the old Roman and Grecian governments, which sure is an error, for if religion and the word of God makes men wiser than their neighbors, and these times have the advantage of all that have gone before us in experience and observation, it is probable that by all these helps, we may better frame rules of government for ourselves than to receive others upon the bare authority of the wisdom, justice, etc. of those heathen commonwealths. Among other things, he advised the people to keep all their magistrates in an equal rank, and not give more honor or power to one than to another, which is easier to advise than to prove, seeing it is against the practice of Israel (where some were rulers of thousands, and some but of tens) and of all nations known or recorded.

WINTHROP'S SPEECH TO THE GENERAL COURT, JULY 3, 1645

I suppose something may be expected from me, upon this charge that is befallen me, which moves me to speak now to you; yet I intend not to intermeddle in the proceedings of the court, or with any of the persons concerned therein. Only I bless God, that I see an issue of this troublesome business. I also acknowledge the justice of the court, and, for mine own part, I am well satisfied, I was publicly charged, and I am publicly and legally acquitted, which is all I did expect or desire. And though this be sufficient for my justification before men, yet not so before the God, who hath seen so much amiss in my dispensations (and even in this affair) as calls me to be humble. For to be publicly and criminally charged in this court, is matter of humiliation, (and I desire to make a right use of it,) notwithstanding I be thus acquitted. If her father had spit in her face, (saith the Lord concerning Miriam,) should she not have been ashamed seven days? Shame had lien upon her, whatever the occasion had been. I am unwilling to stay you from your urgent affairs, yet give me leave (upon this special occasion) to speak a little more to this assembly. It may be of some good use, to inform and rectify the judgments of some of the people, and may prevent such distempers as have arisen amongst us. The great questions that have troubled the country, are about the authority of the magistrates and the liberty of the people. It is yourselves who have called us to this office, and being called by you, we have our authority from God, in way of an ordinance, such as hath the image of God eminently stamped upon it, the contempt and violation whereof hath been vindicated with examples of divine vengeance. I entreat you to consider, that when you choose magistrates, you take them from among yourselves, men subject to like passions as you are. Therefore when you see infirmities in us, you should reflect upon your own, and that would make you bear the more with us, and not be severe censurers of the failings of your magistrates, when you have continual experience of the like infirmities in yourselves and others. We account him a good servant, who breaks not his covenant. The covenant between you and us is the oath you have taken of us, which is to this purpose, that we shall govern you and judge your causes by the rules of God's laws and our own, according to our best skill. When you agree with a workman to build you a ship or house, etc., he undertakes as well for his skill as for his faithfulness, for it is his profession, and you pay him for both. But when you call one to be a magistrate, he doth not profess nor undertake to have sufficient skill for that office, nor can you furnish him with gifts, etc., therefore you must run the hazard of his skill and ability. But if he fail in faithfulness, which by his oath he is bound unto, that he must answer for. If it fall out that the case be clear to common apprehension, and the rule clear also, if he transgress here, the error is not in the skill, but in the evil of the will: it must be required of him. But if the case be doubtful, or the rule doubtful, to men of such understanding and parts as your magistrates are, if your magistrates should err here, yourselves must bear it.

For the other point concerning liberty, I observe a great mistake in the country about that. There is a twofold liberty, natural (I mean as our nature is now corrupt) and civil or federal. The first is common to man with beasts and other creatures. By this, man, as he stands in relation to man simply, hath liberty to do what he lists; it is a liberty to evil as well as to good. This liberty is incompatible and inconsistent with authority, and cannot endure the least restraint of the most just authority. The exercise and maintaining of this liberty makes men grow more evil, and in time to be worse than brute beasts: omnes sumus licentia deteriores. This is that great enemy of truth and peace, that wild beast, which all the ordinances of God are bent against, to restrain and subdue it. The other kind of liberty I call civil or federal, it may also be termed moral, in reference to the covenant between God and man, in the moral law, and the politic covenants and constitutions, amongst men themselves. This liberty is the proper end and object of authority, and cannot subsist without it; and it is a liberty to that only which is good, just, and honest. This liberty you are to stand for, with the hazard (not only of your goods, but) of your lives, if need be. Whatsoever crosseth this, is not authority, but a distemper thereof. This liberty is maintained and exercised in a way of subjection to authority; it is of the same kind of liberty wherewith Christ hath made us free. The woman's own choice makes such a man her husband; yet being so chosen, he is her lord, and she is to be subject to him, yet in a way of liberty, not of bondage; and a true wife accounts her subjection her honor and freedom, and would not think her condition safe and free, but in her subjection to her husband's authority. Such is the liberty of the church under the authority of Christ, her king and husband; his yoke is so easy and sweet to her as a bride's orna-ments; and if through frowardness or wantonness, etc., she shake it off, at any time, she is at no rest in her spirit, until she take it up again; and whether her lord smiles upon her, and embraceth her in his arms, or whether he frowns, or rebukes, or smites her, she ap-prehends the sweetness of his love in all, and is refreshed, supported, and instructed by every such dispensation of his authority over her. On the other side, ye know who they are that complain of this yoke and say, let us break their bands, etc., we will not have this man to rule over us. Even so, brethren, it will be between you and your magistrates. If you stand for your natural corrupt liberties, and will do what is good in your own eyes, you will not endure the least weight of authority, but will murmur, and oppose, and be always striving to shake off that yoke; but if you will be satisfied to enjoy such civil and lawful liberties, such as Christ allows you, then will you quietly and cheerfully submit unto that authority which is set over you, in all the administrations of it, for your good. Wherein, if we fail at any time, we hope we shall be willing (by God's assistance) to hearken to good advice from any of you, or in any other way of God; so shall your liberties be preserved, in upholding the honor and power of authority amongst you.

JOHN COTTON, 1584–1652

[John Cotton, the son of a well-to-do attorney, was born in Derby, Derbyshire, and entered Trinity College, Cambridge, at the age of thir-teen, taking his B.A. in 1603; he later migrated to Emmanuel College, taking his M.A. in 1606. He was chosen fellow and head lecturer of the College, was ordained in 1610 and became vicar of St. Botolph's, in Boston, Lincolnshire, in 1612, receiving degree of B.D. in 1613. For twenty years he was a conspicuous figure in the Church, enjoying a great reputation as a preacher and a theologian, protected from the Laudian power by the favor of powerful persons. He preached* the farewell sermon to Winthrop's fleet in 1630; in 1633 he was at last forced to resign for nonconformity. He came to New England on the same ship with Thomas Hooker, the only other minister in New England who could approach him in reputation and learning. He was immediately chosen teacher of the Boston church. Though coming close to being ruined for the countenance he seemed to give to the teachings of Anne Hutchinson, he recovered himself in time, and remained the dominating figure in the councils of the New England clergy. His many writings on church polity were looked upon both in New England and in England as the standard expositions of the Congregational system, and his more general sermons and writings set the model for New England orthodoxy. For biography, see William Walker, *Ten New England Leaders*, and Cotton Mather, *Magnalia;* bibliography by Julius H. Tuttle in *Bibliographical Essays; A Tribute to Wilberforce Eames*, 1924.

When the New England migration occurred, the Puritan party in England had not yet come to any explicit agreement concerning the form of church organization they intended to set up in place of the episcopalian; the majority of Puritans had some species of Presbyterianism in mind, and they were often very much puzzled as stories of the New England system were carried back to England. They were still more bewildered when they heard rumors of political practices in Massachusetts which were the direct results of the church polity, but which seemed to run counter to the traditions and rights of Englishmen. Lord Say and Seal was a Puritan noble who meditated abandoning England; but Massachusetts did not sound too attractive to him, for there men were admitted to citizenship, regardless of their social position, only when they had become church members, and the noble Lord feared that he or some of his friends might be excluded. Cotton's reply is deferential but firm; he defends the franchise requirement as the very foundation of the Bible Commonwealth. The text is from Thomas Hutchinson, *History of Massachusetts Bay*, Vol. I, 1764, Appendix III.

The second passage, from a volume of Cotton's sermons, illustrates the other side of Puritan political theory, the conception of limitation by fundamental law and basic right. The letter to Lord Say and Seal can be reconciled with this passage only by means of the peculiar doctrine of the covenant found in Winthrop's speech on liberty. The text is from *An exposition upon the 13th Chapter of the Revelation* (London, 1656), pp. 71–73; published after his death, the book declares that the sermons were "Taken from his mouth in Short-writing."]

COPY OF A LETTER FROM MR. COTTON TO LORD SAY AND SEAL IN THE YEAR 1636.

RIGHT honourable,
. . . I am very apt to believe, what Mr. Perkins [1] hath, in one of his prefatory pages to his golden chaine, that the word, and scriptures of God doe conteyne a short *upoluposis*, or platforme, not onely of theology, but also of other sacred sciences, (as he calleth them) attendants, and handmaids thereunto, which he maketh ethicks, eoconomicks, politicks, church-government, prophecy, academy. It is very suitable to Gods all-sufficient wisdome, and to the fulnes and perfection of Holy Scriptures, not only to prescribe perfect rules for the right ordering of a private mans soule to everlasting blessednes with himselfe, but also for the right ordering of a mans family, yea, of the commonwealth too, so farre as both of them are subordinate to spiritual ends, and yet avoide both the churches usurpation upon civill jurisdictions, *in ordine ad spiritualia*,[2] and the commonwealths invasion upon ecclesiasticall administrations, *in ordine* to civill peace, and conformity to the civill state. Gods institutions (such as the government of church and of commonwealth be) may be close and compact, and co-ordinate one to another, and yet not confounded. God hath so framed the state of church government and ordinances, that they may be compatible to any common-wealth, though never so much disordered in his frame. But yet when a commonwealth hath liberty to mould his owne frame (*scripturæ plenitudinem adoro*)[3] I conceyve the scripture hath given full direction for the right ordering of the same, and that, in such sort as may best mainteyne the *euexia*[4] of the church. Mr. Hooker doth often quote a saying out of Mr. Cartwright (though I have not read it in him) that noe man fashioneth his house to his hangings, but his hangings to his house. It is better that the commonwealth be fashioned to the setting forth of Gods house, which is his church: than to accommodate the church frame to the civill state. Democracy, I do not conceyve that ever God did ordeyne as a fitt government eyther for church or commonwealth. If the people be governors, who

shall be governed? As for monarchy, and aristocracy, they are both of them clearly approoved, and directed in scripture, yet so as referreth the soveraigntie to himselfe, and setteth up Theocracy in both, as the best forme of government in the commonwealth, as well as in the church.

The law, which your Lordship instanceth in (that none shall be chosen to magistracy among us but a church member) was made and enacted before I came into the country; but I have hitherto wanted sufficient light to plead against it. 1st. The rule that directeth the choice of supreame governors, is of like æquitie and weight in all magistrates, that one of their brethren (not a stranger) should be set over them, Deut. 17. 15. and Jethroes counsell to Moses was approved of God, that the judges, and officers to be set over the people, should be men fearing God, Exod. 18. 21. and Solomon maketh it the joy of a commonwealth, when the righteous are in authority, and their mourning when the wicked rule, Prov. 29. 21. Jab 34. 30. Your Lordship's feare, that this will bring in papal excommunication, is iust, and pious: but let your Lordship be pleased againe to consider whether the consequence be necessary. *Turpius ejicitur quam non admittitur:* [5] nonmembership may be a just cause of non-admission to the place of magistracy. A godly woman, being to make choice of an husband, may justly refuse a man that is eyther cast out of church fellowship, or is not yet receyved into it, but yet, when shee is once given to him, shee may not reject him then, for such defect. Mr. Humfrey was chosen for an assistant (as I heare) before the colony came over hither: and, though he be not as yet ioyned into church fellowship (by reason of the unsetlednes of the congregation where he liveth) yet the commonwealth doe still continue his magistracy to him, as knowing he waiteth for oppertunity of enioying church fellowship shortly.

When your Lordship doubteth, that this corse will draw all things under the determination of the church, *in ordine ad spiritualia* [2] (seeing the church is to determine who shall be members, and none but a member may have to doe in the government of a commonwealth) be pleased (I pray you) to conceyve, that magistrates are neyther chosen to office in the church, nor doe governe by directions from the church, but by civill lawes, and those enacted in generall corts, and executed in corts of iustice, by the governors and assistants. In all which, the church (as the church) hath nothing to doe: onely, it prepareth fitt instruments both to rule, and to choose rulers, which is no ambition in the church, nor dishonor to the commonwealth, the apostle, on the contrary, thought it a great dishonor and reproach to the church of

Christ, if it were not able to yield able judges to heare and determine all causes amongst their brethren, I Cor. 6. 1. to 5. which place alone seemeth to me fully to decide this question: for it plainely holdeth forth this argument: It is a shame to the church to want able judges of civill matters (as v. 5.) and an audacious act in any church member voluntarily to go for judgment, otherwhere than before the saints (as v. 1.) then it will be noe arrogance nor folly in church members, nor prejudice to the commonwealth, if voluntarily they never choose any civill judges, but from amongst the saints, such as church members are called to be. But the former is cleare: and how then can the latter be avoyded. If this therefore be (as your Lordship rightly conceyveth one of the maine objections if not the onely one) which hindereth this commonwealth from the entertainment of the propositions of those worthy gentlemen, wee intreate them, in the name of the Lord Jesus, to consider, in meeknes of wisdome, it is not any conceite or will of ours, but the holy counsell and will of the Lord Jesus (whom they seeke to serve as well as wee) that overruleth us in this case: and we trust will overrule them also, that the Lord onely may be exalted amongst all his servants. What pittie and griefe were it, that the observance of the will of Christ should hinder good things from us!

But your Lordship doubteth, that if such a rule were necessary, then the church estate and the best ordered commonwealth in the world were not compatible. But let not your Lordship so conceyve. For, the church submitteth itselfe to all the lawes and ordinances of men, in what commonwealth soever they come to dwell. But it is one thing, to submit unto what they have noe calling to reforme: another thing, voluntarily to ordeyne a forme of government, which to the best discerning of many of us (for I speake not of myselfe) is expressly contrary to rule. Nor neede your Lordship feare (which yet I speake with submission to your Lordships better judgment) that this corse will lay such a foundation, as nothing but a mere democracy can be built upon it. Bodine [6] confesseth, that though it be *status popularis*, where a people choose their owne governors; yet the government is not a democracy, if it be administred, not by the people, but by the governors, whether one (for then it is a monarchy, though elective) or by many, for then (as you know) it is aristocracy. In which respect it is, that church government is iustly denied (even by Mr. Robinson [7]) to be democratical, though the people choose their owne officers and rulers.

Nor neede wee feare, that this course will, in time, cast the commonwealth into distractions, and popular confusions. For (under correction) these three things doe not undermine, but doe mutually and strongly mainteyne one another (even those three which wee principally aime at) authority in magistrates, liberty in people, purity in the church. Purity, preserved in the church, will preserve well ordered liberty in the people, and both of them establish well-ballanced authority in the magistrates. God is the author of all these three, and neyther is himselfe the God of confusion, nor are his wayes the wayes of confusion, but of peace. . . .

Now the Lord Jesus Christ (the prince of peace) keepe and bless your Lordship, and dispose of all your times and talents to his best advantage: and let the covenant of his grace and peace rest upon your honourable family and posterity throughout all generations.

Thus, humbly craving pardon for my boldnesse and length, I take leave and rest,

Your Honours to serve in Christ Jesus,

J. C.

LIMITATION OF GOVERNMENT

THIS may serve to teach us the danger of allowing to any mortall man an inordinate measure of power to speak great things, to allow to any man uncontrollableness of speech, you see the desperate danger of it: Let all the world learn to give mortall men no greater power then they are content they shall use, for use it they will: and unlesse they be better taught of God, they will use it ever and anon, it may be make it the passage of their proceeding to speake what they will: And they that have liberty to speak great things, you will finde it to be true, they will speak great blasphemies. No man would think what desperate deceit and wickednesse there is in the hearts of men: And that was the reason why the Beast did speak such great things, hee might speak, and no body might controll him: What, saith the Lord in *Jer.* 3. 5. *Thou hast spoken and done evill things as thou couldst.* If a Church or head of a Church could have done worse, he would have done it: This is one of the straines of nature, it affects boundlesse liberty, and to runne to the utmost extent: What ever power he hath received, he hath a corrupt nature that will improve it in one thing or other; if he have liberty, he will think why may he not use it. Set up the Pope as Lord Paramount over Kings and Princes, and they shall know that he hath power over them, he will take liberty to depose one, and set up another. Give him power to make Laws, and he will approve, and disprove as he list; what he approves is Canonicall,

what hee disproves is rejected: Give him that power, and he will so
order it at length, he will make such a State of Religion, that he that
so lives and dyes shall never be saved, and all this springs from the
vast power that is given to him, and from the deep depravation of
nature. Hee will open his mouth, *His tongue is his owne, who is Lord·
over him,* Psal. 12. 3, 4. It is therefore most wholsome for Magistrates
and Officers in Church and Common-wealth, never to affect more
liberty and authority then will do them good, and the People good;
for what ever transcendant power is given, will certainly over-run those
that give it, and those that receive it: There is a straine in a mans
heart that will sometime or other runne out to excesse, unlesse the
Lord restraine it, but it is not good to venture it: It is necessary therefore, that all power that is on earth be limited, Church-power or
other: If there be power given to speak great things, then look for
great blasphemies, look for a licentious abuse of it. It is counted a
matter of danger to the State to limit Prerogatives; but it is a further
danger, not to have them limited: They will be like a Tempest, if
they be not limited: A Prince himselfe cannot tell where hee will
confine himselfe, nor can the people tell: But if he have liberty to
speak great things, then he will make and unmake, say and unsay,
and undertake such things as are neither for his owne honour, nor
for the safety of the State. It is therefore fit for every man to be studious
of the bounds which the Lord hath set: and for the People, in whom
fundamentally all power lyes, to give as much power as God in his
word gives to men: And it is meet that Magistrates in the Commonwealth, and so Officers in Churches should desire to know the utmost
bounds of their own power, and it is safe for both: All intrenchment
upon the bounds which God hath not given, they are not enlarge-
ments, but burdens and snares; They will certainly lead the spirit
of a man out of his way sooner or later. It is wholsome and safe to
be dealt withall as God deales with the vast Sea; *Hitherto shalt thou
come, but there shalt thou stay thy proud waves:* and therefore if they be
but banks of simple sand, they will be good enough to check the vast
roaring Sea. And so for Imperiall Monarchies, it is safe to know how
far their power extends; and then if it be but banks of sand, which is
most slippery, it will serve, as well as any brazen wall. If you pinch
the Sea of its liberty, though it be walls of stone or brasse, it will
beate them downe: So it is with Magistrates, stint them where God
hath not stinted them, and if they were walls of brasse, they would
beate them downe, and it is meet they should: but give them the liberty
God allows, and if it be but a wall of sand it will keep them: As this

liquid Ayre in which we breath, God hath set it for the waters of the Clouds to the Earth; It is a Firmament, it is the Clouds, yet it stands firme enough, because it keeps the Climate where they are, it shall stand like walls of brasse: So let there be due bounds set, and I may apply it to Families; it is good for the Wife to acknowledg all power and authority to the Husband, and for the Husband to acknowledg honour to the Wife, but still give them that which God hath given them, and no more nor lesse: Give them the full latitude that God hath given, else you will finde you dig pits, and lay snares, and cumber their spirits, if you give them lesse: there is never peace where full liberty is not given, nor never stable peace where more then full liberty is granted: Let them be duely observed, and give men no more liberty then God doth, nor women, for they will abuse it: The Devill will draw them, and Gods providence leade them thereunto, therefore give them no more then God gives. And so for children; and servants, or any others you are to deale with, give them the liberty and authority you would have them use, and beyond that stretch not the tether, it will not tend to their good nor yours: And also from hence gather, and goe home with this meditation; That certainly here is this distemper in our natures, that we cannot tell how to use liberty, but wee shall very readily corrupt our selves: Oh the bottomlesse depth of sandy earth! of a corrupt spirit, that breaks over all bounds, and loves inordinate vastnesse; that is it we ought to be carefull of.

ROGER WILLIAMS, 1604–1683

[Roger Williams, son of a London merchant tailor, attracted the attention of Sir Edward Coke, the great jurist, through whose influence he was elected pensioner at Sutton's Hospital (Charterhouse) in 1621; admitted pensioner at Pembroke College, Cambridge, in 1623, he took his B.A. in 1627. He first landed in New England in 1631, and was chosen teacher of the church of Salem, but objecting that the church had not "separated" from the Church of England, he refused the office and went to Plymouth, where he ministered for a year or so, but was not officially ordained; in 1633 he returned to Salem, was again chosen minister, and accepted the post. Thereupon he began a two-year career of agitation and trouble-making that ended with his banishment in October, 1635. He continued to demand that the churches of New England announce their separation from the Church of England, at a time when all the ingenuity the authorities could muster was being expended in proving that they never had seceded from the true Church of England; he attacked the charter on the ground that the King of England had no title to the land and that the colonists needed only to purchase Massachusetts from the Indians; he denied that a magistrate could tender an oath to an unregenerate man, thus promising to upset the whole judicial system of the colony; finally, when he was being dealt with for these heresies, he broached the idea that the civil magistrates had no power to punish persons for their religious opinions. Sentence of banishment was pronounced upon him in October, 1635, but he was allowed to remain in Salem for the winter on condition that he keep quiet; in January the Court heard that people of Salem were resorting to his house and sent Captain Underhill to arrest him; probably John Winthrop sent him a warning, and he fled to the Narragansett country in the dead of winter (cf. p. 484). Thus he became the founder of Providence, Rhode Island, and the principal guide and statesman for that tumultuous colony. He became a Baptist in 1639, but in a few months renounced even that creed, and for the rest of his life called himself a "seeker," one who was always searching for the pure truth but did not expect to find it in this world. He went to England as agent for Rhode Island in 1643; during the voyage he wrote his *Key into the Language of America;* he was always on particularly good terms with the Indians, and rendered the colonies of Massachusetts Bay and Connecticut great service as ambassador and spy. While in England he became a friend of John Milton and published two books attacking John Cotton as the spokesman for the orthodox theory of persecution. The more important of these, *The Bloudy Tenent of Persecution*, was ordered by Parliament to be burned by the common hangman. John Cotton replied with *The Bloudy Tenent, washed, And made white in the bloud of the Lambe* (London, 1647). Williams secured a charter for the Rhode Island settlements, and in 1651 returned to England once more to defend this charter; on this occasion he published his reply to Cotton's reply, entitled *The Bloody Tenent yet More Bloody: by Mr Cottons endevour to wash it white in the Blood of the Lambe*. He served as governor of Rhode Island from 1654 to 1657, supported himself in his last years by trade with the Indians, and died in poverty as a result of King Phillip's War. Biographies by J. M. Straus, 1894, Edmund J. Carpenter, 1909, James E. Ernst, 1932. This text is from *The Bloudy Tenent*, ed. Samuel L. Caldwell, *Publications of the Narragansett Club*, Vol. III (Providence, 1867).]

THE BLOUDY TENENT OF PERSECUTION

To every Courteous Reader.

WHILE I plead the Cause of *Truth* and *Innocencie* against the bloody *Doctrine* of *Persecution* for cause of *conscience*, I judge it not unfit to give *alarme* to my selfe, and all men to prepare to be *persecuted* or hunted for cause of *conscience*.

Whether thou standest charged with 10 or but 2 *Talents*, if thou huntest any for cause of *conscience*, how canst thou say thou followest the *Lambe* of *God* who so abhorr'd that practice? . . .

Who can now but expect that after so many scores of yeares *preaching* and *professing* of more *Truth*, and amongst so many great *contentions* amongst the very best of *Protestants*, a fierie furnace should be heat, and who sees not now the *fires* kindling?

I confesse I have little hopes till those flames are over, that this Discourse against the *doctrine* of *persecution* for cause of *conscience* should passe currant (I say not amongst the *Wolves* and *Lions*, but even amongst the *Sheep* of *Christ* themselves) yet *liberavi animam meam*,[1] I have not hid within my *breast* my *souls* belief: And although sleeping on the bed either of the pleasures or profits of sinne thou thinkest thy conscience bound to smite at him that dares to waken thee? Yet in the middest of all these *civill* and *spirituall Wars* (I hope we shall agree in these particulars.)

First, how ever the proud (upon the advantage of an higher earth or ground) or'elooke the poore and cry out *Schismatickes, Hereticks*, &c. shall *blasphemers* and *seducers* scape unpunished? &c. Yet there is a sorer punishment in the *Gospel* for despising of *Christ* then *Moses*, even when the despiser of *Moses* was put to death without mercie, *Heb*. 10. 28, 29. He that beleeveth not shall bee damned, *Marke* 16. 16.

Secondly, what ever Worship, Ministry, Ministration, the best and purest are practised without *faith* and true perswasion that they are the true institutions of God, they are sin, sinfull worships, Ministries, &c. And however in Civill things we may be servants unto men, yet in Divine and Spirituall things the poorest *pesant* must disdaine the service of the highest *Prince:* Be ye not the servants of men, I Cor. 14.

Thirdly, without search and triall no man attaines this faith and right perswasion, I *Thes.* 5. Try all things.

In vaine have *English Parliaments* permitted *English Bibles* in the poorest *English* houses, and the simplest man or woman to search the Scriptures, if yet against their soules perswasion from the Scripture, they should be forced (as if they lived in *Spaine* or *Rome* it selfe without the sight of a *Bible*) to beleeve as the Church beleeves.

Fourthly, having tried, we must hold fast, I *Thessal.* 5. upon the losse of a Crowne, *Revel.* 13. we must not let goe for all the flea bitings of the present afflictions, &c. having bought Truth deare, we must not sell it cheape, not the least graine of it for the whole World, no not for the saving of Soules, though our owne most precious; least of all for the bitter sweetning of a little vanishing pleasure.

For a little puffe of credit and reputation from the changeable breath of uncertaine sons of men.

For the broken bagges of Riches on Eagles wings: For a dreame of these, any or all of these which on our death-bed vanish and leave tormenting stings behinde them: Oh how much better is it from the love of Truth, from the love of the Father of lights, from whence it comes, from the love of the Sonne of God, who is the way and the Truth, to say as he, *John* 18. 37. For this end was I borne, and for this end came I into the World that I might beare witnesse to the Truth.

THE ANSWER OF MR. IOHN COTTON OF BOSTON
IN NEW-ENGLAND, . . . PROFESSEDLY MAIN-
TEINING PERSECUTION FOR CAUSE
OF CONSCIENCE.[2]

The *Question* which you put, is, Whether *Persecution* for cause of *Conscience*, be not against the *Doctrine* of *Jesus Christ* the *King of Kings*.

Now by *Persecution* for Cause of *Conscience*, I conceive you meane, either for professing some point of *Doctrine* which you believe in Conscience to be the Truth, or for practising some *Worke* which in *Conscience* you be-lieve to be a *Religious Duty*.

Now in Points of *Doctrine* some are *fundamentall*, without right beliefe whereof a Man cannot be *saved:* Others are *circumstantiall* or lesse principall, wherein Men may differ in judgement, without prejudice of *salvation* on either part.

In like sort, in Points of *Practice*, some concerne the waightier Duties of the *Law*, as, What *God* we worship, and with what kinde of *Worship;* whether such, as if it be *Right*, fellowship with *God* is held; if *Corrupt*, fellowship with Him is lost.

Againe, in Points of *Doctrine* and *Worship* lesse Principall: either they are held forth in a meeke and *peaceable* way, though the Things be *Erroneous* or unlawfull: Or they are held forth with such *Arrogance* and *Impetuousnesse*, as tendeth and reacheth (even of it selfe) to the disturbance of *Civill Peace*.

Finally, let me adde this one distinction more: When we are persecuted for *Conscience* sake, It is either for *Conscience* rightly informed, or for erronious and blind *Conscience*.

These things premised, I would lay down mine
Answer to the Question in certaine *Conclusions*.

First, it is not lawfull to persecute any for *Conscience* sake *Rightly informed;* for in *persecuting* such, *Christ* himselfe is persecuted in them, *Acts* 9. 4.

Secondly, for an *Erronious* and *blind Conscience*, (even in fundamentall and weighty Points) It is not lawfull to persecute any, till after *Admonition* once or twice: and so the Apostle directeth, *Tit.* 3. 10. and giveth the Reason, that in *fundamentall* and principall points of Doctrine or Worship, the Word of *God* in such things is so cleare, that hee cannot but bee convinced in *Conscience* of the dangerous *Errour* of his way, after once or twice *Admonition*, wisely and faithfully dispensed. And then if any one persist, it is not out of *Conscience*, but against *his Conscience*, as the Apostle saith, *vers.* 11. He is subverted and sinneth, being condemned of Himselfe, that is, of his owne *Conscience*. So that if such a Man after such Admonition shall still *persist* in the Errour of his way, and be therefore punished; He is not *persecuted* for Cause of *Conscience*, but for sinning *against* his Owne *Conscience*.

REPLY TO THE AFORESAID ANSWER OF MR. COTTON.

In a CONFERENCE betweene *Truth and Peace*.

Truth. In what *darke corner* of the World (*sweet Peace*) are *we two* met? How hath this present evill *World*

banished *Me* from all the Coasts & Quarters of it?
and how hath the Righteous *God* in judgement taken
Thee from the *Earth*, Rev. 6. 4.

Peace. 'Tis lamentably true (*blessed Truth*) the *founda-*
tions of the *World* have long been out of course: the
Gates of *Earth* and *Hell* have conspired together to in-
tercept our joyfull *meeting* and our holy *kisses:* With what
a wearied, *tyred Wing* have I flowne over *Nations, King-*
domes, Cities, Townes, to finde out precious *Truth?*

Truth. The like enquiries in my flights and travells
have I made for *Peace*, and still am told, she hath left
the *Earth*, and fled to *Heaven*.

Peace. Deare *Truth*, What is the *Earth* but a *dungeon*
of darknesse, where *Truth* is not?

Truth. And what's the *Peace* thereof but a *fleeting*
dreame, thine *Ape* and *Counterfeit?*

Peace. O where's the Promise of the *God* of *Heaven*,
that *Righteousnes* and *Peace* shall *kisse* each other?

Truth. Patience (sweet *Peace*) these *Heavens* and *Earth*
are growing *Old*, and shall be changed like a *Garment*,
Psal. 102. They shall melt away, and be burnt up with
all the *Works* that are therein; and the most high *Eternall*
Creatour, shall gloriously create *New Heavens* and *New*
Earth, wherein dwells *Righteousnesse*, 2 Pet. 3. Our *kisses*
then shall have their *endlesse* date of pure and sweetest
ioyes? till then both *Thou* and *I* must hope, and wait,
and beare the furie of the *Dragons* wrath, whose *mon-*
strous Lies and *Furies* shall with himselfe be cast into the
lake of *Fire*, the *second death*, Revel. 20. . . .

Truth. In the Answer Mr. *Cotton* first layes downe
severall *distinctions* and *conclusions* of his owne, tending to
prove persecution. . . .

Peace. The first distinction is this: By persecution for
cause of *Conscience*, "I conceive you meane either for
professing some point of *doctrine* which you beleeve in
conscience to be the *truth*, or for *practising* some worke which
you beleeve in *conscience* to be a *religious* dutie.["]

Truth. I acknowledge that to molest any person, *Jew*
or *Gentile*, for either professing *doctrine*, or practising *wor-*
ship meerly *religious* or spirituall, it is to persecute him,
and such a person (what ever his *doctrine* or *practice* be
true or *false*) suffereth persecution for *conscience*.

But withall I desire it may bee well observed, that
this *distinction* is not full and complete: For beside this
that a man may be persecuted because he holdeth or

Truth and
Peace rarely
and seldom
meete.

The first
distinction
discussed.

Definition of
persecution
discussed.

practiseth what he beleeves in *conscience* to be a *Truth*,
(as *Daniel* did, for which he was cast into the *Lyons* den,
Dan. 6.) and many thousands of *Christians*, because they
durst not cease to *preach* and *practise* what they beleeved
was by *God* commanded, as the *Apostles* answered (*Acts*
4. & 5.) I say besides this a man may also be persecuted,
because hee dares not be *constrained* to yeeld obedience
to such *doctrines* and *worships* as are by men invented
and appointed. So the three famous *Jewes* were cast into
the fiery furnace for refusing to fall downe (in a *non-con-
formity* to the whole conforming world) before the golden
Image, Dan. 3. 21. So thousands of *Christs witnesses* (and
of late in those bloudy *Marian* dayes) have rather chose
to yeeld their *bodies* to all sorts of *torments*, then to subscribe to *doctrines*, or practise *worships*, unto which the
States and Times (as *Nabuchadnezzar* to his golden *Image*)
have compelled and urged them . . .

Truth. . . . *Gods people* were and ought to be *Noncon-
formitants*, not daring either to be *restrained* from the
true, or *constrained* to *false Worship*, and yet without *breach*
of the Civill or *Citie-peace*, properly so called.

Peace. Hence it is that so many glorious and flourishing
Cities of the World maintaine their *Civill* peace, yea the
very *Americans* & wildest *Pagans* keep the peace of their
Towns or *Cities;* though neither in one nor the other
can any man prove a true *Church* of God in those places,
and consequently no spirituall and heavenly peace: The
Peace *spirituall* (whether true or false) being of a higher
and farre different nature from the Peace of the place
or people, being meerly and essentially *civill* and *humane.*

Truth. O how lost are the sonnes of men in this point?
To illustrate this: The *Church* or *company* of *worshippers*
(whether true or false) is like unto a Body or Colledge
of *Physitians* in a *Citie;* like unto a *Corporation, Society,* or
Company of *East-Indie* or *Turkie-Merchants,* or any other
Societie or *Company* in *London:* which Companies may hold
their *Courts,* keep their *Records,* hold *disputations;* and in
matters concerning their *Societie,* may dissent, divide,
breake into *Schismes* and *Factions,* sue and implead each
other at the *Law,* yea wholly breake up and dissolve
into pieces and nothing, and yet the *peace* of the *Citie*
not be in the least measure impaired or disturbed; because the *essence* of being of the *Citie,* and so the *well-
being* and *peace* thereof is essentially distinct from those
particular *Societies;* the *Citie-Courts, Citie-Lawes, Citie-*

Conscience
will not be
restrained from
its own worship,
nor constrained
to another.

Gods people
must be
Non-conformi-
tants to Evill.

The difference
between
Spirituall and
Civill Peace.

The difference
between the
Spirituall and
Civill State.

punishments distinct from theirs. The *Citie* was before them, and stands absolute and intire, when such a *Corporation* or *Societie* is taken down . . .

Peace. Yea but it is said that the blinde *Pharises* misguiding the subjects of a *Civill State*, greatly sinne against a *Civill State*, and therefore justly suffer *civill punishment;* for shall the *Civill Magistrate* take care of *outsides* only, to wit, of the bodies of men, and not of soules, in labouring to procure their everlasting welfare?

Truth. I answer, It is a *truth*, the mischiefe of a blinde *Pharises* blinde *guidance* is greater then if he acted Treasons, Murders, &c. and the losse of one soule by his seduction is a greater mischiefe then if he blew up Parliaments, and cuts the throats of Kings or Emperours, so pretious is that invaluable Jewell of a Soul, above all the present lives and bodies of all the men in the world! and therefore a firme Justice calling for *eye* for *eye*, *tooth* for *tooth*, *life* for *life;* calls also *soule* for *soule*, which the blindguiding seducing *Pharisee* shall surely pay in that dreadfull Ditch, which the Lord Jesus speakes of, but this sentence against him the Lord Jesus only pronounceth in His *Church*, His *spirituall judicature*, and executes this *sentence* in part at present and hereafter to all eternity: Such a *sentence* no *Civill Judge* can passe, such a *Death* no *Civill sword* can inflict.

Soul killing the chiefest murder. No Magistrate can execute true justice in killing soule for soule, but Christ Jesus who by typicall death in the Law, typed out spirituall in the Gospel.

I answer secondly, *Dead men* cannot be infected, the *civill state*, the *world*, being in a naturall state dead in sin (what ever be the *State Religion* unto which *persons* are forced) it is impossible it should be infected: . . .

A great mistake in most to conceive that dead men, that is, soules dead in sin may be infected by false doctrine.

Moreover as we see in a *common plague* or *infection* the names are taken how many are to dye, and not one more shall be strucke, then the destroying *Angel* hath the names of. So here, what ever be the soule *infection* breathed out from they lying lips of a *plague-sicke Pharisee*, yet the names are taken, not one *elect* or chosen of God shall perish, *Gods sheep* are safe in His *eternall hand* and *counsell*, and he that knowes his *materiall*, knows also his *mysticall stars*, their *numbers*, and calls them every one by *name*, none fall into the *Ditch* on the blinde *Pharises* backe, but such as were *ordained* to that *condemnation*, both *guid* and *followers*, I *Pet.* 2. 8. *Jude* 4. The *vessells* of *wrath* shall breake and split, and only they to the praise of *Gods* eternall *justice*, *Rom.* 9. . . .

All naturall men being dead in sin, yet none die everlastingly but such as are thereunto ordained.

Truth. . . . I observe that he implyes that beside the *censure* of the Lord *Jesus*, in the hands of his *spirituall governours*, for any spirituall evill in *life* or *doctrine*, the *Civill Magistrate* is also to inflict *corporall punishment* upon the contrary minded: whereas

If the Civill
Magistrate be
a Christian,
he is bound to
be like Christ
in saving, not
destroying
mens bodies.

First, if the *Civill Magistrate* be a *Christian*, a *Disciple* or follower of the meeke *Lambe* of *God*, he is bound to be far from destroying the *bodies of men*, for refusing to receive the *Lord Jesus Christ*, for otherwise hee should not know (according to this speech of the *Lord Iesus*) what *spirit* he was of, yea and to be ignorant of the sweet end of the comming of the *Son of Man*, which was not to destroy the *bodies of Men*, but to save both *bodies* and *soules*, *vers.* 55. 56.

The Civill
Magistrate
bound not to
inflict nor to
suffer any
other to
inflict violence,
stripes, or any
corporall
punishment
for evill
against Christ.

Secondly, if the *Civill Magistrate*, being a *Christian*, gifted, *prophesie* in the *Church*, I *Corinth.* 1. 14. although the *Lord Iesus Christ*, whom they in their owne persons hold forth, shall be refused, yet they are here forbidden to call for fire from *heaven*, that is, to procure or inflict any corporall *judgement* upon such *offenders*, remembring the end of the *Lord Iesus* his comming, not to *destroy* mens lives, but to *save* them.

Lastly, this also concernes the *conscience* of the *Civill Magistrate*, as he is bound to preserve the *civill peace* and quiet of the *place* and people under him, he is bound to suffer no man to breake the *Civill Peace*, by laying hands of *violence* upon any, though as vile as the *Samaritanes* for not receiving of the *Lord Iesus Christ*.

Revel. 13
13. Fire from
heaven.
What the
fire from
heaven is
which the
fals prophet
bringeth
downe.

It is indeed the *ignorance* and blind *zeale* of the second *Beast*, the *false Prophet*, *Rev.* 13. 13. to perswade the *civill Powers* of the earth to persecute the Saints, that is, to bring fiery *judgements* upon men in a *judiciall way*, and to pronounce that such *judgements* of *imprisonment, banishment, death*, proceed from Gods righteous *vengeance* upon such *Hereticks*. So dealt divers *Bishops* in *France*, and *England* too in Queene *Maries* dayes with the Saints of God at their putting to death, declaiming against them in their Sermons to the people, and proclaiming that these persecutions even unto death were Gods *just judgements from heaven upon these Heretickes*. . . .

Spirituall
weapons only
effectuall in
spirituall &
soule
causes.

Truth. . . . To batter downe *Idolatry, false worship, heresie, schisme, blindnesse, hardnesse*, out of the *soule* and *spirit*, it is vaine, improper, and unsutable to bring those *weapons* which are used by *persecutors, stocks, whips, prisons, swords, gibbets, stakes*, &c. (where these seem to prevaile with some Cities or Kingdomes, a stronger force sets up againe, what a weaker pull'd downe) but against these *spirituall strong holds* in the soules of men, *Spirituall Artillery* and *weapons* are proper, which are mighty through *God* to subdue and bring under the very *thought* to *obedience*, or else to binde fast the soule with *chaines* of *darknesse*, and to locke it up in the *prison* of *unbeleefe* and hardnesse to *eternity*.

I observe that as *civill weapons* are improper in this businesse, and never able to effect ought in the *soule:* So (although they were proper, yet) they are *unnecessary*, for if as the *Spirit* here saith (and the *Answerer* grants) *spirituall weapons* in the hand of *Church officers* are able and ready to take *vengeance* on all disobedience, that is *able* and mighty, sufficient and ready for the *Lords* worke either to *save* the soule, or to *kill* the soule of whomsoever, be the party or parties opposite, in which respect I may againe remember that speech of *Job*, How hast thou helped him that hath no power? *Job* 26. . . .

Civill weapons not only improper, but unnecessary in spirituall causes.

Will the *Lord Jesus* (did He ever in His owne Person practice, or did he appoint to) joyne to His *Breastplate* of *Righteousnesse*, the *breastplate* of *iron* and *steele?* to the *Helmet* of *righteousnesse* and *salvation* in *Christ*, an helmet and crest of *iron*, *brasse*, or *steel*, a target of wood to His *shield* of Faith? [to] His two *edged sword* comming forth of the mouth of *Jesus*, the *materiall sword*, the worke of Smiths and Cutlers? or a girdle of shooes leather to the girdle of truth, &c. Excellently fit and proper is that *alarme* and *item*, *Psal.* 2. Be *wise* therefore O ye *Kings* (especially those ten *Horns*, *Rev.* 17.) who under pretence of fighting for *Christ Jesus* give their power to the *Beast* against *Him*, and be warned ye *Judges* of the Earth: *Kisse the Son*, that is with *subjection* and *affection*, acknowledge Him only the *King* and *Judge* of *soules* (in that power bequeathed to His *Ministers* and *Churches*) lest if His wrath be kindled, yea but a little, then *blessed* are they that *trust in* Him. . . .

Spirituall Ammunition. Eph. 6. applied *Materiall* and *Spirituall Artillery* unfitly joyned together.

An alarme to civill or earthly Rulers.

Peace. Yea but (say they) the *godly* will not persist in *Heresie* or turbulent *Schisme*, when they are convinced in *Conscience*, &c.

Truth. Sweet *Truth*, if the Civill Court and *Magistracy* must judge (as before I have written) and those Civill Courts are as lawfull, consisting of *naturall men* as of *godly* persons, then what *consequences* necessarily will follow, I have before mentioned. And I adde, according to this *conclusion* it must follow, that, if the most *godly* persons yeeld not to once or twice *Admonition* (as is maintained by the *Answerer*) they must necessarily be esteemed

The doctrine of persecution necessarily and most commonly falls heaviest upon the most godly persons.

obstinate persons, for if they were *godly* (saith he) they would yeeld. Must it not then be said (as it was by one, passing sentence of *Banishment* upon some, whose god-linesse was acknowledged) that he that commanded the *Judge* not to respect the poore in the cause of *judgement*, commands him not to respect the holy or the godly person?

The doctrine of persecution drives the most godly persons out of the world.

Hence I could name the place and time when a *godly* man, a most desirable person for his trade, &c. (yet something different in *conscience*) propounded his willing-nesse and desire to come to dwell in a certaine *Towne* in *New England;* it was answered by the Chiefe of the place, This man differs from us, and wee desire not to be troubled. So that in conclusion (for no other reason in the world) the poore man, though godly, usefull and peaceable, could not be admitted to a Civill Being and Habitation on the Common Earth in that Wildernesse amongst them. . . .

Peace. Mr. *Cotton* concludes with a confident perswasion of having removed the grounds of that great *errour, viz.* that persons are not to be persecuted for cause of *conscience.*

Truth. And I beleeve (deare *Peace*) it shall appear to them that (with feare and trembling at the word of the Lord) examine these passages, that the charge of *errour* reboundeth backe[,] even such an *errour*, as may well bee called the *bloody tenent*, so directly contradicting

The bloody Tenent.

the *spirit* and *minde* and *practice* of the *Prince* of *Peace;* so deeply guilty of the *blood* of soules compelled and forced to *Hypocrisie* in a *spirituall* and *soule rape;* so deeply guilty of the *blood* of the *Soules* under the *Altar*, perse-cuted in all *ages* for the *cause* of *Conscience*, and so de-structive to the *civill peace* and *welfare* of all *Kingdomes, Countries*, and *Commonwealths.*

LETTER TO THE TOWN OF PROVIDENCE,
January, 1655

[Upon his return from England in 1654 Roger Williams found the town of Providence torn by internal dissension; he was instrumental in restoring order, but soon afterwards a paper was circulating among the citizens proclaiming that it was contrary to the Gospel to execute judgment upon transgressors against the public or private weal. Williams thereupon wrote the following letter to the town in order to explain precisely what were the limits he prescribed to the liberal views he had maintained against John Cotton and the authorities of Massachusetts Bay. This text is from *Letters, Publications of the Narragansett Club*, Vol. VI (Providence, 1874), pp. 278–279.]

THAT ever I should speak or write a tittle, that tends to such an infinite liberty of conscience, is a mistake, and which I have ever disclaimed and abhorred. To prevent such mistakes, I shall at present only propose this case: There goes many a ship to sea, with many hundred souls in one ship, whose weal or woe is common, and is a true picture of a commonwealth, or a human combination or society. It hath fallen out sometimes, that both papists and protestants, Jews and Turks, may be embarked in one ship; upon which supposal I affirm, that all the liberty of conscience, that ever I pleaded for, turns upon these two hinges—that none of the papists, protestants, Jews, or Turks, be forced to come to the ship's prayers or worship, nor compelled from their own particular prayers or worship, if they practice any. I further add, that I never denied, that notwithstanding this liberty, the commander of this ship ought to command the ship's course, yea, and also command that justice, peace and sobriety, be kept and practiced, both among the seamen and all the passengers. If any of the seamen refuse to perform their services, or passengers to pay their freight; if any refuse to help, in person or purse, towards the common charges or defence; if any refuse to obey the common laws and orders of the ship, concerning their common peace or preservation; if any shall mutiny and rise up against their commanders and officers; if any should preach or write that there ought to be no commanders or officers, because all are equal in Christ, therefore no masters nor officers, no laws nor orders, nor corrections nor punishments; —I say, I never denied, but in such cases, whatever is pretended, the commander or commanders may judge, resist, compel and punish such transgressors, according to their deserts and merits. This if seriously and honestly minded, may, if it so please the Father of lights, let in some light to such as willingly shut not their eyes.

I remain studious of your common peace and liberty.

Roger Williams.

NATHANIEL WARD, 1578–1652

[Nathaniel Ward was an older man than most of the first ministers in New England and had a much more varied and secular career; these facts must be remembered in accounting for his style, the pe-

culiar quality of his writings, his wit, and his part in formulating the
laws of Massachusetts Bay. He was born at Haverhill, Essex, the son
of a minister; admitted sizar at Emmanuel College, 1596, he took his
B.A. in 1600, his M.A. in 1603. He studied and practised law, traveled
widely on the continent, and became a minister only in 1618. He served
as chaplain to an English factory at Ebling; returning to England he
was curate of St. James's, Picadilly, and of Stondon Massey in Essex.
A participant in the formation of the Massachusetts Bay Company,
he came to New England after he was silenced by Laud in 1634. For
two years he served as minister at Ipswich (of which the Indian name
was Aggawam), resigned in 1636, but remained in Massachusetts until
1646. He drew up the *Body of Liberties* in 1641 (cf. p. 204). Over the
mantel of his house in Ipswich a former occupant is said to have
carved three words representing the sum of Puritan ethics: sobriety,
justice, and piety; Nathaniel Ward added the word laughter. He is
reported to have said at one time, "I have two comforts to live upon:
The one is, in the Perfections of Christ: the other is in the imperfections of all Christians." After his return to England he preached a
sermon before the House of Commons, and in 1648 was made minister
of Shenfield, Essex. He wrote his pamphlet in 1645; it was published
in London in 1647. This text is from the first and third editions. The
full title of the book is:

> *The Simple Cobler of Aggawam in America. Willing to help 'mend his
> Native Country, lamentably tattered, both in the upper-Leather and sole, with
> all the honest stiches he can take.*
> *And as willing never to bee paid for his work, by Old English wonted pay.*
> *It is his Trade to patch all the year long, gratis*
> *Therefore I pray Gentlemen keep your purses.*

It was announced as written by "Theodore de la Guard." Cf. S. E.
Morison, *Builders of the Bay Colony;* J. W. Dean, *Nathaniel Ward,* 1868;
New England Historical & Genealogical Register, XVI, 365; XLI, 282.]

THE SIMPLE COBLER OF AGGAWAM

SATHAN is now in his passions, hee feeles his passion approaching;
he loves to fish in royled waters. Though that Dragon cannot
sting the vitals of the Elect mortally, yet that Beelzebub can fly-blow
their Intellectuals miserably: The finer Religion grows, the finer he
spins his Cobwebs, he will hold pace with Christ so long as his wits
will serve him. Hee sees himselfe beaten out of grosse Idolatries,
Heresies, Ceremonies, where the Light breakes forth with power; he

will therefore bestirre him to prevaricate Evangelicall Truths, and Ordinances, that if they will needs be walking, yet they shall *laborare varicibus*,[1] and not keep their path: he will put them out of time and place; Assassinating for his Engineers, men of Paracelsian [2] parts, well complexioned for honesty; for, such are fittest to Mountebanke his Chimistry into sicke Churches and weake Judgements.

Nor shall hee neede to stretch his strength overmuch in this worke: Too many men having not laid their foundation sure, nor ballasted their Spirits deep with humility and feare, are prest enough of themselves to evaporate their owne apprehensions. Those that are acquainted with Story know, it hath ever been so in new Editions of Churches: Such as are least able, are most busy to pudder in the rubbish, and to raise dust in the eyes of more steady Repayrers. Civill Commotions make room for uncivill practises: Religious mutations, for irreligious opinions: Change of aire, discovers corrupt bodies: Reformation of Religion, unsound mindes. He that hath any well-faced phancy in his Crowne, and doth not vent it now, feares, the pride of his own heart will dub him duns for ever. Such a one will trouble the whole *Israel* of God with his most untimely births, though he makes the bones of his vanity stick up, to the view and griefe of all that are godly wise. The devill desires no better sport then to see light heads handle their heeles, and fetch their carreers in a time, when the Roofe of Liberty stands open.

The next perplexed Question, with pious and ponderous men, will be: What should be done for the healing of these comfortlesse exulcerations. I am the unablest adviser of a thousand, the unworthiest of ten thousand; yet I hope I may presume to assert what follows without just offence.

First, such as have given or taken any unfriendly reports of us *New-English*, should doe well to recollect themselves. We have been reputed a Colluvies of wild Opinionists, swarmed into a remote wildernes to find elbow-roome for our phanatick Doctrines and practises: I trust our diligence past, and constant sedulity against such persons and courses, will plead better things for us. I dare take upon me, to be the Herauld of *New-England* so farre, as to proclaime to the world, in the name of our Colony, that all Familists, Antinomians, Anabaptists, and other Enthusiasts, shall have free Liberty to keep away from us, and such as will come to be gone as fast as they can, the sooner the better.

Secondly, I dare averre, that God doth no where in his word tolerate Christian States, to give Tolerations to such adversaries of his Truth, if they have power in their hands to suppresse them.

Here is lately brought us an Extract of a *Magna Charta*, so called, compiled between the Sub-planters of a *West-Indian* Island; whereof the first article of constipulation, firmely provides free stable-roome and litter for all kinde of consciences, be they never so dirty or jadish; making it actionable, yea, treasonable, to disturb any man in his Religion, or to discommend it, whatever it be. We are very sorry to see such professed profanenesse in *English* Professors, as industriously to lay their Religious foundations on the ruine of true Religion; which strictly bindes every conscience to contend earnestly for the Truth: to preserve unity of spirit, faith and Ordinances, to be all like-minded, of one accord; every man to take his brother into his Christian care: to stand fast with one spirit, with one minde, striving together for the faith of the Gospel: and by no meanes to permit Heresies or erroneous opinions: But God abhorring such loathsome beverages, hath in his righteous judgement blasted that enterprize, which might otherwise have prospered well, for ought *I* know: I presume their case is generally known ere this.

If the devill might have his free option, I beleeve he would ask nothing else, but liberty to enfranchize all other Religions, and to embondage the true; nor should he need: It is much to be feared, that laxe Tolerations upon State-pretences and planting necessities, will be the next subtle Stratagem he will spread, to distate the Truth of God and supplant the peace of the Churches. Tolerations in things tolerable, exquisitely drawn out by the lines of the Scripture, and pensill of the Spirit, are the sacred favours of Truth, the due latitudes of Love, the faire Compartiments of Christian fraternity: but irregular dispensations, dealt forth by the facilities of men, are the frontiers of errour, the redoubts of Schisme, the perillous irritaments of carnall enmity.

My heart hath naturally detested foure things: The standing of the Apocrypha in the Bible; Forrainers dwelling in my Countrey, to crowd out native Subjects into the corners of the Earth; Alchymized coines; Tolerations of divers Religions, or of one Religion in segregant shapes: He that willingly assents to the last, if he examines his heart by daylight, his conscience will tell him, he is either an Atheist, or an Heretique, or an Hypocrite, or at best a captive to some lust: polchpiety is the greatest impiety in the world. True Religion is *Ignis probationis*, which doth *congregare homogenea & segregare heterogenia*.[3]

Not to tolerate things meerly indifferent to weak consciences, argues a conscience too strong: pressed uniformity in these, causes much disunity. To tolerate more than indifferents, is not to deale indifferently with God; He that doth it, takes his Scepter out of His hand,

and bids Him stand by. The power of all Religion and Ordinances, lies in their purity: their purity in their simplicity: then are mixtures pernicious. I lived in a City, where a Papist Preached in one Church, a Lutheran in another, a Calvinist in a third; a Lutheran one part of the day, a Calvinist the other, in the same Pulpit: the Religion óf that place was but motly and meagre, their affections Leopard-like.

If the whole Creature should conspire to doe the Creator a mis-chiefe, or offer him an insolency, it would be in nothing more, then in erecting untruths against his Truth, or by sophisticating his Truths with humane medley's: the removing of some one iota in Scripture, may draw out all the life, and traverse all the Truth of the whole Bible: but to authorise an untruth, by a Toleration of State, is to build a Sconce against the walls of Heaven, to batter God out of his Chaire: To tell a practicall lye, is a great sinne, but yet transient; but to set up a Theoricall untruth, is to warrant every lye that lyes from its root to the top of every branch it hath.

I would willingly hope that no Member of the Parliament hath skil-fully ingratiated himselfe into the hearts of the House, that he might watch a time to midwife out some ungracious Toleration for his own turne, and for the sake of that, some others. I would also hope that a word of generall caution should not bee particularly misapplied. Yet good Gentlemen, looke well about you, and remember how *Tiberius* plaid the Fox with the Senate of *Rome*, and how *Fabius Maximus* cropt his eares for his cunning.

That State is wise, that will improve all paines and patience rather to compose, then tolerate differences in Religion. There is no divine Truth, but hath much Celestiall fire in it from the Spirit of Truth: nor no irreligious untruth, without its proportion of Antifire from the Spirit of Error to contradict it: the zeale of the one, the virulency of the other, must necessarily kindle Combustions. Fiery diseases seated in the spirit, embroile the whole frame of the body; others more ex-ternall and coole, are lesse dangerous. They which divide in Religion, divide in God; they who divide in him, divide beyond *Genus Generalissi-mum*,[4] where there is no reconciliation, without atonement; that is, with-out uniting in him, who is One, and in his Truth, which is also one.

Wise are those men who will be perswaded rather to live within the pale of Truth where they may bee quiet, than in the purliev's, where they are sure to bee hunted ever and anon, doe Authority what it can. Every singular Opinion, hath a singular opinion of it self; and he that holds it, a singular opinion of himselfe, and a simple opinion of all contra-sentients: he that confutes them, must confute all three at once, or else he does nothing; which will not be done without more stirre then the peace of the State or Church can indure.

And prudent are those Christians, that will rather give what may be given, then hazard all by yeelding nothing. To sell all peace of Country, to buy some peace of Conscience unseasonably, is more avarice than thrift, imprudence than patience: they deale not equally, that set any Truth of God at such a rate; but they deale wisely that will stay till the Market is fallen.

My prognosticks deceive me not a little, if once within three seven yeares, peace prove not such a penny worth at most Marts in Christendome, that he that would not lay downe his money, his lust, his opinion, his will, I had almost said the best flower of his Crowne, for it, while he might have had it; will tell his owne heart, he plaid the very ill husband.

Concerning Tolerations I may further assert.

That Persecution of true Religion, and Toleration of false, are the *Jannes* and *Jambres* to the Kingdome of Christ, whereof the last is farre the worst. *Augustines* tongue had not owed his mouth one penny-rent though it had never spake word more in it, but this, *Nullum malum pejus libertate errandi.*[5]

He that is willing to tolerate any Religion, or discrepant way of Religion, besides his owne, unlesse it be in matters meerly indifferent, either doubts of his owne, or is not sincere in it.

He that is willing to tolerate any unsound Opinion, that his owne may also be tolerated, though never so sound, will for a need hang Gods Bible at the Devills girdle.

Every Toleration of false Religions, or Opinions hath as many Errors and sinnes in it, as all the false Religions and Opinions it tolerates, and one sound one more.

That State that will give Liberty of Conscience in matters of Religion, must give Liberty of Conscience and Conversation in their Morall Lawes, or else the Fiddle will be out of tune, and some of the strings cracke.

He that will rather make an irreligious quarrell with other Religions, then try the Truth of his own by valuable Arguments, and peaceable Sufferings; either his Religion, or himselfe is irreligious.

Experience will teach Churches and Christians, that it is farre better to live in a State united, though somewhat Corrupt, then in a State, whereof some Part is Incorrupt, and all the rest divided.

I am not altogether ignorant of the eight Rules given by Orthodox Divines, about giving Tolerations, yet with their favour I dare affirme,

That there is no Rule given by God for any State to give an Affirmative Toleration to any false Religion, or Opinion whatsoever; they must connive in some Cases, but may not concede in any.

That the State of *England* (so farre as my Intelligence serves) might in time have prevented with ease, and may yet without any great difficulty deny both Toleration, and Connivances *salva Republica*.[6]

That if the State of *England* shall either willingly Tolerate, or weakly connive at such Courses, the Church of that Kingdome will sooner become the Devills Dancing-Schoole, then Gods-Temple: The Civill State a Beare-garden, then an Exchange: The whole Realme a Pais base,[7] then an *England*. And what pity it is, that that Country which hath been the Staple of Truth to all Christendome, should now become the Aviary of Errors to the whole World, let every fearing heart judge. . . .

Concerning Novelties of opinions; I shall expresse my thoughts in these briefe passages. First, that Truth is the best boone God ever gave the world: there is nothing in the world, any further then Truth makes it so; it is better than any creat' *Ens* or *Bonum*, which are but Truths twins.[8] Secondly, the least Truth of Gods Kingdome, doth in its place, uphold the whole kingdome of his Truths; Take away the least *vericulum* [9] out of the world, and it unworlds all, potentially, and may unravell the whole texture actually, if it be not conserved by an Arme of extraordinary power. Thirdly, the least Evangelicall Truth, is more worth·than all the Civill Truths in the world, that are meerly so. Fourthly, that Truth is the Parent of all Liberty whether politicall or personall; so much untruth, so much thraldome, *John* 8. 32.

Hence it is, that God is so jealous of his Truths, that he hath taken order in his due Justice: First, that no practicall sin is so sinfull as some errour in judgement; no men so accursed with indelible infamy and dedolent impenitency, as Authours of Heresie. Secondly, that the least Error, if grown sturdy and pressed, shall set open the Spittle-doore of all the squint-ey'd, wry-necked, and brasen-faced Errors that are or ever were of that litter; if they be not enough to serve its turne, it will beget more, though it hath not one crust of reason to maintain them. Thirdly, that, that State which will permit Errors in Religion, shall admit Errors in Policy unavoydably. Fourthly, that that Policy which will suffer irreligious errors, shall suffer the losse of so much Liberty in one kinde or other, I will not exempt *Venice*, *Rhaguse*, the *Nether-lands*, or any.

An easie head may soon demonstrate, that the prementioned Planters,

by Tolerating all Religions, had immazed themselves in the most intolerable confusions and inextricable thraldomes the world ever heard
of. I am perswaded the Devill himselfe was never willing with their
proceedings, for feare it would break his winde and wits to attend such
a Province. I speak it seriously according to my meaning. How all
Religions should enjoy their liberty, Justice its due regularity, Civill
cohabitation morall honesty, in one and the same Jurisdiction, is beyond the Artique of my comprehension. If the whole conclave of Hell
can so compromise, exadverse, and diametriall contradictions, as to
compolitize such a multimonstrous maufrey of heteroclytes and quic-
quidlibets quietly; I trust I may say with all humble reverence, they
can doe more then the Senate of Heaven. My *modus loquendi* [10] pardoned; I entirely wish much welfare and more wisdome to that
Plantation. . . .

Should I not keep promise in speaking a little to Womens fashions,
they would take it unkindly: I was loath to pester better matter with
such stuffe; I rather thought it meete to let them stand by themselves,
like the *Quæ Genus* [11] in the Grammar, being Deficients, or Redundants,
not to bee brought under any Rule[.] I shall therefore make bold for
this once, to borrow a little of their loose-tongue Liberty, and mispend
a word or two upon their long-wasted, but short-skirted patience: a
little use of my stirrup will doe no harme.

> *Ridentem dicere verum, quid prohibet?* [12]
>
> *Gray Gravity it selfe can well beteame,*
> *That Language be adapted to the Theme.*
> *He that to Parrots speaks, must parrotise;*
> *He that instructs a foole, may act th' unwise.*

It is known more then enough, that I am neither Nigard, nor Cinick,
to the due bravery of the true Gentry: if any man mislikes a bully
mong drassock more then I, let him take her for all mee: I honour
the woman that can honour her self with her attire: a good Text
alwayes deserves a fair Margent: I am not much offended, if I see a
trimme, far trimmer than she that wears it: in a word, whatever Christianity or Civility will allow, I can afford with *London* measure: but
when I heare a nugiperous Gentledame inquire what dresse the Queen
is in this week; what the nudiustertian fashion of the Court; I mean
the very newest: with egge to be in it in all haste, what ever it be;
I look at her as the very gizzard of a trifle, the product of a quarter
of a cypher, the epitome of nothing, fitter to be kickt, if she were of a
kickable substance, than either honoured or humoured.

To speak moderately, I truely confesse, it is beyond the ken of my understanding to conceive, how those women should have any true grace, or valuable vertue, that have so little wit, as to disfigure themselves with such exotick garbes, as not onely dismantles their native lovely lustre, but transclouts them into gant bar-geese, ill-shapen shotten shell-fish, Egyptian Hieroglyphicks, or at the best into French flurts of the pastery, which a proper English-woman should scorn with her heeles: it is no marvell they weare drailes on the hinder part of their heads, having nothing as it seems in the fore-part, but a few Squirrills braines, to help them frisk from one ill-favor'd fashion to another.

> *These whimm' Crown'd shees, these fashion-fansying wits,*
> *Are empty thin brain'd shells, and fidling Kits,*

The very troublers and impoverishers of mankind. I can hardly forbeare to commend to the world a saying of a Lady living sometime with the Queen of *Bohemiah*, I know not where she found it, but it is pitty it should be lost.

> *The world is full of care, much like unto a bubble;*
> *Women and care, and care and women, and women and care and trouble.*

The Verses are even enough for such odde pegma's. I can make my self sick at any time, with comparing the dazzling splender wherewith our Gentlewomen were embellished in some former habits, with the gut-foundred goosdome, wherewith they are now surcingled and debauched. We have about five or six of them in our Colony: if I see any of them accidentally, I cannot cleanse my phansie of them for a month after. I have been a solitary widdower almost twelve years, purposed lately to make a step over to my Native Country for a yoke-fellow: but when I consider how women there have tripe-wifed themselves with their cladments, I have no heart to the voyage, lest their nauseous shapes and the Sea, should work too sorely upon my stomach. I speak sadly; me thinks it should break the hearts of Englishmen, to see so many goodly English-women imprisoned in French Cages, peering out of their hood-holes for some men of mercy to help them with a little wit, and no body relieves them.

It is a more common then convenient saying, that nine Taylors make a man: it were well if nineteene could make a woman to her minde: if Taylors were men indeed, well furnished but with meere morall principles, they would disdain to be led about like Apes, by such mymick Marmosets. It is a most unworthy thing, for men that

have bones in them, to spend their lives in making fidle-cases for
futilous womens phansies; which are the very pettitoes of infirmity, the
gyblets of perquisquilion toyes. I am so charitable to think, that most of
that mystery, would work the cheerfuller while they live, if they might
be well discharged of the tyring slavery of mis-tyring women: it is
no little labour to be continually putting up English-women into Out-
landish caskes; who if they be not shifted anew, once in a few moneths,
grow too sowre for their Husbands. What this Trade will answer for
themselves when God shall take measure of Taylors consciences is
beyond my skill to imagine. There was a time when

> *The joyning of the Red-Rose with the White*
> *Did set our State into a Damask plight.*

But now our Roses are turned to *Flore de lices*, our Carnations to
Tulips, our Gilliflowers to pansies, our City-Dames, to an indenomi-
nable Quaemalry of overturcas'd things. Hee that makes Coates for
the Moone, had need take measure every noone; and he that makes
for women, every Moone, to keep them from Lunacy.

I have often heard diverse Ladies vent loud feminine complaints
of the wearisome varieties and chargable changes of fashion: I marvell
themselves prefer not a Bill of redresse. I would *Essex** Ladies would
lead the *Chore*, for the honour of their County and persons; or rather
the thrice honourable Ladies of the Court, whom it best beseemes:
who may wel presume of a *Le Roy le veult* from our sober King, a *Les
Seigneurs ont Assentus* [13] from our prudent Peers, and the like Assentus
from our considerate, I dare not say wife-worne Commons: who I
beleeve had much rather passe one such Bill, than pay so many
Taylors Bills as they are forced to doe.

Most deare and unparallel'd Ladies, be pleased to attempt it: as
you have the precellency of the women of world for beauty and feature;
so assume the honour to give, and not take Law from any, in matter of
attire: if ye can transact so faire a motion among your selves unanimously, I dare say, they that most renite, will least repent. What
greater honour can your Honors desire, then to build a Promontory
president to all foraigne Ladies, to deserve so eminently at the hands
of all the English Gentry, present and to come; and to confute the
opinion of all the wise men in the world; who never thought it possible
for women to doe so good a work.

---

* [*Ward's note, marginal in the original:*] All the Counties and shires of England
have had wars in them since the Conquest, but Essex, which is onely free, and should
be thankful.

[Added in 3ᵈ ed.]—If any man think I have spoken rather merrily than seriously he is much mistaken, I have written what I write with all the indignation I can, and no more then I ought. I confesse I veer'd my tongue to this kinde of Language *de industria* though unwillingly, supposing those I speak to are uncapable of grave and rationall arguments . . .

There is a quadrobulary saying, which passes current in the Westerne world, That the Emperour is King of Kings, the Spaniard, King of Men, the French, King of Asses, the King of *England*, King of Devills: By his leave that first brayed the speech, they are pretty wise Devills and pretty honest; the worst they doe, is to keep their Kings from Divelizing, and themselves from Assing: Were I a King (a simple supposall) I would not part with one good English Divell, for two of the Emperours Kings nor three of the Spaniards Men, nor foure French Asses; if I did, *I* should thinke my selfe an Asse for my labour. *I* know nothing that Englishmen want, but true Grace, and honest pride: let them be well furnisht with those two, I feare they would make more Asses, then *Spaine* can make men, or the Emperour Kings. You will say I am now beyond my latchet; but you would not say so, if you knew how high my latchet will stretch, when I heare a lye with a latchet, that reaches up to his throat that first forged it.

He is a good King that undoeth not his Subjects, by any one of his unlimited Prerogatives: and they are a good People, that undoe not their Prince, by any one of their unbounded Liberties, be they the very least: I am sure either may, and I am sure neither would be trusted, how good soever. Stories tell us in effect, though not in termes, that over-risen Kings, have been the next evills to the world, unto falne Angels; and that over-franchized people, are devills with smooth snaffles in their mouthes. A King that lives by Law, lives by love; and he that lives above Law, shall live under hatred doe what he can. Slavery and Knavery goe as seldome asunder, as Tyranny and Cruelty.

I have a long while thought it very possible, in a time of Peace, and in some Kings Reigne, for disert Statesmen, to cut an exquisite thred between and quite through Kings Prerogatives, and Subjects Liberties of all sorts, so as *Cæsar* might have his due, and People their share, without such sharpe disputes. Good Casuists would case it, and case it, part it and part it, now it, and then it, punctually. *Aquinas*, *Suarez*, or *Valentia*,[14] would have done it long ere this, and they not been Popish, I might have said knavish; for, if they be so any where, it is in their Tractates of Priviledges. Our Common Law doth well, but it must doe better before things doe as they should. There are some *Maximes* in Law, that would bee taught to speak a little more mannerly, or else well *Anti-maxim'd:* we say, the King can doe a Subject no wrong; why may we not say, the Parliament can do the King no wrong? We say, *Nullum tempus occurrit Regi* [15] in taking wrong; why may we not say, *Nullum tempus succurrit Regi* [16] in doing wrong? which I doubt will prove a better Canon, if well examined.

Authority must have power to make and keep people honest; People, honesty to obey Authority; both, a joynt-Councell to keep both safe. Morall Laws, Royall Prerogatives, Popular Liberties, are not of Mans making or giving, but Gods: Man is but to measure them out by Gods Rule: which if mans wisdome cannot reach, Mans experience must mend: And these Essentialls, must not be Ephorized or Tribuned by one or a few Mens discretion, but lineally sanctioned by Supreame Councels. In *pro-re-nascent* occurrences, which cannot be foreseen; Diats, Parliaments, Senates, or accountable Commissions, must have power to consult and execute against intersilient dangers and flagitious crimes prohibited by the light of Nature: Yet it were good if States would let People know so much before hand, by some safe woven *manifesto*, that grosse Delinquents may tell no tales of Anchors and Buoyes, nor palliate their presumptions with pretence of ignorance. I know no difference in these Essentialls, between Monarchies, Aristocracies, or Democracies; the rule and reason will bee found all one, say Schoolemen and Pretorians what they will. And in all, the best Standard to measure Prerogatives, is the Plough-staffe; to measure Liberties, the Scepter: if the tearmes were a little altered into Loyall Prerogatives and Royall Liberties, then we should be sure to have Royall Kings and Loyall Subjects.

> *Subjects their King, the King his Subjects greets,*
> *Whilome the Scepter and the Plough-staffe meets.*

But Progenitors have had them for four and twenty predecessions: that would be spoken in the Norman tongue or Cimbrian, not in the English or Scottish: When a Conquerour turnes Christian, Christianity turnes Conquerour: if they had had them time out of minde of man, before *Adam* was made, it is not a pin to the point in *foro rectæ rationis:* [17] Justice and Equity were before time, and will be after it: Time hath neither Politicks nor Ethicks, good nor evill in it; it is an empty thing, as empty as a *New-English* purse, and emptier it cannot be: a man may break his neck in time, and in a lesse time then he can heale it.

JONATHAN MITCHELL, 1624–1668

[Jonathan Mitchell, the intellectual leader of New England in the second generation, was born at Halifax, Yorkshire, and was brought by his parents to New England in 1635. Graduated from Harvard in 1647, he was chosen to the important post of minister at Cambridge, where he married the widow of his great predecessor, Thomas Shepard. He was the leader of the movement for the Half-Way Covenant, was the tutor and mentor of Increase Mather. This text is from *Nehemiah on the Wall in Troublesome Times* (Cambridge, 1671), an election sermon preached in 1667. Cf. life in Cotton Mather, *Magnalia*, and J. L. Sibley, *Biographical Sketches*.]

NEHEMIAH ON THE WALL

CIVIL rulers] *are especially to seek the welfare of the people of God:* or to seek the welfare of the people over whom they are Rulers, especially when as they are the Lords people. . . .

VSE I. This Point shews us what ought to be the general End and Rule of all the Motions and Actions of Rulers, *viz.* the welfare of the poeple. To that scope *Nehemiah* bends all his Actions and Endeavours; and *Finis est mensura mediorum*, the End serves to measure, regulate, direct and limit the means, and shew what should be done. That *Maxime* of the *Romans* was and is a Principle of right Reason, *Salus Populi Suprema Lex*, (The welfare of the People is the Supreme Law) and is engraven on the Forehead of the Law and Light of *Nature*. Hence it is owned and confirmed by the *Scriptures*, as we see in the Text; and it is easily deducible from the Law of God: for that that is indeed the Law of Nature, is a part of the Eternal Law of God; and the Law of God enjoyns, that in Humane Civil Affairs, things be managed according to right Reason and Equity; and that Rulers, as they are for the people, so they are to make it their main business, and the scope of all their Actions, Laws and Motions, to seek the welfare of the people. There is Sun-light for this Maxime, and it was never doubted nor denied by any that held but to Rational and Moral Principles. Hence this Law being Supreme, it limits all other Laws and Considerations. Hence it is impossible that a people or their Rulers should be bound by any other Law, or Custome, or Consideration whatsoever, to do any thing that is really and evidently contrary to this. If it be indeed contrary or destructive to the welfare of the people, (of the Community they stand charged with) it is impossible they should be bound in *Conscience* to do it.

This is the *Compass* that Rulers are to steer by, and the *Touch-stone* of Right and Wrong in all their Motions, *viz*. What is for or against the Publick good, and the Welfare of the people, *Rom*. 13. 14. That bounds and regulates his whole Ministration. What is for the *Common good*, that and that only you are to do; and all that are set in place of Rule and Government (be they of higher or of lower quality) do stand charged with the welfare of that people, whom they are Rulers over.

I know when it comes to particulars, the doubt will still be, What is for the welfare of the people. One will say, this is most for the common good, another that. But

1. It will help much if this Principle be setled and acknowledged, That in Civil Affairs, the Consideration of the welfare of the whole, is that which shews and determines what is right, and weighs down all other Considerations whatsoever. Men will say, We must do what is right, whatsoever comes of it: *Fiat Justitia ruat Cœlum*. True, but it is most certain it is not right, if it be against the welfare of the people. It is impossible that any thing should be truly right, that is destructive to the common good: for it will constantly hold, *Salus Populi Suprema Lex*.

2. Consider the things wherein the welfare of a people does consist, which are above-mentioned, (*viz*. Religion in the first place, and then their Safety, or the Preservation of their Being, both Personal and Political, and their participation in the Rules and Fruits of Righteousness, Equity, Order and Peace) and that will help to discover and discern what is for the welfare of the people, or for the common good, and what not. There is need of much prudence and wariness in particular Applications and Cases; but those general Principles will hold, That a peoples welfare lies in such things as these, and that Rulers are bound in all their Motions and Actions to seek the welfare of the people, and to do nothing contrary thereunto.

VSE II. Hence see, that difficulties and troubles do not *excuse*, nor should *discourage* Rulers from doing the work of their Places which God calls them unto, or from seeking the welfare of the people: Such things do not excuse, nor should discourage from taking and accepting the Place of Rule when called to it. As they did not *Nehemiah*, though he heard before that their condition was a condition of great affliction and reproach, *Neh*. 1. 3. yet he voluntarily left the Court of *Persia*, to embarque with the *Jews* at *Jerusalem*, when in so stormy a time as this was; and how is he honoured in the Book of God for it? It was a difficult time and task that *Moses* was sent upon, accompanied also with a deep sense of his own infirmity and unfitness, *Exod*. 3. 4. he could not but be slow and backward to such a work; but yet when he was over-backward the Lord grew angry, and chides him into a consent: but (I say) difficulties and troubles should not discourage nor hinder Rulers from doing the work of their Places when set therein, *i.e.* from faithful seeking and acting for the welfare of the people, which is (as we have said) the summary work of the Rulers Place. Consider a little the difficulties that lay upon the *Jews* and their Rulers at this time in *Jerusalem*, after their return from Captivity, and in the dayes of *Nehemiah*.[1]

1. They were a small, weak and despised people, *Nehem.* 4. 1, 2, 4. & 1. 3. & 2. 19. Contempt and reproach is a bitter and killing thing to ingenuous Spirits; yet this they were fain to bear and pass through. It was a *day of small things*, which others, yea even themselves are apt to despise, *Zech.* 4. 10.

2. They were in the midst of Enemies, and Adversaries round about them, of several sorts and Nations; *Sanballat* a *Moabite*, (from *Horonaim* a chief City of *Moab*, *Isa.* 15. 5. *Jer.* 48. 3, 5, 34. called the *Horonite*) and *Tobiah* the Servant, the *Ammonite*, on the East, *Neh.* 2. 10. (*The Servant*, he was Governour of the *Ammonites*, but of a base and servile spirit; some think that of a mean man, he was got into Place, and therefore is called *Tobiah the Servant:* such are often worst, *Prov.* 30. 21, 22.) *Geshem* the *Arabian* (Neh. 6. 1. & 4. 7.) and others on the *South;* and the *Samaritans* on the *North*, Neh. 4. 2. Ezra 4. 9, 10. Thus they were beset round with Adversaries, and Ill-willers, and many Informers and Complainers there were against them, as before in the dayes of *Zerubbabel*, *Ezra* 4. & 5.

3. Their Adversaries did labour to affright them with the Accusation of *Rebellion*, *Neh.* 2. 19. an old *Artifice*, but it was an injurious Calumny, and most groundless Accusation. The building of the Wall of *Jerusalem* for *self-preservation*, had nothing in it of *Rebellion:* but many clamours and stories they raised of that nature, *Neh.* 6. 6, 7, 8. and see their end therein, *ver.* 9. to weaken and discourage them from their work, that their hearts and hands might fail them therein, that was it they aimed at.[2]

4. There were Discontents and Divisions among themselves, *Neh.* 5. 1. Great Complaints of the *Inferiour* sort against their *Superiours;* of the Poor against the Rich; of Brethren against Brethren: yea, there were among themselves that were helpers to their Adversaries, and complied with them, even some *chief men* and others, *Neh.* 6. 17, 18. and thereby, among other evils, it came to pass that nothing could be kept within its due compass, but every thing was carried and reported to their

Adversaries, *ver.* 19. *They uttered my words* (or my matters) *unto him;* and that doubtless not in the fairest dress. Yea, there were some of the Prophets that endeavoured to weaken the hands of faithful *Nehemiah*, and to put discouragement upon him, *Neh.* 6. 10, (This *Shemaiah* is conceived to be the same that is mentioned *Ezra* 8. 16.) 11, 12, 13. (By the way, who would have said that that would have been a sin, which might seem to be a prudent retirement for safety? yea, but for *Nehemiah*, in a case so circumstanced, to act fear and discouragement to the prejudice of his Cause and Work, would have been a sin.) But *ver.* 14. there were also that raised Slanders of others of their *Prophets*, those it's like who were of another minde, *ver.* 7.

5. They were poor, and low, and weak as to outward estate, con-flicting with wants and straits, and many difficulties in that respect, very unable to support themselves, and to bear the Publick Burthens that were then upon them, *Neh.* 5. 2–5. and *ver.* 18. *The bondage was heavy upon this people:* Neh. 9. 37. *We are in great distress.*

6. Hence there was *hard* Work, and *weak* Instruments, ready many times to be discouraged, *Neh.* 4. 10. the Workmen themselves, and those that should joyn hands together to labour and carry on the work, began to mutter and be discouraged, by the difficulty of the work, and their own weakness; *We are not able,* say they, *to carry it on:* At the same time when the Adversaries were high, *president* and threatning, *ver.* 11. their own workmen began to be disheartned and *diffident*, ver. 10. Here was a juncture of discouraging trial. Hence hard shifts they were fain to make to carry on the work, and to put forth them-selves to the utmost, and beyond an ordinary measure, by the care and courage and conduct of good *Nehemiah, ver.* 16, 17. Every one had both his hands full, and they were fain to do two works at once, the work of a *Souldier*, and of a *Labourer*, ver. 18, 21, 22, 23.

7. It was a time of many *fears;* wherein they had many fears among them, and many that heightned those fears: many Reports, Threatnings and fore-speakings of this, and that, to that purpose, *Neh.* 4. 12. *&* 6. 9, 13, 14, 19. It is observeable, that that was the drift and endeavours of Adversaries and Ill-willers, *Fear, fear, fear;* a discouraging *Heart* and *Hand-weakning* carnal *fear.* The great word of *God* to godly Rulers is, *Be strong, and of a good courage,* fear not when in Gods way and work, *Josh.* 1. 6, 7, 9. But the word of *Satan* and his Instruments is, *Fear,* be *afraid,* look upon the danger of being faithful: But (as to man and second Causes) they had many very great causes of fear, many dangers round about them, and to be faithful in duty in a time of fear, proves a difficult task to flesh and blood.

8. Which was worst of all, Among this people of the *Jews* after Captivity, when engaged in Reforming work, there were many sins, disorders and miscarriages, which were provoking unto God, and a great exercise of discouragement to their faithful Leaders; such in *Ezra's* time as made him *blush before God*, and fear what God would do with them, *Ezra* 9. 6, 10, 14. And before that in *Haggai's* time, such neglects of carrying on Temple-work, and of finishing what was begun, as he sharply reproves, yea as God reproved from Heaven, by Drought, Blastings, &c. *Hag.* 1. 2, 5, 6, 9, 10, 11. & 2. 16, 17. And here in *Nehemiahs* time there were faults, evils and distempers found among them, as *Neh.* 5. 1, 6, 7, 9. & 13. 4, 5, 10, 15, 18, 23, 24, 26, 27. not onely matter of *Affliction*, but sinful *Corruptions* and Distempers do sprout up among a Reforming people, and those they have to wrestle with: yet neither did these take them or their Leaders off from their Work, nor utterly overturn it; nor did the Lord cast them off (though he chastened them) but helped them along, though in much infirmity. He was with them at many a dead lift, (*Hag.* 2. 4.) and after *frowns*, yet *smiled* on them again: especially while the Leaders were faithful to search out and testifie against *evil*, and to set upon *duty* when called to it; and the people were willing to hearken to them, and to be reduced and reformed by them: both which may be observed of them all along in the story, *Hag.* 1. 12, 13. *Ezra* 10. 2, 3, 4, 7, 8, 12, 14.

9. Lastly, we may remember the long time wherein this poor people were conflicting and labouring under Difficulties and Infirmities, and what a succession of Difficulties and Troubles did attend them in the Reforming, and Rebuilding work they were upon. From their first Grant by *Cyrus*, unto the beginning of *Nehemiahs* Government (in the twentieth year of *Artaxerxes*) according to the shortest Account, were 82 years (so *Usher* in his *Annals*. *Junius* saith 146. *Lightfoot* saith but 37, but few embrace that.) Almost all that time, & so afterward in the time of *Nehemiahs* Government, they were followed with various Troubles and Exercises (as the story at large tells us) though they had their lucid Intervals, and the Lord still helping in the issue.

Thus that word was made good, *Dan.* 9. 25. that *Jerusalem*, both City and Wall, *should be built again in troublous times*. Yet notwithstanding all this, they went on in their Work with *Courage*, and *Constancy*, and *Confidence* in God, *Neh.* 2. 20. and he did prosper them, not by preventing Difficulties, but by carrying on the Work in their hands through all Difficulties, and in the midst of all their Infirmities. And it is observeable, That every *Tragedy* they passed through, had a glad *Catastrophe;*

every stress had a comfortable issue: God still helped them in the conclusion and upshot of every business, that they came off well at last,
though with much tugging and wrestling, much exercise of Faith and
Patience. So in the Building of the Temple, (thus it went on heavily,
and met with many obstructions, and many Adversaries; yet they got
through at last, to their great joy) *Ezra* 6. 15, 16, 22. So here in the
building of the Wall, *Neh.* 6. 15, 16. & 12. 27, 43. And so in the Reformation of Abuses, *Ezra* 10. *Neh.* 5. & 13. The story of the *Church* in all
Ages, & especially in the Scripture, informs us, that the best and greatest works God hath delighted to carry on through many Difficulties
and Oppositions, and in much felt infirmity of Instruments. The time
of *Moses*, of *David*, of *Israel*, all along in the *Old Testament*, will furnish
us with many Instances of it; yea and also of the *Apostles* in their Work
under the *New Testament*, *Act.* 20. 19. 1 *Cor.* 16. 9. & 3. 3. 2 *Cor.* 11. 23–
28, 29, 30. *Gal.* 4. 13, 14. the glorious Gospel must be preached &
carried on *through Infirmity of the flesh*, i.e. through outward meanness
and affliction of Instruments, yet not therefore to be despised. The
whole Church of God, and every particular concernment thereof, is in
a *Militant* conflicting condition in this world, and it must be no stumbling to us to see it so: it occasions the more exercise of *Faith, Patience,
Prayer, &c.* in the work (as we see in the example of *Nehemiah* all along)
and the more of God to appear in the issue of it, *Neh.* 6. 16.

Go on therefore in the Work of the Lord, and in the Service of your
several Places, and be not taken off by trouble, difficulties, oppositions,
felt infirmities in your selves, weaknesses and distempers in persons and
things round about you, (which will alwayes be.) When were there
work for Patience, Faith, Fortitude, Self-denial, and for the Spirit of a
Souldier, Wrestler, &c. if it were not for such things? We must none
of us say, of one Order or other, I will serve God in my place, and
help build the Wall of *Jerusalem*, if I may do it with ease, and tran-
quility, without trouble, without hazard, without reproaches, and ill
requitals from men. &c. Christ is little beholden to us, if that be all
we will do for him; that is too low for the Spirit of a *good Souldier of
Christ Jesus*, 2. Cor. 6. 4, 5, 8. Yea, now you look like the Ministers of
God, when you cheerfully discharge your Places, though surrounded
and loaden with Afflictions, Distresses, Labours, false Reproaches, &c.
Now you are drest like a Minister, like a Servant of God, and of his
people in Publick Work; and through such things as these, you must
go on in your Work, as the Apostles then did.

WILLIAM STOUGHTON, 1631–1701

[William Stoughton was the second son of Israel Stoughton, who came to New England in 1630, a founder of Dorchester and a large land owner. William graduated from Harvard in 1650, went to Oxford, where he became a fellow of New College and received his M.A. in 1653. He was a curate in Sussex in 1659, was ejected from his church and from his fellowship at the Restoration, and returned to Massachusetts in 1662. He preached at Dorchester, but refused to be ordained, and turned from theology to law and politics. He was an Assistant, 1671–1686; Commissioner of the United Colonies, 1674–1676, 1680–1686; a judge, and an agent of the colony in England, 1676–1679. He was a friend of Joseph Dudley, by whom he was appointed deputy governor in 1686; he remained on Andros's council, but went over to the Revolution in 1688. Named lieutenant governor under the new charter in 1692, he became acting governor in 1694 and was the real head of the colony from then until his death, except for the few months in 1699 and 1700 when Bellomont was in Boston. He was chief justice of the special court which tried and condemned the witches at Salem in 1692, and he is said never to have repented his share in the proceedings. The text is from *New-Englands True Interest; Not to Lie* (Cambridge, 1670), an election sermon preached on April 29, 1668. Cf. Sibley, *Biographical Sketches*.]

NEW–ENGLANDS TRUE INTEREST

A<small>ND</small> here I shall consider that the words of the Text are spoken concerning a People, even the Body of a Nation; and so my endeavour shall be to apply the Truths delivered, unto this present Assembly standing before the Lord this day as the *Body of this People:* Such in several respects is the Capacity of this solemn Congregation, and unto you *as such*, my desire is to speak in the Name of the Lord. For many a day and year, even from our first beginnings hath this word of the Lord been verified concerning us in this Wilderness; *The Lord hath said of* New-England, *Surely they are my People, Children that will not lie, so hath he been our Saviour.* Upon this Basis have all the *Saviourly Undertakings* of the Lord been founded in the midst of us, and upon this bottom do we unto this day abide.

The solemn work of this day is *Foundation-work;* not to lay a new Foundation, but to continue and strengthen, and beautifie, and build

upon that which hath been laid. Give me leave therefore, Honoured
and Beloved, to awaken, and call upon you, in the Name of him who
sends me, with reference unto those *Foundations* that are held forth to
us in the Text, for if these should be *out of course*, what could the
Righteous do? If we should so frustrate and deceive the Lords Expectations, that his Covenant-interest in us, and the Workings of his Salvation be made to cease, then All were lost indeed; Ruine upon Ruine,
Destruction upon Destruction would come, until one stone were not
left upon another. . . .

   Use 1. *Of Information;* to let *New-England* know what that gracious
infinitely wise, holy and awful dispensation of divine Providence is,
under which the Lord hath set us and continued us unto this day. We
must look upon our selves as under a *solemn divine Probation;* It hath been
and it is a Probation-time, even to this whole People. Under great
hopes, and singular eminent Expectations hath the Lord our God
been trying of us, and is yet trying us in the wayes of his Salvation.
There is this *one* voice of all his Providences towards us; they call aloud
unto us in this language of a Probation-time, *To day if this my people
will hear my voice;* To day if they will come up to the Lords Expectations,
and answer his promises; To day, that is, whilest it is a day of Salvation,
whilest the Lord is yet so wonderfully preserving of us, displaying his
Banner over us, holding underneath the Everlasting Arms, and making
us to taste so much of his loving kindness and tender mercies every way.
Divine Expectations frustrated will issue dreadfully, when the Lord
shall make us know his *breach of promise*, Numb. 14. 34. This we must
know, that the Lords promises, and expectations of great things, have
singled out *New-England*, and all sorts and ranks of men amongst us,
above any Nation or people in the world; and this hath been and is a
time and season of eminent trial to us. If I should say that the very
world, or common ordinary Professors expect great things from us at
this day, there is a great deal of weight in it; If I say that the faithful
precious suffering Saints of God in all other places, that have heard of
the Lords Providences towards us, do expect and promise great things
from us, this is farre more; But to mention the Lords own Expectations,
this is most of all, these are certainly most solemn and awfull. Every
Expectation of God is most just and righteous. *Are not my wayes equal?*
saith God, *Ezek.* 18. 29. Yes, most equal, blessed God; Bountiful and
Rich hast thou been in all thy free Bestowings; equal and just art thou
in all thy greatest Expectations. If we do but run over the foremen-
tioned grounds of divine Expectation, it will be sufficient to commit
the judgement of this case even to *our selves*, as *Isa.* 5. 3.

As for special Relation unto God; whom hath the Lord more signally exalted then his people in this Wilderness? The Name and Interest of God, and Covenant-relation to him, it hath been written upon us in Capital Letters from the beginning. God had his *Creatures* in this Wilderness before we came, and his *Rational Creatures* too, a multitude of them; but as to *Sons* and *Children* that are Covenant-born unto God, Are not we the *first* in such a Relation? in this respect we are surely the Lords *first-born* in this Wilderness. Of the poor Natives before we came we may say as *Isa.* 63. 19. *They were not called by the Lords Name, he bear not Rule over them:* But we have been from the beginning, and we are the *Lords.*

As for Extraction and Descent, if we be considered as a *Posterity,* O what Parents and Predecessors may we the most of us look back unto, through whose Loins the Lord hath stretched forth the line of his Covenant, measuring of us out, and taking us in to be a peculiar Portion to himself?

As for Restipulations, and Engagements back again to God; what awfull publick Transactions of this kinde have there been amongst us? Hath not the eye of the Lord beheld us laying *Covenant-Engagements* upon our selves? hath not his ear heard us solemnly *Avouching* him, and him alone, to be our God and Saviour? Hath not a great part of the world been a witness of these things, even of our explicite ownings of, and Covenantings with the Lord as our God, laying this as a foundation-stone in our Building; and of this we may say, It hath been a special Exasperation unto Adversaries and Ill-willers, that despised *New-England* hath laid claim to, and publickly avouched and challenged a special Interest in God above others.

As for our Advantages and Priviledges in a Covenant-state, here time and strength would fail to reckon up what we have enjoyed of this kinde; if any people in the world have been lifted up to heaven as to Advantages and Priviledges, we are the people. Name what you will under this Head, and we have had it. We have had *Moses* and *Aaron* to lead us; we have had Teachings and Instructions, *line upon line, and precept upon precept;* we have had Ordinances and Gospel-dispensations the choicest of them; we have had Peace and Plenty; we have had Afflictions and Chastisements in measure; we have had the Hearts, and Prayers, and Blessing of the Lords people every where; we have had the Eye and Hand of God, watching and working every way for our good; our Adversaries have had their Rebukes, we have had our Encouragements, and a wall of fire round about us. What could have been done more for us then hath been done?

And then in the last place, as to *New-Englands first wayes;* what glorious things might here be spoken, unto the praise of free-grace, and to justifie the Lords Expectations upon this ground? Surely God hath often spoke concerning His Churches here, as in *Jer.* 2. 2. *I remember the kindness of thy youth, &c.* O what were the open Professions of the Lords people that first entred this Wilderness? How did our fathers entertain the Gospel, and all the pure Institutions thereof, and those Liberties which they brought over? What was their Communion and Fellowship in the Administrations of the Kingdome of Jesus Christ? What was the pitch of their Brotherly love, of their Zeal for God and his Wayes, and against wayes destructive of Truth and Holiness? What was their Humility, their Mortification, their Exemplariness? How much of Holiness to the Lord was written upon all their wayes and transactions? God sifted a whole Nation that he might send choice Grain over into this Wilderness. 1st generation now dead + gone

Thus it hath been with us as to grounds of Divine Expectation: And therefore let us in the fear of God learn this great truth to day, and receive the instruction thereof sealed up unto all our souls; *That the great God hath taken up great Expectations of us, and made great Promises to himself concerning us, and this hath been, and is* New-Englands *day and season of Probation.*

WILLIAM HUBBARD, 1621–1704

[William Hubbard, son of a husbandman of Tenring, Essex, came with his family to New England in 1635, and settled at Ipswich. He graduated in the first class at Harvard College, 1642, studied medicine and did not become a minister until 1656, when he was settled as the colleague of Thomas Cobbet at Ipswich. He was a ringleader along with John Wise in the protest against Andros's taxation, 1687; he kept his head during the witchcraft panic. In 1677 he published a history of the Indian wars in New England, and wrote a general history of New England which was based chiefly on Winthrop's manuscript *Journal.* He lived to be one of the oldest and most venerated ministers in the colony, but after his first wife died he shocked his parishioners by marrying his housekeeper in 1694. This text is from *The Happiness of a People In the Wisdome of their Rulers Directing And in the Obedience of their Brethren Attending* (Boston, 1676), a sermon preached on election day, May 3, of that year. Cf. Sibley, *Biographical Sketches;* Sprague, *Annals;* Samuel G. Drake, edition of *A Narrative of the Troubles with the Indians* (Roxbury, 1865).]

THE HAPPINESS OF A PEOPLE

IT WAS Order that gave Beauty to this goodly fabrick of the world, which before was but a confused Chaos, without form and void: Therefore when Job, when he would set out the terribleness of the grave and the dismal state of death, he calls it, the Land of darkness, and the shadow of death without any Order. *Job 10. 22.* For Order is as the soul of the Universe, the life and health of things natural, the beauty and strength of things Artificial. . . . The better to understand this we may consider what Order is? The Schools tell us, it is, *Parium, impariumque; sua cuique; tribuens loca, opta disposito.* Such a disposition of things in themselves equall and unequall, as gives to every one their due and proper place. It suited the wisdom of the infinite and omnipotent Creator, to make the world of differing parts, which necessarily supposes that there must be differing places, for those differing things to be disposed into, which is Order. The like is necessary to be observed in the rational and political World, where persons of differing endowments and qualifications need differing station to be disposed into, the keeping of which, is both the beauty and strength of such a society. Naturalists tell us that beauty in the body arises from an exact symmetry or proportion of contrary humours, equally mixed one with another: so doth an orderly and artificial distribution of diverse materials, make a comely Building, while homogeneous bodyes (as the depths of waters in the Sea, and heaps of sand on the Shore) run into confused heaps, as bodyes uncapable to maintain an order in themselves. So that it appears, whoever is for a parity in any Society, will in the issue reduce things into an heap of confusion. That God who assumes to him self the title of being the God of Glory, is the God of peace, or Order and not of confusion. 1 *Cor.* 14. 33 compar'd with *ver.* 40. He is so in his Palace of the world, as well as in his temple of his Church: in both may be observed a sweet subordination of persons and things, each unto other . . . Look we into the third heavens the high and holy place, as a Royal Pavilion pitched by the Almighty for the recidence of his Glory, although it be furnished with Inhabitants suitable to the nature of that celestial throne, yet are they not all of one rank and order; there are Cherubims as well as Seraphims, Arch-Angels as well as Angels, Thrones and Dominions, as well as Principalityes and Powers. There are also, as in a middle rank, the Spirits of just men made perfect: though no unclean thing may enter in, yet have they not attained their perfection in Glory, but do yet expect an addition of Glory: but in the outward Court, as there are diversity of gifts, so there are of places, and order: some that are to rule and go before, others that are to be subject, and to follow. If we shall but descend and take notice of the firmament, the pavement of that glorious mansion place, although it be the roof of this lower world, may we not there see, one star differing from another in glory? There is placed the Sun, the lord and ruler of the day, as well as the Moon, that rules the night, together with the stars, as the common-people of that upper region, who yet doe immediately veyle their glory, and withdraw their light, when their bridegroom cometh forth of his chamber. In the firmament of the air, may we not see the lofty eagle in his flight far surmounting the little choristers of the valleys? The like disproportion who observes not amongst those creatures that take their pastime in the deep waters, or that range upon the high mountains, hunting for their prey? And hath not the same Almighty Creator and disposer of all things made some of the sons of men as far differing in height of body one from the other, as Saul from the rest of the people. . . . And are not some advanced as high above others in dignity and power, as much as the cedars of Lebanon the low shrubs of the valley? It is not then the result of time or chance, that some are mounted on horseback, while others are left to travell on foot. That some have with the Centurion power to command, while others are required to obey, *the poor and the rich meet together, the Lord is the maker of them both,* The Almighty hath appointed her that sits behind the mill, as well as him that ruleth on the throne. And herein hath he as well consulted the good of humane nature, as the glory of his own wisdome and power: Thoase of the superiour rank, but making a supply of what is wanting in the other: otherwise might not the foolish and ignorant be like to loose themselves in the Wilderness, if others were not as eyes to them [?] The fearful and the weak might be distroyed, if others more strong and valiant, did not protect and defend them. The poor and needy might starve with hunger and cold, were they not fed with the morsells, and warmed with the fleece of the wealthy. Is it not found by experience, that the greatest part of mankind, are but as tools and Instruments for others to work by, rather then any proper Agents to effect any thing of themselves: In peace how would most people destroy themselves by slothfulness and security? In war they would be destroyed by others, were it not for the wisdome and courage of the valliant. If the virtue and valour of the good did not interpose by their authority, to prevent and save, the vice of the bad would bring mischief enough upon places to ruine both, else why is it so frequently intimated in the latter end of the book of Judges, that in those dayes, when there was no king in

Israel, but every man was left to do what seemed right in his own eyes, that these and those enormityes break forth, that violated all Lawes, and offered violence even unto nature itself? . . . Thus if Order were taken away, soon would confusion follow, and every evill work, *James* 3. 16. Nothing therefore can be imagined more remote either from right reason, or true religion, then to think that because we were all once equal at our birth, and shall be again at our death, therefore we should be so in the whole course of our lives. In fine, a body would not be more monstrous and deformed without an Head, nor a ship more dangerous at Sea without a Pilot, nor a floack of sheep more ready to be devoured without a Shepheard, then would humane Society be without an Head, and Leader in time of danger. . . .

In a curious piece of Architecture, that which first offers it self to the view of the beholder, is the beauty of the structure, the proportion that one piece bears to another, wherein the skill of the Architect most shews it self. But that which is most Admirable in sensitive and rational beings, is that inward principle, seated in some one part, able to guid the whole, and influence all the rest of the parts, with an apt and regular motion, for their mutual good and safety. The wisdome of the Creatour was more seen in the breath of life, breathed into the Nostrils of Adam, whereby he became a living soul, then in the feature and beauty of the goodly frame of his body, formed out of the dust, as the Poet speaks, *Os homini sublime dedit* . . . The Architect of that curious piece hath placed the Head in the fore-front, and highest sphear, where are lodged all the senses, as in a Watch-Tower, ready to be improved upon all occasions, for the safety and preservation of the whole. There are placed those that look out at the windows, to foresee evil and danger approaching, accordingly to alarm all the other inferiour powers, to take the signal and stand upon their guard, for defence of the whole. There also is the seat of the Daughters of musick, ready to give audience to all reports and messages that come from abroad; if any thing should occurre or happen nearer home, or further off, imparting either fear of evil, or hope of good: Their work is immediately to dispatch messages through the whole province of nature, to summon all the other Members together, to come in and yield the assistance to prevent the mischief feared, or prepare for the reception of the good promised, or pretended, as the nature of the case may require. Thus are all orders wont to be dispathched and issued from the Cinque ports of the senses in, and about the head, for the benefit and advantage of the whole body. Very fitly therefore in the body politick are the rulers by way of allusion called Heads. And in case of inability to discharge those functions, such societies may not undeservedly be compared to the *Palmists* Idols, that have eyes but see not, and have ears but hear not. Suppose the hands be never so strong for action or the feet never so swift for motion, yet if there be not discretion in the head to discerne, or judgement to determine what is meet to be done for the obviating of evil and danger, or procuring of good, it will be impossible to save such a body from ruine and destruction. If the Mast be never so well strengthened, and the Tackline never so well bound together, yet if there want a skilful Pilot to Steer and Guide, especially in a rough and tempestuous Sea, the lame will soon take the prey.

SAMUEL WILLARD, 1640–1707

[Samuel Willard, born in Concord, was the son of Major Simon Willard, a founder of the town; he graduated from Harvard College in the class of 1659, and preached for a time at Groton until the church and the town were scattered by an Indian attack in 1676. He was then called to the Old South Church in Boston, where he remained until his death, second in importance only to Increase Mather in Eastern Massachusetts. John Dunton said of him, "He's a Man of Profound Notions: Can say what he will, and prove what he says." Though less dictatorial than Increase, his scholarship was probably broader and his mind more philosophical. He delivered a series of sermons over a long period of years expounding in systematic detail the outline of the orthodox theology; the sermons were published after his death in a tremendous folio volume. He was Vice-President of Harvard College from 1701 to 1707, which office was really the headship because their was no President. Cf. Samuel Eliot Morison, *Harvard College in the Seventeenth Century;* Sibley, *Biographical Sketches;* Sprague, *Annals.* This text is from *The Character of a Good Ruler* (Boston, 1694), an election sermon, preached on May 30.]

THE CHARACTER OF A GOOD RULER

WHETHER the Ordination of *Civil Government* be an *Article of the Law of Nature*, and it should accordingly have been established upon the Multiplication of Mankind, although they had retained their Primitive Integrity: Or whether it have only a *Positive right*, and was introduced upon mans *Apostacy;* is a question about which all are not agreed. The equity of it, to be sure, is founded in the Law Natural, and is to be discovered by the light of Nature, being accordingly acknowledged by such as are strangers to Scripture Revelation; and by Christians it is reducible to the first Command in the Second Table of the Decalogue; which is supposed to be a transcript of the Law given to *Adam* at the first, and written upon the Tables of his Heart. For tho', had man kept his first state, the Moral Image Concreated in him, consisting in, *Knowledg, Righteousness, and True Holiness,* would have maintained him in a perfect understanding of, and Spontaneous Obedience to the whole duty incumbent on him, without the need of civil Laws to direct him, or a civil Sword to lay compulsion on him; and it would have been the true Golden Age, which the Heathen *Mythologists* are to Fabulous about. yet even then did the All-Wise God Ordain Orders of Superiority and Inferiority among men, and required an *Honour* to be paid accordingly. But since the unhappy Fall hath Robbed man of that perfection, and filled his heart with perverse and rebellious principles, tending to the Subversion of all Order and the reducing of the World to a *Chaos;* necessity requires, and the Political happiness of a People is concerned in the establishment of Civil Government. The want of it hath ever been pernicious, and attended on with miserable Circumstances. When there was no Governour in *Israel*, but every man did what he would, what horrible outrages, were then perpetrated, though Holy and Zealous *Phinehas* was at that time the High-Priest? and we ourselves have had a Specimen of this in the short *Anarchy* accompanying our late *Revolution.* Gods Wisdom therefore, and his goodness is to be adored in that he hath laid in such a relief for the Children of men, against the mischief which would otherwise devour them; and engraven an inclination on their hearts, generally to comply with it. But this notwithstanding, mens sins may put a curse into their Blessings, & render their remedy to be not better, possibly worse than the Malady. Government is to prevent and cure the disorders that are apt to break forth among the Societies of men; and to promote the civil peace and prosperity of such a people, as well as to suppress impiety, and nourish Religion. For this end there are to be both *Rulers*, and such as are to be *Ruled* by them: and the Weal or Wo of a People mainly depends on the qualifications of those *Rulers*, by whom we are to be Governed. . . .

DOCTRINE

It is of highest Consequence, that Civil Rulers should be Just Men, and such as Rule in the Fear of God. . . .

Civil Rulers are all such as are in the exercise of a rightful Authority over others. These do not all of them stand in one equal Rank, nor are alike influential into Government. There are Supream and Sub-ordinate Powers: and of these also there are some who have a *Legislative*, others an *Executive* Power in their Hands; which two, though they may sometimes meet in the same persons, yet are in themselves things of a different Nature. There are *Superiour Magistrates* in *Provinces*, and such as are of *Council* with them, and *Assembly men*, the *Representatives* of the People. There are *Judges* in Courts, *Superiour* and *Inferiour; Justices* of the *Peace* in their several Precincts: and in each of these Orders there Resides a measure of Authority.

Now, that all these may be *Just*, it is firstly required, that they have a Principle of *Moral Honesty* in them, and Swaying of them: that they *Love Righteousness, and Hate Iniquity:* that they be *Men of Truth*, Exod. 18. 21. for every man will act in his Relation, according to the Principle that Rules in him: so that an Unrighteous man will be an Unrighteous Ruler, so far as he hath an Opportunity.

They must also be acquainted with the Rules of Righteousness; they must know what is Just, and what is Unjust, be *Able Men*, Exod. 18. 21. For, though men may know and not do, yet *without Knowledge the Mind cannot be good.* Ignorance is a Foundation for Error, and will likely produce it, when the man applies himself to act: and if he do right at any time, it is but by guess, which is a very poor Commendation.

Again, he must be one that respects the Cause, and not the persons in all his Administrations, Deut. 1. 17. *Ye shall not respect Persons in Judgment*, &c. if his Affections Oversway his Judgment at any time, they will be a crooked Biais, that will turn him out of the way, and that shall be Justice in one mans case, which will not be so in another.

Farthermore, he must be one whom neither Flattery nor Bribery may be able to remove out of his way, Deut. 16. 19. *Thou shalt not wrest Judgment, thou shalt not Respect Persons, neither take a Gift;* and hence he must be one who hates both Ambition and Covetousness, Exod. 18. 21 *Hating Covetousness;* which word signifies, a *Greedy Desire*, and is applicable to both the fore cited Vices: for if these Rule him, he will never be a just Ruler.

Finally, he must be one who prefers the publick Benefit above all private and separate Interests whatsoever. Every man in his place, owes himself to the good of the whole; and if he doth not so devote himself, he is unjust: and he who either to advance himself, or to be Revenged on another, will push on Injurious Laws, or pervert the true Intention of such as are in Force, is an unjust man: and he who is under the influence of a *Narrow Spirit*, will be ready to do so, as occasion offers.

Nor is this *Justice* to be lookt upon as separate from the *Fear of God*, but as influenced and maintained by it. He therefore that *Ruleth in the Fear of God*, is one who Acknowledgeth God to be his Soveraign, and carries in his heart an Awful Fear of him: who owns his Commission to be from him, and expects ere long to be called to give in an Account of his managing of it: which maketh him to study in all things to please him, and to be afraid of doing any thing that will provoke him.

And accordingly, he is a Student in the Law of God, and *Meditates in it Day and Night;* making it the Rule into which he ultimately resolves all that he doth in his place. We find that in the Old Law, the *King* was to *write a* Copy of it with his own hand, and to make use of it at all times: *Deut.* 17. 18, 19.

If he hath any thing to do in the making of Laws, he will consult a good Conscience, and what may be pleasing to God, and will be far from *framing mischief by a Law.* And if he be to execute any Laws of men, he will not dare to give a judgment for such an one as directly Crosseth the Command of God, but counts it *ipso facto* void, and his Conscience acquitted of his Oath.

Yea the *Fear of God* will make him not to think himself Lawless; nor dare to bear witness, by Laws and Penalties, against sins in others, which he countenanceth and encourageth by living in the Practise of himself: But to use utmost endeavours that his own life may be an exemplification of Obedience, and others may learn by Him, what a Veneration he hath for the Laws that are enacted for the good of Man-kind.

In a word, he is one that will take care to promote *Piety* as well as *Honesty* among men; and do his utmost that the true Religion may be countenanced and established, and that all Ungodliness, as well as Unrighteousness, may have a due Testimony born against it at all times. So he resolves *Psal.* 75. 10. *all the horns of the wicked also will I cut off; but the horns of the righteous shall be exalted.*

It then follows that we enquire of what great moment or consequence it is that these should be such: and there is a three-fold respect in which the high importance of it is to be discovered by us.

1. In respect to the Glory of God.

Civil Rulers are Gods Vicegerents here upon earth; hence they are somtimes honoured with the title of Gods, *Psal.* 82 6. *I have said ye are Gods.* Government is Gods Ordinance; and those that are Vested with it, however *mediately* introduced into it, have their rightful authority from him, Prov. 8. 15, 16. *By me Kings Reign, and Princes Decree Justice. By me Princes Rule, and Nobles, even all the Judges of the Earth,* and they that are from him, should be for him, and ought to seek the Honour of him who is *King of Kings, and Lord of Lords:* which they only then do, when they manage their whole Interest and Power with a Design for his Glory; & accordingly manage themselves in all their Ministrations by the Statutes of his Kingdom; which none will ever do, but they that are *Just, Ruling in the Fear of God.* Righteousness and Religion flourishing in these, will be as a Torch on an Hill, whose Light and Influence will be vastly extensive: every one will be advantaged to see their good works, and to Glorifie God for and in them. Their very Example will have the force of a Law in it, and win many by a powerful Attraction, to the avoiding of sin, and practising of Righteousness. They will be a good Copy, that many will be ambitious to write after: and their faithful Administrations will render them a *Terror to Evil Doers, and an Encouragement to them that do well;* which will advance the very end of Government. Whereas the Evil Deportment, and Ill Management of *Rulers,* who are unjust, and void of the Fear of God, is an open scandal, and of a more pernicious tendency than the wickedness of others; inasmuch as their Example is a discouragement to them that are well disposed, and animates those that are set in their hearts for iniquity, and they are thereby emboldned to shew their heads, and to declare their sin as *Sodom:* hence that Remark of the Psalmist, *Psal.* 12. 8. *The wicked walk on every side, when the vilest men are exalted.* Those that would bear their Testimony against Impiety and Debauchery, are frowned on and neglected; and such as would Nourish them are Countenanced: and either good Laws to suppress them are not provided, or they are laid by as things Obsolete, and of no Service: and thus all Abominations come in upon a People as a Flood, and the Name of God is wofully dishonoured by this means: and hereupon the last and most excellent end of Government comes to be frustrated, and what is there that we can conceive to be of greater weight than this? if this be lost, the Glory of such a people is gone.

2. In regard to the weal of the People over whom they Rule.

A People are not made for Rulers, But Rulers for a People. It is indeed an Honour which God puts upon some above others, when he takes them from among the People, and sets them up to Rule over them, but it is for the Peoples sake, and the Civil felicity of them is the next end of Civil Policy; and the happiness of Rulers is bound up with theirs in it. Nor can any wise men in authority think themselves happy in the Misery of their Subjects, to whom they either are or should be as Children are to their Fathers: We have the Benefit of Government expressed, 1. *Tim.* 2 : 2. *a quiet Life and a peaceable, in all Godliness and honesty.* and it lies especialy with Rulers, under God, to make a People Happy or Miserable. When men can injoy their Liberties and Rights without molestation or oppression; when they can live without fear of being born down by their more Potent Neighbours; when they are secured against Violence, and may be Righted against them that offer them any injury, without fraud; and are encouraged to serve God in their own way, with freedom, and without being imposed upon contrary to the Gospel precepts; now are they an happy People. But this is to be expected from none other but men just and Pious: they that are otherwise, will themselves be oppressours, and they that are influenced by them, and dependent on them, will adde to the grievance. They that should look after them Will Do it fast enough: Yea every one will usurp a License to do so to his Neighbour upon an advantage: and such a people must needs groan under an intollerable burden. Besides, it is a great Truth, that the Mercies and Judgments of God come upon a people, according as their Rulers carry themselves in managing of the Trust which God hath committed to them. Just and Zealous Rulers, are men that *Stand in the Gap*, and keep off Judgments from a sinning people; God *sought* for *one* such, *Ezek.* 22. 30. they *turn away wrath*, when it hath made an inroad, so it is recorded of Phinehas that he did, *Ps.* 106. 30. and God is wont to Bless such a People, as He did *Israel* and *Judah* in the days of *David, Solomon, Jehoshaphat, Hezekiah,* and *Josiah:* wheras when these fall into such sins as God is Provoked at, the People are like to Smart for it. There is such an Influence with the Prevarications of these men, that, in the righteous judgment of God, those under them suffer grievously by it. This the Heathen observed in the course of Providence, and made that remark upon it, *Delirant reges, plectuntur Achivi.* Thus *David* numbers the People, and Seventy Thousand of the men of Israel die for it, 2Sa. 24. Yea such may be the influence of the Male-administration of Rulers, though done without malice, and in an heat of misguided *zeal* for the People of GOD; as *Sauls* act in Slaying the *Gibeonites* is recorded to have been 2 *Sam* 21 2. that the Guilt may ly long upon a Land, and break out in Terrible Judgments a great while after, and not be expiated till the sin be openly confessed, and the Atonement sought unto.

3. With Reference to *Rulers* themselves. It is, as we before Observed, a Dignity put upon them, to be preferred to Government over their Brethren; to have the oversight, not of Beasts, but of Men. But as there is a great Trust devolved on them, so there is an answerable Reckoning which they must be called unto: And however they are setled in Authority by men, yet GOD, who Rules over all, hath put them in only *Durante Bene Plecito:* they are upon their good Behaviour; they are *Stewards*, and whensoever GOD pleaseth, He will call for a Reckoning, and put them out. *GOD sets up, and he pulls down;* and he hath a respect to mens Carriages in his dealings with them. Godly and Zealous *Phinehas* got a Blessing for himself and his Posterity, *Numb.* 25. 11. *&c.* Whereas *Saul* procured for himself a Rejection, and the laying aside and almost Extirpation of his Family. We have this also instanced in *Shebna* and *Eliakim Isa.* 22. 15. *&c.* Yea, what did *Jeroboam*, what did *Ahab*, and many others procure for themselves, by their ill Government, but the utter rooting out of their Names, and Posterity? The *Fourth Generation* may Rue that ever they derived from such Progenitors. The only sure way for Rulers to build up their own Houses, is to be such in their places as *David* was, of whom we have that Testimony, *Psal.* 78. 71, 72. *He brought him to Feed* Jacob *his People, and* Israel *his Inheritance. So he Fed them according to the Integrity of his heart, and guided them by the Skilfulness of his hands.* And although GOD doth not always peculiarly put a Brand in this World upon Impious and Unjust Rulers, yet there is a Tribunal before which they must stand e're long as other men; only their Account will be so much the more Fearful, and Condemnation more Tremendous, by how much they have neglected to take their greater advantages to Glorify GOD, and abused their Power to His Dishonour, by which they had a fairer opportunity than other men.

JOHN WISE, 1652–1725

[John Wise, the son of an indentured servant, graduated from Harvard College in 1673, and began to preach to the people of the Chebacco district, a corner of Ipswich township, in 1680; he was ordained minister of a formally incorporated church there in 1682. He was given ten acres of land, paid £60 a year, one third of it in money and the rest in grain, along with forty cords of wood and eight loads of marsh hay. Almost nothing can be discovered about his life except on the three or four occasions upon which he emerged to take up the cudgels for some cause or other. In 1687 he led the town of Ipswich in fiery protest against taxes levied by Governor Andros without the consent of any legislature, making a speech to the town meeting in which he said, "We had a good God, and a good King, and should do well to stand to our Priviledges." He was arrested, jailed, and fined by Andros. In 1690 he was chaplain of the disastrous expedition against Quebec; he wrote an account of the fiasco with a fine scorn for the amateur militia officers. He helped check the witchcraft panic, and in 1703 was a signer of a petition to clear the names of those that had been condemned. He supported inoculation in 1721, and in his last years agitated for paper money. On every occasion when we get a glimpse of him, Wise is a vigorous, hard-hitting, racy champion of popular causes and the agrarian point of vew. The *Proposals* against which he wrote his two most important tracts were first issued by an association of Boston and Cambridge ministers in 1705; he overwhelmed these proposals with abuse in *The Churches Quarrel Espoused* in 1710, and argued the cause of the independency and autonomy of separate congregations more soberly and learnedly in the *Vindication of the Government of New-England Churches*, 1717. This text is from the first edition of the *Vindication*. Cf. Sibley, *Biographical Sketches*.]

VINDICATION

DEMONSTRATION II

CHAP I.

THE Divine Establishment in Providence of the fore-named Churches in their Order is apparently the Royal assent of the supream Monarch of the Churches, to the grave Decisions of Reason in favour of Mans Natural state of Being, and Original Freedom. For if we should make a new *Survey* of the Constitution before named under the brightest Light of Nature, there is no greater Example of natural Wisdom in any settlement on Earth; for the present and future security of Humane Beings in all that is most Valuable and Grand, then in this. That it seems to me as though Wise and Provident Nature by the Dictates of Right Reason excited by the moving Suggestions of Humanity; and awed with the just demands of Natural Libertie, Equity, Equality, and Principles of Self-Preservation, Originally drew up the Scheme, and then obtained the Royal Approbation. And certainly it is agreeable that we attribute it to God whether we receive it nextly from Reason or Revelation, for that each is equally an Emanation of his Wisdom, *Prov.* 20. 27. The Spirit of Man is the Candle of the Lord, searching all the inward parts of the Belly. There be many larger Volumes in this dark Recess called the Belly to be read by that Candle God has Light up. And I am very well assured the fore named Constitution is a Transcript out of some of their Pages, Joh. 1. 4, 9. *And the Life was the Light of Men, which Lighteth every Man which cometh into the World.* This admirable Effect of Christs Creating Power in hanging out so many Lights to guide man through a dark World, is as Applicable to the Light of Reason, as to that of Revelation. For that the Light of Reason as a Law and Rule of Right, is an Effect of Christ's Goodness, care, and creating Power, as well as of Revelation; though Revelation is Natures Law in a fairer and brighter Edition. This is granted by the *London* Ministers,[1] *P.* 8. *C.* 3. "That, that which is evident by, and consonant to the true Light of Nature, or Natural Reason, is to be accounted, *Jure Divino*, in matters of Religion. But in the further and more distinct management of this Plea; I shall,

1. Lay before the Reader several Principles [of] Natural Knowledge.
2. Apply or Improve them in Ecclesiastical affairs.
3. Inferr from the Premises, a Demonstration that these Churches, if not properly Formed; yet are fairly Established in their present Order by the Law of Nature.

Chap II.

1. I Shall disclose several Principles of Natural Knowledge; plainly discovering the Law of Nature; or the true sentiments of Natural Reason, with Respect to Mans Being and Government. And in this Essay I shall peculiarly confine the discourse to two heads, *viz*

1. Of the Natural (in distinction to the Civil) and then,
2. Of the Civil Being of Man. And I shall Principally take Baron *Puffendorff*[2] for my Chief Guide and Spokes-man.

1. I shall consider Man in a state of Natural Being, as a Free-Born Subject under the Crown of Heaven, and owing Homage to none but God himself. It is certain Civil Government in General, is a very Admirable Result of Providence, and an Incomparable Benefit to Man-kind, yet must needs be acknowledged to be the Effect of Humane Free-Compacts and not of Divine Institution; it is the Produce of Mans Reason, of Humane and Rational Combinations, and not from any direct Orders of Infinite Wisdom, in any positive Law wherein is drawn up this or that Scheme of Civil Government. Government (says the Lord *Warrington*[3]) is necessary—in that no Society of Men can subsist without it; and that Particular Form of Government is necessary which best suits the Temper and Inclination of a People.

Nothing can be Gods Ordinance, but what he has particularly Declared to be such; there is no particular Form of Civil Government
described in Gods Word, neither does Nature prompt it. The Government of the *Jews* was changed five Times. Government is not formed
by Nature, as other Births or Productions; If it were, it would be the
same in all Countries; because Nature keeps the same Method, in
the same thing, in all Climates. If a Common Wealth be changed
into a Monarchy, is it Nature that forms, and brings forth the Monarch?
Or if a Royal Family be wholly Extinct (as in *Noah's* Case, being
not Heir Apparent from Descent from *Adam*) is it Nature that must
go to work (with the King Bees, who themselves alone preserve the
Royal Race in that Empire) to Breed a Monarch before the People
can have a King, or a Government sent over them? And thus we
must leave Kings to Resolve which is their best Title to their Crowns,
whether Natural Right, or the Constitution of Government settled by
Humane Compacts, under the Direction and Conduct of Reason. But
to proceed under the head of a State of Natural Being, I shall more
distinctly Explain the State of Humane Nature in its Original Capacity,
as Man is placed on Earth by his Maker, and Cloathed with many
Investitures, and Immunities which properly belong to Man separately
considered. As,

   1. The Prime Immunity in Mans State, is that he is most properly
the Subject of the Law of Nature. He is the Favourite Animal on
Earth; in that this Part of Gods Image, *viz.* Reason is Congenate with
his Nature, wherein by a Law Immutable, Instampt upon his Frame,
God has provided a Rule for Men in all their Actions, obliging each
one to the performance of that which is Right, not only as to Justice,
but likewise as to all other Moral Vertues, the which is nothing but
the Dictate of Right Reason founded in the Soul of Man. . . . That
which is to be drawn from Mans Reason, flowing from the true Current of that Faculty, when unperverted, may be said to be the Law
of Nature; on which account, the Holy Scriptures declare it written
on Mens hearts. For being indowed with a Soul, you may know from
your self, how, and what you ought to act, Rom. 2. 14. *These having
not a Law, are a Law to themselves.* So that the meaning is, when we
acknowledge the Law of Nature to be the dictate of Right Reason,
we must mean that the Understanding of Man is Endowed with such
a power, as to be able, from the Comtemplation of humane Condition to discover a necessity of Living agreeably with this Law: And
likewise to find out some Principle, by which the Precepts of it, may
be clearly and solidly Demonstrated. The way to discover the Law

of Nature in our own state, is by a narrow Watch, and accurate Contemplation of our Natural Condition, and propensions. Others say this is the way to find out the Law of Nature. *scil.* If a Man any ways doubts, whether what he is going to do to another Man be agreeable to the Law of Nature, then let him suppose himself to be in that other Mans Room; And by this Rule effectually Executed. A Man must be a very dull Scholar to Nature not to make Proficiency in the Knowledge of her Laws. But more Particularly in pursuing our Condition for the discovery of the Law of Nature, this is very obvious to view, *viz.*

1. A Principle of Self-Love, & Self-Preservation, is very predominant in every Mans Being.

2. A Sociable Disposition.

3. An Affection or Love to Man-kind in General. And to give such Sentiments the force of a Law, we must suppose a God who takes care of all Mankind, and has thus obliged each one, as a Subject of higher Principles of Being, then meer Instincts. For that all Law properly considered, supposes a capable Subject, and a Superiour Power; And the Law of God which is Binding, is published by the Dictates of Right Reason as other ways: Therefore says *Plutarch, To follow God and obey Reason is the same thing.* But moreover that God has Established the Law of Nature, as the General Rule of Government, is further Illustrable from the many Sanctions in Providence, and from the Peace and Guilt of Conscience in them that either obey, or violate the Law of Nature. But moreover, the foundation of the Law of Nature with relation to Government, may be thus Discovered. *scil.* Man is a Creature extreamly desirous of his own Preservation; of himself he is plainly Exposed to many Wants, unable to secure his own safety, and Maintenance without the Assistance of his fellows; and he is also able of returning Kindness by the furtherance of mutual Good; But yet Man is often found to be Malicious, Insolent, and easily Provoked, and as powerful in Effecting mischief, as he is ready in designing it. Now that such a Creature may be Preserved, it is necessary that he be Sociable; that is, that he be capable and disposed to unite himself to those of his own species, and to Regulate himself towards them, that they may have no fair Reason to do him harm; but rather incline to promote his Interests, and secure his Rights and Concerns. This then is a Fundamental Law of Nature, that every Man as far as in him lies, do maintain a Sociableness with others, agreeable with the main end and disposition of humane Nature in general. For this is very apparent, that Reason and Society render Man the most potent of all Creatures.

And Finally, from the Principles of Sociableness it follows as a fundamental Law of Nature, that Man is not so Wedded to his own Interest, but that he can make the Common good the mark of his Aim: And hence he becomes Capacitated to enter into a Civil State by the Law of Nature; for without this property in Nature, *viz.* Sociableness, which is for Cementing of parts, every Government would soon moulder and dissolve.

2. The Second Great Immunity of Man is an Original Liberty Instampt upon his Rational Nature. He that intrudes upon this Liberty, Violates the Law of Nature. In this Discourse I shall wave the Consideration of Mans Moral Turpitude, but shall view him Physically as a Creature which God has made and furnished essentially with many Enobling Immunities, which render him the most August Animal in the World, and still, whatever has happened since his Creation, he remains at the upper-end of Nature, and as such is a Creature of a very Noble Character.[4] For as to his Dominion, the whole frame of the Lower Part of the Universe is devoted to his use, and at his Command; and his Liberty under the Conduct of Right Reason, is equal with his trust. Which Liberty may be briefly Considered, Internally as to his Mind, and Externally as to his Person.

1. The Internal Native Liberty of Mans Nature in general implies, a faculty of Doing or Omitting things according to the Direction of his Judgment. But in a more special meaning, this Liberty does not consist in a loose and ungovernable Freedom, or in an unbounded Licence of Acting. Such Licence is disagreeing with the condition and dignity of Man, and would make Man of a lower and meaner Constitution then Bruit Creatures; who in all their Liberties are kept under a better and more Rational Government, by their Instincts. Therefore as *Plutarch* says, *Those Persons only who live in Obedience to Reason, are worthy to be accounted free: They alone live as they Will, who have Learnt what they ought to Will.* So that the true Natural Liberty of Man, such as really and truely agrees to him, must be understood, as he is Guided and Restrained by the Tyes of Reason, and Laws of Nature; all the rest is Brutal, if not worse.[5]

2. Mans External Personal, Natural Liberty, Antecedent to all Humane parts, or Alliances must also be considered. And so every Man must be conceived to be perfectly in his own Power and disposal, and not to be controuled by the Authority of any other. And thus every Man, must be acknowledged equal to every Man, since all Subjection and all Command are equally banished on both sides; and considering all Men thus at Liberty, every Man has a Prerogative to Judge

for himself, *viz*. What shall be most for his Behoof, Happiness and Well-being.

3. The Third Capital Immunity belonging to Mans Nature, is an equality amongst Men; Which is not to be denied by the Law of Nature, till Man has Resigned himself with all his Rights for the sake of a Civil State; and then his Personal Liberty and Equality is to be cherished, and preserved to the highest degree, as will consist with all just distinctions amongst Men of Honour, and shall be agreeable with the publick Good. For Man has a high valuation of himself, and the passion seems to lay its first foundation (not in Pride, but) really in the high and admirable Frame and Constitution of Humane Nature. The Word Man, says my Author, is thought to carry somewhat of Dignity in its sound; and we commonly make use of this as the most proper and prevailing Argument against a rude Insulter, *viz*. *I am not a Beast or a Dog, but am a Man as well as your self*. Since then Humane Nature agrees equally with all persons; and since no one can live a Sociable Life with another that does not own or Respect him as a Man; It follows as a Command of the Law of Nature, that every Man Esteem and treat another as one who is naturally his Equal, or who is a Man as well as he. There be many popular, or plausible Reasons that greatly Illustrate this Equality, *viz*. that we all Derive our Being from one stock, the same Common Father of humane Race. On this Consideration *Bœthius* checks the pride of the Insulting Nobility.

> *Quid Genus et Proavos Strepitis?*
> *Si Primordia Vestra,*
> *Auteremque Deum Spectas,*
> *Nullus Degener Extat*
> *Nisi vitiis Pejora fovens,*
> *Proprium Deserat Ortum.*

> *Fondly our first Descent we Boast;*
> * If whence at first our Breath we Drew,*
> * The common springs of Life we view,*
> *The Airy Notion soon is Lost.*

> *The Almighty made us equal all;*
> * But he that slavishly complyes*
> * To do the Drudgery of Vice,*
> *Denyes his high Original.*

And also that our Bodies are Composed of matter, frail, brittle, and lyable to be destroyed by thousand Accidents; we all owe our Existence to the same Method of propagation. The Noblest Mortal in his Entrance on to the Stage of Life, is not distinguished by any pomp or of passage from the lowest of Mankind; and our Life hastens to the same General Mark: Death observes no Ceremony, but Knocks as loud at the Barriers of the Court, as at the Door of the Cottage. This Equality being admitted, bears a very great force in maintaining Peace and Friendship amongst Men. For that he who would use the Assistance of others, in promoting his own Advantage, ought as freely to be at their service, when they want his help on the like Occasions. *One Good turn Requires another*, is the Common Proverb; for otherwise he must need esteem others unequal to himself, who constantly demands their Aid, and as constantly denies his own. And whoever is of this Insolent Temper, cannot but highly displease those about him, and soon give Occasion of the Breach of the Common Peace. It was a Manly Reproof which *Charactacus* gave the *Romans*. *Num Si vos Omnibus* &c. What! because you desire to be Masters of all Men, does it follow therefore that all Men should desire to be your Slaves, for that it is a Command of Natures Law, that no Man that has not obtained a particular and special Right, shall arrogate to himself a Larger share then his fellows, but shall admit others to equal Priviledges with himself. So that the Principle of Equality in a Natural State, is peculiarly transgressed by Pride, which is when a Man without sufficient reason prefers himself to others. And though as *Hensius*, Paraphrases upon *Aristotle's* Politicks to this Purpose. *viz. Nothing is more suitable to Nature, then that those who Excel in Understanding and Prudence, should Rule and Controul those who are less happy in those Advantages*, &c. Yet we must note, that there is room for an Answer, *scil.* That it would be the greatest absurdity to believe, that Nature actually Invests the Wise with a Sovereignity over the weak; or with a Right of forcing them against their Wills; for that no Sovereignty can be Established, unless some Humane Deed, or Covenant Precede: Nor does Natural fitness for Government make a Man presently Governour over another; for that as *Ulpian* says, *by a Natural Right all Men are born free;* and Nature having set all Men upon a Level and made them Equals, no Servitude or Subjection can be conceived without Inequality; and this cannot be made without Usurpation or Force in others, or Voluntary Compliance in those who Resign their freedom, and give away their degree of Natural Being   And thus we come,

2. To consider Man in a Civil State of Being; wherein we shall observe the great difference betwen a Natural, and Political State; for in the Latter State many Great disproportions appear, or at least many obvious distinctions are soon made amongst Men; which Doctrine is to be laid open under a few heads.

1. Every Man considered in a Natural State, must be allowed to be Free, and at his own dispose; yet to suit Mans Inclinations to Society; And in a peculiar manner to gratify the necessity he is in of publick Rule and Order, he is Impelled to enter into a Civil Community; and Divests himself of his Natural Freedom, and puts himself under Government; which amongst other things Comprehends the Power of Life and Death over Him; together with Authority to Injoyn him some things to which he has an utter Aversation, and to prohibit him other things, for which he may have as strong an Inclination; so that he may be often under this Authority, obliged to Sacrifice his Private, for the Publick Good. So that though Man is inclined to Society, yet he is driven to a Combination by great necessity. For that the true and leading Cause of forming Governments, and yielding up Natural Liberty, and throwing Mans Equality into a Common Pile to be new Cast by the Rules of fellowship; was really and truly to guard themselves against the Injuries Men were lyable to Interchangeably; for none so Good to Man, as Man, and yet none a greater Enemy. So that,

2. The first Humane Subject and Original of Civil Power is the People. For as they have a Power every Man over himself in a Natural State, so upon a Combination they can and do bequeath this Power unto others; and settle it according as their united discretion shall Determine. For that this is very plain, that when the Subject of Sovereign Power is quite Extinct, that Power returns to the People again. And when they are free, they may set up what species of Government they please; or if they rather incline to it, they may subside into a State of Natural Being, if it be plainly for the best. In the *Eastern* Country of the *Mogul*, we have some resemblance of the Case; for upon the Death of an absolute Monarch, they live so many days without a Civil Head; but in that *Interregnum*, those who survive the Vacancy, are glad to get into a Civil State again; and usually they are in a very Bloody Condition when they return under the Covert of a new Monarch; this project is to indear the People to a Tyranny, from the Experience they have so lately had of an Anarchy.

3. The formal Reason of Government is the Will of a Community, yielded up and surrendred to some other Subject, either of one particular Person, or more, Conveyed in the following manner.

Let us conceive in our Mind a multitude of Men, all Naturally Free & Equal; going about voluntarily, to Erect themselves into a new Common-Wealth. Now their Condition being such, to bring themselves into a Politick Body, they must needs Enter into divers Covenants.

1. They must Interchangeably each Man Covenant to joyn in one

lasting Society, that they may be capable to concert the measures of their safety, by a Publick Vote.

2. A Vote or Decree must then nextly pass to set up some Particular species of Government over them. And if they are joyned in their first Compact upon absolute Terms to stand to the Decision of the first Vote concerning the Species of Government: Then all are bound by the Majority to acquiesce in that particular Form thereby settled, though their own private Opinion, incline them to some other Model.

3. After a Decree has specified the Particular form of Government, then there will be need of a New Covenant, whereby those on whom Sovereignty is conferred, engage to take care of the Common Peace, and Welfare. And the Subjects on the other hand, to yield them faithful Obedience. In which Covenant is Included that Submission and Union of Wills, by which a State may be conceived to be but one Person. So that the most proper Definition of a Civil State, is this. *viz.* A Civil State is a Compound Moral Person. whose Will (United by those Covenants before passed) is the Will of all; to the end it may Use, and Apply the strength and riches of Private Persons towards maintaining the Common Peace, Security, and Well-being of all. Which may be conceived as tho' the whole State was now become but one Man; in which the aforesaid Covenants may be supposed under Gods Providence, to be the Divine *Fiat*, Pronounced by God, let us make Man. And by way of resemblance the aforesaid Being may be thus Anatomized.

1. The Sovereign Power is the Soul infused, giving Life and Motion to the whole Body.

2. Subordinate Officers are the Joynts by which the Body moves.

3. Wealth and Riches are the Strength.

4. Equity and Laws are the Reason.

5. Councellors the Memory.

6. *Salus Populi*, or the Happiness of the People, is the End of its Being; or main Business to be attended and done.

7. Concord amongst the Members, and all Estates, is the Health.

8. Sedition is Sickness, and Civil War Death.

4. The Parts of Sovereignty may be considered: So,

1. As it Prescribes the Rule of Action: It is rightly termed *Legislative Power*.

2. As it determines the Controversies of Subjects by the Standard of those Rules. So is it justly Termed Judiciary Power.

3. As it Arms the Subjects against Foreigners, or forbids Hostility, so its called the Power of Peace and War.

4. As it takes in Ministers for the discharge of Business, so it is called the Right of Appointing Magistrates. So that all great Officers and Publick Servants, must needs owe their Original to the Creating Power of Sovereignty. So that those whose Right it is to Create, may Dissolve the being of those who are Created, unless they cast them into an Immortal Frame. And yet must needs be dissoluble if they justly forfeit their being to their Creators.

5. The Chief End of Civil Communities, is, that Men thus conjoyned, may be secured against the Injuries, they are lyable to from their own Kind. For if every Man could secure himself singly; It would be great folly for him, to Renounce his Natural Liberty, in which every Man is his own King and Protector.

6. The Sovereign Authority besides that it inheres in every State as in a Common and General Subject. So farther according as it resides in some One Person, or in a Council (consisting of some Select Persons, or of all the Members of a Community) as in a proper and particular Subject, so it produceth different Forms of Common-wealths, *viz.* Such as are either simple and regular, or mixt.

1. The Forms of a Regular State are three only, which Forms arise from the proper and particular Subject, in which the Supream Power Resides. As,

1. A Democracy, which is when the Sovereign Power is Lodged in a Council consisting of all the Members, and where every Member has the Priviledge of a Vote. This Form of Government, appears in the greatest part of the World to have been the most Ancient. For that Reason seems to shew it to be most probable, that when Men (being Originally in a condition of Natural Freedom and Equality) had thoughts of joyning in a Civil Body, would without question be inclined to Administer their common Affairs, by their common Judgment, and so must necessarily to gratifie that Inclination establish a Democracy; neither can it be rationally imagined, that Fathers of Families being yet Free and Independent, should in a moment, or little time take off their long delight in governing their own Affairs, & Devolve all upon some single Sovereign Commander; for that it seems to have been thought more Equitable, that what belonged to all, should be managed by all, when all had entered by Compact into one Community. The Original of our Government, says *Plato*, (speaking of the *Athenian* Commonwealth) *was taken from the Equality of our Race. Other States there are composed of different Blood, and of unequal Lines, the Consequence of which are disproportionable Soveraignty, Tyrannical or Oligarchycal Sway; under which men live in such a manner, as to Esteem themselves partly*

Lords, and partly Slaves to each other. But we and our Country-men, being all Born Brethren of the same Mother, do not look upon our selves, to stand under so hard a Relation, as that of Lords and Slaves; but the Parity of our Descent incline us to keep up the like Parity by our Laws, and to yield the precedency to nothing but to Superiour Vertue and Wisdom. And moreover it seems very manifest that most Civil Communities arose at first from the Union of Families, that were nearly allyed in Race and Blood. And though Ancient Story make frequent mention of Kings, yet it appears that most of them were such that had an Influence rather in perswading, then in any Power of Commanding. So *Justin* discribes that Kind of Government, as the most Primitive, which *Aristotle* stiles an Heroical Kingdom. *viz.* Such as is no ways Inconsistent with a Democratical State. *De Princip. Reru.* 1. *L.* 1. *C.*

A democracy is then Erected, when a Number of Free Persons, do Assemble together, in Order to enter into a Covenant for Uniting themselves in a Body: And such a Preparative Assembly hath some appearance already of a Democracy; it is a Democracy in *Embrio* properly in this Respect, that every Man hath the Priviledge freely to deliver his Opinion concerning the Common Affairs. Yet he who dissents from the Vote of the Majority, is not in the least obliged by what they determine, till by a second Covenant, a Popular Form be actually Established; for not before then can we call it a Democratical Government, *viz.* Till the Right of Determining all matters relating to the publick Safety, is actually placed in a General Assembly of the whole People; or by their own Compact and Mutual Agreement, Determine themselves the proper Subject for the Exercise of Sovereign Power. And to compleat this State, and render it capable to Exert its Power to answer the End of a Civil State: These Conditions are necessary.

1. That a certain Time and Place be Assigned for Assembling.

2. That when the Assembly be Orderly met, as to Time and Place, that then the Vote of the Majority must pass for the Vote of the whole Body.

3. That Magistrates be appointed to Exercise the Authority of the whole for the better dispatch of Business, of every days Occurrence; who also may with more Mature diligence, search into more Important Affairs; and if in case any thing happens of greater Consequence, may report it to the Assembly; and be peculiarly Serviceable in putting all Publick Decrees into Execution. Because a large Body of People is almost useless in Respect of the last Service, and of many others, as to the more Particular Application and Exercise of Power. Therefore

it is most agreeable with the Law of Nature, that they Institute their Officers to act in their Name, and Stead

2. The Second Species of Regular Government, is an Aristocracy; and this is said then to be Constituted when the People, or Assembly United by a first Covenant, and having thereby cast themselves into the first Rudiments of a State; do then by Common Decree, Devolve the Sovereign Power, on a Council consisting of some Select Members; and these having accepted of the Designation, are then properly invested with Sovereign Command; and then an Aristocracy is formed.

3. The Third Species of a Regular Government, is a Monarchy which is settled when the Sovereign Power is confered on some one worthy Person. It differs from the former, because a Monarch who is but one Person in Natural, as well as in Moral account, & so is furnished with an Immediate Power of Exercising Sovereign Command in all Instances of Government; but the fore named must needs have Particular Time and Place assigned; but the Power and Authority is Equal in each. . . .

An Aristocracy is a dangerous Constitution in the Church of Christ, as it possesses the Presbytery of all Church Power: What has been observed sufficiently Evinces it. And not only so but from the Nature of the Constitution, for it has no more Barrier to it, against the Ambition, Insults, and Arbitrary measures of Men, then an absolute Monarchy. But to abbreviate; it seems most agreeable with the Light of Nature, that if there be any of the Regular Government settled in the Church of God it must needs be.

3. A Democracy. This is a form of Government, which the Light of Nature does highly value, & often directs to as most agreeable to the Just and Natural Prerogatives of Humane Beings. This was of great account, in the early times of the World. And not only so, but upon the Experience of several Thousand years, after the World had been tumbled, and tost from one Species of Government to another, at a great Expence of Blood and Treasure, many of the wise Nations of the World have sheltered themselves under it again; or at least have blendished, and balanced their Governments with it.

It is certainly a great Truth, *scil*. That Mans Original Liberty after it is Resigned, (yet under due Restrictions) ought to be Cherished in all wise Governments; or otherwise a man in making himself a Subject, he alters himself from a Freeman, into a Slave, which to do is Repugnant to the Law of Nature. Also the Natural Equality of Men amongst Men must be duly favoured; in that Government was never Established by God or Nature, to give one Man a Prerogative to insult over another; therefore in a Civil, as well as in a Natural State of Being, a just Equality is to be indulged so far as that every Man is bound to Honour every Man, which is agreeable both with Nature and Religion, 1 Pet. 2. 17. *Honour all Men.*—The End of all good Government is to Cultivate Humanity, and Promote the happiness of all, and the good of every Man in all his Rights, his Life, Liberty, Estate, Honour, &c. without injury or abuse done to any. Then certainly it cannot easily be thought, that a company of Men, that shall enter into a voluntary Compact, to hold all Power in their own hands, thereby to use and improve their united force, wisdom, riches and strength for the Common and Particular good of every Member, as is the Nature of a Democracy; I say it cannot be that this sort of Constitution, will so readily furnish those in Government with an appetite, or disposition to prey upon each other, or imbezle the common Stock; as some Particular Persons may be apt to do when set off, and Intrusted with the same Power. And moreover this appears very Natural, that when the aforesaid Government or Power, settled in all, when they have Elected certain capable Persons to Minister in their affairs, and the said Ministers remain accountable to the Assembly; these Officers must needs be under the influence of many wise cautions from their own thoughts (as well as under confinement by their Commission) in their whole Administration: And from thence it must needs follow that they will be more apt, and inclined to steer Right for the main Point, *viz.* The peculiar good, and benefit of the whole, and every particular Member fairly and sincerely. And why may not these stand for very Rational Pleas in Church Order?

For certainly if Christ has settled any form of Power in his Church he has done it for his Churches safety, and for the Benefit of every Member: Then he must needs be presumed to have made choice of that Government as should least Expose his People to Hazard, either from the fraud, or Arbitrary measures of particular Men. And it is as plain as day light, there is no Species of Government like a Democracy to attain this End. There is but about two steps from an Aristocracy, to a Monarchy, and from thence but one to a Tyranny; an able standing force, and an Ill-Nature, *Ipso facto*, turns an absolute Monarch into a Tyrant; this is obvious among the Roman *Cæsars*, and through the World. And all these direful Transmutations are easier in Church affairs (from the different Qualities of things) then in Civil States. For what is it that cunning and learned Men can't make the World swallow as an Article of their Creed, if they are once invested with an Uncontroulable Power, and are to be the standing Oratours to Mankind in matters of Faith and Obedience?

JOHN BARNARD, 1681–1770

[John Barnard was born in Boston, the son of a housewright and
selectman, educated at the Latin school under Ezekiel Cheever, and
graduated from Harvard College in 1700. While an undergraduate he
was much stimulated by the poetry of Cowley. He joined the North
Church, assisted in the preparation of a pamphlet in defense of Increase and Cotton Mather against the accusations of Robert Calef,
and took his M.A. in 1703. Though for a time regarded as a "tool of the
Mathers," he nevertheless won the esteem and friendship of Benjamin
Colman. He served as chaplain in the melancholy expedition against
Port Royal in 1707; he indulged in a game of cards during this enterprise,
was censured by the Mathers, and though he made public acknowledgment of his fault, turned his affections to the more liberal wing of the
clergy. He went to London, 1709–1710; when he returned he was opposed by the Mathers, but in spite of them was finally settled over a
church at Marblehead in 1716. His influence in the town was large; at
the time of his settlement Marblehead was a straggling fishing village;
he guided not only the spiritual but the material career of his congregation and was instrumental in transforming the town into a thriving sea-
port in the course of his long ministry. He was influential in getting his
friend Holyoke chosen President of Harvard College in 1737. A tall,
energetic figure, he was a scholar, linguist, mathematician, an expert
on ships and shipbuilding, an amateur musician, an upholder of inoculation; he was active in reassembling a library for the college after
the fire of 1764. All told, he was one of the finest examples of the
eighteenth-century New England parson. His autobiography is printed
in *Collections of the Massachusetts Historical Society*, Series 3, V, 177–243.
This text is from *The Throne Established by Righteousness* (Boston, 1734),
an election sermon. Cf. Sibley, *Biographical Sketches*.]

THE THRONE ESTABLISHED BY RIGHTEOUSNESS

1. The first Thing I would observe here is, the *Original* of Government, and whence it takes its Rise. And I doubt not to say, That it is
from God, who is the *God of Order and not of Confusion:* That is to say,
that, upon Supposition that Mankind dwell together in Societies,
which the humane Nature cannot well avoid, it is not a matter of
Liberty and Freedom, and left to the Option and Choice of the Will
of Man, whether there shall be Government, or no, or whether there
shall be **any Rules** for the regulating of that Society; but it has the

stamp of the Divine Authority upon it, and comes to us with a *thus saith the Lord*.

This the Voice of *Nature* plainly declares to us. Forasmuch as the Divine Sovereignty, and unerring Wisdom, has formed, and fitted, the humane Nature for Rule and Government, and necessitated it to it, this may be justly looked upon as the Voice of God to Mankind; because the Almighty's adapting his Creatures to a particular End, is one way of making known His Mind and Will concerning them; and every true dictate of right Reason, is no other than God speaking to his rational Creatures, by the inward Sentiments of their own Mind. Thus 'tis that they, who are destitute of the written Law, *are a Law unto themselves*, as the Apostle expresses it, The Law or Will of God being written upon their Hearts, and legible, in some measure, by the Candle of the Lord, which he hath lighted up within them.

'Tis very evident, the Nature of Man is formed for Government, and necessitated to it, from that Power of Reason and Understanding that is in him, his fixed Bent to Society, and the many Weaknesses and Imperfections that attend him.

Thro' the distinguishing Favour of the Almighty, He has, by His Inspiration, given us Understanding, & made us wiser than the Beasts of the Field, or the Fowls of the Air; and thus He hath formed us capable of acting by Rule, which sufficiently intimates His Will to us, that we are not left to live and range at Large, but that we keep ourselves within due Bounds, and walk by Rule; and this necessarily supposes some certain Rule for us to regulate ourselves by.

And because Society is the natural result of Reason, in a dependent Being, and he must have all in himself, and be Master of an unbounded Understanding, and unlimited Power, or be void of all true Reason and Knowledge, that can subsist by himself without having any Regards to an other; therefore it is necessary, that this rational Agent, who yet falls short of Perfection, should be under Subjection, not only to such Laws as more especially relate to his Conduct to his Maker, but such also as have a more particular Referrence to his Fellow Creature, to whom he stands related, on whom he has some dependance for the necessaries, and conveniencies, of the present Life, and all adapted to the nature of that Society of which he is a part; and this clearly infers the Superiority of Some to give Law, for the well ordering of the Society, and the subjection of all to those Laws, according as they have a special referrence to them: And what is this but Government?

Thus I doubt not but Government would have been necessary to Man, even in a state of Innocency; because Society would then have been as agreable to his rational Nature, and more delightful to his pure Mind, and as necessary to him upon many Accounts, as now; and, in the midst of all his Purity, he would still have remained but a fallible Creature; all of which would have required a Rule suited to direct his Actions, in the several Relations he would sustain, and Businesses he would have been employed in: and this infers Government; tho', probably, very different, in its kind, from what is to be found in the World, in our Day. In short, the *Fifth Commandment*, as well as others, of the moral Law, would have been in force, and obligatory upon the innocent Creature. . . .

However, since Sin has broke in upon the World, and vitiated the humane Nature, there is but so much the more Reason and Necessity for Government among Creatures that are become so very weak, and depraved; to restrain their unruly Lusts, and keep, within due Bounds, the rampant Passions of Men, which else would soon throw humane Society into the last Disorder and Confusion. For if all Men were left to live, and act, as they please, 'tis undoubted, the different Views and Interests, Humours and Passions of Mankind, and these often excited by false Principles, and strongly moved by a corrupt Bias upon the Mind, would unavoidably produce a continual Jarr and Strife, a constant Endeavour in every one to promote his own, and gratify Self, and so a perpetual Preying of the Stronger upon the Weaker; and no Man would be able to call any thing his own, nor be secure of his Life and Limbs, from the Rapine, and Violence, of his Fellow Creature; and by how much the Views, Interest, and Passions of Men, are more numerous, appropriated, and strong, by so much would they become fiercer upon one another than the Beasts of Prey. And does not this necessitate Laws to tame this fierce Creature, to bound his Appetites, & bridle his Passions, that he may not be injurious to his Neighbour! Who is the Man, that would be willing that all the Injury of ungoverned Lust and Passion should fall upon himself? And what is the Result of all this? but that there be a legislative Power, to enact such Laws, and an executive one, to put the Laws in Force, and compel to Obedience to them, lodged somewhere, as shall be best adapted to the Order, and Preservation of the Society. And this is Government. Thus the light of Nature shews us the Reason, and Necessity, of Government; and this Voice of Nature is the Voice of God. Thus 'tis that *vox populi est vox Dei*. . . .

So that we see, the Original of Government is from God, who has taught it, to Mankind, by the Light of natural Reason, † and plainly

† Hence is that of *Hesiod*, Εκ δὲ διὸς βασιλῆες: and thus *Homer*, τ'μη δ'ἐκ διὸς ἐϛι.[1]

required it, in His holy Word. And that there are any, who walk in the Shape of Men, that do not diligently attend to the voice of Reason, nor enquire after Understanding, but sit down contented in the most abject Stupidity, scarce distinguishing themselves from the Brute, by any true Acts of Reason, is no more an Objection to Government's being a true Dictate of Nature, than one Man's shutting his Eyes would be, against the Sun's being risen, when all, who have their Eyes open, walk in the full Light of it.

2. The second thing I proposed to offer something upon, under the Head of Government, was, the *Form* of it. And here the Enquiry is, What Form of Government is chiefly to be regarded by a People? Since Government originates from God, and is of Divine appointment, is there any particular Form of Divine Ordination? Or if not, what Form shall a People put themselves under as most eligible?

To the First of these Enquiries, I think there is no great difficulty in Answering, That I know of no particular Form of Civil Government, that God Himself has, directly, and immediately, appointed, by any clear Revelation of His Mind and Will, to any People whatever. The Scripture speaks of Civil Rulers under the several Denominations that were in use, at that Day; but it no where directs to, and enjoyns, any one Scheme of Civil Government, even upon God's own peculiar favorite People; but we find, when they became a settled Nation, in the Land which God had promised to their Fathers, it was the People's own Choice to come under a *Monarchical* Form of Government, and they said, *Nay, but we will have a King over us; that we also may be like all the Nations, and that our King may Judge us, and go out before us, and fight our Battles.* And tho' there was some manifestation of the Divine Displeasure against them, for their asking a King, yet this was not for their assuming that particular Form of Civil Government, but for their throwing off the *Theocracy,* they and their Fathers, had so long experienced the Benefit of.

So that it is evident God Almighty has left it to the natural Reason of Mankind, in every Nation and Country, to set up that Form, which, upon a thorow Consideration of the Nature, Temper, Inclinations, Customs, Manners, Business, and other Circumstances of a People, may be thought best for them. And hence it is that some Nations have tho't it best for them to keep the Power of Government in the Hands of the Body of the People, while others have thought fit to lodge it in the Hands of their chief Families and Nobles; others again have devolved the Weight of the Government upon a single Person, leaving it wholly with Him to assign what Part, to what Persons, he pleases;

and another People have looked upon it most adviseable, for them. to take a middle way between these Extreams, and have laid up the Honours of Government, in a single Person, as their Supream Head, to flow from him down to all the Members; and then have divided the Weight and Burden of it, between this single Person, a Body of Nobles of his creating, and a Select Assembly of their own choosing; by which Means, Sovereignty is so happily tempered with Righteousness and Mercy, and Will and Pleasure directed and limited by Liberty and Property, as to guard against Tyranny on the one Hand, and Anarchy on the other. Tho' neither of these Schemes, nor any other that may be tho't of, are immediately and directly of Divine Appointment, yet so far as any, or all of them, are the Result of right Reason so far it may be said of them, that they are of God. Thus, the *Powers that be*, be they what they will, meaning Government, *are ordained of God.* And as every People are left to their Liberty to constitute what Form of Civil Gcve.nment, all things considered, may appear best to them, as to any thing to the contrary from the Law of God, so, doubtless, it remains with any civil Society to alter, and change, the Form of their Government, when they see just Reason for it, and all Parties are consenting to it.

But if there be no particular Form of Civil Government appointed by God, and every Nation and People are left to their own Prudence to establish what Form they please, which Form and Scheme is best? If this Enquiry means, What Form is best, considered absolutely, and by it self? I answer, That Form which is best accommodated to all the Ends of Government. What That is, may be tho't an hard Question, and it is not my Business to determine it. Tho' I would observe, that, possibly, it may be a just Answer to the Enquiry, to say, that it is an improper Question; because there can be no Government without a People, or Subject of it; and the good, or ill, Qualities of it, can fall under no Consideration, but as Government stands related to its Subject; so that the Circumstances of a particular People must come into Consideration, to determine what is best. If the Question mean, what Form is relatively best? I answer, That which will suit the People best: which requires a thorow Knowledge of them, their Scituation, Produce, Genius, and the like, to resolve. If still it be insisted on, what Form is best for our selves? To this I answer, were we absolutely free to choose for ourselves, it must be left to the wisest Heads, the greatest Politicians among us, and those best acquainted with the People, and Country, to advise upon it: but as we are not at Liberty now to choose, I can readily Answer, that Form of Civil

Government is best for us, which we are under; I mean the *British Constitution*. And this I can say, not only because we are a dependant Government, but because were I at full Liberty, I should choose to be (as, blessed be God, we are,) of the Number of the happy Subjects of *Great Britain*, whom God hath blessed above all People upon the Face of the Earth, in the Felicity of their Constitution: and I look upon my self happy, that I know not of a single true *New England* Man, in the whole Province, but what readily subscribes to these Sentiments, and hopes we shall continue, to be the genuine Members of that glorious Constitution, thro'out all Ages. . . .

4. I am now to consider what are the great *Ends* of Government. And here I must observe, that the ultimate and supreme Ends of Government, are the same with the last End of all Creatures, and all their Actions; *that God in all things may be glorified:* but then the subordinate End, and that which is the main, as it respects Man, is the common Good of the Society, State or Kingdom.

It is beneath the Dignity of a rational Agent to act for no End; and it is contrary to Reason, and Religion, to propound any but a good one; and the Good aimed at cannot be appropriated to this or that Set or Party, of Men, in the State, without having a suitable Regard to others; but must necessarily extend to the whole Body, otherwise it would soon be subversive of it self. For let us consider the Ends of Government as having Respect either to the Ruler, or Ruled, seperately taken.

If, on the one Hand, we could suppose the Good, Benefit, and Advantage of the Throne, or Ruler, were the sole Ends of Government, this would introduce Tyranny, Oppression, Injustice, and, by Degrees, prove the Overthrow of the State. For while civil Rulers either thro' mistake of their End, or want of Rectitude to act up to it, appropriate all unto themselves, and seek only their own Grandure, the making of their Families, and the gratifying of their own Appetites, and Passions; while their constant Cry is, *give, give,* and they cannot content themselves without their Subjects Vineyard, and snatch his Ewe Lamb from his Bosome, and exert their Authority to suppress all that they think stands in their way; whether by placing them in the Front of the Battle, to fall by a foreign Hand, or proceeding against them with an apparent solemn Form, but real Prostitution, of Justice, or dispatching them with a Bow-string; it is evident that they will be no better than *roaring Lyons, and ranging Bears,* which gradually devour up their Subjects, and their Substance, till there is no more to give, or none to give it: or else, the continual Oppressions, *which make wise Men mad,* will produce such Ferments, and Tumults among

the People, as in Time, to shake off the Yoke, and free themselves
from the Tyrant. . . .

One would be ready to think it hardly possible for any, who are
not destitute of the Understanding of Men, and lost to all true Reverence to the Deity, to entertain such a monstrous Conception, That
God Almighty, the wisest, and the best of Beings, should make whole
Nations of Men, and bring them together in Societies, for no other End,
but the promoting the Honour, the increasing the Riches, and nourishing the Lusts of any single Person, or any particular Sett of Men.

On the other Hand, if the Good of the Subject, considered as distinct from that of the Ruler, were the End of Government, what
would the Consequence of this be, but Anarchy, wild Disorder, and
universal Confusion? Which would be as destructive to Government
as the hottest Tyranny could be. For the civil Rulers of a People
have not only their Interests in many Respects, twisted together with
the Subjects, but some things which belong to them, in a peculiar
Manner, as Rulers, which are very essential to the Support of Government; I mean, their distinguishing Honour, their Authority and Power,
their more special Security, and the like; and if these Interests which
are appropriated to them, should not be duely consulted, in the Administration, their Glory would soon become dim, their Authority be
trampled on, and their Persons liable to the insult of every one that
had more Sense than Understanding, and more of Passion than either:
And any one may easily see where this would End.

So that it is the Good of the whole Community both Rulers and
Ruled in Conjunction, that is the great and main End of Government;
and therefore we find Dr. *Tillotson* [2] thus expressing himself, *The great
End of Government is, to preserve Men in their Rights, against the Encroach-
ments of Fraud and Violence.* To preserve *Men*, not this or that Person,
or this Set of Men, only, but the whole Body of Mankind, and every
individual Member of the Body Politick. Hence I suppose arose that
Maxim, *Salus Populi est suprema Lex*, the Safety and Welfare of the
whole, (not the Subjects only, as some are ready enough to understand it,) is to give Law to the Government, and to be preferred to
the seperate Interest of any particular Person whatever. As the Rights,
Liberties, Defence, Protection, and Prosperity of the Subjects are to
be consulted; so the Honour, Majesty and Authority, of the Ruler
are to be considered as, unitedly the Ends of Government; and tho',
possibly, the first may be tho't the Primary, and the latter the Secondary Ends, yet cannot they well be separated without the Destruction of the Government.

JONATHAN MAYHEW, 1720–1766

[Jonathan Mayhew was born on Martha's Vineyard, where his father, Experience Mayhew, was a famous missionary to the Indians. Graduating from Harvard in 1744, Jonathan Mayhew was from the beginning of his career a radical, an agitator, a dominating figure. His theological opinions were so liberal that when he was ordained at the West Church in Boston, in 1747, only two other ministers would attend; he was a forerunner of Unitarian belief as early as the 1750's, asserted free will, opposed the Great Awakening, fought the growing influence of Episcopalianism, and preached the right of revolution. He was a leader of sentiment against the Stamp Act, and was regarded by Otis and the Adamses as a prophet of the Revolution. A volume of sermons published in 1749 won him a D.D. from Aberdeen. His most famous sermon, *A Discourse concerning Unlimited Submission*, was delivered on January 30, 1750, the anniversary day of the execution of Charles I; this text is from the first edition. Cf. Alden Bradford, *Memoir of the Life and Writings of Rev. Jonathan Mayhew*.]

A DISCOURSE CONCERNING UNLIMITED SUBMISSION

IF WE calmly consider the nature of the thing itself, nothing can well be imagined more directly contrary to common sense, than to suppose that *millions* of people should be subjected to the arbitrary, precarious pleasure of *one single man;* (who has *naturally* no superiority over them in point of authority) so that their estates, and every thing that is valuable in life, and even their lives also, shall be absolutely at his disposal, if he happens to be wanton and capricious enough to demand them. What unprejudiced man can think, that God made ALL to be thus subservient to the lawless pleasure and phrenzy of ONE, so that it shall always be a sin to resist him! Nothing but the most plain and express revelation from heaven could make a sober impartial man believe such a monstrous, unaccountable doctrine, and, indeed, the thing itself, appears so shocking—so out of all *proportion*, that it may be questioned, whether all the *miracles* that ever were wrought, could make it credible, that this doctrine *really* came from God. At present, there is not the least syllable in scripture which gives any countenance to it. The hereditary, indefeasible, divine right of kings, and the doctrine of non-resistance, which is built upon the supposition of such a right, are altogether as fabulous and chimerical, as transubstantiation; or any of the most absurd reveries of ancient or modern visionaries. These notions are fetched neither from divine revelation, nor human reason; and if they are derived from neither of those sources, it is not much matter from *whence they come, or whither they go.* Only it is a pity that such doctrines should be propagated in society, to raise factions and rebellions, as we see they have, in fact, been both in the *last*, and in the *present*, REIGN.

But then, if unlimited submission and passive obedience to the *higher powers*, in all possible cases, be not a duty, it will be asked, "How far are we obliged to submit? If we may innocently disobey and resist in some cases, why not in all? Where shall we stop? What is the measure of our duty? This doctrine tends to the total dissolution of civil government; and to introduce such scenes of wild anarchy and confusion, as are more fatal to society than the worst of tyranny."

After this manner, some men object; and, indeed, this is the most plausible thing that can be said in favor of such an absolute submission as they plead for. But the worst (or rather the best) of it, is, that there is very little strength or solidity in it. For similar difficulties may be raised with respect to almost every duty of natural and revealed religion.—To instance only in two, both of which are near akin, and indeed exactly parallel, to the case before us. It is unquestionably the duty of children to submit to their parents; and of servants, to their masters. But no one asserts, that it is their duty to obey, and submit to them, in all supposeable cases; or universally a sin to resist them. Now does this tend to subvert the just authority of parents and masters? Or to introduce confusion and anarchy into private families? No. How then does the same principle tend to unhinge the government of that larger family, the body politic? We know, in general, that children and servants are obliged to obey their parents and masters respectively. We know also, with equal certainty, that they are not obliged to submit to them in all things, without exception; but may, in some cases, reasonably, and therefore innocently, resist them. These principles are acknowledged upon all hands, whatever difficulty there may be in fixing the exact limits of submission. Now there is at least as much difficulty in stating the measure of duty in these two cases, as in the case of rulers and subjects. So that this is really no objection, at least no reasonable one, against resistance to the *higher powers:* Or, if it is one, it will hold equally against resistance in the other cases mentioned.—It is indeed true, that turbulent, vicious-minded men, may take occasion from this principle, that their rulers may, in some cases, be lawfully resisted, to raise factions and disturbances in the state; and to make resistance where resistance is needless, and therefore, sinful. But is it not equally true, that children and servants of turbulent, vicious minds, may take occasion from this principle, that parents and masters may, in some cases be lawfully resisted, to resist when resistance is unnecessary, and therefore, criminal? Is the principle in either case false in itself, merely because it may be abused; and applied to legitimate disobedience and resistance in those instances, to which it ought not to be applied? According to this way of arguing, there will be no true principles in the world; for there are none but what may be wrested and perverted to serve bad purposes, either through the weakness or wickedness of men.*

* We may very safely assert these two things in general, without undermining government: One is, That no civil rulers are to be obeyed when they enjoin things that are inconsistent with the commands of God: All such disobedience is lawful and glorious; particularly, if persons refuse to comply with any *legal establishment of religion,* because it is a gross perversion and corruption (as to doctrine, worship and discipline) of a pure and divine religion, brought from heaven to earth by the *Son of God,* (the only King and Head of the *christian* church) and propagated through the world by his inspired apostles. All commands running counter to the declared will of the supreme legislator of heaven and earth, are null and void: And therefore disobedience to them is a duty, not a crime. . . . Another thing that may be asserted with equal truth and safety, is, That no government is to be submitted to, at the *expence* of that which is the *sole end* of all government,—the common good and safety of society. Because, to submit in this case, if it should ever happen, would evidently be to set up the *means* as more valuable, and above, the *end:* than which there cannot be a greater solecism and contradiction. The only reason of the institution of civil government; and the only rational ground of submission to it, is the common safety and utility. If therefore, in any case, the common safety and utility would not be promoted by submission to government, but the contrary, there is no ground or motive for obedience and submission, but, for the contrary.

Whoever considers the nature of civil government must, indeed, be sensible that a great degree of *implicit confidence,* must unavoidably be placed in those that bear rule: this is implied in the very notion of authority's being originally a *trust,* committed by the people, to those who are vested with it, as all just and righteous authority is; all besides, is mere lawless force and usurpation; neither God nor nature, having given any man a right of dominion over any society, independently of that society's approbation, and consent to be governed by him—Now as all men are fallible, it cannot be supposed that the public affairs of any state, should be always administred in the best manner possible, even by persons of the greatest wisdom and integrity. Nor is it sufficient to legitimate disobedience to the *higher powers* that they are not so administred; or that they are, in some instances, very ill-managed; for upon this principle, it is scarcely supposeable that any government at all could be supported, or subsist. Such a principle manifestly tends to the dissolution of government; and to throw all things into confusion and anarchy.—But it is equally evident, upon the other hand, that those in authority may abuse their *trust* and power *to such a degree,* that neither the law of reason, nor of religion, requires, that any obedience or submission should be paid to them; but, on the contrary, that they should be totally *discarded;* and the authority which they were before vested with, transferred to others, who may exercise it more to those good purposes for which it is given.—Nor is this principle, that resistance to the *higher powers,* is, in some extraordinary cases, justifiable, so liable to abuse, as many persons seem to apprehend it. For although there will be always some petulant, querulous men, in every state—men of factious,

A PEOPLE, really oppressed to a great degree by their sovereign, cannot well be insensible when they are so oppressed. And such a people (if I may allude to an ancient *fable*) have, like the *hesperian* fruit, a DRAGON for their *protector* and *guardian:* Nor would they have any reason to mourn, if some HERCULES should appear to dispatch him—For a nation thus abused to arise unanimously, and to resist their prince, even to the dethroning him, is not criminal; but a reasonable way of vindicating their liberties and just rights; it is making use of the means, and the only means, which God has put into their power, for mutual and self-defence. And it would be highly criminal in them, not to make use of this means. It would be stupid tameness, and unaccountable folly, for whole nations to suffer *one* unreasonable, ambitious and cruel man, to wanton and riot in their misery. And in such a case it would, of the two, be more rational to suppose, that they that did NOT *resist*, than that they who did, would *receive to themselves damnation.*

---

turbulent and carping dispositions,—glad to lay hold of any trifle to justify and legitimate their caballing against their rulers, and other seditious practices; yet there are, comparatively speaking, but few men of this *contemptible character:* It does not appear but that mankind, in general, have a disposition to be as submissive and passive and tame under government as they ought to be.—Witness a great, if not the greatest, part of the known world, who are now groaning, but not murmuring, under the heavy yoke of tyranny! While those who govern; do it with any tolerable degree of moderation and justice, and, in any good measure act up to their office and character, by being public benefactors; the people will generally be easy and peaceable; and be rather inclined to flatter and adore, than to insult and resist, them. Nor was there ever any *general* complaint against any administration, *which lasted long*, but what there was good reason for. Till people find themselves greatly abused and oppressed by their governors, they are not apt to complain; and whenever they do, in fact, find themselves thus abused and oppressed, they must be stupid not to complain. To say that subjects in general are not proper judges when their governors oppress them, and play the tyrant; and when they defend their rights, administer justice impartially, and promote the public welfare, is as great *treason* as ever man uttered;—'tis treason,—not against one *single* man, but the state—against the whole body politic;—'tis treason against mankind;—'tis treason against common sense; —'tis treason against God. And this impious principle lays the foundation for justifying all the tyranny and oppression that ever any prince was guilty of. The people know for what end they set up, and maintain, their governors; and they are the proper judges when they execute their *trust* as they ought to do it;—when their prince exercises an equitable and paternal authority over them;—when from a prince and common father, he exalts himself into a tyrant—when from subjects and children, he degrades them into the class of slaves;—plunders them, makes them his prey, and unnaturally sports himself with their lives and fortunes——

THIS WORLD AND THE NEXT

THE historian of the New England Puritans frequently has occasion to lament the many dry bones of metaphysics and abstruse theology which he is compelled to turn up in the effort to resurrect a semblance of that extinct species; his construction is bound all too often to resemble one of those grinning skeletons of antediluvian monsters, imperfectly wired together and stored in some museum of paleontology, making altogether too exorbitant a demand upon the imagination of the spectator to carry the conviction that the creature ever lived and breathed and moved. The vast differences between the intellect of the seventeenth century and the present necessitate so much laborious restatement of the abstractions of Puritanism that the flesh and blood realities of the Puritans themselves are lost to view. It is supremely difficult for us to imagine that the doctrine was not always present in their minds as we find it embalmed in a crabbed catechism, and still more difficult for us to understand that to them it was an all pervading sensibility, a depth of feeling, and a way of life, that it was not only of the mind but just as much of the heart and the passions.

When we come to examine the sermons, the words delivered from the pulpits by living men to living ears, we find that the ideas therein discussed were indeed those of the creed, the dogmas of original sin, irresistible grace, and predestination. But they were not developed as points in a formal lecture, or expounded as curious and technical problems; they were not preached as doctrines, or contentions, or theories, but as vivid facts. The systematized theology served primarily as a frame of reference within which the issues of human existence could be confronted immediately. The language employed was not that of the schoolroom and the textbook, but of the streets, of trades, of adventures. The sentences were not bare abstractions, but concrete dramatizations, replete with the imagery of fishing, farming, carpentering, of the city and the meadow, of the seasons and of the moods of men. The method of developing sermons from texts in the Bible strengthened this tendency to concrete and solid presentation; the ministers did not select a doctrine to preach upon, and then hunt texts to support it, but they took this or that text and deciphered its meaning. That man is naturally bound in sin and must hang upon the dispensations of grace from God—this was a dogma; but as

Thomas Hooker preaches, it takes form no longer as a colorless generalization, but as an unforgettable picture:

> You know the Dog must stay till his Master comes in, and when hee
> is come, hee must stay till he sit downe, and till hee cut his meate,
> and hee must not have the meate from his trencher neither, when he
> hath stayed all this while, he hath nothing but the crums. So it is
> with a poore sinner; you must not thinke that God will bee at your
> becke: No, you must bee content with the crums of mercy, and pity,
> and lye under the table til the Lord let the crums fall.[1]

That a regenerate man progresses from the initial stage of illumination
to a fuller and deeper immersion in grace was a tenet of the creed;
but as John Cotton develops it in the passage below, through the
metaphor of a man wading into the waters of a shallow beach and at
last reaching the cool depths, out of sight of land, the paragraph, instead of being a logical proof, becomes an ecstatic prose poem.

The most persistent misunderstanding of the Puritan mind in contemporary criticism results in the charge that it was fatalistic. To one
unfamiliar with the inward power of the belief, who judges merely
upon the external evidence of the doctrine, there seems no conceivable
motive for positive human exertion; the logical inference from the
decrees of predestination and reprobation would seem to be the attitude which Increase Mather is found herein discussing, the frame
of mind in which a man says, "God does not send me grace, I can't
convert myself," and gives over trying. Though the Puritan did indeed
live much of his life by logic, he did not so live all of it or even the
most important part of it. Dialectics and syllogisms do not account
for the driving force of the Massachusetts settlers, or for the vehemence
of the Ironsides' cavalry charges, whose enemies "God made as stubble
to our swords." In these selections Increase Mather disposes of this
question of passivity in what had become the conventional response;
but by his day the zeal was already beginning to decline, and his
answer is probably not the best solution of the problem. Perhaps the
finest statement of the invigorating effects of a philosophy of divine
determination is Oliver Cromwell's account of his thoughts before the
battle of Naseby, when his ranks of "poor, ignorant men" were being
drawn up to face the oncoming host of gallant and flashing cavaliers;
then, says Cromwell, "I could not, riding alone about my business,
but smile out to God in praises, in assurance of victory, because God
would, by things that are not, bring to naught things that are. Of

[1] *The Soules Humiliation* (London, 1638), p. 127.

which I had great assurance, and God did it." [1] How men could work themselves into this frame of mind, combining trust in God's disposing power with an assurance of victory, going through fire and water in order that what was decreed might be fulfilled, what sort of thinking brought them to this conclusion, may appear by the selections in this chapter from the sermons of Thomas Hooker. His exhaustive analysis of the true sight of sin, and his stirring account of the struggle of the saint with inherent evil uncover the sources of that almost titanic energy of which the Puritans were so abundantly possessed. A true sight of sin, he says, consists in perceiving it "clearly" and "convictingly," and the imagery by which he brings home the full brilliance of the clarity and the overwhelming weight of the conviction makes clear why there was little need for him to dwell upon a remote and semi-mythological fall of Adam, or no need whatsoever to entangle his auditors in the subtleties of free will, foreordination and absolute decree. Anyone who ever saw himself as pitilessly as Hooker requires would thereafter spend his days and nights in feverish exertions to lift himself out of such a mire of depravity. When the soul saw its task, thus clearly and convictingly, as a fact, not a theory, then also the need for divine assistance in escaping the clutch of sin was no longer something to be proved by a series of geometrical corollaries but became a desperate hunger gnawing ceaselessly at a man's very vitals. The thrill, the excitement, the challenge of the conflict against Satan would entirely drive out of his mind the suggestion that he might better fold his hands and await the pleasure of God. When we consider how intense, in Puritan eyes, was the warfare of the spirit and the flesh, and how interminable a campaign the true soldier of Christ undertook when he enrolled himself in the regiment of the godly, then we can perhaps gauge the true sublimity of Puritanism as we find Hooker insisting, and his congregation no doubt agreeing, that the awakened sinner should actually be grateful to the minister who by his winged sermons had pierced the doors of his complacency, he should be overjoyed that he had been dragged against all his natural inclinations from the peace and security of a false contentment into the heat and fury of this battle.

Inspired volunteers, going forth under the banners of truth, do not make lazy or half hearted campaigners. But if the religion of the Puritan was intense, it was not foolhardy. He was ecstatic, but not insane. He employed self-analysis, meditation, and incessant soul-searching to drive out sin from one stronghold after another; in every

[1] Charles Firth, *Oliver Cromwell* (London, 1900), p. 127.

siege he had to be not only valiant, but self-controlled, patient, wary, and crafty. It was an entirely subjective struggle; the victories were gained within the soul, and the final triumph could never be won on this side of the grave. Consequently while the saints were occupied internally with the conquest of evil, they could not expect to fare externally any better than others. All men must live among men and as men; whether their souls are filled with the Holy Ghost or not, they must suffer the diseases and decays to which men are subject. The exhilaration of faith is known to the heart of the believer, but, as Samuel Willard explains, those inward supports are remote from public view. Appearances therefore are deceiving, and the saint must keep his wits about him; he must remain calm in the midst of ardor, he must burn with fervor, but always be detached and analytical, to make sure that his agitation is genuinely of the spirit, not of mere human cupidity, and to guard against suffocating the flame with false assurances and outward conformity. Puritanism would make every man an expert psychologist, to detect all makeshift "rationalizations," to shatter without pity the sweet dreams of self-enhancement in which the ego takes refuge from reality. A large quantity of Puritan sermons were devoted to exquisite analyses of the differences between "hypocrites" and saints, and between one kind of hypocrite and another, to exposing not merely the conscious duplicity of evil men, but the abysmal tricks which the subconscious can play upon the best of men. The duty of the Puritan in this world was to know himself—without sparing himself one bit, without flattering himself in the slightest, without concealing from himself a single unpleasant fact about himself.

In the course of this sustained and unmitigated meditation, he perpetually measured himself by the highest imaginable excellency. The Puritan was taught to approve of no act because it was good enough for the circumstances, to rest content with no performance because it was the best that could be done in this or that situation. He knew indeed that life is imperfect, that the purest saints do not ever entirely disentangle themselves from the meshes of corruption, but though perfection was unattainable—even more because it was so—he bent every nerve and sinew to attempting the attainment. The Puritan life might be compared to that of a poet laboring under penalty of death to produce several hundred lines a day, and yet driven by an acute critical sense to despise every passage, every phrase that did not flow from the fountain of fresh and original inspiration. Nothing was to be done by the force of habit, in the facility of mere technical proficiency, by mechanical routine; ideally every moment and every action should reveal radiations of the supernal vitality. So far as men fell short of this ideal, they were contemptible. Over against this transcendent standard, physical existence was inevitably seen as frail, transitory, and unprofitable. When two Harvard students broke through the ice while skating, and were drowned, Increase Mather drew the moral that the times of men are in the hand of God, that no one knows when the blow will fall upon himself, or what lies in wait for him tomorrow or the day after. No trust is to be put in the things of this world, no reliance placed upon material devices. Life is a chronicle of accidents and blunders, reversals and hopes defeated.

But at the same time, if life in the world is a melancholy spectacle, it is not a tale told by an idiot; there is indeed sound and fury, but behind the meaningless futility of appearances there stand the ranks of the eternal verities. The ax-head may slip, as Urian Oakes says, and the skull of an innocent and good man be split; but the Puritan is not thereupon to cry, "Out, out—." The blade was guided by the steady hand of God, and somewhere, somehow there is a reason for this casualty, there must be a justice behind the apparent injustice. Men may not readily see it; like John Winthrop telling of the lady whose linen was burned and whose husband was shortly afterwards slain (p. 137), they may be hard pressed to explain why some events turn out as they do, and be brought time and time again to confess that in this or that series of misfortunes or streaks of luck they can not discover the wisdom of God. Nevertheless, that He who orders all things does order them by the counsel of His perfect reason and that nothing in the world is really chance, accident, or blind fate— this was the constant and unshakable conviction of the Puritan. The one thing he insisted upon, however, was that in order that this conviction might be upheld, no realities should be glossed over, no horror and no agony denied. The assertion was to be made with a clear-eyed perception of things as they do fall out, for weal or for woe.

All events therefore have their reason and their logic. We must strain to the full extent of our capacities to discover the reason and comprehend the logic. But our finite minds can not grasp all things, and our corrupted intellects can not understand all the things we grasp. No matter how much we know, there will always remain a margin to the page of knowledge which we cannot explore; the limits of the universe are not searchable with the human eye. The labor demanded of the intelligent man is that he give over no exertion to account for things, that he never accept without endeavouring to explain, that

he never take a conclusion on trust until he has exhausted all means
to take it on reason; but all the time he must remember that explanation can only go so far, that mortal reason is not God's reason, that
there is always more ignorance to be confessed than certain knowledge
to be enjoyed. The Puritan was completely hospitable to the revolu-
tionizing discoveries made by physical science during the seventeenth
century, but as long as he remained true to the fundamentals of
Puritanism he was not deceived into concluding that man had at
last unriddled the universe.

What the admirable sagacity of future ages may compass as to
thousands of problems within the circle of Sciences, or in that most
noble Art of Chymistry, or the Analysis of the three kingdoms of
nature: the tubes and glasses of our present inventions give us no
sufficient prospect. . . . The learned of this age wonder at the denial
of the motion of the Earth, tho now the truth of it appears clear to
all the generality of the ingenious of *Europe* . . .
Indeed so may posterity deride at these our ages, and the more
ingenious of future times, may stand amazed at our dulness and stupidity about minerals, meteors and the cure of diseases, and many
thousand things besides, about the lustre of stars and precious stones,
which may be as easy to them as letters to us . . . Such rare inventions
may be given in of God to beautifie the glory of the latter days. All
our writings in Divinity, will be like insipid water, to what shall then
appear upon the Stage, . . . and the Artists that shall then be born,
may discover more things in the works of God to be discust and endeavoured to be explained, then they themselves shall arrive to. The
superfine Wisdom and Learned Wits of those acute times will discover
vast regions of darkness and ignorance. There will be a *plus ultra* to
the end of the world . . . if in millions of things we are stunted and
fooled at every turn, that we may cry out with the Satyrist—*Auriculas
Asini quis non habet?* What fearful sots are we in the things before us?
Then what shall dull reason do in the great sublimities and solemnities
of faith, and the doctrine set forth by Infinite Wisdom. [1]

It was in the eighteenth century, along with their reaction against
the religious theory of society, that New Englanders abandoned the
caution inculcated by this passage, and then many of them jumped
as blithely as did the rest of the learned world to the comfortable
conclusion that Sir Isaac Newton had explained the mind of God.
Two hundred years afterwards physics has become more metaphysical
than scholasticism itself, astronomers turn to writing "in Divinity,"
and before our superfine wisdoms loom vast regions of darkness and

[1] Samuel Lee, Χαρὰ της Πισεως, *The Joy of Faith* (Boston, 1687), pp. 212–214.

ignorance, as the visible universe has become once again relative to itself and full of exceedingly deceptive appearances.

Urian Oakes concludes his sermon on providence with an injunction which was constantly delivered from New England pulpits: "labour to be prepared and provided for Disappointments." Put beside this another instruction which was equally recurrent through the sermons of Puritan ministers: "as the things and objects are, great, or mean, that men converse withall; so they are high or low spirited." [1] Take these two rules together—on the one hand, to expect nothing but disappointment in this life, on the other, to cultivate a high-spirited frame of mind by converse with the highest objects of contemplation, and between these two poles the daily life of the Puritans oscillated. John Cotton gives instructions to artisans, farmers, and merchants for the prosecution of their callings, explaining that men should pursue their worldly vocations, but not expect too much from them, should work in them, and yet labor in faith. His requirements would seem full of inconsistencies and impossibilities to one unadjusted to the dual contention of the Puritan synthesis: the fallibility of material existence and the infallibility of the spiritual, the necessity for living in a world of time and space according to the laws of that time and that place, with never once forgetting that the world will pass, be resolved back into nothingness, that reality and permanence belong to things not as they appear to the eye but to the mind.

It is by the Spiritual Operations and Actions of our minds that we meet with the Lord, and have a kind of intercourse with the Almighty, who is a Spirit. For al outward things are for the body, the body for the soul, the soul is nextly for God, and therefore meets as really with him in the Actions of Understanding, as the Eye meets with the Light in Seeing; which no other Creature can do, nor no action of a bodily Creature doth. Our Sences in their sinful and inordinate swervings, when they become means and in-lets of evil from their objects, they meet with the Creature firstly, and there make the jar: It's the beauty of the Object that stirs up to lust by the Eye, the daintiness of the Diet that provokes to intemperance by the tast, the harsh and unkind language that provokes to wrath and impatience by the Ear: But the Mind and Understanding toucheth the Lord directly, meets with his Rule, and with God acting in the way of his Government there, and when it goes off from the Rule as before, and attends its own vanity and folly, it justles with the Almighty, stands in open defyance and resistance against him. [2]

[1] Jonathan Mitchell, *A Discourse of the Glory To which God hath called Believers* (London, 1677), pp. 225–226.

[2] Thomas Hooker, *The Application of Redemption* (London, 1659), pp. 158–159.

The man who is misled by appearances "justles" with God, and is not merely a sinner and a reprobate; he is, still more tragically, a man to whom reality, the order of things "as they be," will never become known. Puritanism was regulated by the possibility of each man's achieving this insight, on whatever level of culture or education he dwelt, with the aid of divine grace; the assumption was that once this comprehension was gained, men would be able to live amid disappointments without being dissappointed, amid deceptions without being deceived, amid temptations without yielding to them, amid cruelties without becoming cruel.

The ideal of conduct thus held out was definitely affirmative. There is very little preaching of hell-fire in seventeenth-century sermons; Hooker's sentences are as far in that direction as any minister went before the beginning of the evangelical revival and the thunderings of Jonathan Edwards. So often are the first Puritans accused of living in fear and trembling under the threat of eternal torment that this point needs to be heavily underscored. That the ministers did not play upon their congregations' nerves by painting the horrors of the pit was because, for one thing no doubt, the sensibilities of people in the seventeenth century were inured to violence. This was still the age in which mothers took their children for a treat to public executions. In part the lack of brimstone sermons is accounted for by the Puritan disinclination to make religion emotional at the cost of judicious analysis and sound intellectual conviction. In converting sinners, said Samuel Willard, we must "imitate God"; we must "first deal with their understandings; to raise the affections, without informing the mind, is a fruitlesse unprofitable labour, and serves but to make zeal without knowledge." [1] But still more fundamentally, Puritan ministers did not bludgeon their people with the bloody club of damnation because their eyes were fixed upon the positive side of religion, upon the beauties of salvation, the glory of God, and the joy of faith. The worst they could imagine for the reprobate was not physical burnings and unslaked thirst, but the deprivation of God's spirit.

There is a great deal goes to the eternal life of a soul, and thou hast none of it; thou wantest the love of God, which is better than life; thou wantest grace which is indeed the inward principle of life in the soul; thou wantest the promise which is the support of the soul here in this life. [2]

[1] *Mercy Magnified on a Penitent Prodigal* (Boston, 1684), p. 150.
[2] *Ibid.*, p. 106.

What were racks and tortures compared to the want of these things? The applications or "uses" of all doctrines stated in the sermons stress continually the note of hope, the possibility that anyone, no matter how immoral or depraved he has been, may yet be saved; it is only with the next century that men are bluntly told how God abhors them and holds them over the pit of Hell as one holds a spider or some loathsome insect over the fire. When the seventeenth-century preacher wanted to arouse men he would tell them not of the irreversible sentence passed upon them in the future world, but would instance afflictions already suffered, or predict those to come, in this world—plagues, fires, earthquakes, and shipwrecks—punishments that men might survive and from which they might profit. This tendency undoubtedly produced some unpleasant characteristics, and gave opportunity for such an egotist as Increase Mather, or for such an egomaniac as his son Cotton, to hurl the vengeance of God at persons or actions they themselves did not happen to like, and even forced solid minds like John Winthrop's to twist coincidences into special interpositions of the deity. The bent of the seventeenth-century Puritan was to portray God as indeed a stern disciplinarian and one not to be trifled with, but nevertheless not as a savage chief exulting in the protracted writhings of his helpless captives. The deity was first and foremost the source of that spirit of peace to which some men might attain, "and sometimes in that unspeakable measure, as that it passeth the understanding of a man to conceive." [1] Not all men would or could reach this light, but no single individual need ever give over the hope that he might discover himself one of the favored, or ever abandon the endeavor to make himself one of them.

Thus the Puritan lived in this world, and tried desperately not to be of it; he followed his calling, plowed his land, laid away his shillings, and endeavored to keep his mind on the future life. He looked upon the physical world as the handiwork of God, and the charms of the universe as His creations, and yet he told himself, "Get thy heart more and more weaned from the Creature, the Creature is empty, its not able to satisfie thee fully, nor make thee happy." [2] He came to New England to make an earthly home, but for many years he looked upon his home, as far as any conscious expression would indicate, entirely in terms of the right ecclesiastical polity and the place of true doctrine; he lived through New England summers, the splen-

[1] John Cotton, *Christ the Fountaine* (London, 1651), p. 102.
[2] Edward Reyner, *The Rule of the New Creature*, appended to Hooker, *The Danger of Desertion* (London, 1641), p. 29.

dors of the fall, he inhaled the sea airs and heard the pine boughs sway,
and he believed he was thinking only of election and serving the will
of God. He reminded himself again and again that "the beauty of
the object stirs up to lust by the Eye."

Samuel Sewall, solid, bulky judge, literal-minded, no match for the
quick wit of Madam Winthrop, would hardly in the wildest stretch
of the imagination be called a poetic soul. He wrote two treatises on
the fulfillment of Biblical prophecies, and worried over the bewildering texts of the Book of Revelations, until we wonder how even a
person who believed that every single letter and dot of punctuation
in the Scripture was directly dictated by God could still spend so
much time so fruitlessly and unimaginatively as in arguing the precise years of the opening of the seven seals, or in trying to decide in
just what thousand years Satan would be bound. These were indeed
Puritan compositions, exhibiting the worst qualities of the Puritan
mind, its slavish literalness, its deficient sense of proportion, its bearing
down upon minutiae with the same emphasis brought to larger and
fundamental points. And then at the end, in asserting that a certain
prophecy might be fulfilled in America, Sewall finds himself justifying
the land itself, as a fit scene for the enactment of God's triumph, and
without quite knowing what he is doing sings a hymn of praise to the
purely physical and sensuous New England. He had been a boy at
Newbury, had played on the beach at Plum Island, and although his
determination had been set upon the other world and his efforts devoted to rendering mystical visions into dull prose, he himself proves
that all this time the beauty of the land, the loveliness of the objects,
had not been entirely lost upon him. He had felt the hectoring wind
on Plum Island, heard the sea-gull, smelt the marshes. The Puritans
were not blind or insensitive. They saw and loved the perch and pick-
erel, the dove and the white oak and the rows of Indian corn; but even
from a world as beautiful and lovely as this they yet hoped to be translated, "to be made partakers of the Inheritance of the Saints in Light."

THOMAS HOOKER, 1586–1647

[Thomas Hooker was probably born in Marfield, Leicestershire, of
yeomen stock. Admitted sizar at Queen's College, Cambridge, he migrated to Emmanuel, taking his B.A. in 1608, his M.A. in 1611. He was
a fellow of Emmanuel College, 1609–1618, acquiring the reputation of a
great teacher and preacher; rector of Esher in Surrey, 1620, lecturer at
St. Mary's, Chelmsford, in Essex, 1626, he was finally forced by Bishop

Laud to retire when he had become one of the most conspicuous leaders of Puritan sentiment in the land. For a year he kept a school at Little Baddow, where John Eliot was his assistant. Cited before the High Commission in 1630, he was given the amount of his bail by devoted followers and fled to Holland. For two years he was minister of an English Puritan church at Delft, then at Rotterdam, where he was associated with the great William Ames. A group of his friends from Chelmsford migrated to New England in a body, and persuaded him to come over to be their pastor. He sailed on the same ship with Stone and Cotton, after various adventures escaping the Anglican authorities, and was ordained pastor of the church at Newtown. In 1635 his congregation asked permission to move to Connecticut and the magistrates refused; in 1636 Hooker led his people to Hartford, apparently in spite of the Massachusetts authorities, who put the best face possible on the secession. For the rest of his life he was the virtual dictator of Connecticut; he returned several times to the Bay, once to be moderator of the synod at which the opinions of Anne Hutchinson were condemned. He was a powerful and dominating figure; Cotton Mather said of him that he could put a King in his pocket. He was one of the most eloquent of Puritan preachers, perhaps the most powerful pulpit orator among the ministers of New England. His manner seems to have been less scholastic and logical than that of Cotton, his style more popular and more ornamented with similes and figures. At the same time he was as great a master of dialectic and argument; his *Survey of the Summe of Church Discipline* is the supreme exposition of the Congregational church polity, couched in the terms and figures of the Ramean logic, and containing a complete expression not merely of New England ecclesiastical theory but of political doctrine and of the philosophical concepts of law, nature, and reason. He has frequently been claimed as an exponent of a more democratic social philosophy than that embraced by the Massachusetts leaders, but this opinion rests upon a misreading of two or three of his utterances; his religious and political opinions were thoroughly orthodox and he maintained them with vigor. See G. L. Walker, *Thomas Hooker*, 1891; Perry Miller, *New England Quarterly*, IV (1931), 663–712. This text is from *The Application of Redemption By the Effectual Work of the Word, and Spirit of Christ, for the bringing home of Lost Sinners to God. The Ninth and Tenth Books*, 2d. edition (London, 1659), pp. 52–66, 210–217, 234–238, 453–459. The sermons in this volume were delivered at Hartford.]

A TRUE SIGHT OF SIN

Wherein this true sight, and apprehension of sin properly discovers it self.

I ANSWER, A true sight of sin hath two Conditions attending upon it; or it appears in two things: We must see sin, 1. Cleerly. 2. Convictingly, what it is in it self, and what it is to us, not in the appearance and paint of it, but in the power of it; not to fadam it in the notion and conceit only, but to see it with Application.

We must see it cleerly in its own Nature, its Native color and proper hue: It's not every slight conceit, not every general and cursorie, confused thought or careless consideration that will serve the turn, or do the work here, we are all sinners; it is my infirmity, I cannot help it; my weakness, I cannot be rid of it; no man lives without faults and follies, the best have their failings, *In many things we offend all.* But alas all this wind shakes no Corn, it costs more to see sin aright than a few words of course; It's one thing to say sin is thus and thus, another thing to see it to be such; we must look wis[e]ly and steddily upon our distempers, look sin in the face, and discern it to the full; the want whereof is the cause of our mistaking our estates, and not redressing of our hearts and waies, *Gal.* 6. 4. *Let a man prove his own work.* Before the Goldsmith can sever and see the Dross asunder from the Gold, he must search the very bowels of the Mettal, and try it by touch, by tast, by hammer, and by fire; and then he will be able to speak by proof what it is; So here. We perceive sin in the crowd and by hearsay, when we attend some common and customary expressions taken up by persons in their common converse, and so report what others speak, and yet never knew the Truth, what either others or we say, but we do not single out our corruptions and survey the loathsomness of them, as they come naked in their own Natures; this we ought to do: There is great ods betwixt the knowledg of a Traveller, that in his own person hath taken a view of many Coasts, past through many Countries, and hath there taken up his abode some time, and by Experience hath been an Eye-witness of the extream cold, and scorching heats, hath surveyed the glory and beauty of the one, the barrenness and meanness of the other; he hath been in the Wars, and seen the ruin and desolation wrought there; and another that sits by his fire side, and happily reads the story of these in a Book, or views the proportion of these in a Map, the ods is great, and the difference of their knowledg more than a little: the one saw the Country really, the other only in the story; the one hath seen the very place, the other only in the paint of the Map drawn. The like difference is there in the right discerning of sin; the one hath surveyed the compass of his whol course, searched the frame of his own heart, and examined the windings and turnings of his own waies, he hath seen what sin is, and what it hath done, how it hath made havock of his peace and comfort, ruinated and laid wast the very Principles of Reason and Nature, and Morality, and made him a terror to himself, when he hath looked over the loathsom abominations that lie in his bosom, that he is afraid to approach the presence of the Lord to bewail his sins, and to crave pardon, lest he should be confounded for them, while he is but confessing of them; afraid and ashamed lest any man living should know but the least part of that which he knows by himself, and could count it happy that himself was not, that the remembrance of those hideous evils of his might be no more; Another happily hears the like preached or repeated, reads them writ or recorded in some Authors, and is able to remember and relate them. The ods is marvelous great. The one sees the History of sin, the other the Nature of it; the one knows the relation of sin as it is mapped out, and recorded; the other the poyson, as by experience he hath found and proved it. It's one thing to see a disease in the Book, or in a mans body, another thing to find and feel it in a mans self. There is the report of it, here the malignity and venom of it.

But how shall we see cleerly the Nature of sin in his naked hue?

This will be discovered, and may be conceived in the Particulars following. Look we at it: First, As it respects God. Secondly, As it concerns our selves. As it hath reference to God, the vileness of the nature of sin may thus appear.

It would dispossess God of that absolute Supremacy which is indeed his Prerogative Royal, and doth in a peculiar manner appertayn to him, as the Diamond of his Crown, and Diadem of his Deity, so the Apostle, *He is God over all blessed for ever,* Rom. 9. 5. All from him and all for him, he is the absolute first being, the absolute last end, and herein is the crown of his Glory. Al those attributes of Wisdom, Goodness, Holiness, Power, Justice, Mercy, the shine and Concurrency of all these meeting together is to set out the unconceivable excellency of his Glorious name, which exceeds all praise, *Thyne is the kingdom, the power and the glory,* the right of all and so the rule of all and the Glory of all belongs to him.

Now herein lyes the unconceavable hainousness of the hellish nature of sin, it would justle the Almighty out of the Throne of his Glorious Soveraignty, and indeed be above him. For the will of man being the chiefest of all his workmanship, all for his body, the body of the soul, the mind to attend upon the will, the will to attend upon God, and to make choyce of him, and his wil, that is next to him, and he onely above that: and that should have been his Throne and Temple or Chair of State, in which he would have Set his Soveraignty for ever. He did in an Especial manner intend to meet with man, and to communicate himself to man in his righteous Law, as the rule of his Holy and righteous will, by which the will of *Adam* should have been ruled and guided to him, and made happie in him; and all Creatures should have served God in man, and been happy by or through him, serving of God being happy in him; But when the will went from under the government of his rule, by sin, *it would be above God, and be happy without him,* for the rule of the law in each command of it, holds forth a three-fold expression of Soveraignty from the Lord, and therein the Soveraignty of all the rest of his Attributes.

1. The Powerful Supremacy of his just will, as that he hath right to dispose of all and authority to command all at his pleasure; *What if God will? Rom.* 9. 22 *My Counsel shall stand and I wil do all my pleasure, Isa.* 46. 10. And as its true of what shal be done upon us, so his wil hath Soveraignty of Command in what should be done by us we are to say *the will of the Lord be done; Davids* warrant was *to do all Gods wils Acts.* 13. 22. and our Saviour himself professeth, *John.* 6. 38. *that he came not to do his own will but the will of him that sent him,* and therfore his wrath and jealousie and judgment will break out in case that be disobeyed.

2. There is also a fulness of wisdom in the law of God revealed to guide & direct us in the way we should walk, *Psal.* 19. 7. *the law of God makes wise the simple,* 2. *Tim.* 3. 15. *it's able to make us wise unto Salvation.*

3. There's a Sufficiency of God to content and satisfy us. *Blessed are they who walk in his wayes, and blessed are they that keep his Testimonies. Psal.* 119. 1. 2. *Great prosperity have they that love the law, and nothing shal offend them,* ver. 16. and in truth there can be no greater reward for doing wel, than to be enabled to do well, he that hath attayned his last end he cannot go further, he cannot be better;

Now by sin we justle the law out of its place, and the Lord out of his Glorious Soveraignty, pluck the Crown from his head, and the Seepter out of his hand, and we say and profess by our practice, there is not authority and power there to govern, nor wisdom to guide, nor good to content me, but I will be swayed by mine own wil and led by mine own deluded reason and satisfied with my own lusts. This is the guise of every graceless heart in the commission of sin; so *Pharaoh who is the Lord? I know not the Lord, nor will I lett Israel go. Exod.* 5. 2. in the time of their prosperity see how the Jews turn their backs and shake off the

authority of the Lord, *we are Lords* (say they) *we will come no more at thee.
Jer.* 2. 31. *and our tongues are our own who shal be Lords over us? Psal.* 12. 4.
So for the wisdom of the world, see how they set light by it as not worth
the looking after it *Jer.* 18. 12. *we wil walk after our own devices & we wil
every one do the imagination of his own evil heart, yea they sett up their own
traditions,* their own Idols and delusions, and Lord it over the law,
making the command of God of none effect Math. 15. 8. 9. So for the goodness
of the word; *Job.* 22. 17. *Mat.* 3. 14. *It is in vayn to serve God and what
profit is there that we have kept his ordinances, yea his Commandemnts are ever
grievous,* Its a grievous thing to the loose person he cannot have his
pleasures but he must have his guilt and gall with them; Its grievous
to the worlding that he cannot lay hold on the world by unjust means,
but Conscience layes hold upon him as breaking the law. Thou that
knowest and keepest thy pride and stubbornness and thy distempers,
know assuredly thou dost justle God out of the Throne of his glorious
Soveraignty and thou dost profess, Not Gods wil but thine own (which
is above his) shall rule thee, thy carnal reason and the folly of thy mind,
is above the wisdome of the Lord and that shal guide thee; to please
thine own stubborn crooked pervers spirit, is a greater good than to
please God and enjoy happines, for this more Contents, thee; That
when thou considerest but thy Course, dost thou not wonder that the
great and Terrible God doth not pash such a poor insolent worm to
pouder, and send thee packing to the pitt every moment.

2. It smites at the Essence of the Almighty and the desire of the
sinner, is not only that God should not be supream but that indeed he
should *not be at all,* and therefore it would destroy the being of Jehovah.
Psal. 81. 15. sinners are called *the haters of the Lord.* John. 15. 24. *they
hated both me and my Father.* Now he that hates endeavours if it be possible the annihilation of the thing hated, and its most certain were it in
their power, they would pluck God out of Heaven the light of his truth
out of their Consciences, and the law out of the Societies and Assemblies
where they live, that they might have elbow room to live as they list.
Nay what ever they hate most and intend, and plott more evil against
in al the world, they hate God most of all, and intend more evil against
him than against all their Enemies besides, because they hate all for
his sake, therefore wicked men *are said to destroy the law Psal.* 126. 119
the Adulterer loaths that law that condemns, uncleaness; the Earth-
worm would destrow that law that forbids Covetousness, they are sayd
to *hate the light* John 3. 21. to hate the Saints and Servants of the Lord
John 15. 18. *the world hates you,* he that hates the Lanthorn for the lights
sake, he hates the light much more, he that hates the faithful because

of the Image of God, and the Grace that appears there, he hates the God of all, Grace and Holiness, most of all, so God to *Zenacharib*, Isa. 37. 28. *I know thy going out and thy Comming in, and thy rage against me,* Oh it would be their content, if there was no God in the world to govern them, no law to curbe them, no justice to punish, no truth to trouble them, Learn therfore to see how far your rebellions reach, It is not arguments you gainsay, not the Counsel of a Minister you reject, the command of a Magistrate ye oppose, evidence of rule or reason ye resist; but be it known to you, you fly in the very face of the Almighty, and it is not the Gospel of Grace ye would have destroyed, but the spirit of Grace, the author of Grace the Lord Jesus, the God of all Grace that ye hate.

It crosseth the whol course of Providence, perverts the work of the Creature and defaceth the beautiful frame, and that sweet correspondence and orderly usefulness the Lord first implanted in the order of things; The Heavens deny their influence, the Earth her strength, the Corn her nourishment, thank sin for that. Weeds come instead of herbs, Cockle and Darnel instead of Wheat, thank sin for that, *Rom.* 8. 22. *The whol Creature* (or Creation) *grones under vanity,* either cannot do what it would or else misseth of that good and end it intended, breeds nothing but vanity, brings forth nothing but vexation, It crooks all things so as that none can straiten them, makes so many wants that none can supply them, *Eccles.* 1. 15. This makes crooked Servants in a family no man can rule them, crooked inhabitants in towns, crooked members in Congregations, ther's no ordering nor joynting of them in that comly accord, and mutual subjection; know they said, *the adversary sin hath done all this.* Man was the mean betwixt God and the Creature to convey all good with all the constancy of it, and therefore when Man breaks, Heaven and Earth breaks all asunder, the Conduit being cracked and displaced there can be no conveyance from the Fountain.

In regard of our selves, see we and consider nakedly the nature of sin, in Four particulars.

Its that which makes a separation between God and the soul, breaks that Union and Communion with God for which we were made, and in the enjoyment of which we should be blessed and happie, *Isai.* 59. 1. 2. *Gods ear is not heavy that it cannot hear nor his hand that it cannot help, but your iniquities have separated betwixt God and you & your sins have hid his face that he wil not hear for he professeth,* Psal. 5. 4. *that he is a God that wills not wickedness neither shal iniquity dwell with him. Into the new Jerusalem shal no unclean thing enter, but without shal be doggs Rev.* 21. 27. The Dogs to their Kennel, and Hogs to their Sty and Mire: but if an

impenitent wretch should come into Heaven, the Lord would go out
of Heaven; *Iniquity shall not dwell with sin.* That then that deprives me
of my greatest good for which I came into the world, and for which I
live and labor in the world, and without which I had better never to
have been born; nay, that which deprives me of an universal good, a
good that hath all good in it, that must needs be an evil, but have all
evil in it: but so doth sin deprive me of God as the Object of my will,
and that wills all good, and therefore it must bring in Truth all evil
with it. Shame takes away my Honor, Poverty my Wealth, Persecution
my Peace, Prison my Liberty, Death my Life, yet a man may still be a
happy man, lose his Life, and live eternally: But sin takes away my
God, and with him all good goes; Prosperity without God will be my
poyson, Honor without him my bane; nay, the word without God
hardens me, my endeavor without him profits nothing at all for my
good. A Natural man hath no God in any thing, and therefore hath no
good.

It brings an incapability in regard of my self to receive good, and an
impossibility in regard of God himself to work my spiritual good, while
my sin Continues, and I Continue impenitent in it. An incapability of
a spiritual blessing, *Why trangress ye the Commandement of the Lord that ye
cannot prosper do what* ye can, 2 Chron. 24. 20. And *He that being often
reproved hardens his heart, shal be consumed suddenly and there is no remedy,*
He that spils the Physick that should cure him, the meat that should
nourish him, there is no remedy but he must needs dye, so that the
Commission of sin makes not only a separation from God, but obstinate
resistance and continuance in it, maintains an infinit and everlasting
distance between God and the soul: So that so long as the sinful
resistance of thy soul continues; God cannot vouchsafe the Comforting
and guiding presence of his grace; because it's cross to the Covenant of
Grace he hath made, which he will not deny, and his Oath which he
will not alter. So that should the Lord save thee and thy Corruption,
carry thee and thy proud vnbeleeving heart to heaven he must nullify
the Gospel, (Heb. 5. 9. *He's the Author of Salvation to them that obey him*)
and forswear himself, (Heb. 3. 18. *He hath sworn unbeleevers shall not enter
into his rest*) he must cease to be just and holy, and so to be God. As *Saul*
said to *Jonathan* concerning *David*, 1 Sam. 20. 30, 31. *So long as the Son
of* Jesse *lives, thou shalt not be established, nor thy Kingdom:* So do thou
plead against thy self, and with thy own soul; So long as these rebellious
distempers continue, Grace and Peace, and the Kingdom of Christ can
never be established in thy heart For this obstinate resistance differs
nothing from the plagues of the state of the damned, when they come to

the highest measure, but that it is not yet total and final, there being some kind of abatement of the measure of it, and stoppage of the power of it. Imagine thou sawest the Lord Jesus coming in the clouds, and heardest the last trump blow, *Arise ye dead, and come to judgment:* Imagine thou sawest the Judg of all the World sitting upon the Throne, thousands of Angels before him, and ten thousands ministring unto him, the Sheep standing on his right hand, and the Goats at the left: Suppose thou heardest that dreadful Sentence, and final Doom pass from the Lord of Life (whose Word made Heaven and Earth, and will shake both) *Depart from me ye cursed;* How would thy heart shake and sink, and die within thee in the thought thereof, wert thou really perswaded it was thy portion? Know, that by thy dayly continuance in sin, thou dost to the utmost of thy power execute that Sentence upon thy soul: It's thy life, thy labor, the desire of thy heart, and thy dayly practice to depart away from the God of all Grace and Peace, and turn the Tomb-stone of everlasting destruction upon thine own soul.

It's the Cause which brings all other evils of punishment into the World, and without this they are not evil, but so far as sin is in them. The sting of a trouble, the poyson and malignity of a punishment and affliction, the evil of the evil of any judgment, it is the sin that brings it, or attends it, *Jer.* 2. 19. *Thine own wickedness shall correct thee, and thy back slidings shall reprove thee, know therefore that it is an evil, and bitter thing that thou hast forsaken the Lord.* Jer. 4. 18. *Thy waies and doings have procured these things unto thee, therefore it is bitter, and reacheth unto the heart.* Take miseries and crosses without sin, they are like to be without a sting, the Serpent without poyson, ye may take them, and make Medicines of them. So *Paul* 1 *Cor.* 15. 55. he plaies with death it self, sports with the Grave. *Oh death, where is thy sting? Oh Grave where is thy Victory? the sting of death is sin.* All the harmful annoyance in sorrows and punishments, further than either they come from sin, or else tend to it, they are rather improvements of what we have than parting with any thing we do enjoy, we rather lay out our conveniences than seem to lose them, yea, they encrease our Crown, and do not diminish our Comfort. *Blessed are ye when men revile you, and persecute you, and speak all manner of evil of you for my sake, for great is your reward in Heaven:* Matth. 5. 11. There is a blessing in persecutions and reproaches when they be not mingled with the deserts of our sins; yea, our momentary short affliction for a good cause, and a good Conscience, works an excessive exceeding weight of Glory. If then sin brings all evils, and makes all evils indeed to us, then is it worse than all those evils.

It brings a Curse upon all our Comforts, blasts all our blessings, the best of all our endeavors, the use of all the choycest of all Gods Ordinances: it's so evil and vile, that it makes the use of all good things, and all the most glorious, both Ordinances and Improvements evil to us. *Hag.* 2. 13. 14. When the Question was made to the Priest; *If one that is unclean by a dead Body touch any of the holy things, shall it be unclean? And he answered, Yea. So is this People, and so is this Nation before me, saith the Lord; and so is every work of their hands, and that which they offer is unclean:* If any good thing a wicked man had, or any action he did, might be good, or bring good to him, in reason it was the Services and Sacrifices wherein he did approach unto God, and perform Service to him, and yet *the Sacrifice of the wicked is an abomination to the Lord*, Prov. 28. 9. and Tit. 1. 15. *To the pure all things are pure; but to the unbeleeving there is nothing pure, but their very Consciences are defiled.* It is a desperate Malignity in the temper of the Stomach, that should turn our Meat and diet into Diseases, the best Cordials and Preservatives into Poysons, so that what in reason is appointed to nourish a man should kill him. Such is the venom and malignity of sin, makes the use of the best things become evil, nay, the greatest evil to us many times; *Psal.* 109. 7. *Let his prayer be turned into sin.* That which is appointed by God to be the choycest means to prevent sin, is turned into sin out of the corrupt distemper of these carnal hearts of ours.

Hence then it follows; *That sin is the greatest evil in the world, or indeed that can be.* For, That which separates the soul from God, that which brings all evils of punishment, and makes all evils truly evil, and spoils all good things to us, that must needs be the greatest evil, but this is the nature of sin, as hath already appeared.

But that which I will mainly press, is, Sin is only opposite to God, and cross as much as can be to that infinite goodness and holiness which is in his blessed Majesty; it's not the miseries or distresses that men undergo, that the Lord distasts them for, or estrangeth himself from them, he is with *Joseph* in the Prison, with the three Children in the Furnace, with *Lazarus* when he lies among the Dogs, and gathers the Crums from the rich Mans Table, yea with *Job* upon the dung-hil, but he is not able to bear the presence of sin: yea, of this temper are his dearest servants, the more of God is in them, the more opposite they are to sin where ever they find it. It was that he commended in the Church of *Ephesus, That she could not bear those that were wicked*, Rev. 2. 3. As when the Stomach is of a pure temper and good strength, the least surfet or distemper that befals, it presently distasts and disburdens it self with speed. So *David* noted to be *a man after Gods own heart*. He professeth, 101. *Psal.* 3. 7. *I hate the work of them that turn aside, he that worketh deceit shall not dwell in my house, he that telleth lyes, shall not tarry in my sight.* But when the heart becomes like the Stomach, so weak it cannot help it self, nor be helped by Physick, desperate diseases and dissolution of the whol follows, and in reason must be expected. Hence see how God looks at the least connivance, or a faint and feeble kind of opposition against sin, as that in which he is most highly dishonored, and he follows it with most hideous plagues, as that indulgent carriage of *Ely* towards the vile behavior of his Sons for their grosser evils, 1 *Sam.* 2. 23. *Why do you such things, It's not well my Sons that I hear such things: It is not well,* and is that all? why, had they either out of ignorance not known their duty or out of some sudden surprisal of a temptation neglected it, it had not been well, but for them so purposedly to proceed on in the practice of such gross evils, and for him so faintly to reprove: The Lord looks at it as a great sin thus feebly to oppose sin, and therefore verse 29. he tells him, *That he honored his Sons above God,* and therefore he professeth, *Far be it from me to maintain thy house and comfort, for he that honors me I wil honor, and he that despiseth me shall be lightly esteemed,* verse 30. Hence it is the Lord himself is called *the holy one of Israel,* 1. Hab. 12. *Who is of purer eyes than to behold evil, and cannot look upon iniquity,* no not in such as profess themselves Saints, though most deer unto him, no, nor in his Son the Lord Jesus, not in his Saints, *Amos,* 8. 7. *The Lord hath sworn by himself, I abhor the excellency of* Jacob; what ever their excellencies, their priviledges are, if they do not abhor sin, God will abhor them, *Jer.* 22. 24. *Though* Coniah *was as the Signet of my right hand, thence would I pluck him.* Nay, he could not endure the appearance of it in the Lord Christ, for when but the reflection of sin (as I may so say) fell upon our Savior, even the imputation of our transgressions to him, though none iniquity was ever committed by him, the Father withdrew his comforting presence from him, and let loose his infinite displeasure against him, forcing him to cry out, *My God, my God, why hast thou forsaken me?*

Yea, Sin is so evil, (that though it be in Nature, which is the good Creature of God) that there is no good in it, nothing that God will own; but in the evil of punishment it is otherwise, for the torments of the Devils, and punishments of the damned in Hell, and all the plagues inflicted upon the wicked upon Earth, issue from the righteous and revenging Justice of the Lord, and he doth own such execution as his proper work, *Isa.* 45. 7. *Is there any evil in the City,* viz. of punishment, *and the Lord hath not done it? I make peace, I create evil, I the Lord do all these things:* It issues from the Justice of God that he cannot but reward every one according to his own waies and works; those are a mans own, the holy one of Israel hath no hand in them; but he is the just Executioner of the plagues that are inflicted and suffered for these; and hence our blessed Savior becoming our Surety, and standing in our room, he endured the pains of the Second death, even the fierceness of the fury of an offended God; and yet it was impossible he could commit the least sin, or be tainted with the least corrupt distemper. And it's certain it's better to suffer all plagues without any one sin, than to commit the least sin, and to be freed from all plagues. Suppose that all miseries and sorrows that ever befel all the wicked in Earth and Hell, should meet together in one soule, as all waters gathered together in one Sea: Suppose thou heardest the Devils roaring, and sawest Hell gaping, and flames of everlasting burnings flashing before thine eyes; it's certain it were better for thee to be cast into those inconceivable torments than to commit the least sin against the Lord: Thou dost not think so now, but thou wilt find it so one day.

MEDITATION

MEDITATION *is a serious intention of the mind whereby wee come to search out the truth, and settle it effectually upon the heart.*

An intention of the mind; when one puts forth the strength of their understanding about the work in hand, takes it as an especial task whereabout the heart should be taken up and that which wil require the whol man, and that to the bent of the best ability he hath, so the word is used *Jos.* 1. 8. *thou shalt not suffer the word to depart out of thy mind, but thou shalt meditate therein day and night,* when either the word would depart away or our corruptions would drive it away, meditation layes hold upon it and wil not let it go, but exerciseth the strength of the attention of his thoughts about it, makes a buisiness of it as that about which he might do his best, and yet fals short of what he should do in it. So *David* when he would discover where the stream and overflowing strength of his affections vented themselves, he points at this practice as that which employes the mind to the ful. *Psal* 119. 197. *Oh how I love thy law, it is my meditation all the day,* love is the great wheel of the soul that sets al on going, and how doth that appear? it is my meditation day and night; the word in the original signifyeth to swim, a man spreads the breadth of his understanding about that work, and layes out himself about the service wherein there is both difficulty and worth.

Serious.] Meditation is not a flourishing of a mans wit, but hath a set bout at the search of the truth, beats his brain as wee use to say, hammers out a buisiness, as the Gouldsmith with his mettal, he heats it and beats it turnes it on this side and then on that, fashions it on both that he might frame it to his mind; meditation is hammering of a truth or poynt propounded, that he may carry and conceive the frame and compass in his mind, not salute a truth as we pass by occasionally but solemnly entertain it into our thoughts; Not look upon a thing presented as a spectator or passenger that goes by: but lay other things aside, and look at this as the work and employment for the present to take up our minds. It's one thing in our diet to take a snatch and away, another thing to make a meal, and sit at it on purpose until wee have seen al set before us and we have taken our fil of al, so we must not cast an eye or glimpse at the truth by some sudden or fleighty apprehension, a snatch and away, but we must make a meal of musing. Therefore the Psalmist makes it the main trade that a Godly man drives, professedly opposite to the carriage of the wicked, whether in his outward or inward work, in his disposition or expression of himself in his common practice; whereas they walk in the corrupt counsels of their own hearts, stand in the way of sinners, not only devise what is naught, but practice and persevere in what they have devised, and sit in the seat of the scorners; A blessed man his rode in which he travels, his set trade *he meditates in the Law of God day and night:* that is the counsel in which he walks, the way in which he stands, the seat in which he sits. Look at this work as a branch of our Christian calling, not that which is left to our liberty, but which is of necessity to be attended and that in good earnest as a Christian duty, which God requires, not a little available to our spiritual welfare.

The end is doubly expressed in the other part of the description.

1. *The searching of the truth.*
2. *The effectual setling of it upon the heart.*

The search of the truth: Meditation is a coming in with the truth or any cause that comes to hand, that we may enquire the ful state of it before our thoughts part with it, so that we see more of it or more clearly and fully than formerly we did, this is one thing in that of the Prophet *Hos.* 6. 3. *Then shall yee know if you follow on to know,* when we track the footsteps of the truth, in al the passages, until we have viewed the whol progresse of it, from truth to truth from point to point. *This it is to dig for wisdom, Prov.* 2. 2. When men have found a mine or a veyn of Silver, they do not content themselves, to take that which is uppermost and next at hand within sight which offers it self upon the surface of the Earth, but they dig further as hoping to find more, because they see somewhat. So meditation rests not in what presents it self to our consideration, but digs deeper gathers in upon the truth, and gaynes more of it then did easily appear at the first, and this it doth.

1. *When it recals things formerly past, sets them in present view before our consideration and judgment* Meditation sends a mans thoughts afar off, cals over and revives the fresh apprehension of things done long before, marshals them al in rank together, brings to mind such things which were happily quite out of memory, & gone from a man, which might be of great use and special help to discover our condition according to the quality of it; may be Conscience starts the consideration but of one sin, but meditation looks abroad, and brings to hand many of the same, and of the like kind and that many dayes past and long ago committed, This distemper now sticks upon a man and brings him under the arrest of Conscience and the condemnation thereof. But saies meditation let me mind you of such and such sins at such and such times, in such and such companies, committed and multiplyed both more and worse than those that now appear so loathsom and so troublesom to you; meditation is as it were the register and remembrancer, that looks over the records of our daily corruptions, and keeps them upon file, and brings them into court and fresh consideration *Job*. 13. 26. *Thou makest me to possess the sins of my youth:* This makes a man to renew the sins of his youth, makes them fresh in our thoughts, as though new done before our eyes. This Interpreters make the meaning of that place *Job*. 14. 17. *My trangression is sealed up in a bag, and thou sewest up mine iniquity,* though God do thus, yet he doth it by this means in the way of his Providence, *i.e.* by recounting and recalling our corruptions to mind, by serious meditation we sew them all up together, we look back to the linage and pedegree of our lusts, and track the abominations of our lives, step by step, until we come to the very nest where they are hatched and bred, even of our original corruption, and body of death, where they had their first breath and being, links al our distempers together from our infancy to our youth, from youth to riper age, from thence to our declining daies. So *David*, from the vileness of his present lusts is led to the wickedness *in which he was warmed*, Psal. 51. 5. This was typed out in the old Law by *the chewing of the cud;* Meditation cals over again those things that were past long before, and not within a mans view and consideration.

Meditation *takes a special Survey of the compass of our present condition, and the Nature of those corruptions that come to be considered:* It's the traversing of a mans thoughts, the coasting of the mind and imagination into every crevis and corner, pryes into every particular, takes a special view of the borders and confines of any corruption or condition that comes to be scanned, *Psal.* 119. 59. *I considered my waies, and turned my feet unto thy testimonies;* he turned them upside down, looked through them as it were; a present apprehension peeps in as it were through the crevis or key-hole, looks in at the window as a man passeth by; but Meditation lifts up the latch and goes into each room, pries into every corner of the house, and surveyes the composition and making of it, with all the blemishes in it. Look as the Searcher at the Sea-Port, or Custom-house, or Ships, satisfies himself not to over-look carelessly in a sudden view, but unlocks every Chest, romages every corner, takes a light to discover the darkest passages. So is it with Meditation, it observes the woof and web of wickedness, the ful frame of it, the very utmost Selvage and out-side of it, takes into consideration all the secret conveyances, cunning contrivements, all bordering circumstances that attend the thing, the consequences of it, the nature of the causes that work it, the several occasions and provocations that lead to it, together with the end and issue that in reason is like to come of it, *Dan.* 12. 4. *Many shall run to and fro, and knowledg shall encrease:* Meditation goes upon discovery, toucheth at every coast, observes every creek, maps out the dayly course of a mans conversation and disposition.

The second End of Meditation is, *It settles it effectually upon the heart.* It's not the pashing of the water at a sudden push, but the standing and soaking to the root, that loosens the weeds and thorns, that they may be plucked up easily. It's not the laying of Oyl upon the benummed part, but the chafing of it in, that suppleth the Joynts, and easeth the pain. It is so in the soul; Application laies the Oyl of the Word that is searching and savory, Meditation chafeth it in, that it may soften and humble the hard and stony heart: Application is like the Conduit or Channel that brings the stream of the Truth upon the soul; but Meditation stops it as it were, and makes it soak into the heart, that so our corruptions may be plucked up kindly by the Roots.

This settling upon the heart appears in a three-fold work.

It affects the heart with the Truth attended, and leaves an Impression upon the Spirit answerable to the Nature of the thing which is taken into Meditation: 2 *Pet.* 2. 8. It's said of *Lot, in seeing and hearing, he vexed his righteous soul.* Many saw and heard the hideous abominations, and were not touched nor affected therewith. No more had he been, but that he vexed and troubled his own righteous soul, because he was driven to a dayly consideration of them which cut him to the quick. The word is observable, it signifies to try by a touch-stone, and to examine, and then upon search to bring the soul upon the rack: therefore the same word is used, *Matth.* 14. 24. *The Ship was tossed by the waves;* the consideration of the abominations of the place raised a tempest of trouble in *Lots* righteous soul. This the wise man calls *laying to the heart,* Eccles. 7. 1, 2. *It's better to go to the house of mourning than to the house of laughter; for this is the end of all men, and the living will lay it to his heart.* When the Spectacle of Misery and Mortality is laid in the grave, yet savory Meditation laies it to a mans heart, and makes it real there in the work of it. The Goldsmith observes that it is not the laying of the fire, but the blowing of it that melts the Mettal: So with Meditation, it breaths upon any Truth that is applied, and that makes it really sink and soak into the soul; and this is the reason why in an ordinary and common course of Providence, and Gods dealing with sinners, (leaving his own exceptions to his own good pleasure) that the most men in the time and work of Conversion have that scorn cast upon them, *that they grow melancholly.* And it's true thus far in the course of ordinary appearance; The Lord usually never works upon the soul by the Ministry of the Word to make it effectual, but he drives the sinner to sad thoughts of heart, and makes him keep an audit in his own soul by serious meditation, and pondering of his waies; otherwise the Word neither affects throughly, nor works kindly upon him.

It keeps the heart under the heat and authority of the Truth that it's taken up withal, by constant attendance of his thoughts. Meditation keeps the Conscience under an arrest, so that it cannot make an escape from the Evidence and Authority of the Truth, so that there is no way, but either to obey the Rule of it, or else be condemned by it. But escape it cannot, Meditation meets and stops al the evasions and sly pretences the fals-hearted person shal counterfeit. If a man should deny his fault, and himself guilty, Meditation will evidence it beyond all gainsaying, by many testimonies which Meditation wil easily cal to mind; remember ye not in such and such a place: upon such an occasion, you gave way to your wicked heart to do thus and thus; you know it, and God knows it, and I have recorded it: If the sinner would lessen his fault, Meditation aggravates it; or if he seem to slight it, and look at it as a matter of no moment, yet Meditation will make it appear, there is greater evil in it, and greater necessity to bestow his thoughts upon it than he is aware of.

Hence it is Meditation laies siege unto the soul, and cuts off al carnal pretences that a wretched self-deceiving hypocrite would relieve himself by; and stil lies at the soul, this you did, at that time, in that place, after that manner; so that the soul is held fast prisoner, and cannot make an escape; but as *David* said, *Psal.* 51. 3. *My sins are ever before me:* Consideration keeps them within view, and will not suffer them to go out of sight and thoughts; and therefore it is *Paul* joyns those two together, 1 *Tim.* 3. 15. *Meditate in these things, and be in them.*

It provokes a man (by a kind of over-bearing power) to the practice of that with which he is so affected: A settled and serious Meditation of any thing, is as the setting open of the Flood-gates, which carries the soul with a kind of force and violence, to the performance of what he so bestows his mind upon; as a mighty stream let out turns the mill. *Phil.* 4. 9. *Think of these things, and do them:* thinking men are doing men. *Psal.* 39. 3. *While I was thus musing, the fire brake out, and I spake:* the busie stirring of Meditation is like the raising of a tempest in the heart, that carries out all the actions of the man by an uncontroulable command. *I considered my waies, and turned my feet unto thy Statutes:* right Consideration, brings in a right Reformation with it.

WANDERING THOUGHTS

THE Marriner, because the Channel is narrow, and the wind somwhat scant, he toucheth in many places, tacks about, and fetcheth many points, but stil because it's to attain the Haven; therfore each man in reason concludes, that was the cause that invited him to al that variety in his course. It's so in the carriage of the soul; the cause why a man fetcheth such a compass, and tacks about in his own contrivements; now this, now that; one while one way, another while this or that presented and pursued busily; yet in the issue we land al our thoughts, and look at the last how to bring in content to such a lust: It's certain the vanity of that lust occasioned and drew the vanity of thy thoughts after it.

The cause being thus conceived, the Cure is fair and easie to comprehend; namely, *Cure these inordinate and raging lusts,* and thence wil follow a stil and quiet composure of mind; purge the stomach if it be foul, and that wil ease the pain of wind in the Head, because that is caused by the fumes that arise from thence. Take off the plummet, or lessen but the weight of it, the minutes though they hurried never so fast before, yet wil not move at all, or at least very slowly and quietly. So here, take off the poyse of the affections, purge away these noysom lusts which carry and command the head, and send up dunghil steams which distemper the mind, and disturb it, and those windy imaginations wil cease, and those thoughts of the mind like the minutes, either wil not move, or move in order and manner as may help and not hinder. Here the great skil and care ought to be to labor the clensing and sanctification of such affections which are most tainted, and where the vein and sourse of original corruption, either through custom, or constitution, or company, hath vented it self most usually, and so hath taken up the soul, and gained, and so exercised greater power over it. For as in bruised or weak parts, all the humors run thither, so commonly this corruption is the sink and drain of the soul, all distempered thoughts, and other inferior lusts, empty themselves, and become Servants unto this. If once the affections had gained such a tast and rellish of the sweetness that is in Christ, and his Truth, that al these baggage and inferior things here below seemed sapless, and that the heart were endeared to him & his Truth, and carried strongly after both: this would carry the thoughts vehemently, & keep them so strongly to both, that they would be so far from wandring away from Christ, that they would not be taken from bestowing the strength of their intentions about him, *Psal.* 119 .97. *Oh how I love thy Law, it is my Meditation all the day;* verse 93. *I will never forget thy Precepts, for thereby thou hast quickened me;* ver. 23. *Princes sate and spake against me, but thy servant did meditate in thy Statutes.* In reason he would have conceived it was high time for him to bethink himself how to prevent their fury, & it would cost him sad thoughts of heart how to provide for his succor and safty; no truly, *Thy servant did meditate in thy law.*

Possess thy heart with an actual consideration, and a holy dread of the glorious presence of the Almighty, who sees and pondereth all thy paths, and therefore wil take an account, and that strictly, of all the outstrainings of thy thoughts when thou comest to give attendance upon him, and to draw neer into his presence, in some peculiar and spiritual Service: There is a kind of heedless wantonness which like a Canker breeds in our Atheistical dispositions, whereby we see not the Rule that should guide us, we lay aside also the consideration of that power that doth rule us, and wil bring us to judgment, and so missing the guide that should shew us the path, and the power that should awe us, and constrain us to keep the rode, a mans mind powrs out it self to every vanity that next offers it self unto its view. Whereas were we aware of his presence, and awed with it, it would cause us to eye him, and attend him in his way and work, wherein he commands us to walk with him. As it is with trewantly Schollers who are sporting and gaming out of their place, and from any serious attendance upon their books, when nothing wil stil them, and force them to their studies, as soon as ever there is but the least inkling of the Master, or any eye they can cast upon his approach, they are all as stil as may be, repair presently to their place, fal close, and let their minds to their work; O Master, Master, our Master is yonder; there follows stilness and attendance presently. Our trewantly and wanton minds are of this temper, we are apt to straggle out of our places, or from giving attendance to those special Services which the Lord cals for at our hands, and to lay out themselves upon things that are not pertinent, and further than we are awed with the apprehension of Gods sight and presence, who cals for the dayly attendance of our thoughts when we draw neer unto him, doth see and observe our carelessness, and wil proceed in Judgment, and execute punishment upon us for it, it's scant possible to hold the bent of our thoughts awfull, to the business we have in hand. It was the Curse which attended *Jonah* when he departed away from the presence of the Lord, and from following his Command, he followed *lying vanities,* Jonah, 2. 8. And it's the peculiar plague which is appointed in the way of Providence, and the Lords righteous proceedings to befal al who bestow not their hearts upon him, *Eph.* 4. 21. *They walk in the vanity of their minds;* and the reason is rendred, *they are strangers from the life of God.* When our thoughts start aside from under the Government of Gods Wisdom, the Rule of Truth and stability, they wander up and down in the waies of error and vanity, and find no end or measure, follow vanity, and become vain, nor can they attain any stability before they return thither. As your vagabond beggars, and vagrant persons in the Country from whence we came, there is no possibility to fasten them to any imployment, or settle them in any place before they come under the eye of Authority, and power of the Magistrate. So fares it with our vagabond and vagrant thoughts; further than they are under the eye of God, and awed with his presence, it's not possible to stop them from the pursuit of vanity, or confine them to setled consideration of that which concerns our duty and comfort. The Rule is one, like it self accompanied with stability and rest; if once we go astray from that, there is neither end nor quiet in error, but restlessness and emptiness. The Sea, while it keeps the Channel, the course is known, and the Marriners can tel how to advantage their passage; but if once it exceeds the banks, no man can tel whither it wil go, or where it will stay. Our imaginations are like the vast Sea, while we eye the

Rule, and are ordered by the Authority of it, we know our compass; but once go off, and we know not whither we shal go, or where we shal stay.

Be watchfully careful to observe the first wandrings and out-strayings of thy thoughts, how they first go off from the attendance to the work in hand, and look off from the matter, thou settest thy self to meditate in; immediately recal them back, bring them to their task again, and set them about their intended work. If often they fly out and follow fresh occasions that Satan or a mans corruptions shal suggest take them at the first turn and often again settle them upon the service, until at last by constant custom our mind and thoughts wil buckle handsomly to their business, after they be kept in by a daily care; I have heard Hunts-men say when they have young dogs, raw and that hath not been entred nor accquainted with their sport, if a fresh game come in view, or some other unexpected prey cross them in their way, they forsake the old sent and follow that which is in their eye, but their manner is to beat them off, and cal them away from that, and then to bring them to the place where they left their former pursuit, and there set them to find the sent afresh, until at last being often checked and constantly trayned up they wil take and attend the first game, so here, with our wandring minds which are not trayned up to this work of meditation, if they begin to fly off and follow a new occasion, suffer not thy thoughts to range, but bring your mind back again, and set it upon the former service, and then by thy constant care and Gods blessing thy mind wil fal in sweetly and go away with the work, or as men use to do with some kind of wand that is warped & bent somwhat much one way, they bend it a little, at the first & there hold it. Bend it & hold it, at last it comes fully to the fashion they desire it. So here often bend and hold thy mind bent to the work in hand, *Heb.* 2. 1. *let us give earnest heed to the things wee have heard;* our roving thoughts are like riven vessels, if the parts be not glewed and the breaches brought together again by strong hand, they wil leak out, so here &c.

REPENTANT SINNERS AND THEIR MINISTERS

Doct. They whose hearts are pierced by the Ministry of the word, they are carryed with love and respect to the Ministers of it.

Men and Brethren, they be words of honor & love, & they spoke them seriously and affectionaley, they mocked them before, and they now embrace them, they cared not what tearms of reproach they cast

upon their persons, they know not now what titles of love and tender-
ness to put upon them, they now fal at their feet as clients, who flouted
them before as enemies, so it was with the jalour *Acts* 16. 30, 31, 34.
how kindly doth he *Paul* and *Silas* whome erewhile he handled so
currishly, beyond the bounds of reason and humanity, he entertains
them in the best room of his house who before thought the worst
place in the prison too good for them. He baths their wounded parts
which he had whipped and stocked before, fears and trembles before
them as his counsellors, whom he handled most harshly before as
Prisoners; he feasts them as his guests whom he had struck as Malefactors; the wind was in another dore, the man is of another mind
yea is another man than he was. God had no sooner opened the heart
of *Lydia* to attend the word but her affections were exceedingly enlarged, towards the dispensers thereof. *Acts* 16. 15. so that the cords
of her loving invitation led *Paul* and held him captive, he professed
she compelled them i.e. by her loving and affectionate expressions, prevailed with them for a stay. And while *Paul* had the *Galathians* under
the Pangs of the new birth and Christ was now *forming in them*, they
professed they *would have plucked out their eyes* and have given them to
the Apostle, *Gal.* 4. 15.

Naaman hath no sooner his leprosy healed, and his heart humbled
and cut off from his corruption, but he professed himself and what
he had is at the devotion of the Prophet, and that not out of comple-
ment but in truth, 2 *Kings* 5. 15. *Take a blessing from thy servant.*

Reasons are two.

They see and know more than formerly they did, when happily the crooked
counsels of others deceived them, and their own carnal reason couzened
and deluded their own souls that they mis-judged the men and their
doctrine also. As that they did not speak the truth, or else had some
crooked and self-seeking ends in what they spak; As either to gratify
other mens humors whom they would please or else to set up their
own persons and praise and esteem in the apprehensions of others as
singular men and more than of an ordinary frame; and therefore
would wind men up to such a high pitch of holiness, and force them
to such a singular care to fly the very appearance of al evil, when
its more than needs and more than God requires, and more than any
man can do but now they find by proof and are forced out of their
own sence and feeling to acknowledg the truth of what they have
spoken, and what they have heard, & themselves also, to be the
faithful embassadors of the Lord Jesus, and therefore worthy to be
believed and attended in their dispensations and honored of al. *So*

Paul 2 Cor. 4. 3. *We hope we are made manifest unto your consciences* Thus the Woman of *Samaria* when our Savior came home to the quick and met with the secrets of her heart, she then fel from her taunting and slighting of our Savior to admiring of him, *Come faith she behould the man that told me al that ever I did, is not he the Christ.* John, 4. 29. Look as *Nabuchadnezzar* said, *Dan.* 4. last, now I know the God of *Daniel* is the true God, *and now I praise the living God,* so when they have been in the fire, and God hath had them upon the anvil, now I know what sin is, now I know what the danger is, now I know what necessity there is to part with sin; when the Patient hath found the relation and direction of the Physitian hath proved real it makes him prize and honor his skil and counsel, for ever; and for ever to have his custom, As the Pythonist was compelled from the power of *Pauls* administration to confess, *these are the Servants of the living God which shew unto us the way of Salvation,* so here.

As they see more and can therefore judge better of the worth of persons and things; *so their conscience now hath more scope, and the light of reason hath more liberty, and allowance to express that they know, and nothing now can withstand and hinder;* for while men are held captive under the power of their lusts and corruptions of their hearts, in which they live, and which for the while they are resolved to follow; though their reason happily do yeild it, and their own hearts and Consciences cannot but inwardly confess it, the persons are holy, the sins are vile which they condemn, and dangers dreadful which they forewarn; yet to profess so much openly to others, and to the world were to judg themselves while they would acquit others, and condemn their own courses, while they should praise and honor the carriages and persons of others, and therefore darken the evidence of the word by carnal cavils and reproaches, stifle the wittness of Conscience, and stop its mouth that it cannot speak out. Thus *Rom.* 1. 18. *they hold down the truth in unrighteousness.* When the truth that is by their judgments assented unto, and by their hearts yeilded, and therefore should break out and give in testimony to the good wayes of God: their corrupt and unrighteous and rebellious hearts hold it prisoner, wil not suffer it either to appear unto others or prevail with themselves; As it fared with the Scribes & Pharisees when the wonder was wrought by *Peter,* say they *Acts,* 4. 16. *that indeed a notable miracle hath been done by them is manifest to all that dwel in Jerusalem, and we cannot deny it (q. d.* they would have done it if they could) *but that it spread no further, let us charge them straitly that they speak no more in this name.* But here when the conscience of a poor sinner is convinced, and the heart wounded, and that resistance and gainsaying distemper is taken off and crushed, now Conscience is in commission and hath his scope & the coast is now clear that reason may be heard, now the broken hearted sinner wil speak plainly, these are the guides that God hath set up, their direction I wil attend, these are the dear and faithful servants of the Lord whom I must honor, and with them I would betrust my soul, not with the blind guides, and false teachers, who daub with untempered morter and are not trustie to God, nor their own souls, and therefore cannot be to me. Oh send for such though in their life time they could not endure the sight, abide the presence, nor allow them a good word, reviled their persons and proceedings and professions, (yea that they wil confess) but it was directly against their own judgment and knowledg and Conscience, myne own heart often gave my tongue the lye, when I did so speak and so disparage their conversation, otherwise I must have condemned mine own course and Conscience also, but the Lord is with them, and the truth is with them, and a Blessing wil undoubtedly follow them. Ask why these poor pierced sinners did not go to the Scribes, they would tel the truth. Oh it was they that deceived us, led and drew us to the commission of this hellish wickedness; we cannot cal them teachers but murtherers, they could never help themselves, therefore not help us.

INSTRUCTION, *Sound contrition and brokenness of heart brings a strange & a sudden alteration into the world, varies the price and valew of things and persons beyond imagination, turnes the market upside down;* makes the things appear as they be, & the persons to be honored and respected as they are in truth, that look what the truth determines, reason approves, and Conscience witnesseth, that account is current in the hearts and apprehensions of those, whose hearts have been pierced with godly sorrow for their sins. Because such judg not by outward appearance as it is the guise of men of corrupt minds, but upon experience, that which they have found and felt in their own hearts, what they have seen and judged in their own spirits, they cannot but see so and judg so of others. Those who were mocked as *men ful of new wine*, are now the precious servants of the Lord, flouted to their faces not long since, now they attend them, honor and reverence them, yea fal at their very feet. It was before men and drunkards, now men and bretheren, the world you see is wel amended but strangely altered. It was said of *John* Baptist the fore-runner of our Savior, and the scope of whose doctrine was mainly to prepare the way for the Lord, it's said of him that *Elias* is come and hath reformed al, set a new face and frame in the profession of the Gospel, *Math.* 17. 11. *Turned the disobedient to the wisdom of the just men, the hearts of children to the fathers,* that though they were so degenerate that *Abraham* would not own them had he been alive, yet when the Ministery of *John* had hammered and melted them for the work of our Savior, they bcame to be wholly altered, their judgments altered and their carriage also. For in truth the reason why men see not the loathsomness of other mens sins, or else have not courage to pass a righteous sentence upon them, It is because they were never convinced to see the Plague sore of their own corruptions, never had their hearts affected with the evil of them in their own experience but their own Conscience was misled out of authority, and stifled that it durst not outwardly condemn that which inwardly they could not but approve. They therefore who either do not see their own evil, or dare not proceed in open judgment to condemn, they wil either not see or not pass a righteous judgment upon others, so *Paul* intimates to *Agrippa, Acts,* 26. 8. 9. *let it not seem strange Oh King for I my self did think I should do many things against the name of Jesus, which I also did. q. d.* whiles thou so continuest thou wilt see as I did, and do as I did, but after God had entered into combate with him and spoken dreadfully to his soul see, he is another man, and of another mind; he destroyed the Churches, *now takes care of them;* he that hated the name and Gospel of Jesus *counts al things dung and dross for the excellent knowledg of Jesus,* the world is well amended but its mervailously altered, and therfore *we have found this man a Pestilent fellow Acts,* 17. 16. he hath subdued the state of the world.

TERROR, *this shewes the dreadful and miserable condition of al those who after al the light that hath been let into their minds, conviction into their Consciences, horror into their hearts touching the evils that have been committed and come now to be discovered unto them, they loath the light that hath layd open their evils, distast those persons and preachers and Christians most, that have dealt most plainly to descover the loathsomness of their distempers,* it shewes the irrecoverable corruption of the mind and heart that grows worst under the best means, and cleaves most to its sins under al the choycest means that would pluck their sins from their heart, and their heart from them, they are either fools or mad men that cannot endure the presence of the Physitian without whose help they could not be cured. This is made an evidence of the estrangment of Gods heart from a people, and an immediate fore-runner of their ruin. *Isa.* 9. 13. 14. 17. *For this people turneth not unto him that smote them, neither do they seek the Lord, therefore the Lord wil cut off from Israel head & tail, branch & rush, one day therfore the Lord shal have no pity on their young men nor mercy on their fatherless, for every one is an Hipocrite.* It takes away al pity in God, al hopes in themselves of any good. After *Pharoah* had many qualmes & recoylings of spirit by *Moses* dealing with him, & the miracles which he had wrought for his repentance, & at last sides it with the hellish stiffness of his own stubborn heart, so that he cannot endure the speech or presence of *Moses* any more, Exod. 10. 28. *get thee from me, see my face no more, for the day thou seest my face thou shalt die*, God sends *Moses* no more, but sends his plagues to destroy his first born he wil not see the face of *Moses* he shal feel the fierceness of the wrath of the Lord.

JOHN COTTON, 1584–1652

[For Cotton's life see p. 207. Cotton's sermons are perfect examples of the Puritan ideal of the plain style. Restrained and self-possessed, meticulously logical and rigorously organized, they stay close to the texts, and use hardly any metaphors or figures but those supplied by the Bible itself.

The texts of the first two selections are from *The New Covenant, or A Treatise, unfolding the order and manner of the giving and receiving of the Covenant of Grace to the Elect* (London, 1654), pp. 44–47, 64–69.

The texts of the third and fourth selections are from *The way of Life* (London, 1641), pp. 104–105, 436–451. These sermons were probably delivered in England.

The text of the fifth selection is from *Christ the Fountaine* (London, 1651), pp. 15–21, 25–30.]

SWINE AND GOATS

ALL THE men in the world are divided into two ranks, Godly or Ungodly, Righteous or Wicked; of wicked men two sorts, some are notoriously wicked, others are Hypocrites: Of Hypocrites two sorts (and you shall find them in the Church of God) some are washed Swine, others are Goats.

1. The *Swine* are those of whom our Saviour Christ saith, *That they returne unto their wallowing in the mire;* like unto these are such men who at the hearing of some Sermon have been stomach sick of their sins, and have rejected their wicked courses, but yet the swines heart remaineth in them, as a Swine when he cometh where the puddle is, will readily lye down in it: so will these men wallow in the puddle of uncleannesse when their conscience is not pricked for the present: But these are a grosser kind of Hypocrites.

2. There is another sort that goe far beyond these, and they are *Goats*, so called, *Matth.* 25. 32, 33. and these are clean Beasts such as chew the cudd, meditate upon Ordinances, and they divide the hoofe, they live both in a generall and particular calling, and will not be idle; they are also fit for sacrifice; what then is wanting? Truly they are not *sheep* all this while, they are but *Goats*, yet a Goat doth loath that which a Swine will readily break into; but where then doe they fall short of the nature of sheep? A difference there is, which standeth principally in these particulars.

1. The Goat is of a Capricious nature, and affecteth Eminency, his gate also is stately, *Prov.* 30. 30. *Agur* reckoneth the He-goat among the 4 things that are comely in going: And they are full of Ambition, they cannot abide swamps and holes, but will be climbing upon the tops of mountains; there is not that plain lowly sheepish frame that attendeth unto the voyce of the Shepheard, to be led up and downe in fresh pastures: they attend upon their ends, and will outshoot God in his own Bowe, and therefore when they have done many things for Christ, he will say unto them, *Depart from me, ye workers of iniquity*. More Eminency they did affect, then they were guided unto. Thus it was with *Jehu*, who in his zeal for God thought to promote himselfe, and herein he will not be perswaded of his sin, and therefore going into crooked wayes, he cometh at length to cleave unto the sins of *Jeroboam* the Son of *Nebat*, who made *Israel* to sin; yet notwithstanding, you may rec[e]ive a Goat into Church-fellowship for all his capricious nature, and he will be a clean creature, and of much good use. The five foolish *Mat.* 25. 2. were all of them *Virgins*, all of them abhorring Idolatry, and all go forth to meet the Bridegroome, and yet they are foolish and never shall you make them wise, to be all for Christ, onely hearing and obeying his voyce.

2. They are of a Rankish nature all of them, specially the old Goats will have an unsavory relish, far from that pleasant sweetnesse that is in a sheep; and herein Hypocrites are greatly different from the sheep of Christ, as the Prophet speaketh, *Ezek.* 34. 21. and they marre the Pastures with their feet, and will be at length mudling the faire waters of the Sanctuary also; and in your best sanctification they fall far short of a sheep-like frame of spirit, diligently to heare the voyce of the Shepheard, this will not be found in the sanctification of the best Hypocrite under Heaven, they may goe far and yet fall away, and this is no Arminianism, but if you search the Scriptures diligently, you will find these things to be true.

HYPOCRITES AND SAINTS

TRULY it is hard to perceive when men differ, and therefore it is not an easie matter to make such use of Sanctification, as by it to beare witnesse unto Justification: [1] and it will be a very hard case and much more difficult, when men cannot feele the presence of spirituall gifts, but want spirituall light: and when they doe finde faith in themselves, they doe finde it in hypocrites also, even in hypocrites also, even faith to seeke the Lord, & faith to waite upon him, and faith to apply him, saying, *My God*, and faith to stay upon the *God of Israel;* and yet these men doe vanish away in hypocrisie; this hypocrites may doe; seeing therefore what easines of errour may befall Christians, whether this or that grace be of the right stampe or no, it will behove Christians to be wary, for even Eagle-eyed Christians will have much adoe so to discerne of sanctification in themselves, before they see their justification, as to cut off all hypocrites from having the like in them, for the sanctified frame of Gods children, and that which seemeth to be like it in hypocrites, both of them spring from the holy Ghost, and both from faith: but now the Spirit of God hath further worke in his own people, beyond what he worketh upon others, though he melteth both, yet hypocrites are melted as iron, which will returne againe to his former hardnes, but his owne people are melted into flesh, which will never returne to his hardnes more, neither can they rest in any measure of softnes unto which they have attained, but still are carryed toward Jesus Christ: so that the one is a temporary faith, and the other persevereth; though both worke in the name of Christ, yet this difference will be found between them, not only when hypocrites come to be blasted, but even in the middest of their profession: As for the faith of the Gospell of Jesus Christ, it is never president of its own power, but his strength lyeth out of himselfe in Christ; whereas hypocrites and legall Christians are confident of their faith, that they can make use of it unto such and such ends, they think they need no more but look up to Christ, and their worke is at an end; and such strength they finde in themselves, as that they doe not feare, but that they shall carry an end all their worke to Gods glory and their own: whereas the strongest faith even of the *Thessalonians* (whose faith was such, as none of all the Churches went before them) if it be not supplyed and strengthened, they know, & the Apostle *Paul* knoweth that it will warpe & shrinke. This may we see by comparing, 1 *Thes.* 1. 3. with *Chap.* 3. 2, 10. And the faithfull people of God, *Isa.* 26. 12. acknowledge Him to *worke all their works for them.* And therefore as there is a reall difference in the presence of the Spirit; so also in the worke of faith in hypocrites, and the children of God, for the one putteth confidence in himselfe in the gift received, and the other in *Jehovah*. This is the first difference of Sanctification.

2. There is Difference also in the Rule whereby they are guided, though both seeke to the word of God & take delight in that, insomuch as you shall not be able to difference them there, yet a great difference there is in the apprehension of the word: the one is so confident of the comfort that he hath in the word, and he will be ready to take it ill at Gods hand, if he finde not acceptance before him: Now the other see the need they have of the Lord to maintaine their comfort for them. This manner of affection we finde in *David*, when the Lord had brought him and his people into a sweet frame and temper of spirit to offer willingly towards the building of the Temple; what saith *David* now? Doth he thinke this to be enough? No, no, but he prayeth to the Lord, 1 *Chron.* 29. 18. *O Lord God of Abraham, Isaack, and Israel our fathers keepe this for ever in the imagination of the thoughts of the heart of thy people, and prepare their heart unto thee.* Thus is he sensible that these comforts would soone faile them, & they should againe waxe barren and uncomfortable. And here is the nature of true Consolation in Christ, to looke up unto the Lord to preserve and maintaine it, and so he is still drawne neerer & neerer to Christ. But now though both attend unto the Word, as their Rule of Sanctification, if you take it in the way, in which the one and the other hold it forth, yet there is a great difference. *Psal.* 119. 6. *Then shall I not be ashamed,* &c. Here is a Rule; what, may not hypocrites walke according to this rule? Truly they professe no lesse, and they think it enough, if they have but a Rule in their eye, and therfore under a spirit of bondage they are confident and say, *What soever the Lord commandeth us, we will heare it and doe it,* Deut. 5. 27. And what saith *Balaam; Though* Balaack *would give me an house full of silver and gold, I cannot goe beyond the Commandement of the Lord,* Numb. 22. 18. and yet he loved the wages of iniquity; and indeed those that undertake so much in their owne strength, they come afterward to be weary of the Lord, and weary of his Commandements: as *Amos* 8. 5. and they say at last, *It is in vaine to serve God, and what profit is it that we have kept his ordinances?* Mal. 3. 14. These are but like washed swine, that will crop grasse for a while in a faire Pasture, but if you keepe them long there, they will not delight in such manner of feeding, but will rather choose to go into the mire; but as for goats they will delight in the Commandments of the Lord, *Isa.* 58. 2. It is not a very hard thing unto them, nor grievous for them to keep solemne fasting dayes together, they come willingly,

they delight to come, therefore the difference will be hardly discovered, and unles you be a Christian of a very cleere discerning, you will not finde the difference.

WADING IN GRACE

FOR further encouragement hereunto, consider that place, *Ezech.* 47. 3, 4, 5. It shewes you the marvailous efficacy of the spirit of Grace in the dayes of the Gospel: First a Christian wades in the rivers of God his grace up to the ankles, with some good frame of spirit; yet but weakly, for a man hath strength in his ankle bones, *Acts* 3. and yet may have but feeble knees, *Heb.* 12. 12. So farre as you walk in the waters, so far are you healed; why then in the next place, he must wade till he come to the knees, goe a thousand Cubits, a mile further, and get more strength to pray, and to walk on in your callings with more power and strength.

Secondly, but yet a man that wades but to the knees, his loynes are not drenched, for nothing is healed but what is in the water. Now the affections of a man are placed in his loynes, God tries the reines; a man may have many unruly affections, though he be padling in the wayes of grace; he may walk on in some eavennesse, and yet have many distempered passions, and may have just cause to complaine of the rottennesse of his heart in the sight of God: why then, thou hast waded but to the knees, and it is a mercy that thou art come so farre; but yet the loynes want healing, why, wade a mile further then; the grace of God yet comes too shallow in us, our passions are yet unmortified, so as we know not how to grieve in measure, our wrath is vehement and immoderate, you must therefore wade untill the *loynes bee girt with a golden girdle;* wade an-end, & think all is not well untill you be so deep, & by this you may take a scantling, what measure of grace is poured out upon you. And if thou hast gone so farre, that God hath in some measure healed thy affections, that thou canst be angry and sin not, &c. it is well, and this we must attain to. But suppose the loyns should be in a good measure healed, yet there is more goes to it then all this; and yet when a man is come thus farre, he may laugh at all temptations, and blesse God in all changes: But yet goe another thousand Cubits, and then you shall swimme; there is such a measure of grace in which a man may swimme as fish in the water, with all readinesse and dexterity, gliding an-end, as if he had water enough to swimme in; such a Christian doth not creep or walk, but he runs the wayes of Gods Commandements; what ever he is to doe or to suffer he is ready for all, so every way drenched in grace, as let God turn him any way, he is never drawn dry.

CHRISTIAN CALLING

WEE are now to speake of living by faith in our outward and temporall life: now our outward and temporall life is twofold, which wee live in the flesh. It is either a civill, or a naturall life, for both these lives we live, and they are different the one from the other: Civill life is that whereby we live, as members of this or that City, or Town, or Commonwealth, in this or that particular vocation and calling.

Naturall life I call that, by which we doe live this bodily life, I meane, by which we live a life of sense, by which we eate and drinke, by which we goe through all conditions, from our birth to our grave, by which we live, and move, and have our being. And now both these a justified person lives by faith; To begin with the former.

A true beleeving Christian, a justified person, hee lives in his vocation by his faith.

Not onely my spirituall life, but even my Civill life in this world, all the life I live, is by the faith of the Son of God: he exempts no life from the agency of his faith, whether he live as a Christian man, or as a member of this or that Church, or Commonwealth, he doth it all by the faith of the Son of God.

Now for opening this point, let me shew you what are those severall acts of faith which it puts forth about our occasions, and vocations, that so we may live in Gods sight therein.

First, Faith drawes the heart of a Christian to live in some warrantable calling; as soone as ever a man begins to looke towards God, and the wayes of his grace, he will not rest, till he find out some warrantable Calling and imployment: An instance you have in the Prodigall son, that after he had received & spent his portion in vanity, and when being pinched, he came home to himself, & comming home to his Father, the very next thing after confession and repentance of his sin, the very next petition he makes, is, *Make mee one of thy hired servants;* next after desire of pardon of sin, then put me into some calling, though it be but of an hired servant, wherein he may bring in God any service; A Christian would no sooner have his sinne pardoned, then his estate to be setled in some good calling, though not as a mercenary slave, but he would offer it up to God as a free-will Offering, he would have his condition and heart setled in Gods peace, but his life setled in a good calling, though it be but of a day-labourer, yet make me as one that may doe thee some service; *Paul* makes it a matter of great thankfulnesse to God, that he had given him ability, and put him in place

where he might doe him service, 1 *Tim.* 1. 12. And in the Law, they
were counted uncleane beasts that did not divide the hoofe into two,
Lev. 11. 3. therefore the Camell, though he chewed the cud, yet because he did not divide the hoofe, hee was counted uncleane; and God
by the Beasts, did signifie to us sundry sorts of men, who were cleane,
who not, as you may see in *Peters* Vision, in *Acts* 10. It shewes you then,
that it is onely a cleane person, that walkes with a divided hoofe, that
sets one foote in his generall, and the other in his particular calling;
he strikes with both, he serves both God and man, else he is an uncleane
beast, if he have no calling but a generall, or if no calling but a particular, he is an uncleane creature; But now as soone as ever faith purifies
the heart, it makes us cleane creatures, *Acts* 15. 9. and our callings doe
not interfeire one upon another, but both goe an end evenly together,
he drives both these plowes at once; *As God hath called every man, so let
him walke*, 1 Cor. 7. 19, 20. This is the cleane worke of faith, hee would
have some imployment to *fill the head and hand with*.

Now more particularly, faith doth warily observe the warrantable-
nesse of its calling.

Three things doth faith finde in a particular calling.

First, It hath a care that it be a *warrantable* calling, wherein we
may not onely aime at our own, but at the publike good, that is a
warrantable calling, *Seek not every man his owne things, but every man the
good of his brother*, 1 *Cor.* 10. 24. *Phil.* 2. 4. Seek one anothers welfare;
faith works all by love, *Gal.* 5. 6. And therefore it will not think it hath
a comfortable calling, unlesse it will not onely serve his owne turne,
but the turn of other men. Bees will not suffer drones among them,
but if they lay up any thing, it shall be for them that cannot work;
he would see that his calling should tend to publique good.

Secondly, Another thing to make a calling warrantable, is, when
God gives a man *gifts* for it, that he is acquainted with the mystery
of it, and hath gifts of body and minde sutable to it: *Prov.* 16. 20. *He
that understands a matter shall finde good;* He that understands his businesse
wisely. God leads him on to that calling, 1 *Cor.* 7. 17. To shew you that
when God hath called me to a place, he hath given me some gifts
fit for that place, especially, if the place be sutable and fitted to me and
my best gifts; for God would not have a man to receive five Talents,
and gaine but two, he would have his best gifts improved to the best
advantage.

Thirdly, That which makes a calling warrantable, is, when it is
attained unto by warrantable and direct *meanes*, when a man enterprises
not a calling, but in the use of such meanes as he may see Gods provi-

dence leading him to it: so *Amos* manifests his calling against the High
Priest, *Amos* 7. 14, 15. *The Lord tooke me, and said unto me, Goe, feed my
people:* So he had a warrant for it, Gods hand led him to it in Gods
Ordinance, and therein he comforted himselfe, whereas another man
that hath taken up such a calling without warrant from God, he deales
ingenuously, *Zach.* 13. 5. and leaves it; to shew you that a man ought
to attend upon his owne warrantable calling. Now faith that hath
respect unto the word of God for all its wayes, he would see his calling
ayming at the publique good, he would see gifts for it, and an open
doore for his entrance into it, hee would not come unto it by deceit
and undermining of others, but he would see the *providence and ordinance*
of God leading him unto it, the counsell of friends, and encouragement
of neighbours; this is the first work of faith.

2. Another work of faith, about a mans vocation and calling, when
faith hath made choyce of a warrantable calling, then he *depends* upon
God for the quickning, and sharpning of his gifts in that calling, and
yet depends not upon his gifts for the going through his calling, but
upon God that gave him those gifts, yea hee depends on God for the
use of them in his calling; faith saith not, Give me such a calling and
turne me loose to it; but faith lookes up to heaven for skill and ability,
though strong and able, yet it looks at all its abilities but as a dead work,
as like braided wares in a shop, as such as will be lost and rust, unlesse
God refresh and renue breath in them. And then if God doe breathe
in his gifts, hee depends not upon them for the acting his work, but
upon Gods blessing in the use of his gifts; though he have never so
much skill and strength, he looks at it as a dead work, unlesse God
breathe in him; and he lookes not at his gifts as breathed onely on by
God, as able to doe the work, unlesse also he be followed by Gods
blessing. *Blessed bee the Lord my strength, that teacheth my hands to warre,
and my fingers to fight, Psal.* 44. 1. He had been trained up to skill that
way, yet he rests onely in Gods teaching of him, *Psal.* 18. 32, 33, 34.
It is the Lord that girds me with strength; he puts strength into his hands,
so that a *Bow of steele is broken with my armes;* And therefore it was that
when he went against *Goliah,* though he had before found good successe in his combats with the Lyon and the Beare, yet he saith not, I
have made my part good enough with them, and so shall I doe with
this man; no, but this is the voyce of faith; *The Lord my God that delivered me out of their hands, he will deliver me out of the hand of this Philistim;*
Hee that gave me strength and skill at that time, hee is the same,
his hand is not shortned: And then what is this Philistim more then one
of them? 1 *Sam.* 17. 37. And so when hee comes in *Goliahs* presence,

and looks in his face, he tels him he comes to him *in the name of the Lord of Hosts;* and hee comes not onely in the Lords name, but he *looks up to him for skill and strength to help;* and therefore saith ver. 40. *The Lord will close thee in my hands;* so that by his owne strength shall no flesh prevaile; *It is in vaine,* saith faith, *to rise early, and goe to bed late, but it is God that gives his beloved rest, Psal.* 127. 1, 2, 3. *Prov.* 3. 5, 6. The strongest Christian is never more foyled, then when he goes forth in strength of gifts received, and his owne dexterity.

Thirdly, We live by faith in our vocations, in that faith, *in serving God, serves men, and in serving men, serves God:* The Apostle sweetly describes it in the calling of servants, *Eph.* 6. 5. to 8. *Not with eye service as men-pleasers, but as the servants of Christ, doing the will of God from the heart with good will, as unto the Lord, and not unto men;* Not so much man, or onely man, but chiefly the Lord; so that this is the work of every Christian man in his calling, even then when he serves man, he serves the Lord; he doth the work set before him, and he doth it *sincerely,* and *faithfully,* so as he may give account for it; and he doth it *heavenly* and *spiritually; He uses the world as if he used it not,* 1 *Cor.* 7. 31. This is not the thing his heart is set upon, hee lookes for greater matters then these things can reach him, he doth not so much look at the world as at heaven. And therefore that which followes upon this, he doth it all *comfortably,* though he meet with little encouragements from man, though the more faithfull service he doth, the lesse he is accepted; whereas an unbeleeving heart would be discontented, that he can finde no acceptance, but all he doth is taken in the worst part; but now if faith be working and stirring, he wil say, *I passe very litle to be judged by you, or by mans judgement,* 1 *Cor.* 4. 3. I passe little what you say, or what you do, God knows what I have done, & so his spirit is satisfied, 1 *Thess.* 2. 6. *We were tender over you, as a Nurse over her childe;* We wrought not for wages, nor for the praise of you, if so, wee had not been the servants of Christ. A man therefore that serves Christ in serving of men, he doth his work sincerely as in Gods presence, and as one that hath an heavenly businesse in hand, and therefore comfortably as knowing God approves of his way and work.

Fourthly, Another act of faith about a mans vocation is this; It *encourageth* a man in his calling to the most homeliest, and difficultest, and most dangerous things his calling can lead and expose himselfe to; if faith apprehend this or that to be the way of my calling, it encourages me to it, though it be never so *homely,* and *difficult,* and *dangerous.* Take you a carnall proud heart, and if his calling lead him to some homely businesse, he can by no meanes embrace it, such homely employments a carnall heart knowes not how to submit unto; but now faith having put us into a calling, if it require some homely employment, it encourageth us to it, he considers, It is my calling, and therefore he goes about it freely, and though never so homely, he doth it as a work of his calling, *Luke* 15. 19. *Make mee one of thy hired servants:* A man of his rank and breeding was not wonted to hired servile work, but the same faith that made him desirous to be in a calling, made him stoop to any work his calling led him to; there is no work too hard or too homely for him, for faith is conscious, that it hath done most base drudgery for Satan. No lust of pride, or what else so insolent, but our base hearts could be content to serve the Devil and nature in it, and therefore what drudgery can be too homely for me to doe for God? *Phil.* 2. 5, 7. *Let the same minde bee in you that was in Christ Iesus, hee made himselfe of no reputation;* he stood not upon it, that he was borne of God, and equall to the most High, but he made himselfe a servant, and of no reputation, and so to serve God, and save men; and when his Father called him to it, he stooped to a very low employment, rose up from Supper, and girded himselfe with a Towell, and washed his Disciples feet, *Iohn* 13. They thought it was a service too homely for him to doe, but he tells them, that even they ought thus to serve one another. So faith is ready to embrace any homely service his calling leads him to, which a carnall heart would blush to be seene in; a faithfull heart is never squeamish in this case, for repentance will make a man revenge himselfe upon himselfe, in respect of the many homely services he hath done for Satan, and so faith encourageth us to the most difficult and homely businesses. *Ezra* 10, 4. *It is a great thing* thou art now about, yet *arise and bee doing, for the matter belongs to thee:* Yea, and though sometimes the work be more dangerous, yet if a man be called to it, faith dares not shrink; It was an hard point that *Herod* was put upon, either now hee must bee prophane, or discover his hypocrisie; now therefore *Iohn* dischargeth his conscience, and though it was dangerous for him to bee so plaine, yet faith encourageth him to it; if it appeare to bee his Calling, faith doth not picke and choose, as carnall reason will doe.

Firstly, Another act of faith, by which a Christian man lives in his vocation, is, That faith *casts all the failings and burthens of his calling upon the Lord;* that is the proper work of faith, it rolls and casts all upon him.

Now there are three sorts of burthens that befall a man in his calling.

1. *Care about the successe of it;* and for this faith casts its care upon

God, 1 *Pet.* 5. 7. *Pro.* 16. 3. *Commit thy workes unto the Lord, and thy thoughts shall be established, Psal.* 55. 22. 24. *Cast thy burthen upon the Lord, and he will deliver thee;* faith will commend that wholly to God.

2. A second burthen, is *feare of danger* that may befall us therein from the hand of man. *Luke* 13. 31. 32. Some bids Christ goe out of the Country, for *Herod* will kill him; what saith Christ to that? *Goe tell that foxe I must worke to day and to morrow, &c.* He casts that upon God and his calling, God hath set me a time, and while that time lasts, my calling will beare me out, and when that time is out, then I shall be perfect.

3. Another burthen, is the burthen of *injuries*, which befalls a man in his calling. I have not hastened that evill day, Lord thou knowest; he had not wronged himselfe nor others in his calling, and therefore all the injuries that befall him in his calling, he desires the Lord to take it into his hands.

Sixtly, Faith hath another act about a mans vocation, and that is, it takes *all successes* that befall him in his calling with *moderation*, hee equally beares good and evill successes as God shall dispense them to him. Faith frames the heart to moderation, be they good or evill, it rests satisfied in Gods gracious dispensation; *I have learned in what estate soever I am, therewith to bee content, Phil.* 4. 11, 12. This he had learned to doe, if God prosper him, he had learned not to be puffed up, and if he should be exposed to want, he could do it without murmuring. It is the same act of unbeleefe, that makes a man murmure in crosses, which puffes him up in prosperity; now faith is like a poyse, it keeps the heart in an equall frame, whether matters fall out well or ill, faith takes them much what alike, faith moderates the frame of a mans spirit on both sides.

Seventhly, The last work which faith puts forth about a mans calling, is this, faith with boldnesse *resignes up* his calling into the hands of God or man; when ever God calls a man to lay downe his calling, when his work is finished, herein the sons of God farre exceed the sons of men; another man when his calling comes to bee removed from him, hee is much ashamed, and much afraid, but if a Christian man be to forgoe his calling, he layes it downe with comfort and boldnesse, in the sight of God and man.

First, *In the sight of God,* 2 *Tim.* 4. 7. *I have fought the fight, I have kept the faith, and finished my course,* and therefore, *henceforth is laid up for me a crowne of righteousnesse, which God according to his righteous* word and promise will give him, as a reward for his sincere and faithfull walking; he lookes up to God, and resignes up his calling into his hand; he

tels *Timothy*, the day of his departure is at hand; and now, this is
matter of strong consolation to him; faith beleeving, that God put
him into his calling, and hath beene helpfull to him hitherto, and
now growne nigh to the period of his calling, here was his comfort,
that he had not throwne himself out of his work; but God cals him
to leave it, and so he leaves it, in the same hand from whom he received it. A man that in his calling hath sought himselfe, and never
looked farther then himselfe, he never comes to lay downe his calling,
but he thinks it is to his utter undoing: a Swine that never did good
office to his owner, till hee comes to lye on the hurdle, he then cryes
out; but a Sheep, who hath many times before yeelded profit, though
you take him and cut his throat, yet hee is as a Lamb dumb before the
shearer; so a carnall man, that never served any man but himselfe,
call him to distresse in it, and he murmures and cries out at it; but
take you a Christian man, that is wonted to serve God in serving of
men, when hee hath beene faithfull and usefull in his calling, he
never layes it downe but with some measure of freedome and boldnesse of spirit; as it was with the three Princes in the furnace, they
would live and dye in Gods service, and therefore God marvailously
assisted them in their worst houres; the soule knows whom it hath
lived upon: This is the life of faith in the upshot of a mans calling,
he layes it downe in confidence of Gods acceptance: and for *man*,
he hath this boldnesse in his dealings with men, he boldly challenges
all the sons of men, of any injury done to them, and he freely offers
them restitution and recompence, if any such there should be: It was
the comfort of *Samuel* when hee was growne old, and the people were
earnest for a King, 1 *Sam.* 12. 3. he saith unto them; Behold, here
am I before you this day, beare witnesse against me this day, *Whose
Oxe or Asse have I taken? &c.* hee makes an open challenge to them
all, and they answered, *Thou hast done us no wrong.* This is the comfort
of a Christian, when he comes to lay downe his calling, he cannot
onely with comfort looke God in the face, but all the sons of men.
There is never a Christian that lives by faith in his calling, but hee
is able to challenge all the world for any wrong done to them, *We
have wronged and defrauded no man*, Acts 20. 26. 2 Cor. 12. We have
done most there, where we are least accepted; that is the happinesse
of a Christian, those who have beene the most weary of him, have
had the least cause.

Vse 1. From hence you see a just reproofe of the infidelity found
in them that live without a calling, they either want faith, or the exercise of faith; if thou beest a man that lives without a calling, though

thou hast two thousands to spend, yet if thou hast no calling, tending to publique good, thou art an uncleane beast; if men walke without a cloven hoofe, they are uncleane: and hast thou a Calling, and art never so diligent in it, it is but *dead worke*, if thou want faith. It likewise reproves such Christians, as consider not what gifts they have for this and that calling; he pleads for himselfe, his wife and children, further then himselfe he respects no calling; and this is want of faith in a Christians calling: or if men rest in the strength of their owne gifts, for the performing of their callings, and will serve God in some things, and themselves and theirs in other some, or if we can tell how to be eye-servants, it is but a dead worke, for want of faith; or if thou lose thy selfe, and thy heart is carnall, and not heavenly minded, thou mayest have faith, but that is but a dead worke. And if thou cast not all thy care and burthen upon God, thou wilt be very dead when ill successes fall out; but had we faith, it would support us in our worst successes; and if better successes come, if faith be wanting, our vaine heart will be lifted up; and if Christians be confounded before God and men, when they are to resigne up their callings, it is a signe that either they have no faith, or it puts not forth life and courage into them; and if it so fall out, know that the root of it springs from an unbeleeving heart.

Vse 2. It is an Use of instruction to every Christian soule that desires to walke by faith in his calling, If thou wouldst live a lively life, and have thy soule and body to prosper in thy calling, labour then to get into a good calling, and therein live to the good of others; take up no calling, but that thou hast understanding in, and never take it unlesse thou mayest have it by lawfull and just meanes, and when thou hast it, serve God in thy calling, and doe it with cheerfulnesse, and faithfulnesse, and an heavenly minde; and in difficulties and dangers, cast thy cares and feares upon God, and see if he will not beare them for thee; and frame thy heart to this heavenly moderation in all successes to sanctifie Gods name; and if the houre and power of darknesse come, that thou beest to resigne up thy calling, let it bee enough that conscience may witnesse to thee, that thou hast not sought thy selfe, nor this world, but hast wrought the Lords workes; thou mayest then have comfort in it, both before God and men.

Vse 3. It is a word of consolation to every such soule, as hath beene acquainted with this life of faith in his calling, Bee thy calling never so meane and homely, and never so hardly accepted, yet, if thou hast lived by faith in thy calling, it was a lively worke in the sight of God, and so it will be rewarded when thy change shall come; Many a Chris-

tian is apt to be discouraged and dismaid if crosses befall him in his
calling, but be not afraid, let this cheare up thy spirit, that what ever
thy calling was, yet thou camest into it honestly, and hast lived in it
faithfully, your course was lively and spirituall, and therefore you may
with courage looke up for recompence from Christ.

PURCHASING CHRIST

1 John 5. 12

He that hath the Son, hath life, and he that hath not the Son, hath not life.

BECAUSE in Scripture phrase, there are more wayes of having Christ
requisite for the knowledge of every soul[,] I thought it therefore
not amisse to open those other wayes by which in Scripture we are said
to have Christ.

Secondly, as therefore we have him first by worshipping of him, so
secondly we have him by purchase; this way of having Christ is expressed to us partly in the parable of the Merchant man, *Matth.* 13. 46,
*Who when he had found a pearle of precious price, he sold all that [he] had and
bought it;* that is one way of having Christ, to purchase him, to buy him:
you have the like also held out in *Esa.* 55. 1, 2. *every one that is a thirst,
come and buy without money or without price,* wherein the Holy Ghost
calleth upon us to receive the Lord Jesus Christ as revealed in his
ordinances, and he makes a solemne proclamation to all, to come to
these waters and buy without money? or how without money? It is true,
should a man offer his house full of Treasure for Christ, it would be
despised *Cant.* 8. 7. and when *Simon Magus* offered to buy the gifts of
the Holy Ghost for money, it was rejected with a curse. *Act.* p. 8, 9, 10,
and if the gift of the Holy Ghoast cannot be bought for money, how
can the Lord Jesus Christ be bought for money?

And yet thus much I say, that many times without laying out of
money, he cannot be had, without parting with money we cannot get
him, the case so stands that sometimes, the holding fast a mans money
lets go the Lord Jesus Christ, you have a famous example in the
Young man, *Matth.* 19. 21. *to* 24. Where our Saviour shewes how hard
a thing it is for a rich man to enter into the Kingdome of Heaven,
because it is hard for a rich man to part with all that he hath, when
God calls for it at his hands, so that without mony sometimes Christ
cannot be had; And yet for mony he cannot be had, it was upon the
point of mony, that the Lord Jesus parted with the *Pharisees, Luke* 16.
11. 12. *If you be unfaithfull with the mammon of iniquity, who will trust you
with true treasure;* if you use not outward things well, who will give you

saving grace in Jesus Christ? so that sometimes for want of spending of money in a right way, many a man looses the Lord Jesus; so that though Christ cannot be had for money, yet sometimes without expence of mony he cannot be had.

For opening of this point there are three Cases in which money must be layed out, or else Christ cannot be had, and in refusing to lay out money, we refuse life in him.

First, when the Lord by some speciall command requires it, as was the case of the young man in the Gospel, there was a speciall commandement given to him, not given to every man, nor to every rich man, nor scarce any man in ordinary course now adayes, yet then given to him; and now to stick for money, and rather lose eternall life then his goods, in such a case as this, he loseth his life in Christ; and upon the same poynt, or the like, broke *Ananias* and *Saphira*, it was the common resolution of the Church of God in that Age to sell all that they had, and to give to the poore, and to live after the same rate that other men did, a like proportion to every man; and to distribute faithfully to every man as every man had need, and as the Apostles saw cause; and when they come and keep back part of the price for which their possessions was sold, you see how bitter a curse from the presence of the Lord fell upon them, they were cut off from the Congregation of Gods people, and it is much to be feared, cut off from the Lord Jesus Christ, and from all hope of eternall life, and to stand as a terrible example to the whole Church of God, to shew what a dangerous thing it is to stand upon termes with Christ, and not to part with money for him; they could not have fellowship with the people of God, unless they parted with all they had, and live upon the common distribution; but this case is not alwayes.

But secondly, there is another time, namely, when in case of persecution the market of Christ goes at so high a rate, that a man cannot have Christ with any comfort in his soule, or peace to his Conscience, or purity of heart or life, unlesse he hazzard all his estate, or a good part of it: In buying and selling of a precious commodity, a good Chapman will have it what ever it cost him: So Christ is sometimes at an higher, and sometimes at a lower rate, but whatever he costs him, he will have him; it is spoken in commendation of the *Hebrews*, that *they suffered joyfully the spoyling of their goods*, Heb. 10. 34. to shew you, that sometimes it comes to that passe, that unlesse a man be content to part with all his goods, he cannot have the recompence of reward, the Lord Jesus Christ to his soule; and therefore the Servants of God have been content to loose all that they had, and willing to resigne up all for the maintaining the integrity of their spirits, and the purity of their hearts and lives in the presence of God, and then let all goe, they can *suffer the spoyle of all joyfully*.

3. It is in case that by Gods providence you be cast to live in such Congregations, where you cannot have the Ordinances of God but at a great charge, as it is the case of many places, that unlesse they be at charge for the Ministery of the Gospel it cannot be had; then we must communicate freely that way, then *be not deceived, God is not mocked, for what a man sowes that shall he also reap*, Gal. 6. 6, 7, 8. Where the Apostle doth encourage men at such a time as this, when the Gospel, cannot be had but at great charge, then lay out liberally for the Gospel of Christ, and he calls it, A sowing to the Spirit; as a man that layes out his money for an earthly commodity, for a good bargaine, he reapes corruption; so he that sowes of the Spirit, shall of the Spirit reape life everlasting. When a man layes out his money unto Spirituall ends, to obtaine the free passage of the Ordinances of Christ, to enjoy the liberty of the Gospel, he thereby sowes to the Spirit, and shall of the Spirit reap life everlasting; for this is the blessing promised unto it, such as so sow, *shall of the Spirit reap life everlasting;* so that when a man out of a good and honest heart, and an hungering desire after Gods Ordinances, shall be willing to be at charge for them, he hath this promise made to him, and it shall be fulfilled, *He shall of the Spirit reap life everlasting.* But yet, when a man hath layed out his money for this end, if he then thinke his money is worthy of Christ, he gets him not; but this is the first way of having Christ by way of Purchase, a seasonable laying out our money for him as God requires it.

Secondly, Christ is to be purchased, not so much by money, as chiefly this purchase must be made by parting with all those many and strong Lusts, and Corruptions, and sinfull rebellions of heart, by which we keep off Christ from comming into our hearts; this is that which the Prophet *Esay* directs us to, *Esa.* 55. 7. *Let the wicked forsake his way, and the unrighteous man his thoughts,* &c. where he tels us what we must give for Christ, for sinne is neither money nor moneys worth; but he makes a good bargaine that parts with his sins, though he should get no Christ for his parting with them. He speakes of the first and principall part of the life of a Christian man, the life of his Justification that springs from pardon of sinne; let a man forsake those sins and lusts that he hath been most carried captive with; let a wicked man forgoe his thoughts and wayes, both his secret and open sins, and let him *then turne to God, and he will abundantly pardon;* then God will receive him graciously, to the justification of life. This is the thing that we must doe, this was the point upon which sundry of them that have been hopefull for Religion, have broken off from Christ, and Christ from them; they have forsooke him, and he left them; *Jehu* stuck upon this very point, he would goe a great way, but when it comes (as he thinkes) to hazzard his title to the Crowne, then he will set up the *golden Calves;* when he saw that all must be parted with, rather then he would forgoe that, without which he could not maintaine his Kingdome, he would rather loose Christ, then venture the losse of that, 2 *King*. 10. 29. 31. *He regarded not to walke in all the Commandements of the Lord*, and then as he cut short with God in reformation, and did not fulfill to walke after the Lord, therefore God cut *Jehu* short of all the hopes of grace that ever he might have attained, to vers. 32. so that if we cut at a scanting with God, and will part with some lusts and corruptions, but not with others, then will God cut you short of all your hopes of eternall life: and it was upon the same termes that *Herod* fell short of Christ, *Mar*. 6. 10. *Luk*. 3. 18. he had done many things according to *Johns* Ministry, but when God would cut him short of *Herodias* his darling Lust, that nothing might lye between God and him, but might now become fit for Christ, because he would not cut himselfe short of *Herodias*, and cut short his reformation there, then this was added to all his other sins, he *shut up* John *in prison*, and afterward cut off his head also; so that when there is any sinne, whether honour or pleasure, or any comfort in this life, that men will not be content to cut themselves short of, it is the way to utter ruine; God will not be abundantly ready to pardon such. And so was it with *Dæmas*, when the love of money did so prevaile with his heart, after he had been much esteemed of the Apostles, and mentioned honourably in their Writings, yet in the end it is said of him, *He hath forsaken me, and loved this present world*, 2 Tim. 4. 10. Love of the world had so prevailed with him, that he fell off from *Paul*, and from the Lord, whose Servant *Paul* was, and from fellowship in the Gospel, and so did not finde Christ; this rule is universally to be followed, and the care of it not to be neglected in any case, that our sins are to be put out of our hearts and hands, as ever we looke to finde Christ, and life in him; notable is that expression recorded in *Judg*. 10. 10. to 16. the people come and *cry to the Lord*, to deliver them out of the hands of their enemies; but they had got to themselves other gods, and now he would deliver them no more; When the people heard that, that God would not deliver them, and could finde no acceptance from him, so long as they continued in such a sinne; they thereupon goe and put away all their Idols, and leaves not one to be seen among them; and when God sees that they had put them away, the text saith, *that his soule was grieved for their misery,* and his bowels rowled within him for them, and he delivered them: So that when men are willing to fore-go their honourable sinnes, their sweet and delightfull sinnes, their profitable sinnes, and those wherewith they have been most captivated; and he knowes one may as well pull their hearts out of their bellies, as some sinnes out of them; but when he sees men are willing to fore-go their most darling delightfull sins, willing to breake off all impediments that stand between God and them, the Soule of God is grieved in such a case, and it pitties him now that such a soule should be without him; and then it will not be long ere God stirres them up meanes of deliverance, and he himselfe will reveale himselfe unto them. Notable is that speech, *Hos.* 14. 3. 8. when they *take words to themselves,* and promise to leave all their evil wayes, whereby they sinne against God, they make this request to God, That *he would take away their iniquities from them;* and least God should answer them, but be you doing something in the meane time; they professe, that for their owne parts they will set about the doing of their iniquities away, and they say; Ashur *shall not save us, and we will have no more to doe with them;* wherein he shewes you, that God lookes not that only his people shall pray him to take away their iniquities, for we may pray so long enough, and not finde it done; but when we desire God to doe it, and set our hearts and hands to it, and now with heart and hand say, *Ashur shall not save us, nor will we say any more to the workes of our hands, Ye are our gods;* then saith God in vers. 4. *I will heale their back-slidings, and will love them freely,* &c. God is then abundantly ready to pardon, when men forsake their owne wayes and thoughts, and throw away the sins that hang about them, God will say of such a people, *I will heale them, and love them freely, mine anger is turned away from them.* And you may presume, when Gods anger is turned away, it is by and through Christ, or else there is no healing; and therefore in vers. 8. *Ephraim* saith, *What have I to doe any more with Idols;* the heart of a Christian, or of a Nation, shall openly acknowledge, that they wil have no more fellowship with these abominations; and then saith God, *I have heard him, and observed him.* God heares us, and understands what we say, and observes us well, and offers to be a covert to us from the storme, when we begin solemnly to abandon such evils, then he heares us, and answers us according to the desire of our hearts; you have many a soule that cryes to God, Take away our iniquity, and many Petitions we put up to God to that purpose; and that sometimes with many bitter moanes, but God heares it not; we pour out our plaints in vaine, and he regards it not; but when we come to God, and desire him not only to take them from us, but begin to consider our owne wayes and iniquities, and to put them from us, out of our hearts and hands, and we wil no more take such bad wayes, as heretofore we have done; we *will no more ride upon horses*, nor run to forreigne Princes for succour; then God heares, and grants graciously whatever his poore people begge at his hands, and answers it according to all the desire of their hearts, then the Lord presently gives us the Lord Jesus Christ, and life and healing in him; and this is the second way of having Christ by purchase. . . .

Fourthly, there is yet something more then all this, a further price to pay, if we mean to purchase Christ; And that is, that we part with all our good parts, and all the good common gifts of grace, which are found sometimes in good nature, and sometimes in the children of the Church, we must part with them all that we may win Christ 1 *Cor.* 3. 18. *If any man among you seem to be wise in this world, let him become a foole that he may be wise:* who ever would be a wise man, (as a wise man he cannot be, if hee have not his part in Christ) he must lay aside his serious and sad deliberation, and communication with flesh and blood, and all things in the way of God, that he thinkes will be prejudiciall, if any man be so wise, as to see this and that danger in a Christian course, let him become a foole; else he shall never become a Christian: if a man will be content to forsake all for Christ, he must first be a foole, and be content to bee counted a foole, and heare every carnall man to count him a foole. And I speak not onely of carnal and civill wisdom, that, that only is to be denyed in this case, but common graces, which many times choakes all the hypocrites in the bosome of the Church; they are commonly choaked upon this point, upon these things they trust, and doe therefore verily beleeve, that this and that interest, God hath in them, and they in God; because they have received such and such gifts from him, and this is the case formerly mentioned, *Matth.* 7. 22, 23. they pleaded their spirituall gifts, though common gifts, and such as may be found in *workers of iniquity*, they *prayed to God*, a common gift; and they *prophesied in his name*, they had prophetical gifts; some measure of the spirit of ministery, and they were able *to cast out devills in Christs name;* now when as men do trust upon these, and settle themselves upon such a change, truly, hereby they loose that power in Christ which else they might have had. Its a wonder to see what a change propheticall gifts will work in a man, 1 *Sam.* 10. 10, 12. he, there *Saul* had a spirit of prophesie came upon him, and the people wondred at it, it works a strange change in a man, and so in the next chap. the 19 and 23 ver. he prophesied til he came at such a place, so that you shall see a man that is trained up in any good order, though

sometimes given to loose company; when once God begins to poure
into him any spirituall gift, to inlighten his mind, and to inlarge his
affection, that hee begins to have some love to, and some joy in the
Word, and some sorrow in hearing of the Word, and some comfort in
meditation: Its wonder to see what a change this will work in the
spirit; he forthwith begins to abandon his loose courses, and sets himselfe to a more strict course, then hee begins to see his acquisite learning
is but a small matter to edification; hee prizes his spirituall gifts, and
hee is able now to doe much; and when a mans heart is thus changed
by propheticall gifts, it workes in a man such confidence in his soule,
that he thinkes all the Congregation shall perish before he can perish,
and if Ministers, may be thus deceived by common gifts and graces,
how much more may their poor hearers bee deceived, when they by
hearing the Word find such comfort, and illumination, and inlarge-
ments, that they thereby finde a great change wrought in them; and
yet if ministers may bee so much deceived, in presuming vainly of
their good estate, which was not so, then much more common Christians: Should any man presume at *Fœlix his trembling, Act.* 24. 25.
At Jehues zeale, 2 *King.* 10. 16. *At Ahabs humiliation,* 1 *King.* 21. 28, 29.
At Herods joy in hearing, you know what became of all these, these be
graces of God, though but common graces, and if the Prophets were
deceived, may not these be deceived also, that have neither Christ
nor any part in him; and therefore a man that would bee sure not to
goe without Christ, nor without life in him; he must not trust in any
spirituall gift he hath received, though his mind be inlightened, sometimes to feare, sometimes to joy, to humiliation, to inlargement, to
zealous reformation, yet rest in none of these, for these you may have
and yet want Christ, and life in him; common graces may and will
deceive you, a man may have all these, and yet not prize Christ, as
his cheifest good; he may have all these, and yet not worship him:
Notwithstanding all these, there may bee some iniquity in their hands
for which cause God will not shew mercy to them: See and observe,
if in the midst of all these you do not *worke some iniquity;* they were
workers of iniquity always at the best, *Matth.* 7. 23. you may be workers
of iniquity, notwithstanding all these; and therefore consider if there
be not some veine of pride, and hypocrisie, and covetousnesse, that
cleaves fast to your hearts, which you allow your selves in, which if
you doe, these very gifts will bee your ship-wracke, your anchor will
breake, and your ship will bee carryed away, and you fall downe in
destruction; but see that your hearts bee cleane, and see that there bee
not an ill thought or way that you allow your selves in, and if so, then

your heart will lay hold upon God, and you will prize Christ, and then it is a signe those gifts you have are not in hypocrisie; for in an hypocrite, they are alwayes found with some sinne, which if a man doe not willfully shut his eyes against hee may see, for our Saviour speakes of such a sinne in them, as the rest of the people of God may know them to be counterfeits, from verse 15 to 23. *You shall know them by this, doe men gather grapes of thornes, or figges of thistles?* have not they their ill haunts, but put away these from you, if you mean to have Christ.

INCREASE MATHER, 1639–1723

[Increase Mather, the most conspicuous figure in the second generation of New Englanders, was born in Dorchester, where his father, Richard, was minister. Educated at home and at the free school in Boston, he entered Harvard in 1651, though he spent most of his college years at Ipswich and Boston under the supervision of John Norton. Taking his B.A. in 1656, he went to England, studied at Trinity College, Dublin, where he received his M.A. in 1658. He became a friend of John Howe, a powerful Independent minister, whose pulpit he filled at Great Torrington, Devonshire. He served as chaplain to the garrison at Guernsey, and had just been called to an important post at Gloucester when the Restoration closed all avenues of advancement to him in England. He returned to Guernsey, then to Boston in 1661, the next year marrying Maria Cotton, daughter of John Cotton. He immediately assumed the role of a leading divine by opposing his father and Jonathan Mitchell on the Half-Way Covenant, though he was finally persuaded to change sides. Installed as teacher of the Second Church in Boston, 1664, he was thereafter strategically located to influence the policies of the colony. In 1674 he was elected fellow of Harvard College and in 1681 refused the presidency because he did not wish to leave his church; in 1685 he accepted it, though he was a nonresident administrator and still devoted much the larger share of his attentions to his church and to colonial affairs. Sent as agent for the colony to England in 1688, he remained abroad for four years, negotiating for the renewal of the charter through the shifting scenes of the Glorious Revolution. At the moment of his triumphant return in 1692, with the governor and the slate of magistrates having been nominated by himself, he was at the apex of his power. Thereafter his influence began to decline: many citizens who had no idea with what he had contended believed he had made too many concessions in securing the charter. In 1701 he was forced to resign the presidency of the College by a law requiring the president to live in Cambridge, but after his defeat Samuel Willard was put in charge under the title of vice-president and the residence requirement was not enforced. Though he gave the court at the Salem witch trials good advice—which they did not take—he and his son Cotton were attacked as though they had been responsible for the miscarriage of justice. Solomon Stoddard of Northampton dominated the Western part of the colony and inaugurated there policies that Mather abhorred. In Boston itself he was bearded by the establishment of the Brattle Street Church under Benjamin Colman in 1699, who instituted certain practices which Mather had opposed. But if his power in his last years was curtailed, he remained a commanding figure, fighting courageously for inoculation in 1721, maintaining the principles of the founders to the last ditch, and yet moving with the times on at least some important questions. In 1718 he and Cotton Mather assisted at the ordination of a Baptist minister. He was a voluminous writer, only surpassed in the number of his publications by Cotton Mather. An exponent of the plain style, he preached solid, logical, and learned sermons. For biography, see Kenneth B. Murdock, *Increase Mather*.

The text of the first selection is from *Awakening Truths Tending to Conversion*, (Boston, 1710) pp. 66–78. The second selection is from *A Discourse Concerning the Uncertainty of the Times of Men* (Boston, 1697), pp. 8–21, 34–36, a sermon delivered at Harvard College after two undergraduates, skating on Fresh Pond, broke through the ice and were drowned. The third selection is from *Practical Truths Tending to Promote the Power of Godliness* (Boston, 1682), pp. 209–212.]

PREDESTINATION AND HUMAN EXERTIONS

THERE are some Sinners so unreasonable, and so wicked. Ask them why they don't reform their Lives, why don't you Turn over a new leaf, and amend your ways and your doings, they will answer, God does not give me Grace. I can't Convert my self, and God does not Convert me. Thus do they insinuate as if God were in fault, and the blame of their Unconversion to be imputed unto him. But as Elihu speaks, *Suffer me a little, and I will shew you what I have yet to say on God's behalf.*

1. I say, God is not bound to give Sinners Grace: He is an absolute Sovereign, and may give Grace or deny Grace to whom he pleaseth. Shall the thing formed, say to him that formed it, why hast thou made me thus? has not the Potter power over the Clay, to make one vessel

unto honour, and another to dishonour? The glorious God has a greater power over his Creatures, than the Potter has over the Clay. Wherefore, *He has Mercy on whom He will have Mercy, and whom He will He hardens,* Rom. 9. 18. If He giveth Grace to any man in the World, it is from His Sovereign good pleasure. Why were such poor Fishermen as *Peter,* and *James,* and *John,* and others, as mean as they, made the Subjects of Saving Grace, when many incomparably beyond them in Learning and Wisdom, have been left to perish in their unbelief? Even so, because so it has seemed good in the sight of Him, who is the Lord of Heaven and Earth, *Math.* 11. 25, 26. Grace is a wonderful gift of God. Sinners are enemies to him, and Rebels against him: Is He bound to bestow such a gift on his Enemies, when it may be too they will not so much as humbly Pray unto him for it[?] Indeed He sometimes has done so. Sinners that never Prayed to him, that never had one thought in their hearts of returning to him, he has miraculously Prevented them with Sovereign Grace. So it was with the Converted Gentiles. Of them the Lord says, *I am sought of them that asked not for me, I am found of them that sought me not, I said, behold me, behold me to a Nation that was not called by my Name,* Isa. 69. 1. Nay, sometimes when Sinners have been in the height of their Resistance and Rebellion, to shew the exceeding Riches of his Grace, God has then Converted them. Thus it was with *Saul* afterwards *Paul,* when he was breathing out Slaughters against the Disciples of the Lord, then did God give him Faith in Christ, without his Praying for it. Thus also those Converts in the Second Chapter of the Acts. Not many days before their Conversion they had been Murdering the Son of God. And just before the Sermon began they were mocking of the Preacher, and yet Converted by that Sermon. Such Instances there have been known in the World, of men that have come to hear a Sermon only to deride it, and yet have been Savingly wrought upon by it. A credible Author reports, that two profane men drinking together, knowing that Mr. *Hooker* was to Preach, one of them said to the other, *Let us go hear how Hooker will baul,* yet was he Converted by that very Sermon, which he went to hear with a Scornful Spirit. And after that had such a love for Mr. *Hooker,* as to remove three thousand Miles, that so he might live under his Ministry. Such Examples are wonderful Evidences of Sovereign Grace.[1]

2. Altho' it is true, (as has been shewed) that Sinners cannot Convert themselves, their *Cannot* is a wilful *Cannot.* Math. 22. 2. *They will not come.* It is not said they *could not* (tho' they could not of themselves come to Christ) but that they *would not* come. If it were in the power

of a Sinner to Convert himself, he would not do it: For he hates Conversion. *It is abomination to fools to depart from evil*, Prov. 13. 19. Psal. 50. 17. *Thou hatest instruction.* If they hate to be Converted they will not chuse it. Prov. 1. 29. *They hated knowledge, and did not chuse the fear of the Lord.* Their hearts are in Love,. and in League with their Lusts, yea they hate to be *turned* from them: They love darkness rather than light, they hate the light, neither come they to the light, *Joh.* 3. 19, 20. Sinners are haters of God: they say and think that they love him, but the Lord knows that they hate him, and therefore they will not repent of their Sins, and believe on Christ. Christ said to the Jews, *You will not come to me that you might have Life*, Joh. 5. 40. No, they would dy first. And why would they not come? The reason of their Aversion is mentioned in v. 42. *I know you, that you have not the Love of God in you.* Their carnal unregenerate Minds were full of enmity against God, and therefore they would not come to Jesus Christ the Son of God. They cannot Convert themselves, and they are not willing that God should Convert them. If Sinners were willing to have Grace and Holiness, why do they not repair to him for it, who alone can give it to them? An hungry man is willing to have bread, therefore he will seek after it, where ever it is to be had. When the Egyptians were hunger bitten, they went to Pharaoh, crying for bread, he bid them go to Joseph, and they did so. Thus if Sinners were willing to be Converted, they would cry to God to turn them: whenas there are many Sinners that did never put up one earnest Prayer to God in their Lives, that he would bestow Converting Grace on them.

3. Sinners can do more towards their own Conversion than they do or will do. They should give *diligence* to make sure of their being effectually called. They should *strive* to enter in at the strait gate. Conversion is the strait gate that leadeth unto Salvation. They should *Labour* not for the meat that perisheth, but for that which endureth to Everlasting Life: but they do not give diligence, they do not strive, they do not labour to obtain Grace and Salvation: Therefore they perish, and perish justly. Prov. 21. 25. *The desire of the slothful kills him, for his hands refuse to labour.* Men say that they desire Grace, and yet their hands refuse to Labour, they will be at no pains to obtain it: And this slothfulness kills them. It proves the death of their Souls. *The Soul of the sluggard desireth and has nothing, but the Soul of the diligent shall be made fat*, Prov. 13. 4. There are several things which Sinners have power to do in order to their own Conversion, & which they ought to do, but they will not.

(1) They have power to avoid those things which are an hindrance

of Conversion. *e.g.* They can if they will forbear the outward Acts of sin. By giving way to sin their hearts are hardned, and their Conversion becomes the more difficult. Heb. 3. 13. *Take heed lest any of you be hardned through the deceitfulness of sin.* But Sinners give way to many sins which they could abstain from, if they would. A Sabbath-breaker can forbear his profaning of the Sabbath. An ungodly Swearer can forbear his profane Oathes, if he will. A Lyar can forbear telling such Lyes. Sinners can avoid the Temptations which will endanger their falling into sin. He that knows that if he goeth to such a place, or into such a company, he will probably be drawn into sin, ought to avoid the Temptation. Prov. 4. 15. *Avoid it, turn from it, and pass away.* The Sinner can do so if he will, but he will not keep out of the way of Temptation. A drunkard will not avoid the Temptation to that his sin. Prov. 23. 31. *Look not on the Wine when it giveth his colour.* He can chuse whether he will look on the wine or no: he has power to refrain, but will not. Thus men by habituating themselves to sin, do what in them is to hinder their own Conversion. Jer. 13. 23. *Can the Ethiopian change his skin, or the Leopard his Spots? then may you also do good that are accustomed to do evil.* Again, Evil Companions hinder Conversion. *Alas! Alas! Alas!* these have been the Eternal ruin of many a Young Man, that was in an hopeful way for Conversion: He has fallen in with vain Companions, they have given him bad Counsel, so have Convictions been stifled, and the motions of Gods holy Spirit quenched in his Soul. The word of the Lord sayes, *Forsake the foolish & Live,* Prov. 9. 6. The Sinner has power to forsake them, but he will not tho' he dies for it.

(2) Sinners have power to wait on God in the use of means which has a tendency to promote Conversion. They can if they will, not only forsake evil Companions, but associate themselves with those that are good: Then are they in the way of Conversion. Prov. 13. 20. *He that walketh with wise men shall be wise, but a Companion of fools shall be destroyed.* That Learned & Holy Man Dr. *Goodwin* [2] in the account which he giveth of his Conversion, declares, That when he was a Young Schollar in the University of *Cambridge,* there were in that *College,* which he belonged unto, a *Number of holy Youth's* (that's his Expression) his associating himself with them was an happy means of furthering the work of Conversion in his Soul. This Unconverted Sinners have power to do. Their feet are as able to carry them to a godly Meeting as to an ungodly one. Reading the Scripture has sometimes been the Means of Conversion. I could tell you of several Learned Jews that were Converted from their Judaism by Reading the 53.

Chapter of Isaiah. The famous Fr. *Junius*,[3] was Converted from his *Atheism* by reading the first Chapter of John's Gospel. He that can read is able to read the Scripture, and Books which promote Godliness in the power of it, but a Sinful Creature chuseth rather to mispend his Time in reading vain Romances, or it may be worse Books. A diligent attendence to the Word of God is the way to obtain Converting Grace. Rom. 10. 17. *Faith comes by hearing, and hearing by the Word of God.* Sinners many Times do not mind what they hear. Nay, it may be they will *Set themselves to sleep when God is speaking to them* by his Minister? And shall they then complain, that they cannot Convert themselves, & that God will not Convert them? Once more, Serious thinking & Consideration on Spiritual and Eternal things is oftentimes blessed unto Conversion. This is what God has given men power to do, if they will use that power. They ought seriously to think what they have done, and what they are, and what their end is like to be. If they would do so, it may be Repentance would be the effect of it. 1 King. 8. 47. *If they shall bethink themselves, and Repent, and make Supplication.* David sayes, *I thought on my wayes, and turned my feet unto thy Testimonies*, Psal. 119. 59. If men would be perswaded *to think seriously*, it may be they would *Turn. How long shall thy vain thoughts lodge within thee?* A Sinner will suffer vain thoughts to lodge within him, but serious & holy thoughts he will give no lodging unto, he will not suffer them to abide in his heart. Serious *Consideration* is a duty incumbent on Sinners. Hag. 1. 5. *Thus sayes the Lord of hosts, Consider your wayes.* Would the Unconverted Sinner, consider sadly what his Sinful wayes have been, what numberless sins he has been guilty of, and what a fountain of sin his heart is, and whither he is going, it may be Conversion would follow upon such serious consideration. Ezek. 18. 28. *Because he considereth and turns away from all his Transgressions.* Yes, if he is set upon *Considering*, there is great hopes that he will Turn, and that he shall live, and not dye. If he will be perswaded to go alone, to think and consider sadly with himself, What is my present Condition? Am I in Christ, or am I not in Christ? If I should dy this Night, What would become of my Soul? In what World must it be to all Eternity? It may be such considerations would issue in Conversion. Sinners should consider of Death, that the thing is certain, and the Time uncertain, and that they run an infinite hazzard if they neglect making sure of an Interest in Christ one day longer. Deut. 32. 29. *O that they were wise, that they would consider their latter end!* And they should *Consider* of the *Eternity* which follows immediately upon death. If they would do that, surely it would affect their Souls. A late Writer (which I have formerly mentioned) speaks of a pious man, that One in Company with him observing a more than ordinary fixedness and concern in his Countenance, asked him, What his thoughts were upon, he then thereupon uttered that Word *For-ever*, and so continued saying nothing but repeating that Word, *For-ever! For-ever! For-ever!* a quarter of an hour together. His Thoughts and Soul was swallowed up with the consideration of ETERNITY. And truly if an Unconverted Sinner would be perswaded to go alone and think seriously of Eternity, if it were but for one quarter of an hour, it may be it would have an Everlasting Impression on his heart. This Sinners can do if they will: And if they will not do as much as this comes to, towards their own Conversion and Salvation, how inexcusable will they be? Their blood will be upon their own heads. Let them no more say, *God must do all, we can do nothing*, and so encourage themselves to Live in a careless neglect of God, and of their own Souls, and Salvation. Most certainly, altho' we cannot say, That if men improve their Natural abilities as they ought to do, that Grace will infallibly follow, yet there will not one Sinner in all the Reprobate World, stand forth at the day of Judgment, and say, Lord, Thou knowest I did all that possibly I could do, for the obtaining Grace, and for all that, Thou didst withold it from me.

MAN KNOWS NOT HIS TIME

THE DOCTRINE at present before us, is,

   That for the most part the Miserable Children of Men, know not their Time.

There are three things for us here briefly to Enquire into. (1.) *What Times they are which Men know not?* (2.) *How it does appear that they are Ignorant thereof.* (3.) The Reason *Why they are kept in Ignorance of their Time.*

Quest. 1. *What Times are they which men know not?*

Ans. 1. *Time is sometimes put for the proper season for Action.* For the fittest season for a man to Effect what he is undertaking. The Seventy Greek Interpreters translate the words KAIRON AUTOU. There is a *Season*, a fit Time for men to go to work in. If they take hold of that nick of opportunity, they will prosper and succeed in their Endeavours. It is a great part of wisdom to know that season. Hence it is said, *A wise mans Heart discerneth both Time and Judgment.* Eccles. 8. 5. but few have that wisdom or knowledge. Therefore it is added in the next verse. *because to every purpose there is Time and Judgment, therefore the misery of man is great upon him.* The meaning is, because men discern not the proper Time for them to Effect what they purpose, their misery is great. If they would attempt such a thing just at such a Time, they would make themselves and others happy, but missing that Opportunity great misery comes upon them. So it is as to Civil Affairs very frequently: Men discern not the proper only season for them to obtain what they desire. Yea, and so it is as to Spirituals. Men are not aware of the proper season wherein they may obtain good for their Souls. There is a price put into their hands to get Wisdom, but they have no heart to know and improve it. There is a day of Grace in which if men seek to God for mercy they shall find it. Isa. 55. 6. *Seek ye the Lord while he may be found.* The most of them that have such a day know it not until their finding Time is past. Thus it was with Israel of old. Jere. 8. 7. *The Stork in the heaven knows her appointed Time, the Turtle, and the Crane, and the Swallow observe the Time of their coming, but my People know not the Judgment of the Lord.* They discerned not the *Judgments,* that is the dispensations of God. They had a Summer of prosperity but did not improve it. There was a Winter of Adversity coming on them, but they knew it not, nor did they use the proper only means to prevent it. So the Jews when Christ was amongst them, had a blessed time if they had known it: but they knew not the things of their peace, in the day of their peace; they knew not the Time of their Visitation.

2. *A man knows not what Changes shall attend him whilest in this World.* Changes of Providence are in the Scripture called *Times.* It is said that the Acts of David, and *the Times that went over him,* and over Israel, and over all the Kingdoms of the Countries, were written by *Samuel,* and *Nathan* the Prophet, and in the Book of *Gad* the *Seer,* meaning the Changes of Providence which they were subject unto. 1 *Chron.* 29. 30. A man knows not whether he shall see good or evil days for the Time to come: he knoweth what his past days have been; but does not know what they shall be for the time to come. It may be he is now in prosperity: he has Friends, Children, Relations, which he takes delight in, he has Health, an Estate, and Esteem in the World, he does not know that he shall have any of these things for the future. Indeed, men in Prosperity are apt to think (as they would have it) that they shall alwayes, or for a long time be so: but very often they find themselves greatly mistaken. The Psalmist confesseth that it was so with him. Psal. 30. 6, 7. *In my prosperity I said, I shall never be moved, Lord, by thy favour, thou hast made my Mountain to stand strong: thou didst hide thy face and I was troubled.* His Enemies were all subdued: his Mountain, that is his Kingdom, especially his Royal Palace in Mount Sion was become exceeding strong, that now he thought all dangers were over, but *Absaloms* unexpected Rebellion involved him and the

whole Land in Trouble. The good People in *Josiahs* time promised
themselves great happiness for many a year under the Government
of such a King as he was. Lam. 4. 20. *Of whom we said under his shadow
we shall Live*. But his sudden Death made a sad Change in all the
Publick Affairs. A man knows not *what* Afflictions shall come upon
him whilest on the earth. This is true concerning particular Persons:
they may know in general, that Afflictions shall attend them in an
evil Sinful World. But what those Afflictions in particular shall be
they know not. Thus the Apostle speaks, Act. 20. 22, 23. *I go bound
in Spirit to Jerusalem, not knowing what things shall befall me there, save that
the holy Spirit witnesseth in every City, saying, that Bonds and Afflictions
abide me*. So that he knew in general that he should meet with Affliction, but not in special what the Affliction would be. So is it true
concerning a People, that they know not what *Times* or *Changes* may
pass over them. Little was it thought that whilest *Hoshea* (who was the
best of all the Nineteen Kings that had Ruled over the Ten Tribes)
was Reigning, a Powerful forreign Enemy should invade the Land
and make them all Slaves. Little did the Jews think that when *Josiah*
was but Thirty nine years old, he should dy before that year was
out, and they never see good day more after his Death. And as men
know not *What* their Changes and Afflictions must be, so neither *When*
they shall come upon them. Whether it will be a long or a short time
before those Changes overtake them. Mar. 13. 35. *You know not when
the Master of the House comes, at even, or at mid-night, or at the Cock crowing,
or in the morning*. Thus a man knoweth not whether the sharpest Afflictions which are reserved for him, shall come upon him in his Youth,
or in his middle age, or in his old age; though for the most part mens
greatest Afflictions overtake them in their old age. Nor can any man
know whether his Afflictions will soon be over or continue for a longer
time. Thus, the Lords People knew that their Captivity in *Babylon*
should last for Seventy years and no longer; but that knowledge was
by divine Revelation. As for some other Persecutions they knew not
how long they would continue. Psal. 74. 9. *There is no more a Prophet,
neither is there any that knows how long*. Those words seem to respect the
Persecution under *Antiochus*, when there was no Prophet.

3. *A man knows not the Time of his Death:* Often it is so, that when
Death falls upon a man, he thinks no more of it, than the Fishes
think of the Net before they are Caught in it; or then the Birds think
of the Snare before they are taken in it, as *Solomon* here speaks. It
useth to be said, (and it is a plain, weighty known Truth) that nothing
is more certain then that every man shall Dy, and nothing more un-

certain than the Time when. Old *Isaac* said, Gen. 27. 2. *Behold, I know not the day of my Death.* Though he Lived above twenty years after he spoke those words, he did not know that he should Live a day longer. A man cannot know how long himself or another shall live. It is true that *Hezekiah* was ascertained that he should not dy before fifteen years were expired. And the Prophet *Jeremy* knew that *Hananiah* should not live a year to an end. Jer. 28. 16. *This year thou shalt Dy, because thou hast Taught Rebellion against the Lord.* But those were extraordinary cases. It is not a usual thing for a man to know before hand how many months or years he shall live in this World: Nor may he desire to know it, but he ought to leave that with God. Although *David* prayed, saying, *Lord make me to know my End, and the number of my Dayes, what it is. Psal.* 39. 4. His meaning is, not that he might know just how many dayes he should live, but that he might be made duely sensible of his own frailty and mortality, and lead his life accordingly. Oftentimes Death is nearest to men when they least think of it; especially it is so with ungodly men: we have an instance of it in *Agag.* He came before *Samuel, delicately, and said, surely the bitterness of death is past.* 1 *Sam.* 15. 32. Little did he think, that within a few hours, he should be cut in pieces. When *Haman* boasted of his being the chief Favourite at Court, and that the Queen had invited no one but the King & himself to a Banquet, he little thought of the destruction which was then preparing for him. When *Belshazzar* was in the beginning of the night drinking and making merry with his profane Companions, he little thought that he should be a dead man before morning; but *that night was Belshazzar slain. Dan.* 5. 30. The Rich Fool in the Gospel dream'd of a long life and merry: He said to his Soul, Eat, Drink and be merry, thou hast Goods laid up for many years. But God said, *This night thy Soul shall be required of thee:* He must appear immediately before the dreadful Tribunal. Luk. 12. 20. Thus we see what Time it is which men know not.

The second thing to be Enquired into, is, *How it does appear that men know not their Time.*

Answ. 1. It is evident, *In that all future Contingencies are known to God only.* Hence Christ said to the Disciples, *It is not for you to know the Times and the Seasons which the Father has put in his own power. Act* 1. 7. Future Times and Contingent Events, the knowledge & disposal of them has God reserved to himself. There are future things which happen necessarily, that a man may know them long before they come to pass: *God has appointed Lights in the Heaven to be for Signs and Seasons.* Gen. 1. 14. These move regularly and unfailably according to that

Order which the Creator has established. Therefore a man may know
infallibly how many hours or minutes such a day or night will be
long before the Time comes; He may know when there will be an
Eclipse of the Sun or of the Moon, twenty, or an hundred years before
it comes to pass: [4] but for Contingent Things, which have no necessary
dependance on the constituted Order of Nature, but upon the meer
Pleasure and Providence of God, they are not known except unto
God, or to them unto whom he shall reveal them. The Lord chal-
lengeth this as his Prerogative. The Idols whom the Heathen worshipped, could not make known future Contingencies. Isa. 41. 22, 23.
*Let them shew us what shall happen, or declare us things for to come, shew the
things that are to come hereafter, that we may know they are Gods.* To do this
was past their skill. The Devil knows many future things which men
are ignorant of; He could foretel *Sauls* ruin, and *Davids* coming to the
Kingdom. Nevertheless, there are many future Events which he has
no knowledge of. Therefore he often deludes those that Enquire of
him with deceitful and uncertain Answers. But as for men they are
ignorant of future things, which most nearly concern themselves, or
their own Families. No man knows so much as who shall be his Heir,
or Enjoy the Estate which he has laboured for. Psal. 39. 6. *Surely
every man walks in a vain shew, he heapeth up riches, and knows not who shall
gather them.* He knows not whether one of his Relations, or a meer
stranger shall possess that Estate which he has taken so much pains,
and disquieted himself so much for the obtaining of it. This meditation made *Solomon* out of Love with this World. He new as much as
any man, and yet he confesseth that he did not know whether the
man that should come after him, and enjoy all that he had Laboured
for, would be a wise man or a fool, Eccles. 2. 18, 19. And he says,
A man knows not that which shall be; for who can tell him when it shall be.
Eccles. 8. 7. He knows neither what nor when it shall be. And again
he saith, *A man cannot tell what shall be; and what shall be after him who
can tell him!* Eccl. 10. 14. This is to be understood concerning Contingent Events. Such as the particular Afflictions which are to befall
a man, or the Time, Place, or manner of his Death.

    2. *The Times of men are ordered according to the Decree of God.* There is
nothing comes to pass in the Earth, but what was first determined by
a wise decree in Heaven. Act. 15. 18. *Known unto God are all his works
from the beginning of the World.* God knows what he has to do. The
Apostle speaks there concerning the Conversion of the Gentiles. This
did God fore-know and decree from the beginning of the World, yea
from all Eternity. The like is to be said concerning every thing which

happens in the World. Not a Sparrow falls to the Ground without his Providence, and therefore not without his decree, the one being an Infallible Effect of the other. He has decreed when and where every man that comes into the World shall be Born; and where he shall live, in what Country, and in what Town; yea, and in what House too. Act. 17. 26. *He has determined the times before appointed, & the bounds of their Habitation.* He has decreed when every man shall dy. Eccl. 3. 2. *There is a Time to be Born, and a Time to Dy.* That is to say, a Time decreed and appointed by God when every man shall be born, and when he shall dy. Nor shall any man live a day longer than the Time which the Lord has appointed for him. Job 14. 5. *His dayes are determined, the number of his months are with thee, thou hast appointed his bounds that he cannot pass.* All the Circumstances attending every mans Death, the place and the manner of it, whether he shall dy by Sickness, or by any other Accident, all is determined in Heaven before it comes to pass on the Earth. Now the decrees of God are Secret things until the Event or some divine Revelation shall discover them. Deut. 29. 29. *Secret things belong unto the Lord our God.* His divine decrees are those secret things, which Himself alone knows. Rom. 11. 34. *For who hath known the mind of the Lord? or, who has been his Counsellor?*

3. *The Conversations of men generally make it manifest, that they know not their Time.* They do many things which they would not do, and they neglect many things which they would certainly practise, if they knew what Times are near them. Math. 24. 43. *If the good man of the house had known in what watch the Theef would come, he would have watched, and would not have suffered his house to be broken up.* Thus men live in a careless neglect of God, and of their own Souls and Salvation, but if they knew that Death will come stealing suddenly upon them, they would watch and pray. Did they know that before the next week, they shall be in another World, they would live after another manner than now they do. Most commonly Persons are light and vain in their Spirits, when heavy Tidings is near to them. Did they know what sad News they shall hear shortly, they would be in a more solemn frame of Spirit. Isa. 5. 12. *The harp and the viol, the tabret, and the pipe, and wine are in their feasts, but they regard not the work of the Lord, neither consider the operation of his hands.* Had they known what work God intended to make with them speedily, they would have minded something else besides their sensual pleasures and delights.

We proceed to Enquire 3. *Whence it is that men know not their Time.*

Answ. It is from God. He will have them to be kept in ignorance and uncertainties about their Time: And this for wise & holy Ends. *e.g.*

1. That so his Children might live by Faith. That so they might live a life of holy dependance upon God continually. They must not know their Times, that so they might Trust in the Lord at all times. God would not have his Children to be anxiously solicitous about future Events, but to leave themselves and theirs with their Heavenly Father, to dispose of all their Concernments, as He in his Infinite Wisdom and Faithfulness shall see good.

2. That their Obedience may be tried. That they may follow the Lord, as it were blind-fold, whithersoever He shall lead them, though they do not see one step of their way before them, as *Abraham* did. Heb. 11. 8. *When he was called to go out into a place which he should after receive for an Inheritance, he obeyed, and went out not knowing whither he went.* We must follow God, tho' we know not what He will do with us, or how He will dispose of us, as to our Temporal Concerns, submitting our selves, yea, our lives and all entirely to the Will of God in every thing. That saying ought to be often in our mouths, *If the Lord will, and we shall live, and do this or that. Jam.* 4. 15.

3. Men must not know their Time, that so they may be ever watchful. Math. 25. 13. *Watch therefore, for you know neither the day nor the hour wherein the Son of Man comes.* The generality of men, if they had it revealed to them (as *Hezekiah*) that they should certainly live so many years, they would in the mean time be careless about their Souls, and the World to come. We see that notwithstanding they are uncertain how short their Time may be, they are regardless about their future eternal Estate. How much more would they be so, if they knew that Death and Judgment were not far off from them?

4. As to some they are kept in Ignorance of their Times, that so they may with the more comfort and composure of Spirit follow the work which they are called unto: That they may with diligence and chearfulness attend the duties of their general and particular Calling; which they could not do, if they knew what Evil Times and Things are appointed for them. The terror of what is coming on them, would be so dismal to them, that they could not enjoy themselves, nor take comfort in any thing they enjoy. As the Apostle speaks to the covetous Jews, Jam. 5. 1. *Go to now you rich men, weep and howl for your miseries that shall come upon you.* So there are many in the World, that would spend their days in weeping and howling, did they but know what is coming on them and theirs. When the Prophet *Elisha* had it revealed to him, that sad things were coming on the Land, by reason of a bloody Neighbour Nation, which would break in upon them, and exercise barbarous Cruelties; the holy man wept at the foreknowledge of it. 2 King. 8. 11.

The man of God wept. So there would be nothing but weeping in many Families, weeping in many Towns, and in some whole Countries, did men but know their Times. Therefore they must be kept in ignorance thereof until the things come upon them. . . .

And now as I have spoken these things to all this Assembly, so let me apply them in a special manner to you the *Scholars* of this *Colledge,* who are here present before the Lord. I am concerned in my Spirit for you. All of you are my Children: And do you think that I can see my Children Drowned, and not be troubled for it? God has come among you this last week, & lessened two of your number by a sad & awful Providence. Do you think these two were greater Sinners than any amongst you. No, no, they were both of them hopeful youths. One of them (young *Eyres*) was an only Son, and a desirable dutiful Son, of a sweet amiable Temper, beloved by every body. He was observed to read the Scriptures constantly every day with great Alacrity. A sign that there was *some good thing in him towards the God of Israel.* As for the other (*Maxwell*) the Rebuke of Heaven in taking him away is the more solemn, in that his pious Relations sent him from far: to be Educated in this Nursery, for Religion and good Literature. I took special notice of him; but could never observe any thing in him, but what was commendable, He was ingenious, and industrious, and I believe truly pious; had he lived, he was like to have been a choice Instrument of Service to the Church of God in his Time. And I am perswaded that his Soul is among the Angels of God. *But if this be done to the green Tree, what shall be done to the Dry?* This fatal blow looks ominously on the poor *Colledge.* Considering some other circumstances; there is cause to fear lest *suddenly* there will be no *Colledge* in *New England;* and this as a sign that ere long there will be no Churches there. I know there is a blessed day to the visible Church not far off; but it is the Judgment of very Learned men, that in the Glorious Times promised to the Church on Earth, *America* will be Hell. And altho there is a number of the Elect of God yet to be born here, I am verily afraid, that in process of Time, *New England* will be the wofullest place in all *America,* as some other parts of the World once famous for Religion, are now the dolefullest on the Earth, perfect Emblems and Pictures of Hell. When you see this little *Academy* fallen to the ground (as now it is shaking and most like to fall) then know it is a terrible thing which God is about to bring upon this Land. In the mean time, you the *Students* here, are concerned to bewail the Breach which the Lord has made among you. If you slight and make light of this hand of the Lord, or do not make a due improvement of it, you may fear, that God has not done with you, but that he has more arrows to shoot amongst you, that shall suddenly strike some of you ere long. But Oh that the Lord would sanctify what has hapned to awaken you unto serious thoughts about Death and Eternity. Who knows but that God may make these sudden Deaths, an occasion of promoting the Salvation, & Eternal Life of some amongst you. It is related concerning *Waldo,* (He from whom the *Waldenses* have that Name given them) [5] that the occasion of his Conversion was the *Sudden Death* of one of his Companions. The sight of that made him serious. He did not know, but that he might *dy suddenly* too, and that he was therefore concerned to be always fit to dy. So did he turn to the Lord, and became a great Instrument of Glory to God and good to his Church. Oh! that it might be so with you.

SLEEPING AT SERMONS

INSTR. 1. *We may here take notice that the nature of man is wofully corrupted and depraved,* else they would not be so apt to sleep when the precious Truths of God are dispensed in his Name, Yea, and men are more apt to sleep then, than at another time. Some woful Creatures, have been so wicked as to profess they have gone to hear Sermons on purpose, that so they might sleep, finding themselves at such times much disposed that way. This argueth as Satans malice, so the great corruption and depravation of the nature of men, whence it is that they are inclined unto evil, and indisposed to the thing that good is. Yea, some will sit and sleep under the best Preaching in the World. When *Paul* was alive, there was not a better Preacher upon the Earth then he. *Austin* [6] had three wishes: one was, that (if the Lord had seen meet) he might see Christ in the flesh: his second wish was, that he might have seen *Paul in the Pulpit;* but notwithstanding *Pauls* being so excellent a Preacher, there were some that could sit and sleep under his Ministry. When Soul-melting Sermons are Preached about Christ the Saviour, about the pardon of sin, about the glory of Heaven, there are some that will sleep under them. When soul-awakening Sermons are Preached, enough to make rocks to rend and to bleed; when the word falls down from Heaven like Thunder, the voice of the Lord therein being very powerful and full of Majesty, able to break the Cedars of *Lebanon,* and to make the wilderness to shake; yet some will sit and sleep under it: such is the woful corruption and desperate hardness of the hearts of the Children of men.

Instr. 2. *Hence see, that there is great danger in those things which men are apt to look upon as little sins, yea as no sins at all.*

As for sleeping at Sermons, some look upon it as no sin; others account it a *peccadillo*, a sin not worth taking notice of, or the troubling themselves about. But my Text sheweth that danger and death is in it. VVe have solemn Instances in the Scripture, concerning those that have lost their lives, because they have been guilty of such miscarriages, as carnal reason will say are but little sins. VVhen there was a man that gathered a few sticks upon the Sabbath day, he was put to death for it; and yet men would be apt to think his sin was not (though indeed it was) very great. Men account it a small matter to add something of their own to the worship of God: but when *Nadab* and *Abihu* did so, *there went out fire from the Lord*, and consumed them to death. VVhen *Vzzah* a good man, did with a pious intention touch the Ark, (which he being no Priest should not have done) *God smote him for his Error, that he dyed by the Ark of God*. Behold! the severity of God, and let us tremble at it. Common sins, which almost every one is guilty of, are accounted small iniquities; but there is exceeding danger in following a multitude to do evil. Sins of Omission are esteemed small, but mens Souls may be thrown into the fire and burned for ever, not only for bearing evil fruit, but because they do not bring forth good fruit, *Mat.* 3. 10. At the last day the Son of God will pronounce a Sentence of eternal death upon thousands of Millions, because they have omitted these and those duties which he required and expected from them. Sinful words are looked upon as small evils by many. How common is it for persons to say, *what shall we be made offenders for a word?* abusing that Scripture which reproveth those that make others offenders for speaking good and faithful words. But doth not the Scripture say, *by thy words thou shalt be condemned, Mat.* 12. 37. Corrupt communications, obscene discourses, unclean lascivious speeches, discover the persons that delight in them to be amongst the number of those that shall (without Repentance) be condemned at the day of *Judgement*, yet there are some that make light of them. Thus concerning those words which some call *Petty Oathes;* some are so profanely ignorant as to think, that they may Swear by *their Faith and Troth*, and that there is no great hurt or danger in it. But there is danger of no less than Damnation for these seemingly little sins, if men shall allow themselves therein, notwithstanding the Commandment of God to the contrary. See the word of the Lord to this purpose, *Jam.* 5. 12. *But above all things Swear not,* (i.e. vainly, or except duely called therunto) *neither by Heaven, neither by the Earth, neither by any other Oath*, therefore not by your Faith or Troth, *lest you fall into condemnation.*

Again, sinful thoughts are esteemed small evils; but I must tell you,

that vain thoughts, and much more vile unclean thoughts, if indulged
and delighted in, may hinder the Salvation of a mans Soul. Witness
that Scripture, *Jer.* 4. 14. *O Jerusalem, wash thine heart from wickedness,
that thou mayest be saved; how long shall thy vain thoughts lodge within thee?*
so that there is more than a little danger, in those evils, which men
account little sins.

URIAN OAKES, 1631–1681

[Urian Oakes, born in England, was brought to Cambridge by his
family, his father being a solid citizen, selectman, and deputy to the
General Court. He graduated from Harvard in 1649, became a teaching fellow and edited the Almanac for 1650. In 1654 he went to England, was given an important pulpit at Tichfield, Hants, from which
he was ejected in 1662. He was headmaster of the Southwark Grammar
school, organized a separate Congregational church at Tichfield, and
was called back to the Cambridge church in 1671. For four years he
was acting president of Harvard College, and in 1680 consented to be
formally installed as president, but died within a year. A little man,
a sharp wit, an excellent Latinist, with genuine learning and a degree
of urbanity, his sermons are among the best of seventeenth-century New
England productions. Cf. Cotton Mather, *Magnalia;* Sibley, *Biographical
Sketches;* Morison, *Harvard College in the Seventeenth Century.* This text is
from *The Soveraign Efficacy of Divine Providence; Overruling and Omnipotently
Disposing and Ordering all Humane Counsels and Affairs, Demonstrated and
Improved* (Boston, 1682), pp. 5–22, 32–37; this sermon, on Ecclesiastes
9 : 11, was delivered at Cambridge on September 10, 1677, on the
occasion of an Artillery election; it shows the mark of careful preparation and polish and constitutes the classic exposition of the Puritan
doctrine of divine concurrence in the operation of natural causes.]

THE SOVERAIGN EFFICACY OF DIVINE PROVIDENCE

D OCT. *That the Successes and Events of Vndertakings and Affairs are not
determined infallibly by the greatest Sufficiency of Men, or Second Causes;
but by the Counsel and Providence of God ordering and governing Time and
Chance according to his own good Pleasure.*

I have endeavoured to comprize and grasp the substance of *Solomon's*
Intendment, in this Doctrinal Conclusion: and shall explicate and
demonstrate the Truth of it (as God shall help) in the following Propositions.

Prop. 1. *Second Causes may have a sufficiency in their Kind, to produce these and those Effects:* an hability, a congruous disposition, or an aptness, yea, a kind of sufficiency in order to the putting forth this and that Act, and the giving Existence to these and those Effects: not indeed an absolute and universal Sufficiency (which can be affirmed of none but Him that is Allsufficient and Omnipotent) but a limited sufficiency, or a sufficiency in their *Kind*, and order: The Sun, to *shine;* the Fire, to *burn* that which is combustible; the Rational Creature to act or effect this or that in a way of *counsel*, and with *freedom of will;* the Swift, to *run;* the strong and valiant, and well-instructed Souldier, to *fight well;* the wise man, to *get his bread* to gather *riches*, to gain *acceptance* among those with whom he hath to do. This is no more than to say, that created Agents and Second Causes, may have the active power and virtue of causes, all that is requisite on their parts in order to the production of their peculiar and appropriate Effects, all that sufficiency that *dependent Beings*, and *second Causes* are capable of. And indeed it belongs to the Infinite Wisdom and Goodness of God to furnish his Creatures with sufficient Ability for the operations and effects He hath made them for: and so He did at *first*, when He made every thing good in its *Kind;* and whatever Defect there is *now* in this respect, it is the fruit & punishment of Sin. Though God is *able* to give Being to things in an immediate way, yet it is his *pleasure* in the course of his Providence to use Means, and to produce many things by the mediation and Agency of second Causes, and so gives *causal virtue* and ability to these and those things in order to the producing of such and such Effects. It is a good observation, that the Lord is pleased, not through any *defect of power* in Himself but out of *the abundance of his goodness* to communicate causal power and virtue to his Creatures, & to honour them with that Dignity that they may be his Instruments, by which He will produce these and those Effects: whereby He takes them, as it were, into partnership & fellowship with Himself in the way of his providential Efficiency, that they may be *Vnder-workers* to, yea *Co-vorkers* with Himself. Hence He gives them an aptitude and sufficiency in their *kind* in order to their respective operations and effects: though some have a greater aptitude & sufficiency than others. But without some degree of such *sufficiency*, nothing can deserve the name of a *Cause;* the very essence whereof consists in its *power, virtue & ability* to produce an *Effect.* A *cause* cannot be a *cause* without an *active power*, or *sufficiency* to give *being* to this or that *Effect.*

Prop. 2. *The Successes, and Events of Affairs and Vndertakings do ordinarily depend in some respects upon the Sufficiency of Second Causes.*

I do not say in the *Observation;* nor is it the meaning of *Solomon,* that Successes and Events of Affairs and Undertakings do not depend at all in an ordinary course, on the sufficiency of Second Causes. For this were to deny and destroy their *causality,* and to make nothing of their *efficiency.* Second causes have their peculiar Influence into their *Effects,* and contribute something to their *Existence:* and to assert the contrary, were to say that Causes are no Causes, and to speak a flat Contradiction. This would be to suppose that the Lord hath set up an Order and course in Nature, in vain; and given to Second Causes a sufficiency *in their Kind,* for *Action,* to no purpose; and to deny the ordinary Providence of God, which is that whereby the Lord observes the Order which He hath set, and that course of Nature which is originally of his own Appointment, whereby one thing depends upon, and receives Being from another. Though the Lord is pleased sometimes upon great and important Occasions, to leave the ordinary Road of Providence, and act beyond and above the usual, stated course of Things; and not to concurre with, and shine upon the endeavours of created Agents, so as to crown them with that success which according to an ordinary course of Providence, might be rationally expected; yet it is not to be imagined that He should ordinarily dispence with the course, and methods of his ordinary Providence: For why then should it be called *ordinary?* God who is the Lord of Hosts, the great Leader Commander & Ruler of Nature, not only *permits,* but also *effectually commands* and causes his whole *Militia,* ordinarily, to *move* and *act* according to their *Natures* and *natural Properties* respectively, without *Countermanding* them, or turning them out of their way. For (as I remember One argues) He will not shew such a dislike to his own workmanship, as ordinarily to cross the Order, and alter the course He hath set in the World. Therefore the meaning of the Text is not, that *Swiftness* conduces nothing to the *winning of the Race,* or *Strength,* to the winning of the *Battel;* or *Wisdom* & *Vnderstanding,* to the getting of *Bread* and *Riches;* or *Prudence, Art,* or *Skill,* to the getting of the *Favour* and *goodwill of Princes,* or *People:* nor, that the *Race* is *never* to the *Swift,* or the *Battel never* to the *Strong;* no nor yet, that the *Race* is not *more frequently* to the *Swift,* and the *Battel usually* to the *Strong, &c.* For the Lord doth most ordinarily award *Success* unto causes of greatest *Sufficiency,* rather than *Disappointment* & *Defeatment.* Otherwise, it would be a very *heartless,* if not a *foolish* Thing (in the eye of Reason) to *use means,* or to think to get the *Race* by *Swiftness,* or *Bread* by *Labour* and *Diligence,* or *Favour* by *dexterous* & *prudent Behaviour;* or *Learning,* by *Study* and *Industry;* or to *win the Battel* by good *Conduct,* and *Courage,* and *numbers of men.* Yea then *Wis-*

dom would not be better than *Folly;* nor *Strength* more desirable than *Weakness;* nor *Diligence* more beneficial & available than *Idleness,* and *sitting still.* This therefore is evident, that the Issues and Events of Undertakings do *in some respect, ordinarily,* depend upon the *Sufficiency* of *Second Causes;* insomuch as the greatest probability of Success (according to an ordinary providence, and in the eye of Reason) is ordinarily on the side of Causes that are most sufficient in their kind of Efficiency.

Prop. 3. *Second Causes, though of greatest Sufficiency in their kind, have not the certain Determination of Successes & Events in their own Hands: but may be frustrated & disappointed.*

Though the Successes and Events of Undertakings ordinarily depend upon the sufficiency of Second Causes; yet they are not infallibly determined thereby. Created Agents have not Events in their own Hands, but may be disappointed: they cannot warrant the Events of their Undertakings, or Success of their Counsels and Endeavours; but may be defeated of their Hopes and Expectations. Thus no man hath the absolute command of the Issue & success of his own Undertakings. He may be sure of this or that Event, if the Lord *Promise* it to him, or *Reveal* it to be *His Pleasure* to give such Success to such Endeavours: but he cannot be secured of it from, or by any *Sufficiency* of his own. He may, as a wise man, foresee & say, what in an ordinary course of Providence is rationally to be expected; but cannot warrant the Success of his Undertakings, or carv out what Event he pleases, to himself. His Prudence, and Providence, and Diligence, and *Sufficiency for Action,* cannot assure him of the *Event,* or determin the Success on his side. And there is that Demonstration of it, that created Agents of the greatest *Sufficiency,* are sometimes disappointed. Two Things I would say here,

1. *Agents of greatest Sufficiency are subject to Disappointment, as well* (I do not say, as much, or as ordinarily and often, but as well) *as Agents of less sufficiency.* The Ablest Men in any kind may miss of the Success they expect, as well as weaker men. That Men of great Sufficiency in this or that way, may be defeated of their Ends and Hopes, *Solomon* from his own Experience, assures us, in the Text: and who is it that upon his own observation cannot set his Seal to what He asserts? He gives five Instances. 1. *The Race is not to the Swift:* not profitable, or successful to him always; but sometimes pernicious, & destructive. Many agood Runner runs Himself into mischief and Ruine. Thus *Asahel,* that is said to be as light of foot as a wild Roe, ran after *Abner* so fast, that he lost his Life in that overhasty pursuit. 2 *Sam.* 2. 18–23.

There are Times when men that are swift would run from danger, and cannot: they have neither power to run, nor success in attempting it, *Jer.* 46, 6. Sometimes the Flight perisheth from the Swift, and he that is swift of foot, or that rideth the Horse, though it be at full speed, cannot deliver himself, *Amos* 2. 14, 15. It is not absolutely in the power of the swiftest man to escape danger, or win the prize by Running. 2. *The Battel is not to the Strong.* There is *in Bello Alea, the Chance of Warre,* as they use to speak. There is, as it were, a kind of Lottery, a great Uncertainty in Warre. Great Armies are sometimes defeated by small and inconsiderable Forces; the great Host of *Midian,* by *Gideon's* three hundred men; the Garrison of the *Philistines* by *Jonathan,* and his Armour-Bearer. This hath been often observed in the World. Sometimes strong and valiant Men are overthrown by those that are in strength farre inferiour to them; *great Goliah,* by *little David.* Well might *David* say, as *Psal.* 33. 16, 17. *There is no King saved by the multitude of an host: a mighty man is not delivered by much strength. An Horse is a vain thing for safety: neither shall he deliver any by his great strength.* There are Times, when *the mighty Ones are beaten down,* Jer. 46. 5. & *The mighty cannot deliver himself, or the strong strengthen himself; but the couragious among the mighty is put to flight,* Amos 2. 14, 16. Sometimes the strong melt like water at approaching danger, and the stouthearted are spoiled and sleep their sleep, and the men of might cannot find their hands, to make the least Defence, or Resistance, *Psal.* 76. 5.

3. *Bread is not to the Wise.* Wise men are not able to get their Livelihood, but have much adoe to make a shift to get a bare Subsistence in the world; and, it may be, are forc'd to beg for it, or be beholding to the Charity of others. There have been strange Instances of very wise, and worthy Persons, that have been reduced to such a Condition. Some of you know the famous Story, *Date Obolum,* or (as others have it) *Panem Belisario.*[1] *David* was put to beg his Bread of *Nabal,* 1. *Sam.* 25. & *Paul* was often in Hunger and Thirst, 2 *Cor.* 11. 27.

4. *Riches are not to men of Vnderstanding.* Sometimes indeed, wise men get Estates and gather Riches; and one would think they should be best accomplish'd for it: and yet it so falls out, that some understanding Men cannot thrive in the World and grow rich, notwithstanding all their Endeavours. So it is, that many men of great Understanding and rational Forecastings and Contrivances to gather wealth, though they lay out their Parts and their Hearts this way, and would be rich, yet they cannot; but are strangely defeated. You read of the *poor* wise man, *Eccles.* 9. 15. Many men of great Understandings are too wise, and of too great Spirits to labour after wealth; or if they do,

their designs are unsuccessful. 5. *Favour is not to men of Skill.* Many
very wise, and knowing, & skillful men, and experienced in Affairs,
and prudent also in their Deportment, yet cannot get, or keep the
Favour of Princes or People. Some Expositors on the Place, instance
in *Joseph*, that was envied, and hated, and sold by his Brethren, &
also lost the favour of *Potiphar* (though He managed the Affairs of
his House prudently and prosperously, and deserved well at his Hands)
and was cast into Prison by him. *David*, that was hated and persecuted
by *Saul*; *Daniel*, that was cast into the Lions Den, though *an excellent
Spirit was found in Him*, and great Prudence and Faithfulness in managing the Affairs of the Empire; and before that, though He had been
in great Favour and Esteem in *Nebuchadnezzar*'s time, yet afterwards
in the Reign of *Belshazzar*, He lived obscure, and as it were buried
at Court, as Mr. *Cartwright* gathers from *Dan*. 5. 11, 12, 13. Many
wise, and learned, and Ingenious Men cannot get the Favour of men,
or keep it, when they have. The *poor* wise man delivered the City,
and yet no man remembred that same poor man, *Eccl*. 9. 15. *Belisarius*
(whom I mentioned before) was a most prudent, experienced, faithful
General under the Emperour *Justinian*, that had won Him many
Battels, reduced many Cities & Countryes to his Obedience and approved Himself for a most loyal, and worthy Subject, & yet after all
his Services, even in *that* Emperour's Time, was through Envy, falsely
accused, for ought appears by the Story, had his Eyes put out, and was
forced to stand daily in the Temple of *Sophia*, where He held out his
wooden dish, begging his Bread, and useing those words, *Give a little
Bread to* Belisarius, *whom his Virtue & Valour hath raised; and Envy depressed, & cast down again.* Other Scripture Testimonies and Instances,
besides those in the Text, might be produced, if it were needful. But
every observing man's experience may furnish him with Demonstrations of his Truth, *That Agents of greatest Sufficiency among men are subject
to Disappointments, as well as those of less Sufficiency.* Again,

2. *Agents of little, or no Sufficiency, succeed sometimes in their Undertakings; when those of greater Sufficiency, miscarry & meet with Disappointment.* There is many times one Event to both as *Solomon* speaks *Eccl*.
9. 2. when the ablest Agents are frustrated, as well as the weakest:
and there is sometimes a better Event to weaker Agents, & Instruments; they prosper in their way, when abler men are disappointed.
The Race is *sometimes* to the Slow, and the Swift lose the Prize. The
Battel is *sometimes* to the Weak; and the Strong are put to flight: as
we have many Instances both in Scripture and common History.
Weak and simple people have bread enough sometimes, when wise

men are in want of their daily bread. *Nabal* had good store, when *David* was hard put to it. Men of shallow heads grow rich and get great Estates, when men of understanding can thrive at no Hand. *Solomon* tells us of the *poor* wise man; and our Saviour in that Parable, *Luk.* 12. 16, 20. tells us of a *rich Fool.* It is ordinarily seen in the World, that the thriving men in Estates, are none of the most understanding & judicious. Many a man hath this world-craft, that yet is a man of no deep or solid Understanding. So, many weak, worthless, ignorant, empty Persons find Favour with Princes and People: when men of Skill, & Learning, & great worth are neglected and despised. This is an Evil under the Sun, & an Error that proceeds from the Ruler, a great miscarriage in Government, that *Folly is set in great dignity* (Fools are favoured and advanced) *and the Rich,* i.e. men of rich Endowments for Wisdom and Piety, *sit in low places,* i.e. are depressed and discountenanced; *Servants are upon Horses,* men of poor servile Spirits and Conditions, are set up and honoured, *and Princes,* i.e. men of great worth, *walking as Servants upon the Earth.* Eccl. 10. 5, 6, 7. So that it appeares plainly, that Success doth not alwayes wait upon the Counsels and Actions of Persons of great Sufficiency; but they may suffer Disappointment, when others are prosperous: Which demonstrates that the Issues and Events of Undertakings and Affairs are not determined infallibly by the Qualifications & accomplishments of created Agents, and Second Causes.

Prop. 4. *The Defeat & Disappointment of Agents of great Sufficiency in their kind, is from the Hapning of* Time *&* Chance *unto them.*

Some read it (and the Original will bear it) *because,* or *for* Time and Chance happeneth to them all. For Explication.

1. By *Time,* understand not barely the *Duration,* or *spate* of Time, which hath no such determining Influence into humane Affairs. But Time *so & so Circumstanced.* Time is sometimes as much as a special *Season* or *Opportunity,* when there is a concurrence of Helps, means, and advantages for the furthering the Designs and undertakings of men. By *Time* sometimes, we are to understand such a *Nick,* or *Juncture* of time, wherein there is a coincidence of Difficulties, disadvantages, & hindrances to the effecting of any Business. And this seems the meaning of *Solomon* in the Text. An adverse or *evil Time,* Ec. 9. 12. Sometimes the Times favour the Enterprizes of men, Sometimes they frown upon them. At one time, wise and good men stand up for the Defence of their Country and Liberties thereof, and prosper in it; the Times favour them, there is a concurrence of all manner of Furtherances and advantages: at another time, they may endeavour it,

and the Times frown upon them, the Spirit and Humour of the People is degenerated; and they swim against the stream, & are lost in the Attempt. And we say, *Such a Man was worthy of better Times*, had been a brave man, if He had lived in better Times, his worth had been more known and prized, and He would have had better. success. So when the Time of Judgment upon a People, is come, then wrath ariseth against them without remedy; and then the *strong man* may fight for the defence of such a Country; and *the wise man* endeavour to deliver the City: but all in vain; they shall miscarry in the Undertaking. *Aben Ezra* (as *Mercer* tells us) referres this to the *Conjunctions*, and *Aspects* of the Starres, by which He apprehended these inferiour Things were governed. We are sure there are certain Periods, and Revolutions of Time, respecting the Prosperity, or Adversity of Nations, Countries, Cities, Churches, Families, Persons. As Time is set to all the Successes, so to all the Defeats and disappointments of men; and when this Time comes, no Sufficiency of man can withstand Disappointments.

2. By *Chance*, Understand contingent and casual Events. Many things fall out between the *Cup*, and the *Lip;* or otherwise than expect or imagine, or can possibly foresee. Some Event chops in, and interposeth unexpectedly, to cross a man's Designs, & defeat his Hopes & rational Expectations. When *Saul* and his men were compassing *David* and his men, and ready to take them, then comes a Messenger to *Saul*, saying, *Haste & come: for the* Philistines *have Invaded the Land*. 1 Sam. 23. 27. When *Haman* had plotted the Ruine of the *Jews*, and brought his Design near to an Issue, then the King cannot sleep but calls for the Book of the Records of the Chronicles, and they read to Him of the good Service of *Mordecai*, in discovering the Treason that was plotted against his Person; and one thing falls in after another, to defeat *Haman's* cruel design, and ruine the whole fabrick of his strong built, and almost perfected Contrivance In this sence *Time* and *Chance* happens to men of greatest Sufficiency, which they cannot either foresee, (*Eccl* 9. 12.) or prevent, or help themselves against them when they come upon them: and hereby their Counsels, and Undertakings are defeated and ruined sometimes.

Prop. 5. *Time and Chance which happens to men in the way of their Vndertakings, is effectually ordered & governed by the Lord*. God is the Lord of Time, and Orderer, and Governour of all Contingences. Time and Chance that further or hinder the Designs of men, are under the Rule and Management of the Lord. His Counsel sets the *Times*, appoints the *Chances;* His Providence dispenses the *Times*, and frames the *Chances*, that befall men. The Lord hath in his own power the Dispensation of *Times*, Eph. 1. 10. *The Times and Seasons He hath put in his own power*, Act. 1. 7. He hath such a Dominion over the Times, that *He changeth Times and Seasons*, according to his own pleasure. *Dan.* 2. 31. *My Times* (saith *David*, Ps. 31. 15. *are in thy Hands*. He means the state and condition of his *Times;* his Prosperities, and Adversities; his Successes, and Disappointments; and universally, whatever should befall him in the Times that should pass over Him. Moreover, all the Chances that happen to men, as the Scripture but now mentioned shews, are in the Hand of God. *My Times* i.e. the Chances of my Times. No Contingency, or Emergency, or Accident so casual, but it is ordered & governed by the Lord. The Arrow that was shot at a venture, and smote *Ahab* throw the joints of his Harness, was directed at him by the Hand of God. So in that case of Man-slaughter, and killing a man casually, as if a man be hewing Wood, and his hand fetcheth a stroke with the Axe, to cut down a Tree, and the head slippeth from the helve, and lighteth upon his Neighbour, that he die, *Deut.* 19. 5. God is said in that case, to *deliver* that man that is slain, *into his hand*, Exod. 21. 13. God ordereth that sad event. All Casualties in the World, are guided by the steady Hand of the great God. *Thou* (saith *David*, Ps. 16. 5.) *maintainest my Lot*. The Lord makes and disposes the Lot, or Chance of every man, whatever it is. He hath appointed all Times and Chances in his *Eternal* Counsel; and in *Time* executes accordingly, in the course of his Providence.

Prop. 6. *The great God hath the absolute and infallible Determination of the Successes and Events of all the Operations & Vndertakings of created Agents & Second Causes, in his own Power*. His Counsel and soveraign Will appoints what they shall be, and his Providence (which is not determined by any Second Cause: but is the Determiner of them all) Executes accordingly. And it must needs be so, if you consider these two Particulars,

1. *God is the Absolute First Cause, and Supream Lord of all*. Of Him, and to Him, and through Him are all Things, *Rom.* 11. 36. He that understands any thing of God indeed, knows this to be a Truth. Here we might be large; as they that are acquainted with the Doctrine of *Creation* and *Providence*, in *Conservation* and *Gubernation* of all Things, will readily apprehend: for here we might shew you, 1. That God is the absolute first Cause of all the causal power and virtue that is in Creatures. He gives them power to act, furnisheth them with a Sufficiency for their Operations. He gives Swiftness to the Runner; Skill, and Strength, and Courage, to the Souldier.

Sustaining force, [handwritten annotation]

2. That He supports, and continues the active power of the crea-ture. He continues Swiftness, Wisdom, Strength, Courage, as He pleaseth. If He withdraw, all is gone. The Swift is lame, or slow-footed, the Strong is weak & timorous, the Wise is foolish and besotted, the man of Skill, is a meer Bungler at any thing. 3. That He doth by a *previous Influx* excite and stirre up, and actuate the active power of the Creature, and set all the wheels agoing. For the most operative, active created Virtue, is not a *pure Act:* but hath some *Potentiality* mixed with it; and therefore cannot put forth it self into Action, unless it be set agoing by the *first Cause.* And the creature cannot be the absolute *first Cause* of any *physical action.* In Him we live, and move, *Act.* 17. 28. Again. 4. That He determines and applyes Second Causes to the Objects of their Actions. When they stand, as it were, *in Bivio,* as it is said of *Nebuchadnezzar,* when he was marching with his Army He *stood at the parting of the way, at the head of the two wayes, to use Divination,* as doubting which way he had best to march; whether to *Jerusalem,* or some other way, *Ezek.* 21. 21, 22. Then the Lord casts the Scale and the Lot, & determines them this way, and not another. He doth not only stir up Second Causes to act at large, and set them agoing, and leave it to their own Inclination, whither they shall go, & what they shall do: but He leads them forth, and determines them to this, or that Object. 5. That He *cooperates,* and workes *jointly* with Second Causes, in producing their Effects. As He *predetermins* Second Causes, so He *concurres* with them in their Operations. And this *Præ-determination,* and *Concurse* is so necessary; that there can be no real Effect produced by the Creature without it. And it is a Truth also, that when God Improves Second Causes for the production of any Effect, He so concurres with them, that He doth withall most im-mediately, intimously, and without Dependence upon these Causes by which He acts, produce the *Entity,* or *Esse* of the Effect. If this be considered, it will appear that created Agents, are as it were, God's Instruments, that act as they are acted by Him; and cannot move of themselves. The busy, bustling, proud *Assyrian* was so, *Is.* 10. 15. 6. *That all the Ataxy, Disorder, Irregularity, moral Evil that is found in the Actions of Rational Agents, is by His Permission.* If it were not the Pleasure of God to permit it, no Sin should be in the World, nor in the Actions of Men. Though there is no *Legal* Permission, or allowance of it; (for the Law of God forbids it) yet there is a *Providential* Permission of it. God could have kept it out of his World. 7. *That He limits and sets Bounds to the Actions of Second Causes: what they shall do, and how farre they shall proceed in this or that way.* He set bounds to Satan, when he

had Commission to afflict *Job*. He limits, and restrains the Eruptions of the Wrath & Rage of the Churches Adversaries, *Ps.* 76. 10. He sets bounds to the sinfull Actions of Men: He regulates and governs all the Actions of Second Causes, as to time, place, degrees, and all manner of Circumstances. He is not the *Author:* but He is the *Orderer* of Sin it self. 8. *That He serves Himself, and his own Ends of all Second Causes.* He makes them all in all their Operations subservient to his own Designs: and that not only natural, but rational Agents, that act by Counsel. And not only such of them as are his professed willing Servants. Many serve God's ends beside their Intentions, and against their wills. I will do this and that saith God, by the *Assyrian, howbeit he meaneth not so*, Is. 10. 6, 7. Wicked men and Devils do God's will against their own will, and beside their Intentions. *Ye thought Evil against me* (saith *Joseph* to his Brethren) *but God meant it for good &c.* Gen. 50. 20. God elicites what good He pleases out of the actions of his Creatures. Whatever this or that Agent proposeth to himself, yet God alwayes attaineth His Ends. He serves Himself of the very Sins of his Creatures, and brings good out of them. He makes that which is not *Bonum honestum*, to be *Bonum conducibile:* [2] and though Sin is not good; yet, as God orders the matter, it is good, in order to many holy Ends, that Sin should be in the World, as *Austin observes*.

9. *That He useth means in themselves* unfit, *and improves Agents of themselves* insufficient, *to bring about his own Purposes & produce marveilous Effects.* Yea, and it is as easy with Him to do any thing by weak and insufficient, as by the ablest & most accomplished Instruments. *There is no restraint to the Lord to Save by many, or by few.* 1 Sam. 14. 6. *It is nothing with Him to help, whether with many, or with them that have no power.* 2 Chron. 14. 11. Despicable Instruments, sometimes, do great Things in His Hand. 10. *That He renders the aptest means ineffectual, and the Vndertakings of the most sufficient Agents unsuccessful, when He pleases.* He hath a *Negative Voice* upon all the Counsels and Endeavours, and Active Power of the Creature. He can stop the Sun in its course, and cause it to withdraw its shining; He can give check to the Fire, that it shall not burn; & to the hungry Lions, that they shall not devour: and He can order it so, that the men of might shall *sleep their sleep, and not find their Hands.* He can break the Ranks of the most orderly Souldiers, take away courage from the stoutest hearts, send a pannick Fear into a mighty Host, and defeat the Counsels of the wisest Leaders and Conducters. He can blow upon, and blast the likeliest Undertakings of the ablest Men. In a word: the Lord being the Absolute First Cause, and supream Governour of all his Creatures, and all their

Actions; though He hath set an Order among his Creatures, this shall be the cause of that effect, &c. yet He himself is not tied to that Order; but Interrupts the course of it, when He pleases. The Lord reserves a Liberty to Himself to interpose, and to Umpire matters of Success and Event, contrary to the Law and common Rule of Second Causes. And though He ordinarily concurreth with Second Causes according to the Law given and Order set; yet sometimes there is in his Providence a Variation and Digression. Though He hath given Creatures power to act; and Man, to act as *a Cause by Counsel*, and hath furnished him with active Abilities; yet He hath not made any Creature *Master of Events;* but reserves the Disposal of Issues, and Events to Himself. Herein the absolute Soveraignty and Dominion of God appears.

2. *Otherwise, the Lord might possibly suffer real Disappointment, and be defeated of his Ends in some Instances.* He might be cross'd in his Designs, if any of his Creatures could doe what they will, without absolute Dependence upon Him. He could not be sure of his Ends, & what He designs in the World, if He had not command of all Events that may further or hinder them. If there were any active power in Creatures that He cannot controll; or any one event that is out of his Reach, and absolutely in the Creature's power, exempted from his providential Command, it would be possible that He might be defeated of his Ends, and so far unhappy, as to his *voluntary Happiness*, which results from his having his *Pleasure done* in the World, and compassing all his Ends in the works of Creation and Providence. God hath made all Things, ruleth all Things, and manageth all Things according to the Counsel of his Will, in a way of subserviency to Himself, and his own Occasions: which He could not do universally and infrustrably, if He had not the absolute and infallible Determination of all Events in his own Hand. *But His Counsel shall stand, and He will do all his Pleasure:* Is. 46. 10. Thus much for the Explication, and Confirmation of the Doctrine.

USE I. Of Instruction, in these Particulars.

1. *We see what a poor dependent, nothing-Creature Proud Man is:* Depending absolutely upon God for his Being, Actions, and the Success of them. Men of greatest Sufficiency cannot get their own Bread, or bring any thing to effect in their own strength. Let their Abilities be what they will (*Swiftness*, for the *Race; Strength*, for the *Battel; Wisdom*, for getting their *Bread, &c.*) yet they shall stand them in no stead without the concurrence and Blessing of God. Man saith, he will do this and that: but he must ask God leave first. He saith, To day or to morrow I will go to such a place, and buy and sell, & get gain; whereas he knows

not what shall be: but it shall certainly be as the Lord will. *The way of man is not in himself; it is not in man that walketh to direct his steps*, nor perform any thing that he purposeth, without divine Concurrence, or Permission. He hath not the Success of any of his actions in his own power; nor doth he know that any thing he doth shall prosper. One would wonder poor *dependent* man should be so *proud!* Any little thing lifts him up. When the Souldier on such occasions as these, is in his Bravery, in his military Garb drest up for the purpose, with his *Buffe Coat*, his *Scarfe*, his *rich Belt*, his *Arms, a good Horse under him*, O what a goodly Creature is he in his own Eyes! and what wonders can he do in his own conceit! and yet he hath as absolute need of God's Assistance, if he go forth to Battel, as any naked, unarmed man. He cannot move a step, or fetch his next breath, or bring his hand to his mouth, or leap over a straw, or do any thing, without help from God, *in whose hand his breath is, and whose are all his wayes* Dan. 5. 23. It's strange to see how the hearts of men are lifted up with nothing! *O cease ye from Man: for wherein is he to be accounted of?*

2. *We see that there is, and there is not* Chance *in the World*. Chance there is, in respect of Second Causes: (so some things fall out Κατα Συγκυριαν as our Saviour speaks *Luk*. 10. 31.) but no Chance as to the first Cause. That piece of *Atheism*, and *Heathenism* ascribing things to *Fortune* and *Chance*, is hardly rooted out of the minds of men, that are or should be better instructed and informed. The *Philistines* when they were plagued, could not tell whether *God* had done it, or a meer *Chance* happened to them, 1 *Sam*. 6. 9. They understood not, that what was *a Chance to them*, was ordered by the *Providence of God*. Truth is, Chance is something that falls out beside the Scope, Intention, and foresight of *Man*, the Reason and cause whereof may be hid from him; and so it excludes the Counsel of *Men;* but it doth not exclude the Counsel and Providence of *God;* but is ordered and governed thereby. And it is so farre from being *Chance* to God, that there is as much (if not more) of the Wisdom, and Will, and Power of God appearing in matters of Chance and Contingency, as in any other Events.

3. *We see here something of the Power, and Greatness, and Glory of God appearing in his Efficiency, whereby He works all in all*. As He is himself Independent, so all Things have an absolute Dependence on Him. He gives Success, or causeth Disappointment, as he pleaseth. So that men are wholly beholden to Him for all the good they enjoy: for Victory, for Bread, for Riches, for Favour and Acceptance, for all. Nothing comes to pass without his Permission, if it be *moral Evil;* without his Concurse and cooperation, yea, Predetermination, if it be *moral* or

physical Good, or *penal Evil*. In him we live and move, and have our Being. The Counsels of the ablest Statesmen, how rational soever, shall not prosper without him: Ministers, how sufficient soever, pious, learned, industrious, zealous, shall convert no man, edify no man, comfort & establish no man, without Him. 1 *Cor.* 3. 6, 7. Though Scholars study hard, they shall make no proficiency without the Blessing of God. The Merchant may trade, and project rationally, and yet shall not grow rich upon it, unless God give him success. It is God that maketh *Zebulum rejoice in his Going out, and Issachar in his Tents:* that crowns the labours of Seamen, Merchants, and Husbandmen with Success. *Except the Lord build the House* &c Ps. 127. 1. *Training Days, Artillery Days*, tho' of great use, and very necessary; yet are all in vain, unless the Lord bless. He must instruct, and teach, and accomplish you; otherwise the help of your expert Officers, and your own endeavours to learn War, will signify nothing. And when valiant Souldiers come to fight; whatever Skill, and Strength, and Courage, and Conduct, and Advantages they have, yet they will be worsted, if the Lord do not give Success. We should learn hence to admire the Power and Greatness of God. It is a lamentable thing, that He that doth all, is thought to do nothing! He can work without Means, by insufficient Means; & blast the ablest Instruments: and yet is little minded in the World. God gives forth a Challenge to Idols, *Do good*, if you can, *or do evil*. Isai. 41. 23. It is God's Prerogative to do good or evil, i.e. not the evil of *Sin* (which argues Defect and Impotency; and comes not within the compass of Omnipotency to do it) but of *Punishment*. God only can give good, or award bad Success; and *Reward* or *Correct* and punish his Creatures that way. *Who is he that saith* (what Man or Angel?) *& it* cometh to pass, when the Lord commandeth it not? Lam. 3. 37. O see, and adore the Greatness of God in this respect! He works all in all. . . .

First, Whatever your own Sufficiencie may be, yet acknowledge God thankfully, as if you had been wholly Insufficient: for your Sufficiencie is of God, and He could have disappointed notwithstanding. The ground of our Unthankfulness for all good Issues and Events of Affairs and Undertakings, is, because we do not see the good Hand of God dispensing all to us. We make too *little* of God, and too *much* of our selves; either by thinking we deserve better than God hath done for us (Hence a proud Heart is never thankful to God or Man) or by thinking we have done all, or more than we have done, toward the getting of this or that Mercy. We put our selves too much in the place of God; as if it were in our power to make our Endeavours Successful, and to give a

good Effect and Issue to them, according to *our* Desire. We get up into
God's Throne, and usurp upon his Prerogative, and assume that which
is peculiar to Him, when we presume we can bring any thing to pass,
or do any thing successfully in our Own strength. If we make our selves
the only and absolute *first Causes* of our good Success; no marvel we
make our selves the *last End* also, and deny God the glorie. O do not
ascribe good Success to your own Wit, and Parts, and Policy, and
Industrie, and say, my Nimbleness hath won the Race; my Conduct
and Courage hath won the Battel; my Wisom hath gotten me this
Bread; my Understanding hath heaped up this Wealth; my Dexteritie,
and Skill, and Complaisance, and agreeable Conversation hath procured me the Favour of Rulers or People; my Parts or Study hath
given me this Learning. Say not with the Vapouring *Assyrian, By the
Strength of My Hand I have done it, and by My Wisdom: for I am Prudent.*
Isa. 10. 13. Let not this be so much as the secret Language of your
Hearts. Say not, as *Nebuchadnezzar, This is great Babylon, which I have
built,* and so derogate from God that works all in all; lest He turn you
a grazing, as He did him, with the Beasts of the Field, and teach you
better Manners by some severe Correction. Do not *Sacrifice to your own
Nets, and burn Incense to your Drags; as if by them your portion were fat,
and meat plenteous* (Hab. 1. 16.) but ascribe all to God. There is that deep
Wickedness in the Hearts of Men, that if they get any thing by any
Fraud, and crafty fetches, and overreaching of their Brethren, in a
sinful way, they will be too readie to attribute *that* to the Providence
and Blessing of God, and say, it was God's Providence that cast it in
upon them; when they have been craftily and sinfully designing it,
and bringing it about: but when they have gotten any thing honestly,
by their Wisdom and Prudence, and Industrie, they are too ready to
forget Providence, and ascribe all to themselves. See the Evil of this,
and remember that no People in the World have greater cause of
Thankfulness than we have to God, who hath governed *Time* and
Chance on our behalf marvellously. O Bless Him for good Success, not
only when you cannot but acknowledge your own *Insufficiency;* but also
when you have apprehensions of the greatest *Sufficiency* of Second
Causes. And *Blessed for ever be the Lord, who hath Pleasure in the Prosperity
of his Servants,* Psal. 35. 27.

Secondly, *Acknowledge God also in all your Frustrations and Disappointments, so as to resent his Disposals and Dispensations towards you in a* gracious
manner. We have met with manie Disappointments in the late Warre,
and in other respects. We should see God in all. When He blasts our
Corn, defeats our *Souldiers,* frowns upon our *Merchants,* and we are

disappointed; now acknowledge the Hand of God, Ordering *Time,* and *Chance* according to his Good Pleasure. Justifie God in all, and bear such Frustrations patientlie. When you have done your Dutie, be quiet, though the Event doth not answer your Endeavours, and Hopes. Take heed of quarrelling at GOD's Disappointments. Do you know VVhom you have to do with? *I was dumb, I opened not my mouth; because Thou didst it.* Psal. 89. 9. If we look at faultie Instruments, or at meer Chance onely, we shall be apt to murmur. It is the observation of One, *That the Reason why men are more apt to fly out into Cursings and Blasphemies for their bad Luck (as they call it) in those Vnlawful Games of Cards, and Dice, than in other Exercises, that are governed by Art and Skill, ariseth partly from the very nature of those Games: because when they have tried their Lot or Chance over and over, and their Expectation is deceived, they think that that Power that governs the Lot or Chance, is Adverse to them. They cannot blame their own Art or Skill, when no Art can infallibly determine the Event; but curse their bad Fortune.* And if we look at Disappointments, as our bad *Fortune* and *Chance* onely, looking no further, we shall be apt to fret and quarrel: but if we do indeed see God ordering our Lot for us, it may and ought to silence us. When Magistrates have done their Duty, according to the Law of God, and of the Country, and endeavoured faithfully to give check & stop to the Inundation of *Profaneness* and *Heresy;* and yet the bad Genius of the Times, and degenerous Humour of the People, and this or that Emergency happens, that frustrates the Success of their Counsels and Endeavours; truly they may sit down and mourn indeed; but yet humbly submit to the All-disposing Providence of God. When Ministers have laboured faithfully, and yet Israel is not gathered, and their Labours seem to be in vain, not successful in converting Sinners; they may weep in secret indeed; but yet patiently bear the Unsuccessfulness of their Ministry from the Hand of God. When Souldiers have shewed themselves valiant, and faithful, and done what they can; and yet are worsted: They must acknowledge God's Hand in it, and that *the Battel is the Lord*'s. 1 Sam. 17. 47. who governeth the Warre, and determins the Victory on what side He pleaseth. All men have *Briars* and *Thorns* springing up in the way of their Callings, as well as Husbandmen; and meet with Difficulties and Crosses therein. Get the Spirit *David* had 2 *Sam.* 15. 25, 26. and so acknowledge God in every thing, as to submit humbly to his Disposals, even when they are Adverse, and cross to your Desires and Expectations.

Thirdly, *Be always Prepared for Disappointments.* Do not promise your selves Success from the Sufficiency of Second Causes: God may determine otherwise. . . . Events are not in the Creatures power. The

Lord sometimes disappoints men of greatest Sufficiency, overrules and
controlls their Counsels and Endeavours, and blasts them strangely.
Time and *Chance* happens to them. If *Adam* had stood; though he would
not have had the Determination of Events & Successes in his own hand;
yet God would have determined them for him according to his hearts-
desire: and he should never have been disappointed. But since the Fall,
as no Man hath power to determine Events (which is God's Prerogative) so it is just with God that every man should meet with Crosses
and Disappointments; and this is the Fruit of the Curse, under which
all natural men ly: and as for the People of God; though they are
delivered from the Curse of the Law, in the *Formality* of it; so that nothing befalls them *as a Curse*, how *cross* soever it be: yet they are not yet
absolutely delivered from the *Matter* of the Curse, as appears by the
Afflictions they meet with, and Death it self. And indeed it makes
sometimes for the glory of God, to disappoint Men of greatest Abilities.
When men do not see and own God; but attribute Success to the
Sufficiency of Instruments, It's time for God to maintain his own Right
(as Dr. *Preston*[3] speaks) and shew that He gives, or denies Success,
according to His own good Pleasure. God is much seen in Controlling
the ablest Agents, & blasting their Enterprizes; yea more, many times,
than in backing them, & blessing their Endeavours in an ordinary
Course of Providence. Herein the *Wisdom* of God is much seen. It is
best, sometimes, it should be so, with respect to God's Int'rest and
Glory. His *Power* also appears in giving Check to the Ablest Instruments, and turning all their Designs another way than they Intended.
His *Mercy* also to his People, is seen herein; for it is best for them,
in some Cases, to be defeated and disappointed. His *Justice* also appears herein, in his correcting and punishing the Self-confident, sinful
Creature with unexpected Disappointments. So that it is our Wisdom, to look for Changes and Chances, some Occurrents and Emer-
gencies that may blast our Undertakings, that Faith and Prayer may
be kept agoing, and lest if such Frustrations befall us unexpectedly, we
either fly out against God, or faint and sink in Discouragements. At
the first going out of our Forces, in the beginning of the Warre, what
great Apprehensions were there of speedy Success and ending of the
Warre; that it was but going and Appearing, and the Enemy would
be faced down: As if the first News from our Souldiers should be,
Venimus, Vidimus, Vicimus.[4] And several times after, great probability
of concluding that unhappy War; and yet all disappointed, contrary
to Expectation.[5] VVhen there is therefore greatest Probability of Success, yet remember there may be Disappointment; and provide for it,

that you may not be surprised thereby. This may be good Counsel to men of projecting Heads, that are wont to be very confident that they see their way farre before them: but they do not know what *Time* and *Chance* may happen: This may check the Confidence of Man, and teach us not to promise our selves great Things, or build upon this or that Event or Enjoyment for time to come. Labour to be prepared and provided for Disappointments.

JOSHUA MOODY, 1633–1697

[Joshua Moody was born in Ipswich, Suffolk; his father was a saddler, who migrated to Ipswich, Massachusetts, in 1634, and then to Newbury. He graduated from Harvard College in 1653, was a teaching fellow in 1655; in 1658 he began to preach in Portsmouth, New Hampshire, though he could not get a church formally organized until 1671. In 1682 he became a popular hero by stoutly resisting the attempts of Governor Cranfield to force him to administer the sacraments according to the rites of the Church of England. He was sentenced to six months in jail, served thirteen weeks, and was forbidden to preach. He came to Boston, assisted James Allen at the First Church, declined the presidency of Harvard and a call from New Haven. Still living in Boston in 1688–1689, he was a leader of the revolution against Andros. He resisted the witchcraft frenzy, actually aiding two of the accused to escape. He returned to Portsmouth in 1693. Cf. Sibley, *Biographical Sketches;* Sprague, *Annals.* This text is from *Souldiery Spiritualized, Or the Christian Souldier Orderly, and Strenuously Engaged in the Spiritual Warre* (Cambridge, 1674), an artillery election sermon preached in Boston on June 1, 1674; it is unusual among Puritan sermons for the elaborate and sustained metaphor upon which it is built. Not only does Moody portray the whole of human existence under the figure of war and battle, but he takes up in succession the technical commands of the parade ground and of formation and develops a spiritual significance for each.]

SOULDIERY SPIRITUALIZED

As FOR my manner of speaking in the using of many Metaphorical Expressions, and Allusions unto the Calling, Postures, and motions of Souldiers . . . though it may possibly grate upon some Critical and captious Ears, yet I hope it will be at least excusable or tolerable to your selves. . . . Had I been to handle the same Head of Divinity on another occasion and before another Auditor, I could and should have sought out other words, . . . I conceive a man should take Measure of his Theam to cut out his Language by, and make it up something according to the mode of his Auditory. . . .

The Lord takes care to make us spiritual in all our Imployments, by spiritualizing all our Imployments. Yea, all our Relations and Conditions, as well as Imployments, are so improved to our Hands by the Spirit of God in his Word as that they may be useful both as Monitors and Helpers to mind us of, and further us in those matters that are of most solemn and momentous, because of Eternal concernment . . . From the King upon the Throne to the Hewer of wood and drawer of water, the Lord is in his word teaching us by such familiar and known *Metaphors* taken from those Callings that we are versed in, in so much that all sorts of men may say concerning the voice of God in his word, as they in another Case Acts. 2. 8. 11. How is it that we hear from thence in our own Tongue wherein we have been bred, and in the proper *dialect* of those Imployments to which we have been bred, the wonderful Counsels of God declared to us: the Lords manner of speaking as it helps us to the understanding of what he saith, so his love and Care therein should quicken us to the practice of what we understand. . . .

Know, that *Death our Enemy* is upon a *swift* and *speedy march* towards us, and we are hastening toward him, and therefore must necessarily meet quickly, between this and that the Time is but short, over a few dayes (*moments* it may be) the day will discover what we have been, and done. We are now all of us *training up* under the *doctrine* and *Discipline* of the *Lords House*, and possibly (you, probably) in this Life he may put us to the Trial what we have gained, some such *plunge* we may be brought unto, as wherein we shall have occasion to use all the Skill that ever we have had an opportunity of getting. He may call us to *combate* with *Persecution*, *Poverty*, *Reproach*, Bereavements of Relations, &c. or at the utmost Death will try us all, *Death*, (I say,) which among men of all *Ages* and *Sexes* takes *promiscuously* according to the *Commission* which the *Lord of Life and Death* hath given it, though ordinarily, those that are in the Front are nextly for present Service, who *discharge*, and *Fall off*, and make way for the next to be *Front*.[1] So *one Generation passeth away, and another comes in its Room* Eccl. 1. 4. ever in motion, going off, and coming on the *stage* each hour and movement. I may not unfitly liken the *whole Race of Mankind*, or all the men in the world to a *well-Marshall'd* Army, (*well Marshall'd* I say, for notwithstanding all the *seeming*, and in themselves the real *Confusions* that there are, the Lord orders all *wisely*, and at the end will

discover when all is put together, *beautifully* too) upon a *march* to meet
with *Death*, where the *first Rank discharge*, (yea, and are *discharged* too)
Fall off, yea, *Fall down*, never to return or rise more, and then the next
is first, and so on: there are *Old men*, *middle-Aged*, and *Young ones*, in the
Front, *Center*, and *Rear* of the *Army*, The *Old Fall off*, the *middle-Aged*
Advance, the *Younger* are *drawing* after, now though sometimes here and
there one of the *younger ones* may be pickt out of the *Reer* by a Shott out
of *Deaths murthering piece*, yet we commonly say, and truly, *Young ones*
may die, but Old ones must. It's a usual word of Command among
you, *The First Rank make ready*, they especially should be ready; but it
is a duty for us all to *watch and pray alwayes*, that we may be *accounted*
worthy to stand when the Son of man shall come. Let all our *Care*
and *motion* through-out our whole Life tend to the fitting us for a
safe, Honourable, and comfortable Exit at last, that when we come to
look *Death* in the *Face*, or to *look back*, (and we should often *look back*)
upon our *Life past*, we may neither be *afraid*, nor *ashamed to die*.

SAMUEL WILLARD, 1640–1707

[For life of Willard see p. 250. The first selection is from *The Child's*
Portion (Boston, 1684), pp. 66–70. The second selection is from *The*
High Esteem Which God hath of the Death of his Saints (Boston, 1683),
pp. 14–18, a funeral sermon upon John Hull, the famous mintmaster
of the colony, the father-in-law of Samuel Sewall. The third selection
is from *The Peril of the Times Displayed* (Boston, 1700), pp. 90–93; the
passage is representative of the wails over the moral declension of
New England that make up a large part of most sermons at the end
of the seventeenth century.]

SAINTS NOT KNOWN BY EXTERNALS

1. The reason why the Children of God are so little regarded here
in the World; it is because the World knows not who they are, nor
what they are born unto: Their great Glory for the present is within;
outwardly they look like other men, they eat, drink, labour, converse
in earthly imployments, as others do; the communion which they
have with God in all of these, is a secret thing: They are Sick, Poor,
Naked, Distressed like other men; those inward supports which they
have under all those exercises, are remote from publick view: They
dy, and are buried under the Clods, and their bodyes putrifie and
rot like other men; and none see those joyes that their souls are entred

into, nor that guard of Angels which comes as a Convoy, and carryes them into *Abraham's* bosom: Nay, they have their sins, their spots, their imperfections and weaknesses here, as well as other men; but their tears, repentance, secret mournings, and renewals of Faith, and restorings to peace and soul-comfort, are secret.

And hence,

Though the Righteous Man be indeed surpassingly more excellent than his neighbour, yet is he not thought so to be: Whereas, did the World see and understand, whose sons they are, what inheritances they are the undoubted heirs of, and what are those Gloryes they shall ere long be made to possess, it would alter their opinion, and make them afraid of them, and not dare to do them any wrong. How fearful was *Abimestech* of *Abraham*, when God did but tell him he was a Prophet? *Gen.* 20. 7, 8.

2. Here we see the reason why the People of God are often so doubtful, disquiet, discontent, and afraid to dy (I put things together) The ground of all this is because they do not as yet see clearly what they shall be: It would be a matter of just wonderment to see the Children of God so easily and often shaken, so disturbed and perplexed in hours of Temptation, were it not from the consideration, that they at present know so little of themselves or their happiness: Sometimes their sonship it self doth not appear to them, but they are in the dark, at a loss about the evidencing of it to the satisfaction of their own minds; and from hence it is that many doubtings arise, and their souls are disquieted. Sometimes their present sufferings look bigger in their thoughts, than the conceptions or apprehensions which they entertain of their future Glory, these things being near, and the other looked on at a distance, and hence they out-weigh, in their rash judgements, and now they are disquiet and discontent, and say with him, *Psal.* 73. 13. *I have cleansed my heart in vain, and washed my hands in innocency.* And usually in their good frames, they apprehend more of the sweetness of present Communion with God in his Ordinances, than of that blessed immediate communion in Glory; and this makes them, with good *Hezekiah*, to turn away their faces from the messages of death and change: All these things are arguments of the weak sight and dark thoughts which we here have of the things of another world: which yet, it is the holy pleasure of God, that it shall be so a while, for the advancing of his own ends in his Saints.

3. Learn hence a reason why the present sufferings of God's Children can neither argue against, nor yet prejudice their felicity: for the time is not yet come wherein they are to appear like themselves: *Joseph's*

prisoned condition, and prison robes set him never the further off from his preferment in *Pharaoh*'s Court; but were indeed the very harbingers of it: When the appointed time for the manifestation of the Sons of God shall come, he can fetch them out in hast, change them in the twinkling of an eye, and cloath them upon with all that excellency and splendid Glory, whereby, they who were but the other day lying among the pots, shall with their dazling lustre outshine the Sun in the Firmament. It is the Almighty's good pleasure, that their life, for the present, should be hid with Christ in God: But yet he hath his time, and will take his opportunity to reveal and make it known.

4. This teacheth us that the Glory of the sons of God must needs be wonderfully and astonishingly great: For why? Have they not already in hand, that which surpasses the knowledge of all the world, and which is in value transcendently more worth than all the Crowns and Kingdoms, and Gloryes of it? Do they not live upon, and satisfie their souls with marrow and fatness here, *Psal.* 63. 5. Are they not here replenished with the fatness of God's house? *Psal.* 36. 8. Who, but he that enjoys it, can declare what an happiness it is to enjoy peace with God, and fellowship with Christ, assurance of his love, and consolation of his spirit? Who, but he that hath felt it, can tell what it is to have the love of God shed abroad in his heart, and in his Soul to hear the sweet voice of Pardon, and promises of Glory? to ly all night in the bosom of Christ, and have his left hand underneath his head, and his right hand imbracing of him? And yet he that knows all this doth not know what he shall be: These are but the displayes of the outward Temple, or holy place; what then is to be seen in the holy of Holies? These are but drops, and rivulets which come in Pipes, and in little portions; how glorious a thing then must it needs be to dwel at the fountain, and swim for ever in those bankless, and bottomless Oceans of Glory? How happy then are the dead in Christ, who are now seeing, tasting, knowing and experiencing these things?

THE DEATH OF A SAINT

1. *When the Saints die let us mourn:* And there is no greater Argument to be found that we should excite our selves to mourn by, then the remembrance that they were *Saints:* it should more effect our hearts at the thoughts of this that they were *Saints*, then that they were our Father, or Mother, or Brethren, or nearest or dearest Friends, for this is that which makes their loss to be greater than any other Relation doth or can; others are natural, but these are pious Tears that

are shed upon this account: Another Man may be a private loss when
he is gone, his Family or his Neighbours, or Consorts may miss him;
but a *Saint*, though he be a private Christian, is yet, when he dies a,
publick loss, and deserves the *tears of Israel;* how much more than
when he hath been a Saint providentially put into a capacity of being,
and by Grace helpt and enabled to be a publick benefit by the Orb
he moved in? when a Saint *Dies* there is manifold ground of Mourning;
there is then a Pillar pluckt out of the Building, a Foundation Stone
taken out of the Wall, a Man removed out of the Gap; and now it
is to be greatly feared that God is departing, and *Calamities* are coming,
and are not these *things* to be lamented?

2. *When the Saints die beware of irregular Mourning:* though we are
to lament their Death, yet we must beware that it be after the right
manner: a dying Saint may say to his weeping Friends that stand
round about, wringing their hands, after the same Language that
Christ did to those weeping Women, *Luk.* 23. 27, 28, 29. *Daughters
of Jerusalem, weep not for me, but for your selves, and your Children,* &c.
It is we and not they that are indangered and endamaged by it: we
may therefore weep for our selves, and there is good reason for it,
but to mourn for them is superfluous. Is their Death precious in Gods?
let it not be miserable in our esteem: and tell me you whose hearts
throb, and eyes run over with sorrow, is it not a precious thing to
be asleep in Jesus? to ly in the lap of his providence, and rest from the
labours and sorrows of a troublesome World? to be laid out of the
noise of the whistling Winds, and feel none of the impetuosity of
those Storms and Tempests that are blowing abroad? to be out of the
sight and hearing of the rolling and dashing waves of the roaring Sea?
to sleep out the rest of the tempestuous night of this World, standing
in the inner Chamber of Gods Providence, in answer to that sweet
invitation? *Isai.* 26. 22. *Come my People, enter into thy Chambers, and
shut thy doors about thee,* &c. . . .

3. *Is the death of the Saints precious in Gods sight? let it be so in ours too.*
They are not to be accounted for contemptible things which God sets
an high value upon; and it is our wisdom to think and speak of persons and things as God doth: we ought not to slight the death of the
righteous, and speak meanly of it, as of a thing that is little momentous:
I am sure their arrival at Heaven is there taken notice of as a thing
worthy of observation; and shall not their departure be regarded?
they are welcomed into the Palace of delight with *Panegyricks;* and
shall then be hence dismissed with no more but a sorry saying, there
is now a good Man gone, and he will be missed in the Family, or

the Church to which he once belonged? we should embalm the memory of the Saints with the sweet smelling Spices that grew in their own Gardens, and pick the chiefest Flowers out of those Beds to strew their Graves withal; we should remember and make mention of them with honourable thoughts and words: and though it be now grown a Nickname of contempt among wicked and prophane Men, yet count it the most orient Jewel in their Crown, the most odoriferous and pleasant Flower in their Garland, that we can say of them that they lived and died Saints; all other Eschutcheons will either wear away, or be taken down, every other monument will become old, and grow over with the Moss of time, and their Titles, though cut in Brass, will be Canker-eaten and illegible: this onely will endure and be fresh and Flourishing, when Marble it self shall be turned into common dust.

Such an one it is whom we have now lost; and Oh that we knew how great a loss we have sustained in him! they are little things to be put into the account, and weigh but light in the commendations we have to give him; to say, This Government hath lost a Magistrate; this Town hath lost a good Benefactor; this Church hath lost an honourable Member; his Company hath lost a worthy Captain; his Family hath lost a loving and kind Husband, Father, Master; the Poor have lost a Liberal and Merciful Friend; that nature had furnished him with a sweet and affable Disposition, and even temper; that Providence had given him a prosperous and Flourishing Portion of this Worlds Goods; that the love and respect of the People had lifted him up to places of honour and preferment; this, this outshines them all; that he was a Saint upon Earth; that he lived like a Saint here, and died the precious Death of a Saint, and now is gone to rest with the Saints in glory: this hath raised those Relicks of his above common dust, and made them precious dust. When Conscience of duty stimulated me to perform my part of his Exequies, and put me upon it to do him honour at his Death; methoughts Justice required, and envy it self would not nibble at this Character: and if the Tree be to be known by its Fruits, his works shall praise him in the Gates: For his constant and close secret Communion with God (which none but Hypocrites are wont to do with the sound of a Trumpet) such as were most intimate with him, have known and can testifie: the care which he had to keep up constant Family Worship, in reading of the Scriptures, and praying in his Family (from which no business publick or private could divert him) was almost now unparalleld; the honourable respect he bore to God's holy Ordinances, by diligently attending upon them, and esteeming highly of God's Servants for their work sake, and care that he used to live the Truths which he heard from time to time, was very singular: the exemplariness of his Life and Converse among Men, and the endeavours which he used to shew forth the Graces of the Spirit, not being ashamed of Christ, nor being willing to be a shame unto him; let all that knew him bear witness of: his meek boldness in reproving Sin, and gentle faithfulness in endeavouring to win Sinners as he had opportunity, is known to such as lay in his way: His constancy in all these whiles times have changed, and many Professors have degenerated, when he strove to grow better as the times grew worse, will speak the sincerity of his Profession: his living above the World, and keeping his heart disentangled, and his mind in Heaven, in the midst of all outward occasions and urgency of Business, bespake him not to be of this World, but a Pilgrim on the Earth, a Citizen of Heaven: In a word, he was a true *Nathaniel*.

But God hath taken him from us, and by this stroak given us one more sad prognostick of misery a coming: when there are but a few Saints in the World, and those die apace too, what is to be thought to be at the door? I dare say his Death was precious in Gods sight, and he had some holy end in taking him away just now, who might probably have lived many years, and done much more service for God in his Generation: I shall not make it my work to Prophesie; the Lord grant we do not all know it too soon to our cost. Mean time let us have such in remembrance, and labour to be followers of them who through Faith and Patience do now inherit the promises, and that will be the best way to divert the Omen: Let us account the *Saints* precious whiles they live, and God will not begrutch them to us: but if we by contempt, obloquy, and wickedly grieving their *Righteous Souls*, make their lives a burden to them; if they cannot live in honour among Men, they shall die in favour with God, and he will make their death a precious gain to them, though it be a direful presage of a great inundation of sad Calamities coming upon those whom they leave behind them.

DEGENERATING NEW ENGLAND

I confess that it must be granted, that in the best times, and in places where the power of Godliness is most flourishing, there have been, and will be those that have not the fear of God before their eyes: there were so in the times of the greatest *Reformation* that we read of in the Book of God. In this world we must expect that

Wicked men will be mixed with the Godly, and such as will dare to shew their wickedness in their Lives, and not be afraid *to Transgress in a Land of Uprightness.* But when such are not countenanced, but due testimony is born against them; when they are contemned in the places where they live, and a note of infamy and scandal is put upon them; this will not be charged on such a people for *Apostasy:* But when such sins grow frequent, and those that have taken on themselves a name of being Religious, begin to indulge themselves herein; and men that allow themselves in such things are not *Reproached* for it, but are in as good Credit as the best, it then becomes a bad symptom, and saith that the times are declining and perilous. Much more when such as these will undertake to justify, and patronize such things: and are there not sad complaints made on this account? I shall here instance only in some that are more notorious. Are not Gods *Sabbaths* wofully neglected? How little care is there used in making of due preparation for them? How wofully can such as would be esteemed Godly, encroach upon holy time, and be engaged, either in secular business, or in vain Company, and possibly in publick houses, when they should be at home, in their Closets, or with their Families, Sanctifying of Gods day, and shewing of the *Honourable esteem* they have for it? And I am well satisfyed, that *where the strict Observation of Gods Sabbath is lost, there the Power of Godliness is gone.* How much complaint is there made of woful *Dishonesty* in their dealings, practised by such as can talk high of their Religion? How many fallacious tricks they can use in their Commerce? How deceitful in their Labour? How false to their words and promises? as if dissembling and lying were no reproach to the name of Christians. How many *Intemperate Church Members* are there reported to be, who spend their precious time in frequenting Publick Houses, and keeping of loose and lewd Company? who can come to the *Lords Table* on the Sabbath, and wrong themselves by excessive Drinking on the week days? How much *Animosity, Contention,* and implacable bitterness of Spirit, breaking forth in indecent words and carriages, between such as are bound in the strongest Evangelical ties to *Love one another, and meekly to bear with each others infirmities?* How much raising, spreading, and receiving of *Slanders* and *Defamations* one of another; contrary to that Charity which ought to *Cover a Multitude of sins?* These, and a great many more of like nature, . . . so far as they spread and prevail, and begin to grow common, are an ill Omen; for, they are indisputable denials of the power of Godliness, at least in the vigour of it, in those who are Guilty of them, for *that teacheth men to Live Soberly, Righteously and Godly.*

SAMUEL SEWALL, 1652–1730

[Samuel Sewall's father first came to New England in 1634, but returned to England, where Samuel was born. The family came back to New England after the Restoration. Samuel graduated from Harvard College in 1671 and was chosen fellow shortly afterwards; for a few years he hesitated between the ministry and a more secular calling, but his mind was made up for him when he married Hannah, the daughter of John Hull, the wealthiest man in the colony; from that time Sewall was a man of substance, with an estate to administer, and with leisure to devote to learned hobbies and the public service. He was manager of the colony's printing press, 1681–84, deputy in the General Court, 1683, a member of the council, 1684–86. In England in 1688, he was of assistance to Increase Mather in the charter negotiations. A member of the council under the new charter, 1692 to 1725; he was a judge in the special court at Salem which tried and executed the supposed witches, and he was of so heroic a mold that five years later he could make public acknowledgment of his error. A justice of the superior court in 1692, he was promoted to judge of probate for Suffolk County, 1715, and from 1718 to 1728 was chief justice of the colony. Sewall's literary fame rests upon his *Diary*, but in his lifetime he published several items. Meditating upon the evil of negro slavery, he wrote and published a small pamphlet, *The Selling of Joseph*, 1700, the first antislavery tract in America. His favorite study was that of Biblical prophecies and their fulfillments; this text is from one of his pamphlets on the meaning of the Book of Revelation, *Phænomena quædam Apocalyptica ad Aspectum Novi Orbis configurata. Or, some few Lines towards a description of the New Heaven As It makes to those who stand upon the New Earth* (Boston, 1697).]

PHÆNOMENA

CAPT. *John Smith* in his History published *Anno* 1624. affirms that he found *New-England* well inhabited with a goodly, strong, and well proportioned People. And the Proverb is, *Shew me the Man, and not the Meat.* And if men can be contented with the Food and Raiment intended in 1 *Tim.* 6. 8. they need not fear subsisting where *Ash, Chesnut, Hazel, Oak* & *Walnut* do naturally and plentifully grow. But for this, let Mr. *Morden* be consulted, to whom *N. E* is beholden for the fair Character given them in his Geographie. It is remarkable, that Mr. *Parker*, who was a successfull Schoolmaster at *Newbury* in *Barkshire*, in the happy days of Dr. *Twisse;* was much about this time preaching and Proving at *Ipswich* in *Essex*, That the Passengers came over upon good Grounds, and that GOD would multiply them as He did the Children of *Israel*. His Text was *Exod.* 1. 7. As Mr. *Nicolas Noyes*, who was an Auditor, and is yet living, lately informed me. Mr. *Parker* was at this time; 1634. principally concerned in beginning *Newbury*, where the Learned and Ingenious Mr. *Benjamin Woodbridge*, Dr. *Twisse's* Successor, had part of his Education under his Unckle *Parker*. *Mary Brown* (now *Godfry*) the First-born of *Newbury*, is yet alive; and is become the Mother and Grandmother of many children. And so many have been born after her in the Town, that they make two Assemblies, wherein GOD is solemnly worshipped every Sabbath Day. And

Besides all that have issued out to begin other Plantations.

As long as *Plum Island* shall faithfully keep the commanded Post; Notwithstanding all the hectoring Words, and hard Blows of the proud and boisterous Ocean; As long as any Salmon, or Sturgeon shall swim in the streams of *Merrimack;* or any Perch, or Pickeril, in *Crane-Pond;* As long as the Sea-Fowl shall know the Time of their coming, and not neglect seasonably to visit the Places of their Acquaintance: As long as any Cattel shall be fed with the Grass growing in the Medows, which do humbly bow down themselves before *Turkie-Hill;* As long as any Sheep shall walk upon *Old Town Hills*, and shall from thence pleasantly look down upon the River *Parker*, and the fruitfull *Marishes* lying beneath; As long as any free and harmless Doves shall find a White Oak, or other Tree within the Township, to perch, or feed, or build a careless Nest upon; and shall voluntarily present themselves to perform the office of Gleaners after Barley-Harvest; As long as Nature shall not grow Old and dote; but shall constantly remember to give the rows of Indian Corn their education, by Pairs: So long shall Christians be born there; and being first made meet, shall from thence be Translated, to be made partakers of the Inheritance of the Saints in Light.

Volume I

Chapter I—History

THOMAS SHEPARD

1. Shepard is referring to the years 1629 and 1630, when Parliament had been dissolved, the Laudians securely entrenched in power, and the outlook for Puritans apparently become hopeless; during these years "this great enterprise," the Massachusetts Bay Company, was formed and the migration undertaken. Shepard is writing eighteen years later when the Puritan and parliamentary cause seems to have triumphed, and he must remind his English critics how desperate the situation seemed in 1630.

2. These sentences summarize the intolerable dilemma which the Puritans confronted in 1630, when they were striving to reform the Church of England and yet at the same time not to separate from it or to allow themselves to be forced into the position of "schismatics." The "distinctions" by which Puritans strove to "salve" their consciences were those between the substance and accidents of a true church; they insisted that the Church of England was "true" in substantials, but corrupt in accidentals, such as the episcopal hierarchy. Since the authorities more and more insisted that the bishops and the rituals were essential to the Church of England, it became increasingly difficult for the Puritans to maintain their fine distinctions. The migration to Massachusetts was the only solution for this problem except open revolution.

JOHN WINTHROP

1. Isaac Allerton (1586–1659), an original member of the Plymouth group, the business man and financier of the colony; he later became engaged in somewhat shady trading deals and withdrew from Plymouth to New Haven.

2. John Endecott (1589–1665), governor of the outpost at Salem, continued to be one of the magistrates after Win-

throp's arrival, and after Winthrop's death was several times governor; a stern Puritan of the most uncompromising variety, he cut down the Maypole at Merry Mount, caused Winthrop and the government considerable embarrassment when he cut the red cross out of the English flag because it was a Popish emblem, and as governor wrote his name in blood by his persecution of the Quakers.

3. Samuel Skelton (1584–1634), the colleague of Francis Higginson in the ministry of the church at Salem.

4. Nahumkeck was the Indian name for Salem.

5. Winthrop always speaks of himself in the third person.

6. Sir Henry Vane (1613–1662), son of a member of the Privy Council, came to Boston in 1635, and was elected governor in 1636 as a tribute rather to his high social station and influential connections than to his wisdom or experience. His conduct in New England exhibits the worst side of his erratic character; in his subsequent career he was to reveal more lofty and more courageous qualities, though he always was an incurable idealist and visionary, winning the admiration of John Milton and the scorn of Oliver Cromwell. Though not a Regicide, he was leader of the most radical republican sentiment among the Puritans, opposed the Restoration, and was executed on Tower Hill in 1662.

7. Hugh Peter (1598–1660), a vigorous and pugnacious Puritan, one of the first investors in the Massachusetts Bay Company, came to New England in 1635 and was established as minister at Salem, where he reorganized the church shattered by Roger Williams's heresies. He returned to England in 1641 and had a spectacular career as an Independent minister, army chaplain, and rabble-rouser; so conspicuous did he become that upon the Restoration he was executed, though he, like Vane, had not been an actual Regicide.

8. Thomas Dudley (1576–1653), sec-

ond in command to Winthrop, a former soldier and steward to the earl of Lincoln; he was governor in 1634, 1640, 1645, and 1650. A hard, single-minded man, he represents, as against Winthrop, the narrower and harsher features of early Puritanism.

9. See account of John Wilson (1588–1667), p. 552.

10. John Haynes (1594–1654), a man of substance from Essex, came to New England in the same ship with Hooker and Cotton; governor of Massachusetts in 1635, he was a follower of Hooker, moved to Connecticut in 1637, was chosen first governor of Connecticut and served in that office every alternate year until his death.

11. Though perhaps disguised to modern ears by the technical theological jargon, the purport of these opinions is fairly clear. The standard Protestant doctrine was that men were saved by their faith in Christ, not by their works, that Christ had fulfilled the law, satisfied the vengeance of God, and that His righteousness was "imputed" to the saints for their salvation. The legal imputation of Christ's virtue to the credit of man was called "justification"; that is, a man was justified before the tribunal of God because Christ had satisfied God's indictment against him. A justified man was expected thereafter to conduct himself in a Christian manner, or at least to strive to do so; his conduct, after his justification, was called his "sanctification." According to the orthodox view, in the moment of justification the regenerate man received an ability to pursue more or less perfectly a sanctified course of life. The evocation of such an ability was understood to be a work of the Holy Ghost. At the same time, though the impetus might come from the Divine Spirit, though a spiritual power might be thus conveyed into the soul, the individuality of the saint was deemed inviolate, and his effort toward sanctification was to proceed from his own exertions. Regeneration, so to speak, took off the chains that bound a man in sin; thereafter he was to labor as an individual, under the guidance of his own intelligence, to fulfill the law of God.

The theory of Mrs. Hutchinson, though seeming close to the orthodox version, was of a vitalistic, mystical character; by maintaining that "the Holy Ghost dwells in a justified person" she concluded that the saint in the moment of justification received an influx of energy which overwhelmed and obliterated his individuality, carrying him along on a wave of ecstasy; consequently she argued that it made no difference whether he achieved any sanctification whatsoever, that his good or bad conduct cast no light on his salvation, which was a matter entirely of inward spiritual ravishment. Whatever virtues he achieved in his life were not wrought by his own volition, but by the power of the divine spirit working in him. He was merely to surrender his will to the promptings and propulsions from within. In Winthrop's eyes, these doctrines led to the abandonment of all individual moral responsibility, to an ethical anarchy and an uncontrollable self-righteousness which might have very dangerous social consequences.

12. John Wheelwright (1592–1679), B.A., Sidney Sussex College, Cambridge, 1615; M.A., 1618. A brother-in-law of Anne Hutchinson, he emigrated to New England in 1636. After his banishment in 1637 he founded Exeter, New Hampshire; returned to England, 1656–1662; his sentence revoked by the Massachusetts government, he came back to New England and served as minister at Salisbury, 1662–1679.

13. I.e., Winthrop, in this year serving as deputy-governor.

14. I.e., John Wilson. For the distinction between "pastor" and "teacher," see p. 386.

15. Newtown was the original name for Cambridge.

16. According to the Congregational theory of church polity, a synod was not a legislative body, but merely a gathering of learned men for the purposes of discussion and clarification; their decisions were theoretically not binding upon any particular congregation unless the congregation chose to endorse them. Presbyterian Puritans, who upheld the compulsory power of synods (hence Milton's line, "New Presbyter is but Old Priest

writ large"), had criticized the Congregational polity for its lack of a central controlling power, and had predicted that in a crisis the Congregational churches would fall apart. In such works as Shepard and Allin's *Defence of the Answer*, the Congregationalists insisted that the Word of God was so clear that when the ministers would gather to formulate its teachings the results of their deliberations would win instant consent from all right-minded men. In 1637 the majority of the church of Boston were devoted to Mrs. Hutchinson, and upon the success or failure of the synod in bringing that church to the true doctrine depended the success or failure of the whole Bible Commonwealth. When the Antinomians refused to accept the conclusions of the synod the government was compelled to step in and proceed against them as persons opposing the obvious and explicit principles of the true religion. As long as the "advisory" synods of New England were thus backed by the force of the civil authority, they were able to keep the churches in line; after the charter was repealed and the government was no longer willing to enforce Congregational uniformity, the churches were left to their own devices.

17. John Davenport (1597–1670), along with Cotton and Hooker one of the most powerful of New England ministers, came to Boston in 1635, led his followers to New Haven, which colony he dominated until its unification with Connecticut; he then accepted a call from the First Church of Boston, 1668, where his coming precipitated a quarrel that split the church.

18. The formidable list of these errors is in Charles Francis Adams, *Antinomianism in the Colony of Massachusetts Bay* (Boston, 1894), pp. 95–124.

19. The contention that the charter of the Massachusetts Bay Company gave the government power to settle all cases without the possibility of an appeal to the King's courts was certainly unjustified; yet it was doggedly maintained and was the principal reason for the virtual independence enjoyed by the colony of Massachusetts Bay until the charter was revoked in 1684.

20. From the orthodox point of view, Mrs. Hutchinson's admission that she believed she had received special revelations direct from God was proof positive that she had been inspired by evil powers; the canon of revelation was believed closed with the book of Revelation, and though God might continue to betray his wishes and commands in the government of the world and the disposition of particular events, no mortal was any longer to receive commands from Him in so many words. If the possibility of continued revelation from God direct to individuals had been admitted, any man or woman might have claimed divine sanction for any conceivable notion.

21. The scene here described must have been the most dramatic and tragic in the history of New England: Mrs. Hutchinson, arraigned before the church, most of the congregation having been her followers in the beginning of the struggle but now turned against her through the masterful strategy of John Winthrop and the pressure of outside opinion, hearing the sentence pronounced against her by her beloved minister, John Cotton, upon whose words she had hung in England, whom she had followed to New England, and from whom she believed she had derived her teachings. John Cotton's role in the drama leaves much to be explained. If he did not actually proclaim what Mrs. Hutchinson thought he did, he must have used many incautious phrases, and when the storm had gathered he abandoned her entirely. His condemning her before the whole congregation must have been for her like turning the knife in a wound. His position at the moment was extremely precarious, and it was only by his opportune bending to the victorious party and his carrying out their sentence against Anne Hutchinson that he retained his influence in the community. For a moment during the crisis he meditated moving to New Haven; Roger Williams later accused him of contemplating a "separation" from the churches of Massachusetts, and Cotton endeavored to defend himself in what is one of the lamest apologies ever penned by a righteous man (*Master John Cotton's*

Answer to Master Roger Williams, ed. J. Lewis Diman, *Publications of the Narragansett Club,* II, 79–85).

22. The moderation of the militia on this occasion is a tribute to the moral power of religion among the rank and file of the first generation; it was almost unprecedented in the days of "Merrie England" for a thousand Englishmen to gather in one place without drunkenness or quarrelling. By the end of the century the ministers were unanimously complaining that training days were anything but occasions for sober drill.

23. The servant's reply is the closest approach to the humorous in the *Journal,* but to the aristocratic Winthrop the remark did not appear funny, for he wrote in the margin of his manuscript, "insolent."

24. The synod of 1648 drew up the final codification of the New England church polity in *The Cambridge Platform.*

EDWARD JOHNSON

1. Reference to manner in which it was required by law in England that Sunday should be celebrated; in 1618 James I published a declaration permitting dancing, archery, May games, and other sports on Sundays; Charles I endeavored to force the clergy to read this "Booke of Sports" from their pulpits. Many Puritan clergymen were suspended for refusing.

2. The fleeing ministers were disguised as seamen in order to escape from the Court of High Commission, before which many of them were indicted for nonconformity.

3. The "Lady Arrabella," Arbella Johnson, daughter of the earl of Lincoln; she and her husband, Isaac Johnson, sailed with the fleet in 1630, the flagship being named in her honor. They were the wealthiest of the emigrants; both died within a few months of the landing.

4. John Norton (1606–1663), B.A., Peterhouse, Cambridge, 1624; M.A., 1627; came to New England with Shepard in 1635; was ordained teacher at Ipswich; called to the First Church of Boston to succeed Cotton, 1652; along with Governor Endecott he was the leader of

the persecution of the Quakers; in 1662 he went as agent for the colony to England, failed to get the expected results, and died an unpopular man.

5. Münster, a town in Germany in which there was a famous outbreak of Anabaptists in 1534; these Anabaptists, convinced that they were God's chosen people, attempted to set up a reign of the saints by putting all the unregenerate to the sword. Münster was a byword for the horrors of direct inspiration, and the possibility that Anne Hutchinson's followers might resort to the Anabaptists' tactics was always present in the minds of the Massachusetts authorities.

6. Cambridge.

7. A slur upon the English army under Cromwell, which, being recruited from many sects, was enforcing a policy of toleration in England at the time Johnson was writing.

COTTON MATHER

1. Persons born in America of European race; a word used at this time most frequently in the West Indies, so that Mather means in particular students coming to Harvard from the West Indies.

2. "Drove forth the eminent pious heroes to withstand so many misfortunes, to undertake so many labors," Vergil, *Aeneid,* I, 9, slightly altered.

3. John Foxe (1516–1587), English Protestant, author of *Acts and Monuments of these latter and perillous Dayes,* in Latin, 1559; in English, 1563; written in exile at Strasbourg during the reign of Queen Mary, the book is a chronicle of the sufferings and martyrdoms of English Protestants. It was read thoroughly by all Puritans of the seventeenth century.

4. John Wyckliffe (*c.* 1320–1384), medieval reformer, who attacked the corruption of the medieval clergy, the supremacy of the Pope, asserted the supremacy of the scriptures as a rule of faith, attacked the theory of transubstantiation; he was regarded by Protestants as a forerunner of the Reformation.

5. Peter Heylin (1600–1662), Anglican clergyman, chaplain to Charles I, violent partisan of Laud, and embittered foe of Puritanism.

6. John Owen (1616–1683), leading Independent minister, chaplain to Cromwell, Vice-Chancellor of Oxford, 1651–1659, minister of a non-conformist church in London after the Restoration. He was invited to come to New England, was a friend and correspondent of many of the New England divines, though in 1669 he wrote to New England reproving the churches for their persecution of Quakers. Reference to *Inquiry concerning Evangelical Churches*, *Works*, ed. Gold, XV, 209.

7. "That they acknowledge themselves never to be perfect."

8. "He calls her fair, not absolutely, but fair among women, that is to say with a distinction, so that she may thereby be more restrained, and may know her deficiencies."

9. For Ramus and his influence in New England see Introduction, pp. 28–39.

10. "Among the many favours with which you have enriched me, this I shall keep in remembrance, which thanks to you I learned through your reply at Poissey, that of the fifteen centuries since Christ, the first is truly golden and that the rest, the further they are removed the more they are wretched and degenerate; therefore when I had free choice, I preferred the golden age." This was the famous statement by which Ramus publicly announced his conversion to Protestantism, 1561.

11. "Remote regions."

12. "Outer darkness."

13. James Howell (c. 1594–1666), author of *Epistolae Ho-Elianae*.

14. "An anthology."

15. "History is the witness of time, the messenger of antiquity, the light of truth, the life of memory, the magistrate of life" (Cicero, *De Oratore*, II, 9.)

16. "Rather to be admired than imitated."

17. "A pleasant, faithful and accurate writer." Justus Lipsius (1547–1606), a humanist, scholar, and editor, who chiefly devoted himself to making available the teachings of classical Stoicism.

18. "Sweeter than honey." Photius was patriarch of Constantinople, ninth century; Colerus is Johann Coler, German theologian of the sixteenth century.

19. "A prudent writer, if ever there was one."

20. "Seems to have surpassed all Greek and Latin authors."

21. "In him alone (to speak of historians) the Roman people had a genius worthy of their empire."

22. "Great wars, the storming of cities, kings put to flight and captured."

23. Probably a grammarian of Alexandria at the end of the first century.

24. "Historians are to be read with moderation and kindness, and it is to be remembered that they can not be in all circumstances like Lynceus."

25. Louis Aubery, Seigneur du Maury, d. 1687.

26. "History is the narrative of great actions with praise or blame."

27. "I believe it is the principal function of history not to be silent respecting virtues, and to hold up before depravity, both in word and deed, the dread of infamy with posterity."

28. The name sometimes applied to himself by Claude Saumaise, or Salmasius (1588–1653), the learned scholar with whom Milton disputed.

29. Virgilius of Salzburg was condemned by Pope Zachary, 745, for a treatise on the Antipodes contending that there is another world underneath the earth.

30. Konrad Schlüsselberg (1543–1619), Lutheran theologian.

31. "It is most proper to History, to praise eminent deeds."

32. Professor Murdock interprets this obscure phrase as the equivalent of our "fail to see the woods for the trees."

33. Daniel Chaumier (c. 1570–1621), André Rivet (1573–1651), French Calvinist writers.

34. Howell, *Epistolae*, Bk. 1, Sect. 4, Letter xxi.

35. "It is offensive to God when anyone who is like him, excelling in virtue, is dishonoured, or praise given to the contrary."

36. Jacques Auguste de Thou (1553–1617), French historian.

37. "Much that is most false and unworthy."

38. "The simplest style of writing."

39. "Memoirs of ecclesiastical transactions."

40. "Just as salt discreetly sprinkled on food flavors it, and adds to the pleasure of the relish, so if you mingle a little of antiquity, the oration is made more lovely."

41. "I beg pardon for this self-praise."

42. "Every writer is in error about his own writings."

43. Professor Murdock indicates the explanation for this sentence in a passage from William Lambarde, *Perambulation of Kent* (1570), ed. 1826, p. 233: "Our speech at this day (for the most part) consisteth of words of one sillable. Which thing Eramus observing, merily in his Ecclesiast, compareth the English toong to a Dogs barking, that soundeth nothing els, but Baw, waw, waw, in Monosillable."

44. "In a long work."

45. "Before speaking of the thing, a little about myself."

46. "Deliver me from a man of one occupation."

47. "Mistakes."

48. "Egostistical discourse."

49. "He was so incapable of envy that if he came upon any elegant expression of another's it pleased him not less than if it had been his own."

50. I.e., members of the High-Church party in the Church of England.

51. Heinrich Cornelius Agrippa (1487–1535), attacked by the Inquisition for his *De Vanitate et Incertitude Scientiorum*, 1531.

52. "Happy he whom the Lord signalized with this honor, that he may have the most evil men for his enemies."

53. "This I wish, now my verse pleases me" (Martial, *Epig.* VI, 61. 4).

54. A play on words, roughly thus: "He received the stones, to whom Christ was a rock." An example of the bad taste of which Cotton Mather was too capable.

55. Wyckliffe's epitaph, Speed, *History*, ed. 1614, p. 610, or Fuller, *Church History*, ed. 1837, I, 494: "The Devells Instrument, Churches Enemy, Peoples Confusion, Hereticks Idoll, Hypocrites Mirrour, Schismes Broacher, Hatreds Sower, Lyes Forger. Flatteries Sinke: who at his death despaired like Cain,

and stricken by the horrible judgment of God, breathed forth his wicked soule to the dark mansion of the black devell."

56. Reference to Solomon Stoddard and the ministers of the Connecticut valley under his leadership, who at the time Mather wrote were inaugurating a change in the church polity whereby all persons in a town not openly scandalous should not only be admitted to the church but also brought to both sacraments. In the next decade Stoddard and the Mathers carried on an acrimonious pamphlet controversy about this question.

57. James Ussher (1581–1656), Anglican clergyman of Calvinistic tenets, Archbishop of Armaugh, a leading moderate who strove to reconcile Anglicans and Puritans and was thoroughly respected by his Puritan opponents.

58. Stephen Marshall (1594–1655), English Puritan, advocate of the Presbyterian polity, but of a more moderate sort than the Scotch variety.

59. Jeremiah Burroughs (1594–1655), Independent divine, a spokesman along with John Owen for Cromwell's policy of toleration.

60. "No one is more oppressive than the ignorant man, because he thinks nothing done correctly unless he does it himself," Terence, *Adelphi*, ll. 98–99.

61. "What am I? Nothing. Who am I? No one. But the Grace of Christ makes what I am, what I live, what I do."

Chapter II—The State and Society

JOHN WINTHROP

1. Reference to the followers of Peter Waldo (fl. 1170) in the Piedmont, a medieval sect that resisted the authority of Rome in the thirteenth and fourteenth centuries and ultimately became merged with the Protestants; they were of great value in Protestant polemic because they could always be cited as an example of a pure and true church existing before Luther and supplying a long tradition for Protestantism.

2. Winthrop is here using one of the favorite arguments of the non-separating Congregational theorists, the contention that the Reformed Churches of the Con-

Notes

tinent and the Church of England were "true" churches, even though they maintained a Presbyterian or Episcopalian form of government; the imperfections of their government were to be regarded as unfortunate handicaps which eventually they were certain to overcome, because if they really lived up to their profession of basing their religion upon the Bible they would inevitably reorganize their churches according to the Congregational plan. Therefore, Winthrop is arguing, the settlers of New England, still members of the Church of England and maintaining fellowship with the Protestant Churches of Europe, will realize in America what the others profess but do not yet practice.

3. Note the extension of the doctrine of the covenant between God and the individual saint to include also a theoretical covenant between God and the people as a whole. The doctrine was the foundation for the Puritan theory of social cohesion, of the unified society bound together as one man by an irrevocable covenant with God Himself.

4. In the Congregational polity only those were admitted who could give evidence before the congregation that they bore the visible marks of regeneration upon them.

5. A reference to the heresy broached by Roger Williams two years before. With characteristic generosity, Winthrop is insinuating that in spite of his errors Williams might still be a genuine Christian (cf. Bradford's similar judgment, p. 111), though Winthrop is clear that Williams's errors merited banishment, however holy Williams himself might be.

6. Winthrop here witnesses the first stirrings of libertarian sentiments among the people and the emergence of the purely political attitude toward fundamental law that was ultimately to replace the more complex religious theory of the dual origin of government in the social compact and in the divine covenant.

7. The result of this action was the "Body of Liberties," drawn up by Nathaniel Ward and adopted by the General Court in 1641.

JOHN COTTON

1. William Perkins (1558–1602), one of the greatest of English Calvinists, fellow of Christ's College, Cambridge, influential preacher and pamphleteer; his works were read throughout Protestant countries and in New England.

2. "In order towards things spiritual."

3. "I speak of the plenitude of scripture."

4. "Vigour."

5. "More unseemly to be ejected than not to be admitted."

6. Jean Bodin (1530–1596), French political philosopher.

7. John Robinson, pastor of the Scrooby congregation; being a Separatist and a leader of the most extreme Congregationalists, Robinson might be expected to stress the more democratic features of the polity; hence the effectiveness of Cotton's insisting, first, that by the principles of a purely secular theorist, Bodin, Congregational theory is not democratic, and second, that even by its most radical exponent it is not made into a popular government.

ROGER WILLIAMS

1. "I have liberated my soul."

2. Cotton wrote this statement of the orthodox position in answer to questions addressed to him by a Baptist; the paper fell into Williams's hands and he used it as the text to be refuted in *The Bloudy Tenent*, by means of a dialogue between "Truth" and "Peace."

NATHANIEL WARD

1. "Labour with straddlings."

2. Paracelsus (1490–1541), the famous German physician, had the reputation for being an honest and good but misguided man; he was frequently cited in religious controversy as the supreme example of a well-meaning but dangerous person.

3. True religion is "the fire of proof" which doth "unite the homogeneous and separate the heterogeneous."

4. "The most generic genus."

5. "No evil is worse than liberty for the erring."

6. "Without violation of the state."

7. A "low country," i.e. Holland, where a certain toleration of various Protestant sects was permitted; Holland was a commercial rival of England at the time Ward was writing, and his scornful reference was an appeal to English prejudices.

8. I.e., nothing in the world exists any further than Truth gives it its existence; Truth itself is better than any entity or any good thing, because any created thing derives its being from Truth, and is therefore Truth's "twin."

9. A small javelin.

10. "Mode of speaking."

11. "In what gender."

12. "To speak truth laughing, what hinders?"

13. Traditional formulas for the assents of the King and of the House of Lords to an act of Parliament.

14. Catholic theologians.

15. "No occasion opposes the King."

16. "No occasion assists the King."

17. "In the forum of right reason"; i.e., the prerogatives of the King and the liberties of the subject are so old that they were originally formulated in the Norman or ancient British language, but their validity rests not upon even the most ancient tradition, but upon the dictates of right reason, for time, from the point of view of eternal truth, is a conception as empty of significance as a New England purse is empty of money.

JONATHAN MITCHELL

1. Mitchell's long analysis of the plight of Israel in the days of Nehemiah is clearly a discussion of the condition of New England in 1667; this sermon illustrates the fashion in which New England theorists maintained the exact analogy of the Lord's people in New England with the chosen people of the Old Testament, and therefore endeavored to apply the social and political precedents of Palestine to America.

2. A reference to the charges being levied against Puritan New England by Anglicans and Royalists after the Restoration.

JOHN WISE

1. Reference to the platform for the attempted unification of the Independent and Presbyterian churches drawn up in London, 1690. Increase Mather, then in England negotiating for the charter, had assisted in the preparation of this declaration, and he and Cotton were constantly citing it in an effort to prove to English and European Protestants that the New England way was not a peculiar or provincial system. Consequently enemies of the Mathers found it strategic to quote to the London ministers against the Mathers whenever possible; the founders of the Brattle Street Church and Solomon Stoddard had already shown Wise the advantage of this maneuver.

2. Samuel Pufendorf, 1632–1694, German theologian and philosopher, author of De Jure Naturæ et Gentium, one of the chief sources for eighteenth-century conceptions of natural law; it was translated into English by Basil Kennett, 1703. Wise leans heavily upon it throughout his argument.

3. Probably Archibald Johnston, Lord Warrington, Scottish judge and statesman.

4. Note that at this point Wise is simply setting aside all consideration of man as basically corrupted and inherently depraved, thus marking his departure from traditional Puritan theology.

5. Compare this statement with Winthrop's theory (p. 207), in which divine grace must assist reason before man can submit himself to the rule of justice and equity.

JOHN BARNARD

1. "From the divine King"; "Is it not from Zeus?"

2. John Tillotson (1630–1694), Archbishop of Canterbury, famous preacher of the moderate Anglican party, led the movement toward the simple, clear style in pulpit oratory and toward common-sense ethics and comprehensible teaching instead of theological complexities and intricate doctrines; that Barnard should quote Tillotson was equivalent to wearing the badge of the liberal school of thought.

Chapter III—This World and the Next

JOHN COTTON

1. See note, p. 766, for the distinction between justification and sanctification. It was probably Cotton's preaching in the vein represented by this passage that led Mrs. Hutchinson to conclude that sanctification or righteous behavior had nothing to do with whether or not one was saved, and from Cotton's strong insistence upon considering the motives from which good conduct springs rather than the goodness of the actions themselves she derived the dangerous idea that the quality of one's actions was of no consequence and that all one need be concerned about was being informed with the true spirit.

INCREASE MATHER

1. Such examples also give point to Hooker's remarks on the attitude of converted sinners toward the ministers who have wrought their repentance, pp. 309–314.

2. Dr. Thomas Goodwin (1600–1680), Independent divine, a leader of the Independent party in the Westminster Assembly, friend of Cotton and Davenport.

3. Franz Junius (1545–1602), French Huguenot divine.

4. Mather's admission that eclipses of the sun and moon follow a regular and "unfailable" course and therefore may be predicted with certainty, with his restriction of God's unpredictable actions to the realm of "contingent things," indicates the beginning of clerical concessions to the scientific account of the universe.

5. Waldo and Waldenses, cf. note p. 770.

6. St. Augustine.

URIAN OAKES

1. "Bread for Belisarius."

2. "An honest good," i.e., intrinsically good; "an expedient good," i.e., conducible to good.

3. Dr. John Preston (1587–1628), famous Puritan divine and leader, Master of Emmanuel College, 1622; he exerted a profound influence on the first generation of New England Puritans, many of whom studied under him at Cambridge, all of whom read his works; from his sermons the New England ministers derived the particular features of their doctrine of the Covenant of Grace.

4. "We came, we saw, we conquered" —a paraphrase of Caesar's famous message.

5. Reference to King Philip's War, 1674–1676, in which the male population of New England was decimated.

JOSHUA MOODY

1. Reference to the battle tactics employed at the period, when reloading took time; troops were drawn up in three ranks, the first firing at the command "discharge," retiring to the rear to load their weapons at the command "fall off"; the second rank would then fire and retire, the third in turn, and the first rank be back in action once more.

I. HISTORICAL BACKGROUND

Inevitably a bibliography in which so many divisions obtain must occasionally seem arbitrarily constructed. Additional historical items will be found in Sections IV (Manners) and V (Biography). From the earliest times New England has been more felicitously interpreted by historians than by any other single group. The number of important studies, from those of Thomas Hutchinson to those of Charles McL. Andrews, runs to a formidable length.

A. Primary Sources

Only sources of colonial history which deal with the Puritan colonies have been included.

Acts and Resolves, Public and Private, of the Province of the Massachusetts Bay, The, Boston, 1869–1922, 21 vols. (Records from 1691.)

Andrews, Charles McL., ed., *Narratives of the Insurrections, 1675–1690,* Original Narratives Series, New York, 1915; 1959.

Bartlett, John R., ed., *Records of the Colony of Rhode Island and Providence Plantations, in New England,* Providence, 1856–1865, 10 vols.

Bishop, George, *New-England Judged, Not by Man's, but the Spirit of the Lord,* London, 1661. Second part, London, 1667. Both parts, London, 1703. (Quaker attack on the Puritan regime.)

Bradford, William, "A Description and Historical Account of New England in verse; from a MS.," *Collections of the Massachusetts Historical Society,* first series, III (1794), 77–84.

—— *History of Plymouth Plantation, 1606–1646.* First printed in *Collections of the Massachusetts Historical Society,* fourth series, III (1856); the best edition is that of Worthington C. Ford, Boston, 1912; in Original Narratives Series, ed. William T. Davis, New York, 1908; 1959. Cf. *Of Plymouth Plantation,* ed., Samuel Eliot Morison with a "Modern (*not* modernized) text," notes, and an extended introduction. New York, 1952.

Calder, Isabel M., ed., *Colonial Captivities, Marches and Journeys,* New York, 1935.

Child, Major John, *New-Englands Jonas cast up at London,* London, 1647. Reprinted

in *Collections of the Massachusetts Historical Society,* second series, IV (1816), 107–120.

Church, Benjamin, *Entertaining Passages Relating to Philip's War which Began in the Month of June, 1675,* Boston, 1716. Frequently reprinted; ed. Henry M. Dexter, Boston, 1865–1867, 2 vols.

Clarke, John, *Ill News from New-England; Or, A Narative of New-Englands Persecution,* London, 1652; reprinted in *Collections of the Massachusetts Historical Society,* fourth series, II (1854), 1–113. (An attack upon orthodox Puritanism by an Anabaptist.)

Donnan, Elizabeth, ed., *Documents Illustrative of the History of the Slave Trade to America,* Washington, 1930–1935, 4 vols. (Vol. I, 1441–1700; important contribution to colonial economic history.)

Dow, George F., ed., *Records and Files of the Quarterly Courts of Essex County, Massachusetts* [*1636–1692*], Salem, 1911–1921, 8 vols.

Drake, Samuel G., ed., *The Old Indian Chronicle; being a Collection of Exceeding Rare Tracts,* Boston, 1836.

Dreuillettes, Father Gabriel, "Narrative of a Journey to New England, 1650," *The Jesuit Relations and Allied Documents . . . 1610–1791* (ed. Reuben G. Thwaites, Cleveland, 1896–1901, 73 vols.) XXXVI, 83–111.

Dudley, Thomas, "Letter to the Countess of Lincoln," in Joshua Scottow, *Massachusetts,* pp. 36–47; Boston, 1696; also in *Collections of the Massachusetts Historical*

Society, first series, Vol. VIII (1802); *Collections of the New Hampshire Historical Society*, Vol. IV (1834), 224–249; Force, *Tracts*, Vol. II, No. 4; Young, *Chronicles of the First Planters*. (Written in the first year of the settlement, the latter remains fresh and vivid with the very flavor of the early months.)

Force, Peter, *Tracts and Other Papers Relating Principally to the Origin, Settlement, and Progress of the Colonies in North America*, Washington, 1836–1846, 4 vols; New York, 1947.

Foxcroft, Thomas, *Observations Historical and Practical, on the Rise and Primitive State of New-England*, Boston, 1730. (Celebration of the first centennial of Massachusetts Bay.)

Gookin, Daniel, "An Historical Account of the Doings and Sufferings of The Christian Indians in New England, in the years 1675, 1676, 1677," *Transactions and Collections of the American Antiquarian Society*, II (1836), 423–534.

—— *Historical Collections of the Indians in New England* (preface dated 1674), Boston, 1792; also in *Collections of the Massachusetts Historical Society*, first series, I (1792), 141–227.

Gorton, Samuel, *Simplicities Defence against Seven-Headed Policy*, London, 1646; Force, *Tracts*, Vol. IV (1846), No. 6. (A heated but inchoate onslaught upon the Puritan regime by a religious visionary.)

Groome, Samuel, *A Glass For the People of New-England*, London, 1676; reprinted in *Magazine of History*, XXXVII (1929), No. 3, 1–44. (A Quaker tract against the Massachusetts Bay Colony.)

Haller, William, ed., *The Leveller Tracts, 1647–1653*, New York, 1944.

Hart, Albert B., ed., *American History Told by Contemporaries*, New York, 1897–1929, 5 vols. (Vols. I and II cover the Puritan period.)

Higginson, Francis, *New-England Plantation; Or, A Short and True Description of the Commodities and Discommodities of that Countrey*, London, 1630; *Collections of the Massachusetts Historical Society*, first series, I (1792), 117–124; Force, *Tracts*, Vol. I, No. 12; Young, *Chronicles*, pp. 239–267, with introduction; *Proceedings of the Massachusetts Historical Society*, LXII (1930), 301–321. (Written by the first

minister at Salem, who came with the advance guard in 1629; the initial reactions of Englishmen to the new scene.)

—— *A True Relacion of the Last Voyage to New England*, MS. prepared 1629; first printed in Hutchinson, *A Collection of Papers*, Boston, 1769; also in Young, *Chronicles*, pp. 213–239; *Proceedings of the Massachusetts Historical Society*, LXII (1930), 281–299. (Journal of the voyage of the advance contingent of the Massachusetts Bay Colony in 1629.)

Hoadly, Charles J., ed., *Records of the Colony and Plantation of New Haven, from 1638 to 1649*, Hartford, 1857.

—— *Records of the Colony or Jurisdiction of New Haven, from May, 1653, to the Union*, Hartford, 1858.

Howgil, Francis, *The Popish Inquisition Newly Erected in New-England*, London, 1659. (Quaker attack on New England orthodoxy.)

Hubbard, William, *A General History of New-England, from the Discovery to MDCLXXX*. First printed from MS. in *Collections of the Massachusetts Historical Society*, second series, Vols. V–VI (1815); best edd., Boston, 1848, 1878. (Written in 1680 at the request of and by subsidy from the General Court, it is based chiefly on Bradford and Winthrop, but inserts some items not found elsewhere. It was used by Cotton Mather and Thomas Prince in compiling their histories.)

—— *A Narrative of the Troubles with the Indians In New-England*, Boston, 1677; ed. Samuel G. Drake, Roxbury, Mass., 1865, 2 vols.

Hutchinson, Thomas, comp., *A Collection of Original Papers Relative to the History of the Colony of Massachusets-Bay*, Boston, 1769; reprinted Albany, 1865, 2 vols. (An invaluable collection, containing documents of fundamental importance, the originals of which were lost at the time of the Revolution.)

Jensen, Merrill, ed., *English Historical Documents*, Vol. IX; *American Colonial Documents to 1776*, New York, 1955. (Contains basic documents and a useful bibliography of both primary and secondary works relating to American colonial history, 1607–1776.)

Johnson, Edward, *A History of New-England. From the English planting in the*

Yeere 1628, untill the Yeere 1652 . . . [better known by its running-title:] *The Wonder-working Providence of Sions Saviour in New England*, London, 1654; ed. William F. Poole, Andover, Mass., 1867; *Collections of the Massachusetts Historical Society*, second series, Vols. II, III, IV, VII, VIII (1814–1819); reprinted, 1826, 1846; ed. J. F. Jameson, Original Narratives Series, New York, 1910; 1959. (A history of the migration and first two decades of settlement, written by a layman, a militia captain, and a settler of the town of Woburn. It is valuable in that it represents the point of view of the rank and file, although in a florid style not characteristically Puritan.)

Josselyn, John, *An Account of Two Voyages to New-England*, London, 1675; reprinted in *Collections of the Massachusetts Historical Society*, third series, III (1833), 211–354. (Not a Puritan, the author is sometimes refreshingly critical of men and manners.)

—— *New-Englands Rarities Discovered: in Birds, Beasts, Fishes, Serpents, and Plants of that Country*, London, 1672; reprinted, ed. E. Tuckerman, *Transactions and Collections of the American Antiquarian Society*, IV (1860), 133–238.

Lechford, Thomas, "Note-Book Kept by Thomas Lechford, Esq., Lawyer, In Boston, Massachusetts Bay, From June 27, 1638, to July 29, 1641," ed. E. E. Hale, *Transactions and Collections of the American Antiquarian Society*, Vol. VII (1885). (Lechford, no Puritan, was a lawyer who came to Massachusetts to make a living; he could not overcome the Puritan prejudice against lawyers, and was debarred for trying to influence a jury. Leaving wife and goods, he returned to England. An invaluable firsthand record of daily life in New England.)

—— *Plain Dealing; Or, Newes from New-England*, London, 1642; reissued in 1644 with a new title; printed in *Collections of the Massachusetts Historical Society*, third series, III (1833), 55–128; also ed. J. H. Trumbull, in *Library of New England History*, No. 4, Boston, 1867. (An attack on Puritans, but surprisingly judicious.)

Lincoln, Charles H., ed., *Narratives of the Indian Wars, 1675–1699*, Original Narratives Series, New York, 1913.

MacDonald, William, ed., *Select Charters and Other Documents Illustrative of American History, 1606–1775*, New York, 1899.

Mason, John, *A Brief History of the Pequot War*, first printed in part in Increase Mather, *A Relation*, 1677; reprinted by Thomas Prince (who identified the author), Boston, 1736; ed. Charles Orr, *History*, Cleveland, 1897; *Collections of the Massachusetts Historical Society*, second series, VIII (1819), 120–153.

Masters, John, "Letter to Lady Barrington and Others, March 14, 1630/1," *New England Historical and Genealogical Register*, XCI (1937), 68–71.

Mather, Cotton, *A Brief Account of the State of the Province of the Massachusetts-Bay in New-England, Civil and Ecclesiastical*, Boston, 1717.

—— *Magnalia Christi Americana*, London, 1702; reprinted, ed. Thomas Robbins, Hartford, 1853–1855, 2 vols. (The *omnium gatherum* of seventeenth-century New England, which could appropriately be listed under every section in this bibliography. A work of monumental scholarship that is amazingly accurate and perceptive. Cf. Preface, *Selections from Cotton Mather*, ed. K. B. Murdock, New York, 1926, for best critical estimate.)

—— "Political Fables" (MS. *ca.* 1692), *Collections of the Massachusetts Historical Society*, third series, Vol. I (1825), 126–133; *The Andros Tracts*, Boston, 1868–1874, II, 325–332; reprinted in part, Murdock, *Selections*, pp. 363–371, with introduction. (In the form of beast fables Mather defends the government of New England under Phips against his detractors.)

—— *The Present State of New-England*, Boston, 1690.

Mather, Increase, *A Brief History of the Warr With the Indians in New-England*, Boston, 1676; reprinted, ed. S. G. Drake, under the title *The History of King Philip's War*, Boston and Albany, 1862.

—— *A Relation Of the Troubles which have hapned in New-England, By Reason of the Indians there*, Boston, 1677; ed. S. G. Drake, under the title *Early History of New England*, Albany, 1864.

Morton, George, comp., *Mourt's Relation*. First published as *A Relation or Journall of the beginning and proceedings of the English Plantation setled at Plimoth*, London,

1622; abbreviated in *Purchas his Pilgrims*, London, 1625, Bk. X, ch. iv; *Collections of the Massachusetts Historical Society*, first series, VIII (1802), 203–239; second series, IX (1822), 26–73; ed. Henry M. Dexter, Boston, 1865. (A minute diary of events from November, 1620, to December, 1621, and probably the joint work of Bradford and Winslow. It is continued by Winslow as *Good Newes from New-England*, London, 1624. Often reprinted.)

Morton, Nathaniel, *New-England's Memoriall*, Cambridge, 1669; facsimile ed. by Arthur Lord, Boston, Club of Odd Volumes, 1903.

Morton, Thomas, *New English Canaan*, Amsterdam, 1637; ed. Charles F. Adams, Boston, 1883. (A riotous attack on the Puritans by a gentleman of questionable antecedents who clashed with the authorities of both Plymouth and Massachusetts Bay, and was expelled for conduct which they considered both immoral and dangerous.)

Noble, John, ed., *Records of the Court of Assistants of the Colony of the Massachusetts Bay, 1630–1692*, Boston, 1901–1904, 2 vols.; Vol. III, ed. John F. Cronin, 1928.

Penhallow, Samuel, *History of the Wars of New England*, Boston, 1726; Cincinnati, 1859.

Prince, Thomas, *A Chronological History of New-England In the Form of Annals*, Boston, 1736–1755, 2 vols.; reprinted in *Collections of the Massachusetts Historical Society*, second series, VII (1818), 189–295.

Public Records of the Colony of Connecticut, The, Hartford, 1850–1890, 15 vols. Vols. 1–3, ed. J. H. Trumbull; vols. 4–15, ed. C. J. Hoadly. (Vols. 1–7 contain records from 1636 to 1735.)

Records of the Colony of New Plymouth in New England, Boston, 1855–1861, 12 vols. in 10. Vols. 1–8, ed. Nathaniel B. Shurtleff; vols. 9–12, ed. David Pulsifer.

Records of the Suffolk County Court, 1671–1680, Publications of the Colonial Society of Massachusetts, Vols. XXIX, XXX (1933). Introduction by Zechariah Chafee, Jr.

Rowlandson, Mary (White), *The Sovereignty & Goodness of God, Together, with the Faithfulness of His Promises Displayed*, 2nd ed., Cambridge, 1682; facsimile reprint, ed. H. S. Nourse and J. E. Thayer, Lancaster, Mass., 1903; ed. Frederick L.

Weis, Boston, 1930. Reprinted frequently under title, *The Narrative of the Captivity . . . of Mrs. Mary Rowlandson*.

Scottow, Joshua, *Massachusetts; Or, The first Planters of New-England, The End and Manner of their coming thither, and Abode there*, Boston, 1696.

—— *A Narrative Of The Planting of the Massachusets Colony Anno 1628*, Boston, 1694; reprinted in *Collections of the Massachusetts Historical Society*, fourth series, IV (1858), 279–330.

Shurtleff, Nathaniel B., ed., *Records of the Governor and Company of the Massachusetts Bay*, Boston, 1853–1854, 5 vols. in 6. (Covering the period 1628–1686.)

Smith, John, *Advertisements For the unexperienced Planters of New-England, or any where*, London, 1631; reprinted in *Collections of the Massachusetts Historical Society*, third series, III (1833), 1–53. ("Promotion" literature designed to draw settlers to New England.)

—— *A Description of New England: or the Observations, and Discoveries, of Captain John Smith*, London, 1616; reprinted in *Collections of the Massachusetts Historical Society*, third series, VI (1837), 95–140.

Stearns, Raymond P., ed., "Correspondence of John Woodbridge, Jr., and Richard Baxter," *New England Quarterly*, X (1937), 557–583.

Ward, Ned, *A Trip to New-England*, London, 1699; reissued by the Club for Colonial Reprints, ed. G. P. Winship, Providence, 1905. (A libellous pamphlet with amusing passages on the peccadilloes of New Englanders.)

White, John, *The Planters Plea; or, The Grounds of Plantations examined*, London, 1630; facsimile, ed. Marshall H. Saville, The Sandy Bay Historical Society, Rockport, Mass., 1930; reprinted in *Proceedings of the Massachusetts Historical Society*, LXII (1929), 367–425. (A defense of the project for settling Massachusetts Bay, written by an English minister, and published while the fleet was on the water.)

Whitmore, William H., ed., *The Andros Tracts: being a Collection of Pamphlets and Official Papers*, Boston, 1868–1874, 3 vols. (A collection of original narratives concerning the Andros regime, 1686–1689, and the revolution of 1689; important

sources for general history and for political theory and tradition.)

Williams, John, *The Redeemed Captive,
returning to Zion*, Boston, 1707; reprinted
constantly; Springfield, Mass., 1908, with
bibliography. (The most popular of all
narratives of captivity, a "best seller"
for a century.)

Winslow, Edward, *Good Newes from
New-England*, London, 1624; abbreviated
in *Purchas his Pilgrims*, London, 1625, Bk.
X, ch. v; reprinted in *Collections of the
Massachusetts Historical Society*, first series,
VIII (1802), 239–276; also second series,
IX (1822), 74–104; also fourth series, I
(1852), 195–218 (where it is presented in
hendecasyllabic couplets as well as in
prose, from the London, 1648, edition).
Reprinted in Edward Arber, *The Story of
the Pilgrim Fathers*, London, 1897.

—— *Hypocrisie Unmasked: by A true Re-
lation of the Proceedings of the Governour and
Company of the Massachusets against Samuel
Gorton*, London, 1646; ed. H. M. Chapin,
Providence, 1916.

—— *New-Englands Salamander, discovered by an irreligious and scornefull Pamphlet,
called New-Englands Jonas*, London, 1647;
reprinted in *Collections of the Massachusetts
Historical Society*, third series, II (1830),
110–145. (A reply to Major John Child,
in defense of Massachusetts.)

Winthrop, John, *Winthrop's Journal
"History of New England," 1630–1649*, ed.
James K. Hosmer, Original Narratives
Series, New York, 1908, 2 vols.; the best
edition is that of James Savage, Boston,
1825–1826. (Invaluable account from the
pen of the first governor of Massachusetts
Bay Colony.)

Wood, William, *New Englands Prospect*,
London, 1634, 1635, 1639; ed. C. Deane,
Boston, 1865; ed. H. W. Boynton, Boston,
1898.

Young, Alexander, ed., *Chronicles of the
First Planters of the Colony of Massachusetts
Bay, from 1623 to 1636*, Boston, 1846.

—— *Chronicles of the Pilgrim Fathers . . .
from 1602 to 1625*, Boston, 1841.

B. SECONDARY WORKS

Consult also Section II B of this bibliography.

Adams, Brooks, *The Emancipation of
Massachusetts*, Boston, 1887; Houghton-
Mifflin paperback with introduction by
Perry Miller, 1962. (A vigorous onslaught,
inspired by a militant liberalism, upon
what the author calls the tyranny of the
Puritan priest.)

Adams, Charles Francis, *Three Episodes
of Massachusetts History*, Boston, 1892, 2
vols. (The best account of the Antinomian
affair.)

Adams, Elizabeth L., "The Wars of
New England," *More Books*, XV (1940),
87–101. (An analysis of a manuscript
version of Penhallow's history.)

Adams, James Truslow, *The Founding of
New England*, Boston, 1921. (An interpretation in terms of "economic and
imperial relations," confessedly hostile to
the Puritan way of thought.)

—— *Revolutionary New England, 1691–
1776*, Boston, 1923.

Akagi, Roy H., *The Town Proprietors of
the New England Colonies . . . 1620–1770*,
Philadelphia, 1924.

Andrews, Charles McL., *The Beginnings
of Connecticut, 1632–1662*, New Haven, 1934.

—— *The Colonial Background of the
American Revolution*, New Haven, 1924;
Yale paperback, 1959.

—— *The Colonial Period*, New York,
1912. (Excellent brief summary.)

—— *The Colonial Period of American
History*, IV vols., New Haven, 1934–1938.
(The standard history; the culmination
of a lifetime of work by the foremost
authority on the field.)

—— *Colonial Self-Government, 1652–
1689* (*The American Nation*, Vol. V), New
York, 1904.

—— *The Fathers of New England*, New
Haven, 1919. Vol. VI of *Chronicles of
America*, ed. Allen Johnson. (Popular
presentation.)

—— *Our Earliest Colonial Settlements*,
New York, 1933.

—— *The Rise and Fall of the New Haven
Colony*, Publications of the Tercentenary Com-
mission of the State of Connecticut, New
Haven, 1936.

—— *The River Towns of Connecticut*, Baltimore, 1889.

Arnold, Samuel G., *History of the State of Rhode Island and Providence Plantations*, 4th ed., New York, 1894, 2 vols.

Bailyn, Bernard, "The Apologia of Robert Keayne," *William and Mary Quarterly*, VII (1950), 568–587. (A study of the New England merchant and the Puritan ethic.)

—— "Kinship and Trade in Seventeenth-Century New England," *Explorations in Entrepreneurial History*, VI (1953–1954), no. 4.

——, and Lotte Bailyn, *Massachusetts Shipping, 1697–1714: A Statistical Study*, Cambridge, 1959. (A statistical study of the Massachusetts shipping registry.)

—— *The New England Merchants in the Seventeenth Century*, Cambridge, 1955. (Economic history in human terms.)

Banks, Charles E., *The Planters of the Commonwealth . . . 1620–1640*, Boston, 1930.

Barnes, Viola F., *The Dominion of New England*, New Haven, 1923. (The Andros regime, 1686–1689.)

—— "Richard Wharton, A Seventeenth Century New England Colonial," *Publications of the Colonial Society of Massachusetts*, XXVI (1927), 238–270.

Beard, Charles A., and Mary R., *The Rise of American Civilization*, New York, 1927, 2 vols.; revised and enlarged, 1933. (Brilliant study of American development, stressing chiefly social and economic aspects; the section on New England is regrettably brief.)

Bebb, Evelyn D., *Noncomformity and Social and Economic Life, 1660–1800*, London, 1935.

Becker, Carl L., *Beginnings of the American People*, New York, 1915; Cornell Univeristy Press paperback, 1958.

Bining, Arthur C., *British Regulation of the Colonial Iron Industry*, Philadelphia, 1933.

Boorstin, Daniel J., *The Americans: the Colonial Experience*, New York, 1958.

Bowen, Richard Le Baron, *Early Rehoboth: Documented Historical Studies of Families and Events in This Plymouth Colony Township*, 4 vols., Concord, N. H., 1945–1950. (A model of local history.)

—— *The Providence Oath of Allegiance and Its Signers, 1651–1652*, Providence, 1943.

—— *Rhode Island Colonial Money and Its Counterfeiting, 1647–1726*, Concord, N. H., 1942.

—— "The 1690 Tax Revolt of Plymouth Colony Towns," *Register, New England Historical and Genealogical Society*, CXII (1958), 4–14; reprinted in *Collected Papers: Armorial, Genealogical and Historical*, Rehoboth, 1959.

Buffinton, Arthur H., "The Isolationist Policy of Colonial Massachusetts," *New England Quarterly*, I (1928), 158–177.

—— "The Massachusetts Experiment of 1630," *Publications of the Colonial Society of Massachusetts*, XXXII (1937), 308–320.

Burrage, Champlin, *The Early English Dissenters in the Light of Recent Research*, Cambridge, Eng., 1912, 2 vols.

Burrage, Henry S., *The Beginnings of Colonial Maine 1602–1658*, Portland, 1914.

Byington, Ezra H., *The Puritan as a Colonist and Reformer*, Boston, 1899.

—— *The Puritan in England and New England*, Boston, 1896.

Calder, Isabel M., *The New Haven Colony*, New Haven, 1934. (An admirable and definitive study.)

Cambridge Modern History, The, Vol. VII, 2nd ed., New York, 1924. Chapter I, "The Colonies, 1607–1700"; Chapter II, "The Colonies, 1700–1763." ("Cheap edition," 1934, without bibliographies.)

Campbell, Mildred, "Social Origins of Some Early Americans," *Seventeenth-Century America: Essays in Colonial History*, ed., James Morton Smith, Chapel Hill, 1959, 63–89. (It was the "middling people" that provided the bulk of English migration to America in the second half of the seventeenth century.)

Carman, Harry J., *Social and Economic History of the United States*, Boston, 1930. Vol. I, *From Handicraft to Factory, 1500–1820*.

Caulkins, Frances M., *History of New London, Connecticut*, New London, 1852. (A good history of an important town.)

Channing, Edward, *History of the United States*. Vol. I (New York, 1905), *The Planting . . . 1000–1660*; Vol. II (1908), *A Century of Colonial History, 1660–1760*.

Clark, George N., *The Later Stuarts*.

1660–1714, Oxford, 1934. (The best handbook for English background; excellent bibliography.)

Clarke, Mary Patterson, *Parliamentary Privilege in the American Colonies*, New Haven, 1943.

Crouse, Nellis M., "Causes of the Great Migration," *New England Quarterly*, V (1932), 3–36.

Curti, Merle, *The Growth of American Thought*, New York and London, 1943; 1951. (A social history of American thought.)

Dexter, Henry M., *The England and Holland of the Pilgrims*, Boston, 1905.

Dorfman, Joseph, *The Economic Mind in American Civilization 1609–1865*, New York, 1946. (See Vol. I, Book 1, "Colonial America.")

Douglas, Charles H. J., *The Financial History of Massachusetts*, New York, 1892.

Dow, George F., and John H. Edmonds, *The Pirates of the New England Coast, 1630–1730*, Salem, 1923.

Dow, George F., "Shipping and Trade in Early New England," *Proceedings of the Massachusetts Historical Society*, LXIV (1932), 185–210.

—— "The Topsfield Copper Mines," *Proceedings of the Massachusetts Historical Society*, LXV (1933), 570–580.

Doyle, John A., *The English in America*. Vols. II and III, *The Puritan Colonies*, London, 1887.

Dunn, Richard S., "Seventeenth Century English Historians," *Seventeenth-Century America: Essays in Colonial History*, ed,, James Morton Smith, Chapel Hill, 1959, 195–225. (Traces the separate evolutions of the English and American historical tradition.)

Ellis, Arthur B., *History of the First Church in Boston, 1630–1880*, Boston, 1881.

Ellis, George E., *The Puritan Age and Rule in the Colony of the Massachusetts Bay, 1629–1685*, New York, 1888.

Field, Edward, ed., *State of Rhode Island and Providence Plantations*, Boston, 1902, 3 vols.

Foote, Henry W., *Annals of King's Chapel*, Boston, 1882–1896, 2 vols.

French, Allen, *Charles I and the Puritan Upheaval: A Study of the Causes of the Great Migration*, London, 1955; Boston, 1956.

Friedman, Lee M., *Early American Jews*, Cambridge, 1934.

Friis, Herman R., "A Series of Population Maps of the Colonies and the United States, 1625–1790," *Geographical Review*, XXX (1940), 463–470.

Fullerton, Kemper, "Calvinism and Capitalism," *Harvard Theological Review*, XXI (1928), 163–195.

Goodman, Abram Vossen, *American Overture: Jewish Rights in Colonial Times*, Philadelphia, 1947.

Gottfried, Marion H., "The First Depression in Massachusetts," *New England Quarterly*, IX (1936), 655–678.

Graham, Ian C. C., *Colonists from Scotland: Emigrants to North America, 1707–1783*, Ithaca, 1956.

Greene, Evarts B., *Provincial America, 1690–1740*, New York, 1905. (Vol. VI in *The American Nation: A History*, ed. A. B. Hart.)

Greene, Evarts B., and Virginia D. Harrington, *American Population before the Federal Census of 1790*, New York, 1932. (The best available data.)

Greene, Lorenzo Johnson, *The Negro in Colonial New England, 1620–1776*, New York, 1942.

Griffith, Ernest S., *History of American City Government; The Colonial Period*, New York, 1938. (Institutional and political history.)

Gutstein, Morris A., *The Story of the Jews of Newport, 1658–1908*, New York, 1936.

Hall, Albert H., "How Massachusetts Grew, 1630–1642," *Publications of the Cambridge Historical Society*, XXI (1936), 14–49.

Halsey, Abigail Fithian, *In Old Southampton*, New York, 1940. (From the founding by men from Lynn, Massachusetts [1640], through the Revolutionary War.)

Hansen, Marcus L., *The Atlantic Migration, 1607–1860*, Cambridge, 1940; Harper Torchbook edition, 1961.

Hart, Albert B., ed., *Commonwealth History of Massachusetts*, New York, 1927–1930, 5 vols.

Hartley, E. N., *Ironworks on the Saugus: The Lynn and Braintree Ventures of the Company of Undertakers of the Ironworks in New England*, Norman, 1957. (The story of iron-making in seventeenth-century America.)

Hill, Hamilton A., *History of the Old South Church*, Boston, 1890, 2 vols. (One of the most valuable of local church histories, covering the period 1669–1884.)

Holmes, Abiel, *The Annals of America*, Cambridge, 1805; 2nd ed. 1829. (Vol. I, 1492–1732.)

Hooker, Roland M., *The Colonial Trade of Connecticut, Publications of the Tercentenary Commission of the State of Connecticut*, 1936.

Howard, Leon, "The Puritans in Old and New England," *Anglo-American Cultural Relations in the Seventeenth and Eighteenth Centuries*, Leon Howard and Louis B. Wright, Los Angeles, 1959, ch. I.

Hutchinson, Thomas, *The History of the Colony of Massachusetts-Bay*, Boston, 1764–1828, 3 vols.; ed. Lawrence S. Mayo, Cambridge, 1936, 3 vols. (Both a history and a source book; indispensable; should be used in the Mayo ed.)

—— "Additions to Thomas Hutchinson's *History of Massachusetts-Bay*," ed. Catherine Barton Mayo, *Proceedings of the American Antiquarian Society*, LIX (1949), 13–74.

Jernegan, Marcus W., *The American Colonies, 1492–1750. A Study of Their Political, Economic and Social Development*, New York, 1929. (Vol. I in *Epochs of American History*. The best one-volume survey of the period, extremely compact; the bibliographies cull the best works published before 1929.)

—— *Laboring and Dependent Classes in Colonial America, 1607–1783*, Chicago, 1931; 1960.

Johnson, Edgar A. J., "Some Evidence of Mercantilism in the Massachusetts-Bay," *New England Quarterly*, I (1928), 371–396.

Jones, Howard M., "The Colonial Impulse: An Analysis of the 'Promotion' Literature of Colonization," *Proceedings of the American Philosophical Society*, XC (1946), 131–161.

—— "Origins of the Colonial Idea in England," *Proceedings of the American Philosophical Society*, LXXXV (1941–1942), 448–465.

Kennedy, William H. J., "Catholics in Massachusetts before 1750," *Catholic Historical Review*, XVII (1931), 10–28.

Kimball, Gertrude S., *Providence in Colonial Times*, Boston, 1912.

Labaree, Leonard W., "The Royal Governors of New England," *Publications of the Colonial Society of Massachusetts*, XXXII (1936), 120–131.

Leach, Douglas Edward, *Flintlock and Tomahawk: New England in King Philips' War*, New York, 1958.

Lothrop, Samuel K., *A History of the Church in Brattle Street, Boston*, Boston, 1851.

Love, William DeLoss, *The Colonial History of Hartford*, Hartford, 1914.

—— *Samson Occom, and the Christian Indians of New England*, Boston, 1900.

McCutcheon, Roger P., "Americana in English Newspapers, 1648–1660," *Publications of the Colonial Society of Massachusetts*, XX (1920), 84–96.

McElroy, John W., "Seafaring in Seventeenth-Century New England," *New England Quarterly*, VIII (1935), 331–364.

MacFarlane, Ronald O., "The Massachusetts Bay Truck-Houses in Diplomacy with the Indians," *New England Quarterly*, XI (1938), 48–65.

McKay, George L., *Early American Currency—Some Notes on the Development of Paper Money in the New England Colonies*, New York, 1944.

Marcus, Jacob Rader, ed., *American Jewry Documents: 18th Century, Primarily Hitherto Unpublished Manuscripts*, Cincinnati, 1959.

—— *Early American Jewry, 1649–1794*, Philadelphia, 1951. (Based on examination of personal and business letters.)

Maurer, Oscar Edward, *A Puritan Church and Its Relation to Community, State, and Nation. Addresses Delivered in Preparation for the Three Hundredth Anniversary of the Settlement of New Haven*, New Haven, 1938.

Mitchell, Mary H., *History of the United Church of New Haven, 1742–1792*, New Haven, 1942.

Mood, Fulmer, *The English Geographers and the Anglo-American Frontier in the Seventeenth Century*, University of California Publications in Geography, Vol. 6, No. 9, 363–396; Berkeley and Los Angeles, 1944. (A stimulating survey of the work of the geographers and its relation to the promotional literature of the seventeenth century.)

Moody, Robert Earle, "A Re-Examination of the Antecedents of the Massachusetts Bay Company's Charter of 1629," *Publications of the Massachusetts Historical Society*, LXIX (1947–1950), 1956, 56–80.

Morison, Samuel Eliot, *Builders of the Bay Colony*, Boston, 1930; Cornell paperback. (A history and interpretation of New England Puritanism in a series of brilliant biographical portraits; an essential book; counters many of the theories of J. T. Adams, and establishes and defines the essentially religious motivation of the settlement.)

—— "The Mayflower's Destination, and the Pilgrim Fathers' Patents," *Transactions of the Colonial Society of Massachusetts*, XXXVIII (1959), 387–413.

—— "New Light Wanted on the Old Colony," *William and Mary Quarterly*, XV (1958), 359–364.

—— "The Pilgrim Fathers, Their Significance in History," *Transactions of the Colonial Society of Massachusetts*, XXXVIII (1959), 364–379.

Morse, Jarvis M., "John Smith and His Critics: A Chapter in Colonial Historiography," *Journal of Southern History*, I (1935), 123–137.

Murdock, Kenneth B., "Clio in the Wilderness: History and Biography in Puritan New England," *Church History*, XXIV (1955), 221–238. (The best exposition of the Puritan view of history.)

—— "William Hubbard and the Providential Interpretation of History," *Proceedings of the American Antiquarian Society*, LII (1942), 15–37.

Neal, Daniel, *The History of New-England*, London, 1720; 2nd ed., 1747, 2 vols.

—— *The History of the Puritans*, London, 1732–1738, 4 vols.; later editions. (Superseded in factual range by subsequent works, yet still one of the best interpretations of the Puritan mind.)

Nettels, Curtis P., *The Roots of American Civilization: A History of Colonial Life*, New York, 1938. (The economic structure of colonial culture.)

Newton, Arthur P., *The Colonising Activities of the English Puritans*, New Haven, 1914.

Noe, Sydney P., "The Coinage of Massachusetts Bay Colony," *Proceedings of the American Antiquarian Society*, LX (1950), 11–20.

—— *The Pine Tree Coinage of Massachusetts*, New York, 1952. (Numismatic Notes and Monographs, No. 125.)

Notestein, Wallace, *The English People on the Eve of Colonization, 1603–1630*, New York, 1954; Harper Torchbook edition, 1962. (Social history at its best; early 17th century English society anatomized.)

O'Brien, Michael J., *Pioneer Irish in New England*, New York, 1937.

Oldmixon, John, *The British Empire in America*, London, 1708, 2 vols. Vol. I: "The History of New England," pp. 25–116.

Osgood, Herbert L., *The American Colonies in the Eighteenth Century*, New York, 1924, 3 vols. (A standard history, particularly concerned with political aspects.)

—— *The American Colonies in the Seventeenth Century*, New York, 1904–1907, 3 vols.

Palfrey, John G., *A Compendious History of New England*, Boston, 1858–1890, 5 vols. (As detailed as was possible at the time; largely superseded by later works, but still valuable as a work of reference.)

Park, Charles E., "Friendship as a Factor in the Settlement of Massachusetts," *Proceedings of the American Antiquarian Society*, N.S. XXVIII (1918), 51–62.

Perley, Sidney, *The History of Salem, Massachusetts*, Salem, 1924. (Vol. I, covering 1626–1637.)

Phillips, James Duncan, *Salem in the Eighteenth Century*, Boston, 1937.

—— *Salem in the Seventeenth Century*, Boston, 1933.

Richman, Irving B., *Rhode Island: A Study in Separatism*, Boston, 1905.

—— *Rhode Island: Its Making and Its Meaning*, New York, 1902.

Robbins, Chandler, *A History of the Second Church, or Old North, in Boston*, Boston, 1852.

Rose, John Holland, A. P. Newton, and E. A. Benians, *The Cambridge History of the British Empire*, Vol. I: *The Old Empire from the Beginnings to 1783*, Cambridge, Eng., 1929.

Rosenberry, Lois K. Mathews, *The Expansion of New England*, Boston, 1909.

Rose-Troup, Frances, *John White, the Founder of Massachusetts*, New York, 1930. (Detailed, but injudicious.)

—— *The Massachusetts Bay Company and Its Predecessors*, New York, 1930. (Neither complete nor entirely accurate.)

Rossiter, Clinton, *Seedtime of the Republic: The Origin of the American Tradition of Political Liberty*, New York, 1953. (Summary background of colonial history and conditions of life.)

Rowse, A. L., *The Elizabethans and America*, New York, 1959. (Tendentious history in the grand manner, basically unsympathetic to the Puritans and New England.)

Sachse, William L., *The Colonial American in Britain*, Madison, 1956.

Saltonstall, William G., *Ports of Piscataqua*, Cambridge, 1941.

Savelle, Max, *The Foundations of American Civilization*, New York, 1942. (Emphasis on the diplomatic aspects of early American history and on the relation of the continental colonies to the British West Indies.)

Scudder, Townsend, *Concord, American Town*, Boston, 1947.

Seybolt, Robert Francis, *The Town Officials of Colonial Boston, 1634–1775*, Cambridge, 1939. (An attempt to straighten out and correct the *Reports of the Record Commissioners of the City of Boston*.)

Shannon, Fred A., *Economic History of the People of the United States*, New York, 1934.

Shipton, Clifford K., "The New England Clergy of the 'Glacial Age,'" *Publications of the Colonial Society of Massachusetts*, XXXII (1937), 24–54.

—— "Immigration to New England, 1680–1740," *Journal of Political Economy*, LXIV (1936), 225–239.

—— "The New England Frontier," *New England Quarterly*, X (1937), 25–36.

Sly, John F., *Town Government in Massachusetts, 1620–1930*, Cambridge, 1930.

Stearns, Raymond P., "The New England Way in Holland," *New England Quarterly*, VI (1933), 747–792.

—— "The Weld-Peter Mission to England," *Publications of the Colonial Society of Massachusetts*, XXXII (1936), 188–246.

Stoughton, John, *History of Religion in England, from the Opening of the Long Parliament*, 4th ed., London, 1901, 8 vols. (The most readable and generally useful account of the English background.)

Sutherland, Stella H., *Population Distribution in Colonial America*, New York, 1936.

Sylvester, Herbert M., *Indian Wars of New England*, Boston, 1910, 3 vols.

Tillyard, E. M., *The Elizabethan World Picture*, London, 1943.

Trefz, Edward K., "The Puritans' View of History," *Boston Public Library Quarterly*, IX (1957), 115–136. (Belief in the Providence of God demanded an objective history of His workings.)

Trumbull, Benjamin, *A Complete History of Connecticut, Civil and Ecclesiastical*, New Haven, 1818, 2 vols.; new ed., New London, 1898. (Both a history and a source book; invaluable.)

Turner, Frederick J., "The First Official Frontier of the Massachusetts Bay," *Publications of the Colonial Society of Massachusetts*, XVII (1915), 250–271.

Usher, Roland G., *The Pilgrims and Their History*, New York, 1918.

Van de Wetering, John, "Thomas Prince's Chronological History," *William and Mary Quarterly*, XVIII (1961), 546–557.

Wakeman, Henry O., *The Church and the Puritans, 1570–1660*, London, 1887. (A convenient brief survey of religious background for the Puritan migration.)

Walker, George L., *History of the First Church in Hartford, 1633–1883*, Hartford, 1884.

Waters, Thomas F., *Ipswich in the Massachusetts Bay Colony*, Ipswich, 1905–1917, 2 vols. (A good history of an important town.)

Weeden, William B., *Economic and Social History of New England, 1620–1789*, Boston, 1890, 2 vols. (Still the best attempt at a complete treatment of the subject; badly organized, but a mine of information.)

Welles, Lemuel A., *The History of the Regicides in New England*, New York, 1927.

—— *The Regicides in Connecticut*, Publications of the Tercentenary Commission of the State of Connecticut, New Haven, 1935.

Wertenbaker, Thomas Jefferson, *The Puritan Oligarchy: The Founding of American Civilization*, New York, 1947.

Winsor, Justin, ed., *The Memorial History of Boston, 1630–1880*, Boston, 1880–1881, 4 vols.

—— *Narrative and Critical History of America*, Boston, 1884–1889, 8 vols. (Still useful; each chapter includes an essay on authorities which is often an excellent guide to source material.)

Wright, Louis B., *The Atlantic Frontier:*

Colonial American Civilization, 1607–1763, New York, 1947; London ed'n., 1949, *The Colonial Civilization of North America.*

—— *Middle-Class Culture in Elizabethan England*, Chapel Hill, 1935. (Indispensable for social and cultural backgrounds.)

—— *Religion and Empire: The Alliance between Piety and Commerce in English Expansion, 1558–1625*, Chapel Hill, 1943. (Demonstrates the importance of the religious motives in exploration and settlement of America.)

II. THEORIES OF THE STATE AND SOCIETY

The most important single form of publication concerned with the theory of society was the election sermon, the discourse delivered annually to the General Court on the day of the election. Political and social issues were often discussed in the annual sermons delivered on the occasion for the electing of officers to the Ancient and Honorable Artillery Company of Boston. A complete list of these sermons would swell the pages of this bibliography beyond the point of usefulness, and only those of special importance are here listed. For further guidance to the sermons, consult in Section B: Roberts, Swift, Vail, and Whitman.

A. Primary Sources

Expressions of Puritan political and social theory are to be found scattered through sermons, journals, and letters. Very few works were dedicated solely to this particular theme, so that a complete bibliography of passages of this sort would involve a repetition of almost all the titles mentioned in these lists. Consult in addition to the items here, those listed in section III A 2, for sermons devoted to ecclesiastical polity, all of which contain statements on the relation of Church and State, the basic social problem for Puritan theorists. (For convenience the following abbreviations are used in this section: AES (Artillery Election Sermon); MES (Massachusetts Election Sermon); CES (Connecticut Election Sermon).

Appleton, Nathaniel, *The Origin of War examin'd and applied*, Boston, 1733. (AES)

Barnard, John, *The Throne Established by Righteousness*, Boston, 1734. (MES)

Belcher, Joseph, *The Singular Happiness Of such Heads Or Rulers, As Are able to Choose out their Peoples Way*, Boston, 1701. (MES)

Belcher, Samuel, *An Essay Tending to Promote the Kingdom of our Lord Jesus Christ*, Boston, 1707. (MES)

Book of the General Laws For the People within the Jurisdiction of Connecticut, The, Cambridge, 1673. (Codification of the laws after the union of Connecticut and New Haven.)

Breck, Robert, *The Only Method to Promote the Happiness of a People and their Prosperity*, Boston, 1728. (MES)

Buckingham, Thomas, *Moses and Aaron. God's Favour To His Chosen People, in Leading them by the Ministry of Civil & Ecclesiastical Rulers, Well Qualified for the Offices they are Called to Execute*, New London, 1729. (CES for 1728.)

Bulkeley, Gershom, *The People's Right to Election Or Alteration of Government in Connecticott*, Philadelphia, 1689; *Collections of the Connecticut Historical Society*, I (1860), 57–75; *Andros Tracts*, II, 83–109.

—— *Will and Doom, or The Miseries of Connecticut by and under an Usurped and Arbitrary Power* [1692]; *Collections of the Connecticut Historical Society*, III (1895), 69–269. (One of the most pronounced expressions of the radical implications of Puritan theory.)

Bulkley, John, *The Necessity of Religion*

in Societies, New London, 1713. (CES.
Next to pamphlets of Wise, this is the
best of early eighteenth-century treatises.)

Burnham, William, *God's Providence In
Placing Men In their Respective Stations &
Conditions Asserted & Shewed*, New Lon-
don, 1722. (CES)

Cobbet, Thomas, *The Civil Magistrates
Power In matters of Religion Modestly De-
bated*, London, 1653. (One of the best
statements of the Puritan theory of
Church and State, by the first minister at
Lynn.)

Colman, Benjamin, *Faith Victorious*, Boston, 1702. (AES)

Cotton, John, *An Abstract Of Laws and
Government. Wherein as in a Mirrour may be
seen the wisdome & perfection of the Government of Christs Kingdome*, London, 1641;
1655. Reprinted in Thomas Hutchinson,
A Collection of Original Papers, 1769; Force,
Tracts, III, No. 9. (This code, known
as "Moses His Judicials," was never
adopted by the colony of Massachusetts,
but became the fundamental law for the
stricter colony of New Haven. It formu-
lates the extreme religious program in
society and law, but should be compared
with that actually adopted by the Massachusetts General Court from the pen of
Nathaniel Ward. Cf. Worthington C.
Ford, "Cotton's 'Moses His Judicials,'"
*Proceedings of the Massachusetts Historical
Society*, second series, XVI (1903), 274–
284; Isabel Calder, "John Cotton's
'Moses His Judicials,'" *Publications of the
Colonial Society of Massachusetts*, XXVIII
(1935), 86–94.

—— *The Bloudy Tenent, washed, And
made white in the bloud of the Lambe*, London,
1647. (Reply to Roger Williams; the
classic Puritan statement on the question
of toleration.)

—— *The Controversie Concerning Liberty
of Conscience in Matters of Religion, Truly
stated, and distinctly and plainly handled*, London, 1646.

—— "Copy of a Letter from Mr. Cotton to Lord Say and Seal in the Year
1636," in Thomas Hutchinson, *The History of the Colony*, ed. Mayo, I, 414–417.

—— *A Discourse about Civil Government
in a New Plantation Whose Design is Religion*,
Cambridge, 1663. (Perhaps the fundamental text for understanding the social

objectives of orthodox Puritanism. Written for the guidance of the New Haven
Colony, it was intended for the planters
who wished to create a society still more
perfect than that of Massachusetts Bay.
It was published after Cotton's death,
and was long attributed to John Davenport, who saw it through the press; cf.
Isabel M. Calder, "The Authorship of 'A
Discourse,'" *American Historical Review*,
XXXVII, 267–269.)

—— *A Letter to Mr. [Roger] Williams*,
London, 1643; ed. Reuben A. Guild, *Publications of the Narragansett Club*, I (1866),
285–311.

Cutler, Timothy, *The Firm Union of a
People Represented*, New London, 1717.
(CES)

Danforth, Samuel, *A Brief Recognition
of New-Englands Errand into the Wilderness*,
Cambridge, 1671. (MES for 1670.)

Davenport, John, *A Sermon Preach'd at
the Election . . . 1699*, Boston, 1670; reprinted in *Publications of the Colonial Society
of Massachusetts*, X (1907), 1–6. (MES for
1669.)

Davis, Andrew M., ed., *Tracts Relating
to the Currency of the Massachusetts Bay,
1682–1720*, Boston, 1902.

—— *Colonial Currency Reprints, 1682–
1751*, Boston, 1910–1911, 4 vols.

Dummer, Jeremiah, *A Defence of the
New-England Charters*, London, 1721;
Boston, 1721, and later. (Essential for an
understanding of the fashion in which
seventeenth-century Puritan theory
merges by degrees into the Whig theory
of the eighteenth century.)

Eliot, Jared, *Give Cesar his Due; Or, The
Obligations that Subjects are under to their
Civil Rulers*, New London, 1738. (CES. A
work that marks the complete domestica-
tion of the theories of Locke and Puf-
fendorf in eighteenth-century Puritan
theory.)

Eliot, John, *The Christian Commonwealth:
or, The Civil Policy of The Rising Kingdom
of Jesus Christ*, London, 1659; republished
in *Collections of the Massachusetts Historical
Society*, third series, IX (1846), 127–164.
(Published immediately after the Restoration, this book was extremely impolitic
in its assertion of radical Puritan tendencies, and was therefore condemned by the
General Court of Massachusetts. The

action was rather a piece of strategy than a disapproval of the ideas. The book is therefore an expression of theories that reached their fullest development during the period of the English Civil Wars, that were thereafter checked and to some extent driven underground, but that remain in the background of New England thought, to reappear in the work of Wise, Mayhew, and the Revolutionary pamphleteers.)

Farrand, Max, ed., *The Book of the General Lawes and Libertyes* (1648), Cambridge, 1929. (Cf. also review by T. F. T. Plucknett, *New England Quarterly*, III (1930), 156–159.

Fitch, James, *An Holy Connexion; Or a true Agreement Between Jehovahs being a Wall of Fire to his People, and the Glory in the midst thereof*, Cambridge, 1674. (CES)

Hancock, John, *Rulers should be Benefactors*, Boston, 1722. (MES)

Higginson, John, *The Cause of God and his people in New-England*, Cambridge, 1663. (MES)

Hooke, William, *New Englands Teares, for Old Englands Feares*, London, 1641. (Expresses New England's attitude toward the Civil Wars in England. It is also valuable as an expression of the Puritan feeling concerning war.)

Hooker, Thomas, "Rev. Thomas Hooker's Letter, in Reply to Governor Winthrop," *Collections of the Connecticut Historical Society*, I (1860), 1–18. (An angry letter, the result of a dispute between Connecticut and Massachusetts, wherein Hooker roundly asserts his political philosophy.)

Mather, Cotton, *Durable Riches*, Boston, 1695.

—— *Fair Dealing*, Boston, 1716.

Mather, Eleazer, *A Serious Exhortation to the Present and Succeeding Generation in New-England*, Cambridge, 1671; Boston, 1678.

Mather, Increase, *A Discourse Concerning the Danger of Apostacy*, Boston, 1679; 1685. (A review and summary of the state of New England; MES for 1677.)

—— *The Great Blessing of Primitive Counsellours*, Boston, 1693. (MES)

—— *The Surest way to the Greatest Honour*, Boston, 1699. (MES. The third of four election sermons Mather preached.)

—— *The Excellency of a Publick Spirit*, Boston, 1702.

Mayhew, Jonathan, *A Discourse concerning Unlimited Submission and Non-Resistance to the Higher Powers*, Boston, 1750; reprinted J. W. Thornton, *The Pulpit of the American Revolution*, Boston, 1860. (The final statement of Puritan radicalism in eighteenth-century terms.)

Mitchel, Jonathan, *Nehemiah on the Wall in Troublesom[e] Times*, Cambridge, 1671. (MES for 1667.)

Moody, Joshua, *Souldiery Spiritualized, or the Christian Souldier Orderly, and Strenuously Engaged in the Spiritual Warre, And So fighting the good Fight*, Cambridge, 1674. (AES)

Moss, Joseph, *An Election Sermon . . . frequent Readings and Studying the Scriptures and the Civil Law of the Common Wealth, is Needful and Profitable for Rulers*, New London, 1715. (CES. One of the best statements of theory of social compact.)

Noyes, James, *Moses and Aaron: Or, The Rights of Church and State*, London, 1661.

Noyes, Nicholas, *New-Englands Duty and Interest, To be an Habitation of Justice*, Boston, 1698. (MES)

Oakes, Urian, *New-England Pleaded with, And pressed to consider the things which concern her Peace, at least in this her Day*, Cambridge, 1673.

Oxenbridge, John, *New-England Freemen Warned and Warmede; To be Free indeed having an Eye to God in their Elections*, Boston, 1673. (MES for 1671.)

Pemberton, Ebenezer, *The divine Original and Dignity of Government Asserted*, Boston, 1710. (MES)

Prince, Thomas, *The People of New-England Put in mind of the Righteous Acts of the Lord to Them and their Fathers, and Reasoned with concerning them*, Boston, 1730. (MES)

Richardson, John, *The Necessity of a Well Experienced Souldiery*, Cambridge, 1679. (AES for 1675.)

Shepard, Thomas, "Thomas Shepard's Election Sermon, in 1638," *New England Historical and Genealogical Register*, XXIV (1870), 361–366. (MES. One of the best statements of the original political ideal.)

Somers, John, *The Security of Englishmen's Lives; Or, The Trust, Power and Duty of the Grand Juries of England*, London, 1718; frequently reprinted.

Stoddard, Solomon, *The Way for a People to Live Long in the Land that God Hath given them*, Boston, 1703. (MES)

Stoughton, William, *New-Englands True Interest; Not to Lie*, Cambridge, 1670. (MES for 1668.)

Wadsworth, Benjamin, *Rulers Feeding & Guiding their People*, Boston, 1716. (MES)

Whitmore, William H., *A Bibliographical Sketch of the Laws of the Massachusetts Colony from 1630 to 1686*, Boston, 1890. (Contains the "Body of Liberties," the code written by Nathaniel Ward and adopted by the General Court in 1641.)

—— ed., *The Colonial Laws of Massachusetts. Reprinted from the Edition of 1672*, Boston, 1887; 1890.

Willard, Samuel, *The Character Of a Good Ruler*, Boston, 1694. (MES)

—— *The Man of War*, Boston, 1699. (AES)

—— *The Only sure way to prevent threatned Calamity*, Boston, 1684. (MES for 1682.)

Williams, Roger, *The Bloudy Tenent of Persecution, for cause of Conscience, discussed, in A Conference betweene Truth and Peace*, London, 1644; ed. Samuel L. Caldwell, *Publications of the Narragansett Club*, Vol. III, 1867.

—— *The Bloody Tenent yet More Bloody: by Mr Cottons endevour to wash it white in the Blood of the Lambe*, London, 1652; ed. S. L. Caldwell, *Publications of the Narragansett Club*, Vol. IV, 1870.

—— *The Hireling Ministry None of Christs*, London, 1652.

—— *Mr. Cottons Letter Lately Printed, Examined and Answered*, London, 1644; ed. R. A. Guild, *Publications of the Narragansett Club*, I (1866), 313–396.

Williams, William, *A Plea for God, and An Appeal to the Consciences of a People Declining in Religion*, Boston, 1719. (MES)

Winthrop, John, "A Modell of Christian Charity," *Winthrop Papers, Collections of the Massachusetts Historical Society*, third series, VII (1838), 31–48; *The Winthrop Papers*, Massachusetts Historical Society, Boston, 1931, II, 282–295. (Written on the *Arbella* during the voyage to New England in 1630.)

Wise, John, *The Churches Quarrel Espoused*, Boston, 1710.

—— *A Vindication of the Government of New England Churches*, Boston, 1767; reprinted in "Scholars' Facsimiles and Reprints," ed. Perry Miller, Gainesville, Fla., 1958. (Reissues of both titles in one volume, Boston, 1772; 1862.)

Woodward, John, *Civil Rulers are God's Ministers, for the People's Good*, Boston, 1712.

B. SECONDARY WORKS

Puritan social and economic theory was so inextricably woven into the religious doctrine that few works were ever written specifically on the subject. Many titles in Section III also contain observations on social thought.

Aldrich, Peleg E., "John Locke and the Influence of His Works on American Thought," *Proceedings of the American Antiquarian Society*, April, 1879, 22–39.

Allen, Neal W., ed., *Province and Court Records of Maine*. Vol. IV: *The Court Records of York County, Maine, 1692–1711*, Portland, 1958.

Andrews, Charles M., "On Some Early Connecticut History," *New England Quarterly*, XVII (1944), 3–24. (Connecticut's unbroken tradition of orthodoxy and responsible self-government based on a narrow franchise of free men.)

Baldwin, Alice M., *The New England Clergy and the American Revolution*, Durham, 1928. (An able history of the development of Puritan thought into the Whig philosophy of the Revolution.)

Blodgett, John T., "The Political Theory of the Mayflower Compact," *Publications of the Colonial Society of Massachusetts*, XII (1911), 204–213.

Boorstin, Daniel J., "The Puritan Tradition: Community Above Ideology," *Commentary*, XXVI (1958), 288–299.

Borgeauc, Charles, *The Rise of Modern Democracy in Old and New England*, London, 1894.

Brauer, Jerald C., "Puritan Mysticism

and the Development of Liberalism," *Church History*, XIX (1950), 151–170.

Brennan, Ellen E., "The Massachusetts Council of the Magistrates," *New England Quarterly*, IV (1931), 54–93. (An excellent analysis of early government, contending that by 1644 political leadership had ceased to be responsible to God and had been made responsible to the freeman.)

Brockunier, Samuel H., *The Irrepressible Democrat: Roger Williams*, New York, 1940.

Brown, B. Katherine, "Freemanship in Puritan Massachusetts," *American Historical Review*, LIX (1954), 865–883.

—— "A Note on the Puritan Concept of Aristocracy," *Mississippi Valley Historical Review*, XLI (1954), 105–112. (What Cotton, Winthrop and other Puritan leaders meant by aristocracy has a close relationship to what we call democracy.)

Brown, Robert E., *Middle-Class Democracy and the Revolution in Massachusetts, 1691–1780*. Ithaca, 1955.

Buck, Edward, *Massachusetts Ecclesiatical Law*, New York, 1866.

Buffinton, Arthur H., "The Puritan View of War," *Publications of the Colonial Society of Massachusetts*, XXVIII (1935), 67–86.

Burrage, Champlin, *The Church Covenant Idea*, Philadelphia, 1904.

Calder, Isabel M., "John Cotton and the New Haven Colony," *New England Quarterly*, III (1930), 82–94.

Chafee, Zechariah, Jr., "Colonial Courts and the Common Law," *Proceedings of the Massachusetts Historical Society*, LXVIII (1944–1947), 1952, 132–159.

—— "Records of the Rhode Island Court of Equity," *Publications of the Colonial Society of Massachusetts*, XXXV (1942–1946), 91–118.

Cobb, Sanford H., *The Rise of Religious Liberty in America: A History*, New York, 1902.

Cook, George Allen, *John Wise: Early American Democrat*, New York, 1952. (All and more than there is to be known about John Wise.)

Davis, Andrew M., *Currency and Banking in the Province of the Massachusetts-Bay*, New York, 1901, 2 vols.

Davis, Charles T., "Some Thoughts on Early Colonial Development," *Proceedings of the Massachusetts Historical Society*, LXIV (1932), 507–515. (Legal development in New England.)

Dexter, Henry M., *As To Roger Williams, and his "Banishment" from the Massachusetts Plantation*, Boston, 1876. (A vigorous statement of what was the orthodox view toward such a man as Williams in the seventeenth century; valuable for securing the proper perspective upon Williams' liberalism.)

Dickinson, John, "Economic Regulations and Restrictions on Personal Liberty in Massachusetts," *Proceedings of the Pocumtuck Valley Historical Association*, VII (1929), 485–525.

Dunn, Richard S., "John Winthrop, Jr., and the Narragansett Country," *William and Mary Quarterly*, XIII (1956), 68–86.

—— "John Winthrop, Jr., Connecticut Expansionist: The Failure of His Designs on Long Island, 1663–1675," *New England Quarterly*, XXIX (1956), 3–26.

Earle, Alice M., *Curious Punishments of Bygone Days*, Chicago, 1896.

East, Robert A., "Puritanism and New Settlement," *New England Quarterly*, XVII (June), 255–264.

Eisenger, Chester E., "The Puritans' Justification for Taking the Land," *Essex Institute Historical Collections*, LXXXIV (1948), 131–143.

Ernst, James E., *The Political Thought of Roger Williams*, Seattle, 1929.

Eusden, John Dykstra, *Puritan Lawyers, and Politics in Early Seventeenth-Century England*, New Haven, 1958.

Farrand, Max, "Massachusetts Laws of 1660," *Publications of the Colonial Society of Massachusetts*, XXVII (1932), 194–197.

Farrell, John T., "The Early History of Rhode Island's Court System," *Rhode Island History*, IX (1950), 65–71, 103–117; X (1951), 14–27.

Figgis, John N., *The Divine Right of Kings*, 2nd ed., London, 1914.

Ford, Worthington C., and Albert Matthews, "Bibliography of the Laws of the Massachusetts Bay, 1641–1776," *Publications of the Colonial Society of Massachusetts*, IV (1910), 291–480.

Fowler, David H., "Connecticut's Freemen: The First Forty Years," *William and Mary Quarterly*, XV (1958), 312–333.

French, Allen, "The Arms and Military Training of our Colonizing Ancestors," *Proceedings of the Massachusetts Historical Society*, LXVII, 3–21.

Frese, Joseph Raphael, "Early Parliamentary Legislation on Writs of Assistance [1660–1696]," *Transactions of the Colonial Society of Massachusetts*, XXXVIII (1959), 318–359.

Gierke, Otto von, *Natural Law and the Theory of Society, 1500–1800*, Cambridge, Eng., 1934, 2 vols.; Beacon paperback. (Introduction by Ernest Barker.)

Gooch, George P., *The History of English Democratic Ideas in the Seventeenth Century*, ed. H. J. Laski, London, 1927; Harper Torchbook edition, 1959.

Goodman, Leonard S., "Mandamus in the Colonies—The Rise of the Superintending Power of American Courts," *American Journal of Legal History*, I (1957), 308–335; II (1958), 1–34.

Goodspeed, Charles Eliot, "Extortion, Captain Turner, and the Widow Stolion," *Transactions of the Colonial Society of Massachusetts*, XXXVIII (1959), 60–79. (Magistrates dictated the wages paid to workmen, prices of commodities and percentage of profit allowed to merchants.)

Gough, J. W., *The Social Contract*, Oxford, 1937.

Gray, Stanley, "The Political Thought of John Winthrop," *New England Quarterly* III (1930), 681–705.

Greene, Evarts B., *Religion and the State: The Making and Testing of an American Tradition*, New York, 1941.

Greene, Maria L., *The Development of Religious Liberty in Connecticut*, Boston, 1905.

Grinnell, Frank W., "John Winthrop and the Constitutional Thinking of John Adams," *Proceedings of the Massachusetts Historical Society*, LXIII (1931), 91–119.

Haffenden, Philip S., "The Anglican Church in Restoration Colonial Policy," *Seventeenth-Century America: Essays in Colonial History*, ed., James Morton Smith, Chapel Hill, 1959, 166–191.

—— "The Crown and the Colonial Charters, 1675–1688," *William and Mary Quarterly*, XV (1958), 297–311, 452–466.

Haller, William, Jr., *The Puritan Frontier: Town Planting in New England*

Colonial Development 1630–1660. Studies in History, Economics and Public Law, No. 568, New York, 1951.

Harper, Lawrence A., *The English Navigation Laws: A Seventeenth-Century Experiment in Social Engineering*, New York, 1939.

Harris, Marshall, *Origin of the Land Tenure System in the United States*, Ames, 1953.

Haskins, George L., "Codification of Law in Colonial Massachusetts: A Study in Comparative Law," *Indiana Law Review*, 30 (1954–1955), 1–18.

—— *Law and Authority in Early Massachusetts: A Study in Tradition and Design*, New York, 1960. (A discussion of law and order in provincial and local government 1630–1648.)

Hedges, James B., *The Browns of Providence Plantations: Colonial Years*, Cambridge, 1952. (Studies in economic history.)

Hilkey, Charles J., *Legal Development in Colonial Massachusetts, 1630–1686*, New York, 1910.

Hirsch, Elizabeth F., "John Cotton and Roger Williams: Their Controversy Concerning Religious Liberty," *Church History*, X (1941), 38–51.

Hoon, Elizabeth, *The Organization of the English Customs System 1696–1786*, New York, 1938.

Howe, Mark DeWolfe, and Louis F. Eaton, Jr., "The Supreme Judicial Power in the Colony of Massachusetts Bay," *New England Quarterly*, XX (1947), 291–316. (A brilliant study correcting traditional misconceptions of the struggle between magistrates and deputies over the negative voice in matters of judicature.)

Hudson, Winthrop S., "Puritanism and the Spirit of Capitalism," *Church History*, XVIII (1949), 3–17. (An illuminating criticism of Weber and Tawney.)

Jacobson, Jacob M., ed., *The Development of American Political Thought: A Documentary History*, New York, 1932.

Jeffrey, William, Jr., "Early New England Court Records: A Bibliography of Published Materials," *Boston Public Library Quarterly*, VI (1954), 160–184; reprinted in *American Journal of Legal History*, I (1957), 119–147.

Johnson, Edgar A. J., *American Economic*

Thought in the Seventeenth Century, London, 1932.

—— "Economic Ideas of John Winthrop," *New England Quarterly*, III (1930), 235–250.

Jordan, Wilbur K., *The Development of Religious Toleration in England*, 4 vols., Cambridge, 1932–1940.

Labaree, Leonard Woods, *Conservatism in Early American History*, New Haven, 1948.

Lauer, Paul E., *Church and State in New England*, Baltimore, 1892.

Leach, Douglas Edwards, "The Military System of Plymouth Colony," *New England Quarterly*, XXIV (1951), 342–364.

Levitan, Tina, "Hebraic Mortar," *American Hebrew*, CLVII, Feb. 27, 1948, 2, 15. (The Old Testament as a source for colonial democratic processes.)

Lokken, Roy N., "The Concept of Democracy in Colonial Political Thought," *William and Mary Quarterly*, XVI (1959), 568–580.

Lord, Arthur, "The Mayflower Compact," *Proceedings of the American Antiquarian Society*, N.S. XXX (1920), 278–294.

McElroy, Paul Simpson, "John Wise: The Father of American Independence," *Essex Institute Historical Collections*, LXXXI (1945), 201–226. (Wise's contribution to the cause of civil liberty.)

McIlwain, Charles H., "The Transfer of the Charter to New England, and its Significance in American Constitutional History," *Proceedings of the Massachusetts Historical Society*, LXIII (1931), 53–64.

Matthews, Nathan, "The Results of the Prejudice Against Lawyers in Massachusetts in the 17th Century," *Massachusetts Law Quarterly*, XIII (May, 1928), 73–94.

Mead, Sidney E., "From Coercion to Persuasion: Another Look at the Rise of Religious Liberty and the Emergence of Denominationalism," *Church History*, XXV (1950), 317–337.

Merrian, Charles E., *A History of American Political Theories*, New York, 1903; 1926.

Mesnard, Pierre, *L'Essor de la Philosophie Politique au XVIe Siècle*, Paris, 1936.

Miller, John C., "Religion, Finance, and Democracy in Massachusetts," *New England Quarterly*, VI (1933), 29–58. (Establishes a connection between emotionalism of the frontier awakening with back-country hostility to urban financial control.)

Miller, Perry, "Religion and Society in the Early Literature: The Religious Impulse in the Founding of Virginia," *William and Mary Quarterly*, 3rd series, V (1948), 492–522; VI (1949), 24–51; reprinted in *Errand into the Wilderness*, Cambridge, 1956, 99–140.

—— "Thomas Hooker and the Democracy of Early Connecticut," *New England Quarterly*, IV (1931), 663–712; reprinted in *Errand into the Wilderness*, Cambridge, 1956; (Examination of claims for democratic origins of Connecticut in the light of orthodox Puritan theory.)

Mook, H. Telfer, "Training Day in New England," *New England Quarterly*, XI (1938), 675–697.

Morgan, Edmund S., "The Case against Anne Hutchinson," *New England Quarterly*, X (1937), 635–649.

Morris, Richard B., *Government and Labor in Early America*, New York, 1946.

—— "Legalism *versus* Revolutionary Doctrine in New England," *New England Quarterly*, IV (1931), 195–215. (Data on the low estate in which most lawyers were held in Massachusetts during the early colonial period.)

—— "Massachusetts and the Common Law: The Declaration of 1646," *American Historical Review*, XXXI (1926), 443–453.

——, and Jonathan Grossman, "The Regulation of Wages in Early Massachusetts," *New England Quarterly*, XI (1938), 470–500.

—— *Studies in the History of American Law, with Special Reference to the Seventeenth and Eighteenth Centuries*, New York, 1930.

Mosse, George L., *The Holy Pretence: A Study in Christianity and Reason of State from William Perkins to John Winthrop*, Oxford, 1957. (A study of the attempt to reconcile Christian ethic and political exigencies.)

Niebuhr, Richard, "The Idea of Covenant and American Democracy," *Church History*, XXIII (1954), 126–135.

Noble, John, "Notes on the Trial and Punishment of Crimes in . . . the Time of the Colony," *Publications of the Colonial Society of Massachusetts*, III (1900), 51–66.

Page, Elwin L., *Judicial Beginnings in New Hampshire 1640–1700*, Concord, N. H., 1959. (Based on original trial court records and the printed sources.)

Park, Charles E., "Excommunication in Colonial Churches," *Publications of the Colonial Society of Massachusetts*, XII (1911), 321–332.

—— "Two Ruling Elders of the First Church in Boston," *Publications of the Colonial Society of Massachusetts*, XIII (1912), 82–95.

Parkes, Henry B., "John Cotton and Roger Williams Debate Toleration, 1644–1652," *New England Quarterly*, IV (1931), 735–756.

Pound, Roscoe, "Puritanism and the Common Law," *American Law Review*, XLV (1911), 811–829.

Reed, Susan M., *Church and State in Massachusetts, 1691–1740*, Urbana, Ill., 1914.

Reinsch, Paul S., *English Common Law in the Early American Colonies*, University of Wisconsin, Bulletin II, No. 4, in Economics, Political Science, and History, 1899.

Roberts, Oliver A., *History of the Military Company of the Massachusetts*, Boston, 1895–1901, 4 vols.

Robertson, D. B., *The Religious Foundations of Leveller Democracy*, New York, 1951. (A significant contribution to understanding the essentially religious character of left-wing Puritanism.)

Savelle, Max, *Seeds of Liberty: The Genesis of the American Mind*, New York, 1948. (Cultural patterns, 1740–1760.)

Schapiro, Jacob S., *Social Reform and the Reformation*, New York, 1909.

Schenk, W., *The Concern for Social Justice in the Puritan Revolution*, London and New York, 1948. (Religious propulsion of Puritan thought to achieve an equitable social order.)

Scott, Kenneth, *Counterfeiting in Colonial America*, New York, 1957.

Seidman, Aaron B., "Church and State in the Early Years of the Massachusetts Bay Colony," *New England Quarterly*, XVIII (1945), 211–233.

Seybolt, Robert F., "The Ministers at the Town Meetings in Colonial Boston," *Publications of the Colonial Society of Massachusetts*, XXXII (1938), 300–304.

Sharp, Morrison, "Leadership and Democracy in the Early New England System of Defense," *American Historical Review*, L (1945), 244–260.

Shipton, Clifford K., "Puritanism and Modern Democracy," *New England Historical and Genealogical Register*, CI (1947), 181–198.

Silver, Rollo G., "Financing the Publication of Early New England Sermons," *Studies in Bibliography: Papers of the Bibliographic Society of the University of Virginia*, XI (1958), 163–178.

Simpson, Alan, "How Democratic Was Roger Williams?" *William and Mary Quarterly*, XIII (1956), 56–67.

—— *Puritanism in Old and New England: A Study in the Politics of Enthusiasm*, Chicago, 1955; University of Chicago paperback.

—— 'Saints in Arms. English Puritanism as Political Utopianism," *Church History*, XXIII (1954), 119–125. (A study of Puritan fanaticism.)

Slafter, Edmund, *John Checkley: or, The Evolution of Religious Toleration in Massachusetts Bay*, Boston, 1897, 2 vols.

Smith, Abbot E., *Colonists in Bondage*, Chapel Hill, 1941.

Smith, Chard Powers, "Church and State in Wethersfield, 1696–1699," *New England Quarterly*, XXIX (1956), 82–87. (Control of church and state by the freemen.)

Smith, Joseph H., *Appeals to the Privy Council from the American Plantations*, New York, 1950. (An examination of the appellate jurisdiction of the Privy Council over the courts of the American colonies.)

Stead, George A., "Roger Williams and the Massachusetts-Bay," *New England Quarterly*, VII (1934), 235–257.

Stearns, Raymond P., "John Wise of Ipswich Was No Democrat in Politics," *Essex Institute Historical Collections*, Jan., 1961.

Story, Irving C., "John Wise: Congregational Democrat," *Pacific University Bulletin* XXXVI (1939), No. 3. (An analysis of the *Vindication of New England Churches*.)

Swift, Lindsay, "The Massachusetts Election Sermons," *Publications of the Colonial Society of Massachusetts*, I (1895), 388–451.

Tawney, Richard H., *Religion and the Rise of Capitalism*, New York, 1926; 1952; New American Library paperback. (An able and superbly written book, presenting the economic background of the Protestant movement, with a section on New England in particular.)

—— "Religious Thought on Social and Economic Questions in the Sixteenth and Seventeenth Centuries," *Journal of Political Economy*, XXXI (1923), 461–493,. 637–674, 804–825.

Vail, Robert W. G., "A Check List of New England Election Sermons," *Proceedings of the American Antiquarian Society*, XLV (1935), 233–266.

Weis, Frederick L., *The Colonial Clergy and the Colonial Churches of New England*, Lancaster, Mass., 1936. (A compendium of short biographical sketches.)

Whitman, Zechariah G., *An Historical Sketch of the Ancient and Honourable Artillery Company*, Boston, 1820; 1842.

Wigmore, John H., editor-in-chief, *Select Essays in Anglo-American Legal History*, Boston, 1907–1909, 3 vols.

Winslow, Ola Elizabeth, *Meetinghouse Hill: 1630–1783*, New York, 1952.

(Origins of American democracy lie in the town meetings. The town, not the church, owned the meetinghouse and paid the minister's salary.)

Wolford, Thorp L., "The Laws and Liberties of 1648: The First Code of Laws Enacted and Printed in English America," *Boston University Law Review*, XXVIII (1948), 426–463.

Woodhouse, Arthur S. P., *Puritanism and Liberty, University of Toronto Quarterly*, IV, No. 3, 1935; London, 1950.

Wright, Benjamin F., Jr., *American Interpretations of Natural Law*, Cambridge, 1931.

Wright, Harry A., "The Technique of Seventeenth Century Indian-Land Purchases," *Essex Institute Historical Collections*, LXXVII (1941), 185–197.

Zagorin, Perez, *A History of Political Thought in the English Revolution*, London, 1954. (A Marxian interpretation.)

—— "The Social Interpretation of the English Revolution," *Journal of Economic History*, Sept., 1959.

Ziff, Larzer, "The Social Bond of the Church Covenant," *American Quarterly*, X (1958), 454–462.

III. PURITAN RELIGIOUS THOUGHT

In this section are listed the more important works illustrating the Puritans' general view of the world and of life. Most of them are naturally sermons or theological treatises, yet in them can be found pronouncements upon the various problems of human existence, practical and philosophical.

A. Primary Sources

Since a full list of the original sources for a history of Puritan religious thought would include almost all the publications of Puritan spokesmen, only those items are mentioned that are particularly apt.

1. The General View

Adams, Charles F., ed., *Antinomianism in the Colony of Massachusetts Bay, 1636–1638*, Boston, 1894. (A collection of the materials relating to the trial and expulsion of Anne Hutchinson; indispensable for an understanding of the philosophical issues of Puritanism. Footnotes not always reliable.)

Allin, James, *Man's Self Reflection a Means to Further his Recovery from His Apostasy from God*, Cambridge, 1680. (A

discussion of the rôle of introspection in Puritan life.)

Ames, William, *Conscience with the Power and Cases thereof . . . Translated out of Latine into English, for more publique benefit*, London, 1643. (This and the following were the standard handbooks on theology and ethics in seventeenth-century New England. They are compact, methodical outlines of the official creed.)

—— *The Marrow of Sacred Divinity, Drawne out of the Holy Scriptures, and the Interpreters thereof, and brought into Method,*

London, 1638[?]. (Translated from the Latin *Medulla Sacrae Theologiae*, 1623.)

Brattle, William, *Compendium Logicæ Secundum Principia D. Renati Cartesii Plerumque Efformatum, et Catechistice Propositum*, Boston, 1735. (The first American text on logic; used as a text at Harvard as late as 1765.)

Bulkeley, Peter, *The Gospel-Covenant; or the Covenant of Grace opened*, 2nd ed., London, 1651. (The most important exposition of the concept of the covenant, a fundamental idea in New England Puritan thought.)

Bulkley, John, *The Usefulness of Reveal'd Religion, to Preserve and Improve that which is Natural*, New London, 1730. (Extremely important document for the transition from seventeenth-century Puritanism to eighteenth-century rationalism.)

Chauncy, Charles, *Enthusiasm Described and Caution'd Against*, Boston, 1742.

—— *A Letter from a Gentleman in Boston to Mr. George Wishart*, Edinburgh, 1742; reprinted, *Clarendon Historical Society Reprints*, first series, No. 7, Edinburgh, 1883. (A description of the Great Awakening.)

—— *Seasonable Thoughts on the State of Religion in New-England*, Boston, 1743. (Against Whitefield and enthusiasts of the Great Awakening.)

Checkley, John, *Choice Dialogues, between a Godly Minister and an Honest Countryman, concerning Election and Predestination*, Boston, 1720.

Clarke, Samuel, *A Mirrour or Looking-Glasse both for Saints, and Sinners*, London, 1646. (A contemporary estimate of the Antinomian heresy.)

Colman, Benjamin, *God Deals with us as Rational Creatures*, Boston, 1723.

—— *A Humble Discourse of the Incomprehensibleness of God*, Boston, 1715; 1740; Northampton, 1804.

Cooper, William, *Man humbled by being compar'd to a Worm*, Boston, 1732.

Cotton, John, *A Briefe Exposition with Practicall Observations upon The Whole Book of Ecclesiastes*, London, 1654. (A skeleton outline of a series of sermons; probably Cotton's own notes. Since Ecclesiastes is more than any other book of the Bible concerned with what might be called secular issues, this work is a mine of information on Puritan attitudes that are seldom discussed in the more strictly theological writings.)

—— *An Exposition upon the Thirteenth Chapter of the Revelation*, London, 1656.

—— *Gods Mercie mixed with his Justice*, London, 1641; reprinted in "Scholars' Facsimiles and Reprints," ed. Perry Miller, Gainesville, Fla., 1958. (A succinct statement of Puritan thought on one of the central problems.)

—— *Gods Promise To His Plantation*, London, 1630; *Old South Leaflets*, No. 53; cf. E. D. Mead, *Proceedings of the Massachusetts Historical Society*, I, 101–115. (The valedictory sermon delivered as the fleet was to set sail in 1630; succinct expression of the Puritan aim in migrating to the new world.)

—— *Milk for Babes, Drawn out of the Breasts of both Testaments, chiefly for the spirituall nourishment of Boston babes in either England, but may be of like use for any Children*, London, 1646; Cambridge, 1656. (Catechism for children; the theology is expressed in simplest terms.)

—— *The New Covenant; Or, a Treatise, unfolding the order and manner of the giving and receiving of the Covenant of Grace to the Elect*, London, 1654.

—— *The way of Life*, London, 1641. (A series of readable sermons, it is the best literary statement, in the least technical terms, of the Puritan code.)

Dudley, Paul, *An Essay On The Merchandize of Slaves & Souls of Men; . . . With an Application Thereof to the Church of Rome*, Boston, 1731.

Dummer, Jeremiah, *A Discourse on the holiness of the Sabbath-day*, Boston, 1704. (Valuable for definitions of positive and natural law; for many important ideas at the turn of the century.)

Fitch, James, *The first Principles of the Doctrine of Christ*, Boston, 1679. (The best succinct summary of the creed and philosophy of the New England variety of Calvinism.)

Flynt, Josiah, "The Worlds Eternity is an Impossibility," *Almanack*, Cambridge, 1666.

Frere, W. H., and C. E. Douglas, *Puritan Manifestoes*, London, 1907; 1954.

Haller, William, ed., *Tracts on Liberty in the Puritan Revolution, 1638–1647*, New York, 1934, 3 vols.

Haller, William, and Godfrey Davies, eds., *The Leveller Tracts, 1647–1653*, New York, 1944.

Hanbury, Benjamin, ed., *Historical Memorials Relating to the Independents or Congregationalists, from their Rise to the Restoration*, London, 1839–1844, 3 vols. (A collection of copious extracts from the writings of Congregationalists, including many of the New England apologists. It provides a text for many books not easily available, and enables New England thought to be seen as part of a whole movement in English religious life.)

Hoar, Leonard, *The Sting of Death and Death Unstung*, Boston, 1680.

Hooke, William, *New-Englands Sence, of Old-England and Irelands Sorrowes*, London, 1645.

Hooker, Thomas, *The Application of Redemption By the Effectual Work of the Word and Spirit of Christ, for the bringing home of Lost Sinners to God*, London, 1657; 1659. (Sermons delivered at Hartford; the summary of Hooker's doctrine and spirit.)

—— *The Soules Exaltation*, London, 1638.

—— *The Soules Humiliation*, 2nd ed., London, 1638.

—— *The Soules Implantation*, London, 1637.

—— *The Soules Preparation for Christ*, London, 1632.

(These four works, which logically run *Preparation, Humiliation, Implantation*, and *Exaltation*, are the masterpieces of the most impassioned orator in the first generation of preachers. They were probably written before Hooker left England. They constitute the most minute and searching analysis of the soul and the process of spiritual regeneration, the most coherent and sustained expression of the essential religious experience ever achieved by the New England divines.) Sermons selected from the *Application, Preparation*, and *Implantation* reprinted in *Redemption, Three Sermons*, ed. Everett H. Emerson, Gainesville, Fla., 1956.)

Johnson, Samuel, *Samuel Johnson . . . His Career and Writings*, ed. Herbert and Carol Schneider, New York, 1929, 4 vols.

Mather, Cotton, *Fair Weather*, Boston, 1691.

—— *The Faith of the Fathers*, Boston, 1699.

—— "A Letter on the late Disputes about the Trinity," preface to Thomas Bradbury, *Necessity of Contending for Revealed Religion*, Boston, 1720.

—— *A Man of Reason*, Boston, 1718.

—— *Manuductio ad Ministerium*, Boston, 1726; New York, 1938. (Handbook for preachers.)

—— *Reason Satisfied: and Faith Established*, Boston, 1712.

—— *Reasonable Religion*, Boston, 1700.

—— "To the Reader," *The Boston Ephemeris*, 1683.

Mather, Increase, *Angelographia*, Boston, 1696.

—— *Awakening Truths Tending to Conversion*, Boston, 1710.

—— *A Call from Heaven To the Present and Succeeding Generations*, Boston, 1679.

—— *A Discourse Proving that the Christian Religion, Is the only True Religion*, Boston, 1702.

—— *The Doctrine of Divine Providence, opened and applyed*, Boston, 1684.

—— *Practical Truths Tending to Promote the Power of Godliness*, Boston, 1682.

—— *Some Important Truths About Conversion*, London, 1674; Boston, 1684.

—— *Soul-Saving Gospel Truths*, Boston, 1703; 1712.

—— *The Times of men are in the hand of God*, Boston, 1675.

Mayhew, Experience, *A Discourse shewing that God dealeth with Men As with Reasonable Creatures*, Boston, 1720.

Mitchell, Jonathan, *A Discourse of the Glory To which God hath called Believers By Jesus Christ*, London, 1677; Boston, 1721.

More, Paul Elmer, and Frank L. Cross, *Anglicanism: The Thought and Practice of the Church of England, Illustrated from the Religious Literature of the Seventeenth Century*, Milwaukee, Wis., 1935. (The most convenient source for tenets of the Puritans' opponents.)

Morgan, Joseph, *The History of the Kingdom of Basruah*, Boston, 1715; reprinted with three formerly unpublished letters, Cambridge, 1946. (An allegory of man's fall and redemption.)

Morton, Charles, *The Spirit of Man*, Boston, 1693.

Norton, John, *The Heart of N-England rent at the Blasphemies of the Present Generation*, Cambridge, 1659. (Condemnation of the Quakers.)

—— *The Orthodox Evangelist*, London, 1654. (Compact statement of the whole system of theology.)

Oakes, Urian, *The Soveraign Efficacy of Divine Providence*, Boston, 1682.

Parker, Thomas, *The Copy of a Letter Written . . . to His Sister*, London, 1650; Boston, 1925.

Pemberton, Ebenezer, *Sermons and Discourses on Several Occasions*, ed. Benjamin Colman, London, 1727. (A collection of the writings of one of the best minds in New England in the first two decades of the eighteenth century.)

Powicke, Frederick J., ed., *Some Unpublished Correspondence of the Reverend Richard Baxter and the Reverend John Eliot, 1656-1682*, Manchester, Eng., 1931.

Prince, Thomas, *Morning Health No Security Against the Sudden Arrest of Death before Night*, Boston, 1727.

Prince, Thomas, Jr., ed., *The Christian History, containing Accounts of the Revival and Propagation of Religion in Great-Britain & America*, Boston, 1744-1745, 2 vols. (America's first religious periodical; the literary repository for the revivalist wing of the New England clergy in the Great Awakening, opposed to Charles Chauncy.)

Robinson, John, *Works*, ed. Robert Ashton, Boston, 1851, 3 vols. (The writings of the pastor of the Pilgrim congregation in England and Holland, who, though he did not come to America, exerted a great influence on the thought of New England.)

Sewall, Samuel, *Phænomena quædam Apocalyptica*, Boston, 1697; 1727.

—— *Proposals Touching the Accomplishment of Prophecies*, Boston, 1713.

—— "Samuel Sewall and the New England Company," *Proceedings of the Massachusetts Historical Society*, LXVII (1941-1944), 1945, 55-110. (Sewall's account book when he was disbursing agent for a London missionary society, ed. George P. Winship.)

Shepard, Thomas, "Letter to Hugh Peter," *American Historical Review*, IV (1898), 105.

—— *New Englands Lamentation for Old Englands present errours, and divisions, and their feared future desolations if not timely prevented*, London, 1645. (New England attitude toward religious developments in England during the Civil Wars.)

—— *Works*, ed. John Albro, Boston, 1853, 3 vols. (The collected writings of one of the four major figures in the first generation of New England divines.)

Shepard, Thomas, Jr., *Eye-Salve; Or, A Watch-Word From our Lord Jesus Christ unto his Churches*, Cambridge, 1673.

Sherman, John, "A brief Essay to promote a religious improvement of this preceding Calendar," *Almanack*, Cambridge, 1677.

—— "A Monitory Advertisement," *Almanack*, Cambridge, 1676.

Stoddard, Solomon, *The Duty of Gospel-Ministers to preserve a People from Corruption*, Boston, 1718.

Thacher, Thomas, *A Fast of God's Chusing*, Boston, 1678.

"Tracts Relating to the Attempts to Convert to Christianity the Indians of New England," *Collections of the Massachusetts Historical Society*, third series, Vol. IV, 1834. (John Eliot, *The Day-Breaking*, 1647; Thomas Shepard, *The Clear Sunshine*, 1648; Edward Winslow, comp., *The Glorious Progress*, 1649; Henry Whitfield, *The Light appearing*, 1651; *Strength out of Weakness*, 1652; John Eliot and Thomas Mayhew, *Tears of Repentance*, 1653; John Eliot, *A Late and Further Manifestation*, 1655.)

Wadsworth, Benjamin, *Christ's Fan in his hand, separating the wheat & chaff*, Boston, 1722.

—— *An Essay on the Decalogue, or Ten Commandments*, Boston, 1719.

—— *True Piety the best Policy for Times of War*, Boston, 1722.

—— *The Way of life opened in the everlasting Covenant*, Boston, 1712.

Ward, Nathaniel, *The Simple Cobler of Aggawam in America*, London, 1647; ed. David Pulsifer, Boston, 1843; Ipswich Historical Society, 1906.

Wheelwright, John, *John Wheelwright. His Writings*, ed. Charles H. Bell, Boston, 1876. (The life and writings of a minister expelled from Massachusetts Bay for his friendship with the Antinomian party.)

Willard, Samuel, *The Barren Fig Trees Doom*, Boston, 1691.

—— *A Brief Discourse of Justification*, Boston, 1686.

—— *A Brief Reply to Mr. George Kieth*, Boston, 1703.

—— *The Child's Portion; Or, The Unseen Glory Of the Children of God, Asserted, and proved*, Boston, 1684.

—— *A Compleat Body of Divinity in Two Hundred and Fifty Expository Lectures*, Boston, 1726. (The *summa* of New England theology; the first folio printed in America; an immense repository, which makes dull reading, but is the authoritative reference book for the orthodox position on all points of the creed.)

—— *The Heart Garrisoned; Or, The Wisdome, and Care of the Spiritual Souldier above all things to safeguard his Heart*. Cambridge, 1676.

—— *The High Esteem Which God hath of the Death of his Saints*, Boston, 1683. (Sermon occasioned by the death of John Hull.)

—— *The Peril of the Times Displayed; Or, The Danger of Mens taking up with a Form of Godliness, But Denying the Power of it*, Boston, 1700.

Williams, Roger, *Experiments of Spiritual Life & Health, And their Preservatives*, London, 1652; Providence, 1863.

—— *George Fox Digg'd out of his Burrowes*, Boston, 1676; ed. J. L. Dimon, *Publications of the Narragansett Club*, Vol. V (1872). (Although the apostle of religious liberty, Williams attacked Quakers furiously.)

Wolfe, Don, ed., *Leveller Manifestoes of the Puritan Revolution*, New York, 1944.

2. The Way of the Churches

Barnard, John, *The Lord Jesus Christ the only, and Supream Head of the Church*, Boston, 1738. (Important sermon, marking the ultimate outcome of the ecclesiastical polity, where the Congregational system is actually claimed to give liberty of conscience.)

Cotton, John, *The Keyes of the Kingdom of Heaven, and Power thereof, according to the Word of God*, London, 1644.

—— *The Way of Congregational Churches Cleared*, London, 1648. (The best statement in historical terms of the sources, background, and development of the New England polity.)

Davenport, John, *An Answer of the Elders of the severall Churches in New-England unto Nine Positions sent over to them*, London, 1643. (Written in 1639, it is the first attempt to systematize the principles of the New England ecclesiastical order.)

The Power of Congregational Churches Asserted and Vindicated, London, 1672.

Hooker, Thomas, *A Survey of the Summe of Church-Discipline*, London, 1648. (The most profound, philosophical, and reasoned statement of the practical program of New England Puritanism. Indispensable.)

Mather, Cotton, *Ratio Discipline Fratrum Nov-Anglorum*, Boston, 1726; ed. T. C. Upham, Portland, 1829. (The best crystallization of a century of ecclesiastical development in New England.)

Mather, Increase, *The Divine Right of Infant-Baptisme Asserted and Proved from Scripture And Antiquity*, Boston, 1680.

—— *The Order of the Gospel, Professed and Practised by the Churches of Christ in New-England, Justified*, Boston, 1700.

—— *A Dissertation, wherein The Strange Doctrine Lately Published in a Sermon, The Tendency of which, is, to Encourage Unsanctified Persons (which such) to Approach the Holy Table of the Lord, is Examined and Confuted*, Boston, 1708. (Attack on Solomon Stoddard.)

Mather, Richard, *An Apologie of the Churches in New-England for Church-Covenant*, London, 1643.

—— *Church-Government and Church-Covenant Discussed*, London, 1643. (Cf. T. J. Holmes, *Proceedings of the American Antiquarian Society*, N.S. XXXIII (1923), 291–296.)

Mather, Samuel, *An Apology For the Liberties of the Churches in New England: To which is prefix'd, A Discourse concerning Congregational Churches*, Boston, 1738.

Perkins, William, *Of the Calling of the Ministrie: Two Treatises. Describing the duties and Dignities of that Calling*, London, 1606; *Works*, 1618, III, 429–463. (Perkins was regarded as one of the greatest of theologians by New Englanders, and his works were standard texts; this treatise enunciates the Puritan conception of the role and function of the minister.)

Shepard, Thomas, and John Allin, *A Defence of the Answer made unto the Nine Questions or Positions sent from New-England*, London, 1648.

Stoddard, Solomon, *An Appeal to the Learned. Being A Vindication of the Right of Visible Saints to the Lords Supper, Though they be destitute of a Saving Work of God's Spirit on their Hearts: Against the Exceptions of Mr. Increase Mather*, Boston, 1709.

—— *The Doctrine of Instituted Churches Explained and Proved from the Word of God*, London, 1700. (A reply to Increase

Mather's *The Order of the Gospel*, this work initiated the so-called Stoddardean doctrine: that all who professed belief in saving grace might therefore partake of the Lord's Supper.)

—— *The Inexcusableness of Neglecting The Worship of God, under A Pretence of being in an Unconverted Condition*, Boston, 1708. (A statement of Stoddard's theories of church polity, marking a departure from the orthodox platform, and the beginning of a bitter controversy with Increase Mather.)

B. SECONDARY WORKS

There are few substantial studies of Puritan thought before the present century. Particularly within the last generation an effort has been made to examine and appraise Puritan thought as a chapter in intellectual history. This section of the bibliography should be supplemented by Section II B.

Akers, Charles, "The Making of a Religious Liberal: Jonathan Mayhew and the Great Awakening," *New England Social Studies Bulletin*, XI, No. 3 (Mar., 1954), 18–25.

Armstrong, Maurice W., "English, Scottish and Irish Backgrounds of American Presbyterianism, 1689–1729," *Journal of the Presbyterian Historical Society*, XXXIV (1956), 3–18.

Atkins, Gaius Glenn, and Frederick L. Fagley, *History of American Congregationalism*, Boston and Chicago, 1942. (A popular and not always critical account.)

Bacon, Leonard W., *A History of American Christianity*, New York, 1897.

Banks, Charles E., "Religious 'Persecution' as a Factor in the Emigration to New England," *Proceedings of the Massachusetts Historical Society*, LXVIII (1934–1935), 136–151.

Bartlett, Irving H., "The Puritans as Missionaries," *Boston Public Library Quarterly*, II (1950), 99–118.

Beardsley, Frank G., *A History of American Revivals*, New York, 1912.

Becker, Carl L., *The Heavenly City of the Eighteenth-Century Philosophers*, New Haven, 1932; Yale paperback. (A brilliant analysis of eighteenth-century rationalism, interpreting it as a new attempt to realize the Augustinian City of God on earth. This study of the religious overtones of eighteenth-century thought helps to make

comprehensible the tendencies of the seventeenth century.)

Benz, Ernest, "The Pietist and Puritan Sources of Early Protestant Missions," *Church History*, XXI (1951), 28–55. (Cotton Mather's correspondence with A. H. Francke and with missionaries from Halle.)

Boardman, George N., *A History of New England Theology*, New York, 1899. (An analysis of the theological systems, but with very limited attention to the historic settings of the New England doctrine.)

Brauer, Jerald C., "Reflections on the Nature of English Puritanism," *Church History*, XXIII (1954), 99–108. (A succinct and penetrating article.)

Buranelli, Vincent, "Colonial Philosophy," *William and Mary Quarterly*, XVI (1959), 343–362.

Calamandrei, Mauro, "Neglected Aspects of Roger Williams' Thought," *Church History*, XXI (1952), 239–256. (Argues that Roger Williams was not a man of the Renaissance nor of the Enlightenment, but a Puritan, Biblicist, and Millenarian.)

Cambridge Modern History, The, Chapters valuable for intellectual background: Vol. II (1903), Chap. xi, "Calvinism and the Reformed Church"; Chap. xix, "Tendencies of European Thought in the Age of the Reformation"; Vol. III (1905), Chap. xxii, "Political Thought in the

Bibliographies

liii

Sixteenth Century"; Vol. IV (1906), Chap. xxvii, "Descartes and Cartesianism"; Vol. V (1907), Chap. xi, "Religious Toleration in England"; Chap. xxiii, "European Science in the Seventeenth and Early Years of the Eighteenth Century"; Chap. xxiv, "Latitudinarianism and Pietism"; Vol. VI (1909), Chap. xxiii, "English Political Philosophy in the Seventeenth and Eighteenth Centuries."

Cambridge Platform of 1648, The; Tercentenary Commemoration, ed. Henry Wilder Foote, Boston, 1949. (Articles by F. L. Fagley, H. W. Foote, P. Miller, R. Bainton, A. C. McGiffert, Jr., A. Bradford and J. B. Conant.)

Catholic Cyclopedia, The, New York, 1907–1914, 6 vols. (Extremely useful, particularly for doctrinal history.)

Choisy, Eugene, and others, *Études sur Calvin et le Calvinisme*, Paris, 1935. (A volume of studies by many European authorities, on the foliation of Calvin, presenting many parallels to New England developments.)

Clark, George N., *The Seventeenth Century*, Oxford, 1929; Galaxy paperback. (An excellent survey of general conditions and intellectual currents.)

Clark, Henry W., *History of English Nonconformity*, London, 1911–1913, 2 vols.

Cragg, G. R., *From Puritanism to the Age of Reason: A Study of Changes in Religious Thought Within the Church of England, 1660–1700*, New York, 1950.

—— *Puritanism in the Period of the Great Persecution, 1660–1688*, New York, 1957.

Cremeans, Charles Davis, *The Reception of Calvinistic Thought in England*, Urbana, 1949. (A valuable study in the transmission of ideas.)

Cross, Arthur L., *The Anglican Episcopate and the American Colonies*, New York, 1902. (Chapters 6 and 7 deal with Mayhew and the Chandler-Chauncy controversies.)

Dale, Robert W., *History of English Congregationalism*, London, 1907.

Davenport, Frederick M., *Primitive Traits in Religious Revivals*, New York, 1905.

Davies, Godfrey, "Arminian versus Puritan in England, *ca.* 1620–1640," *Huntington Library Bulletin*, No. 5 (1934), 157–179.

Davies, Horton, *The Worship of the English Puritans*, London, 1948.

De Jong, Peter Y., *The Covenant Idea in New England Theology, 1620–1847*, Grand Rapids, 1946.

Dexter, Henry M., *The Congregationalism of the Last Three Hundred Years, as Seen in its Literature*, New York, 1880. (The monumental achievement of the greatest of Congregational historians, liberal but inevitably biased in favor of Puritanism. An immense bibliography of Congregational literature, both English and American, the fruit of years of research, is of great value.)

Dickens, A. G., *Lollards and Protestants in the Diocese of York, 1509–1558*, London, 1959. (An important study in the transmission of ideas. Documents an unbroken dissenting tradition from Lollardy to Puritanism.)

Drury, Clifford M., "Presbyterian Beginnings in New England and the Middle Colonies," *Journal of the Presbyterian Historical Society*, XXXIV (1956), 19–35.

Dunning, Albert E., *Congregationalists in America. A popular history of their origin, belief, polity, growth, and work*, Boston, 1894; New York, 1902.

Eames, Wilberforce, "Early New England Catechisms," *Proceedings of the American Antiquarian Society*, N.S. XII (1897–1898), 76–182.

Emerson, Everett H., "Calvin and Covenant Theology," *Church History*, XXV (1956), 136–144.

—— "Thomas Hooker and the Reformed Theology: The Relationship of Hooker's Conversion Preaching to Its Background," *Church History*, XXIV (1955), 369–370. (Abstract of doctoral dissertation.)

Emery, Samuel H., *The Ministry of Taunton*, Boston, 1853, 2 vols. (Reprints of sermons of William Hooke, Samuel Danforth, and Ephraim Judson.)

Faust, Clarence H., "The Decline of Puritanism," *Transitions in American Literary History*, cf. Harry Hayden Clark, Durham, N.C., 1953, 1–48.

—— Clarence H., and Thomas H. Johnson, *Jonathan Edwards*, American Writers Series, New York, 1935; American Century paperback. (Selections from sermons, treatises, and letters; bibliography; discussion of intellectual and literary background.)

Felt, Joseph B., *Ecclesiastical History of New England; comprising not only Religious, but also Moral, and other Relations*, Boston, 1855–1862, 2 vols. (A sprawling, ill-digested amassing of material, valuable for the amount of first-hand material quoted and the immense if unorganized knowledge of local history.)

Fenn, William W., *The Christian Way of Life . . . in the History of Religion in New England*, London, 1924.

—— "John Robinson's Farewell Address," *Harvard Theological Review*, XIII (1920), 236–251.

—— "The Marrow of Calvin's Theology," *Harvard Theological Review*, II (1909), 323–339. (Excellent.)

—— "The Revolt against the Standing Order," *Religious History of New England*, King's Chapel Lectures, Cambridge, 1917.

Fisher, George P., *History of Christian Doctrine*, New York, 1906. (Excellent handbook for the history of theology.)

Foote, Henry Wilder, "The Significance and Influence of the Cambridge Platform of 1648," *Proceedings of the Massachusetts Historical Society*, LXIX (1947–1950), 1956, 81–101.

Ford, Worthington C., "New England Catechisms," *Proceedings of the Massachusetts Historical Society*, LXII (1930), 28–29.

Foster, Frank H., "The Eschatology of the New England Divines," *Bibliotheca Sacra*, XLIII (1886), 6–19.

—— *A Genetic History of the New England Theology*, Chicago, 1907. (The best study of theological development. Unfortunately it devotes but one chapter to the period before Jonathan Edwards.)

Foster, Herbert D., "International Calvinism through Locke and the Revolution of 1688," *American Historical Review*, XXXII (1927), 475–499. (A penetrating study, demonstrating how Calvinism, filtered through Locke, eventuates in Lockean political philosophy.)

Frere, Walter H., *The English Church in the Reigns of Elizabeth and James I*, London, 1904. (Very useful for English religious backgrounds.)

Garrett, C. H., *The Marian Exiles*, Cambridge, Eng., 1938. (Reveals the continental influences on the Elizabethan settlement.)

Gaustad, Edwin Scott, *The Great Awakening in New England*, New York, 1957.

Gohdes, Clarence, "Aspects of Idealism in Early New England," *Philosophical Review*, XXXIX (1930), 537–555. (Points out the influence of the Cambridge Platonists in New England.)

Gordon, George A., *Humanism in New England Theology*, Boston, 1920.

Grabo, Norman S., "The Poet to the Pope: Edward Taylor to Solomon Stoddard," *American Literature*, XXXII (1960), 197–201. (Taylor urges Stoddard to lay down his innovations that threatened the peaceful order of New England churches.)

Griffiths, Olive M., *Religion and Learning: A Study in English Presbyterian Thought from the Bartholomew Ejections (1662) to the Foundation of the Unitarian Movement*, Cambridge, Eng., 1935. (An excellent study, tracing the steps of development whereby Calvinism becomes Unitarian rationalism; a parallel movement to that in New England, which is much illuminated by the comparison.)

Hall, Thomas C., *The Religious Background of American Culture*, Boston, 1930. (A brilliant and often penetrating history, maintaining the questionable thesis that English Puritanism contains an element of thought inherited from Wycliff which is antagonistic to Calvinism.)

Haller, William, "John Foxe and the Puritan Revolution," *The Seventeenth Century: Studies in the History of English Thought . . .*, R. F. Jones et al., Stanford, 1948. (The *Book of Martyrs*, a powerful force on shaping Puritan thought on the church in history.)

—— *Liberty and Reformation in the Puritan Reformation*, New York, 1955. (A continuation to 1649 of the earlier study on the rise of Puritanism.)

—— *The Rise of Puritanism, or the Way to the New Jerusalem as Set Forth in Pulpit and Press . . . 1570–1643*, New York, 1938; Harper Torchbook edition 1957. (This book with the succeeding volume [supra] make a brilliant contribution to our knowledge of the inner life and dynamism of the Puritan movement.)

Hallowell, Richard P., *The Quaker Invasion of Massachusetts*, Boston, 1883.

Haroutunian, Joseph, *Piety versus Moralism: The Passing of the New England Theology*, New York, 1932.

Hastings, James, ed., *Encyclopedia of Religion and Ethics*, New York, 1908–1914, 13 vols. (Very useful; bibliographies given.)

Hazard, Paul, *La Crise de la Conscience Européenne, 1680–1715*, Paris, 1935, 3 vols.

Heimert, Alan, "Puritanism, The Wilderness, and the Frontier," *New England Quarterly*, XXVI (1953), 361–382.

Henson, Herbert H., *Studies in English Religion in the Seventeenth Century*, London, 1903. (Extremely useful and stimulating.)

Hornberger, Theodore, "Benjamin Coleman and the Enlightenment," *New England Quarterly*, XII (1939), 227–240.

—— "Samuel Lee (1625–1691), A Clerical Channel for the Flow of New Ideas to Seventeenth Century New England," *Osiris*, I (1936), 341–355.

Hunt, John, *Religious Thought in England from the Reformation to the End of Last Century*, London, 1870–1873, 3 vols.

Hutton, William H., *The English Church from the Accession of Charles I to the Death of Anne, 1625–1714*, London, 1903.

Jones, Adam L., *Early American Philosophers*, New York, 1898.

Jones, Rufus M., *Mysticism and Democracy in the English Commonwealth*, Cambridge, 1932. (Chapter on "Seeker Movement" is valuable for Williams and New England mysticism.)

—— *The Quakers in the American Colonies*, London, 1911.

——*Studies in Mystical Religion*, London, 1909.

Knappen, Marshall M., *Tudor Puritanism: A Chapter in the History of Idealism*, Chicago, 1939. (An immensely valuable book for understanding the medieval and international character of the Puritan mind.)

——, ed., *Two Elizabethan Puritan Diaries*, Chicago, 1933. (The introduction contains one of the best analyses of the Puritan character yet in print; it rebuts the thesis of Weber and Tawney.)

Lecky, William E. H., *History of the Rise and Influence of the Spirit of Rationalism in Europe*, New York, 1866, 2 vols. (Although antipathetic to the religious point of view, this classic work is still essential to an understanding of the evolution of seventeenth-century New England into eighteenth.)

Lee, Umphrey, *The Historical Backgrounds of Early Methodist Enthusiasm*, New York, 1931.

Levy, Babette May, *Preaching in the First Half Century of New England History*, Hartford, 1945.

Lowenherz, Robert J., "Roger Williams and the Great Quaker Debate,". *American Quarterly*, XI (1959), 157–165.

Lydekker, John Wolfe, "The New England Company, the First Missionary Society. Some Account of Its Foundation and Early History," *Historical Magazine of the Protestant Episcopal Church*, XIV (1944), 107–127.

McClellan, B., "Two Shepherds Contending," *New England Quarterly*, XXVII (1954), 455–472. (The correspondence of J. Ashley, Minister at the Deerfield (1732–1780) with Father Jean Baptiste Sainte Pe, one of the Jesuit leaders in Canada.)

McClurkin, Paul T., "Presbyterianism in New England Congregationalism," *Journal of the Presbyterian Historical Society*, XXXI (1953), 245–254: XXXII (1954), 109–114.

McCulloch, Samuel C., "The Foundation and Early Work of the Society for the Propagation of the Gospel in Foreign Parts, *Huntington Library Quarterly*, VIII (1945), 241–258.

McGiffert, Arthur C., Sr., *Protestant Thought Before Kant*, New York, 1929; 1951; Harper Torchbook edition, 1962. (An excellent handbook; Chapter VIII on seventeenth-century Protestantism, and the section in Chapter IX on the New England theology, are especially useful.)

McGiffert, Arthur C., Jr., *Jonathan Edwards*, New York, 1932.

McGinn, Donald, *The Admonition Controversy*, New Brunswick, 1949. (A study of the beginning of the Puritan movement.)

MacKinnon, James, *Calvin and the Reformation*, London, 1936. (Probably the most convenient one volume survey of "Calvinistic" backgrounds.)

McLachlan, H. J., *Socinianism in 17th-Century England*, Oxford, 1951.

Maclear, James Fulton, "The Heart of New England Rent: The Mystical Element in Early Puritan History," *Mississippi Valley Historical Review*, XLII (1956), 621–652.

—— " 'The True American Union' of Church and State: The Reconstruction of the Theocratic Tradition," *Church History*, XXVIII (1959), 41–62.

Masson, David, *The Life of John Milton*, London, 1859–1894, 7 vols.; New York, 1946. (Still one of the most useful studies of the background of English religious history.)

Michaelsen, Robert S., "Changes in the Puritan Concept of Calling or Vocation," *New England Quarterly*, XXVI (1953), 315–336. (The changes within the Puritan concept of vocation in England helped produce Defoe's "complete trades-man"; in America they contributed to the "wisdom" of Poor Richard and *The Way to Wealth*.)

Micklem, Nathaniel, ed., *Christian Worship: Studies in its History and Meaning*, by Members of Mansfield College, Oxford, 1936.

Miller, Perry, "The End of the World," *William and Mary Quarterly*, VIII (1951), 171–191; reprinted with some modifications in *Errand into the Wilderness*, Cambridge, 1956, 217–239.

—— "From Edwards to Emerson," *New England Quarterly*, XIII (1940), 589–617; reprinted in *Errand into the Wilderness*, Cambridge, 1956, 184–203. (The Puritan effort to confront face to face the blinding image of divinity in the physical world.)

—— "The Half-Way Covenant," *New England Quarterly*, VI (1933), 676–715.

—— "The Marrow of Puritan Divin-ity," *Publications of the Colonial Society of Massachusetts*, XXXII (1938), 247–300; reprinted in *Errand into the Wilderness*, Cambridge, 1956, 48–98. (Analysis of the theory of the covenant in Puritan theology and society; elements of rationalism were already in Puritan thought by 1630, differentiating New England theology from Calvinism and moving in the direc-tion of eighteenth-century points of view.)

—— *The New England Mind: From Colony to Province*, Cambridge, 1953; Beacon paperback, 1961.

—— *The New England Mind: The Seventeenth Century*, New York, 1939; re-issued with "correction of the more egregious misprints," Cambridge, 1954; Beacon paperback, 1961.

—— *Orthodoxy in Massachusetts, 1630–1650: A Genetic Study*, Cambridge, 1933; Beacon paperback. (A study of the religious objectives of the New England Puritans in terms of their origins in England.)

—— "The Puritan Theory of the Sacra-ments in Seventeenth Century New Eng-land," *Catholic Historical Review*, XXII (1937), 409–425.

—— "Solomon Stoddard, 1643–1729," *Harvard Theological Review*, XXXIV (1941), 277–320. (His contribution to religious thought.)

Morais, Herbert M., *Deism in Eighteenth Century America*, New York, 1934. (A pioneer work, which lists the names and the writings of American deists, but does not go very deeply into the analysis of intellectual currents.)

Morgan, Edmund S., "The Puritans' Marriage with God," *South Atlantic Quarterly*, XLVIII (1949), 107–112.

Morison, Samuel E., *The Puritan Pro-naos: Studies in the Intellectual Life of New England in the Seventeenth Century*, New York, 1936; a second edition with minor revisions, *The Intellectual Life of Colonial New England*, New York, 1956; Cornell paperback. (A lively and readable survey of Puritan intellectual life, valuable for discussion of education and curriculum, but untrustworthy on literature and more philosophical aspects.)

—— "Those Misunderstood Puritans," *Forum*, LXXXV (1931), 142–147.

Mosse, George L., "Puritan Radical-ism and the Enlightenment," *Church His-tory*, XXIX (1960), 424–439. (Breaks new ground in tracing the contribution of radical Puritanism—Ranters and Seekers among others—to English deism.)

Mozley, J. F., *John Foxe and His Book*, New York, 1940. (A sympathetic exami-nation of the author of the *Book of Martyrs*, the most widely read of all Protestant histories and one which the

Puritans considered peculiarly their own.)

Murdock, Kenneth B., "The Puritan Tradition in American Literature," Chapter V in *The Reinterpretation of American Literature*, ed. Norman Foerster, New York, 1928.

New Cambridge Modern History, The, Cambridge, Eng., 1957—. (Does not supplant *The Cambridge Modern History*, but valuable interpretations for intellectual background in those volumes published, are Vol. II (1958), ed. G. R. Elton, Chapter XII, Part 2, "Intellectual Tendencies: Science," by A. R. Hall, and Chapter XIII, "Schools and Universities," by Denys Hay, 386–414; Vol. V (1961), ed. F. L. Casten, Chapter III, "The Scientific Movement," by A. R. Hall, and Chapter IV, "Philosophy," by W. Van Leyden, 47–95.)

New Schaff-Herzog Encyclopedia of Religious Knowledge, The, New York, 1908–1912, 12 vols.

Nuesse, Celestine Joseph, *The Social Thought of American Catholics, 1634–1829*, Westminster, Md., 1945.

Nuttall, Geoffrey F., *The Holy Spirit in Puritan Faith and Experience*, Oxford, 1946. (Emphasizes the mystical and "experiential" nature of the Puritan religion.)

Paradise, S. H., "Religion in Essex County," *Americana*, XXIX (1935), 181–227.

Parrington, Vernon L., *Main Currents in American Thought*, New York, 1927–1930, 3 vols.; 1955; one vol. edition, 1939; Harvest paperback. Vol. I: *The Colonial Mind*. (A noble work inspired by a militant liberalism, consequently hostile and unsympathetic to Puritanism; based upon lamentably insufficient familiarity with the sources, and therefore to be read for stimulation, not for fact or accuracy.)

Pattison, Mark, "Tendencies of Religious Thought in England, 1680–1750," in *Essays*, Oxford, 1889, 2 vols., Vol. I, 42–119.

Pickman, Edward M., "The Collapse of the Scholastic Hierarchy in Seventeenth Century France," *Proceedings of the Massachusetts Historical Society*, LXIV (1931), 212–249. (The break-up of the scholastic world; valuable for understanding the background of Puritan intellectual history.)

Platner, John W., "The Congregationalists," *Religious History of New England*, King's Chapel Lectures, Cambridge, 1917. (Excellent.)

Plooij, Daniel, *The Pilgrim Fathers from a Dutch Point of View*, New York, 1932. (New material on the sustained interest of the emigrants from Holland in those left at Leyden.)

Plum, Harry Grant, *Restoration Puritanism*, Chapel Hill, 1943.

Porter, H. C., *Reformation and Reaction in Tudor Cambridge*, Cambridge, Eng., 1958. (A literate, informal study based largely on secondary sources.)

Randall, John H., *The Making of the Modern Mind*, Boston, 1926. (Excellent handbook for the general intellectual background.)

(Ray), Sister Mary Augustina, *American Opinion of Roman Catholicism in the Eighteenth Century*, New York, 1936.

Riley, Arthur J., "Catholicism and the New England Mind," *Publications of the Colonial Society of Massachusetts*, XXXIV (1943), 389–399.

—— *Catholicism in New England to 1788*, Washington, 1936.

Riley, I. Woodbridge, *American Philosophy: The Early Schools*, New York, 1907; 1959. (Excellent as far as it goes, but not sympathetic to Puritanism in general; it sacrifices a study of the whole thought to a concentration upon individual figures. Now outdated.)

—— *American Thought from Puritanism to Pragmatism and Beyond*, New York, 1915.

Robertson, John M., *A Short History of Freethought, Ancient and Modern*, London, 2nd ed., 1906, 2 vols. (Vol. II, Chapter 17, "Early Freethought in the United States.")

Rowley, William E., "The Puritans' Tragic Vision," *New England Quarterly*, XVII (1944), 394–417.

Rupp, E. G., *Studies in the Making of the English Protestant Tradition: Mainly in the Reign of Henry VIII*, Cambridge, Eng., 1958.

Schafer, Thomas A., "Jonathan Edwards's Conception of the Church," *Church History*, XXIV (1955), 51–66.

Schirmer, Walter F., *Antike, Renaissance und Puritanismus*, 2nd ed., München, 1933.

Schneider, Herbert W., *The Puritan*

Mind, New York, 1930; Ann Arbor paperback. (A philosophical interpretation.)

Sencourt, Robert, (pseud.,) *Outflying Philosophy*, London, 1925. (Stimulating essay on seventeenth-century thought, particularly on Sir Thomas Browne, but valuable for religious background.)

Shipton, Clifford K., "The Hebraic Background of Puritanism," *Publications of the American Jewish Historical Society*, XLVII (1958), 140–153.

—— "A Plea for Puritanism," *American Historical Review*, XL (1935), 460–467.

Sisson, Rosemary A., "William Perkins, Apologist for the Elizabethan Church of England," *Modern Language Review*, XLVII (1952), 495–502.

Smith, Chard Powers, *Yankees and God*, New York, 1954. (A popular history of New England culture and Puritanism from the seventeenth to, twentieth century.)

Smyth, Egbert C., "The 'New Philosophy' against which students at Yale College were warned in 1714," *Proceedings of the American Antiquarian Society*, N.S. XI (1896–1897), 251–252.

Solt, Leo F., "Anti-Intellectualism in the Puritan Revolution," *Church History*, XXV (1956), 306–316.

Stearns, Raymond Phineas, *Congregationalism in the Dutch Netherlands: The Rise and Fall of the English Congregational Classes 1621–1635*, Chicago, 1940.

—— "The New England Way in Holland," *New England Quarterly*, VI (1933), 747–792.

Stephen, Leslie, *History of English Thought in the Eighteenth Century*, London, 1876, 2 vols. (The first chapters are useful as supplying a background for intellectual developments in early eighteenth-century New England.)

Sweet, William Warren, *Religion in Colonial America*, New York, 1942. (The Americanization of Christianity through the democratic impulse of the Great Revival.)

—— *The Story of Religions in America*, New York, 1930; 1939.

Tomas, V., "The Modernity of Jonathan Edwards," *New England Quarterly*, XXV (1952), 60–84.

Townsend, Harvey G., *Philosophical Ideas in the United States*, New York, 1934.

(A popular presentation, not too reliable; the bibliography is excellent.)

Tracy, Joseph, *The Great Awakening: A History of the Revival of Religion in the Time of Edwards and Whitefield*, Boston, 1841. (Useful for the extracts from diaries, letters, colonial newspapers, etc.)

Trefz, Edward K., "Satan as the Prince of Evil. The Preaching of New England Puritans," *Boston Public Library Quarterly*, VII (1955), 3–22.

—— "Satan in Puritan Preaching," *Boston Public Library Quarterly*, VIII (1956), 71–84, 148–159.

Trinterud, Leonard J., *The Forming of an American Tradition. A Re-examination of Colonial Presbyterianism*, Philadelphia, 1949. (Emphasizes the New England influence on the colonial church.)

—— "The New England Contribution to Colonial American Presbyterianism," *Church History*, XVII (1948), 32–43.

—— "The Origins of Puritanism," *Church History*, XX (1951), 37–57. (Finds the origins in a native tradition.)

Troeltsch, Ernst, *The Social Teaching of the Christian Churches* (trans. Olive Wyon), London, 1931, 2 vols.; London and Glencoe, Ill., 1949; Harper Torchbook edition 1960. (A monumental work, emphasizing the social implications of religious and ecclesiastical groups; the section on New England is unfortunately based upon very slight familiarity with American sources.)

Tufts, James H., "Edwards and Newton," *The Philosophical Review*, XLIX (1940), 609–622. (Edwards and the "new" science.)

Tulloch, John, *Rational Theology and Christian Philosophy in England in the Seventeenth Century*, London, 1872, 2 vols. (Still the best survey of the growth of rational religious thought in England.)

Turnbull, G. H., "John Drury's Correspondence with the Clergy of New England about Ecclesiastical Peace," *Publications of the Colonial Society of Massachusetts*, XXVIII (1947–1951), 1959, 18–21.

Tuttle, Julius H., "William Whiston and Cotton Mather," *Publications of the Colonial Society of Massachusetts*, XIII (1912), 197–204.

Uhden, Herman F., *The New England Theocracy: A History of the Congregationalists in New England to the Revivals of 1740*, Boston, 1858. (Translation from the German edition of 1842.)

Voegelin, Erich, *Ueber die Form des Amerikanischen Geistes*, Tübingen, 1928.

Waddington, John, *Congregational History*, London, 1869–1880, 5. vols. (The most complete study of English origins and contemporary parallels of the ecclesiastical order.)

Walker, George L., *Some Aspects of the Religious Life of New England, with Special Reference to Congregationalists*, Boston, 1897.

Walker, Williston, *A History of the Congregational Churches in the United States*, New York, 1894. (American Church History Series. The standard short history; not so extensive on some subjects as Dexter, but more even and judicious.)

Webb, Clement C. J., *Studies in the History of Natural Theology*, Oxford, 1915.

Weber, Max, *The Protestant Ethic and the Spirit of Capitalism* (translated by Talcott Parsons), New York, 1930; London, 1948; Scribner's paperback. (The classic interpretation of Protestantism from the economic point of view; it argues that Puritanism came into being as the discipline for a rising capitalist class, and is to be interpreted as a middle-class movement.)

Weis, Frederick L., "The New England Company of 1649 and Its Missionary Enterprises, *Publications of the Colonial Society of Massachusetts*, XXXVIII (1947–1951), 1959, 134–218.

White, Eugene C., "Decline of the Great Awakening in New England, 1741–1746," *New England Quarterly*, XXIV (1951), 35–52.

Whiting, Charles E., *Studies in English Puritanism from the Restoration to the Revolution*, New York, 1931. (The best work for English backgrounds after 1660.)

Willey, Basil, *The Seventeenth Century Background*, London, 1934; Anchor paperback. (A challenging interpretation of various aspects of the century's thought, that may err on the side of a somewhat too intuitive grasp, but supplies a number of stimulating ideas that promise to be fruitful if applied more particularly to Puritan history.)

Williams, George, "The Wilderness and Paradise in the History of the Church," *Church History*, XXVIII (1959), 3–24; reprinted with minor revisions in *Wilderness and Paradise in Christian Thought*, New York, 1961. (Important for understanding the concept of the wilderness in Puritan thought.)

Winslow, Ola Elizabeth, "The Religion of Roger Williams," *Bulletin of the Congregational Library*, VIII (1957), 5–13.

Wood, T., *English Casuistical Divinity during the 17th Century*, London, 1952.

Worthley, Harold Field, "The Colonial Diaconate: an Example of the Allocation and Exercise of Authority in the Particular Churches of New England," *Proceedings of the Unitarian Historical Society*, Vol. XII, Part II (1959), 27–52.

—— "The Massachusetts Convention of Congregational Ministers: an Historical Essay," *Proceedings of the Unitarian Historical Society*, Vol. XII, Part I (1958), 49–103.

Young, Edward J., "Subjects for Master's Degree in Harvard College from 1655 to 1791," *Proceedings of the Massachusetts Historical Society*, XVIII (1881), 119–151.

Ziff, Larzer, "The Salem Puritans in the 'Free Aire of a New World' ", *Huntington Library Quarterly*, XX (1956–1957), 373–384. (Reasserts the influence of Plymouth on the church polity of Salem and subsequently the other churches of the Bay.)

❧ INDEX

Volume I

Adams, John, 277.

Adams, Samuel, 277.

Adams, William, minister of Dedham, 9.

Addison, Joseph, 76; on poetry, 78.

Agrarianism, defended in New England, 257.

Agriculture, in New England, 377.

Allen, James, minister of Boston, 367.

Allerton, Isaac, Pilgrim, xix, 126.

Allin, John, minister of Dedham, 87; co-author of *Defence*, 118; preaches at Cambridge, 142.

Almanacs, 350.

Alsted, Johann Heinrich, German Protestant theologian, 47 n.

Ames, William, English Puritan theologian, 291; importance in America, 47 n.; on prose style, 66–67.

Anabaptists, *see* Baptists.

Anaxagoras, 22 n.

Andrewes, Lancelot, Anglican bishop, prose style of, 69–70.

Andros, Sir Edmund, governor of New England, 243, 246; his taxes protested, 257; opposed by Moody, 367.

Anglicanism, xxiv, xxv, 208, 367; Puritan origin in, 5–6; tenets of, common to Puritanism, 7–11, 88; divergencies from Puritanism, 41–55, 86; opposed by Mayhew, 277.

Anglicans, xix, 165, 178, 184, 185; objections to Quakers, 11; characteristics of prose style, 68–70.

Antinomianism, 10, 14–15, 84, 156–157, 160, 185, 227; objections to, by Willard, 36 n.; by Shepard, 118; by Winthrop, 126; Winthrop's account of, 129–143.

Aquinas, Saint Thomas, 26, 35 n., 235.

Arabella (*Arbella*), the, xxii, 126, 149.

Aristides, 22.

Aristocracy, defined by Wise, 268.

Aristophanes, 22.

Aristotle, 31; scholastic discipline of, 28; grudge against, by Ramists, 33, 74; syllogisms, 33–34; quoted, 263, 267.

Assistants, court of, *see* Magistrates.

Augustine, Saint, 230.

Bacon, Francis, inductive method of, 28.

Ball, John, English prelate, 87; reply to, by Shepard and Allin, 118–122.

Baptists, xxii, 15, 139–140, 160, 185, 225, 227, 335.

Barnard, John, minister of Marblehead, 193; biographical sketch, 270; *Throne Established, 270–276*.

Baxter, Richard, English nonconformist divine, 178.

Bay Psalm Book, 77.

Belcher, Jonathan, governor of Massachusetts, interest in literature, 76.

Belisarius, 354.

Bellomont, Earl of, *see* Coote.

Beverages, xxii, 2.

Bible, the, Puritan dependence on, 4, 10, 26, 41–57, 66, 79, 182 187; Geneva version of, 68; King James version of, 68.

Blackwall, Thomas, English scholar, 76.

Blaxton (or Blackstone), William, early settler, 149.

Bodin, Jean, French political economist, 211.

Boethius, 262.

Books and reading, *see* Libraries.

Boston Latin School, 141, 334.

Bradford, John, Protestant martyr, 119.

Bradford, William, governor of Plymouth, 485; biographical sketch, 90–91; *History*, 82–83, 87–89, 90, *91–117*; on style, 74.

Bradstreet, Simon, governor of Massachusetts, 150.

Brattle, Thomas, merchant of Boston, 24 n.

Brattle, William, minister of Cambridge, 20.

Brewster, William, Plymouth founder, 83, 88, 90, 103; mourned by Bradford, 112–113; sketch of, by Bradford, 113–116.

Bucer, Martin, German theologian, 165.

Bulkeley, Peter, minister of Concord, 133; theories of government, 190.

Burroughs, Jeremiah, English divine, xxiv, 178, 770.

Calef, Robert, writer on witchcraft, 270.

Calvin, John, metaphysics of, 32.

Revised January, 1970

ḥARPER 🔥 ꜩORCḥBOOKS

American Studies: General

CARL N. DEGLER: Out of Our Past: *The Forces that Shaped Modern America*   CN/2
ROBERT L. HEILBRONER: The Limits of American Capitalism   TB/1305
JOHN HIGHAM, Ed.: The Reconstruction of American History   TB/1068
JOHN F. KENNEDY: A Nation of Immigrants. *Illus. Revised and Enlarged. Introduction by Robert F. Kennedy*   TB/1118
GUNNAR MYRDAL: An American Dilemma: *The Negro Problem and Modern Democracy. Introduction by the Author.*
    Vol. I TB/1443;   Vol. II TB/1444
GILBERT OSOFSKY, Ed.: The Burden of Race: *A Documentary History of Negro-White Relations in America*   TB/1405
ARNOLD ROSE: The Negro in America: *The Condensed Version of Gunnar Mydral's* An American Dilemma   TB/3048

American Studies: Colonial

BERNARD BAILYN: The New England Merchants in the Seventeenth Century   TB/1149
ROBERT E. BROWN: Middle-Class Democracy and Revolution in Massachusetts, 1691–1780. *New Introduction by Author*   TB/1413
JOSEPH CHARLES: The Origins of the American Party System   TB/1049

American Studies: The Revolution to 1900

GEORGE M. FREDRICKSON: The Inner Civil War: *Northern Intellectuals and the Crisis of the Union*   TB/1358
WILLIAM W. FREEHLING: Prelude to Civil War: *The Nullification Controversy in South Carolina, 1816-1836*   TB/1359
HELEN HUNT JACKSON: A Century of Dishonor: *The Early Crusade for Indian Reform.* ‡ *Edited by Andrew F. Rolle*   TB/3063
RICHARD B. MORRIS, Ed.: Alexander Hamilton and the Founding of the Nation. *New Introduction by the Editor*   TB/1448
RICHARD B. MORRIS: The American Revolution Reconsidered   TB/1363
GILBERT OSOFSKY, Ed.: Puttin' On Ole Massa: *The Slave Narratives of Henry Bibb, William Wells Brown, and Solomon Northup* ‡   TB/1432

American Studies: The Twentieth Century

WILLIAM E. LEUCHTENBURG: Franklin D. Roosevelt and the New Deal: 1932-1940. † *Illus.*   TB/3025
WILLIAM E. LEUCHTENBURG, Ed.: The New Deal: *A Documentary History* +   HR/1354

Asian Studies

WOLFGANG FRANKE: China and the West: *The Cultural Encounter, 13th to 20th Centuries. Trans. by R. A. Wilson*   TB/1326
L. CARRINGTON GOODRICH: A Short History of the Chinese People. *Illus.*   TB/3015
BENJAMIN I. SCHWARTZ: Chinese Communism and the Rise of Mao   TB/1308

Economics & Economic History

PETER F. DRUCKER: The New Society: *The Anatomy of Industrial Order*   TB/1082
ROBERT L. HEILBRONER: The Great Ascent: *The Struggle for Economic Development in Our Time*   TB/3030
W. ARTHUR LEWIS: The Principles of Economic Planning. *New Introduction by the Author*°   TB/1436

Historiography and History of Ideas

J. BRONOWSKI & BRUCE MAZLISH: The Western Intellectual Tradition: *From Leonardo to Hegel*   TB/3001
WILHELM DILTHEY: Pattern and Meaning in History: *Thoughts on History and Society.*° *Edited with an Intro. by H. P. Rickman*   TB/1075
J. H. HEXTER: More's Utopia: *The Biography of an Idea. Epilogue by the Author*   TB/1195
ARTHUR O. LOVEJOY: The Great Chain of Being: *A Study of the History of an Idea*   TB/1009

History: Medieval

F. L. GANSHOF: Feudalism   TB/1058
DENYS HAY: The Medieval Centuries °   TB/1192
HENRY CHARLES LEA: A History of the Inquisition of the Middle Ages. ‖ *Introduction by Walter Ullmann*   TB/1456

† The New American Nation Series, edited by Henry Steele Commager and Richard B. Morris.
‡ American Perspectives series, edited by Bernard Wishy and William E. Leuchtenburg.
a History of Europe series, edited by J. H. Plumb.
§ The Library of Religion and Culture, edited by Benjamin Nelson.
‖ Researches in the Social, Cultural, and Behavioral Sciences, edited by Benjamin Nelson.
⅀ Harper Modern Science Series, edited by James R. Newman.
° Not for sale in Canada.
+ Documentary History of the United States series, edited by Richard B. Morris.
# Documentary History of Western Civilization series, edited by Eugene C. Black and Leonard W. Levy.
A The Economic History of the United States series, edited by Henry David et al.
¶ European Perspectives series, edited by Eugene C. Black.
** Contemporary Essays series, edited by Leonard W Levy.
* The Stratum Series, edited by John Hale.

1

History: Renaissance & Reformation

JACOB BURCKHARDT: The Civilization of the Renaissance in Italy. *Introduction by Benjamin Nelson and Charles Trinkaus. Illus.* Vol. I TB/40; Vol. II TB/41

JOEL HURSTFIELD: The Elizabethan Nation TB/1312

ALFRED VON MARTIN: Sociology of the Renaissance. ° *Introduction by W. K. Ferguson* TB/1099

J. H. PARRY: The Establishment of the European Hegemony: 1415-1715: *Trade and Exploration in the Age of the Renaissance* TB/1045

History: Modern European

MAX BELOFF: The Age of Absolutism, 1660-1815 TB/1062

ALAN BULLOCK: Hitler, A Study in Tyranny. ° *Revised Edition. Illus.* TB/1123

JOHANN GOTTLIEB FICHTE: Addresses to the German Nation. *Ed. with Intro. by George A. Kelly* ¶ TB/1366

H. STUART HUGHES: The Obstructed Path: *French Social Thought in the Years of Desperation* TB/1451

JOHAN HUIZINGA: Dutch Cviilization in the 17th Century and Other Essays TB/1453

JOHN MCMANNERS: European History, 1789-1914: *Men, Machines and Freedom* TB/1419

FRANZ NEUMANN: Behemoth: *The Structure and Practice of National Socialism, 1933-1944* TB/1289

A. J. P. TAYLOR: From Napoleon to Lenin: *Historical Essays* ° TB/1268

H. R. TREVOR-ROPER: Historical Essays TB/1269

Philosophy

HENRI BERGSON: Time and Free Will: *An Essay on the Immediate Data of Consciousness* ° TB/1021

G. W. F. HEGEL: Phenomenology of Mind. ° || *Introduction by George Lichtheim* TB/1303

H. J. PATON: The Categorical Imperative: *A Study in Kant's Moral Philosophy* TB/1325

MICHAEL POLANYI: Personal Knowledge: *Towards a Post-Critical Philosophy* TB/1158

LUDWIG WITTGENSTEIN: The Blue and Brown Books ° TB/1211

LUDWIG WITTGENSTEIN: Notebooks, 1914-1916 TB/1441

Political Science & Government

C. E. BLACK: The Dynamics of Modernization: *A Study in Comparative History* TB/1321

DENIS W. BROGAN: Politics in America. *New Introduction by the Author* TB/1469

KARL R. POPPER: The Open Society and Its Enemies *Vol. I: The Spell of Plato* TB/1101 *Vol. II: The High Tide of Prophecy: Hegel, Marx, and the Aftermath* TB/1102

CHARLES SCHOTTLAND, Ed.: The Welfare State ** TB/1323

JOSEPH A. SCHUMPETER: Capitalism, Socialism and Democracy TB/3008

PETER WOLL, Ed.: Public Administration and Policy: *Selected Essays* TB/1284

Psychology

LUDWIG BINSWANGER: Being-in-the-World: *Selected Papers. || Trans. with Intro. by Jacob Needleman* TB/1365

MIRCEA ELIADE: Cosmos and History: *The Myth of the Eternal Return* § TB/2050

SIGMUND FREUD: On Creativity and the Unconscious: *Papers on the Psychology of Art, Literature, Love, Religion.* § *Intro. by Benjamin Nelson* TB/45

J. GLENN GRAY: The Warriors: *Reflections on Men in Battle. Introduction by Hannah Arendt* TB/1294

WILLIAM JAMES: Psychology: *The Briefer Course. Edited with an Intro. by Gordon Allport* TB/1034

Religion

TOR ANDRAE: Mohammed: *The Man and his Faith* TB/62

KARL BARTH: Church Dogmatics: *A Selection. Intro. by H. Hollwitzer. Ed. by G. W. Bromiley* TB/95

NICOLAS BERDYAEV: The Destiny of Man TB/61

MARTIN BUBER: The Prophetic Faith TB/73

MARTIN BUBER: Two Types of Faith: *Interpenetration of Judaism and Christianity* TB/75

RUDOLF BULTMANN: History and Eschatalogy: *The Presence of Eternity* TB/91

EDWARD CONZE: Buddhism: *Its Essence and Development. Foreword by Arthur Waley* TB/58

H. G. CREEL: Confucius and the Chinese Way TB/63

FRANKLIN EDGERTON, Trans. & Ed.: The Bhagavad Gita TB/115

M. S. ENSLIN: Christian Beginnings TB/5

M. S. ENSLIN: The Literature of the Christian Movement TB/6

HENRI FRANKFORT: Ancient Egyptian Religion: *An Interpretation* TB/77

IMMANUEL KANT: Religion Within the Limits of Reason Alone. *Introduction by Theodore M. Greene and John Silber* TB/67

GABRIEL MARCEL: Homo Viator: *Introduction to a Metaphysic of Hope* TB/397

H. RICHARD NIEBUHR: Christ and Culture TB/3

H. RICHARD NIEBUHR: The Kingdom of God in America TB/49

SWAMI NIKHILANANDA, Trans. & Ed.: The Upanishads TB/114

F. SCHLEIERMACHER: The Christian Faith. *Introduction by Richard R. Niebuhr.* Vol. I TB/108 Vol. II TB/109

Sociology and Anthropology

KENNETH B. CLARK: Dark Ghetto: *Dilemmas of Social Power. Foreword by Gunnar Myrdal* TB/1317

KENNETH CLARK & JEANNETTE HOPKINS: A Relevant War Against Poverty: *A Study of Community Action Programs and Observable Social Change* TB/1480

GARY T. MARX: Protest and Prejudice: *A Study of Belief in the Black Community* TB/1435

ROBERT K. MERTON, LEONARD BROOM, LEONARD S. COTTRELL, JR., Editors: Sociology Today: *Problems and Prospects* || Vol. I TB/1173; Vol. II TB/1174

GILBERT OSOFSKY: Harlem: The Making of a Ghetto: *Negro New York, 1890-1930* TB/1381

PHILIP RIEFF: The Triumph of the Therapeutic: *Uses of Faith After Freud* TB/1360

GEORGE ROSEN: Madness in Society: *Chapters in the Historical Sociology of Mental Illness.* || *Preface by Benjamin Nelson* TB/1337